BRIEF TABLE OF CONTENTS

OB SKILLS WORKBOOK

The **OB Skills Workbook** is an end-of-text learning resource complete with a wide variety of cases, experiential exercises, and self-assessments to enrich and extend student learning.

JOSSEY-BASS/PFEIFFER CLASSROOM COLLECTION

Selected from the best of the Jossey-Bass and Pfeiffer publications, this collection includes the Kouzes and Posner Leadership Practices Inventory, and exercise selections from the Pfeiffer Annual Editions.

CASES FOR CRITICAL THINKING

The **Cases for Critical Thinking** section contains 18 cases, with each developed to explore issues, concepts and applications for a text chapter.

EXPERIENTIAL EXERCISES

A portfolio of 42 **Experiential Exercises** helps students engage in teamwork and experience practical aspects of each chapter.

SELF-ASSESSMENTS

A set of 22 **Self-assessments** that involves students in exploring their personal managerial tendencies and perspectives.

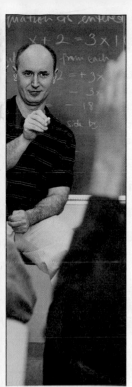

The first person to invent a car that runs on water...

... may be sitting right in your classroom! Every one of your students has the potential to make a difference. And realizing that potential starts right here, in your course.

When students succeed in your course—when they stay on-task and make the breakthrough that turns confusion into confidence—they are empowered to realize the possibilities for greatness that lie within each of them. We know your goal is to create an environment where students reach their full potential and experience the exhilaration of academic success that will last them a lifetime. *WileyPLUS* can help you reach that goal.

Wiley**PLUS** is an online suite of resources—including the complete text—that will help your students:

- come to class better prepared for your lectures
- get immediate feedback and context-sensitive help on assignments and quizzes
- track their progress throughout the course

"I just wanted to say how much this program helped me in studying... I was able to actually see my mistakes and correct them. ... I really think that other students should have the chance to use *WileyPLUS*."

Ashlee Krisko, *Oakland University*

www.wileyplus.com

88% of students surveyed said it improved their understanding of the material. *

FOR INSTRUCTORS

WileyPLUS is built around the activities you perform in your class each day. With WileyPLUS you can:

Prepare & Present
Create outstanding class presentations using a wealth of resources such as PowerPoint™ slides, image galleries, interactive simulations, and more. You can even add materials you have created yourself.

Create Assignments
Automate the assigning and grading of homework or quizzes by using the provided question banks, or by writing your own.

Track Student Progress
Keep track of your students' progress and analyze individual and overall class results.

Now Available with WebCT and Blackboard!

"It has been a great help, and I believe it has helped me to achieve a better grade."

Michael Morris,
Columbia Basin College

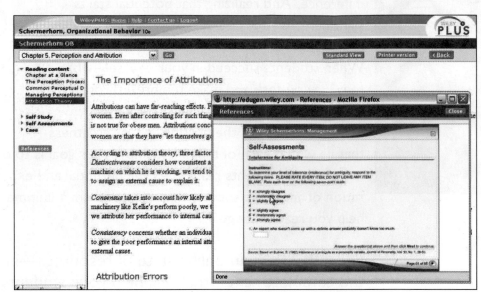

FOR STUDENTS

You have the potential to make a difference!
WileyPLUS is a powerful online system packed with features to help you make the most of your potential and get the best grade you can!

With WileyPLUS you get:

• A complete online version of your text and other study resources.

• Problem-solving help, instant grading, and feedback on your homework and quizzes.

• The ability to track your progress and grades throughout the term.

For more information on what *WileyPLUS* can do to help you and your students reach their potential, please visit www.wileyplus.com/experience.

82% of students surveyed said it made them better prepared for tests. *

*Based on 7000 responses to student surveys in academic year 2006–2007.

Organizational Behavior

Tenth Edition

BICENTENNIAL
1807
⊛WILEY
2007
BICENTENNIAL

THE WILEY BICENTENNIAL—KNOWLEDGE FOR GENERATIONS

*E*ach generation has its unique needs and aspirations. When Charles Wiley first opened his small printing shop in lower Manhattan in 1807, it was a generation of boundless potential searching for an identity. And we were there, helping to define a new American literary tradition. Over half a century later, in the midst of the Second Industrial Revolution, it was a generation focused on building the future. Once again, we were there, supplying the critical scientific, technical, and engineering knowledge that helped frame the world. Throughout the 20th Century, and into the new millennium, nations began to reach out beyond their own borders and a new international community was born. Wiley was there, expanding its operations around the world to enable a global exchange of ideas, opinions, and know-how.

For 200 years, Wiley has been an integral part of each generation's journey, enabling the flow of information and understanding necessary to meet their needs and fulfill their aspirations. Today, bold new technologies are changing the way we live and learn. Wiley will be there, providing you the must-have knowledge you need to imagine new worlds, new possibilities, and new opportunities.

Generations come and go, but you can always count on Wiley to provide you the knowledge you need, when and where you need it!

WILLIAM J. PESCE
PRESIDENT AND CHIEF EXECUTIVE OFFICER

PETER BOOTH WILEY
CHAIRMAN OF THE BOARD

Organizational Behavior

Tenth Edition

John R. Schermerhorn, Jr.

OHIO UNIVERSITY

James G. Hunt

TEXAS TECH UNIVERSITY

Richard N. Osborn

WAYNE STATE UNIVERSITY

BICENTENNIAL
1807
WILEY
2007
BICENTENNIAL

John Wiley & Sons, Inc.

Executive Publisher	Don Fowley
Senior Acquisitions Editor	Kimberly Mortimer
Associate Editor	Jennifer Conklin
Editorial Assistant	Carissa Marker
Executive Marketing Manager	Amy Scholz
Media Editor	Allison Morris
Production Manager	Dorothy Sinclair
Senior Production Editor	Sandra Dumas
Senior Designer	Madelyn Lesure
Creative Director	Harry Nolan
Illustration Editor	Anna Melhorn
Photo Department Manager	Hilary Newman
Photo Editor	Tara Sanford
Photo Researcher	Katherine Bendo
Production Management Services	Ingrao Associates
Cover Image	Don Hammond/Design Pics/Corbis

This book was set in 10/12 ITC Garamond Light by Prepare and printed and bound by R.R. Donnelly (Jefferson City). The cover was printed by R.R. Donnelly (Jefferson City).

This book is printed on acid-free paper.

ISBN 13 978-0-470-08696-4

Printed in the United States of America.

10 9 8 7 6 5 4 3 2 1

About the Authors

Dr. John R. Schermerhorn, Jr. is the Charles G. O'Bleness Professor of Management in the College of Business at Ohio University, where he teaches graduate and undergraduate courses in management. Dr. Schermerhorn earned a Ph.D. in organizational behavior from Northwestern University, an MBA (with distinction) in management and international business from New York University, and a BS in business administration from the State University of New York at Buffalo. He has taught at Tulane University, the University of Vermont, and Southern Illinois University at Carbondale, where he also served as Head of the Department of Management and Associate Dean of the College of Business Administration. Because of his commitment to instructional excellence and curriculum innovation, Ohio University has named Dr. Schermerhorn a University Professor. This is the university's highest campus-wide honor for excellence in undergraduate teaching. Dr. Schermerhorn's international experience also adds a unique global dimension to his teaching and textbooks. He holds an honorary doctorate from the University of Pécs in Hungary. He has also served as a Visiting Professor of Management at the Chinese University of Hong Kong, as on-site Coordinator of the Ohio University MBA and Executive MBA programs in Malaysia, and as Kohei Miura visiting professor at the Chubu University of Japan. Presently he is Adjunct Professor at the National University of Ireland at Galway, a member of the graduate faculty at Bangkok University in Thailand, and advisor to the Lao-American College in Vientiane, Laos. An enthusiastic scholar, Dr. Schermerhorn is a member of the Academy of Management, where he served as chairperson of the Management Education and Development Division. In addition, educators and students alike know him as author of *Management 9e* (Wiley, 2008) and senior co-author of *Organizational Behavior 9/e* (Wiley, 2005), and *Core Concepts of Organizational Behavior* (Wiley, 2004). Finally, Dr. Schermerhorn has also published numerous articles, such as in the *Academy of Management Journal, Academy of Management Review, Academy of Management Executive, Organizational Dynamics, Asia-Pacific Journal of Management*, and the *Journal of Management Development*. Dr. Schermerhorn serves as a guest speaker at colleges and universities, lecturing on developments in higher education for business and management, as well as on manuscript development, textbook writing, and instructional approaches and innovations.

Dr. James G. (Jerry) Hunt is the Paul Whitfield Horn Professor of Management, Professor of Health Organization Management, Former Director, Institute for Leadership Research, and former department chair of Management, Texas Tech University. He received his PhD and master's degrees from the University of Illinois after completing a BS (with honors) at Michigan Technological University.

Dr. Hunt has co-authored an organization theory text and *Core Concepts of Organizational Behavior* (Wiley, 2004) and has authored or co-authored three leadership monographs. He founded the Leadership Symposia Series and co-edited the eight volumes based on the series. He is former editor of the *Journal of Management* and *The Leadership Quarterly*. He has presented or published some 200 articles, papers, and book chapters, and among his better-known books are *Leadership: A New Synthesis*, published by Sage, and *Out-of-the-Box Leadership,* published by JAI. The former was a finalist for the Academy of Management's 1993 Terry Distinguished Book Award. Recently, Dr. Hunt received the Distinguished Service Award from the Academy of Management, the Sustained Outstanding Service Award from the Southern Management Association, and the Barnie E. Rushing, Jr. Distinguished Researcher Award from Texas Tech University for his long-term contributions to management research and scholarship. He has lived and taught in England, Finland, and Thailand, and taught in China.

Dr. Richard N. Osborn is the Wayne State University Distinguished Professor of Management in the School of Business Administration and formerly a Board of Governors Faculty Fellow. He has received teaching awards at Southern Illinois University at Carbondale and Wayne State University, and he has also taught at Arizona State University, Monash University (Australia), Tulane University, University of Munich, and the University of Washington. He received a DBA from Kent State University after earning an MBA at Washington State University and a BS from Indiana University. With over 200 presentations and publications, he is a charter member of the Academy of Management Journals Hall of Fame. Dr. Osborn is a leading authority on international alliances in technology-intensive industries and is co-author of an organization theory text as well as *Basic Organizational Behavior* (John Wiley & Sons, 1995, 1998). He has served as editor of international strategy for the *Journal of World Business* and Special Issue Editor for *The Academy of Management Journal*. He serves or has served as a member of the editorial boards for *The Academy of Management Journal, The Academy of Management Review, Journal of High Technology Management, The Journal of Management, Leadership Quarterly,* and *Technology Studies,* among others. He is very active in the Academy of Management, having served as divisional program chair and president, as well as the Academy representative for the International Federation of Scholarly Associations of Management. Dr. Osborn's research has been sponsored by the Department of Defense, Ford Motor Company, National Science Foundation, Nissan, and the Nuclear Regulatory Commission, among others. In addition to teaching, Dr. Osborn spent a number of years in private industry, including a position as a senior research scientist with the Battelle Memorial Institute in Seattle, where he worked on improving the safety of commercial nuclear power.

Preface

Global warming, terrorism, ethnic conflict, poverty, discrimination, unemployment, illiteracy. . . these are among the many issues and problems we face. But how often do we stop and recognize our responsibilities for problem solving and positive action? In so many ways, and as suggested by the cover of this book, the future of the world rests in our hands. What we do today will have a lasting impact on tomorrow. And whether we are talking about families, communities, nations, or the organizations in which we work and volunteer, the core question remains: How can we join together to have a positive and lasting impact? Look again at the cover. The hands and the globe are not just artistic expressions. They are symbolic of a great opportunity. The world is in our hands, and if those hands do the right things together, wonderful things are possible.

That message is a fitting place to begin *Organizational Behavior*, Tenth Edition. Everyone wants to have a useful and satisfying job and career; everyone wants all the organizations of society—small and large businesses, hospitals, schools, governments, nonprofits, and more—to perform well. In this context the lessons of our discipline are strong and applicable. Armed with an understanding of organizational behavior, great things are possible as people work, pursue careers, and contribute to society through positive personal and organizational accomplishments.

We believe in organizational behavior as a foundation discipline rich with insights for career and life skills. As educators, we believe our job is to bring to the classroom and to our students the great power of knowledge, understanding, and inquiry that characterizes our discipline and its commitment to understanding human behavior in organizations. What our students do with their talents will not only shape the contributions of the institutions of society but also fundamentally alter lives around the globe. Our goal must be to help them gain the understanding that can help them become leaders of tomorrow's organizations.

Organizational Behavior, Tenth Edition, is dedicated to our students, in whose hands rest the real keys to the future. While retaining an emphasis on the fundamentals of organizational behavior, the theme for the new edition is one of learning, understanding, and teamwork in a global context. This theme reflects the challenges of a society that expects high performance and high quality of work life to go hand in hand. It embraces ethics and social responsibility as fundamental to any measures of individual and organizational accomplishments. It respects the talents of workforces increasingly rich in demographic and cultural diversity. And, it recognizes full well the everyday imprint of the forces of globalization.

John R. Schermerhorn Jr.
Ohio University

James G. (Jerry) Hunt
Texas Tech University

Richard N. Osborn
Wayne State University

About This Book

Organizational Behavior, Tenth Edition, brings to its readers the solid and complete content core of prior editions, the exciting "OB Skills Workbook," and many revisions, updates, and enhancements that reflect today's dynamic times.

Organization

The most significant change that past users will note is a rearrangement of the table of contents. The book still covers the discipline in an orderly progression from individuals to groups to leadership and processes to organizations. As always, chapters are written to allow for all chapters and parts to be used out of sequence at the instructor's prerogative.

Content

All chapters and parts have been updated to reflect new research findings and current applications and issues. For this edition, and in response to feedback, we have also rearranged chapters and adjusted content to best reflect developments and directions in the discipline as well as the realities of today's workplaces and career challenges. The major changes were made to strengthen the research component, expand and refocus the chapters dealing with individual behavior and performance, and more fully treat the emerging directions in leadership research and thinking. These changes to the tenth edition are reflected in the following sections and chapters.

Part 1—Organizational Behavior Today:
   Primer on Research Methods now follows Chapter 1.
Part 2—Individuals and Performance:
   Chapter 2 updated and titled—Values, Personality, and Individual Differences.
   Chapter 3 added new content and titled—Emotions, Attitudes, and Job Satisfaction.
   Chapter 4 updated and titled—Perception, Attribution, and Learning.
   Chapter 5 updated and titled—Motivation Theories.
   Chapter 6 updated and titled—Motivation and Job Design
   Chapter 7 updated and titled—Rewards and Performance Management
Part 4—Leadership and Organizational Processes:
   Chapter 11 updated and titled—Leadership Theories.
   Chapter 12 added new content and titled—Emerging Leadership Perspectives.

Ethics Focus

To help students anticipate, understand, and confront the ethical challenges of work and careers today we have added a special feature in each chapter—*Ethics in OB*. This feature presents a situation or issue from an actual case or news report and asks a question of the student reader that requires personal reflection on the ethics and ethics implications. Examples include: "Oprah Builds Leadership Academy for South Africa's Young Women," "The Green Corporation May be More than Public Relations," and "Presenteeism: How Coming in Sick Affects Business."

Research Focus

To better communicate the timely research foundations of OB, new content has been added to a popular feature, *Research Insights,* that is found in each chapter. Each Research Insight overviews an article from a respected journal (such as *Academy of Management Journal* and *Journal of Applied Psychology*). Sample topics include attitudes and performance, ethical behavior, cross-cultural intelligence, and workplace identities, among others. For those who want to give research a special focus in their course, the primer on Research Methods in Organizational Behavior is now included after the Introductory text chapter.

Leadership Focus

To remind students that there are many positive leadership role models available for study, the *Leaders on Leadership* feature is included in each chapter. This feature offers short examples of real leaders, their experiences and perspectives— including Deborah Lee – "Hard Work Leads Deborah L. Lee to the Top," Sarah Blakely – "Spanx Queen Leads from Bottom Line," and Jeff Bezos – "Pizzas Guide Teams and Teamwork at Amazon.com." Each leader vignette is followed by a study question that asks students to further consider and personally apply the implications of the leadership example.

Applications Focus

To assist students with applying the insights of OB to real situations and management problems, two new chapter features have been added to this edition. *Mastering Management* boxes provide insights from practicing managers and recognized organizations. Examples include: "Google's Ten Rules," "Developing Human Capital," and "Ways to Harness Team Diversity." *OB Savvy* boxes summarize major findings and applications. Examples include: "Seven steps to positive norms," "How to create a high-performing team," and "Developing your emotional intelligence."

Pedagogy

As always, a primary goal in writing this book is to create a textbook that appeals to the student reader, while still offering solid content. Through market research surveys and focus groups with students and professors, we continue to learn what features worked best from previous editions, what can be improved, and what can be added to accomplish this goal both effectively and efficiently. Our response is a selection of pedagogical elements that include popular elements from the last edition as well as ones new to this edition.

- **Chapter Opening**—includes a *Chapter at a Glance* section with *Study Topics/Learning Objectives*—linked to the end-of-chapter Summary, and a *short opening vignette* that leads the reader into chapter text.

- **Inside the Chapter**—includes a variety of *thematic embedded boxes* previously noted: *Leaders on Leadership, Ethics in OB, Research Insight, OB Savvy,* and *Mastering Management*. These all highlight relevant, timely, and global themes and situations using the events and examples. In addition, each chapter includes two or more *Margin Photo Essays* that provide further short examples highlighting events and issues. To assist with chapter study and test preparation, each chapter has a running *Margin Glossary* and *Margin List Identifiers*.

- **End of Chapter**—includes a *Study Guide* to help students review and test their mastery of chapter content. Key components are: *Chapter Summary* (keyed to opening *Chapter at a Glance topics*), *Key Terms*, and a *Self-Test*—with multiple choice, short response, and essay questions. Also included is *OB in Action* which is a guide to selections of cases, exercises, and assessments from the OB Skills Workbook and on-line materials that link to chapter material.

The OB Skills Workbook: Featuring The Jossey-Bass/Pfeiffer Collection

The end-of-text **OB Skills Workbook** has become a hallmark feature of the textbook, and it has been updated and expanded for the new edition. In addition to a selection of *cases, exercises,* and *assessments* that can be used at the instructor's convenience, *The Jossey-Bass Pfeiffer Collection* is included. This collection offers the popular Kouzes and Posner *Student Leadership Practices Inventory* and six other selections from Pfeiffer training annuals. These materials are further opportunities to extend the OB learning experience in creative and helpful ways.

New Student and Instructor Support

Organizational Behavior, Tenth Edition, is supported by a comprehensive learning package that assists the instructor in creating a motivating and enthusiastic environment.

Instructor's Resource Manual The Instructor's Resource Manual offers helpful teaching ideas, advice on course development, sample assignments, and chapter-by-chapter text highlights, learning objectives, lecture outlines, class exercises, lecture notes, answers to end-of-chapter material, and tips on using cases.

Test Bank This comprehensive Test Bank (available on the instructor portion of the website) will consist of over 200 questions per chapter. Each chapter will have true/false, multiple choice, and short answer questions. The questions are designed to vary in degree of difficulty to challenge your OB students.

The **Computerized Test Bank** is for use on a PC running Windows. It contains content from the Test Bank provided within a test-generating program that allows instructors to customize their exams.

PowerPoint   This robust set of lecture/interactive PowerPoints is provided for each chapter to enhance your students' overall experience in the OB classroom. The PowerPoint slides can be accessed on the instructor portion of the website and include lecture notes to accompany each slide.

Web Quizzes   An online study guide with online quizzes, varying in level of difficulty designed to help your students evaluate their individual progress through a chapter, available on the student portion of the website. Here students will have the ability to test themselves with 15–25 questions per chapter (including true-false and multiple choice questions).

Pre- and Post-Lecture Quizzes   Included in **WileyPLUS,** the Pre- and Post-Lecture Quizzes consist of 10-15 questions (multiple choice and true/false) per chapter, varying in level of detail and difficulty, that focus on the key terms and concepts within each chapter, so that professors can evaluate their students' progress from before the lecture to after it.

Personal Response System   The Personal Response System questions (PRS or "Clickers") for each chapter of the Organizational Behavior 10th edition textbook are designed to spark discussion/debate in the OB classroom. For more information on PRS, please contact your local Wiley sales representative.

Companion Website   The text's website at http://www.wiley.com/college/schermerhorn contains myriad tools and links to aid both teaching and learning, including nearly all of the resources described above.

Business Extra Select Online Courseware System   http://www.wiley.com/college/bxs. Wiley has launched this program that provides an instructor with millions of content resources from an extensive database of cases, journals, periodicals, newspapers, and supplemental readings. This courseware system lends itself extremely well to the integration of real-world content within Organizational Behavior to enable instructors to convey the relevance of the course content to their students.

Videos

Lecture Launcher: Short video clips tied to the major topics in organizational behavior are available. These clips, available in WileyPLUS or on DVD, provide an excellent starting point for lectures or for general class discussion. Teaching notes for using the video clips are available on the Instructor's portion of the Web site.

Art Imitates Life: Using Movies and Music in Organizational Behavior   Prepared by Robert L. Holbrook, *Ohio University.* Interested in integrating pop culture into your OB course? Looking for ways of integrating the humanities (movies and music) into your classroom? Dr. Holbrook provides innovative teaching ideas for integrating these ideas into your classroom experience. This instructor's supplement is available exclusively for adopters.

Please contact your local Wiley sales representative for additional information on the OB Video Program.

WileyPLUS

WileyPLUS provides an integrated suite of teaching and learning resources, along with a complete online version of the text, in one easy-to-use Web site. **WileyPLUS** will help you create class presentations, create assignments, and automate the assigning and grading of homework or quizzes, track your students' progress, and administer your course. Also includes mp3 downloads of the key chapter topics, providing students with audio module overviews, team evaluation tools, experiential exercises, student self-assessments, flashcards of key terms, and more! For more information, go to http://www.wiley.com/college/wileyplus.

Contributors

Cases for Critical Thinking

Barry R. Armandi, *State University of New York*, David S. Chappell, *Ohio University*, Bernardo M. Ferdman, *Alliant International University*, Placido L. Gallegos, *Southwest Communications Resources, Inc.* and the *Kaleel Jamison Consulting Group. Inc.*, Carol Harvey, *Assumption College*, Ellen Ernst Kossek, *Michigan State University*, Barbara McCain, *Oklahoma City University*, Mary McGarry, *Empire State College*, Marc Osborn, *R&R Partners Phoenix, AZ*, Franklin Ramsoomair, *Wilfrid Laurier University*, Hal Babson and John Bowen of *Columbus State Community College.*

Experiential Exercises and Self-Assessment Inventories

Barry R. Armandi, *State University of New York, Old Westbury*, Ariel Fishman, *The Wharton School, University of Pennsylvania*, Barbara K. Goza, *University of California, Santa Cruz*, D.T. Hall, *Boston University*, F.S. Hall, *University of New Hampshire*, Lady Hanson, *California State Polytechnic University, Pomona*, Conrad N. Jackson, *MPC, Inc.*, Mary Khalili, *Oklahoma City University*, Robert Ledman, *Morehouse College*, Paul Lyons, *Frostburg State University*, J. Marcus Maier, *Chapman University*, Michael R. Manning, *New Mexico State University*, Barbara McCain, *Oklahoma City University*, Annie McKee, *The Wharton School, University of Pennsylvania*, Bonnie McNeely, *Murray State University*, W. Alan Randolph, *University of Baltimore*, Joseph Raelin, *Boston College*, Paula J. Schmidt, *New Mexico State University*, Susan Schor, *Pace University*, Timothy T. Serey, *Northern Kentucky University*, Barbara Walker, *Diversity Consultant*, Paula S. Weber, *New Mexico Highlands University*, Susan Rawson Zacur, *University of Baltimore*.

Acknowledgments

Organizational Behavior, Tenth Edition, benefits from insights provided by a dedicated group of management educators from around the globe who carefully read and critiqued draft chapters of this edition. We are pleased to express our appreciation to the following colleagues for their contributions to this new edition.

William Bommer, *Cleveland State University*
H. Michal Boyd, *Bentley College*
Mark Fichman, *Carnegie Mellon University*
Dean Frear, *Wilkes University*
Eric Lamm, *Boston College*
Daniel McAllister, *University of Nevada, Las Vegas*
Christopher Neck, *Virginia Tech*
Joel Rudin, *Rowan University*
Ted Shore, *California State University, San Marcos*
Robert Steel, *University of Michigan, Dearborn*
Ron Stone, *Keller Graduate School of DeVry University*
Ed Tomlinson, *John Carroll University*
Tony Urban, *Rutgers University*

We also thank those reviewers who contributed to the success of previous editions.

Merle Ace
Chi Anyansi-Archibong
Terry Armstrong
Leanne Atwater
Forrest Aven
Steve Axley
Abdul Aziz
Richard Babcock
David Baldridge
Michael Banutu-Gomez
Robert Barbato
Richard Barrett
Nancy Bartell
Anna Bavetta
Robb Bay
Hrach Bedrosian
Bonnie Betters-Reed

Gerald Biberman
Melinda Blackman
Lisa Bleich
Mauritz Blonder
Dale Blount
G. B. Bohn
Pat Buhler
Gene E. Burton
Roosevelt Butler
Ken Butterfield
Joseph F. Byrnes
Michal Cakrt
Tom Callahan
Daniel R. Cillis
Nina Cole
Paul Collins
Ann Cowden

Deborah Crown
Roger A. Dean
Robert Delprino
Emmeline De Pillis
Pam Dobies
Delf Dodge
Dennis Duchon
Michael Dumler
Ken Eastman
Norb Elbert
Theresa Feener
Janice M. Feldbauer
Claudia Ferrante
Dalmar Fisher
J. Benjamin Forbes
Cynthia V. Fukami
Normandie Gaitley

Daniel Ganster
Joe Garcia
Virginia Geurin
Robert Giambatista
Manton Gibbs
Eugene Gomolka
Barbara Goodman
Stephen Gourlay
Frederick Greene
Richard Grover
Bengt Gustafsson
Peter Gustavson
Lady Alice Hanson
Don Hantula
Kristi Harrison
William Hart
Nell Hartley
Neil J. Humphreys
David Hunt
Eugene Hunt
Howard Kahn
Harriet Kandelman
Paul N. Keaton
Andrew Klein
Leslie Korb
Peter Kreiner
Donald Lantham
Jim Lessner
Les Lewchuk
Kristi M. Lewis
Robert Liden
Beverly Linnell
Kathy Lippert
Michael London
Michael Lounsbury
Carol Lucchesi

David Luther
Lorna Martin
Tom Mayes
Douglas McCabe
James McFillen
Jeanne McNett
Charles Milton
Herff L. Moore
David Morand
David Morean
Sandra Morgan
Paula Morrow
Richard Mowday
Linda Neider
Judy C. Nixon
Regina O'Neill
Dennis Pappas
Edward B. Parks
Robert F. Pearse
Lawrence Peters
Prudence Pollard
Joseph Porac
Samuel Rabinowitz
Franklin Ramsoomair
Clint Relyea
Bobby Remington
Charles L. Roegiers
Steven Ross
Michael Rush
Robert Salitore
Terri Scandura
Mel Schnake
Holly Schroth
L. David Schuelke
Richard J. Sebastian
Anson Seers

William Sharbrough
R. Murray Sharp
Allen N. Shub
Sidney Siegal
Dayle Smith
Mary Alice Smith
Walter W. Smock
Pat Sniderman
Ritch L. Sorenson
Shanthi Srinivas
Paul L. Starkey
Ronni Stephens
Ron Stone
Tom Thompson
Sharon Tucker
Nicholas Twigg
Ted Valvoda
Joyce Vincelette
David Vollrath
Andy Wagstaff
W. Fran Waller
Charles Wankel
Edward Ward
Fred A. Ware, Jr.
Andrea F. Warfield
Harry Waters, Jr.
Joseph W. Weiss
Deborah Wells
Robert Whitcomb
Donald White
Bobbie Williams
Barry L. Wisdom
Wayne Wormley
Barry Wright
Kimberly Young
Raymond Zammuto

We are grateful for all the hard work of the supplements authors, who worked to develop the comprehensive ancillary package described above. We thank Molly Pepper for preparing the Instructor's Resource Guide, Dianne Weinstein for creating the Test Bank, Paula Buchanan for creating the web quizzes, Brad Cox for developing the PowerPoint Presentations, Deniz Hackner for developing the Pre- and Post-Lecture quizzes, and Sandi Dinger for writing the scripts for the mp3 summaries. We'd also like to thank Lenie Holbrook for his insightful creativity in putting together the *Art Imitates Life* guide.

As always, the support staff at John Wiley & Sons was most helpful in the various stages of developing and producing this edition. We would especially like to thank Kim Mortimer (Acquisitions Editor), Judith Joseph (Associate

Publisher), and Jennifer Conklin (Associate Editor) for their extraordinary efforts in support of this project. They took OB to heart and did their very best to build a high performance team in support of this book. We thank everyone at Wiley for maintaining the quest for quality and timeliness in all aspects of the book's content and design. Special gratitude goes to Maddy Lesure as the creative force behind the new design. We also thank Sandra Dumas, and Ingrao Associates for their excellent production and design assistance, Allie Morris for overseeing the media development, and Amy Scholz for leading the marketing campaign. Thank you everyone!!

Brief Contents

Contents

Organizational Behavior

Tenth Edition

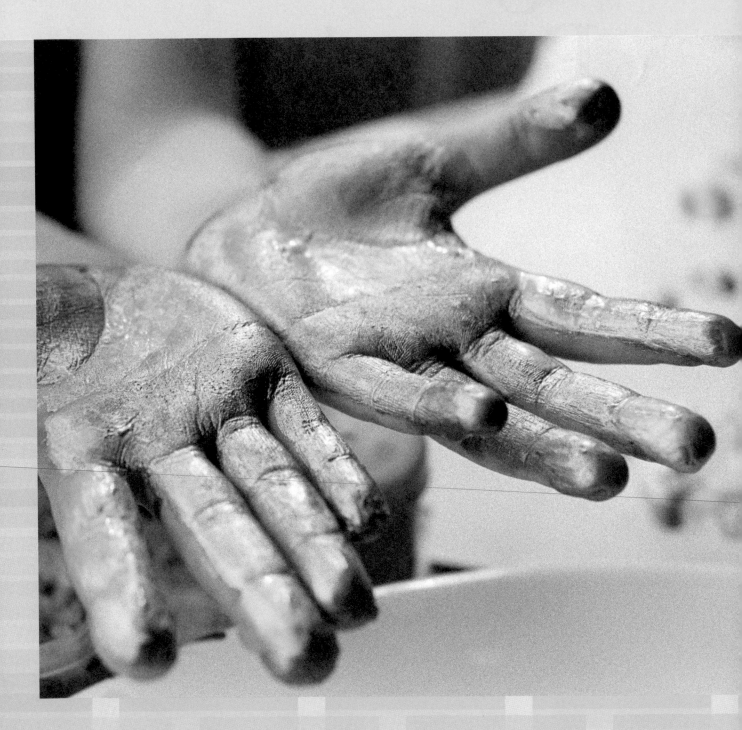

Introducing Organizational Behavior

Chapter at a Glance

People do make the difference in how well our organizations perform. Chapter 1 introduces organizational behavior as a useful knowledge base for career success in today's dynamic work environments. As you read, *keep in mind these study topics.*

INTRODUCING ORGANIZATIONAL BEHAVIOR

- Organizational Behavior
- Scientific Foundations of Organizational Behavior
- Shifting Paradigms of Organizational Behavior

ORGANIZATIONS AS WORK SETTINGS

- Organizational Purpose, Mission, and Strategy
- Organizational Environments and Stakeholders
- Organizational Cultures
- Diversity and Multiculturalism

ORGANIZATIONAL BEHAVIOR AND MANAGEMENT

- The Management Process
- Managerial Activities, Roles, and Networks
- Managerial Skills and Competencies
- Moral Management

LEARNING ABOUT ORGANIZATIONAL BEHAVIOR

- Learning and Experience
- Learning Guide to *Organizational Behavior 10/E*

CHAPTER 1 STUDY GUIDE

People make the difference

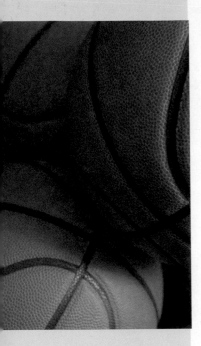

D o you remember the controversy created when the NBA introduced a new basketball? Some called it the ball that just didn't bounce.

You wouldn't think a new basketball would make much of a difference. But this one did. In fact, it set the executives running the National Basketball Association back on their heels. When the NBA introduced a new microfiber ball, they thought its consistent bounce would be the pathway toward better shooting, higher scoring, and improved player statistics. Instead, the new synthetic ball was met with skepticism and even outright scorn by players who preferred the traditional leather ball. LeBron James, Shaquille O'Neal, and Jason Kidd were among those who publicly declared their dislike for the new ball.

The players' union was quick to file a grievance, claiming that the surface of the new ball contributed to increased skin abrasions. The old ball, with its leather construction, was praised as a better alternative, and the NBA was faced with a dilemma—stick with the new ball or revert back to the old one. How did the NBA get in this spot?

The answer rests with this comment by NBA Commissioner David Stern when he announced the return to the leather ball: "We've got to do the right thing here. And, of course the right thing is to listen to our players." And listen he did, but some might say a bit late in the process.

Complaints were that the NBA didn't spend enough time getting player input before making a decision to switch to the new ball. Houston player Rafer Alston said: "They said, 'The ball's here. This is what we're going to use.'. . . There was never a reason or anything." As for Stern, he said: "Whether it's a day late or not, we're dealing with this . . . In hindsight we could have done a better job."[1]

> " . . . we're dealing with this. In hindsight we could have done a better job."

Introducing Organizational Behavior

Stern's lesson in the case of the NBA's attempt to introduce a new basketball is a classic one: when it comes to dealing with people in organizations, it's always better to interact before you act. And when the NBA tinkered with the basketball, it was striking at the core of player performance. As LeBron James said when the smoke cleared and the leather ball was back: "For the league to be successful, obviously the players have to be happy. The basketball is the most important thing to us."[2]

Whether your career unfolds in entrepreneurship, corporate enterprise, public service, or any other occupational setting, it is always worth remembering that people are the basic building blocks of organizational success. Organizations do well when the people in them work hard, individually and collectively, to achieve high performance. Creating success in and by organizations, therefore, requires respect for people, including their needs, talents, and aspirations, and an understanding of the dynamics of human behavior in complex organizational systems.

This book is about people, everyday people like you and like us, who work and pursue careers in today's new and highly demanding settings. It is about people who seek fulfillment in their lives and jobs in a variety of ways and in uncertain times. It is about the challenges of ethics, globalization, technology utilization, diversity, work-life balance, and other issues of the new workplace. And this book is also about how our complex environment requires people and organizations to learn and to continuously develop themselves in the quest for high performance and promising futures.

Organizational Behavior

In this challenging era of work and organizations, the body of knowledge we call "organizational behavior" offers many insights of great value. Called OB for short, **organizational behavior** is the study of human behavior in organizations. It is an academic discipline devoted to understanding individual and group behavior, interpersonal processes, and organizational dynamics with the goal of improving the performance of organizations and the people in them. Learning about OB can help you develop a better work-related understanding about yourself and others; it is a knowledge platform that can expand your potential for career success in the dynamic, shifting, and complex new workplaces of today—and tomorrow.

■ **Organizational behavior** is the study of individuals and groups in organizations.

Scientific Foundations of Organizational Behavior

As far back as a century ago, consultants and scholars were giving increased attention to the systematic study of management. Although the early focus was initially on physical working conditions, principles of administration, and industrial engineering principles, the interest had broadened by the 1940s to include the human factor. This gave impetus to research dealing with individual attitudes, group dynamics, and the relationships between managers and workers. From this foundation the discipline of organizational behavior emerged as a discipline devoted to scientific understanding of individuals and groups in organizations, and of the performance implications of organizational processes, systems, and structures.[3]

Interdisciplinary Body of Knowledge   Organizational behavior is an interdisciplinary body of knowledge with strong ties to the behavioral sciences—psychology, sociology, and anthropology—as well as to allied social sciences such as economics and political science. OB is unique, however, in its goals of integrating the diverse insights of these other disciplines and applying them to real-world problems and opportunities. The ultimate goal of OB is to improve the performance of people, groups, and organizations and to improve the quality of work life overall.

Use of Scientific Methods   The field of organizational behavior uses scientific methods to develop and empirically test generalizations about behavior in organizations. OB scholars often propose and test through scientific methods **models**—simplified views of reality that attempt to identify major factors and forces underlying real-world phenomenon. These models link **independent variables**— presumed causes—with **dependent variables**—outcomes of practical value and interest.

Figure 1.1 describes research methods commonly used. Scientific thinking is important to OB researchers and scholars for these reasons: (1) the process of data collection is controlled and systematic; (2) proposed explanations are carefully

■ **Models** are simplified views of reality that attempt to explain real-world phenomena.

■ **Independent variables** are presumed causes that influence dependent variables.

■ **Dependent variables** are outcomes of practical value and interest.

Figure 1.1   Research methods in organizational behavior.

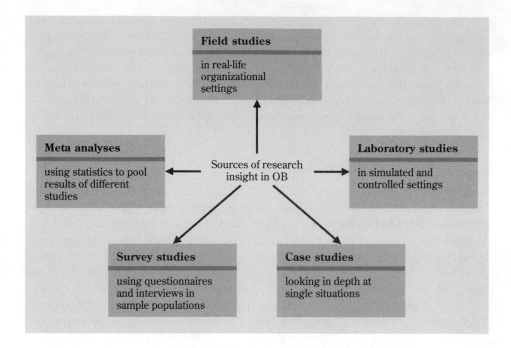

tested; and (3) only explanations that can be scientifically verified are accepted. Research concepts and designs in OB are explained further in the primer on "Research Methods in Organizational Behavior" included after this chapter.

Focus on Application   As already suggested, the science of organizational behavior focuses on applications that can make a real difference in how organizations and people in them perform. For example, in this book you will find models that summarize current understanding about such dependent variables as task performance, job satisfaction, organizational citizenship behavior, ethical behavior, absenteeism, turnover, and organizational effectiveness. The practical questions addressed by the discipline of OB and addressed in this book include these: How should rewards such as merit pay raises be allocated? How can jobs be designed for high performance? What are the ingredients of successful teamwork? How can organizational cultures be changed? Should decisions be made by individual, consultative, or group methods? What is the best way to achieve "win-win" outcomes in a negotiation? Why do people become satisfied and dissatisfied with their work and employers? What influences ethical and socially responsible behavior in and by organizations?

Contingency Thinking   Rather than assuming that there is one "best" or universal answer to questions such as those just posed, OB recognizes that management practices must be tailored to fit the exact nature of each situation. One of the most accepted conclusions of scientific research to date is that there is no one best way to manage people and organizations. Said a bit differently, there are no cookie-cutter solutions that can be universally applied to common organizational problems. An essential responsibility of the science of organizational behavior, in fact, is to create and test models that offer evidence-based foundations for decision making and action.[4]

One of the ways evidence-based thinking manifests itself in OB is through a **contingency approach**, in which researchers identify how different situations can best be understood and handled. For example, in a time of increasing globalization, we need to better understand the influence of cultural differences on how OB theories and concepts apply in different countries.[5] Although it is relatively easy to conclude that what works well in one culture may not work as well in another, it is far harder to specify exactly how cultural differences affect things like motivation, job satisfaction, and ethical behavior. Yet, this is exactly the type of understanding that the contingency approach in organizational behavior seeks to accomplish. Many important contingencies in organizational behavior are considered in this book.

■ The **contingency approach** seeks ways to meet the needs of different management situations.

Shifting Paradigms of Organizational Behavior

Contingencies are especially relevant in the complex workplaces of today, ones that look and act very differently from those of the past. Organizations are displaying new features, they approach work processes in new ways, they face dynamic and changing environments, and they serve customer and client markets with different tastes, values, and needs. Things have been especially dramatic in both the nature and pace of change. One consultant has called it a "revolution that feels something like this: scary, guilty, painful, liberating, disorienting, exhilarating, empowering, frustrating, fulfilling, confusing, and challenging. In other words, it feels very much like chaos."[6]

This sense of revolution derives from many forces. Among them we have to recognize shifting paradigms and the need to make good choices in a context that includes these trends:[7]

- *Commitment to ethical behavior:* Highly publicized scandals involving unethical and illegal business practices prompt concerns for ethical behavior in the workplace; there is growing intolerance for breaches of public faith by organizations and those who run them.
- *Importance of human capital:* A dynamic and complex environment poses continuous challenges; sustained success is earned through knowledge, experience, and commitments of people as valuable human assets of organizations.
- *Demise of command-and-control:* Traditional hierarchical structures are proving incapable of handling new environmental pressures and demands; they are being replaced by flexible structures and participatory work settings that fully value human capital.
- *Emphasis on teamwork:* Organizations today are less vertical and more horizontal in focus; driven by complex environments and customer demands, work is increasingly team based with a focus on peer contributions.
- *Pervasive influence of information technology:* As computers penetrate all aspects of the workplace, implications for workflows, work arrangements, and organizational systems and processes are far-reaching.
- *Respect for new workforce expectations:* The new generation of workers is less tolerant of hierarchy, more informal, and less concerned about status; organizations are paying more attention to helping members balance work responsibilities and personal affairs.
- *Changing careers:* The new realities of a global economy find employers using more "offshoring" and "outsourcing" of jobs; more individuals are now working as independent contractors rather than as traditional full-time employees.

Human Rights Campaign

If you go to the Web site for the Human Rights Campaign, you might find article leads like these: *Leading the Fight Against Hate and Violence . . . Have You Experienced Discrimination . . . Equally Speaking.* This civil rights organization's mission is: "working to achieve gay, lesbian, bisexual and transgender equality." The nonprofit scores employers on their records in offering domestic partner benefits, enacting nondiscrimination policies, and supporting GLBT issues.

MASTERING MANAGEMENT

GOOGLE'S TEN GOLDEN RULES

Google isn't the only organization whose success rises and falls with how well it manages knowledge workers. But it is consistently good at it. Here are Google's tips for becoming a better manager of knowledge workers. Can you think of anything else to add?

1. Hire by committee—make sure recruits talk to their future colleagues.
2. Cater to their every need—make it easy, not hard, for them to perform.
3. Pack them in—put people to work close to one another.
4. Make coordination easy—use technology to keep people talking together.
5. Eat your own dog food—make use of company products.
6. Encourage creativity—allow freedom to come up with new ideas.
7. Strive for consensus—remember: "many are better than the few."
8. Don't be evil—live tolerance and respect.
9. Data drive decisions—do the analysis and stay on track.
10. Communicate effectively—hold many stay-in-touch meetings.[8]

Organizations as Work Settings

In order to understand this complex field of forces, we need to begin with the nature of "organizations" as social phenomena. Simply stated, an **organization** is a collection of people working together in a division of labor to achieve a common purpose. This definition describes everything from clubs, voluntary organizations, and religious bodies to entities such as small and large businesses, labor unions, schools, hospitals, and government agencies. All such organizations share certain common features that can help us better understand and deal with them.

Organizations are collections of people working together to achieve a common purpose.

Organizational Purpose, Mission, and Strategy

The core *purpose* of an organization may be stated as the creation of goods or services for customers. Nonprofit organizations produce services with public benefits, such as health care, education, judicial processing, and highway maintenance. Large and small for-profit businesses produce consumer goods and services such as automobiles, banking, travel, gourmet dining, and accommodations. Yet, as we all know, just how such purposes are pursued by organizations of the same type can vary widely from one to the other. One way these differences are reflected is in the sense of "mission."

As Robert Reich states in his description of the company of the future: "Talented people want to be part of something that they can believe in, something that confers meaning on their work, on their lives—something that involves a mission."[9] *Mission statements* are written statements that describe and help focus the attention of organizational members and external constituents on the core purpose.[10] Ideally, they should communicate to employees, customers, and other audiences a sense of uniqueness for an organization and its products and services. And they should provide a vision and sense of future aspiration.[11] The pharmaceutical giant Merck states that its mission is to "discover, develop, manufacture

Leaders on Leadership

HARD WORK LEADS DEBORAH L. LEE TO THE TOP

It was hard work and a long road that eventually led Deborah Lee to the top job as Chairman and CEO of Black Entertainment Television (BET). Now Lee is not

only heading up the firm for which she was past first general counsel, but she's also center stage as an executive in the competitive cable industry. Lee says that BET seeks to grow from its base of 83 million homes. She wants the network to maintain its core audience while also expanding its non-black viewers—currently running about 30 percent and becoming more global. In leading the firm toward more growth, she says that "it's not about change as much as evolution."

Lee was hand picked for the top job by BET founder and past CEO, Robert L. Johnson. She comes in with years of experience with the firm. Yet, she is also ready to make her own mark by building on past successes with her own ideas. And about being at the top, she adds: ". . . to be able to be the final decision maker and put together a great team, which I have, and watch this network grow even more, which it is doing, is enormously satisfying."[12]

What are the challenges of assuming a leadership position previously held by someone who was highly successful in the role, and, as in Lee's case, perhaps even the founder of the organization?

and market a broad range of innovative products to improve human and animal health." The Maytag Corporation's mission is "to improve the quality of home life by designing, building, marketing and servicing the best appliances in the world." Apple Computer Inc. says that its mission is "bringing the best possible personal computing experience to students, educators, creative professionals, businesses and consumers around the world."[13]

Given a sense of purpose and mission, organizations pursue *strategies* to accomplish them. A **strategy** is a comprehensive plan that guides an organization to operate in ways that allow it to outperform competitors. The variety of mergers, acquisitions, joint ventures, global alliances, and even restructurings and divestitures found in business today are examples of corporate strategies to achieve and sustain advantage in highly competitive environments.[14]

Although organizations need good strategies, strategy alone is no guarantee of success. Sustainable high performance is achieved only when strategies are well implemented. And it is in respect to implementation that understanding organizational behavior becomes especially important. After all, things happen in organizations because people working individually and in groups make them happen; as the chapter subtitle indicates, people make the difference. Armed with an understanding of the dynamics of behavior in organizations provided by OB, managers are well prepared to mobilize and activate human capital and talents to best implement strategies to fulfill the organization's mission and purpose.

Strategy guides organizations to operate in ways that outperform competitors.

Organizational Environments and Stakeholders

The concept of strategy places great significance on the relationship between an organization and its external environment. As shown in Figure 1.2, organizations are dynamic **open systems** that obtain resource inputs from the environment and transform them into finished goods or services that are returned to the environment as outputs.

If everything works right from an open systems perspective, customers and clients in the environment value the organization's outputs and create a continuing demand for them; suppliers value the organization as their customer and continue to provide needed resources; employees value their work opportunities and continue to infuse the transformation processes with their energies and intellects. All of this allows the organization to sustain operations and, hopefully, prosper over the long run. But if and when any aspect of this value chain breaks down, an organization's performance can suffer, and its livelihood may become threatened. In the extreme case the organization can even be forced out of existence.

One way to describe and analyze the complex environment of organizations is in terms of **stakeholders**—people, groups, and institutions that are affected by and thus have an interest or "stake" in an organization's performance. It is common in OB to recognize customers, owners, employees, suppliers, regulators, and local communities among the key stakeholders of organizations. Although an organization should operate in ways that best serve the interests of all stakeholders, the reality is that conflicting interests among multiple stakeholders often create challenges for organizational decision makers. For example, customers increasingly want value pricing and high-quality products; owners are concerned about profits and returns on investments; employees are concerned about jobs, security, and employment conditions; suppliers are interested in contracts and on-time payments; regulators are interested in legal compliance; and local communities are concerned about organizational citizenship and community support.

Open systems transform human and material resource inputs into finished goods and services.

Stakeholders are people and groups with an interest or "stake" in the performance of the organization.

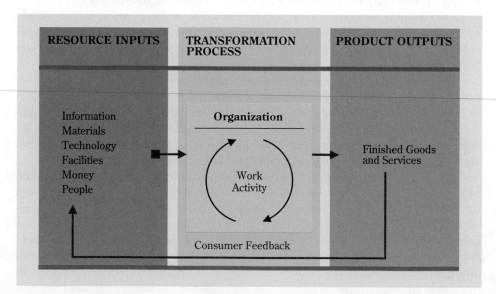

Figure 1.2   Organizations as open systems.

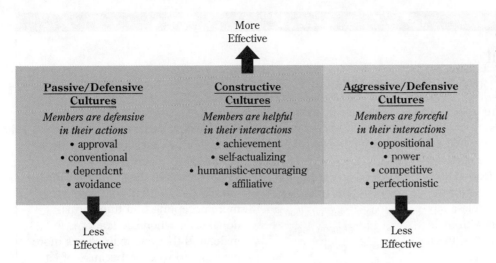

Figure 1.3 Insights on organizational cultures. *Source:* Developed with permission from "The Organizational Culture Inventory," published by Human Synergistics International (Plymouth, Michigan).

Organizational Cultures

In the internal environment of organizations, the shared beliefs and values that influence the behavior of organizational members create what is called the **organizational culture**.[15] Organizations with "strong cultures" operate with a clear vision of the future that is supported by well-developed and well-communicated beliefs and values. The internal environments of organizations with strong and positive cultures often include a high-performance orientation, emphasis on teamwork, encouragement of risk taking, and emphasis on innovation.[16]

Figure 1.3 shows an approach for mapping organizational cultures developed by Human Synergistics.[17] Using an instrument called the Organizational Culture Inventory, or OCI, people describe the behaviors and expectations that make up the prevailing cultures of their organizations.[18] The OCI maps use these results to describe three alternative types of organizational cultures. In a *constructive culture,* members are encouraged to work together in ways that meet higher order human needs. In a *passive/defensive culture,* members tend to act defensively in their working relationships, seeking to protect their security. In an *aggressive/ defensive culture,* members tend to act forcefully in their working relationships to protect their status and positions.

Among these three types of organizational cultures, the constructive culture would be most associated with high-performance organizations. In constructive cultures, researchers find that people tend to work with greater motivation, satisfaction, teamwork, and performance. In passive/defensive and aggressive/defensive cultures, motivation tends to be lower and work attitudes less positive.[19] The expectation is that people prefer constructive cultures and behave within them in ways that fully tap the value of human capital, promoting both high-performance results and personal satisfaction.

Diversity and Multiculturalism

Within the internal environments of organizations, **workforce diversity** describes the presence of individual differences based on gender, race and ethnicity, age, able-bodiedness, and sexual orientation.[20] As used in OB, the term **multiculturalism** refers to pluralism, and to respect for diversity and individual differences.[21]

Organizational culture is a shared set of beliefs and values within an organization.

Workforce diversity describes how people differ in age, race, ethnicity, gender, physical ability, and sexual orientation.

Multiculturalism refers to pluralism and respect for diversity in the workplace.

Research Insight
Women Might Make Better Leaders

No one doubts there are good and bad leaders of both genders. But research by Alice Eagley and her colleagues at Northwestern University suggests that women may be more likely than men to use leadership styles that result in high performance by followers. In a meta-analysis of 45 studies dealing with male and female leadership styles, the researchers found that women are more likely than men to lead by inspiring, exciting, mentoring, and stimulating creativity. These behaviors have "transformational" qualities that build stronger organizations through innovation and teamwork. Women also score higher on rewarding positive performance, while men score higher in punishing and correcting mistakes. Eagley and her colleagues explain these findings in part by the fact that followers are more accepting of a transformational style when the leader is female, and that the style comes more naturally to women because of its emphasis on nurturing. They also suggest that because women may have to work harder than men to succeed, their leadership skills are better developed.[21A]

POSSIBLE LEADERSHIP STRENGTHS OF WOMEN
- More "transformational"
- Good at mentoring
- Very inspiring
- Encourage creativity
- Show excitement about goals
- Reward positive performa

And in this respect, consultant R. Roosevelt Thomas makes the point that when it comes to people and their diversity, positive organizational cultures tap the talents, ideas, and creative potential of all members.[22]

The demographic trends driving workforce diversity in American society are well recognized.[23] There are more women working than ever before in our history, with women taking a bit more than half of new jobs being created.[24] The proportion of African-Americans, Hispanics, and Asians in the labor force is increasing. By the year 2060, people of color will constitute the majority of the U.S. population, and close to 30 percent of the population will be Hispanic.[25]

But trends alone are no guarantee that diversity will be fully valued, respected, and used in the sense of multiculturalism as described by Thomas and others.[26] A key element in any organization that embraces multiculturalism is **inclusivity**—the degree to which the culture respects and values diversity and is open to anyone who can perform a job, regardless of their diversity attributes.[27] *Valuing diversity* is a core OB theme that is central to this book and the new workplace.[28] Yet, valuing diversity in practice still must be considered a work in progress. For example, the latest data show women earning only about 73 cents per dollar earned by men, and holding only 11 CEO jobs and 6.7% of top-paying jobs at *Fortune* 500 companies. They also show women of color holding only 1.7% of corporate officer positions and 1% of top-paying jobs in the *Fortune* 500.[29]

Inclusivity is the degree to which an organization's culture respects and values diversity.

Organizational Behavior and Management

Regardless of your career direction, the field of organizational behavior will some day become especially important as you try to master the special challenges of working as a **manager**, someone whose job it is to directly support the work efforts of others. An **effective manager** is one whose organizational unit, group, or team consistently achieves its goals while members remain capable, committed, and enthusiastic. This definition focuses attention on two key outcomes: **task performance**—the quality and quantity of the work produced or the services provided by the work unit as a whole; and **job satisfaction**—how people feel about their work and the work setting. OB is quite clear in that managers should be held accountable for both results. Just as a valuable machine should not be allowed to break down for lack of proper maintenance, the performance potential of human resources should never be lost or compromised for lack of proper care.

■ **Managers** are responsible for supporting the work efforts of other people.

■ An **effective manager** is one who helps others achieve high levels of both performance and satisfaction.

■ **Task performance** is the quantity and quality of work produced.

■ **Job satisfaction** is a positive feeling about one's work and work setting.

The Management Process

Being a manager is a unique challenge that carries distinct performance responsibilities that link closely with the field of organizational behavior. Managers help other people get important things done in timely, high-quality, and personally satisfying ways. In the new workplaces of today this is accomplished more through "helping" and "supporting" than through traditional notions of "directing" and "controlling." Indeed, the word "manager" is increasingly being described by such terms as "coordinator," "coach," or "team leader."

Among the ways that managerial work has been described and taught is through the four functions shown in Figure 1.4: planning, organizing, leading, and

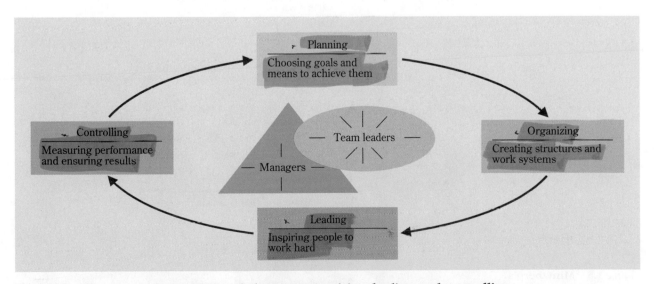

Figure 1.4 The management process of planning, organizing, leading, and controlling.

controlling. They form a framework for managerial action that involves these actions and responsiblities:[30]

■ **Planning** sets objectives and identifies the actions needed to achieve them.

- **Planning**—defining goals, setting specific performance objectives, and identifying the actions needed to achieve them
- **Organizing**—creating work structures and systems, and arranging resources to accomplish goals and objectives

■ **Organizing** divides up tasks and arranges resources to accomplish them.

- **Leading**—instilling enthusiasm by communicating with others, motivating them to work hard, and maintaining good interpersonal relations

■ **Leading** creates enthusiasm to work hard to accomplish tasks successfully.

- **Controlling**—ensuring that things go well by monitoring performance and taking corrective action as necessary

■ **Controlling** monitors performance and takes any needed corrective action.

Managerial Activities, Roles, and Networks

Anyone serving as a manager or team leader faces a very demanding and complicated job that has been described by researchers in the following terms.[31] Managers work long hours. A workweek of more than the standard 40 hours is typical. The length of the workweek increases at higher managerial levels, and heads of organizations often work the longest hours. Managers are busy people. Their work is intense and involves doing many different things on any given workday.

The busy day of a manager includes a shifting mix of incidents that demand immediate attention, with the number of incidents being greatest for lower-level managers. Managers are often interrupted. Their work is fragmented and variable; many tasks must be completed quickly; managers work mostly with other people, and often spend little time working alone. Managers are communicators and spend a lot of time getting, giving, and processing information in face-to-face and electronic exchanges, and in formal and informal meetings.

In what has become a classic study of managerial behavior, Henry Mintzberg described how these activities are enacted in a set of 10 managerial roles, falling into the three categories shown in Figure 1.5.[32] A manager's *interpersonal roles* involve working directly with other people, hosting and attending official cere-

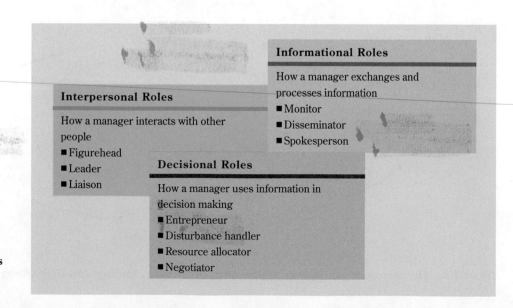

Figure 1.5   Mintzberg's ten roles of effective managers.

Informational Roles

How a manager exchanges and processes information
- Monitor
- Disseminator
- Spokesperson

Interpersonal Roles

How a manager interacts with other people
- Figurehead
- Leader
- Liaison

Decisional Roles

How a manager uses information in decision making
- Entrepreneur
- Disturbance handler
- Resource allocator
- Negotiator

monies (figurehead), creating enthusiasm and serving people's needs (leader), and maintaining contacts with important people and groups (liaison). The *informational roles* involve managers exchanging information with other people, seeking relevant information (monitor), sharing it with insiders (disseminator), and sharing it with outsiders (spokesperson). A manager's *decisional roles* involve making decisions that affect other people, seeking problems to solve and opportunities to explore (entrepreneur), helping to resolve conflicts (disturbance handler), allocating resources to various uses (resource allocator), and negotiating with other parties (negotiator).

Good interpersonal relationships are essential to managerial success in all these roles. Managers and team leaders should be able to develop, maintain, and work well in networks involving a wide variety of people, both inside and outside the organization.[33] These include task networks (of specific job-related contacts), career networks (of career guidance and opportunity resources), and social networks (of trustworthy friends and peers).[34]

Managerial Skills and Competencies

A skill is an ability to translate knowledge into action that results in a desired performance. Robert Katz divides the essential managerial skills into three categories: technical, human, and conceptual.[35] He further suggests that the relative importance of these skills varies across the different levels of management. Technical skills are considered more important at entry levels of management, where supervisors and team leaders must deal with job-specific problems. Senior executives are concerned more with issues of organizational purpose, mission, and strategy. They deal with broader, more ambiguous, and longer-term decisions that require conceptual skills to increase in importance. Human skills, which are strongly grounded in the foundations of organizational behavior, are consistently important across all managerial levels.

Technical Skills A **technical skill** is an ability to perform specialized tasks. Such ability derives from knowledge or expertise gained from education or experience. This skill involves proficiency at using select methods, processes, and procedures to accomplish tasks. Perhaps the best current example is skill in using the latest communication and information technologies. In the high-tech workplaces of today, technical proficiency in word processing, database management, spreadsheet analysis, e-mail, and communication networks is often a hiring prerequisite. Some technical skills require preparatory education, whereas others are acquired through specific training and on-the-job experience.

Human Skills Central to managerial work and team leadership are **human skills**, or the ability to work well with other people. They emerge as a spirit of trust, enthusiasm, and genuine involvement in interpersonal relationships. A person with good human skills will have a high degree of self-awareness and a capacity for understanding or empathizing with the feelings of others. People with this skill are able to interact well with others, engage in persuasive communications, deal successfully with disagreements and conflicts, and more.

An important new emphasis in this area of human skills is **emotional intelligence** (EI), defined by Daniel Goleman as the ability to understand and deal with emotions. EI, with its emphasis on managing emotions both personally and

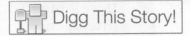
■ **Technical skill** is an ability to perform specialized tasks.

■ **Human skill** is the ability to work well with other people.

■ **Emotional intelligence** is the ability to manage oneself and one's relationships effectively.

OB SAVVY 1.1

Developing Your Emotional Intelligence

- Self-awareness—ability to understand your own moods and emotions
- Self-regulation—ability to think before acting and to control disruptive impulses
- Motivation—ability to work hard and persevere
- Empathy—ability to understand the emotions of others
- Social skill—ability to gain rapport with others and build good relationships

in relationships with others, is now considered an important leadership competency.[36] Goleman's research suggests that a leader's emotional intelligence contributes significantly to his or her leadership effectiveness. Important dimensions of emotional intelligence that can and should be developed by any manager are shown in OB Savvy 1.1. Human skills such as EI are indispensable in the new age of organizations, where traditions of hierarchy and vertical structures are giving way to lateral relations and peer structures.

Conceptual Skills   Managers should be able to view the organization or situation as a whole so that problems are always solved for the benefit of everyone concerned. This capacity to analyze and solve complex and interrelated problems is a **conceptual skill**. It involves the ability to see and understand how the whole organizational system works and how the parts are interrelated. Conceptual skill is used to identify problems and opportunities, gather and interpret relevant information, and make good problem-solving decisions that serve the organization's purpose.

◼◼ Conceptual skill is the ability to analyze and solve complex problems.

Moral Management

Having the essential managerial skills is one thing; using them correctly to get things done in organizations is quite another. And when it comes to ethics and morality, scholar Archie B. Carroll draws a distinction between immoral managers, amoral managers, and moral managers.[37]

The *immoral manager* doesn't subscribe to any ethical principles, making decisions and acting in any situation to simply take best personal advantage. This manager essentially chooses to behave unethically. One might describe the disgraced executives behind various headlines in these terms. The *amoral manager*, by contrast, fails to consider the ethics of a decision or behavior. This manager acts unethically at times but does so unintentionally. Common forms of unintentional ethics lapses that we all must guard against include prejudice that derives from unconscious stereotypes and attitudes, showing bias based on in-group favoritism, claiming too much personal credit for one's performance contributions, and favoring those who can benefit you.[38] Finally, the *moral manager* is one who incorporates ethics principles and goals into his or her personal behavior. For this manager, ethical behavior is a goal, a standard, and even a matter of routine.

Think about this. Carroll believes that the majority of managers tend to act amorally, being well intentioned but often failing to take ethical considerations into account when taking action and making decisions. A review article by Terry Thomas and his colleagues suggests that this pattern most likely applies to the general membership of organizations.[39] They describe the "ethics center of gravity" shown in Figure 1.6 as one that can be moved positively through moral leadership—a "virtuous" shift—or negatively through amoral leadership. The authors also present the concept of **ethics mindfulness** as

◼◼ Ethics mindfulness is an enriched awareness that causes one to consistently behave with ethical consciousness.

OPRAH BUILDS LEADERSHIP ACADEMY FOR SOUTH AFRICA'S YOUNG WOMEN

What does the richest woman in entertainment have to do with organizational behavior? A lot if you're Oprah Winfrey, with a net worth $1.5 billion and counting, when you donate $40 million to establish a leadership academy for young women in South Africa. Upon attending the launch ceremony of the Oprah Winfrey Leadership Academy, Winfrey said: "I wanted to give this opportunity to girls who had a light so bright that not even poverty could dim that light." Girls are selected competitively; they must show both academic excellence and leadership potential, as well as come from households with incomes under $787 per month. About Winfrey's commitment, Nelson Mandela, first president of non-apartheid South Africa said: "The key to any country's future is in educating its youth. Oprah is therefore not only investing in a few young individuals, but in the future of our country." As for Winfrey, her intention is to build yet another school for both young men and young women. She believes that through education "one can change the face of a nation."[40]

Oprah Winfrey's philanthropy and goals are noble, but how can organizations and their members contribute in everyday ways in order to join with her in changing the world through education and leadership development?

an "enriched awareness" that causes one to behave with an ethical consciousness from one decision or behavioral event to another. They describe a leader's responsibilities for communicating ethics values that help build organizational cultures within which ethics mindfulness is the norm. In this view, a moral manager or moral leader always acts as an ethical role model, communicates ethics values and messages, and champions ethics mindfulness. This results in the "virtuous shift" shown in the figure and in organizational culture within which people act ethically as a matter of routine.

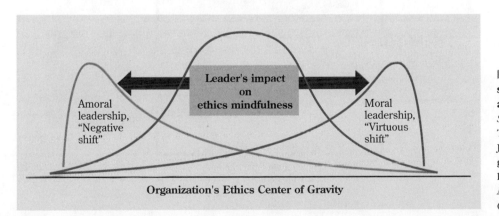

Figure 1.6 Moral leadership, ethics mindfulness, and the virtuous shift.
Source: Developed from Terry Thomas, John R. Schermerhorn Jr., and John W. Dinehart, "Strategic Leadership of Ethical Behavior in Business," *Academy of Management Executive*, 18 (May 2004), pp. 56–66.

Learning about Organizational Behavior

Learning is an enduring change in behavior that results from experience.

Lifelong learning is continuous learning from everyday experiences.

Organizational learning is the process of acquiring knowledge and using information to adapt successfully to changing circumstances.

Learning can be defined as an enduring change of behavior that results from experience. Our new and rapidly developing knowledge-based economy places a great premium on learning by organizations as well as individuals. Only the learners, so to speak, will be able to maintain the pace and succeed in a constantly changing environment. At the individual level, the concept of **lifelong learning** is important. It involves learning continuously from day-to-day work experiences; conversations with colleagues and friends; counseling and advice provided by mentors, success models, training seminars, and workshops; and other daily opportunities. At the organizational level, consultants and scholars emphasize **organizational learning** as the process of acquiring knowledge and using information to adapt successfully to changing circumstances.[41] Just like individuals, organizations must be able to change continuously and positively while searching for new ideas and opportunities.

Learning and Experience

Figure 1.7 shows how the content and activities of the typical OB course can fit together in an experiential learning cycle.[42] The learning sequence begins with initial experience and subsequent reflection. It grows as theory building takes place to try to explain what has happened. Theory is then tested through future behavior. Books and course activities should complement one another and help you move through the phases of the learning cycle. With practice, you can make the cycle part of your commitment to continued personal and career development.

Notice that the figure assigns to you a substantial responsibility for learning. Along with your instructor, we can offer examples, cases, and exercises to provide you with initial experience. We can even stimulate your reflection and theory building by presenting concepts and discussing their research and practical

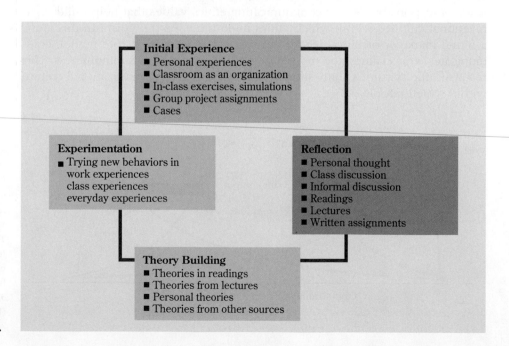

Figure 1.7   Experiential learning in an OB course.

implications. Sooner or later, however, you must become an active participant in the process; you and only you can do the active experimentation required to complete the learning cycle.

Learning Guide to *Organizational Behavior 10/E*

The chapters in *Organizational Behavior 10/E* are presented in building-block fashion. *Part 1* introduces the discipline and context of OB, including its research methods. *Part 2* focuses on individual behavior and performance, while *Part 3* addresses group behavior and teamwork. *Part 4* covers leadership and the processes of OB, including power and politics, decision making, communication, conflict, and negotiation. *Part 5* examines the organizational context in respect to cultures, structures, designs, strategic choices, and change. Finally, the *OB Skills Workbook* provides many active learning opportunities to analyze readings and cases, engage in experiential exercises, and complete skills-assessment inventories to advance your learning. As you move forward with *OB 10/E* and with your study of organizational behavior, remember that

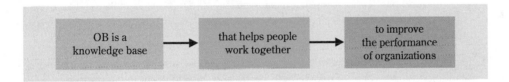

OB is a knowledge base → that helps people work together → to improve the performance of organizations

Chapter 1   Study Guide

What is organizational behavior and why is it important?

- Organizational behavior is the study of individuals and groups in organizations. OB is an applied discipline based on scientific methods and on using a contingency approach, recognizing that management practices must fit the situation.

- Shifting paradigms of OB derive from forces representing a commitment to ethical behavior, importance of human capital, emphasis on teams, influence of information technology, new workforce expectations, and changing careers.

What are organizations like as work settings?

- An organization is a collection of people working together in a division of labor for a common purpose—to produce goods or services for society.

- As open systems, organizations interact with their environments to obtain resources that are transformed into outputs returned to the environment for consumption.

Summary

- Organizations pursue strategies that facilitate the accomplishment of purpose and mission; the field of OB is an important foundation for effective strategy implementation.

- Key stakeholders in the external environments of organizations include customers, owners, suppliers, regulators, local communities, and employees.

- The organizational culture is the internal "personality" of the organization, including the beliefs and values that are shared by members.

- Positive organizational cultures place a high value on workforce diversity and multiculturalism, emphasizing respect and inclusiveness of all members.

What is the nature of managerial work?

- Managers in the new workplace are expected to act more like "coaches" and "facilitators" than as "bosses" and "controllers."

- An effective manager is one whose work unit, team, or group accomplishes high levels of performance that are sustainable over the long term by enthusiastic workers.

- The four functions of management are planning—to set directions; organizing—to assemble resources and systems; leading—to create workforce enthusiasm; and controlling—to ensure desired results.

- Managers fulfill a variety of interpersonal, informational, and decisional roles while working with networks of people both inside and outside of the organization.

- Managerial performance is based on a combination of essential technical, human, and conceptual skills.

How do we learn about organizational behavior?

- Learning is an enduring change in behavior that results from experience.

- True learning about organizational behavior involves a commitment to continuous lifelong learning from one's work and everyday experiences.

- Organizational learning is the process of acquiring knowledge and utilizing information to adapt successfully to changing circumstances.

- Most organizational behavior courses use multiple methods and approaches that take advantage of the experiential learning cycle.

Key Terms

Conceptual skill (p. 16)
Contingency approach (p. 7)
Controlling (p. 14)
Dependent variables (p. 5)
Effective manager (p. 13)
Emotional intelligence (p. 15)
Ethics mindfulness (p. 16)
Human skill (p. 15)
Inclusivity (p. 12)
Independent variables (p. 5)

Job satisfaction (p. 13)
Leading (p. 14)
Learning (p. 18)
Lifelong learning (p. 18)
Managers (p. 13)
Models (p. 5)
Multiculturalism (p. 11)
Open system (p. 10)
Organizational behavior (p. 5)
Organizational culture (p. 11)

Organizational learning (p. 18)
Organizations (p. 8)
Organizing (p. 14)
Planning (p. 14)
Stakeholders (p. 10)
Strategy (p. 9)
Task performance (p. 13)
Technical skill (p. 15)
Workforce diversity (p. 11)

Multiple Choice

1. Which of the following issues is most central to the field of organizational behavior? (a) ways to improve advertising for a new product (b) ways to increase job satisfaction and performance among employees (c) creation of new strategy for organizational growth (d) design of a new management information system.

2. What is the best description of the setting facing organizational behavior today? (a) Command-and-control is in. (b) The new generation expects much the same as the old. (c) Empowerment is out. (d) Work–life balance concerns are in.

3. The term "workforce diversity" refers to differences in race, age, gender, ethnicity, and _____ among people at work. (a) social status (b) personal wealth (c) able-bodiedness (d) political preference.

4. Which statement about OB is most correct? (a) OB seeks "one-best-way" solutions to management problems. (b) OB is a unique science that has little relationship to other scientific disciplines. (c) OB is focused on using knowledge for practical applications. (d) OB is so modern that it has no historical roots.

5. In the open-systems view of organizations, such things as technology, information, and money are considered _____. (a) transformation elements (b) feedback (c) inputs (d) outputs

6. In strategic management, the discipline of organizational behavior is most essential in terms of _____. (a) developing strategies (b) clarifying mission statements (c) implementing strategies (d) identifying organizational purpose

7. According to the Organizational Culture Inventory (OCI), an organization in which members are encouraged to work together in ways that meet higher order human needs is classified as having a _____ culture. (a) constructive (b) motivational (c) passive (d) high achievement

8. Which word best describes an organizational culture that embraces multiculturalism and in which workforce diversity is highly valued? (a) inclusivity (b) effectiveness (c) dynamism (d) predictability

9. The management function of _____ is concerned with creating enthusiasm for hard work among organizational members. (a) planning (b) motivating (c) controlling (d) leading

10. In the management process, _____ is concerned with measuring performance results and taking action to improve future performance. (a) disciplining (b) organizing (c) leading (d) controlling

11. Among Mintzberg's ten managerial roles, acting as a figurehead and liaison are examples of _____ roles. (a) interpersonal (b) informational (c) decisional (d) conceptual

12. According to current views of managerial work, it is highly unlikely that an effective manager will _____. (a) engage in extensive networking (b) have good interpersonal skills (c) spend a lot of time working alone (d) be good at solving problems

13. When a manager moves upward in responsibility, Katz suggests that _____ skills decrease in importance and the _____ skills increase in importance. (a) human, conceptual (b) conceptual, emotional (c) technical, conceptual (d) emotional, human

14. A person with high emotional intelligence would be strong in _____, the ability to think before acting and control disruptive impulses. (a) motivation (b) perseverance (c) self-regulation (d) empathy

15. Which statement about learning is *not* correct? (a) Learning is a change in behavior that results from experience. (b) People learn; organizations do not. (c) Experiential learning is common in OB courses. (d) Lifelong learning is an important personal responsibility for career development.

Short Response

16. What are the key characteristics of OB as a scientific discipline?
17. What does "valuing diversity" mean in the workplace?
18. What is an effective manager?
19. How would Henry Mintzberg describe a typical executive's workday?

Applications Essay

20. Carla, a college junior, is participating in a special "elementary education outreach" project in her local community. Along with other students from the business school, she is going to spend the day with fourth- and fifth-grade students and introduce them to the opportunities of going to college. One of her tasks is to lead a class discussion of the question: "How is the world of work changing today?" Help Carla out by creating an outline for her of the major points that she should try to develop with the students.

These learning activities from *The OB Skills Workbook* are suggested for Chapter 1.

OB in Action

CASE	EXPERIENTIAL EXERCISES	SELF-ASSESSMENT
■ 1. Panera Bread Company	■ 1. My Best Manager ■ 2. Graffiti Needs ■ 3. My Best Job	■ 1. Managerial Assumptions ■ 2. A Twenty-First-Century Manager

Plus—special learning experiences from *The Jossey-Bass/Pfeiffer Classroom Collection*

Primer   Research Foundations of Organizational Behavior

Organizational behavior, or "OB" as we call it, is an applied social science that combines basic theory and practical applications. Because the discipline deals with people in organizations, you will find many sources that provide commentary and advice on OB-related issues. Some are based on solid scientific methods and concepts, while others are speculative. You may find it difficult to decide what to believe and what to dismiss. In order to make good decisions about OB insights and applications you must understand the elements of good theory and be able to ask good questions.

Theory in OB

In a very broad sense, a theory is simply a story of what to look for, how the things you are looking at are related, and why the pieces do or do not fit together into some meaningful tale. The purpose of a theory is to explain and predict. The better the theory, the better the explanation and prediction. More formally stated, a **theory** is a set of systematically interrelated concepts and hypotheses that are advanced to explain and predict phenomena.[1]

In OB some scholars also incorporate an applications aspect. That is, a good theory also can be applied with confidence. John Miner is one of those who has outlined some bases for judging theory in OB.[2] These include:

- A **theory** is a set of systematically interrelated concepts, definitions, and hypotheses that are advanced to explain and predict phenomena.

1. It should aid in understanding, permit prediction, and facilitate influence.
2. There should be clear boundaries for application.
3. It should direct efforts toward important, high-priority items.
4. It should produce generalizable results beyond a single setting.
5. It should be tested using clearly defined concepts and operational measures.
6. It should be both internally consistent and consistent with studies derived from it.
7. It should be stated in understandable terms.

Now that is a very tall order for any theory, and we know of no theory in OB that passes muster on all accounts. Clearly some are better than others. Some theories are pretty good at explanation but lousy at prediction, while others do a reasonable job of prediction but do not facilitate influence. For example, if circumstances are highly similar, predicting an individual will repeat a behavior is a sound bet. Unfortunately, this prediction is rarely supported by a theory explaining why the individual acted in a given manner in the first place. As a manager, even if you know that an individual will repeat a behavior, you also need to know how to change it. And so it goes.

The bottom line is that theory and research go together. The theory tells one what to look for, and the research tells what was found. What was found also tells us what to look for again. It is important to realize that we may not see what we do not conceptualize. But it is equally important to note that for an acceptable theory, others must understand, see, and verify what we see and understand. Among OB researchers this process of seeing, understanding, and verifying is generally accomplished through the scientific method.

Scientific Method

A key part of OB research foundations is the **scientific method**, which involves four steps. First, a *research question* or *problem* is specified. Then one or more *hypotheses* or explanations of what the research parties expect to find are formulated. These may come from many sources, including previous experience and careful review of the literature covering the problem area. The next step is the creation of a *research design*—an overall plan or strategy for conducting the research to test the hypothesis(es). Finally, *data gathering, analysis*, and *interpretation* are carried out.[3]

The Vocabulary of Research

The previous discussion conveyed a quick summary of the scientific method. It's important to go beyond that summation and further develop a number of aspects of the scientific method. Before doing that, we consider the vocabulary of research. Knowing that vocabulary can help you feel comfortable with several terms used in OB research as well as help in our later discussion.[4]

Variable   A **variable** is a measure used to describe a real-world phenomenon. For example, a researcher may count the number of parts produced by workers in a week's time as a measure of the workers' individual productivity.

Hypothesis   Building on our earlier use of the term, we can define a **hypothesis** as a tentative explanation about the relationship between two or more variables. For example, OB researchers have hypothesized that an increase in supervisory participation will increase productivity. Hypotheses are "predictive" statements. Once supported through empirical research, a hypothesis can be a source of direct action implications. Confirmation of the above hypothesis would lead to the following implication: If you want to increase individual productivity in a work unit, increase the level of supervisory participation.

Dependent Variable   The **dependent variable** is the event or occurrence expressed in a hypothesis that indicates what the researcher is interested in explaining. In the previous example, individual performance was the dependent variable of interest. OB researchers often try to determine what factors appear to predict increases in performance.

■ The **scientific method** involves four steps: the research question or problem, hypothesis generation or formulation, the research design, and data gathering, analysis, and interpretation.

■ A **variable** is a measure used to describe a real-world phenomenon.

■ A **hypothesis** is a tentative explanation about the relationship between two or more variables.

■ A **dependent variable** is the event or occurrence expressed in a hypothesis that indicates what the researcher is interested in explaining.

Independent Variable   An **independent variable** is the event or occurrence that is presumed by a hypothesis to affect one or more other events or occurrences as dependent variables. In the example of individual performance, supervisory participation is the independent variable.

Intervening Variable   An **intervening variable** is an event or occurrence that provides the linkage through which an independent variable is presumed to affect a dependent variable. It has been hypothesized, for instance, that participative supervisory practices "independent variable" improve worker satisfaction "intervening variable" and therefore increase performance "dependent variable".

Moderator Variable   A **moderator variable** is an event or occurrence that, when systematically varied, changes the relationship between an independent variable and a dependent variable. The relationship between these two variables differs depending on the level—for instance, high/low, young/old, male/female—of the moderator variable. To illustrate, consider again the previous example of the individual performance hypothesis that participative supervision leads to increased productivity. It may well be that this relationship holds true only when the employees feel that their participation is real and legitimate—a moderator variable. Likewise, it may be that participative supervision leads to increased performance for Canadian workers but not those from Brazil—here, country is a moderator variable.

Validity   **Validity** is concerned with the degree of confidence one can have in the results of a research study. It is focused on limiting research errors so that results are accurate and usable.[5] There are two key types of validity: internal and external. *Internal validity* is the degree to which the results of a study can be relied upon to be correct. It is strongest when alternative interpretations of the study's findings can be ruled out.[6] To illustrate, if performance improves with more participative supervisory practices, these results have a higher degree of internal validity if we can rule out the effects of differences in old and new machines.

External validity is the degree to which the study's results can be generalized across the entire population of people, settings, and other similar conditions.[7] We cannot have external validity unless we first have internal validity; that is, we must have confidence that the results are caused by what the study says they are before we can generalize to a broader context.

Reliability   **Reliability** is the consistency and stability of a score from a measurement scale. There must be reliability for there to be validity or accuracy. Think of shooting at a bull's-eye. If the shots land all over the target, there is neither reliability (consistency) nor validity (accuracy). If the shots are clustered close together but outside the outer ring of the target, they are reliable but not valid. If they are grouped together within the bull's-eye, they are both reliable and valid.[8]

Causality   **Causality** is the assumption that change in the independent variable caused change in the dependent variable. This assumption is very difficult to prove in OB research. Three types of evidence are necessary to demonstrate causality: (1) the variables must show a linkage or association; (2) one variable must precede the other in time; and (3) there must be an absence of other causal factors. [9] For example, say we note that participation and performance increase

---

- An **independent variable** is the event or occurrence that is presumed by a hypothesis to affect one or more other events or occurrences as dependent variables.

- An **intervening variable** is an event or occurrence that provides the linkage through which an independent variable is presumed to affect a dependent variable.

- A **moderator variable** is an event or occurrence that, when systematically varied, changes the relationship between an independent variable and a dependent variable.

- **Validity** is the degree of confidence one can have in the results of a research study.

- **Reliability** is the consistency and stability of a score from a measurement scale.

- **Causality** is the assumption that change in the independent variable has caused change in the dependent variable.

together—there is an association. If we can then show that an increase in participation has preceded an increase in performance and that other factors, such as new machinery, haven't been responsible for the increased performance, we can say that participation probably has caused performance.

Research Designs

As noted earlier, a **research design** is an overall plan or strategy for conducting the research to test the hypothesis(es). Four of the most popular research designs are laboratory experiments, field experiments, case studies, and field surveys.[10]

■ A **research design** is an overall plan or strategy for conducting research to test a hypothesis.

Laboratory Experiments

Laboratory experiments are conducted in an artificial setting in which the researcher intervenes and manipulates one or more independent variables in a highly controlled situation. Although there is a high degree of control, which, in turn, encourages internal validity, since these studies are done in an artificial setting, they may suffer from a lack of external validity.

To illustrate, assume we are interested in the impact of three different incentive systems on employee absenteeism: (1) a lottery with a monetary reward; (2) a lottery with a compensatory time-off reward; and (3) a lottery with a large prize, such as a car. The researcher randomly selects individuals in an organization to come to an office to take part in the study. This randomization is important because it means that variables that are not measured are randomly distributed across the subjects so that unknown variables shouldn't be causing whatever is found. However, often it is not possible to obtain subjects randomly in organizations since they may be needed elsewhere by management.

The researcher is next able to randomly select each worker to one of the three incentive systems as well as a control group with no incentive system. The employees report to work in their new work stations under highly artificial but controlled conditions, and their absenteeism is measured both at the beginning and end of the experiment. Statistical comparisons are made across each group, considering before and after measures.

Ultimately, the researcher develops hypotheses about the effects of each of the lottery treatments on absenteeism. Given support for these hypotheses, the researcher could feel with a high degree of confidence that a given incentive condition caused less absenteeism than did the others since randomized subjects, pre- and posttest measures, and a comparison with a control group were used. However, since the work stations were artificial and the lottery conditions were highly simplified to provide control, external validity could be questioned. Ideally, the researcher would conduct a follow-up study with another design to check for external validity.

■ A **laboratory experiment** is conducted in an artificial setting in which the researcher intervenes and manipulates one or more independent variables in a highly controlled situation.

Field Experiments

Field experiments are research studies that are conducted in a realistic setting. Here, the researcher intervenes and manipulates one or more independent variables and controls the situation as carefully as the situation permits.

■ A **field experiment** is a research study that is conducted in a realistic setting, whereby the researcher intervenes and manipulates one or more independent variables and controls the situation as carefully as the situation permits.

Applying the same research question as before, the researcher obtains management permission to assign one incentive treatment to each of three similar organizational departments, similar in terms of the various characteristics of people. A fourth control department keeps the current payment plan. The rest of the experiment is similar to the laboratory study except that the lottery treatments are more realistic but also less controlled. Also, it may be particularly difficult to obtain random assignment in this case since it may disrupt day-to-day work schedules, and so on. When random assignment is not possible, the other manipulations may still be possible. An experimental research design without any randomization is called a *quasi-experimental design* and does not control for unmeasured variables as well as a randomized design.

Case Studies

A **case study** is an in-depth analysis of one or a small number of settings.

Case studies are in-depth analyses of one or a small number of settings. Case studies often are used when little is known about a phenomenon and the researcher wants to examine relevant concepts intensely and thoroughly. They can sometimes be used to help develop theory that can then be tested with one of the other research designs. Returning to the participation and performance example, one might look at one or more organizations and intensely study organizational success or failure in designing or implementing participation. You might look for differences in how employees and managers define participation. This information could provide insights to be investigated further with additional case studies or other research designs.

A major strength of case studies is their realism and the richness of data and insights they can provide. Some disadvantages are their lack of control by the researcher, the difficulty of interpreting the results because of their richness, and the large amount of time and cost that may be involved.

Field Surveys

A **field survey** is a research design that relies on the use of some form of questionnaire for the primary purpose of describing and/or predicting some phenomenon.

Field surveys typically depend on the use of some form of questionnaire for the primary purpose of describing and/or predicting some phenomenon. Typically, they utilize a sample drawn from some large population. A key objective of field surveys is to look for relationships between or among variables. Two major advantages are their ability to examine and describe large populations quickly and inexpensively, and their flexibility. They can be used to do many kinds of OB research, such as testing hypotheses and theories and evaluating programs. Field surveys assume that the researcher has enough knowledge of the problem area to know the kinds of questions to ask; sometimes, earlier case studies help provide this knowledge.

A key disadvantage of field surveys is the lack of control. The researcher does not manipulate variables; even such things as who completes the surveys and their timing may not be under the researcher's control. Another disadvantage is the lack of depth of the standardized responses; thus, sometimes the data obtained are superficial.

Data Gathering and Analysis

Once the research design has been established, we are ready for data gathering, analysis, and interpretation—the final step in the scientific method. Four common OB data-gathering approaches are interviews, observation, questionnaires, and nonreactive measures.[11]

Interviews

Interviews involve face-to-face, telephone, or computer-assisted interactions to ask respondents questions of interest. Structured interviews ask the respondents the same questions in the same sequence. Unstructured interviews are more spontaneous and do not require the same format. Often a mixture of structured and unstructured formats is used. Interviews allow for in-depth responses and probing. They are generally time consuming, however, and require increasing amounts of training and skill, depending on their depth and amount of structure.

■■■ An **interview** involves face-to-face, telephone, or computer-assisted interactions to ask respondents questions of interest.

Observation

Observation involves watching an event, object, or person and recording what is seen. Sometimes, the observer is separate from the participants and events and functions as an outside researcher. In other cases, the observer participates in the events as a member of a work unit. In the latter case, observations are summarized in some kind of diary or log. Sometimes, the observer is hidden and records observations behind one-way glass or by using hidden cameras and the like.

■■■ **Observation** involves watching an event, object, or person and recording what is seen.

Two advantages of observation are that (1) behavior is observed as it occurs rather than being obtained by asking people after the fact, and (2) the observer can often obtain data that subjects can't or won't provide themselves. A couple of disadvantages are cost and the possible fallibility of observers, who sometimes do not provide complete and accurate data.

Questionnaires

Questionnaires ask respondents for their opinions, attitudes, perceptions, and/or descriptions of work-related matters. They are usually based on previously developed instruments. Typically, a respondent completes the questionnaire and returns it to the researcher. Questions may be open ended, or they may be structured with true-false or multiple-choice responses.

■■■ **Questionnaires** ask respondents for their opinions, attitudes, perceptions, and/or descriptions of work-related matters.

Advantages of questionnaires include the relatively low cost and the fact that the anonymity that often accompanies them may lead to more open and truthful responses. Some disadvantages are the low response rates, which may threaten the generalizability of the results, and the lack of depth of the responses.

Nonreactive Measures

Nonreactive measures are used to obtain data without disturbing the setting being studied. Sometimes, these are termed *unobtrusive measures* since they are designed not to intrude in a research situation. Nonreactive measures can focus on such things as physical traces, archives, and hidden observation. A kind of physical trace occurred when John Fry at 3M distributed test batches of Post-it Notes to 3M employees and discovered that they were using them at higher rates than 3M's leading adhesive product—Scotch Tape.[12] Archives are records that an organization keeps as a part of its day-to day activities; for example, minutes and daily production counts.

■■■ **Nonreactive measures** are used to obtain data without disturbing the setting.

A major advantage of nonreactive measures is that they don't disturb the research setting and so avoid the reaction of a respondent to a researcher. One possible disadvantage is their indirectness; incorrect inferences may be drawn from nonreactive measures. They work best in combination with more direct measures.

Data Analysis and Interpretation

Once the data have been gathered, they need to be *analyzed*. The most common means of analysis involves some kind of statistical approach, ranging from simple counting and categorizing to sophisticated multivariate statistical techniques.[13] It's beyond our scope to discuss this area beyond simply emphasizing its importance. However, various statistical tests are often used to examine support for hypotheses, to check for the reliability of various data-gathering approaches, and to provide information on causality and many other aspects of analysis.

After systematic analysis has been performed, the researcher *interprets* the results and prepares a report.[14] Sometimes, the report is used in-house by management; other times, the results are reported at various conferences and published in journals. Ultimately, many of the results in the OB area appear in textbooks like this one.

Ethical Considerations in Research

Given our emphasis on ethical considerations throughout this book, it is appropriate to end our discussion of OB research with a look at its ethical considerations. These ethical considerations involve rights of four broad parties involved in research in general and in OB research in particular: society, subjects, clients, and researchers.[15]

In terms of *societal rights*—those of the broadest of the parties involved in OB research—three key areas exist: the right to be informed, the right to expect objective results, and the right to privacy or to be left alone. Subjects of research also have rights: the right to choose (to participate or not), to safety, and to be informed. The rights of the client involve two primary concerns: the right to expect high-quality research and the right of confidentiality. Finally, two rights of the researcher stand out: the right to expect ethical client behavior and the right to expect ethical subject behavior.

All of these rights need to be communicated and adhered to by all parties. Indeed, various organizations conducting research are increasingly endorsing codes of ethics to codify such rights. Two particular organizations that have codes of ethics for research covering OB and related areas are the American Psychological Association and the Academy of Management.

Key Terms

Chapter 2

Values, Personality, and Individual Differences

People are different

Chapter at a Glance

Chapter 2 introduces the importance of values, personality, stress, and individual differences in the study of today's work settings. As you read Chapter 2, *keep in mind these study topics.*

CHAPTER 2 STUDY GUIDE

Otto Duffner opened the Bei Otto German restaurant with a small bakery and later a butcher shop and delicatessen in Bangkok, Thailand, in July 1984. It has enjoyed steady growth amid much competition ever since.

Otto says: "As Germans, we follow a strict way of life, well organized, tough and orderly, which is very different from the easy-going Thai way both in life and in business . . . simply saying, like the people here do, Mai Pen Rai (never mind) isn't good enough. I hate this attitude in terms of business." Otto enjoys what he is doing, even if sometimes it involves different origins, cultures, countries, languages, values, and backgrounds. He still wants to keep personal contact with his customers as well as listen to and talk with them. According to Otto, "Customers can instinctively feel whether someone welcomes them, treats them well, or just wants to relieve them of their money."

> **"Customers can instinctively feel whether someone welcomes them, treats them well, or just wants to relieve them of their money."**

Thai people comprise about 40% of his customers; another 10% are from other Asian countries such as Japan and Korea. The rest are Westerners, frequently people living in Bangkok who are employed by embassies and international firms, and tourists. Otto works about 80 hours each week. For Otto, "My hobby is my business."

Otto Duffner and his German restaurant in Thailand illustrates well the notions of values, culture, personality, and individual differences in OB. Each of these is extremely important in helping you understand organizational behavior.[1]

Values

Individual Values

■■■ **Values** can be defined as broad preferences concerning appropriate courses of action or outcomes.

Values can be defined as broad preferences concerning appropriate courses of action or outcomes. As such, values reflect a person's sense of right and wrong or what "ought" to be.[2] "Equal rights for all" and "People should be treated with respect and dignity" are representative of values. Values tend to influence attitudes and behavior. For example, if you value equal rights for all and you go to work for an organization that treats its managers much better than it does its workers, you may form the attitude that the company is an unfair place to work; consequently, you may not produce well or may perhaps leave the company. It is likely that if the company had had a more egalitarian policy, your attitude and behaviors would have been more positive.

Sources of Values Parents, friends, teachers, siblings, education, experience, and external reference groups are all value sources that can influence individual values.

Leaders on Leadership

CULTURAL INTEGRATOR

Carlos Ghosn, the 51-year old CEO of Nissan, is also president and CEO of Renault, Nissan's French partner. He thus adds a home in Paris to his current one in Tokyo. He plans to spend 40% of his time in Paris, 40% in Tokyo, and 20% in the United States (where Nissan has an assembly plant) and the rest of the world. He is also on the boards of Sony, IBM, and Alcoa and emphasizes a "hands on" approach with his firms. This is a difficult assignment for any automotive CEO, but Ghosn's background as the "Boss from Beyond" should suit him well. He earlier lived in Lebanon but was born in Brazil and spoke Portuguese; he then moved to France, where he again led an unusual life. His earlier years were spent mastering cultures and values that were different from each other and from those of Japan and the United States. He is known for his no-nonsense manner and his lack of guile. He wants everything quantified, including measuring and benchmarking. He even formed SWAT teams to deal with low-quality autos from Nissan's newly opened U.S. operation.

Ghosn believes strongly in stretch goals and so far has been very successful in meeting them. The question now is how successful he will ultimately be in dealing with the French, Japanese, and American cultures.[3]

Questions: Compare and contrast the Japanese, French, and U.S. cultures and values and explain some implications for Ghosn's CEO.

Indeed, peoples' values develop as a product of the learning and experience they encounter from various sources in the cultural setting in which they live. As learning and experiences differ from one person to another, value differences result. Such differences are likely to be deep seated and difficult (though not impossible) to change; many have their roots in early childhood and the way a person has been raised.[4]

Types of Values   The noted psychologist Milton Rokeach has developed a well-known set of values classified into two broad categories.[5] **Terminal values** reflect a person's preferences concerning the "ends" to be achieved; they are the goals an individual would like to achieve during his or her lifetime. Rokeach divides values into 18 terminal values and 18 instrumental values as summarized in Figure 2.1. **Instrumental values** reflect the "means" for achieving desired ends. They represent how you might go about achieving your important end states, depending on the relative importance you attached to the instrumental values.

Illustrative research shows, not surprisingly, that both terminal and instrumental values differ by group (for example, executives, activist workers, and union members).[6] These preference differences can encourage conflict or agreement when different groups have to deal with each other.

■■ **Terminal values** reflect a person's preferences concerning the "ends" to be achieved.

■■ **Instrumental values** reflect a person's beliefs about the means for achieving desired ends.

Figure 2.1   Rokeach value survey.

Terminal Values	Instrumental Values
A comfortable life (and prosperous)	Ambitious (hardworking)
An exciting life (stimulating)	Broad-minded (open-minded)
A sense of accomplishment (lasting contibution)	Capable (competent, effective)
A world at peace (free of war and conflict)	Cheerful (lighthearted, joyful)
A world of beauty (beauty of nature and the arts)	Clean (neat, tidy)
Equality (brotherhood, equal opportunity)	Courageous (standing up for beliefs)
Family security (taking care of loved ones)	Forgiving (willing to pardon)
Freedom (independence, free choice)	Helpful (working for others' welfare)
Happiness (contentedness)	Honest (sincere, truthful)
Inner harmony (freedom from inner conflict)	Imaginative (creative, daring)
Mature love (sexual and spiritual intimacy)	Independent (self-sufficient, self-reliant)
National security (attack protection)	Intellectual (intelligent, reflective)
Pleasure (leisurely, enjoyable life)	Logical (rational, consistent)
Salvation (saved, eternal life)	Loving (affectionate, tender)
Self-respect (self-esteem)	Obedient (dutiful, respectful)
Social recognition (admiration, respect)	Polite (courteous, well mannered)
True friendship (close companionship)	Responsible (reliable, dependable)
Wisdom (mature understanding of life)	Self-controlled (self-disciplined)

Another frequently used classification of human values has been developed by psychologist Gordon Allport and his associates. These values fall into six major types:[7]

Allport's six value categories

- *Theoretical*—interest in the discovery of truth through reasoning and systematic thinking
- *Economic*—interest in usefulness and practicality, including the accumulation of wealth
- *Aesthetic*—interest in beauty, form, and artistic harmony
- *Social*—interest in people and love as a human relationship
- *Political*—interest in gaining power and influencing other people
- *Religious*—interest in unity and in understanding the cosmos as a whole

Once again, groups differ in the way they rank order the importance of these values as shown in the following:[8]

- *Ministers*—religious, social, aesthetic, political, theoretical, economic
- *Purchasing executives*—economic, theoretical, political, religious, aesthetic, social
- *Industrial scientists*—theoretical, political, economic, aesthetic, religious, social values

The previous value classifications have had a major impact on the values literature, but they were not specifically designed for people in a work setting. A more recent values schema, developed by Bruce Maglino and associates, is aimed at people in the workplace:[9]

Maglino and associates' value categories

- *Achievement*—getting things done and working hard to accomplish difficult things in life

- *Helping and concern for others*—being concerned for other people and with helping others
- *Honesty*—telling the truth and doing what you feel is right
- *Fairness*—being impartial and doing what is fair for all concerned

These four values have been shown to be especially important in the workplace; thus, the framework should be particularly relevant for studying values in OB.

In particular, values can be influential through **value congruence**, which occurs when individuals express positive feelings upon encountering others who exhibit values similar to their own. When values differ, or are *incongruent,* conflicts over such things as goals and the means to achieve them may result. Maglino and colleagues' value schema was used to examine value congruence between leaders and followers. The researchers found greater follower satisfaction with the leader when there was such congruence in terms of achievement, helping, honesty, and fairness values.[10]

Value congruence occurs when individuals express positive feelings upon encountering others who exhibit values similar to their own.

Patterns and Trends in Values   We should also be aware of applied research and insightful analyses of values trends over time. Daniel Yankelovich, for example, is known for his informative public opinion polls among North American workers, and William Fox has prepared a carefully reasoned book analyzing values trends.[11] Both Yankelovich and Fox note movements away from earlier values, with Fox emphasizing a decline in such shared values as duty, honesty, responsibility, and the like, while Yankelovich notes a movement away from valuing economic incentives, organizational loyalty, and work-related identity. The movement is toward valuing meaningful work, pursuit of leisure, and personal identity and self-fulfillment. Yankelovich believes that the modern manager must be able to recognize value differences and trends among people at work. For example, he reports finding higher productivity among younger workers who are employed in jobs that match their values and/or who are supervised by managers who share their values, reinforcing the concept of value congruence.

In a nationwide sample, managers and human resource professionals were asked to identify the work-related values they believed to be most important to individuals in the workforce, both now and in the near future.[12] The nine most popular values named were recognition for competence and accomplishments, respect and dignity, personal choice and freedom, involvement at work, pride in one's work, lifestyle quality, financial security, self-development, and health and wellness. These values are especially important for managers because they indicate some key concerns of the new workforce. Even though each individual worker places his or her own importance on these values, and even though the United States today has by far the most diverse workforce in its history, this overall characterization is a good place for managers to start when dealing with workers in the new workplace. It is important to remember, however, that although values are individual preferences, many tend to be shared within cultures and organizations.

Values across National Cultures

The word "culture" is frequently used in organizational behavior in connection with the concept of corporate culture, the growing interest in workforce diversity, and the broad differences among people around the world. Specialists tend to agree that **culture** is the learned, shared way of doing things in a particular society. It is the way, for example, in which its members eat, dress, greet and treat one another,

Culture is the learned and shared way of thinking and acting among a group of people or society.

teach their children, solve everyday problems, and so on.[13] Geert Hofstede, a Dutch scholar and consultant, refers to culture as the "software of the mind," making the analogy that the mind's "hardware" is universal among human beings.[14] But the software of culture takes many different forms. We are not born with a culture; we are born into a society that teaches us its culture. And because culture is shared among people, it helps to define the boundaries between different groups and affect how their members relate to one another.

Cultures vary in their underlying patterns of values and attitudes. The way people think about such matters as achievement, wealth and material gain, and risk and change may influence how they approach work and their relationships with organizations. A framework developed by Geert Hofstede offers one approach for understanding how value differences across national cultures can influence human behavior at work. The five dimensions of national culture in his framework can be described as follows:[15]

Hofstede's dimensions of national cultures

▬ **Power distance** is the willingness of a culture to accept status and power differences among its members.

▬ **Uncertainty avoidance** is the cultural tendency to be uncomfortable with uncertainty and risk in everyday life.

▬ **Individualism-collectivism** is the tendency of a culture's members to emphasize individual self-interests or group relationships.

▬ **Masculinity-femininity** is the degree to which a society values assertiveness or relationships.

▬ **Long-term/short-term orientation** is the degree to which a culture emphasizes long-term or short-term thinking.

1. **Power distance** is the willingness of a culture to accept status and power differences among its members. It reflects the degree to which people are likely to respect hierarchy and rank in organizations. Indonesia is considered a high-power-distance culture, whereas Sweden is considered a relatively low-power-distance culture.

2. **Uncertainty avoidance** is a cultural tendency toward discomfort with risk and ambiguity. It reflects the degree to which people are likely to prefer structured versus unstructured organizational situations. France is considered a high uncertainty avoidance culture, whereas Hong Kong is considered a low uncertainty avoidance culture.

3. **Individualism-collectivism** is the tendency of a culture to emphasize either individual or group interests. It reflects the degree to which people are likely to prefer working as individuals or working together in groups. The United States is a highly individualistic culture, whereas Mexico is a more collectivist one.

4. **Masculinity-femininity** is the tendency of a culture to value stereotypical masculine or feminine traits. It reflects the degree to which organizations emphasize competition and assertiveness versus interpersonal sensitivity and concerns for relationships. Japan is considered a very masculine culture, whereas Thailand is considered a more feminine culture.

5. **Long-term/short-term orientation** is the tendency of a culture to emphasize values associated with the future, such as thrift and persistence, or values that focus largely on the present. It reflects the degree to which people and organizations adopt long-term or short-term performance horizons. South Korea is high on long-term orientation, whereas the United States is a more short-term-oriented country.

The first four dimensions in Hofstede's framework were identified in an extensive study of thousands of employees of a multinational corporation operating in more than 40 countries.[16] The fifth dimension of long-term/short-term orientation was added from research using the Chinese Values Survey conducted by cross-cultural psychologist Michael Bond and his colleagues.[17] Their research suggested the cultural importance of Confucian dynamism, with its emphasis on persistence, the ordering of relationships, thrift, sense of shame, personal steadiness, reciprocity, protection of "face," and respect for tradition.[18]

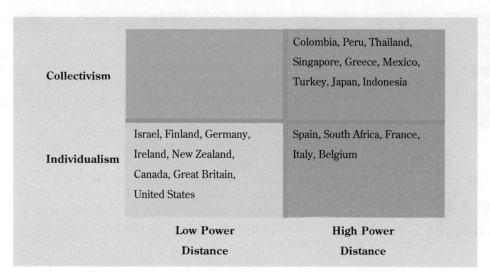

Figure 2.2 Sample country clusters on Hofstede's dimensions of individualism-collectivism and power distance.

When using the Hofstede framework, it is important to remember that the five dimensions are interrelated, not independent.[19] National cultures may best be understood in terms of cluster maps or collages that combine multiple dimensions. For example, Figure 2.2 shows a sample grouping of countries based on individualism–collectivism and power distance. Note that high power distance and collectivism are often found together, as are low power distance and individualism. Whereas high collectivism may lead us to expect a work team in Indonesia to operate by consensus, the high power distance may cause the consensus to be heavily influenced by the desires of a formal leader. A similar team operating in more individualist and low-power-distance Great Britain or America might make decisions with more open debate, including expressions of disagreement with a leader's stated preferences.

At the national level, cultural value dimensions, such as those identified by Hofstede, tend to influence the previously discussed individual sources of values. The sources, in turn, tend to share individual values which are then reflected in the recipients' value structures. For example, in the United States the sources would tend to be influenced by Hofstede's low-power-distance dimensions (along with his others, of course), and the recipients would tend to interpret their own individual value structures through that low-power-distance lens. Similarly, people in other countries or societies would be influenced by their country's standing on such dimensions.

Personality

Joining values and culture for consideration in this chapter is the important aspect of personality.

What Is Personality?

The term **personality** encompasses the overall combination of characteristics that captures the unique nature of a person as that person reacts and interacts with others. As an example, think of a person who was the billionaire founder of a fast-growing, high-tech computer company by the time he was 30; who in his senior year in high school had turned selling newspapers into enough of a business to buy a BMW; who told his

Personality represents the overall profile, or combination of characteristics, that captures the unique nature of a person as that person reacts and interacts with others.

ETHICS IN OB

CHINESE JUDGES OVERWHELMED BY CORRUPTION CASES

China's courts are facing a critical shortage of judges as they try to cope with increasing numbers of corruption cases. Prosecutors indicted more than 30,000 officials on corruption charges during one recent year, and the amount of embezzled money recovered increased more than 60%.

Jia Chunwang, the country's chief prosecutor, claims that work-related crime in some industries and areas has occurred in large numbers. He also says: "The methods are ever-more cunning."

Charges were brought against all sections of government at local and provincial levels, including transportation, health care, and education. The Chinese courts heard more than 24,000 cases of embezzlement, dereliction of duty, and bribery, including the cases of six officials at the ministerial level who were later sentenced to prison terms.

Mr. Chunwang said that many of the best-trained, most experienced judges were retiring or leaving for private industry. He didn't say whether the government had plans to expand the court work force or would offer higher salaries to retain people.[21]

Question: How is it that China's problem sounds as if it could have taken place in the United States or other Western countries even though China is a communist country and has Eastern traditions?

management team that his daughter's first words were "Daddy—kill-IBM, Gateway, Compaq"; who learned from production mistakes and brought in senior managers to help his firm; and who is so private he seldom talks about himself. In other words, think of Michael Dell, the founder of Dell Computer, and of his personality.[20]

Personality combines a set of physical and mental characteristics that reflect how a person looks, thinks, acts, and feels. Sometimes attempts are made to measure personality with questionnaires or special tests. Frequently, personality can be inferred from behavior alone, such as by the actions of Michael Dell. Either way, personality is an important individual characteristic for managers to understand. An understanding of personality contributes to an understanding of organizational behavior in that we expect a predictable interplay between an individual's personality and his or her tendency to behave in certain ways.

Personality and Development

Just what determines personality? Is personality inherited or genetically determined, or is it formed by experience? You may have heard someone say something like, "She acts like her mother." Similarly, someone may argue that "Bobby is the way he is because of the way he was raised." These two arguments illustrate the nature/nurture controversy: is personality determined by heredity—that is, by genetic endowment—or by one's environment? As Figure 2.3 shows, these two forces actually operate in combination. Heredity consists of those factors that are determined at conception, including physical characteristics, gender, and personality factors. Environment consists of cultural, social, and situational factors.

The impact of heredity on personality continues to be the source of considerable debate. Perhaps the most general conclusion we can draw is that heredity sets the limits on just how much personality characteristics can be developed; en-

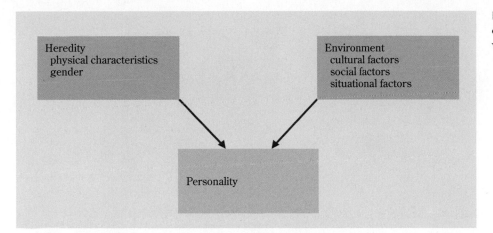

Figure 2.3 Heredity and environmental linkage with personality.

vironment determines development within these limits. For instance, a person could be born with a tendency toward authoritarianism, and that tendency could be reinforced in an authoritarian work environment. These limits appear to vary from one characteristic to the next, and across all characteristics there is about a 50–50 heredity-environment split.[22]

As we show throughout this book, *cultural values and norms* play a substantial role in the development of an individual's personality and behaviors. Contrast the individualism of U.S. culture with the collectivism of Mexican culture, for example.[23] Social factors reflect such things as family life, religion, and the many kinds of formal and informal groups in which people participate throughout their lives—friendship groups, athletic groups, and formal workgroups. Finally, the demands of differing *situational factors* emphasize or constrain different aspects of an individual's personality. For example, in class you are likely to rein in your high spirits and other related behaviors encouraged by your personality. However, at a sporting event, you may be jumping up, cheering, and loudly criticizing the referees.

The **developmental approaches** of Chris Argyris, Daniel Levinson, and Gail Sheehy systematically examine the ways personality develops across time. Argyris notes that people develop along a continuum of dimensions from immaturity to maturity, as shown in Figure 2.4. He believes that many organizations treat mature adults as if they were still immature and that this creates many problems in terms of bringing out the best in employees. Levinson and Sheehy maintain that an individual's personality unfolds in a series of *stages* across time. Sheehy's model, for example, talks about three stages—ages 18–30, 30–45, and 45–85+. Each of these has a crucial impact on the worker's employment and career, as we show in Chapter 7. The implications are that personalities develop over time and require different managerial responses. Thus, the needs and other personality aspects of people initially entering an organization change sharply as they move through different stages or toward increased maturity.[24]

Personality and the Self-Concept

Collectively, the ways in which an individual integrates and organizes the previously mentioned personality aspects and the traits they contain is referred to as **personality dynamics**. It is this category that makes personality more than just the sum of the separate traits. A key personality dynamic in your study of OB is the self-concept.

▇ **Developmental approaches** are systematic models of ways in which personality develops across time.

▇ **Personality dynamics** are the ways in which an individual integrates and organizes social traits, values and motives, personal conceptions, and emotional adjustment.

Figure 2.4   Argyris's maturity–immaturity continuum.

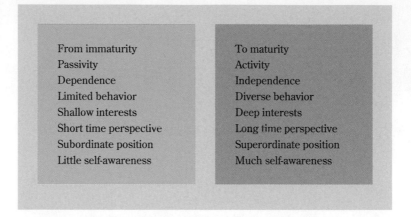

From immaturity
Passivity
Dependence
Limited behavior
Shallow interests
Short time perspective
Subordinate position
Little self-awareness

To maturity
Activity
Independence
Diverse behavior
Deep interests
Long time perspective
Superordinate position
Much self-awareness

Self-concept is the view individuals have of themselves as physical, social, and spiritual or moral beings.

We can describe the **self-concept** as the view individuals have of themselves as physical, social, and spiritual or moral beings.[25] It is a way of recognizing oneself as a distinct human being. A person's self-concept is greatly influenced by his or her culture. For example, Americans tend to disclose much more about themselves than do the English; that is, an American's self-concept is more assertive and talkative.[26]

Two related—and crucial—aspects of the self-concept are self-esteem and self-efficacy. *Self-esteem* is a belief about one's own worth based on an overall self-evaluation.[27] People high in self-esteem see themselves as capable, worthwhile, and acceptable and tend to have few doubts about themselves. The opposite is true of a person low in self-esteem. Some OB research suggests that whereas high self-esteem generally can boost performance and satisfaction outcomes, when under pressure, people with high self-esteem may become boastful and act egotistically. They may also be overconfident at times and fail to obtain important information.[28]

Self-efficacy, sometimes called the "effectance motive," is a more specific version of self-esteem; it is an individual's belief about the likelihood of successfully completing a specific task. You could be high in self-esteem yet have a feeling of low self-efficacy about performing a certain task, such as public speaking.

How Personalities Differ

Big Five Personality Traits

Numerous lists of personality traits—enduring characteristics describing an individual's behavior—have been developed, many of which have been used in OB research and can be looked at in different ways. A key starting point is to consider the personality dimensions that recent research has distilled from extensive lists into what is called the "Big Five":[29]

The Big Five personality dimensions

- *Extraversion*—outgoing, sociable, assertive
- *Agreeableness*—good-natured, trusting, cooperative
- *Conscientiousness*—responsible, dependable, persistent
- *Emotional stability*—unworried, secure, relaxed
- *Openness to experience*—imaginative, curious, broad-minded

Research Insight
Military Cadets' Narcissism and Emergent Leadership

Some 200 military cadets in the National Defence College of Finland rated members of their platoons and themselves on a variety of variables, including the quality of their leadership behaviors. They also completed standardized personality questionnaires measuring the bright or "benign" aspects of the trait related to high self-esteem and psychological health and the dark or "maladaptive" aspects related to exploitativeness, seen as eventually leading to derailment as a leader.

Bright Side	Egotism	
	→	Good
	Self-Esteem	
Dark Side	Manipulativeness	
	→	Poor
	Impression Management	

The most highly-rated leaders reflected the bright side of narcissism while suppressing the dark side. Emergent leaders were found to be high in egotism and self-esteem but low in manipulativeness and impression management, as shown here. Big Five personality factors, discussed below, were marginal in their ability to predict emergent leadership. Support of these bright and dark sides of narcissism led the authors to recommend that peer evaluations should routinely be used for military and possibly other leaders. [29A]

Standardized personality tests determine how positively or negatively an individual scores on each of these dimensions. For instance, a person scoring high on openness to experience tends to ask lots of questions and to think in new and unusual ways. You can consider a person's individual personality profile across the five dimensions. In terms of job performance, research has shown that conscientiousness predicts job performance across five occupational groups of professions—engineers, police, managers, salespersons, and skilled and semi-skilled employees. Predictability of the other dimensions depends on the occupational group. For instance, not surprisingly, extraversion predicts performance for sales and managerial positions.

A second approach to looking at OB personality traits is to divide them into social traits, personal conception traits, and emotional adjustment traits, and then to consider how those categories come together dynamically. [30]

Social Traits

Social traits are surface-level traits that reflect the way a person appears to others when interacting in various social settings. Problem-solving style, based on the work of Carl Jung, a noted psychologist, is one measure representing social traits. [31] It reflects the way a person goes about gathering and evaluating information in solving problems and making decisions.

Information gathering involves getting and organizing data for use. Styles of information gathering vary from sensation to intuitive. *Sensation-type individuals*

Social traits are surface-level traits that reflect the way a person appears to others when interacting in various social settings.

prefer routine and order and emphasize well-defined details in gathering information; they would rather work with known facts than look for possibilities. By contrast, *intuitive-type individuals* prefer the "big picture." They like solving new problems, dislike routine, and would rather look for possibilities than work with facts.

The second component of problem solving, *evaluation,* involves making judgments about how to deal with information once it has been collected. Styles of information evaluation vary from an emphasis on feeling to an emphasis on thinking. *Feeling-type individuals* are oriented toward conformity and try to accommodate themselves to other people. They try to avoid problems that may result in disagreements. *Thinking-type individuals* use reason and intellect to deal with problems and downplay emotions.

When these two dimensions (information gathering and evaluation) are combined, four basic problem-solving styles result: sensation–feeling (SF), intuitive–feeling (IF), sensation–thinking (ST), and intuitive–thinking (IT), together with summary descriptions as shown in Figure 2.5.

Research indicates that there is a fit between the styles of individuals and the kinds of decisions they prefer. For example, STs (sensation–thinkers) prefer analytical strategies—those that emphasize detail and method. IFs (intuitive–feelers) prefer intuitive strategies—those that emphasize an overall pattern and fit. Not surprisingly, mixed styles (sensation–feelers or intuitive–thinkers) select both analytical and intuitive strategies. Other findings also indicate that thinkers tend to have higher motivation than do feelers and that individuals who emphasize sensations tend to have higher job satisfaction than do intuitives. These and other findings

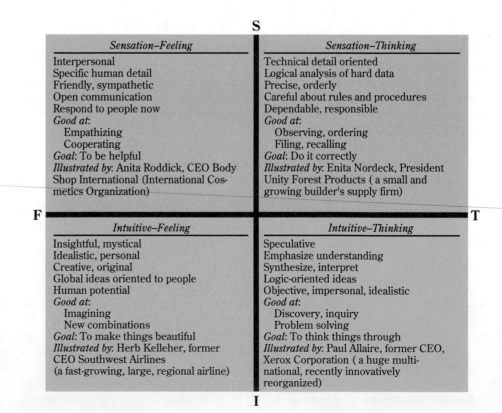

Figure 2.5   Four problem-solving style summaries.

suggest a number of basic differences among different problem-solving styles, emphasizing the importance of fitting such styles with a task's information processing and evaluation requirements.[32]

Problem-solving styles are most frequently measured by the (typically 100-item) *Myers-Briggs Type Indicator (MBTI)*, which asks individuals how they usually act or feel in specific situations. Firms such as Apple, AT&T, and Exxon, as well as hospitals, educational institutions, and military organizations, have used the Myers-Briggs for various aspects of management development.[33]

Personal Conception Traits

The *personal conception traits* represent the way individuals tend to think about their social and physical setting as well as their major beliefs and personal orientation concerning a range of issues.

Locus of Control   The extent to which a person feels able to control his or her own life is concerned with a person's internal–external orientation and is measured by Rotter's locus of control instrument.[34] People have personal conceptions about whether events are controlled primarily by themselves, which indicates an internal orientation, or by outside forces, such as their social and physical environment, which indicates an external orientation. Internals, or persons with an internal locus of control, believe that they control their own fate or destiny. In contrast, externals, or persons with an external locus of control, believe that much of what happens to them is beyond their control and is determined by environmental forces.

In general, externals are more extraverted in their interpersonal relationships and are more oriented toward the world around them. Internals tend to be more introverted and are more oriented toward their own feelings and ideas. Figure 2.6 suggests that internals tend to do better on tasks requiring complex information processing and learning as well as initiative. Many managerial and professional jobs have these kinds of requirements.

Authoritarianism/Dogmatism   Both "authoritarianism" and "dogmatism" deal with the rigidity of a person's beliefs. A person high in **authoritarianism** tends to adhere rigidly to conventional values and to obey recognized authority. This person is concerned with toughness and power and opposes the use of subjective feelings. An individual high in **dogmatism** sees the world as a threatening place. This person regards legitimate authority as absolute and accepts or rejects others according to how much they agree with accepted authority. Superiors who possess these latter traits tend to be rigid and closed. At the same time, dogmatic subordinates tend to want certainty imposed upon them.[35]

From an ethical standpoint, we can expect highly authoritarian individuals to present a special problem because they are so susceptible to authority that in their eagerness to comply they may behave unethically.[36] For example, we might speculate that many of the Nazis who were involved in war crimes during World War II were high in authoritarianism or dogmatism; they believed so strongly in authority that they followed unethical orders without question.

Machiavellianism   The third personal conceptions dimension is Machiavellianism, which owes its origins to Niccolo Machiavelli. The very name of this sixteenth-century author evokes visions of a master of guile, deceit, and opportunism

Locus of control is the extent to which a person feels able to control his or her own life and is concerned with a person's internal–external orientation.

Authoritarianism is a tendency to adhere rigidly to conventional values and to obey recognized authority.

Dogmatism leads a person to see the world as a threatening place and to regard authority as absolute.

Figure 2.6   Some ways in which internals differ from externals.

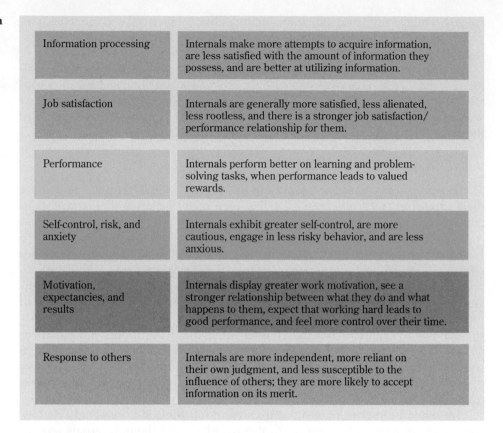

Information processing	Internals make more attempts to acquire information, are less satisfied with the amount of information they possess, and are better at utilizing information.
Job satisfaction	Internals are generally more satisfied, less alienated, less rootless, and there is a stronger job satisfaction/ performance relationship for them.
Performance	Internals perform better on learning and problem-solving tasks, when performance leads to valued rewards.
Self-control, risk, and anxiety	Internals exhibit greater self-control, are more cautious, engage in less risky behavior, and are less anxious.
Motivation, expectancies, and results	Internals display greater work motivation, see a stronger relationship between what they do and what happens to them, expect that working hard leads to good performance, and feel more control over their time.
Response to others	Internals are more independent, more reliant on their own judgment, and less susceptible to the influence of others; they are more likely to accept information on its merit.

in interpersonal relations. Machiavelli earned his place in history by writing *The Prince,* a nobleman's guide to the acquisition and use of power.[37] The subject of Machiavelli's book is manipulation as the basic means of gaining and keeping control of others. From its pages emerges the personality profile of a Machiavellian—someone who views and manipulates others purely for personal gain.

Psychologists have developed a series of instruments called Mach scales to measure a person's Machiavellian orientation.[38] A high-Mach personality is someone who tends to behave in ways consistent with Machiavelli's basic principles. Such individuals approach situations logically and thoughtfully and are even capable of lying to achieve personal goals. They are rarely swayed by loyalty, friendships, past promises, or the opinions of others, and they are skilled at influencing others.

Research using the Mach scales provides insight into the way high and low Machs may be expected to behave in various situations. A person with a "cool" and "detached" high-Mach personality can be expected to take control and try to exploit loosely structured environmental situations but will perform in a perfunctory, even detached, manner in highly structured situations. Low Machs tend to accept direction imposed by others in loosely structured situations; they work hard to do well in highly structured ones. For example, we might expect that, where the situation permitted, a high Mach would do or say whatever it took to get his or her way. In contrast, a low Mach would tend to be much more strongly guided by ethical considerations and would be less likely to lie or cheat or to get away with lying or cheating.

Self-Monitoring

A final personal conceptions trait of special importance to managers is self-monitoring. **Self-monitoring** reflects a person's ability to adjust his or her behavior to external, situational (environmental) factors.[39]

High self-monitoring individuals are sensitive to external cues and tend to behave differently in different situations. Like high Machs, high self-monitors can present a very different appearance from their true self. In contrast, low self-monitors, like their low-Mach counterparts, are not able to disguise their behaviors—"what you see is what you get." There is also evidence that high self-monitors are closely attuned to the behavior of others and conform more readily than do low self-monitors.[40] Thus, they appear flexible and may be especially good at responding to the kinds of situational contingencies emphasized throughout this book. For example, high self-monitors should be especially good at changing their leadership behavior to fit subordinates with more or less experience, tasks with more or less structure, and so on.

▪▪▪ **Self-monitoring** reflects a person's ability to adjust his or her behavior to external situational (environmental) factors.

Emotional Adjustment Traits

The **emotional adjustment traits** measure how much an individual experiences emotional distress or displays unacceptable acts. Often the person's health is affected. Although numerous such traits are cited in the literature, a frequently encountered one especially important for OB is the Type A/Type B orientation.

▪▪▪ **Emotional adjustment traits** measure how much an individual experiences emotional distress or displays unacceptable acts.

Type A and Type B Orientation To get a feel for this orientation, take the following quiz and then read on.[41] Circle the number that best characterizes you on each of the following pairs of characteristics.

Casual about appointments	1 2 3 4 5 6 7 8	Never late
Not competitive	1 2 3 4 5 6 7 8	Very competitive
Never feel rushed	1 2 3 4 5 6 7 8	Always feel rushed
Take one thing at a time	1 2 3 4 5 6 7 8	Try to do many things
Do things slowly	1 2 3 4 5 6 7 8	Do things fast
Express my feelings	1 2 3 4 5 6 7 8	Hold in my feelings
Many outside interests	1 2 3 4 5 6 7 8	Few outside interests

Total your points for the seven items in the quiz. Multiply this total by three to arrive at a final score. Use this total to locate your Type A/Type B orientation on the following list.

Final Points	A/B Orientation
Below 90	B
90–99	B+
100–105	A−
106–119	A
120 or more	A+

■ **Type A orientations** are characterized by impatience, desire for achievement, and a less competitive nature than Type B.

Individuals with a **Type A orientation** are characterized by impatience, desire for achievement, and perfectionism. In contrast, those with a **Type B orientation** are characterized as more easygoing and less competitive in relation to daily events.[42]

Type A people tend to work fast and to be abrupt, uncomfortable, irritable, and aggressive. Such tendencies indicate "obsessive" behavior, a fairly widespread—but not always helpful—trait among managers. Many managers are hard-driving, detail-oriented people who have high performance standards and thrive on routine. But when such work obsessions are carried to the extreme, they may lead to greater concerns for details than for results, resistance to change, overzealous control of subordinates, and various kinds of interpersonal difficulties, which may even include threats and physical violence. In contrast, Type B managers tend to be much more laid back and patient in their dealings with co-workers and subordinates.

■ **Type B orientations** are characterized by an easygoing and less competitive nature than Type A.

Personality and Stress

■ **Stress** is tension from extraordinary demands, constraints, or opportunities.

It is but a small step from a focus on the emotional adjustment traits of Type A/Type B orientation to consideration of the relationship between personality and stress. We define **stress** as a state of tension experienced by individuals facing extraordinary demands, constraints, or opportunities. As we show, stress can be both positive and negative and is an important fact of life in our present work environment.[43]

An especially important set of stressors includes personal factors, such as individual needs, capabilities, and personality.[44] Stress can reach a destructive state more quickly, for example, when experienced by highly emotional people as discussed in Chapter 3 or by those with low self-esteem. People who perceive a good fit between job requirements and personal skills seem to have a higher tolerance for stress than do those who feel less competent as a result of a person-job mismatch.[45] Also, of course, basic aspects of personality are important. This is true not only for those with Type A orientation, but also for the Big Five dimensions of neuroticism or negative affectivity; exroversion or positive affectivity (as discussed in Chapter 3); and openness to experience, which suggests the degree to which employees are open to a wide range of experience likely to involve risk taking and making frequent changes.[46]

Sources of Stress

Any look toward your career future in today's dynamic times must include an awareness that stress is something you, as well as others, are sure to encounter.[47]

■ **Stressors** are things that cause stress.

Stressors are the wide variety of things that cause stress for individuals. Some stressors can be traced directly to what people experience in the workplace, whereas others derive from nonwork and personal factors.

■ **Work stressors** are the things that arise at work to create stress.

Work Stressors   Without doubt, work can be stressful, and job demands can disrupt one's work-life balance. A study of two-career couples, for example, found some 43 percent of men and 34 percent of women reporting that they worked more hours than they wanted to.[48] We know that **work stressors** can arise from many sources—from excessively high or low task demands, role conflicts or ambiguities, poor interpersonal relations, or career progress that is either too slow or too fast. A list of common stressors includes the following:

Possible work-related stressors

- *Task demands*—being asked to do too much or being asked to do too little
- *Role ambiguities*—not knowing what one is expected to do or how work performance is evaluated

- *Role conflicts*—feeling unable to satisfy multiple, possibly conflicting, performance expectations
- *Ethical dilemmas*—being asked to do things that violate the law or personal values
- *Interpersonal problems*—experiencing bad relationships or working with others with whom one does not get along
- *Career developments*—moving too fast and feeling stretched; moving too slowly and feeling stuck on a plateau
- *Physical setting*—being bothered by noise, lack of privacy, pollution, or other unpleasant working conditions

Life Stressors   A less obvious, though important, source of stress for people at work is the *spillover effect* that results when forces in their personal lives "spill over" to affect them at work. Such **life stressors** as family events (e.g., the birth of a new child), economic difficulties (e.g., the sudden loss of a big investment), and personal affairs (e.g., a separation or divorce) can all be extremely stressful. Since it is often difficult to completely separate work and nonwork lives, life stressors can affect the way people feel and behave on their jobs as well as in their personal lives.

■ **Life stressors** are things that arise in our personal lives to create stress.

Stress and Performance

Even though we tend to view and discuss stress from a negative perspective, it isn't always a negative influence on our lives. Indeed, there are two faces to stress—one positive and one negative.[49] **Constructive stress**, or *eustress,* acts in a positive way. It occurs at moderate stress levels by prompting increased work effort, stimulating creativity, and encouraging greater diligence. You may know such stress as the tension that causes you to study hard before exams, pay attention, and complete assignments on time in a difficult class. **Destructive stress**, or *distress,* is dysfunctional for both the individual and the organization. One form is the **job burnout** that shows itself as loss of interest in and satisfaction with a job due to stressful working conditions. When a person is "burned out," he or she feels exhausted, emotionally and physically, and thus unable to deal positively with work responsibilities and opportunities. Even more extreme reactions sometimes appear in news reports of persons who attack others and commit crimes in what is known as "desk rage" and "workplace rage." Too much stress can overload and break down a person's physical and mental systems, resulting in absenteeism, turnover, errors, accidents, dissatisfaction, reduced performance, unethical behavior, and even illness. Stanford scholar and consultant Jeffrey Pfeffer, for example, criticizes organizations that suffer from such excessive practices for creating toxic workplaces.[50] A toxic company implicitly says this to its employees: "We're going to put you in an environment where you have to work in a style and at a pace that is not sustainable. We want you to come in here and burn yourself out. Then you can leave.[51]

■ **Constructive stress** has a positive impact on both attitudes and performance.

■ **Destructive stress** has a negative impact on both attitudes and performance.

■ **Job burnout** shows itself as loss of interest in and satisfaction with a job because of stressful working conditions.

Stress and Health

As is well known, stress can impact a person's health. It is a potential source of both anxiety and frustration, which can harm the body's physiological and psychological well-being over time.[52] Health problems associated with stress include heart attacks, strokes, hypertension, migraine headache, ulcers, substance abuse, overeating, depression, and muscle aches. Managers and team leaders should be alert to signs of excessive stress in themselves and their co-workers. Key symptoms to look for are changes from normal patterns—changes from regular attendance to absenteeism, from punctuality to tardiness, from diligent work to careless work, from a positive attitude to a negative attitude, from openness to change to resistance to change, or from cooperation to hostility.

Stress Management

■■ Stress prevention involves minimizing the potential for stress to occur.

Stress prevention is the best first-line strategy in the battle against stress. It involves taking action to keep stress from reaching destructive levels in the first place. Work and life stressors must be recognized before one can take action to prevent their occurrence or to minimize their adverse impacts. Persons with Type A personalities, for example, may exercise self-discipline; supervisors of Type A employees may try to model a lower-key, more relaxed approach to work. Family problems may be partially relieved by a change of work schedule; simply knowing that your supervisor understands your situation may also help to reduce the anxiety caused by pressing family concerns.

■■ Stress management takes an active approach to dealing with stress that is influencing behavior.

■■ Personal wellness involves maintaining physical and mental health to better deal with stress when it occurs.

Once stress has reached a destructive point, special techniques of **stress management** can be implemented. This process begins with the recognition of stress symptoms and continues with actions to maintain a positive performance edge. The term "wellness" is increasingly used these days. **Personal wellness** involves the pursuit of one's job and career goals with the support of a personal health promotion program. The concept recognizes individual responsibility to enhance and maintain wellness through a disciplined approach to physical and mental health. It requires attention to such factors as smoking, weight, diet, alcohol use, and physical fitness. Organizations can benefit from commitments to support personal wellness. A University of Michigan study indicates that firms have saved up to $600 per year per employee by helping them to cut the risk of significant health problems.[53] Arnold Coleman, CEO of Healthy Outlook Worldwide, a health fitness consulting firm, states: "If I can save companies 5 to 20 percent a year in medical costs, they'll listen. In the end you have a well company and that's where the word 'wellness' comes from."[54]

■■ Employee assistance programs provide help for employees who are experiencing stressful personal problems.

On the organizational side, there is more and more emphasis today on **employee assistance programs** designed to provide help for employees who are experiencing personal problems and the stress associated with them. Common examples include special referrals on situations involving spousal abuse, substance abuse, financial difficulties, and legal problems. In such cases, the employer is trying to at least make sure that the employee with a personal problem has access to information and advice on how to get the guidance and perhaps even treatment needed to best deal with it. Organizations that build positive work environments and make significant investments in their employees are best positioned to realize the benefits of their full talents and work potential. As Pfeffer says: "All that separates you from your competitors are the skills, knowledge, commitment, and abilities of the people who work for you. Organizations that treat people right will get high returns."[55] That, in essence, is what the study of organizational behavior is all about.

Individual Differences and Diversity

A majority of *Fortune* 500 companies, including Colgate Palmolive, Corning, and Quaker Oats, are now providing incentives for executives to deal successfully with workforce diversity.[56] **Workforce diversity** refers to the presence of individual human characteristics that make people different from one another.[57] More specifically, this diversity comprises key demographic differences among members of a given workforce, including gender, race and ethnicity, age, and able-bodiedness. Sometimes they also encompass other factors, such as marital status, parental status, and religion.[58] The challenge is how to manage workforce diversity in a way that both respects the individual's unique perspectives and contributions and promotes a shared sense of organization vision and identity.

Workforce diversity has increased in both the United States and Canada as it has in much of the rest of the world. For example, in the United States, between 2000 and 2010, the number of females in the workforce has been predicted to increase by 15 percent so that more than 62 percent of the women in the United States are expected to be working in 2010. Also, the number of African Americans has been predicted to increase by 26 percent and the number of Hispanics by 43 percent. At the same time, those 40 and older are projected to make up more than one-half of the labor force.

All of this is in sharp contrast to the traditionally younger, mostly white American male labor force. Canadian and U.K. trends for women are similar.[59]

As the workforce becomes increasingly diverse, the possibility of stereotyping and discrimination increases, and managing diversity becomes more important. **Stereotyping** occurs when one thinks of an individual as belonging to a group or category—for instance, elderly person—and the characteristics commonly associated with the group or category are assigned to the individual in question—for instance, older people are not creative. **Demographic characteristics** are the background variables (e.g., age, gender) that help shape what a person becomes over time. They may serve as the basis of stereotypes that obscure individual differences and prevent people from getting to know others as individuals and accurately assessing others' performance potential. If you believe that older people are not creative, for example, you may mistakenly decide not to assign a very inventive 60-year-old person to an important task force.

Discrimination against certain people in the organization is not only a violation of U.S., Canadian, and European Union (EU) laws, but it is also counterproductive because it prevents the contributions of people who are discriminated against from being fully applied. Many firms are increasingly recognizing that a diverse workforce that reflects societal differences helps bring them closer to their customers.

Equal Employment Opportunity

Equal employment opportunity involves both workplace nondiscrimination and affirmative action. Employment decisions are nondiscriminatory when there is no intent to exclude or disadvantage legally protected groups. *Affirmative action* is a set of remedial actions designed to compensate for proven discrimination or correct for statistical imbalances in the labor force (e.g., local workers are 90 percent Hispanic, and your organization employs only 10 percent Hispanics).[60]

The most comprehensive statute prohibiting employment discrimination is Title VII of the Civil Rights Act of 1964. This act prohibits employers from discrim-

Workforce diversity is differences based on gender, race and ethnicity, age, and able-bodiedness.

Stereotyping occurs when one thinks of an individual as belonging to a group or category (e.g., elderly person), and the characteristics commonly associated with the group or category are assigned to the individual in question.

Demographic characteristics are the background variables (e.g., age, gender) that help shape what a person becomes over time.

inating against any individual with respect to compensation, terms, or conditions of employment because of race, color, religion, sex, or national origin. Affirmative action plans are required of federal government agencies and federal contractors, as well as of organizations found to be in noncompliance with equal employment opportunity provisions. Many organizations also have implemented voluntary affirmative action plans.[61]

Affirmative action is legally driven by federal, state and provincial, and local laws, as well as by numerous court cases. It requires written reports containing plans and statistical goals for specific groups of people in terms of such employment practices as hiring, promotions, and layoffs.[62]

Demography and Individual Differences

Demographic characteristics may be thought of in both current terms—for example, an employee's current medical status—and historical terms—for instance, where and how long a person has worked at various jobs. Demographic characteristics of special interest from equal employment opportunity and workplace diversity considerations include gender, age, able-bodiedness, and race and ethnicity.

Gender   The research on working women in general tells us that there are very few differences between men and women that affect job performance (see OB Savvy 2.1). Thus, men and women show no consistent differences in their problem-solving abilities, analytical skills, competitive drive, motivation, learning ability, or sociability. However, women are reported to be more conforming and to have lower expectations of success than do men. And women's absenteeism rates tend to be higher than those of men. This latter finding may change, however, as we see men starting to play a more active role in raising children; absenteeism is also likely to be less frequent as telecommuting, flexible working hours, and the like become more prevalent.[63] With respect to pay, women's earnings have risen slowly from 59 percent of men's in 1975 to as high as 76 percent more recently.[64] Certainly, this rise is not consistent with the large increase of women in the labor force since 1970.[65]

We have summarized a number of individual differences between men and women in the workplace and generally found few differences. Now, following recent researchers and recognizing the controversial nature of data, we summarize conclusions about differences between men and women as leaders.[66] We focus on three leadership questions: (1) What are differences in men's and women's leadership behaviors? (2) Is there prejudice against female leaders? (3) What are some leadership prospects for women?

Differences in Leader Behaviors   First, women tend to be more democratic and less autocratic than men, but not by much. Second, women tend to engage in more transformational behavior and deliver more rewards for good performance than do men.

Prejudice Against Females   Prejudice toward female leaders can come when conforming to their gender (communal) role would produce a failure to meet requirements of the leader role, and conforming

OB SAVVY 2.1

Tips for Dealing with Male and Female Managers

- Do not assume that male and female managers differ in personal qualities.
- Make sure that policies, practices, and programs minimize gender differences in managers' job experiences.
- Do not assume that management success is more likely for either females or males.
- Recognize that there will be excellent, good, and poor managers within each gender.
- Understand that success requires the best use of human talent, regardless of gender.

to the leader role would produce a failure to meet requirements of their gender role. The latter can result in lesser rewards for appropriate leadership behavior than a man would receive.

Leadership Prospects   In spite of the prejudice that still exists, the outlook for women's leadership participation is promising. More and more women are entering leadership positions in industrialized countries. Also, organizations can gain from putting women in leadership positions because it enhances the leadership pool.

Age   The research findings concerning age are particularly important given the aging of the workforce. The number of people age 50 and older has been predicted to increase by nearly 50 percent between 2000 and 2010.[67] Older workers are susceptible to being stereotyped as inflexible and undesirable in other ways. In some cases, workers as young as age 40 are considered to be "old" and complain that their experience and skills are no longer valued. Age-discrimination lawsuits are increasingly common in the United States.[68] Such discrimination also operates in Britain, where 44 percent of older managers say they have experienced age discrimination.[69] On the other hand, small businesses in particular tend to value older workers for their experience, stability, and low turnover rates. Research is consistent with these preferences and also shows lower avoidable absences among older workers.[70] Finally, to the extent that age is linked to experience or job tenure, there is a positive relationship between seniority and performance. More experienced workers tend to have low absence rates and relatively low turnover.

Able-Bodiedness   Even though recent studies report that disabled workers do their jobs as well as, or better than, nondisabled workers, nearly three-quarters of severely disabled persons are reported to be unemployed. Almost 80 percent of those with disabilities say they want to work.[71] Once again, the expected shortage of traditional workers is predicted to lead to a reexamination of hiring policies. More firms are expected to give serious consideration to hiring disabled workers, particularly given that the cost of accommodating these workers has been shown to be low.[72]

Racial and Ethnic Groups   Consistent with some current literature, we use the term "racial and ethnic groups" to reflect the broad spectrum of employees of differing ethnicities or races who make up an ever-increasing portion of the new workforce.[73] Of particular significance in the American workplace is diversity reflected in an increasing proportion of African Americans, Asian Americans, and Hispanic Americans.[74] The Hudson Institute projects this to be 32 percent by 2020.[75] The potential for stereotypes and discrimination to adversely affect career opportunities and progress for members of these and other minority groups must be recognized.

Even though employment decisions based on demographic differences are allowable under Title VII if they can be justified as bona fide occupational qualifications reasonable to normal business operations, race cannot be one of these. Case law has shown that these qualifications are always extremely difficult to justify.[76] The job of flight attendant is a case in point. When the airlines failed to show why men could not perform flight attendant duties as well as females, gender restrictions on hiring were lifted.

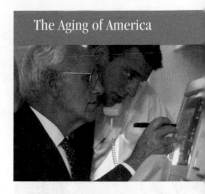

The Aging of America

A recent survey showed that more than half of the 150 executives surveyed regarding the retirement loss of a lot of experienced talent showed that 55% are very or somewhat concerned about impending retirements of key employees. Most also said their firms are taking steps to compensate for this loss. Nearly 60% have begun or enhanced succession-planning programs, and 45% are boosting recruitment and retention efforts. More than one-third are focusing on mentoring programs, and 25% are asking potential or actual retirees to serve as consultants or trainers. However, only 15% are increasing salaries or bonuses.

Thai Kids Under Stress

The Thai Ministry of Public Health revealed recently that more than a million Thai children are suffering from too much stress. Experts say this overload includes too many study hours, less time to play, and hearing parents discuss current economic and political issues. Child stress is becoming a problem, as evidenced by the long lines of children waiting to consult psychiatrists in some government hospitals. Authorities claim society requires the children to be too highly competitive. It is recommended that parents should not equate learning simply with studying. Children also can learn from doing enjoyable and fun activities, say experts.

■■ **Aptitude** represents a person's capability of learning something.

■■ **Ability** reflects a person's existing capacity to perform the various tasks needed for a given job.

Before leaving this section on demographic differences, it is important to reiterate the following:

- Demographic variables are important to consider in order to respect and best deal with the needs or concerns of people of different genders, ethnic backgrounds, ages, and so forth.
- However, these differences are too easily linked with stereotypes, which must be avoided.
- Demography is not a good indicator in seeking good individual–job fits. Rather, aptitude/ability, personality, and values and attitudes are what count.

Aptitude and Ability

Moving beyond demographic differences, let's consider aptitude and ability. **Aptitude** refers to a person's capability of learning something, whereas **ability** refers to a person's existing capacity to perform the various tasks needed for a given job and includes both relevant knowledge and skills.[77] In other words, aptitudes are potential abilities, whereas abilities are the knowledge and skills that an individual currently possesses.

Aptitudes and abilities are important considerations for a manager when initially hiring or selecting candidates for a job. We are all acquainted with various tests used to measure mental aptitudes and abilities. Some of these provide an overall intelligent quotient (IQ) score (e.g., the Stanford-Binet IQ Test). Others provide measures of more specific competencies that are required of people entering various educational programs or career fields. You have probably taken the ACT or SAT college entrance tests. Such tests are designed to facilitate the screening and selection of applicants for educational programs or jobs. In addition to mental aptitudes and abilities, some jobs, such as firefighters and police, require tests for physical abilities. Muscular strength and cardiovascular endurance are two of many physical ability dimensions.[78]

For legal purposes, demonstrated evidence must be presented that those scoring more favorably on the tests will tend to be more successful in their educational program, career field, or job performance than those with lower scores. In other words, there must be a fit between specific aptitudes and abilities and job requirements. If you want to be a surgeon, for instance, and cannot demonstrate good hand-eye coordination, there will not be a good ability–job fit. Such a fit is so important that it is a core concept in Chapter 8 on performance management and rewards.

Managing Diversity and Individual Differences

The concept of managing diversity in organizations emphasizes appreciation of differences in creating a setting where everyone feels valued and accepted. This is true not only in the United States but also in Canada, EU countries, and several countries in Asia.[79] Only the details differ. Managing diversity assumes that groups will retain their own characteristics and will shape the firm as well as be shaped by it, creating a common set of values that will strengthen ties with customers, enhance recruitment, and the like. Sometimes diversity management is resisted because of fear of change and discomfort with differences. To deal with this resistance, some countries, such as Canada, have laws designed to encourage the management of diversity at the provincial level through employment equity legislation.[80]

So how do managers and firms deal with all this? To convey the flavor of what some of the more progressive employers have done, let's now consider the Big

GAINING BACK "STEP-OUT" OR "OFF-RAMP" FEMALE EMPLOYEES

Female professional or managerial level employees are in increasingly short supply due to temporarily leaving the work force. One way of dealing with this shortage is through such programs as Personal Pursuits, sponsored by Deloitte & Touche USA, which allows up to a five-year hiatus. Though negotiated with each person individually, this program is similar to that of other professional firms such as Ernst & Young, among others. As a manager, such a program should be of interest to you personally or in your managerial role with appropriate subordinates.

- Those at the manager level and above who serve clients and who have been with the firm for the last two years are eligible if they have received favorable performance ratings during that time.
- While they can step-out for up to five years, they cannot leave to take a job (without approval) or start a business.
- There is an assigned mentor who provides career counseling and helps the step-out with current training and accreditation.
- The mentor serves as a liaison to help with the transition and to find a new internal position.
- During the step-out period, the person can take on subsidized training and ad hoc work assignments.
- The firm continues to pay for membership and licensing in the usual professional associations.[81A]

Four accounting and professional services firm Ernst and Young (EY).[81] EY has a very strong presence throughout the United States and Canada.

A key aspect is a very strong push from the board chair and CEO on down, including from positions specifically designated to manage various aspects of what EY terms "inclusiveness." At the same time there are two strong measurement tools—balanced score card and what EY terms "ethnicity snapshot"—and each manager and employee has inclusiveness as part of his or her performance evaluation. The intent has been to provide an inclusiveness culture from the partner level on down and one that strives for continuous improvement.

EY's pervasive implementation of such inclusiveness aspects includes real world recruiting, including at the traditionally black colleges; ethnic affinity groups—African American, Hispanic, Asian Pacific Islander; various kinds of inclusiveness awareness and minority conferences and workshops; a push for supplier diversity; executive mentoring and internal minority networking; affinity groups for community service; provision for minorities to be equitably represented at all levels; and an emphasis on working with a leading minority accounting and professional services firm on minority recruiting.

EY thus serves as an inclusiveness benchmark throughout the United States and Canada. Its benchmarking even extends to a large bank in Thailand, which has a similarly focused minority program.

Chapter 2   Study Guide

Summary

What are value differences among individuals, and in relation to national culture?

- Values are broad preferences concerning courses of action or outcomes.
- Rokeach divides 18 values into terminal values (preferences concerning ends) and instrumental values (preferences concerning means).
- Allport and his associates identify six value categories, ranging from theoretical to religious.
- Maglino and his associates classify values into achievement, helping and concern for others, honesty, and fairness.
- There have been societal changes in value patterns away from economic and organizational loyalty and toward meaningful work and self-fulfillment.
- Hofstede's five national culture values dimensions are power distance, individualism–collectivism, uncertainty avoidance, masculinity–femininity, and long-term/short-term orientation.
- Culture is the learned and shared way of doing things in a society; it represents deeply ingrained influences on the way people from different societies think, behave, and solve problems.

What is personality?

- Personality captures the overall profile, or combination of characteristics, that represents the unique nature of an individual as that individual interacts with others.
- Personality is determined by both heredity and environment; across all personality characteristics, the mix of heredity and environment is about 50–50.

How do personalities differ?

- The Big Five personality traits consist of extraversion, agreeableness, conscientiousness, emotional stability, and openness to experience.
- A useful personality framework consists of social traits, personal conception traits, emotional adjustment traits, and personality dynamics, where each category represents one or more personality dimensions.

How are personality and stress related?

- Stress emerges when people experience tensions caused by extraordinary demands, constraints, or opportunities in their jobs.
- Personal stressors derive from personality type, needs, and values; they can influence how stressful different situations become for different people.

- Work stressors arise from such things as excessive task demands, interpersonal problems, unclear roles, ethical dilemmas, and career disappointments.

- Non-work stress can spill over to affect people at work; non-work stressors may be traced to family situations, economic difficulties, and personal problems.

- Stress can be managed by prevention—such as making adjustments in work and non-work factors; it can also be dealt with through personal wellness—taking steps to maintain a healthy body and mind capable of better withstanding stressful situations.

What is the relationship between individual differences and workforce diversity?

- Workforce diversity is the mix of gender, race and ethnicity, age, and able-bodiedness in the workforce.

- Workforces in the United States, Canada, and Europe are becoming more diverse, and valuing and managing such diversity is becoming increasingly more important to enhance organizational competitiveness and provide individual development.

- Demographic differences are background characteristics that help shape what a person has become.

- Gender, age, race and ethnicity, and able-bodiedness are particularly important demographic characteristics.

- The use of demographic differences in employment is covered by a series of federal, state/provincial, and local laws outlawing discrimination.

- Demographic differences can be the basis for inappropriate stereotyping that can influence workplace decisions and behaviors.

- Aptitude is a person's capability of learning something.

- Ability is a person's existing capacity to perform the various tasks needed for a given job.

- Aptitudes are potential abilities.

- Both mental and physical aptitudes and abilities are used in matching individuals to organizations and jobs.

- Managing diversity and individual differences involves striving for a match among the firm, specific jobs, and the people recruited, hired, and developed, while recognizing an increasingly diverse workforce.

- Increasing workforce diversity is provided for by equal employment opportunity, through nondiscrimination and affirmative action; ethical considerations; local, national, and global competitive pressures; and a projected change in the nature of the workforce.

- Once a match between organizational and job requirements and individual characteristics is obtained, it is necessary to manage the increasing diversity in the workforce.

- Firms now use a wide variety of practices in managing workforce diversity: interactive networks, recruitment, education, development, promotion, pay, and assessment among others.

Key Terms

Ability (p. 54)
Aptitude (p. 54)
Authoritarianism (p. 45)
Constructive stress (p. 49)
Culture (p. 37)
Demographic
    characteristics (p. 51)
Destructive stress (p. 49)
Developmental approaches
    (p. 41)
Dogmatism (p. 45)
Emotional adjustment traits
    (p. 47)
Employee assistance
    programs (p. 51)
Individualism-collectivism
    (p. 38)

Instrumental values
    (p. 35)
Job burnout (p. 49)
Life stressors (p. 49)
Locus of control (p. 45)
Long-term/short-term
    orientation (p. 38)
Masculinity-femininity
    (p. 38)
Personality (p. 39)
Personality dynamics
    (p. 41)
Personal wellness (p. 50)
Power distance (p. 38)
Self-concept (p. 42)
Self-monitoring (p. 47)
Social traits (p. 43)

Stereotyping (p. 51)
Stress (p. 48)
Stress management (p. 50)
Stress prevention (p. 50)
Stressors (p. 48)
Terminal values (p. 35)
Type A orientation (p. 48)
Type B orientation (p. 48)
Uncertainty avoidance
    (p. 38)
Values (p. 34)
Value congruence (p. 37)
Workforce diversity
    (p. 51)
Work stressors (p. 48)

Self-Test 2

Multiple Choice

1. Values in the United States _____. (a) are largely unchanged across time (b) have moved away from earlier values (c) are virtually the same as attitudes (d) tend not to be shared within cultures and organizations

2. Values are _____. (a) similar to personality variables (b) used in place of abilities (c) related to aptitudes (d) similar to attitudes

3. _____ is the study of how people in different cultures use persistence, the ordering of relationships, thrift, sense of shame, personal steadiness, reciprocity, protection of "face," and respect for tradition to communicate. (a) Confucian dynamism (b) The Whorfian hypothesis (c) Proxemics (d) Domestic multiculturalism

4. One would expect to find respect for authority and acceptance of status differences in cultures with high _____. (a) power distance (b) individualism (c) uncertainty avoidance (d) aggressiveness

5. Asian countries such as Japan and China are described on Hofstede's dimensions of national culture as generally high in _____. (a) uncertainty avoidance (b) short-term orientation (c) long-term orientation (d) individualism

6. The Big Five framework consists of _____. (a) five aptitudes and abilities (b) five demographic characteristics (c) extraversion, agreeableness, strength, emotional stability, and openness to experience (d) extraversion, agreeableness, conscientiousness, emotional stability, and openness to experience

7. Personality dynamics is represented by _____. (a) self-esteem and self-efficacy (b) Type A/Type B orientation (c) self-monitoring (d) Machiavellianism

8. Task demands and ethical dilemmas are examples of _____ stressors, while a Type A personality is a _____ stressor. (a) work-related; personal (b) work-related; non-work (c) non-personal; personal (d) real; imagined

9. Stress that comes from not knowing or understanding what you are expected to do is caused by the stressor of _____. (a) role conflict (b) task demands (c) interpersonal problems (d) role ambiguity

10. Which is an example of stress management by using the personal wellness strategy? _____. (a) role negotiation (b) empowerment (c) regular physical exercise (d) flexible hours

11. In the United States, Canada, the European Union, and much of the rest of the world, the workforce is _____. (a) becoming more homogeneous (b) more highly motivated than before (c) becoming more diverse (d) less motivated than before

12. Stereotyping occurs when one thinks of an individual _____. (a) as different from others in a given group (b) as possessing characteristics commonly associated with members of a given group (c) as like some members of a given group but different from others (d) as basically not very competent

13. Managing diversity and affirmative action are _____. (a) similar terms for the same thing (b) both mandated by law (c) different but complementary (d) becoming less and less important

14. Aptitudes and abilities are divided into _____. (a) stereotypes (b) physical and mental (c) mental and personality (d) aggressive and passive

15. Demographic differences _____. (a) are especially valuable in selecting workers (b) are based on aptitudes and abilities (c) are the background variables that help shape what a person becomes over time (d) are important personality aspects

Short Response

16. Why is the individualism–collectivism dimension of national culture important in OB?
17. How do power-distance values affect management practices across cultures?
18. In what ways are demographic characteristics important in the workplace?
19. How might stress influence individual performance?

Applications Essay

20. Your boss is trying to figure out how to get the kinds of people she needs for her organization to do well, while at the same time dealing appropriately with an increasing number of non-white female and male workers. She has asked you to respond to this concern. Prepare a short report with specific suggestions for your boss.

These learning activities from *The OB Skills Workbook* are suggested for Chapter 2.

OB in Action

CASE	EXPERIENTIAL EXERCISE	SELF-ASSESSMENT
■ 2. Crossing Borders	■ 8. Prejudice in Our Lives ■ 10. Alligator River Story	■ 5. Personal Values

Plus—special learning experiences from *The Jossey-Bass/Pfeiffer Classroom Collection*

Chapter 3

Emotions, Attitudes, and Job Satisfaction

Chapter at a Glance

OB has increasingly been emphasizing emotional aspects in addition to cognitive factors. As you read Chapter 3, *keep in mind these study topics.*

FOUNDATIONS OF EMOTIONS AND MOODS

Functions Served by Emotions

Major Emotions and Their Subcategories

Self-conscious versus Social Emotions

Positive and Negative Affectivity

EMOTIONS AND MOODS IN ACTION

Affective Events Theory

Emotional Labor

Emotional Intelligence

Emotions and Organizational Behavior

Emotions and Culture

ATTITUDES

Attitudes and Behavior

Attitudes and the Workplace

Attitudes and Cognitive Consistency

JOB SATISFACTION

Concepts and Measures

Job Satisfaction and Performance

It's not only how people think but how they feel

Zach Johnson, holding the lead at one over par in the 2007 Masters golf tournament, slouched in the locker room, averting his eyes from a television because he was afraid that Tiger Woods would overcome the lead he held. He didn't steal a peek until Woods's shot missed the hole. Finally, the tears started to come. Queried earlier by a fan as to how he was feeling, Johnson replied: "My legs are numb from the knees down. . . . I'm not sure they're still attached to my body."

The setup at the Masters was polarizing. Some players felt it was the ultimate test, while others reviled it for the numbing difficulty that drained away much of the excitement of the traditional Masters tournaments.

Although this was only Johnson's second major tour victory, he had a history of never being afraid to win. In the past, he had shown strong determination against long odds in football, golf, soccer, and a three-point basketball shooting contest. His emotions had always served him well.[1]

Foundations of Emotions and Moods

Affects is a generic term that covers a broad range of feelings that individuals express.

Moods are less intense as compared with emotions, and they frequently lack a contextual stimulus.

Emotions are intense feelings directed at someone or something.

As noted earlier, emotions, moods, and some of their related concepts have become increasingly important in the study of organizational behavior. We start our discussion of this increasingly important topic area by defining emotions and their relatives and showing the relationships among them. Here, Figure 3.1 shows emotions, moods, values, and attitudes and uses affects as an umbrella term encompassing all of these.[2]

Affects is a generic term that covers a broad range of feelings that individuals express.[3] Affects encompass emotions, moods, attitudes, and values. **Emotions** are intense feelings that are directed at someone or something. Emotions always have an object, something triggers them. **Moods** are less intense as compared with emotions, and frequently, although not always, lack a contextual stimulus.

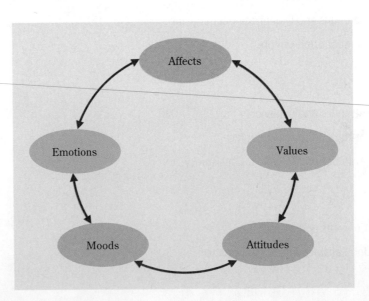

Figure 3.1 **Relationships among affects and related feelings.**

Emotions are argued to be more fleeting than moods. Someone may say or do something to you that leads to a quick and intense positive or negative reaction from you. That feeling will probably quickly pass, whereas a mood is likely to remain for several hours, or maybe even days, and is not likely to be directed at a specific person or event.

Sometimes, of course, an emotion can change into a mood, and a positive or negative mood can develop into a longer-term emotion. Emotions and moods mutually influence each other. Finally, emotions tend to be contagious. We mimic the emotions expressed by others.

Attitudes and values tend to be more stable than emotions and moods, with values the most stable of all. As the figure shows, each of these affects the others, and in total they reflect a wide range of thoughts and feelings in the workplace.

Since values are stable, as we indicated in Chapter 2, they can affect work attitudes, emotions, and moods. For instance, if you value job challenge, you will probably tend to have a negative attitude toward a run-of-the-mill assembly-line job.

Also, attitudes can influence moods and emotions in much the same way. If you really like your job, you are more likely to have positive emotions about it than if you don't. Also, you are probably likely to experience more positive moods about it than if you didn't have such a positive attitude.

Ultimately, it is even possible over time that your values might change in response to your attitudes, emotions, and moods concerning your job. For instance, you might start out feeling that your job is just a job and doesn't do much in terms of fulfilling your values. Then, you may discover some challenges that encourage positive emotions and moods, you develop positive job satisfaction, and eventually come to see the job as meeting one or more of your values. In other words, as Figure 3.1 shows, emotions and moods can influence attitudes, and attitudes, in turn, can influence values.

Functions Served by Emotions

Emotions are a double-edged sword.[4] Some, such as Charles Darwin, have argued that emotions are useful in a person's survival process. For instance, the emotion of excitement encourages you to deal with situations requiring high levels of energy, such as those you encounter during school and job assignments. At the same time, too much energy exertion can tire you out. Anger is another example: often it is bad; however, if channeled correctly, it can stop someone from taking advantage of you. Even a positive emotion, such as empathy, while usually helpful, can sometimes cause the person with whom you originally empathized to take advantage of the situation.

Major Emotions and Their Subcategories

Researchers have identified six major categories of emotions, each of which generally includes some subcategories. These categories are anger, fear, joy, love, sadness, and surprise.[5] While the categories are distinct from each other, the subcategories within each are fairly similar. For example, anger may contain disgust and envy, among other subcategories; fear may contain alarm and anxiety; joy may contain cheerfulness and contentment; love may contain affection, longing, and lust; sadness may contain disappointment, neglect, and shame; surprise, however, contains no subcategories.

Let's Have Fun!

Lou Piniella has been ejected 57 times from baseball games in his 19-year managerial career. However, when he was hired as the Chicago Cubs' new manager, he said: "We're going to have some fun. It's going to be nice and relaxed here." He says this even though the pressure to win is as great as it's always been. Of course, his amused players aren't completely sold and are taking bets on his first meltdown. Even so, the climate at the Cubs' 2007 preseason training camp was upbeat, purposeful, and even relaxed. Piniella takes over from a laid-back previous manager as part of an extreme makeover of a conservative team. Among other things, there are 17 new faces and, for the first time, advertising on the ivy-covered outfield walls at Wrigley Field. The thinking is that the hiring of Piniella, regardless of his emotions, is a signal the Cubs are serious about winning, and the move has already helped in the recruiting of free agents.

Leaders on Leadership

GREEN, UPSIDE DOWN AND INSIDE OUT

Yvon Chouinard, a French Canadian who was born in rural Maine, is the founder of Patagonia, a 35-year-old outdoor clothing and equipment company headquartered in California. His firm is green and all business, "but it's business conducted upside down and inside out." In short, it is radical. The 68-year-old Chouinard says: "I don't think we're going to be here 100 years from now as a society, or maybe even as a species." He looks more like a river guide than an executive.

He captures his feeling about running a business in his book, *Let My People Go Surfing*. It is a green-business primer and memoir. Patagonia has reused materials and, among other things, provided on-site day care, flextime, and maternity and paternity leave on the way to becoming a $270-million-dollar business. Patagonia's philosophy has been not to emphasize making money but to stress doing things right, and the profits will follow. Chouinard believes people should be able to wash travel clothes in a cooking pot or sink, hang them out to dry, and still be presentable on a plane ride home.

Patagonia has more than 900 applicants for every job opening, and Chouinard is a perfectionist. The firm's current CEO says that while Chouinard has an "easygoing persona, he does demand excellence. People would run through walls for him." Chouinard claims: "I'm a very happy person, I never get depressed, even though I know everything's going to hell."[5A]

Question: How is it that Chouinard has been so successful in starting and running his business?

Self-conscious versus Social Emotions

Self-conscious emotions help individuals stay aware of and regulate their relationships with others.

Social emotions refer to individuals' feelings based on information external to themselves.

Self-conscious emotions come from internal sources and social emotions come from external sources.[6] Shame, guilt, embarrassment, and pride are the internal emotions. It is argued that **self-conscious emotions** help individuals stay aware of and regulate their relationships with others. **Social emotions** refer to individuals' feelings based on information external to themselves; they include *pity, envy,* and *jealousy*. An example is feeling envy or perhaps jealousy because a co-worker received a promotion you were hoping for.

Positive and Negative Affectivity

Positive affectivity are those who have a tendency to be perpetually positive.

Negative affectivity are those who are "down" most of the time.

As we have shown, current moods can be affected by many different events. However, there are also relatively stable tendencies to experience positive or negative feelings.[7] Those who are high in **positive affectivity** have a tendency to be perpetually positive. For them, the glass is nearly always half full. In contrast, those with **negative affectivity** are "down" most of the time; they tend to experience negative moods in a wide range of settings and under many different conditions.

These negative people are perpetual pessimists who may perform poorly themselves and also interfere with the performance of others. They tend to create a negative climate in terms of decision making and team performance and are often targets of aggression from co-workers.

Emotions and Moods in Action

Affective Events Theory

As you have read our previous discussion you may have wondered if there is a model that would tie together and extend understanding of people's emotional reactions on the job and how these reactions influence those people. Not surprisingly, there is, as shown in Figure 3.2.[8]

The left-hand side indicates how the work environment and work events have an influence on your feelings. These feelings can be expressed through hassles and uplifts. Emotional labor requirements, discussed further below, refer to the extent individuals have to work hard to show what they see as being appropriate emotions for their jobs. Salespeople and flight attendants are two examples. It is very important that people in these lines of work put on happy faces regardless of how they feel. Thus, the term "labor" comes in—doing this is not easy.

We have all experienced hassles and uplifts on the job, sometimes many of these during a work day. People respond to these positive and negative experiences through positive and negative emotional reactions. Personality enters in primarily through the positive and negative affectivity personality components, where positive and negative reactions tend to be enhanced or cut back depending on the component. Mood can also influence the reactions. Your mood at a given time can exaggerate the nature of the emotions you experience as a result

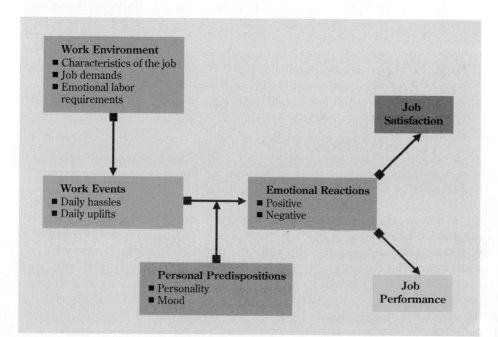

Figure 3.2   Affective Events Theory.

of an event. For example, if you have just been laid off, you are likely to feel worse than you would otherwise when a colleague says something to you that was meant as a neutral comment.

These affective reactions, in turn, are predicted to influence on-the-job reactions such as satisfaction and perhaps even performance. There is strong research support especially for job satisfaction.[9] The moral is that managers should pay lots of attention to affective factors such as moods and emotions.

Emotional Labor

Emotional disso-nance is inconsistencies between emotions we feel and emotions we project.

Emotional labor and its components are important enough topics to be treated in their own right. Being "on" all the time with your emotions is an effort, whether or not the way you act out emotions reflects your true feelings. A discrepancy between the two is called **emotional dissonance**—inconsistencies between emotions we feel and emotions we project.[10]

Emotional labor is a situation where a person displays organizationally desired emotions during interpersonal transactions at work.

As mentioned earlier, this dissonance is where the term emotional *labor* comes from. Formally defined, **emotional labor** is a situation where a person displays organizationally desired emotions during interpersonal transactions at work.[11]

Deep acting is trying to modify your true inner feelings based on display rules.

Deep acting and surface acting are two terms reflecting ways of dealing with emotional dissonance. **Deep acting** is trying to modify your true inner feelings based on display rules, and **surface acting** is hiding your inner feelings and forgoing emotional expressions as a response to display rules.[12]

Surface acting is hiding your inner feelings and forgoing emotional expressions as a response to display rules.

Emotional Intelligence

All of us are familiar with cognitive ability and intelligence, or IQ, which have been measured for over 100 years and which we discussed in Chapter 2. However, a concept that has only recently begun to be recognized is emotional intelligence, or EI. EI was touched on in Chapter 1. EI is one's ability to understand and manage one's own feelings and emotions and the feelings and emotions of others.[13]

EI includes the following factors:[14]

1. Appraisal and expression of emotions in yourself: your ability to understand your own emotions and to express these naturally.
2. Appraisal and recognition of emotions in others: your ability to perceive and understand emotions of others.
3. Regulation of emotions in yourself: your ability to regulate your own emotions.
4. Use of emotions to facilitate performance: your ability to use emotions by directing them toward constructive activities and improved performance (e.g., encouraging better performance from yourself).

Essentially, EI argues that if you are good at knowing and managing your own emotions and are good at reading others' emotions, you may perform better in your own job. There is some support for this intuitive argument. For example, entrepreneurs who can read others earn more money than others less skilled at such readings. Similarly, Chinese factory workers with high co-worker EI ratings received higher performance ratings from their supervisors.[15] Also, EI is a quality that has separated more successful presidents (such as Roosevelt, Kennedy, and Reagan) from those who were less successful (such as Johnson, Carter, and Nixon).[16]

Even more interesting findings were shown in a study that combined EI with IQ. Rather than emphasizing separate findings, the results showed that EI could compensate for those with lower IQs. In other words, high emotional intelligence partially compensated for low cognitive intelligence. Similarly, emotional intelligence mattered less for those with high levels of cognitive intelligence.[17]

EI continues to receive increasing attention. As it does, it seems reasonable to expect more research, and such research is likely to be of the more complex type just summarized.

Emotions and Organizational Behavior

We can conclude the above discussion by focusing first on organizational behavior and then on culture. In terms of OB we are particularly concerned about leadership, motivation, customer service, and gender differences—areas that convey the flavor and reinforce the current increasing managerial emphasis on the importance of increasing the importance of emotions.

Leadership   As we will discuss in Chapter 11 and Chapter 12, astute leaders can use emotions to develop charismatic and transformational leadership. There is lots of research evidence supporting this argument.[18]

Motivation   Affective Events Theory, discussed earlier in this chapter, suggests that employees emphasize emotions, along with more cognitive aspects, in performing their jobs. They can become both cognitively and emotionally committed in their activity in pursuit of a goal.[19]

Customer service   One of the areas most obviously connected to emotions and moods is customer service. Emotional dissonance is especially likely here, as is the experience of **emotional contagion**. In this case, the customer catches the emotions of the salesperson. When those emotions are positive, there is evidence customers shop longer. Of course, this contagion can work both ways.[20]

▬ **Emotional contagion** is when the customer catches the emotions of the salesperson.

MASTERING MANAGEMENT

IMPROVING YOUR SOCIAL IQ

Daniel Goleman discusses social intelligence which he defines as, "being able to read a situation to know how to make a good impression and being able to sense another's feelings and intentions" (p. 10). You should recognize two things about this definition: first, being able to sense another's feelings and intentions is often termed "empathy" and second, the definition is remarkably similar to emotional intelligence.

Below we paraphrase five suggestions by Goleman to improve your listening skills on the way to becoming more empathetic.

• Commit yourself to listening well.
• Get feedback from great listeners who know you well.
• Be watchful. Recognize when you are most likely to trigger the habit you are attempting to change, such as interrupting a person. Work on avoiding the urge to interrupt.
• Think of failures as opportunities and try to handle the failure better the next time.
• Don't ever stop practicing.[21]

Gender differences In the case of gender differences, there is some evidence that management expects men and women to display different emotions. Women report having to suppress more negative feelings and emphasize more positive feelings than men in similar positions.[22]

There are numerous other OB applications of emotions and moods, and you can probably think of many. However, the applications mentioned above convey the flavor and reinforce the current increasing managerial emphasis on the importance of appreciating the power of emotions.

Emotions and Culture

The frequency and intensity of emotions has been shown to vary across cultures. In mainland China, for example, research suggests that people report fewer positive and negative emotions than those in other cultures. Also, such emotions are less intense than what others report. However, Taiwanese Chinese report more positive and fewer negative emotions than those in mainland China.[23]

In contrast, we can say that people's interpretations of cultures appear to be similar across cultures. The major emotions mentioned previously, such as happiness, joy, and love, are all valued positively. However, enthusiasm is valued in the United States while Chinese consider negative emotions as more useful. Also, in Japan and China, unlike in the United States, pride is considered undesirable.[24]

At the same time, the norms for expression vary across cultures. For example, in collectivist cultures (emphasizing group relationships) emotional displays are seen as being concerned with the person expressing the emotion, while people in individualistic cultures such as the United States tend not to think that another's emotional expression is directed at them.[25]

Display rules govern the degree to which it is appropriate for people from different cultures to display their emotions similarly.

Finally, informal standards, called **display rules**, govern the degree to which it is appropriate for people from different cultures to display their emotions similarly. Great Britain encourages downplaying emotions, while Mexicans are much more demonstrative in public. Wal-Mart's emphasis on friendliness, for example, has been found not to work in Germany. There, serious German shoppers have been shown not to like Wal-Mart's friendly greeters and helpful personnel. In Israel shoppers equate smiling cashiers with inexperience, so cashiers are encouraged to look somber.[26]

The message from all this for managers is to be especially sensitive to the way emotions are displayed in other cultures. Often such emotions do not mean what they do in the United States.

Attitudes

As Figure 3.1 showed, another affective component besides emotion and mood is attitude. Attitudes are strongly influenced by values and are acquired from the same sources as values: friends, teachers, parents, role models, and culture. Attitudes focus on specific people or objects, whereas values have a more general focus and are more stable than attitudes. "Employees should be allowed to participate" is a value; your positive or negative feeling about your job because of the participation it allows is an attitude. Formally defined, an **attitude** is a predisposition to respond in a positive or negative way to someone or something in one's environment. For example, when you say that you "like" or "dislike" someone or something, you are

Attitude is a predisposition to respond in a positive or negative way to someone or something in one's environment.

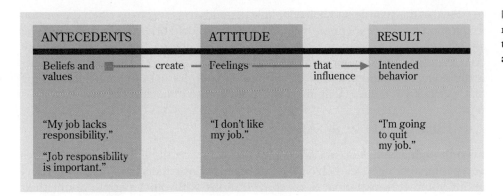

Figure 3.3 A work-related example of the three components of attitudes.

expressing an attitude. It's important to remember that an attitude, like a value, is a hypothetical construct; that is, one never sees, touches, or actually isolates an attitude. Rather, attitudes are *inferred* from the things people say, informally or in formal opinion polls or through their behavior.

Figure 3.3 shows attitudes as accompanied by antecedents and results.[27] The beliefs and values antecedents in the figure form the **cognitive component** of an attitude: the beliefs, opinions, knowledge, or information a person possesses. **Beliefs** represent ideas about someone or something and the conclusions people draw about them; they convey a sense of "what is" to an individual. "My job lacks responsibility" is a belief shown in the figure. Note that the beliefs may or may not be accurate. "Job responsibility is important" is a corresponding aspect of the cognitive component, which reflects an underlying value.

The **affective component** of an attitude is a specific feeling regarding the personal impact of the antecedents. This is the actual attitude itself, such as "I don't like my job." The **behavioral component** is an intention to behave in a certain way based on your specific feelings or attitudes. This intended behavior is a result of an attitude and is a predisposition to act in a specific way, such as "I'm going to quit my job."

Attitudes and Behavior

You should recognize that the link between attitudes and behavior is tentative. An attitude results in *intended* behavior; this intention may or may not be carried out in a given circumstance.

In general, the more specific attitudes and behaviors are, the stronger the relationship. For example, say you are a French Canadian webmaster and you are asked about your satisfaction with your supervisor's treatment of French Canadian webmasters. You also indicate the strength of your intent to look for another webmaster job in a similar kind of organization within the next six months. Here, both the attitude and the behavior are specifically stated (they refer to French Canadian webmasters, and they identify a given kind of organization over a specific time period). Thus, we would expect to find a relatively strong relationship between these attitudes and how aggressively you actually start looking for another webmaster job.

It is also important that a good deal of freedom be available to carry out the intent. In the example just given, the freedom to follow through would be sharply restricted if the demand for webmasters dropped substantially.

Cognitive components reflect the beliefs, opinions, knowledge, or information a person possesses and values of an attitude.

Beliefs represent ideas about someone or something and the conclusions people draw about them.

Affective component of an attitude is a specific feeling regarding the personal impact of the antecedents.

Behavioral component is an intention to behave in a certain way based on your specific feelings or attitudes.

Finally, the attitude and behavior linkage tends to be stronger when the person in question has had experience with the stated attitude. For example, assuming you are a business administration or management major, the relationship between your course attitude and/or your intent to drop the course and your later behavior of actually doing so would probably be stronger in your present OB course than in the first week of your enrollment in an advanced course in nuclear fission.[28]

Attitudes and the Workplace

Even though attitudes do not always predict behavior, the link between attitudes and potential or intended behavior is important for managers to understand. Think about your work experiences or conversations with other people about their work. It is not uncommon to hear concerns expressed about someone's "bad attitude." These concerns typically reflect displeasure with the behavioral consequences with which the poor attitude is associated. Unfavorable attitudes in the form of low job satisfaction can result in costly labor turnover, absenteeism, tardiness, and even impaired physical or mental health. One of the manager's responsibilities, therefore, is to recognize attitudes and to understand both their antecedents and their potential implications.

Attitudes and Cognitive Consistency

■ Cognitive dissonance describes a state of inconsistency between an individual's attitude and behavior.

Leon Festinger, a noted social psychologist, uses the term **cognitive dissonance** to describe a state of inconsistency between an individual's attitudes and his or her behavior.[29] Let's assume that you have the attitude that recycling is good for the economy, but you don't recycle. Festinger predicts that such an inconsistency results in discomfort and a desire to reduce or eliminate it by (1) changing the underlying attitude, (2) changing future behavior, or (3) developing new ways of explaining or rationalizing the inconsistency.

Two factors that influence which of the above choices tend to be made are the degree of control a person thinks he or she has over the situation and the magnitude of the rewards involved. In terms of control, if your boss won't let you recycle office trash, you would be less likely to change your attitude than if you voluntarily chose not to recycle. You might instead choose the rationalization option. Rewards, if they are high enough, tend to reduce your feeling of inconsistency: if I'm rewarded even though I don't recycle, the lack of recycling must not be so bad after all.

Job Satisfaction

We now move from a discussion of attitudes in general to a very specific job attitude—job satisfaction.

Concepts and Measures

Recall that job satisfaction is the degree to which individuals feel positively or negatively about their jobs. It is an attitude or emotional response to one's tasks as well as to the physical and social conditions of the workplace. At first glance, and from the perspective of Herzberg's two-factor theory (Chapter 5), some aspects of job satisfaction should be motivational and lead to positive employment relationships and high levels of individual job performance. But as we will discuss, the issues are more complicated than this conclusion suggests.

On a daily basis, managers must be able to infer the job satisfaction of others by careful observation and interpretation of what they say and do while going about their jobs. Sometimes it is also useful to examine more formally the levels of job satisfaction among groups of workers, especially through formal interviews or questionnaires. Increasingly, other methods are being used as well, such as focus groups and computer-based attitude surveys.[30]

Among the many available job satisfaction questionnaires that have been used over the years, two popular ones are the Minnesota Satisfaction Questionnaire (MSQ) and the Job Descriptive Index (JDI).[31] Both address aspects of satisfaction with which good managers should be concerned for the people reporting to them. For example, the MSQ measures satisfaction with working conditions, chances for advancement, freedom to use one's own judgment, praise for doing a good job, and feelings of accomplishment, among others. The five facets of job satisfaction measured by the JDI are

- *The work itself*—responsibility, interest, and growth
- *Quality of supervision*—technical help and social support
- *Relationships with co-workers*—social harmony and respect
- *Promotion opportunities*—chances for further advancement
- *Pay*—adequacy of pay and perceived equity vis-à-vis others.

Job Satisfaction and Performance

The importance of job satisfaction can be viewed in the context of two decisions people make about their work. The first is the decision to belong—that is, to join and remain a member of an organization. The second is the decision to perform—that is, to work hard in pursuit of high levels of task performance. Not everyone who belongs to an organization performs up to expectations.

The decision to belong concerns an individual's attendance and longevity at work. In this sense, job satisfaction influences *absenteeism,* or the failure of people to go to work. In general, workers who are satisfied with the job itself have more regular attendance and are less likely to be absent for unexplained reasons than are dissatisfied workers. Job satisfaction can also affect *turnover,* or decisions by people to terminate their employment. Simply put, dissatisfied workers are more likely than satisfied workers to quit their jobs.[32]

What is the relationship between individual job satisfaction and individual performance? There is considerable debate on this issue, with three alternative points of view evident: (1) satisfaction causes performance, (2) performance causes satisfaction, and (3) rewards cause both performance and satisfaction.[33]

Argument: Satisfaction Causes Performance   If job satisfaction causes high levels of performance, the message to managers is quite simple: to increase employees' work performance, make them happy. Research, however, indicates that no simple and direct link exists between individual job satisfaction at one point in time and work performance at a later point. This conclusion is widely recognized among OB scholars, even though some evidence suggests that the relationship holds better for professional or higher-level employees than for nonprofessionals or those at lower job levels. Job satisfaction alone is not a consistent predictor of individual work performance.

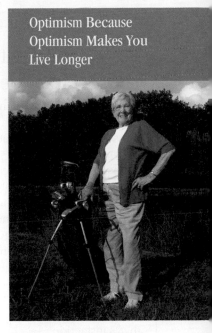

Optimism Because Optimism Makes You Live Longer

A recent study by researchers at Yale and at Miami University in Ohio looked at how positive or negative attitudes toward aging affected longevity. They found that people who viewed aging positively lived an average of 71/2 years longer. These people focused on the good things they had gained, including careful attention to role models. What couldn't we do with an extra 71/2 years of life?

Research Insight
Linking Employee Satisfaction and Firm Performance

One of the important lines of inquiry in organizational behavior research has dealt with the relationship between job satisfaction and performance. Recent research by Benjamin Schneider and his associates with aggregated organizational data indicates that the causal priorities in this relationship are complex and deserving of further research attention. Using longitudinal data collected from large companies during 1987–1995, they measured return on assets (ROA), earnings per share (EPS), and various components of job satisfaction. Analysis showed that satisfaction with pay and security and overall job satisfaction were related to subsequent firm performance. But, also, firm performance appeared to cause overall job satisfaction and satisfaction with security. Schneider and colleagues interpret these results as indicating a complex relationship between employee job satisfaction and firm performance that includes elements of reciprocity. They call attention to the abbreviated model shown in the accompanying figure. Note, especially, the reciprocal relationships between performance and satisfaction and satisfaction and performance.[33A]

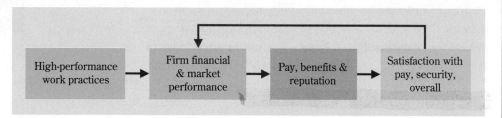

Argument: Performance Causes Satisfaction   If high levels of performance cause job satisfaction, the message to managers is quite different. Rather than focusing first on peoples' job satisfaction, attention should be given to helping people achieve high performance; job satisfaction would be expected to follow. Research indicates an empirical relationship between individual performance measured at a certain time period and later job satisfaction. A basic model of this relationship, based on the work of Edward E. Lawler and Lyman Porter, maintains that performance accomplishment leads to rewards that, in turn, lead to satisfaction.[34] In this model, rewards are intervening variables; that is, they "link" performance with later satisfaction. In addition, a moderator variable—perceived equity of rewards—further affects the relationship. The moderator indicates that performance will lead to satisfaction only if rewards are perceived as equitable. If an individual feels that his or her performance is unfairly rewarded, the performance-causes-satisfaction argument will not hold.

Argument: Rewards Cause Both Satisfaction and Performance   This final argument in the job satisfaction–performance controversy is the most compelling. It suggests that a proper allocation of rewards can positively influence both performance and satisfaction. The key word in the previous sentence is "proper." Research indicates that people who receive high rewards report higher job satisfaction. But research also indicates that performance-contingent rewards influence a person's work performance. In this case, the size and value of the reward vary in proportion to the level of one's performance accomplishment. Large rewards are given for high performance; small or no rewards are given for low performance. And whereas giving a low performer only small rewards initially may lead to dissatisfaction, the expectation is that the individual will make efforts to improve performance in order to obtain greater rewards in the future.

A More Complex View At the same time, as the Research Insight and the OB Savvy 3.1 features for this chapter suggest, relationships become more complex and provide more insight when we move from the individual employee and individual performance level to the organizational or firm level, take time into account, and consider a number of separate components of satisfaction and performance.

The point is that to truly understand the relationship between satisfaction and performance, a manager needs to use a more sophisticated model. The model should consider variables other than simply performance and satisfaction, should focus across time, and should go beyond the individual level of analysis.

OB SAVVY 3.1
Job Satisfaction and Performance

The relationship between job satisfaction and performance is a complex one, as shown below:
- Job satisfaction alone is not a consistent predictor of individual work performance.
- However, individual performance can lead to rewards that, in turn, lead to individual satisfaction (if the rewards are equitable).
- Well-managed rewards can positively influence both individual satisfaction and performance.

High-performance work practices (such as employee involvement, total quality management, and human resource systems) lead to better firm (financial and market) performance, which leads to better working conditions (pay, benefits, reputation); better conditions create positive employee satisfaction components (pay, security, overall) that encourage employee behaviors that feedback and contribute further to firm performance.[34A]

ETHICS IN OB

CANCER BATTLER HUNTS FOR DEEPER SATISFACTION

Willie Leftwich, a former hard-charging Washington, D.C., attorney, has battled cancer and has taken on a new profession. He is now hunched over a spinning wheel, giving form to a clay pot. This abrupt change is part of his soul-searching after he was declared cancer free, and he reassessed his values. This values reassessment came from seeing children fighting for their lives and from seeing doctors, nurses, and cancer survivors giving generously of their time and energy to help those fighting with cancer.

He was struck by the meaninglessness of his high-flying legal career and looked in new directions for a path that would provide deeper satisfaction. He finally found the path through the potter's wheel. Along the way he befriended other potters and thought seriously about bringing pleasure to someone else through taking a lump of clay and making something attractive and functional. "I'm happier than I've ever been. Had it not been for cancer, I probably wouldn't have become a potter and experienced the same satisfaction and meaning in life that I've found working in clay."[35A]

Question: How might you explain this former attorney's new found job satisfaction in terms of discussion of job satisfaction and performance in the text?

Chapter 3   Study Guide

Summary

What are foundations of emotions and moods?

- Affects is a generic term that covers a broad range of feelings that individuals express.

- Emotions are intense feelings that are directed at someone or something.

- Moods are less intense as compared with emotions and frequently, although not always, lack a contextual emphasis.

- Values are relatively stable and can affect work attitudes, emotions, and moods.

- Also, attitudes can influence moods and emotions in much the same way as values.

- Social emotions refer to individuals' feelings based on information external to themselves and include pity, envy, scorn, and jealousy. Self-conscious emotions come from internal sources, help individuals stay aware of and regulate their relationships with others, and include shame, guilt, embarrassment, and pride.

- There are people who are high in positive affectivity or negative affectivity and who tend to be "up" or "down," respectively, most of the time.

What are emotions and moods in action?

- Affective Events Theory (AET) relates characteristics of the job, job demands, and emotional labor requirements to daily hassles and uplifts. These are related to positive and negative emotional reactions, while being moderated by high and low affectivity, personal predispositions, and moods, and are ultimately associated with job satisfaction and performance.

- Emotional labor is a situation where a person displays organizationally desired emotions during interpersonal transactions at work.

- Emotional dissonance is the discrepancy between true feelings and organizationally desired transactions and often characterized by deep acting, to try to modify true inner feelings, or by surface acting to hide one's true inner feelings.

- Emotional Intelligence is one's ability to detect and manage emotional cues and information.

- Astute leaders, using selected emotions, can be perceived as charismatic by their followers.

- Emotional contagion, where a customer catches the emotion from the salesperson, is especially important in customer service.

- Management tends to expect women to suppress negative feelings and emphasize positive feelings more than men.

- Display rules govern the degree to which it is appropriate for people from different cultures to display their emotions similarly.

What are attitudes?

- Attitudes are predispositions to respond positively or negatively to someone or something in one's environment; attitudes are influenced by values but are more specific.

- Individuals desire consistency between their attitudes and their behaviors.

- Attitudes are important because they indicate predispositions toward behaviors.

What is job satisfaction?

- Job satisfaction is the degree to which individuals feel positively or negatively about their jobs.

- There are five facets of job satisfaction:
  - The work itself
  - Quality of supervision
  - Relationships with co-workers
  - Promotion opportunities
  - Pay

- There are three arguments relating to individual job satisfaction and individual performance:
  - Satisfaction causes performance.
  - Performance causes satisfaction.
  - Rewards cause both satisfaction and performance.

- There is also research that uses longitudinal, aggregated organizational data across time: these data show that high performance work practices lead to a firm's financial and market performance, which leads to pay, benefits, and reputation, which leads to overall satisfaction with pay and security, and which, in turn, reciprocally influences a firm's financial and market performance.

Key Terms

Affective component (p. 69)

Affects (p. 62)

Attitude (p. 68)

Behavioral component (p. 69)

Beliefs (p. 69)

Cognitive component (p. 69)

Cognitive dissonance (p. 70)

Deep acting (p. 67)

Display rules (p. 68)

Emotional contagion (p. 67)

Emotional dissonance (p. 66)

Emotional labor (p. 67)

Emotions (p. 62)

Moods (p. 62)

Negative affectivity (p. 64)

Positive affectivity (p. 64)

Self-conscious emotions (p. 64)

Social emotions (p. 64)

Surface acting (p. 67)

Self-Test 3

Multiple Choice

1. Emotions are _____. (a) generic terms that cover a broad range of feelings that individuals express; (b) intense feelings that are directed at someone or something; (c) less fleeting than moods; (d) more stable than values.

2. Emotions and moods influence _____. (a) attitudes; (b) aptitudes; (c) environment; (d) demographics

3. Social emotions _____. (a) come from external sources; (b) are represented by happiness; (c) come from internal sources; (d) include pity and cheerfulness

4. Affective Events Theory _____. (a) is the same as emotional labor; (b) includes daily hassles and daily uplifts; (c) includes only positive reactions; (d) is the same as emotional intelligence

5. Deep acting _____. (a) is trying to modify your true inner feelings based on display rules; (b) includes appraisal and recognition of emotions in others; (c) matters much for intelligence; (d) appears to be related to physical strength

6. Leadership _____. (a) links emotions to charismatic leadership; (b) relates charisma to Affective Events Theory; (c) is linked directly to emotional dissonance; (d) is similar to display rules

7. Emotions _____. (a) are similar to emotional contagion; (b) are expressed similarly by Taiwanese and Mainland Chinese; (c) emphasize display rules; (d) vary across cultures.

8. Attitudes tend to _____. (a) follow values; (b) be stronger than values; (c) be unrelated to behavior; (d) be more general than values

9. Attitudes _____. (a) focus on specific people or objects; (b) do not need to be inferred; (c) represent carried-out behavior; (d) are the same as aptitudes

10. Antecedents and results _____. (a) represent the noncognitive component of attitudes; (b) are not related to attitudes; (b) are usually not intended; (c) are not emphasized much in OB; (d) are stronger when a person has had experience with them

11. Cognitive dissonance _____. (a) describes a state of consistency between a person's attitude and behavior; (b) describes a state of inconsistency between a person's attitude and behavior; (c) is restricted to emotional feelings; (d) is related to display rules

12. Job satisfaction _____. (a) is strongly related to performance; (b) is inconsistently related to performance; (c) is related to performance through values; (d) is related to performance by means of attitudes

13. Job satisfaction _____. (a) does not include facets; (b) includes performance; (c) is a job aptitude; (d) has a complex relationship to performance

14. Job satisfaction _____. (a) is best if considered at one point in time; (b) emphasizes cognitive dissonance; (c) sometimes has reciprocal relationships with performance; (d) is usually related to intellectual capital

15. Performance _____. (a) may cause satisfaction; (b) is less important than satisfaction; (c) is more important than aptitude; (d) is related to body size

Short Response

16. What are the relationships among affect, emotions, moods, attitudes, and values?

17. Compare and contrast positive and negative aspects of anger and empathy.

18. Briefly discuss five facets of job satisfaction and their importance.

19. Briefly discuss attitudes and cognitive dissonance.

Applications Essay

20. Your boss has the impression that "satisfied workers are productive workers" and has asked you to check this out. Prepare a short report with recommendations for your boss.

These learning activities from *The OB Skills Workbook* are suggested for Chapter 3.

OB in Action

CASE	EXPERIENTIAL EXERCISE	SELF-ASSESSMENT
■ 3. SAS Institute	■ 4. What Do You Value in Your Work? ■ 5. My Asset Base	■ 4. Global Readiness Index ■ 5. Personal Values

Plus—special learning experiences from *The Jossey-Bass/Pfeiffer Classroom Collection*

Chapter 4

Perception, Attribution, and Learning

Chapter at a Glance

A particularly striking thing about the current American OB landscape is the importance of perception and its cousins attribution and learning. As you read Chapter 4, *keep in mind these study topics*.

THE PERCEPTION PROCESS

Factors Influencing Perception

Stages of the Perceptual Process

Response to the Perceptual Process

COMMON PERCEPTUAL DISTORTIONS

Stereotypes or Prototypes

Halo Effects

Selective Perception

Projection

Contrast Effects

Self-Fulfilling Prophecies

MANAGING PERCEPTIONS

Impression Management

Distortion Management

ATTRIBUTION THEORY

The Importance of Attributions

Attribution Errors

Attributions across Cultures

INDIVIDUAL LEARNING

Reinforcement

Social Learning Theory

CHAPTER 4 STUDY GUIDE

It's in the eye of the beholder

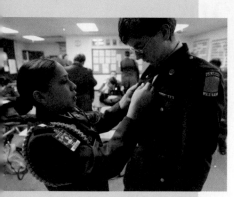

Becky Rangel, a 4-foot-10-inch, 17-year-old brigade commander at Seagonville, Texas, High School, is the new face of Junior ROTC (JROTC) in many large urban programs. She is the senior commander of JROTC programs for 19 Dallas high schools.

Female, and often a minority group member, these leaders now represent some 53 percent of the Dallas program. Six or seven students commanding Dallas Independent School District cadet brigades recently were females.

Often stereotyped as "jalapenos", "pickles," or "cucumbers" by some of the other students, particularly females, they are also seen as role models by many, including young males. Indeed, Becky has strengthened the way she is perceived and has belied the prevailing female stereotype by doing 62 pushups a minute, becoming a National Honor Society parliamentarian, and being chosen for the varsity soccer and cross-country teams. She has clearly overcome the tendency of Hispanic male students not to follow females and can now bark orders with the best of them. To all this, Becky's reply is. "You know what, I'm making something of myself."

These opportunities have occurred since the ROTC reorganization in 1972. Colonel Arthur L. Holmes Jr., director of Army Instruction for the Atlanta Public Schools, argues: "It's a success story. This country just needs to brace itself; it's coming—females are going to be in these leadership roles."[1A]

It's obvious from all this that perception, and its cousins—attribution and learning—are very important. This increasing importance makes it necessary to understand the topics addressed in this chapter.

> ## "You know what, I'm making something of myself."

The Perception Process

A spectacular completed pass during the 1982 National Football Conference championship game helped propel Joe Montana, former San Francisco 49er quarterback, into the legendary status he enjoys today. The reverse effect apparently occurred for Danny White, the Dallas Cowboys' quarterback. He fumbled in the final minute of the same game and never obtained the status of his predecessor, Roger Staubach, even though White took the Cowboys to the championship game three years in a row.[1]

This example illustrates the notion of **perception**, the process by which people select, organize, interpret, retrieve, and respond to information from the world around them.[2] This information is gathered from the five senses of sight, hearing, touch, taste, and smell. As Montana, White, and Staubach can attest, perception and reality are not necessarily the same thing. The perceptions or responses of any two people are also not necessarily identical, even when they are describing the same event.

■ **Perception** is the process through which people receive, organize, and interpret information from their environment.

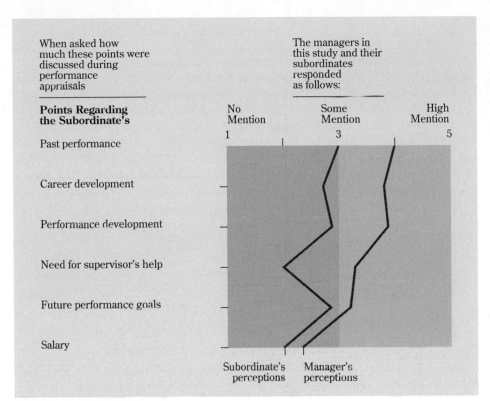

Figure 4.1   Contrasting perceptions between managers and their subordinates: the case of the performance appraisal interview.

Through perception, people process information inputs into responses involving feelings and action. Perception is a way of forming impressions about oneself, other people, and daily life experiences. It also serves as a screen or filter through which information passes before it has an effect on people. The quality or accuracy of a person's perceptions, therefore, has a major impact on his or her responses to a given situation.

Perceptual responses are also likely to vary between managers and subordinates. Consider Figure 4.1, which depicts contrasting perceptions of a performance appraisal between managers and subordinates. Rather substantial differences exist in the two sets of perceptions; the differences can be significant. In this case managers who perceive that they already give adequate attention to past performance, career development, and supervisory help are unlikely to give greater emphasis to these points in future performance appraisal interviews. In contrast, their subordinates are likely to experience continued frustration because they perceive that these subjects are not being given sufficient attention.

Factors Influencing Perception

The factors that contribute to perceptual differences and the perceptual process among people at work, which are summarized in Figure 4.2, include characteristics of the *perceiver*, the *setting*, and the *perceived*.

Figure 4.2   Factors influencing the perceptual process.

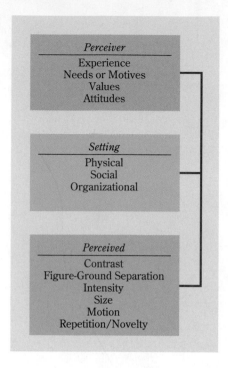

The Perceiver   A person's past experiences, needs or motives, personality, and values and attitudes may all influence the perceptual process. A person with a strong achievement need tends to perceive a situation in terms of that need. If you see doing well in class as a way to help meet your achievement need, for example, you will tend to emphasize that aspect when considering various classes. In the same way a person with a negative attitude toward unions may react antagonistically when local union officials make routine visits to the organization. These and other perceiver factors influence the various aspects of the perceptual process.

The Setting   The physical, social, and organizational context of the perceptual setting also can influence the perceptual process. Kim Jeffrey, the CEO of Nestlés Perrier, was perceived by his subordinates as a frightening figure when he gave vent to his temper and had occasional confrontations with them. Before he was promoted, however, Jeffrey's flare-ups had been tolerable; when he became CEO, they caused intimidation, so his subordinates were afraid to express their opinions and recommendations. Fortunately, after he received feedback about this problem, he was able to change his subordinates' perceptions in the new setting.[3]

The Perceived   Characteristics of the perceived person, object, or event—such as contrast, intensity, figure-ground separation, size, motion, and repetition or novelty—are also important in the perceptual process. For example, one mainframe computer among six PCs or one man among six women will be perceived differently than one of six mainframe computers or one of six men—where there is less contrast. Intensity can vary in terms of brightness, color, depth, sound, and the like. A bright red sports car stands out from a group of gray sedans; whispering or shouting stands out from ordinary conversation.

This concept is known as figure-ground separation: it depends on which image is perceived as the background and which as the figure. For an illustration, look at Figure 4.3. What do you see? Faces or a vase?

In the matter of size, very small or very large people tend to be perceived differently and more readily than average-sized people. Similarly, in terms of motion, moving objects are perceived differently than stationary objects. And, of course, advertisers hope that ad repetition or frequency will positively influence people's perception of a product. Television advertising blitzes for new models of personal computers are a case in point. Finally, the novelty of a situation affects its perception. A purple-haired teenager is perceived differently than a blond or a brunette, for example.

Figure 4.3   Figure-ground illustration.

Stages of the Perceptual Process

So far we have discussed key factors influencing the perceptual process. Now we will look at the stages involved in processing the information that ultimately determines a person's perception and reaction, as shown in Figure 4.4. The information-processing stages are divided into information attention and selection, organization of information, information interpretation, and information retrieval.

Attention and Selection   Our senses are constantly bombarded with so much information that if we don't screen it, we quickly become incapacitated with information overload. *Selective screening* lets in only a tiny proportion of all the information available. Some of the selectivity comes from controlled processing—consciously deciding what information to pay attention to and what to ignore. In this case the perceivers are aware that they are processing information. Think about the last time you were at a noisy restaurant and screened out all the sounds but those of the person with whom you were talking.

In contrast to controlled processing, screening can also take place without the perceiver's conscious awareness. For example, you may drive a car without

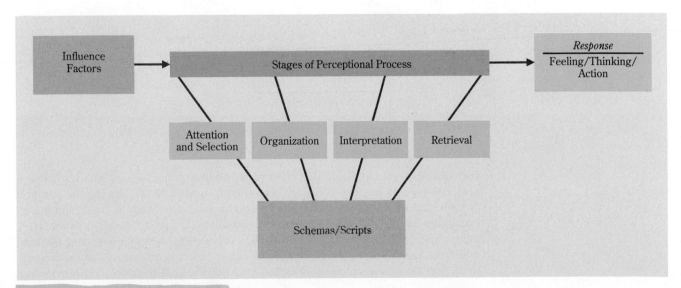

Figure 4.4   The perceptual process.

Research Insight
Perceptions of Organizational and Supervisor Support and Perceived Individual Subordinate Performance

Rhoades and Eisenberger examined the possibility that supervisors' perceptions that were supported by the organization might lead them, in turn, to treat subordinates supportively, with positive consequences for subordinates, perceived supervisor support, perceived organizational support, and various aspects of performance. The researchers surveyed 248 full-time employees of a chain of large discount appliance and electronics firms; the employees completed the survey on company time. The researchers also surveyed 71 supervisors of the subordinates completing the questionnaires.

The results were strongly supportive of the authors' hypotheses based on their initial arguments: Organizational support notions may be expanded to include support provided to subordinates as a way in which supervisors reciprocate perceived favorable treatment from the organization. Perceptions by supervisors that the organization valued their contributions and cared about their well being were shown to be related to subordinates' perceptions of supervisor support. Such support, in turn, was found to be related to subordinates' perceptions of organizational support, in-role performance (e.g., this employee meets formal requirements of the job), and extra-role performance (e.g., this employee goes out of his or her way to help new employees). These findings support the argument that the organization's supportive treatment of supervisors may be useful for increasing subordinates' perceived organizational support as well as subordinate performance. Perceptions on the part of both supervisors and subordinates were clearly important to these findings.

Subordinate-perceived supervisor support was found to be an intervening variable between supervisor-perceived organizational support and subordinate-perceived organizational support, and also for both in-role and extra-role performance.[3A]

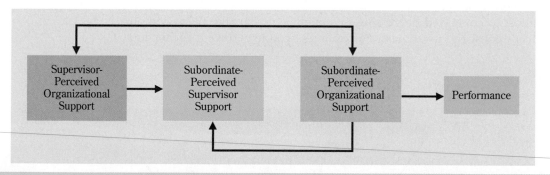

consciously thinking about the process of driving; you may be thinking about a problem you are having with your coursework instead. While driving the car, you are affected by information from the world around you, such as traffic lights and other cars, but you do not pay conscious attention to that information. Such selectivity of attention and automatic information processing works well most of the time when you drive, but if a nonroutine event occurs, such as an animal darting onto the road, you may have an accident unless you quickly shift to controlled processing.

Organization   Even though selective screening takes place in the attention stage, it is still necessary to find ways to organize the information efficiently. **Schemas** help us do this. Schemas are cognitive frameworks that represent organized knowledge about a given concept or stimulus developed through experience.[4] A *self schema* contains information about a person's own appearance, behavior, and personality. For instance, a person with a decisiveness schema tends to perceive himself or herself in terms of that aspect, especially in circumstances calling for leadership.

■■■ **Schemas** are cognitive frameworks that represent organized knowledge about a given concept or stimulus developed through experience.

Person schemas refer to the way individuals sort others into categories, such as types or groups, in terms of similar perceived features. The term "*prototype,*" or "*stereotype,*" is often used to represent these categories; it is an abstract set of features commonly associated with members of that category. Once the prototype is formed, it is stored in long-term memory; it is retrieved when it is needed for a comparison of how well a person matches the prototype's features. For instance, you may have a "good worker" prototype in mind, which includes hard work, intelligence, punctuality, articulateness, and decisiveness; that prototype is used as a measure against which to compare a given worker. Stereotypes may be regarded as prototypes based on such demographic characteristics as gender, age, able-bodiedness, and racial and ethnic groups. The chapter opener, for example, refers to female brigade commanders in stereotypic terms.

A *script schema* is defined as a knowledge framework that describes the appropriate sequence of events in a given situation.[5] For example, an experienced manager would use a script schema to think about the appropriate steps involved in running a meeting. Finally, *person-in situation schemas* combine schemas built around persons (self and person schemas) and events (script schemas).[6] Thus, a manager might organize his or her perceived information in a meeting around a decisiveness schema for both himself or herself and a key participant in the meeting. Here, a script schema would provide the steps and their sequence in the meeting; the manager would push through the steps decisively and would call on the selected participants periodically throughout the meeting to respond decisively. Note that although this approach might facilitate organization of important information, the perceptions of those attending might not be completely accurate because the decisiveness element of the person-in-situation schema did not allow the attendees enough time for open discussion.

As you saw in Figure 4.4, schemas are not important just in the organization stage; they also affect other stages in the perception process. Furthermore, schemas rely heavily on automatic processing to free people up to use controlled processing as necessary. Finally, as we will show, the perceptual factors described earlier as well as the distortions to be discussed shortly, influence schemas in various ways.

Interpretation   Once your attention has been drawn to certain stimuli and you have grouped or organized this information, the next step is to uncover the reasons behind the actions. That is, even if your attention is called to the same information and you organize it in the same way your friend does, you may interpret it differently or make different attributions about the reasons behind what you have perceived. For example, as a manager, you might attribute compliments from a friendly subordinate to his being an eager worker, whereas your friend might interpret the behavior as insincere flattery.

Leaders on Leadership

RICK WARREN: SUPERSTAR LEADER

Rick Warren is a 51-year-old Southern California minister who also has a best-selling book (26 million copies at last count), *The Purpose Driven Life*. He has been called secular America's favorite evangelical Christian. He is also a protégé of the late management guru Peter Drucker, and he has entertained Jack Welch at his home. Just after Hurricane Kat-rina hit in 2005, Warren went on the Larry King television show to describe relief work being done by the churches. As an evangelical Christian, Warren represents some 30 to 50 million Americans.

Warren calls himself a "spiritual entrepreneur" and preaches to more than 20,000 church attendees each Sunday. He has built Saddleback Valley Community Church in Lake Forest, California, into one of the biggest religious institutions in America. He is in charge of an annual budget of $30 million with 300 employees and a 120-acre campus. He wants to bring together conservative and liberal Protestants, fix Africa, and move Christianity in America from self-centeredness to unselfishness.

Warren challenges people to think big but be patient about results. According to Warren, most people set their goals too low and try to accomplish them too quickly. He emphasizes giving up control so an organization can grow, and he delegates accordingly. He uses roughly 3,300 small groups organized a myriad of ways. He claims to be uninterested in operations and to be neither well organized nor disciplined.

One of his large goals is to defeat poverty, illiteracy, and disease in Africa. Warren travels extensively and has taken special interest in Rwanda. He wants to make Rwanda the first "purpose driven nation." Although his message is orthodox, he has been attacked by other evangelicals.

Drucker has called the rise of megachurches, such as Warren's, the most significant social phenomenon of the last 30 years. Whether one agrees or not, most would say he is certainly one of the greatest religious entrepreneurs of his generation.[6A]

Question: Are Rick Warren's goals reachable given the way you perceive that he leads his organization?

Retrieval   So far, we have discussed the stages of the perceptual process as if they all occurred at the same time. However, to do so ignores the important component of memory. Each of the previous stages forms part of that memory and contributes to the stimuli or information stored there. The information stored in our memory must be retrieved if it is to be used. This leads us to the retrieval stage of the perceptual process summarized in Figure 4.4.

All of us at times have trouble retrieving information stored in our memories. More commonly, memory decays, so that only some of the information is retrieved. Schemas play an important role in this area. They make it difficult for people to remember things not included in them. For example, based on your prototype about the traits comprising a "high-performing employee" (hard work, punctuality, intelligence, articulateness, and decisiveness), you may overestimate these traits and underestimate others when you are evaluating the performance of a subordinate whom you generally consider good. Thus, you may overestimate the person's decisiveness since it is a key part of your high-performance prototype.

Indeed, people are as likely to recall nonexistent traits as they are to recall those that are really there. Obviously, this distortion can cause major problems in terms of performance appraisals and promotions, not to mention numerous other interactions on and off the job. Such prototypes, though, allow you to "chunk" information and reduce overload. Thus, prototypes though, are a double-edged sword.

Response to the Perceptual Process

Throughout this chapter, we have shown how the perceptual process influences numerous OB responses. Figure 4.4 classifies such responses into thoughts, feelings, and actions. For example, in countries such as Mexico, bosses routinely greet their secretaries with a kiss, and that is expected behavior. In contrast, in this country your thoughts and feelings might be quite different about such behavior. You might very well perceive this as a form of sexual harassment. As you cover the other OB topics in the book, you also should be alert to the importance of perceptual responses covering thoughts, feelings, and actions.

Common Perceptual Distortions

Figure 4.5 shows some common kinds of distortions that can make the perceptual process inaccurate and affect the response. These are stereotypes and prototypes, halo effects, selective perception, projection, contrast effects, and the self-fulfilling prophecy.

Stereotypes or Prototypes

Earlier, when discussing person schemas, we described stereotypes, or prototypes, as useful ways of combining information in order to deal with information overload. At the same time, we pointed out how stereotypes can cause inaccuracies in

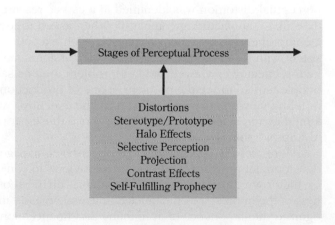

Figure 4.5 Distortions occurring in perceptual process stages.

retrieving information, along with some additional problems. In particular, stereotypes obscure individual differences; that is, they can prevent managers from getting to know people as individuals and from accurately assessing their needs, preferences, and abilities. We compared these stereotypes with research results and showed the errors that can occur when stereotypes are relied on for decision making. Nevertheless, stereotypes continue to exist at the board of directors' level in organizations. A survey of 133 *Fortune* 500 firms showed that female directors were favored for membership on only the relatively peripheral public affairs committees in these organizations. Males were favored for membership on the more important compensation, executive, and finance committees, even when the females were equally or more experienced than their male counterparts.[7]

Both managers and employees need to be sensitive to stereotypes; they must also attempt to overcome them and recognize that an increasingly diverse workforce can be a truly competitive advantage.

Halo Effects

■ **Halo effect** occurs when one attribute of a person or situation is used to develop an overall impression of the person or situation.

A **halo effect** occurs when one attribute of a person or situation is used to develop an overall impression of the individual or situation. Like stereotypes, these distortions are more likely to occur in the organization stage of perception. Halo effects are common in our everyday lives. When meeting a new person, for example, a pleasant smile can lead to a positive first impression of an overall "warm" and "honest" person. The result of a halo effect is the same as that associated with a stereotype, however: individual differences are obscured.

Halo effects are particularly important in the performance appraisal process because they can influence a manager's evaluations of subordinates' work performance. For example, people with good attendance records tend to be viewed as intelligent and responsible; those with poor attendance records are considered poor performers. Such conclusions may or may not be valid. It is the manager's job to try to get true impressions rather than allowing halo effects to result in biased and erroneous evaluations.

Selective Perception

■ **Selective perception** is the tendency to single out for attention those aspects of a situation, person, or object that are consistent with existing beliefs, values, and needs.

Selective perception is the tendency to single out those aspects of a situation, person, or object that are consistent with one's needs, values, or attitudes. Its strongest impact occurs in the attention stage of the perceptual process. This perceptual distortion was identified in a classic research study involving executives in a manufacturing company.[8] When asked to identify the key problem in a comprehensive business policy case, each executive selected a problem consistent with his or her functional area work assignments. For example, most marketing executives viewed the key problem area as sales, whereas production people tended to see the problem as one of production and organization. These differing viewpoints would affect how the executive would approach the problem; they might also create difficulties once these people tried to work together to improve things.

More recently, 121 middle- and upper-level managers attending an executive development program expressed broader views in conjunction with an emphasis on their own function. For example, a chief financial officer indicated an awareness of the importance of manufacturing, and an assistant marketing manager recognized the importance of accounting and finance along with each of their own functions.[9] Thus, this more current research demonstrated very little perceptual selectivity. The researchers were not, however, able to state definitively what accounted for the differing results.

These results suggest that selective perception is more important at some times than at others. Managers should be aware of this characteristic and test whether or not situations, events, or individuals are being selectively perceived. The easiest way to do this is to gather additional opinions from other people. When these opinions contradict a manager's own, an effort should be made to check the original impression.

Projection

Projection is the assignment of one's personal attributes to other individuals; it is especially likely to occur in the interpretation stage of perception. A classic projection error is illustrated by managers who assume that the needs of their subordinates and their own coincide. Suppose, for example, that you enjoy responsibility and achievement in your work. Suppose, too, that you are the newly appointed manager of a group whose jobs seem dull and routine. You may move quickly to expand these jobs to help the workers achieve increased satisfaction from more challenging tasks because you want them to experience things that you, personally, value in work. But this may not be a good decision. If you project your needs onto the subordinates, individual differences are lost. Instead of designing the subordinates' jobs to best fit their needs, you have designed their jobs to best fit your needs. The problem is that the subordinates may be quite satisfied and productive doing jobs that seem dull and routine to you. Projection can be controlled through a high degree of self-awareness and empathy—the ability to view a situation as others see it.

Contrast Effects

Earlier, when discussing the perceived, we mentioned how a bright red sports car would stand out from a group of gray sedans because of its contrast. This perceptual distortion also can occur when, say, a person gives a talk following a strong speaker or is interviewed for a job following a series of mediocre applicants. We can expect a **contrast effect** to occur when an individual's characteristics are contrasted with those of others recently encountered who rank higher or lower on the same characteristics. Clearly, both managers and employees need to be aware of the possible perceptual distortion the contrast effect may create in many work settings.

Self-Fulfilling Prophecies

A final perceptual distortion is the **self-fulfilling prophecy**—the tendency to create or find in another situation or individual that which you expected to find in the first place. A self-fulfilling prophecy is sometimes referred to as the "Pygmalion effect," named for a mythical Greek sculptor who created a statue of his ideal mate and then made her come to life.[10] His prophecy came true! Through self-fulfilling prophecy you also may create in the work situation that which you expect to find.

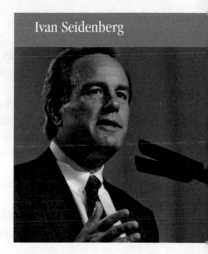

Ivan Seidenberg

Ivan Seidenberg is the current CEO and chair of the communications giant Verizon. He actively projects his feelings about emphasizing "the right thing to do" through the actions of his employees. He is a role model, and he and his employees successfully illustrate such things as philanthropy, supporting minority-owned businesses, and actively recruiting minority employees.

■■ **Projection** is the assignment of personal attributes to other individuals.

■■ **Contrast effects** occur when an individual's characteristics are contrasted with those of others recently encountered, who rank higher or lower on the same characteristics.

■■ **Self-fulfilling prophecy** is the tendency to create or find in another situation or individual that which one has expected to find.

OB SAVVY 4.1

Creating Positive Self-Fulfilling Prophecies for Employees

To develop the valuable skill of creating positive self-fulfilling prophecies for your employees:
- Be aware that positive and optimistic approaches to your subordinates can lead them to positive self-fulfilling prophecies.
- Create a warmer interpersonal climate between your subordinates and you.
- Give more performance feedback to subordinates—make it as positive as possible, given their actual performance.
- Spend lots of time helping subordinates learn job skills.
- Provide more opportunities for subordinates to ask questions.

Self-fulfilling prophecies can have both positive and negative results for you as a manager. Suppose you assume that your subordinates prefer to satisfy most of their needs outside the work setting and want only minimal involvement with their jobs. Consequently, you are likely to provide simple, highly structured jobs designed to require little involvement. Can you predict what response the subordinates would have to this situation? Their most likely response would be to show the lack of commitment you assumed they would have in the first place. Thus your initial expectations are confirmed as a self-fulfilling prophecy.

Self-fulfilling prophecies can have a positive side, however (see OB savvy 4.1). Students introduced to their teachers as "intellectual bloomers" do better on achievement tests than do their counterparts who lack such a positive introduction. A particularly interesting example of the self-fulfilling prophecy is that of Israeli tank crews. One set of tank commanders was told that, according to test data, some members of their assigned crews had exceptional abilities but others were only average. In reality, the crew members had been assigned randomly so that the two test groups were equal in ability. Later the commanders reported that the so-called exceptional crew members performed better than the "average" members. As the study revealed, the commanders had paid more attention to and praised the crew members for whom they had the higher expectations.[11] The self-fulfilling effects in these cases argue strongly for managers to adopt positive and optimistic approaches toward all people at work.

Managing Perceptions

To be successful, managers must understand the perceptual process, the stages involved, and the impact the perceptual process can have on their own and others' responses. They must also be aware of what roles the perceiver, the setting, and the perceived have in the perceptual process. Particularly important with regard to the perceived is the concept of impression management—for both managers and others.

Impression Management

Impression management is a person's systematic attempt to behave in ways that will create and maintain desired impressions in the eyes of others. First impressions are especially important and influence how people respond to one another. Impression management is influenced by such activities as associating with the "right people," doing favors to gain approval, flattering others to favorably impress them, taking credit for a favorable event, apologizing for a negative event while seeking a pardon, agreeing with the opinions of others, downplaying the severity of a negative event, and doing favors for others.[12] Successful managers learn how to use these activities to enhance their own images, and they are sensitive to their use by their subordinates and others in their organizations. In this context, job titles are particularly important.

Distortion Management

During the attention and selection stage, managers should be alert to balancing automatic and controlled information processing. Most of their responsibilities, such as performance assessment and clear communication, will involve controlled processing, which will take time away from other job responsibilities. Along with more controlled processing, managers need to be concerned about increasing the frequency of observations and about getting representative information rather than simply responding to the most recent information about a subordinate or a production order, for instance. Some organizations, including 911 systems, have responded to the need for representative and more accurate information by using current technology. In addition, managers should not fail to seek out disconfirming information that will help provide a balance to their typical perception of information.

The various kinds of schemas as well as prototypes and stereotypes are particularly important at the information organizing stage. Managers should strive to broaden their schemas or should even replace them with more accurate or complete ones.

At the interpretation stage, managers need to be especially attuned to the impact of attribution on information; we discuss this concept further in the next section. At the retrieval stage, managers should be sensitive to the fallibility of memory. They should recognize the tendency to overrely on schemas, especially on prototypes or stereotypes that may bias information storage and retrieval.

Throughout the entire perception process, managers should be sensitive to the information distortions caused by halo effects, selective perception, projection, contrast effects, and self-fulfilling prophecies in addition to the distortions caused by stereotypes and prototypes.

Geoffrey Orsak

Dr. Orsak would like to change the name of Southern Methodist University's school of engineering—something like the Institute of Ingenuity and Creativity has a nice ring. In so doing, he wants to change the image that engineering is just for gearheads, nerds, and geeks. He's trying to recruit students such as head cheerleaders, football quarterbacks, Eagle Scouts, and others with natural leadership abilities. He believes people have to start doing things differently because of our rapidly changing world.

Attribution Theory

Earlier in the chapter we mentioned attribution theory in the context of perceptual interpretation. **Attribution theory** aids in this interpretation by focusing on how people attempt to (1) understand the causes of a certain event, (2) assess responsibility for the outcomes of the event, and (3) evaluate the personal qualities of the people involved in the event.[13] In applying attribution theory we are especially concerned with whether an individual's behavior has been internally or externally caused. Internal causes are believed to be under an individual's control—you believe Jake's performance is poor because he is lazy. External causes are seen as coming from outside a person—you believe Kellie's performance is poor because her machine is old.

The Importance of Attributions

Attributions can have far-reaching effects. For example, over their lifetimes, obese women don't accumulate as much net worth as slender women. Even after

Attribution theory is the attempt to understand the cause of an event, assess responsibility for outcomes of the event, and assess the personal qualities of the people involved.

ETHICS IN OB

JACK McCONNELL, MD

Jack McConnell, a well-known physician, moved to Hilton Head, South Carolina, to retire. He soon discovered he needed to keep busy and perceived that a large number of the resort island's low-income residents had no health care. So he started a free medical clinic to serve them. He was able to attract recently retired physicians and nurses back to work where they could ...."practice medicine the way they were taught to practice" [before managed care].

The clinic, opened in 1994, recently had more than 30,000 patient visits. This success is influenced by the large number of "retired" medical personnel and Dr. McConnell's persuasiveness. The persuasiveness involved not only attracting the medical people but convincing the legislature to amend traditional licensing and malpractice procedures. He also convinced contractors to donate their construction services. His model has been used throughout the United States and he is in the process of starting a clinic in Africa.[13A]

Question: Knowing what you do about perception, how might you use the text's perceptual model to help explain Dr. McConnell's desire for and ultimate success in establishing a clinic when he was retired and dealing with legislators, contractors, and medical personnel?

controlling for such things as health and marital status, women pay a heavy economic penalty for being obese. However, the same is not true for obese men. Attributions concerning obese men are that they are wealthy and successful, whereas attributions concerning obese women are that they have "let themselves go." For obese women, internal attributional causes seem to be operating to their detriment.[14]

According to attribution theory three factors influence this internal or external determination: distinctiveness, consensus, and consistency. *Distinctiveness* considers how consistent a person's behavior is across different situations. If Jake's performance is low, regardless of the machine on which he is working, we tend to give the poor performance an internal attribution; if the poor performance is unusual, we tend to assign an external cause to explain it.

Consensus takes into account how likely all those facing a similar situation are to respond in the same way. If all the people using machinery like Kellie's perform poorly, we tend to give her performance an external attribution. If other employees do not perform poorly, we attribute her performance to internal causation.

Consistency concerns whether an individual responds the same way across time. If Jake has a batch of low-performance figures, we tend to give the poor performance an internal attribution. In contrast, if Jake's low performance is an isolated incident, we attribute it to an external cause.

Attribution Errors

In addition to these three influences, two errors have an impact on internal versus external determination—the *fundamental attribution error* and the *self-serving*

Cause of Poor Performance by Their Subordinates	Most Frequent Attribution	Cause of Poor Performance by Themselves
7	Lack of *ability*	1
12	Lack of *effort*	1
5	Lack of *support*	23

Figure 4.6   **Health care managers' attributions of causes for poor performance.**

bias.[15] Figure 4.6 provides data from a group of health care managers. When supervisors were asked to identify, or attribute, causes of poor performance among their subordinates, the supervisors more often chose the individual's internal deficiencies—lack of ability and effort—rather than external deficiencies in the situation—lack of support. This demonstrates the **fundamental attribution error**—the tendency to underestimate the influence of situational factors and to overestimate the influence of personal factors in evaluating someone else's behavior. When asked to identify causes of their own poor performance, however, the supervisors overwhelmingly cited lack of support—an external, or situational, deficiency. This indicates the **self-serving bias**—the tendency to deny personal responsibility for performance problems but to accept personal responsibility for performance success.

> ▬ **Fundamental attribution error** is the tendency to underestimate the influence of situational factors and to overestimate the influence of personal factors in evaluating someone else's behavior.

> ▬ **Self-serving bias** is the tendency to deny personal responsibility for performance problems but accept personal responsibility for performance success.

To summarize, we tend to overemphasize other people's internal personal factors in their behavior and to underemphasize external factors in other people's behavior. In contrast, we tend to attribute our own success to our own internal factors and to attribute our failure to external factors.

The managerial implications of attribution theory can be traced back to the fact that perceptions influence responses. For example, a manager who believes that subordinates are not performing well and perceives the reason to be an internal lack of effort is likely to respond with attempts to "motivate" the subordinates to work harder; the possibility of changing external, situational factors that may remove job constraints and provide better organizational support may be largely ignored. This oversight could sacrifice major performance gains. Interestingly, because of the self-serving bias, when they evaluated their own behavior, the supervisors in the earlier study indicated that their performance would benefit from having better support. Thus the supervisors' own abilities or willingness to work hard were not believed to be at issue.

Attributions across Cultures

Research on the self-serving bias and fundamental attribution error has been done in cultures outside the United States with unexpected results.[16] In Korea, for example, the self-serving bias was found to be negative; that is, Korean managers attribute workgroup failure to themselves—"I was not a capable leader"—rather than to external causes. In India the fundamental attribution error overemphasizes external rather than internal causes for failure. Still another interesting cultural twist on the self-serving bias and fundamental attribution error is suggested by an example of a Ghanian woman who was the only female sea captain in the fleet.

The difficulty of her becoming a captain was reinforced by Africans' tendency to attribute negative consequences—driving away fish and angering mermaids into creating squalls—to women but apparently not to men. Why these various differences occurred is not clear, but differing cultural values appear to play a role. Finally, there is some evidence that U.S. females may be less likely to emphasize the self-serving bias than males.[17]

Certain cultures, such as that of the United States, tend to overemphasize internal causes and underemphasize external ones. Such overemphasis may result in negative attributions toward employees. These negative attributions, in turn, can lead to disciplinary actions, negative performance evaluations, transfers to other departments, and overreliance on training rather than focusing on such external causes as lack of workplace support.[18] Employees, too, take their cues from managerial misattributions and, through negative self-fulfilling prophecies, may reinforce managers' original misattributions. Employees and managers alike can be taught attributional realignment to help deal with such misattributions.[19]

Individual Learning

So far we have emphasized the importance of perception and attribution theory in understanding OB. Now we turn to still another important process: learning. Learning was defined in Chapter 1 as a relatively permanent change in behavior occurring as a result of experience. The change and experience aspects are very important. The change must not simply be temporary and the experience must result from continued contact in one's current setting. Short-lived performance changes on the job will not do. Note that there is both individual and organizational learning, and here we emphasize individual learning.

In this section we are concerned with individual learning from two perspectives. The first perspective is reinforcement. The second one is **social learning**, including learning from an observational modeling and the vicarious learning perspective that involves perception and attribution aspects.

Social learning theory uses modeling or vicarious learning to acquire behavior through observing and imitating others by means of perception and attribution.

Reinforcement

In OB, reinforcement has a very specific meaning that has its origin in some classic studies in psychology.[20] **Reinforcement** is the administration of a consequence as a result of a behavior. Managing reinforcement properly can change the direction, level, and persistence of an individual's behavior. To understand this idea we need to review some of the concepts of conditioning and reinforcement you learned in your basic psychology course. We will then move on to applications.

Reinforcement is the administration of a consequence as a result of behavior.

Classical and Operant Conditioning   Recall that Ivan Pavlov studied classical conditioning. **Classical conditioning** is a form of learning through association that involves the manipulation of stimuli to influence behavior. The Russian psychologist "taught" dogs to salivate at the sound of a bell by ringing the bell when feeding the dogs. The sight of the food naturally caused the dogs to salivate. Eventually, the dogs "learned" to associate the bell ringing with the presentation of meat and to salivate at the ringing of the bell alone. Such "learning" through association is so common in organizations that it is often ignored until it causes con-

Classical conditioning is a form of learning through association that involves the manipulation of stimuli to influence behavior.

siderable confusion. Take a look at Figure 4.7. The key is to understand a stimulus and a conditioned stimulus. A **stimulus** is something that incites action and draws forth a response (the meat for the dogs). The trick is to associate one neutral potential stimulus (the bell ringing) with another initial stimulus that already affects behavior (the meat). The once-neutral stimulus is called a *conditioned stimulus* when it affects behavior in the same way as the initial stimulus. In Figure 4.7 the boss's smiling becomes a conditioned stimulus because of its linkage to his criticisms.

Operant conditioning, popularized by B. F. Skinner, is an extension of the classical case to much more practical affairs.[21] It includes more than just a stimulus and a response behavior. **Operant conditioning** is the process of controlling behavior by manipulating its consequences. Classical and operant conditioning differ in two important ways. First, control in operant conditioning is via manipulation of consequences. Second, operant conditioning calls for examining antecedents, behavior, and consequences. The *antecedent* is the condition leading up to or "cueing" behavior. For example, in Figure 4.7, an agreement between the boss and the employee to work overtime as needed is an antecedent. If the employee works overtime, this would be the *behavior*, while the *consequence* would be the boss's praise.

A boss who wants a behavior, such as working overtime, to be repeated, must manipulate the consequences. The basis for manipulating consequences is E. L. Thorndike's law of effect.[22] The **law of effect** is simple but powerful: behavior that results in a pleasant outcome is likely to be repeated, while behavior that results in an unpleasant outcome is not likely to be repeated. The implications of this law are rather straightforward. If, as a supervisor, you want more of a behavior, you must make the consequences for the individual positive.

Note that the emphasis is on consequences that can be manipulated rather than on consequences inherent in the behavior itself. OB research often emphasizes specific types of rewards that are considered from the reinforcement perspective to influence individual behavior. *Extrinsic rewards* are positively valued work outcomes that are given to the individual by some other person. They are important external reinforcers or environmental consequences that can substantially influence a per-

Stimulus is something that incites action.

Operant conditioning is the process of controlling behavior by manipulating, or "operating" on, its consequences.

Law of effect is the observation that behavior resulting in a pleasing outcome is likely to be repeated; behavior that results in an unpleasant outcome is not likely to be repeated.

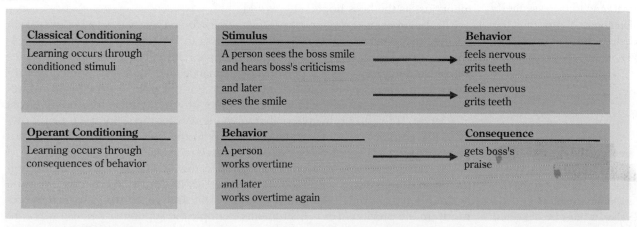

Figure 4.7   Differences between classical and operant conditioning approaches for a boss and subordinate.

Figure 4.8   A sample of extrinsic rewards allocated by managers.

Contrived Rewards: Some Direct Cost		Natural Rewards: No Direct Cost	
refreshments	promotion	smiles	recognition
piped-in music	trips	greetings	feedback
nice offices	company car	compliments	asking advice
cash bonuses	paid insurance	special jobs	
merit pay increases	stock options		
profit sharing	gifts		
office parties	sport tickets		

son's work behaviors through the law of effect. Figure 4.8 presents a sample of extrinsic rewards that managers can allocate to their subordinates.[23] Some of these rewards are contrived, or planned, rewards that have direct costs and budgetary implications. Examples are pay increases and cash bonuses. A second category includes natural rewards that have no cost other than the manager's personal time and efforts. Examples are verbal praise and recognition in the workplace.

Reinforcement Strategies   We now bring the notions of classical conditioning, operant conditioning, reinforcement, and extrinsic rewards together to show how the direction, level, and persistence of individual behavior can be changed. This combination is called **OB Mod** after its longer title of **organizational behavior modification**. OB Mod is the systematic reinforcement of desirable work behavior and the nonreinforcement or punishment of unwanted work behavior. OB Mod includes four basic reinforcement strategies: positive reinforcement, negative reinforcement (or avoidance), punishment, and extinction.[24]

Positive Reinforcement   B. F. Skinner and his followers advocate **positive reinforcement**—the administration of positive consequences that tend to increase the likelihood of repeating the desirable behavior in similar settings. For example, a Texas Instruments manager nods to a subordinate to express approval after she makes a useful comment during a sales meeting. Obviously, the boss wants more useful comments. Later, the subordinate makes another useful comment, just as the boss hoped she would.

To begin using a strategy of positive reinforcement, we need to be aware that positive reinforcers and rewards are not necessarily the same. Recognition, for example, is both a reward and a potential positive reinforcer. Recognition becomes a positive reinforcer only if a person's performance later improves. Sometimes, rewards turn out not to be positive reinforcers. For example, a supervisor at Boeing might praise a subordinate in front of other group members for finding errors in a report. If the group members then give the worker the silent treatment, however, the worker may stop looking for errors in the future. In this case, the supervisor's "reward" does not serve as a positive reinforcer.

To have maximum reinforcement value, a reward must be delivered only if the desired behavior is exhibited. That is, the reward must be contingent on the desired behavior. This principle is known as the **law of contingent reinforcement**. In the previous Texas Instruments example the supervisor's praise was contingent on the subordinate's making constructive comments. Finally, the reward must be given as soon as possible after the desired behavior. This is known as the

■ Organizational behavior modification (OB Mod) is the systematic reinforcement of desirable work behavior and the non-reinforcement or punishment of unwanted work behavior.

■ Positive reinforcement is the administration of positive consequences that tend to increase the likelihood of repeating the behavior in similar settings.

■ Law of contingent reinforcement is the view that for a reward to have maximum reinforcing value, it must be delivered only if the desired behavior is exhibited.

law of immediate reinforcement.[25] If the TI boss had waited for the annual performance review to praise the subordinate for providing constructive comments, the law of immediate reinforcement would be violated.

Now that we have presented the general concepts, it is time to address two important issues of implementation. First, what do you do if the behavior approximates what you want but is not exactly on target? Second, is it necessary to provide reinforcement each and every time? These are issues of shaping and scheduling, respectively.

Shaping   If the desired behavior is specific in nature and is difficult to achieve, a pattern of positive reinforcement, called shaping, can be used. **Shaping** is the creation of a new behavior by the positive reinforcement of successive approximations leading to the desired behavior. For example, new machine operators in the Ford Motor casting operation in Ohio must learn a complex series of tasks in pouring molten metal into castings in order to avoid gaps, overfills, or cracks.[26] The molds are filled in a three-step process, with each step progressively more difficult than its predecessor. Astute master craftspersons first show neophytes how to pour the first step and give praise based on what they did right. As the apprentices gain experience, they are given praise only when all of the elements of the first step are completed successfully. Once the apprentices have mastered the first step, they progress to the second. Reinforcement is given only when the entire first step and an aspect of the second step are completed successfully. Over time, apprentices learn all three steps and are given contingent positive rewards immediately for a complete casting that has no cracks or gaps. In this way behavior is shaped gradually rather than changed all at once.

Scheduling Positive Reinforcement   Positive reinforcement can be given according to either continuous or intermittent schedules. **Continuous reinforcement** administers a reward each time a desired behavior occurs. **Intermittent reinforcement** rewards behavior only periodically. These alternatives are important because the two schedules may have very different impacts on behavior. In general, continuous reinforcement elicits a desired behavior more quickly than does intermittent reinforcement. Thus, in the initial training of the apprentice casters, continuous reinforcement would be important. At the same time, continuous reinforcement is more costly in the consumption of rewards and is more easily extinguished when reinforcement is no longer present. In contrast, behavior acquired under intermittent reinforcement lasts longer upon the discontinuance of reinforcement than does behavior acquired under continuous reinforcement. In other words, it is more resistant to extinction. Thus, as the apprentices master an aspect of the pouring, the schedule is switched from continuous to intermittent reinforcement.

As shown in Figure 4.9, intermittent reinforcement can be given according to fixed or variable schedules. *Variable schedules* typically result in more consistent patterns of desired behavior than do fixed reinforcement schedules. *Fixed-interval schedules* provide rewards at the first appearance of a behavior after a given time has elapsed. *Fixed-ratio schedules* result in a reward each time a certain number of the behaviors have occurred. A *variable-interval schedule* rewards behavior at random times, while a *variable-ratio schedule* rewards behavior after a random number of occurrences. For example, as the apprentices perfect their technique for a stage of pouring castings, the astute masters switch to a variable-ratio reinforcement.

Law of immediate reinforcement states that the more immediate the delivery of a reward after the occurrence of a desirable behavior, the greater the reinforcing effect on behavior.

Shaping is the creation of a new behavior by the positive reinforcement of successive approximations to the desired behavior.

Continuous reinforcement is a reinforcement schedule that administers a reward each time a desired behavior occurs.

Intermittent reinforcement is a reinforcement schedule that rewards behavior only periodically.

Figure 4.9   Four types of intermittent reinforcement schedules.

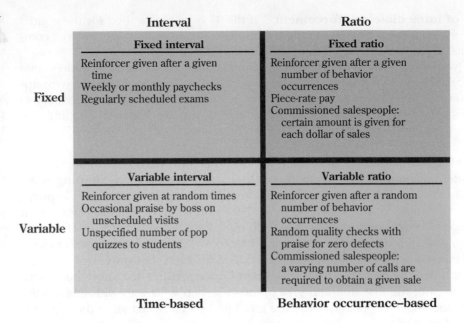

	Interval	Ratio
Fixed	**Fixed interval** Reinforcer given after a given time Weekly or monthly paychecks Regularly scheduled exams	**Fixed ratio** Reinforcer given after a given number of behavior occurrences Piece-rate pay Commissioned salespeople: certain amount is given for each dollar of sales
Variable	**Variable interval** Reinforcer given at random times Occasional praise by boss on unscheduled visits Unspecified number of pop quizzes to students	**Variable ratio** Reinforcer given after a random number of behavior occurrences Random quality checks with praise for zero defects Commissioned salespeople: a varying number of calls are required to obtain a given sale
	Time-based	**Behavior occurrence–based**

Let's look at an example from the Ed Mosely Auto-Mall, Brownfield, Texas.[27] The new operations manager had decided to contribute to the community by offering rewards for high school classroom attendance and good grades. The Mall set up the following schedule during each of the six-week high school grading periods:

Each "A" grade received three entries toward a lottery.

Each "B" grade received one entry.

Each perfect attendance record received two entries.

Shortly after the end of each grading period there was a drawing for three computers based on the number of certified entries. After the last of the 6-week periods each of the previous periods' computer winners was given a key. One of the keys would start a new Mustang, which served as the overall prize in a separate drawing. Additionally, there were prizes to the classroom and the school each computer winner attended and to the school that the car winner attended.

Now let's consider the possible reinforcement program being used. We can argue that the variable-ratio schedule used for the computers rewarded behavior after a random number of entries was drawn from the ones originally contributed by the eligible students. The reinforcement program for the car was similar except that there was only one drawing for the key rather than three. Under variable-ratio schedules the results are similar to playing a slot machine. You keep playing because you have no idea when, or if, you will hit the jackpot. Lotteries similar to the one conducted by the Mosely Auto-Mall have been used by a variety of organizations.[28]

Negative Reinforcement (Avoidance)   A second reinforcement strategy used in OB Mod is **negative reinforcement** or avoidance—the withdrawal of negative consequences, which tends to increase the likelihood of repeating the desirable behavior in similar settings. For example, a manager at McDonald's regularly nags a worker about his poor performance and then stops nagging when the worker does not fall behind one day. We need to focus on two aspects here: the negative consequences followed by the withdrawal of these consequences when

■■■ **Negative reinforcement** is the withdrawal of negative consequences, which tends to increase the likelihood of repeating the behavior in a similar setting; it is also known as avoidance.

desirable behavior occurs. The term "negative reinforcement" comes from this withdrawal of the negative consequences. This strategy is also sometimes called *avoidance* because its intent is for the person to avoid the negative consequence by performing the desired behavior. For instance, we stop at a red light to avoid a traffic ticket, or a worker who prefers the day shift is allowed to return to that shift if she performs well on the night shift.

Punishment A third OB Mod strategy is punishment. Unlike positive reinforcement and negative reinforcement, punishment is intended not to encourage positive behavior but to discourage negative behavior. Formally defined, **punishment** is the administration of negative consequences or the withdrawal of positive consequences that tend to reduce the likelihood of repeating the behavior in similar settings. The first type of punishment is illustrated by a Burger King manager who assigns a tardy worker to an unpleasant job, such as cleaning the restrooms. An example of withdrawing positive consequences is a Burger King manager who docks the employee's pay when she is tardy.

> **Punishment** is the administration of negative consequences that tend to reduce the likelihood of repeating the behavior in similar settings.

Some scholarly work illustrates the importance of punishment by showing that punishment administered for poor performance leads to enhanced performance without a significant effect on satisfaction. However, punishment seen by workers as arbitrary and capricious leads to very low satisfaction as well as low performance.[29] Thus, punishment can be handled poorly, or it can be handled well. Of course, the manager's challenge is to know when to use this strategy and how to use it correctly.

Finally, punishment may be offset by positive reinforcement received from another source. It is possible for a worker to be reinforced by peers at the same time that the worker is receiving punishment from the manager. Sometimes the positive value of such peer support is so great that the individual chooses to put up with the punishment. Thus, the undesirable behavior continues. As many times as an experienced worker may be verbally reprimanded by a supervisor for playing jokes on new employees, for example, the "grins" offered by other workers may well justify continuation of the jokes in the future.

Does all of this mean that punishment should never be administered? Of course not. The important things to remember are to administer punishment selectively and then to do it right.

Extinction The final OB Mod reinforcement strategy is **extinction**—the withdrawal of the reinforcing consequences for a given behavior. For example, Jack is often late for work, and his co-workers cover for him (positive reinforcement). The manager instructs Jack's co-workers to stop covering for him, withdrawing the reinforcing consequences. The manager has deliberately used extinction to get rid of an undesirable behavior. This strategy decreases the frequency of or weakens the behavior. The behavior is not "unlearned"; it simply is not exhibited. Since the behavior is no longer reinforced, it will reappear if reinforced again. Whereas positive reinforcement seeks to establish and maintain desirable work behavior, extinction is intended to weaken and eliminate undesirable behavior.

> **Extinction** is the withdrawal of the reinforcing consequences for a given behavior.

Summary of Reinforcement Strategies Figure 4.10 summarizes and illustrates the use of each OB Mod strategy. They are all designed to direct work behavior toward practices desired by management. Both positive and negative reinforcement are used to strengthen the desirable behavior of improving work quality when it occurs. Punishment is used to weaken the undesirable behavior of high

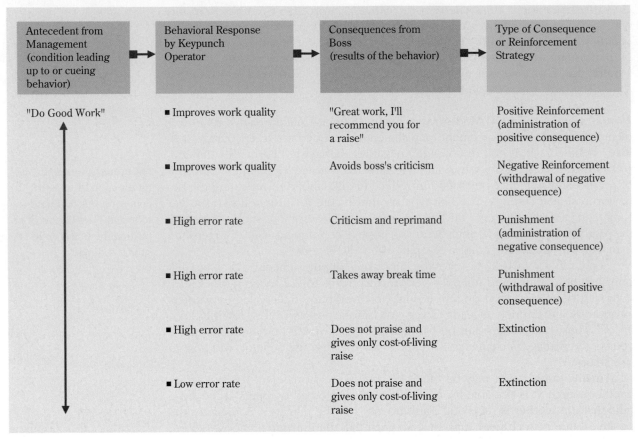

Antecedent from Management (condition leading up to or cueing behavior)	Behavioral Response by Keypunch Operator	Consequences from Boss (results of the behavior)	Type of Consequence or Reinforcement Strategy
"Do Good Work"	■ Improves work quality	"Great work, I'll recommend you for a raise"	Positive Reinforcement (administration of positive consequence)
	■ Improves work quality	Avoids boss's criticism	Negative Reinforcement (withdrawal of negative consequence)
	■ High error rate	Criticism and reprimand	Punishment (administration of negative consequence)
	■ High error rate	Takes away break time	Punishment (withdrawal of positive consequence)
	■ High error rate	Does not praise and gives only cost-of-living raise	Extinction
	■ Low error rate	Does not praise and gives only cost-of-living raise	Extinction

Figure 4.10   Applying reinforcement strategies.

error rates and involves either administering negative consequences or withdrawing positive consequences. Similarly, extinction is used deliberately to weaken the undesirable behavior of high error rates when it occurs. Note also, however, that extinction is used inadvertently to weaken the desirable behavior of low error rates. Finally, these strategies may be used in combination as well as independently.

Ethics and Reinforcement   The effective use of reinforcement strategies can help manage human behavior at work. Testimony to this effect is found in the application of these strategies in many large firms, such as General Electric, and even in small firms, such as Mid-America Building Maintenance. Mid-America, a janitorial services firm in Wichita, Kansas, provides an incentive program to employees who work 90 consecutive workdays without an absence.[30] Reinforcement strategies are also supported by the growing number of consulting firms that specialize in reinforcement techniques.

Managerial use of these approaches is not without criticism, however. For example, some reports on the "success" of specific programs involve isolated cases that have been analyzed without the benefit of scientific research designs. It is hard to conclude definitively whether the observed results were caused by reinforcement dynamics. In fact, one critic argues that the improved performance may well have occurred only because of the goal setting involved—that is, because specific performance goals were clarified, and workers were individually held accountable for their accomplishment.[31]

Another major criticism rests with the potential value dilemmas associated with using reinforcement to influence human behavior at work. For example, some critics maintain that the systematic use of reinforcement strategies leads to a demeaning and dehumanizing view of people that stunts human growth and development.[32] A related criticism is that managers abuse the power of their position and knowledge by exerting external control over individual behavior. Advocates of the reinforcement approach attack the problem head on: they agree that behavior modification involves the control of behavior, but they also argue that behavior control is an irrevocable part of every manager's job. The real question is how to ensure that any manipulation is done in a positive and constructive fashion.[33]

Social Learning Theory

An extension of reinforcement and operant conditioning is social learning theory, sometimes described in vicarious or modeling terms. Both reinforcement theory and social learning behaviors are functions of their consequences. However, social learning theory emphasizes the existence of observational learning and the importance of perception and attribution. Individuals respond to how their perceptions and attributions help define consequences, and not to the objective consequences as such. Although the consequences of reinforcement call for direct reinforcement, for social learning theory they are less direct. Let's explore this idea more specifically.

Social learning is achieved through the reciprocal interactions among people, behavior, and environment. Figure 4.11 illustrates and elaborates on this individualized view of learning drawn from the work of Albert Bandura.[34] According to the figure, the individual uses modeling or vicarious learning to acquire behavior by observing and imitating others. The person then attempts to acquire these behaviors by modeling them through practice. In a work situation, the model may be a manager or co-worker who demonstrates desired behaviors. Mentors or senior workers who befriend younger and more inexperienced protégés can also be important models. Indeed, some have argued that a shortage of

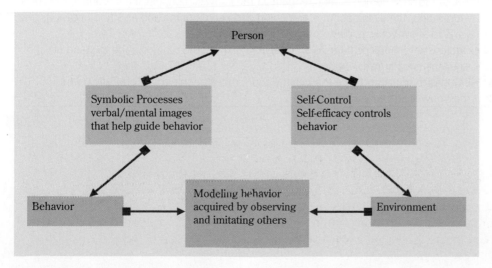

Figure 4.11   Social learning model.

mentors for women in senior management has been a major constraint to their progression up the career ladder.[35]

The symbolic processes depicted in Figure 4.11 are also important in social learning. Words and symbols used by managers and others in the workplace can help communicate values, beliefs, and goals and thus serve as guides to individual's behavior. For example, a "thumbs up" or other signal from the boss lets you know your behavior is appropriate. At the same time, the person's self-control is important in influencing his or her own behavior. **Self-efficacy**—the person's belief that he or she can perform adequately in a situation—is an important part of such self-control. People with self-efficacy believe that they have the necessary abilities for a given job, that they are capable of the effort required, and that no outside events will hinder them from attaining their desired performance level.[36] In contrast, people with low self-efficacy believe that no matter how hard they try, they cannot manage their environment well enough to be successful. For example, if you feel self-efficacy as a student, a low grade on one test is likely to encourage you to study harder, talk to the instructor, or do other things to enable you to do well the next time. In contrast, a person low in self-efficacy would probably drop the course or give up studying. Of course, even people who are high in self-efficacy do not control their environment entirely.

■ **Self-efficacy** is the person's belief that he or she can perform adequately in a situation.

MASTERING MANAGEMENT

ETHICS AND SOCIAL LEARNING THEORY

As this chapter shows, social learning theory emphasizes the importance of modeling and vicarious learning. People respond to how their perceptions and attributions help define consequences. Here are tips to use social learning to emphasize ethics.

- Across different religions, political spectrums, and genders, emphasize the widely-held core values that shape ethics: honesty, responsibility, respect, fairness, and compassion.
- Recognize that which is unethical is untruthful or disrespectful, or irresponsible, or unfair, or lacking in compassion – the opposite of any of those first mentioned.
- Demonstrate the importance of social modeling and mentoring through your body language and actual ethical "doing."
- Related to such demonstration, engage in the conversation, get the discourse, the communication, the dialog about ethics going and keep it going and also find occasions and ways to allow your people to practice these things.
- Demonstrate moral courage as a "catalyst" to strengthen the courage to stand up and say, "this is what really matters."
- Emphasize the importance for wealthy and famous people to act ethically because of their power and access.[36A]

Chapter 4   Study Guide

Summary

What is the perception process?

- Individuals use the perceptual process to pay attention to and to select, organize, interpret, and retrieve information from the world around them.

- The perceptual process involves the perceiver, the setting, and the perceived.

- Responses to the perceptual process involve thinking, feeling, and action classifications.

What are common perceptual distortions?

- Stereotypes or prototypes: an abstract set of features commonly associated with members of a given category.

- Halo effects: one attribute of a person or situation is used to develop an overall impression of the person or situation.

- Selective perception: the tendency to single out for attention those aspects of a situation or person that reinforce or emerge and are consistent with existing beliefs, values, and needs.

- Projection: assignments of personal attributes to other individuals.

- Contrast effects: when an individual's characteristics are contrasted with those of others recently encountered who rank higher or lower on the same characteristics.

How can perceptions be managed?

Managing perception involves:

- Impression management of the self and others

- Managing the information attention and selection stages

- Managing the information organizing stage

- Managing the information interpretation stage

- Managing the information storage and retrieval stage

- Being sensitive to effects of the common perceptual distortions

What is attribution theory?

- Attribution theory involves emphasis on the interpretation stage of the perceptual process and consideration of whether individuals' behaviors result primarily from external causes or from causes internal to the individuals.

- Three factors influence an external or internal causal attribution: distinctiveness, consensus, and consistency.

- Two errors influencing an external or internal causal attribution are the fundamental attribution error and self-serving bias.

- Attributions can be managed by recognizing a typical overemphasis on internal causes of behavior and an underemphasis on external causes.

- An overemphasis on internal causes tends to lead to assignments of failure, disciplinary actions, negative performance evaluations, and the like.

- An underemphasis on external causes tends to lead to lack of workplace support.

What is individual learning?

- Learning is an enduring change in behavior and results from experience.

- Learning can be split into reinforcement and social learning perspectives.

- Reinforcement theories emphasize the means through which the process of controlling an individual's behavior by manipulating its consequences takes place.

- The foundation of reinforcement is the law of effect, which states that behavior will be repeated or extinguished depending on whether the consequences are positive or negative.

- Positive reinforcement is the administration of positive consequences that tend to increase the likelihood of a person's repeating a behavior in similar settings.

- Positive reinforcement should be contingent and immediate, and it can be scheduled continuously or intermittently depending on resources and desired outcomes.

- Negative reinforcement (avoidance) is used to encourage desirable behavior through the withdrawal of negative consequences for previously undesirable behavior.

- Punishment is the administration of negative consequences or the withdrawal of positive consequences, both of which tend to reduce the likelihood of repeating an undesirable behavior in similar settings.

- Extinction is the withdrawal of reinforcing consequences for a given behavior.

- While the consequences of reinforcement call for direct reinforcement, those for social learning are less direct.

- Social learning theory recognizes learning that is achieved through the reciprocal interactions among people, behavior, and environment.

- Social learning theory uses modeling or vicarious learning to acquire behavior through observing and imitating others by means of perception and attribution.

- Both reinforcement and social learning theory are functions of their consequences.

- However, social learning theory emphasizes the existence of observational learning and the importance of perception and attribution.

- Individuals respond to how their perceptions and attributions help define consequences and not to the objective consequences as such.

- For social learning theory the consequences are less direct than for reinforcement.

Key Terms

Attribution theory (p. 91)
Classical conditioning
   (p. 94)
Continuous reinforcement
   (p. 97)
Contrast effects (p. 89)
Extinction (p. 99)
Fundamental attribution
   error (p. 93)
Halo effect (p. 88)
Intermittent reinforcement
   (p. 97)
Law of contingent
   reinforcement (p. 96)

Law of effect (p. 95)
Law of immediate
   reinforcement (p. 97)
Negative reinforcement
   (p. 98)
Operant conditioning
   (p. 95)
Organizational behavior
   modification (OB mod)
   (p. 96)
Perception (p. 80)
Positive reinforcement
   (p. 96)
Projection (p. 89)

Punishment (p. 99)
Reinforcement (p. 94)
Schemas (p. 85)
Selective perception
   (p. 88)
Self-efficacy (p. 102)
Self-fulfilling prophecy
   (p. 89)
Self-serving bias (p. 93)
Shaping (p. 97)
Social learning (p. 94)
Stimulus (p. 95)

Multiple Choice

Self-Test 4

1. Perception is the process by which people _____ information. (a) generate (b) retrieve (c) transmute (d) transmogrify

2. Which is not a perceptual process stage? _____ (a) attention/selection (b) interpretation (c) follow-through (d) retrieval

3. Which of the following is not a perceptual distortion? _____ (a) stereotypes/prototypes (b) the Barnum effect (c) the halo effect (d) the contrast effect

4. Perceptual distortions _____. (a) are quite rare (b) are quite common (c) affect only the interpretation stage (d) make the perceptual process more accurate

5. Which does not influence internal or external attribution of causation? _____. (a) distinctiveness (b) consensus (c) contrast (d) consistency

6. In the fundamental attribution error, the influence of _____. (a) situational factors is overestimated (b) personal factors is underestimated (c) self-factors is overestimated (d) situational factors is underestimated

7. Overemphasizing internal causes can lead to _____. (a) additional workplace support (b) training to correct deficiencies (c) promotion of managers (d) positive self-fulfilling prophecies

8. Attribution _____. (a) is a trait managers are born or not born with (b) lends itself to training (c) is almost impossible to manage (d) is strongly related to participative management.

9. Stereotypes _____. (a) are similar to prototypes (b) are not important in today's organizations (c) are more hurtful than helpful (d) have become important only recently.

10. Internal causes of employee behavior _____. (a) are more accurate than external causes (b) are emphasized especially outside the United States (c) reflect halo effects (d) lead to assignment of failure to a given employee

11. A heavy emphasis on external causes can lead to _____. (a) lack of workplace support (b) a heavy training emphasis (c) being sensitive to effects of common perceptual distortions (d) strong workplace support

12. Negative reinforcement _____. (a) is similar to punishment (b) seeks to discourage undesirable behavior (c) seeks to encourage desirable behavior (d) is also known as escapism.

13. OB Mod emphasizes _____. (a) the systematic reinforcement of desirable work behavior (b) noncontingent rewards (c) noncontingent punishment (d) extinction in preference to positive reinforcement.

14. Punishment _____. (a) may be offset by positive reinforcement from another source (b) generally is the most effective kind of reinforcement (c) is especially important in today's workplace (d) emphasizes the withdrawal of reinforcing consequences for a given behavior.

15. A major difference between reinforcement and social learning theory is _____. (a) reinforcement recognizes the existence of vicarious learning, and social learning does not (b) reinforcement recognizes objective consequences while social learning theory emphasizes how individuals perceive and define consequences (c) reinforcement emphasizes modeling behavior while social learning theory does not (d) there is no major difference between reinforcement and social learning theory

Short Response

16. Draw and briefly discuss the text's model of the perceptual process.

17. Select two perceptual distortions, briefly define them, and show how they influence the perceptual process.

18. Briefly compare and contrast classical conditioning and operant conditioning.

19. Briefly compare and contrast reinforcement with social learning theory.

Applications Essay

20. Your boss has recently heard a little about attribution theory and has asked you to explain it to him in more detail, focusing on its possible usefulness in managing his department. How do you address his request?

These learning activities from *The OB Skills Workbook* are suggested for Chapter 4.

OB in Action

CASE	EXPERIENTIAL EXERCISES	SELF-ASSESSEMNT
■ 4. MAGREC, Inc.	■ 9. How We View Differences ■ 10. Alligator River Story	■ 6. Intolerance for Ambiguity

Plus—speical learning experiences from *The Jossey-Bass Pfeiffer Classroom Collection*

Chapter 5

Motivation Theories

Chapter at a Glance

It's hard to achieve something if you aren't willing to put forth the effort. Chapter 5 focuses on a core question in management and organizational behavior: when and under what conditions are people highly motivated to work? As you read, *keep in mind these study topics*.

Achievement requires effort

Wall Street Journal columnist Carol Hymowitz opened an article written about successful female executives with this sentence: "Reach for the top—and don't eliminate choices too soon or worry about the myth of balance."

One of the first leaders Hymowitz mentions in her article is Carol Bartz, executive chairman of the board of the noted software firm Autodesk. In an interview with Hymowitz, Bartz points out a pressing and common issue. Women often suffer from guilt, inappropriately she believes, as they pursue career tracks. In her own case she has both a demanding career and a family. And in both respects she says that she's found happiness.

Andrea Jung, seen here and chairman and CEO of Avon products, agrees with Bartz that women have to work long hours and meet the challenges of multiple demands as they work their way to the top. For Jung this includes lots of international travel, overnight flights, and jet lag. She makes no bones about the fact that sacrifices are real: missed family gatherings, children's school functions, and more. But she also

considers the trade-offs worthwhile, saying: "If you're comfortable with your choices, that's the definition of peace."

Nancy Peretsman is managing director and executive vice president of the investment bank Allen & Company. She laments that many young women believe they have to trade career advancement for fulfillment in their personal lives. Not so, says Peretsman, who has a top job and a family that includes teenage daughters. She says: "No one will die if you don't show up at every business meeting or every school play."

As for Hymowitz's conclusions, one stands out clearly. She finds that the lessons from women at the top of the corporate ladder come down to these: setting goals, persevering, accepting stretch assignments, obtaining broad experiences, focusing on strengths, not weaknesses, and being willing to take charge of one's own career.

That advice seems well voiced. It also seems appropriate for anyone, be they man or woman, seeking career and personal success in today's corporate world.[1]

> ## "If you are comfortable with your choices, that's the definition of peace."

What Is Motivation?

The opening voices from women at the top of the corporate ladder raise interesting issues. Among them is "motivation." The featured corporate leaders all work very hard, have high goals, and are realistic about the trade-offs between career and family. It's easy and accurate to say that they are highly motivated. But how much do we really know about motivation and the conditions under which people, ourselves included, become highly motivated to work hard . . . at school, in our jobs, and in our leisure and personal pursuits?

Motivation Defined

By definition, **motivation** refers to the individual forces that account for the direction, level, and persistence of a person's effort expended at work. *Direction* refers to an individual's choice when presented with a number of possible alternatives (e.g., whether to pursue quality, quantity, or both in one's work). *Level* refers to the amount of effort a person puts forth (e.g., to put forth a lot or very little). *Persistence* refers to the length of time a person sticks with a given action (e.g., to keep trying or to give up when something proves difficult to attain).

Motivation refers to forces within an individual that account for the level, direction, and persistence of effort expended at work.

Types of Motivation Theories

There are many available theories of motivation, and they can be divided into two broad categories: content theories and process theories.[2] Theories of both types contribute to our understanding of motivation to work, but none offers a complete explanation. In studying a variety of theories, our goal is to gather useful insights that can be integrated into motivational approaches that are appropriate for different situations.

Content theories of motivation focus primarily on individual needs—that is, physiological or psychological deficiencies that we feel a compulsion to reduce or eliminate. The content theories try to explain work behaviors based on pathways to need satisfaction and the influence of blocked needs. This chapter discusses Maslow's hierarchy of needs theory, Alderfer's ERG theory, McClelland's acquired needs theory, and Herzberg's two-factor theory.

Content theories profile different needs that may motivate individual behavior.

Process theories of motivation focus on the thought or cognitive processes that take place within the minds of people and that influence their behavior. Whereas a content approach may identify job security as an important individual need, a process approach would probe further to identify why the person decides to behave in certain ways relative to available rewards and work opportunities. Three process theories discussed in this chapter are equity theory, expectancy theory, and goal-setting theory.

Process theories examine the thought processes that motivate individual behavior.

Motivation across Cultures

Before examining specific motivation theories, an important caveat should be noted. Although motivation is a key concern in organizations everywhere, the theories are largely developed from a North American perspective. As a result, they are subject to cultural limitations and contingencies.[3] Indeed, the determinants of motivation and the best ways to deal with it are likely to vary considerably across the cultures of Asia, South America, Eastern Europe, and Africa, as well as North America. For example, an individual financial bonus might prove "motivational" as a reward in one culture, but not in another. Thus, in researching, studying, and using motivation theories we should be sensitive to cross-cultural issues. We must avoid being parochial or ethnocentric by assuming that people in all cultures are motivated by the same things in the same ways.[4]

Needs Theories of Motivation

Content theories, as noted earlier, suggest that motivation results from our attempts to satisfy important needs. They suggest that managers should be able to understand individual needs and to create work environments that respond positively to them. Each of the following theories takes a slightly different approach in addressing this challenge.

Hierarchy of Needs Theory

■■■ Maslow's **hierarchy of needs theory** offers a pyramid of physiological, safety, social, esteem, and self-actualization needs.

■■■ **Higher-order needs** in Maslow's hierarchy are esteem and self-actualization.

■■■ **Lower-order needs** in Maslow's hierarchy are physiological, safety, and social.

Abraham Maslow's **hierarchy of needs theory**, depicted in Figure 5.1, identifies five levels of individual needs. They range from self-actualization and esteem needs at the top, to social, safety, and physiological needs at the bottom.[5] The concept of a needs "hierarchy" assumes that some needs are more important than others and must be satisfied before the other needs can serve as motivators. For example, physiological needs must be satisfied before safety needs are activated, safety needs must be satisfied before social needs are activated, and so on.

Maslow's model is easy to understand and quite popular. But research evidence fails to support the existence of a precise five-step hierarchy of needs. If anything, the needs are more likely to operate in a flexible rather than in a strict, step-by-step sequence. Some research suggests that **higher-order needs** (esteem and self-actualization) tend to become more important than **lower-order needs**

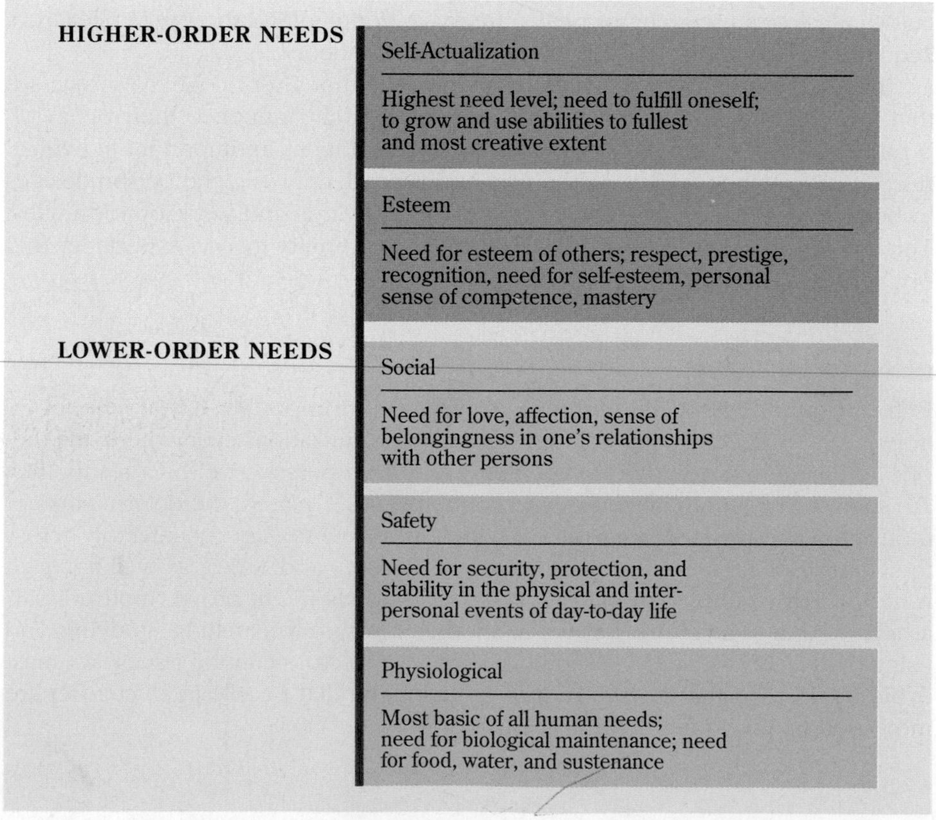

HIGHER-ORDER NEEDS

Self-Actualization

Highest need level; need to fulfill oneself; to grow and use abilities to fullest and most creative extent

Esteem

Need for esteem of others; respect, prestige, recognition, need for self-esteem, personal sense of competence, mastery

LOWER-ORDER NEEDS

Social

Need for love, affection, sense of belongingness in one's relationships with other persons

Safety

Need for security, protection, and stability in the physical and interpersonal events of day-to-day life

Physiological

Most basic of all human needs; need for biological maintenance; need for food, water, and sustenance

Figure 5.1   Higher-order and lower-order needs in Maslow's hierarchy of needs.

(psychological, safety, and social) as individuals move up the corporate ladder.[6] Studies also report that needs vary according to a person's career stage, the size of the organization, and even geographic location.[7] There is also no consistent evidence that the satisfaction of a need at one level decreases its importance and increases the importance of the next-higher need.[8] And findings regarding the hierarchy of needs vary when this theory is examined across cultures. For instance, social needs tend to take on higher importance in more collectivist societies, such as Mexico and Pakistan, than in individualistic ones like the United States.[9]

ERG Theory

Clayton Alderfer's **ERG theory** is also based on needs, but it differs from Maslow's theory in three main respects.[10] First, ERG theory collapses Maslow's five needs categories into three: **existence needs**—desires for physiological and material well being; **relatedness needs**—desires for satisfying interpersonal relationships; and **growth needs**—desires for continued personal growth and development. Second, ERG theory emphasizes a unique *frustration-regression* component. An already satisfied lower-level need can become activated when a higher-level need cannot be satisfied. Thus, if a person is continually frustrated in his or her attempts to satisfy growth needs, relatedness needs can again surface as key motivators. Third, unlike Maslow's theory, ERG theory contends that more than one need may be activated at the same time.

The supporting evidence for ERG theory is encouraging, even though further research is needed.[11] In particular, ERG theory's allowance for regression back to lower-level needs is a valuable contribution to our thinking. It may help to explain why in some settings, for example, worker complaints focus mainly on wages, benefits, and working conditions—things relating to existence needs. Although these needs are important, their importance may be exaggerated because the workers cannot otherwise satisfy relatedness and growth needs in their jobs. This is an example of how ERG theory offers a more flexible approach to understanding human needs than does Maslow's hierarchy.

Acquired Needs Theory

In the late 1940s psychologist David I. McClelland and his co-workers began experimenting with the Thematic Apperception Test (TAT) as a way of measuring human needs.[13] The TAT is a projective technique that asks people to view pictures and write stories about what they see. For example, McClelland showed three executives a photograph of a man looking at family photos arranged on his work desk. One executive wrote of an engineer who was daydreaming about a family outing scheduled for the next day. Another described a designer who had picked up an idea for a new gadget from remarks made by his family. The third described an engineer who was intently working on a bridge stress problem that he seemed sure to solve because of his confident look.[14]

McClelland identified themes through such TAT stories that he believed correspond to needs that are acquired over time as a result of our life experiences. **Need for achievement (nAch)** is the desire to do something better or more efficiently, to solve problems, or to master complex tasks. **Need for affiliation (nAff)** is the desire to establish and maintain friendly and warm relations with

■ Alderfer's **ERG theory** identifies existence, relatedness, and growth needs.

■ **Existence needs** are desires for physiological and material well-being.

■ **Relatedness needs** are desires for satisfying interpersonal relationships.

■ **Growth needs** are desires for continued personal growth and development.

■ **Need for achievement (nAch)** is the desire to do better, solve problems, or master complex tasks.

■ **Need for affiliation (nAff)** is the desire for friendly and warm relations with others.

Leaders on Leadership

LEADING CHANGE BY FILLING A FOUNDER'S SHOES

You may not recognize this name: Leon Gorman. But you most likely recognize the company he led for 34 years: L. L. Bean. And according to Gorman, if his grandfather and the firm's founder L. L. (Leon Leonwood) Bean had had their way, the company might not be around today, let alone still serving as an icon of mail-order success. L. L., he says, was resistant to change. When presented with new ideas to increase sales or speed order processing he would say: "I'm eating three meals a day, and I can't eat four."

After his grandfather died, Leon Gorman took over as president and brought in a new leadership perspective and lots of growth—from $5 million in yearly sales to over $1.2 billion. While leading change, he stuck to L. L.'s core values. As the story goes, his grandfather gave immediate refunds upon learning that many of his first 100 hunting shoes were defective. No questions were asked; customers came first—the L. L. Bean way. Such values were a guide as Gorman led the firm through major growth using professional management practices. The results speak for themselves, and Bean's employees remain committed to quality, customers, and the great outdoors.[12]

Taking over a leadership position from someone who had held the job for a long time, and perhaps very successfully, can be daunting. Can you think of any special challenges that Leon Gorman had to master on his pathway toward leadership success at L. L. Bean, Inc.?

■■■ **Need for power (nPower)** is the desire to control others and influence their behavior.

others. **Need for power (nPower)** is the desire to control others, to influence their behavior, or to be responsible for others.

In terms of practical applications, McClelland encouraged managers to learn how to identify the presence of nAch, nAff, and nPower in themselves and in others, since each need can be linked with a set of work preferences. Someone with a high need for achievement will prefer individual responsibilities, challenging goals, and performance feedback. Someone with a high need affiliation is drawn to interpersonal relationships and opportunities for communication. Someone with a high need for power seeks influence over others and likes attention and recognition.

Since these three needs are acquired, McClelland also believed it may be possible to teach people to develop need profiles required for success in various types of jobs. His research indicated, for example, that a moderate to high need for power that is stronger than a need for affiliation is linked with success as a senior executive. The high nPower creates the willingness to exercise influence and control over others; the lower nAff allows the executive to make difficult decisions without undue worry over being disliked.[15]

Research lends considerable insight into the need for achievement in particular, and it includes some interesting applications in developing nations. For example, McClelland trained businesspeople in Kakinda, India, to think, talk, and act like high achievers by having them write stories about achievement and participate in a business game that encouraged achievement. The businesspeople also met with successful entrepreneurs and learned how to set challenging goals for their own businesses. Over a two-year period following these activities, the participants from the Kakinda study engaged in activities that created twice as many new jobs as those who hadn't received the training.[16]

Two-Factor Theory

Frederick Herzberg took yet another approach to examining the link between individual needs and motivation. He began by asking workers to report the times they felt exceptionally good about their jobs and the times they felt exceptionally bad about them.[17] The researchers noticed that people talked about very different things when they reported feeling good or bad about their jobs. Herzberg explained these results using the **two-factor theory**, also known as the motivator-hygiene theory, because this theory identifies two different factors as primary causes of job satisfaction and job dissatisfaction.

Hygiene factors are sources of job dissatisfaction, and they are associated with the job context or work setting. That is, they relate more to the environment in which people work than to the nature of the work itself. The two-factor theory suggests that job dissatisfaction results when hygiene factors are poor. But it also suggests that improving the hygiene factors will only decrease job dissatisfaction; it will not increase job satisfaction. Among the hygiene factors shown on the left in Figure 5.2, perhaps the most surprising is salary. Herzberg found that a low base salary or wage makes people dissatisfied, but that paying more does not necessarily satisfy or motivate them.

Motivator factors, shown on the right in Figure 5.2, are sources of job satisfaction. These factors are related to job content—what people actually do in their work. They include such things as a sense of achievement, opportunities for

Herzberg's **two-factor theory** identifies job context as the source of job dissatisfaction and job content as the source of job satisfaction.

Hygiene factors in the job context are sources of job dissatisfaction.

Motivator factors in the job content are sources of job satisfaction.

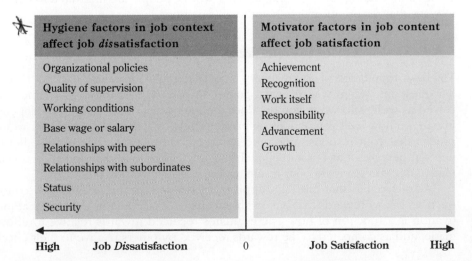

Hygiene factors in job context affect job *dis*satisfaction	Motivator factors in job content affect job satisfaction
Organizational policies	Achievement
Quality of supervision	Recognition
Working conditions	Work itself
Base wage or salary	Responsibility
Relationships with peers	Advancement
Relationships with subordinates	Growth
Status	
Security	

High   Job *Dissatisfaction*   0   Job Satisfaction   High

Figure 5.2   Sources of dissatisfaction and satisfaction in Herzberg's two-factor theory.

personal growth, recognition, and responsibility. According to the two-factor theory, the presence or absence of satisfiers or motivators to people's jobs is the key link to satisfaction, motivation, and performance. When motivator factors are minimal, low job satisfaction decreases motivation and performance; when motivator factors are substantial, high job satisfaction raises motivation and performance.

Job satisfaction and job dissatisfaction are separate dimensions in the two-factor theory. Taking action to improve a hygiene factor, such as by giving pay raises or creating better physical working conditions, will not make people satisfied with their work; it will only prevent them from being dissatisfied on these matters. To improve job satisfaction, Herzberg suggests the technique of *job enrichment* as a way of building satisfiers into job content. This technique is given special attention in the next chapter as a job design alternative. For now, the implication is well summarized in this statement by Herzberg: "If you want people to do a good job, give them a good job to do."[18]

OB scholars have long debated the merits of the two-factor theory, with special concerns being directed at failures to confirm the theory through additional research.[19] It is criticized as being method bound, or only replicable when Herzberg's original methods are used. This is a serious criticism, since the scientific approach valued in OB requires that theories be verifiable under different research methods.[20] Yet, the distinction between hygiene and motivator factors has been a useful contribution to OB. As will be apparent in the discussions of job designs and alternative work schedules in the next chapter, the notion of two factors—job content and job context—has a practical validity that adds useful discipline to management thinking.

Equity Theory of Motivation

What happens when you get a grade back on a written assignment or test? How do you interpret your results, and what happens to your future motivation in the course? Such questions fall in the domain of the first process theory of motivation to be discussed here—**equity theory**. As applied to the workplace through the writing of J. Stacy Adams, equity theory argues that any perceived inequity becomes a motivating state of mind; in other words, people are motivated to behave in ways that restore or maintain equity in situations.[21]

▇ Adams's **equity theory** posits that people will act to eliminate any felt inequity in the rewards received for their work in comparison with others.

Equity and Social Comparisons

The basic foundation of equity theory is social comparison. Think back to the earlier questions. When you receive a grade, do you try to find out what others received as well? And when you do, does the interpretation of your grade depend, in part, on how well your grade compared to those of others? Equity theory would predict that your response upon receiving a grade will be based on whether or not you perceive it as fair and equitable. Furthermore, that determination is only made after you compare your results with those received by others.

Adams argues that this logic applies equally well to the motivational consequences of any rewards that one might receive at work. Adams believes that motivation is a function of how one evaluates received rewards relative to efforts made, and as compared to the rewards received by others relative to their efforts made. A key word in this comparison is "fairness," and as you might expect, any feelings of unfairness or perceived inequity are uncomfortable. They create a state of mind we are motivated to eliminate.

Equity Theory Predictions

Perceived inequity occurs when someone believes that the rewards received for his or her work contributions compare unfavorably to the rewards other people appear to have received for their work. The basic equity comparison can be summarized as follows:

$$\frac{\text{Individual Outcomes}}{\text{Individual Efforts}} \quad \genfrac{}{}{0pt}{}{>}{<} \quad \frac{\text{Others' Outcomes}}{\text{Others' Efforts}}$$

Felt negative inequity in this equation exists when an individual feels that he or she has received relatively less than others have in proportion to work inputs. *Felt positive inequity* exists when an individual feels that he or she has received relatively more than others have. When either feeling exists, the theory states that people will be motivated to act in ways that remove the discomfort and restore a sense of felt equity. In the case of perceived negative inequity, for example, people are likely to respond by engaging in one or more of the following behaviors:

- Change work inputs (e.g., reduce performance efforts).
- Change the outcomes (rewards) received (e.g., ask for a raise).
- Leave the situation (e.g., quit).
- Change the comparison points (e.g., compare self to a different co-worker).
- Psychologically distort the comparisons (e.g., rationalize that the inequity is only temporary and will be resolved in the future).
- Take actions to change the inputs or outputs of the comparison person (e.g., get a co-worker to accept more work).

Research on equity theory indicates that people who feel they are overpaid (perceived positive inequity) are likely to try to increase the quantity or quality of their work, whereas those who feel they are underpaid (perceived negative inequity) are likely to try to decrease the quantity or quality of their work.[22] The research is most conclusive with respect to felt negative inequity. It appears that people are less comfortable when they are underrewarded than when they are overrewarded.

You can view the equity comparison as intervening between the allocation of rewards and the ultimate motivational impact for the recipient

$$\text{reward received} \rightarrow \text{equity comparison} \rightarrow \text{motivational impact.}$$

A reward given by a team leader and expected to be highly motivational to a team member, for example, may or may not work as intended. Unless the reward is perceived as fair and equitable in comparison with the results for other teammates, the reward may create negative equity dynamics and work just the opposite of what the team leader expected. Equity theory reminds us that the motivational value of rewards is determined by the individual's interpretation in the context of social comparison. It is not the reward-giver's intentions that count;

JL Lane

Entrepreneurship flourishes among some college students. While participating in a study abroad program sponsored by Wake Forest University, Jennifer Woodsmall found some interesting handbags in Vietnam. That led her to start JL Lane, importer of handbags made by Vietnamese women. It wasn't easy, but Woodsmall successfully marketed the bags while pursuing a double major in psychology and religion.

■ **Organizational justice** is an issue of how fair and equitable people view workplace practices.

■ **Procedural justice** is the degree to which rules are always properly followed to implement policies.

■ **Distributive justice** is the degree to which all people are treated the same under a policy.

it is how the recipient perceives the reward that will determine actual motivational outcomes. OB Savvy 5.1 offers ideas on how people cope with such equity dynamics.

The processes associated with equity theory and its predictions about motivation are subject to cultural contingencies. The findings and predictions reported here are particularly tied to individualistic cultures in which self-interest tends to govern social comparisons. In more collectivist cultures, such as those of many Asian countries, the concern often runs more for equality than equity. This allows for solidarity with the group and helps to maintain harmony in social relationships.[23]

Equity Theory and Organizational Justice

One of the basic elements of equity theory is the fairness with which people perceive they are being treated. This raises an issue in organizational behavior known as **organizational justice**—how fair and equitable people view the practices of their workplace. In ethics, the justice view of moral reasoning considers behavior to be ethical when it is fair and impartial in the treatment of people. Organizational justice notions are important in OB, and in respect to equity theory, they emerge along three dimensions.[24]

Procedural justice is the degree to which the rules and procedures specified by policies are properly followed in all cases to which they are applied. In a sexual harassment case, for example, this may mean that required formal hearings are held for every case submitted for administrative review. **Distributive justice** is the degree to which all people are treated the same under a policy, regardless of race, ethnicity, gender, age, or any other demographic characteristic. In a sexual harassment case, this might mean that a complaint filed by a man against a woman would receive the same consideration as one filed by a woman against a man. **Interactional justice** is the degree to which the people affected by a decision are treated with dignity and respect.[25] Interactional justice in a sexual harassment case, for example, may mean that both the accused and accusing parties believe they have received a complete explanation of any decision made.

Among the many implications of equity theory, those dealing with organizational justice also must be considered. The ways in which people perceive they are being treated at work with respect to procedural, distributive, and interactional justice are likely to affect their motivation. And it is their perceptions of these justice types, often made in a context of social comparison, that create the ultimate motivational influence.

OB SAVVY 5.1

Steps for Managing Equity Dynamics

- Recognize that equity comparisons are inevitable in the workplace.
- Anticipate felt negative inequities when rewards are given.
- Communicate clear evaluations of any rewards given.
- Communicate an appraisal of performance on which the reward is based.
- Communicate comparison points appropriate in the situation.

■ **Interactional justice** is the degree to which the people are treated with dignity and respect in decision affecting them.

■ Vroom's **expectancy theory** argues that work motivation is determined by individual beliefs regarding effort/performance relationships and work outcomes.

Expectancy Theory of Motivation

Another of the process theories of motivation is Victor Vroom's **expectancy theory**. It posits that motivation is a result of a rational calculation—people will do what they can do when they want to do it.

ETHICS IN OB

THE "GREEN" CORPORATION
MAY BE MORE THAN PUBLIC RELATIONS

Billionaire Richard Branson has pledged $3 billion from the profits of the transportation businesses—airlines and railroads included—of his Virgin Group companies. His goal is to help combat global warming by investing in sustainable energy that reduces the use of coal and oil. He's not alone in his commitment to corporate "greening." Nike has invested millions to find a way to produce its "air" sneakers without sulfur hexaflouride (SF_6), which is a greenhouse gas. And Patagonia's CEO, Yvon Chouinard, helped found the non-profit 1% For the Planet. Its members contribute 1 percent of their sales to nonprofit environmental organizations such as Amazon Watch, San Diego Coastkeeper, and Rainforest Relief.

Large multinational corporations (MNCs) are coming on board with sustainability agendas. Global giant Unilever makes public its contributions to carbon dioxide and hazardous waste, and it funds projects in many countries to fight the ills of water shortages, poverty, and climate change. At a national level, you may hear of "green GDP," a measure that deducts from traditional GDP the cost of environmental damage. And yet there are many businesses and countries that have been slow to join the commitment to going green.[26]

Why might some executives and leaders be motivated by environmental concerns while others lag? How can such tendencies be explained by theories of motivation?

Expectancy Terms and Concepts

In expectancy theory and as summarized in Figure 5.3, a person is motivated to the degree that he or she believes that (1) effort will yield acceptable performance (expectancy), (2) performance will be rewarded (instrumentality), and (3) the value of the rewards is highly positive (valence). Each of the key underlying concepts or terms is defined as follows:[27]

- **Expectancy** is the probability assigned by an individual that work effort will be followed by a given level of achieved task performance. Expectancy would equal zero if the person felt it were impossible to achieve the given performance level; it would equal one if a person were 100 percent certain that the performance could be achieved.

- **Instrumentality** is the probability assigned by the individual that a given level of achieved task performance will lead to various work outcomes. Instrumentality also varies from 0 to 1. Strictly speaking, Vroom's treatment of instrumentality would allow it to vary from −1 to +1. We use the probability definition here and the 0 to +1 range for pedagogical purposes; it is consistent with the instrumentality notion.

- **Valence** is the value attached by the individual to various work outcomes. Valences form a scale from −1 (very undesirable outcome) to +1 (very desirable outcome).

Expectancy is the probability that work effort will be followed by performance accomplishment.

Instrumentality is the probability that performance will lead to various work outcomes.

Valence is the value to the individual of various work outcomes.

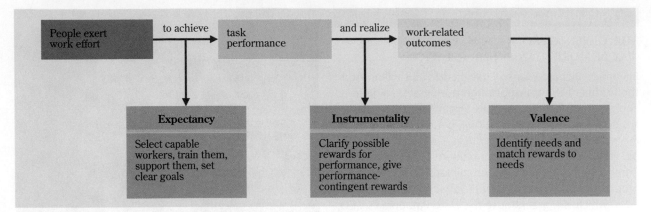

Figure 5.3   Key terms and managerial implications of Vroom's expectancy theory.

Vroom posits that motivation, expectancy, instrumentality, and valence are related to one another by the equation

$$\text{Motivation} = \text{Expectancy} \times \text{Instrumentality} \times \text{Valence}.$$

The multiplier effect in this equation is significant. It means that the motivational appeal of a given work path is sharply reduced whenever any one or more of these factors approaches the value of zero. Conversely, for a given reward to have a high and positive motivational impact as a work outcome, the expectancy, instrumentality, and valence associated with the reward all must be high and positive.

Expectancy Theory Predictions

Suppose that a manager is wondering whether or not the prospect of earning a merit pay raise will be motivational to an employee. Expectancy theory predicts that motivation to work hard to earn the merit pay will be low if *expectancy* is low—a person feels that he or she cannot achieve the necessary performance level. Motivation will also be low if *instrumentality* is low—the person is not confident a high level of task performance will result in a high merit pay raise. Motivation will also be low if *valence* is low—the person places little value on a merit pay increase. And motivation will be low if any combination of these exists. Thus, the multiplier effect advises managers to act to maximize expectancy, instrumentality, and valence when seeking to create high levels of work motivation. A zero at any location on the right side of the expectancy equation will result in zero motivation.

Expectancy Implications and Research

Expectancy logic argues that managers should always try to intervene actively in work situations to maximize work expectancies, instrumentalities, and valences that support organizational objectives.[28] To influence expectancies, the advice is to select people with proper abilities, train them well, support them with needed resources, and identify clear performance goals. To influence instrumentality, the advice is to clarify performance-reward relationships, and then to confirm or live up to them when rewards are actually given for performance accomplishments. To influence valences, the advice is to identify the needs that are important to each individual and then try to adjust available rewards to match these needs.

DEVELOPING HUMAN CAPITAL

Competency is a performance driver, and knowing that one has or is developing the right competencies to do well in a job and career can be a powerful motivator. How well are you doing at building a strong portfolio of executive competencies? Jump-start your thinking by using this framework developed from ideas in a *Harvard Business Review* article by Boris Groysberg, Andrew N. McLean, and Nitin Nohria.[31]

- General Management Human Capital—build skills and competencies in resource acquisition, cultivation, and allocation, including human resource management.
- Strategic Human Capital—build expertise dealing with strategic situations such as cutting costs, driving growth, and dealing with cyclical markets.
- Relationship Human Capital—build capabilities to act based on networking with others with whom you have strong working relationships.
- Industry Human Capital—build familiarity with technologies, customers, regulations, suppliers, and competition specific to an industry.
- Company-Specific Human Capital—build knowledge about internal workings of the organization, its policies, practices, and culture.

A great deal of research on expectancy theory has been conducted.[29] Even though the theory has received substantial support, specific details, such as the operation of the multiplier effect, remain subject to some question. In addition, expectancy theory has proven interesting in terms of helping to explain some apparently counterintuitive findings in cross-cultural management situations. For example, a pay raise motivated one group of Mexican workers to work fewer hours. They wanted a certain amount of money in order to enjoy things other than work, rather than just getting more money in general. A Japanese sales representative's promotion to manager of a U.S. company adversely affected his performance. His superiors did not realize that the promotion embarrassed him and distanced him from his colleagues.[30]

Goal-Setting Theory of Motivation

Some years ago a Minnesota Vikings' defensive end gathered up an opponent's fumble. Then, with obvious effort and delight, he ran the ball into the wrong end zone. Clearly, the athlete did not lack motivation. Unfortunately, however, he failed to channel his energies toward the right goal. Similar problems in goal direction are found in many work settings. Goals are important aspects of motivation, and yet they often go unaddressed. Without clear goals, employees may suffer direction problems; when goals are both clear and properly set, employees may be highly motivated to move in the direction of goal accomplishment.

Motivational Properties of Goals

Goal setting is the process of developing, negotiating, and formalizing the targets or objectives that a person is responsible for accomplishing.[32] Over a number of years Edwin Locke and his associates have developed a comprehensive framework linking goals to performance. Research on goal setting is now quite

Blue Man Group

Three performers are slathered in brilliant blue greasepaint. They never speak. What they do are things like twirl a canvas while spitting paint on it to create a work of art, or play music by drumming on instruments made from PVC pipe, or make rhythmic noises by chomping on cereal. And while all this is great fun, there is a lot of creativity and effort behind the entertainment package. The motivated performers and creators of Blue Man Group blend a mix of "comedy, music and multi-media artistry" into a unique art form.

Research Insight
Conscious and Subconscious Goals Interact for Motivational Impact

Writing in the *Journal of Applied Psychology*, Alexander D. Stajkovic, Edwin A. Locke, and Eden S. Blair note that the literature on goal-setting theory and motivation is well established, but they point out that it deals only with conscious motivation. In two empirical studies they attempt to link this set of findings with a body of literature in social psychology concerned with subconscious goal motivation.

One of the key findings of research on goal-setting theory is that difficult goals lead to higher performance than do general "do your best" or easy goals when performance feedback, goal commitment, and task knowledge are present. A research stream of social psychology literature deals with the subconscious activation of goals by primers found in environments in which goals are regularly pursued. Using this background, the researchers' stated purpose "was to link subconscious and conscious goals by empirically examining the interaction between the two."

A pilot study and a main study were conducted with samples of undergraduate and graduate students at a university in the Midwest. Study participants were divided into two groups, with one group receiving a "priming" treatment where subjects did setup work involving identification or use of achievement-related words before they completed a performance task. In the second, or "no prime" group, only achievement-neutral words were identified or used in the setup work prior to the performance task.

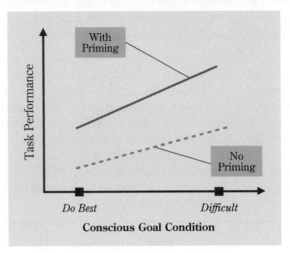

Conscious Goal Condition

In both studies the results confirmed predictions from goal-setting theory by showing that "difficult" conscious goals increased performance relative to "easy" and "do your best" goal-setting conditions. Additionally, the researchers found that subjects in primed subconscious conditions performed better than did those in unprimed subconscious conditions on both "difficult" and "do your best" goals. In other words, primed subconscious goals had positive interactions with conscious goals for both difficult and do your best goals.

The overall conclusions from these studies show that more research is needed on the links between conscious and subconscious goals with task performance. But the initial findings are favorable in suggesting that when both types of goals are used together, their motivational impact is increased.[32A]

extensive. Indeed, more research has been done on goal setting than on any other theory related to work motivation.[33] Nearly 400 studies have been conducted in several countries, including Australia, England, Germany, Japan, and the United States.[34] The basic precepts of goal-setting theory remain an important source of advice for managing human behavior in the work setting.

Goal-Setting Guidelines

Managerially speaking, the implications of research on goal setting can be summarized in the following guidelines:[35]

- *Difficult goals are more likely to lead to higher performance than are less difficult ones.* If the goals are seen as too difficult or impossible, however, the relationship with performance no longer holds. For example, you will likely perform better as a financial services agent if you have a goal of selling 6 annuities a week than if you have a goal of selling 3. But if your goal is selling 15 annuities a week, you may consider that impossible to achieve, and your performance may well be lower than what it would be with a more realistic goal.

- *Specific goals are more likely to lead to higher performance than are no goals or vague or very general ones.* All too often people work with very general goals such as the encouragement to "do your best." Research indicates that more specific goals, such as selling six computers a day, are much more motivational than a simple "do your best" goal.

- *Task feedback, or knowledge of results, is likely to motivate people toward higher performance by encouraging the setting of higher performance goals.* Feedback lets people know where they stand and whether they are on course or off course in their efforts. For example, think about how eager you are to find out how well you did on an examination.

- *Goals are most likely to lead to higher performance when people have the abilities and the feelings of self-efficacy required to accomplish them.* The individual must be able to accomplish the goals and feel confident in those abilities. To take the financial services example again, you may be able to do what is required to sell 6 annuities a week and feel confident that you can. If your goal is to sell 15, however, you may believe that your abilities are insufficient to the task, and thus you may lack the confidence to work hard enough to accomplish it.

- *Goals are most likely to motivate people toward higher performance when they are accepted and there is commitment to them.* Participating in the goal-setting process helps build acceptance and commitment; it creates a sense of "ownership" of the goals. But, goals assigned by someone else can be equally effective when the assigners are authority figures that can have an impact, and when the subordinate can actually reach the goal. According to research, assigned goals most often lead to poor performance when they are curtly or inadequately explained.

Goal Setting and MBO

When we speak of goal setting and its motivational potential, the concept of **management by objectives**, or **MBO**, immediately comes to mind. MBO is a process of joint goal setting between a supervisor and a subordinate.[36] The process involves managers working with their team members to establish performance goals and to make plans that are consistent with higher-level work unit and organizational objectives. This unlocks the motivational power of goal setting as just discussed. And when done throughout an organization, MBO also helps clarify the hierarchy of objectives as a series of well-defined means-ends chains.

Figure 5.4 shows a comprehensive view of MBO. Notice how the process allows managers to make use of goal-setting principles. The joint supervisor and subordinate discussions are designed to extend participation from the point of establishing initial goals to the point of evaluating results in terms of

management by objectives, or **MBO** is a process of joint goal setting between a supervisor and a subordinate.

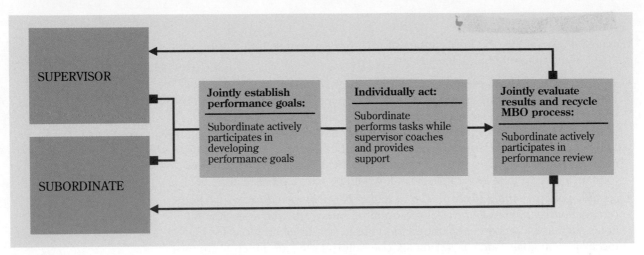

Figure 5.4   How the management by objectives process works.

goal attainment. In addition, however, a successful MBO system calls for careful implementation. Not only must workers have the freedom to carry out the required tasks, but managers should also be prepared to actively support workers' efforts to achieve the agreed-upon goals.

Although a fair amount of research based on case studies of MBO success is available, reports from scientifically rigorous studies have shown mixed results.[37] MBO has much to offer, both as a general management practice and as an application of goal-setting theory. But it is by no means easy to start an MBO program and keep it going. Some reported difficulties with the process include too much paperwork required to document goals and accomplishments, too much emphasis on goal-oriented rewards and punishments, as well as too much focus on top-down goals, goals that are easily stated and achieved, and individual instead of group goals.

Chapter 5   Study Guide

Summary

What is motivation?

- Motivation is an internal force that accounts for the level, direction, and persistence of effort expended at work.

- Content theories—including the work of Maslow, Alderfer, McClelland, and Herzberg— focus on locating individual needs that influence behavior in the workplace.

- Process theories, such as equity and expectancy theory, examine the thought processes that affect decisions made by workers about alternative courses of action.

- Although motivation is of universal interest and importance, specific aspects of work motivation may vary from one culture to the next.

What are the needs theories of motivation?

- Maslow's hierarchy of needs theory views human needs as activated in a five-step hierarchy ranging from physiological (lowest), to safety, to social, to esteem, to self-actualization (highest).

- Alderfer's ERG theory collapses the five needs into three: existence, relatedness, and growth; it maintains that more than one need can be activated at a time.

- McClelland's acquired needs theory focuses on the needs for achievement, affiliation, and power, and it views needs as developed over time through experience and training.

- Herzberg's two-factor theory links job satisfaction to motivator factors, such as responsibility and challenge, associated with job content; it links job dissatisfaction to hygiene factors, such as pay and working conditions, associated with job context.

What is the equity theory of motivation?

- Equity theory points out that social comparison takes place when people receive rewards.

- Any felt inequity in social comparison will motivate people to behave in ways that restore a sense of perceived equity to the situation.

- When felt inequity is negative—that is, when the individual feels unfairly treated—he or she may decide to work less hard in the future or to quit a job for other, more attractive opportunities.

- Organizational justice is an issue of how fair and equitable people view workplace practices; it is described in respect to distributive, procedural, and interactive justice.

What is the expectancy theory of motivation?

- Vroom's expectancy theory describes motivation as a function of an individual's beliefs concerning effort-performance relationships (expectancy), work-outcome relationships (instrumentality), and the desirability of various work outcomes (valence).

- Expectancy theory states that Motivation = Expectancy × Instrumentality × Valence, and argues that managers should make each factor positive in order to ensure high levels of motivation.

What is the goal-setting theory of motivation?

- Goal setting is the process of developing, negotiating, and formalizing performance targets or objectives.

- Research supports predictions that the most motivational goals are challenging and specific, allow for feedback on results, and create commitment and acceptance.

- The motivational impact of goals may be affected by individual difference moderators such as ability and self-efficacy.

- Management by objectives is a process of joint goal setting between a supervisor and worker; is an action framework for applying goal-setting theory in day-to-day management practice and on an organization-wide basis.

Key Terms

Content theories (p. 111)
Distributive justice (p. 118)
Equity theory (p. 116)
ERG theory (p. 113)
Existence needs (p. 113)
Expectancy (p. 119)
Expectancy theory (p. 118)
Growth needs (p. 113)
Hierarchy of needs theory
    (p. 112)
Higher-order needs
    (p. 112)

Hygiene factors (p. 115)
Instrumentality (p. 119)
Interactional justice (p. 118)
Lower-order needs (p. 112)
Management by objectives
    (MBO) (p. 123)
Motivation (p. 111)
Motivator factors (p. 115)
Need for achievement
    (nAch) (p. 113)
Need for affiliation (nAff)
    (p. 113)

Need for power (nPower)
    (p. 114)
Organizational justice
    (p. 118)
Procedural justice (p. 118)
Process theories (p. 111)
Relatedness needs (p. 113)
Two-factor theory (p. 115)
Valence (p. 119)

Self-Test 5

Multiple Choice

1. Motivation is defined as the level and persistence of _____. (a) effort (b) performance (c) need satisfaction (d) performance instrumentalities

2. A content theory of motivation is most likely to focus on _____. (a) organizational justice (b) instrumentalities (c) equities (d) individual needs

3. A process theory of motivation is most likely to focus on _____. (a) frustration-regression (b) expectancies regarding work outcomes (c) lower-order needs (d) higher-order needs

4. According to McClelland, a person high in need achievement will be _____. (a) guaranteed success in top management (b) motivated to control and influence other people (c) motivated by teamwork and collective responsibility (d) motivated by challenging but achievable goals

5. In Alderfer's ERG theory, the _____ needs best correspond with Maslow's higher-order needs of esteem and self-actualization. (a) existence (b) relatedness (c) recognition (d) growth

6. Improvements in job satisfaction are most likely under Herzberg's two-factor theory when _____ are improved. (a) working conditions (b) base salary (c) co-worker relationships (d) opportunities for responsibility

7. In Herzberg's two-factor theory _____ factors are found in job context. (a) motivator (b) satisfier (c) hygiene (d) enrichment

8. In equity theory, the _____ is a key issue. (a) social comparison of rewards and efforts (b) equality of rewards (c) equality of efforts (d) absolute value of rewards

9. In equity motivation theory, felt negative inequity _____. (a) is not a motivating state (b) is a stronger motivating state than felt positive inequity (c) can be as strong a motivating state as felt positive inequity (d) does not operate as a motivating state

10. A manager's failure to enforce a late-to-work policy the same way for all employees is a violation of _____ justice. (a) interactional (b) moral (c) distributive (d) procedural

11. In expectancy theory, _____ is the probability that a given level of performance will lead to a particular work outcome. (a) expectancy (b) instrumentality (c) motivation (d) valence

12. In expectancy theory, _____ is the perceived value of a reward. (a) expectancy (b) instrumentality (c) motivation (d) valence

13. Expectancy theory posits that _____. (a) motivation is a result of rational calculation (b) work expectancies are irrelevant (c) need satisfaction is critical (d) valence is the probability that a given level of task performance will lead to various work outcomes.

14. Which goals tend to be more motivating? _____ (a) challenging goals (b) easy goals (c) general goals (d) no goals

15. The MBO process emphasizes _____ as a way of building worker commitment to goal accomplishment. (a) authority (b) joint goal setting (c) infrequent feedback (d) rewards

Short Response

16. What is the frustration-regression component in Alderfer's ERG theory?
17. What does job enrichment mean in Herzberg's two-factor theory?
18. What is the difference between distributive and procedural justice?
19. What is the multiplier effect in expectancy theory?

Applications Essay

20. While attending a business luncheon, you overhear the following conversation at a nearby table. Person A: "I'll tell you this: if you satisfy your workers' needs, they'll be productive." Person B: "I'm not so sure; if I satisfy their needs, maybe they'll be real good about coming to work but not very good about working really hard while they are there." Which person do you agree with and why?

These learning activities from *The OB Skills Workbook* are suggested for Chapter 5.

OB in Action

CASE	EXPERIENTIAL EXERCISES	SELF-ASSESSMENT
▪ 5. It Isn't Fair	▪ 4. What Do You Value in Work?	▪ 7. Two-Factor Profile
	▪ 11. Teamwork and Motivation	
	▪ 12. The Downside of Punishment	
	▪ 17. Annual Pay Raises	

Plus—special learning experiences from *The Jossey-Bass/Pfeiffer Classroom Collection*

Chapter 6

Motivation and Job Design

Chapter at a Glance

It's not always easy, but creating a good person-job fit has a big performance impact. Chapter 6 extends the study of motivation into job designs, technology, and alternative work schedules. As you read, *keep in mind these study topics.*

JOB-DESIGN APPROACHES
Scientific Management

Job Enlargement and Job Rotation

Job Enrichment

DESIGNING JOBS TO INCREASE MOTIVATION
Job Characteristics Model

Social Information Processing

Practical Questions and Answers

TECHNOLOGY AND JOB DESIGN
Automation and Robotics

Flexible Manufacturing Systems

Electronic Offices

Workflow and Process Reengineering

ALTERNATIVE WORK ARRANGEMENTS
Compressed Work Weeks

Flexible Working Hours

Job Sharing

Telecommuting

Part-Time Work

CHAPTER 6 STUDY GUIDE

It's about person-job fit

I magine a job like this—no problem taking personal time during normal work hours, able to start and quit at times convenient for you, few mandatory meetings, able to work from home. It's not fiction; it's a fact at Best Buy, where the firm's ROWE (short for Results-Only Work Environment) program has changed the rules for many staffers at the firm's Minneapolis headquarters. *Business Week* calls it a *post-geographic workplace* that gives people the freedom "to work wherever they want, whenever they want, as long as they get their work done." It's an output-focused and results-oriented, not a rules-driven culture. So, how does it work?

Well, great, if you ask those participating. Chad Achen, online order manager, has been known to leave early for a movie matinee; Kelly McDevitt, online promotions manager, leaves in the early afternoon to pick her son up from school; Mark Wells, e-learning specialist, sleeps late whenever he wants. And it's also great if you look at the numbers.

> **"The old way of managing and looking at work isn't going to work anymore."**

Voluntary turnover decreased from between 52 percent and 90 percent among divisions adopting ROWE; average productivity increased by 35 percent. Senior Vice President J. T. Thompson became a believer. "For years . . . I was always looking to see if people were here," he says. "I should have been looking at what they were getting done." For her part, Cari Ressler, a co-sponsor of ROWE and a human resource manager, says: "The old way of managing and looking at work isn't going to work anymore. We want to revolutionalize the way work gets done."

But naysayers exist too. One letter writer responded to the *Business Week* article with this comment: "The lack of fixed schedules at Best Buy cannot exist in the long term in a competitive global economy." Another asks: "Can you design metrics that measure the effect of one member needing a quick answer from another and having to chase them down because they don't know whether they're going to be in the office or at a movie?"[1]

Job-Design Approaches

When you think about the Best Buy example, you have to realize that such flexible work practices are not possible for all jobs and situations. But the basic goal applies everywhere—achieving a good fit between the job to be done and the person who is best able to do it. When a good fit exists, we would expect it more likely that the person is highly motivated in his or her job, and high performing. You might think of it in terms of this equation:

$$\text{Person} + \text{Job Fit} = \text{Motivation and Performance.}$$

One of the ways to pursue this goal is by proper **job design**. This is the process through which managers plan and specify job tasks and the work arrangements that allow them to be accomplished. Figure 6.1 shows three major alternative job design

Job design is the process of defining job tasks and the work arrangements to accomplish them.

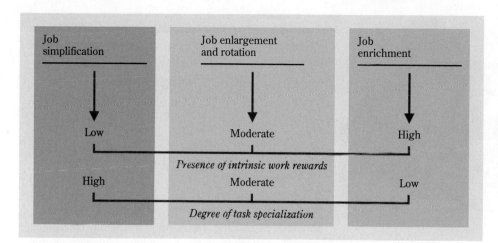

Figure 6.1   **A continuum of job-design strategies.**

approaches, and it also indicates how they differ in the way required tasks are defined and in the motivation provided for the worker. In this sense, the "best" job design is always one that meets organizational requirements for high performance, offers a good fit with individual skills and needs, and provides valued opportunities for job satisfaction.

Scientific Management

The history of scholarly interest in job design can be traced in part to Frederick Taylor's work with *scientific management* in the early 1900s.[2] Taylor and his contemporaries wanted to create management and organizational practices that would increase people's efficiency at work. Their approach was to study a job carefully, break it into its smallest components, establish exact time and motion requirements for each task to be done, and then train workers to do these tasks in the same way over and over again. Taylor's principles of scientific management can be summarized as follows:

1. Develop a "science" for each job that covers rules of motion, standard work tools, and supportive work conditions.
2. Hire workers with the right abilities for the job.
3. Train and motivate workers to do their jobs according to the science.
4. Support workers by planning and assisting their work using the job science.

These early efforts were forerunners of current industrial engineering approaches to job design that emphasize efficiency. Such approaches attempt to determine the best processes, methods, workflow layouts, output standards, and person-machine interfaces for various jobs. A good example is found at United Parcel Service (UPS), where calibrated productivity standards carefully guide workers. At regional centers, sorters must load vans at a set number of packages per hour. After analyzing delivery stops on regular van routes, supervisors generally know within a few minutes how long a driver's pickups and deliveries will take. Engineers devise precise routines for drivers, who save time by knocking on customers' doors rather than looking for doorbells. Handheld computers further enhance delivery efficiencies. At UPS, such scientific management approaches generate significant increases in productivity.

PRESENTEEISM: HOW COMING IN SICK AFFECTS BUSINESS

You wake up and you're feeling even worse than the day before. Sniffling, sneezing, coughing, you make your way to work, hoping to get through the day as best as you can. Fine, but what about everyone that you'll come into contact with that day, and what about the impact your "presenteeism"—going to work sick—can have on office productivity? Brett Gorovsky of CCH, a business information resource, says that when people come to work sick it "can take a very real hit on the bottom line." His firm reports that 56 percent of executives in one poll considered this a problem; that figure is up some 17 percent in a two-year period. Estimates are that the cost of lost productivity is as much as $180 billion annually. WebMD reports a study claiming that the cost of lost productivity could be higher than what might be paid out in authorized sick days. But the fact remains: many of us work sick because we have to if we want to be paid.[3]

What are the ethics of coming to work sick and sharing our illnesses with others? And from the organization's side of things, what are the ethics of not providing benefits sufficient to allow employees to stay home from work when they aren't feeling well?

■ **Job simplification** standardizes tasks and employs people in very routine jobs.

Today, the term **job simplification** is used to describe a scientific management approach to job design that standardizes work procedures and employs people in clearly defined and highly specialized tasks. The machine-paced automobile assembly line is a classic example. Why is it used? Typically, the answer is to increase operating efficiency by reducing the number of skills required to do a job, by being able to hire low-cost labor, by keeping the needs for job training to a minimum, and by emphasizing the accomplishment of repetitive tasks. However, the very nature of such jobs creates potential disadvantages as well. These include loss of efficiency in the face of lower quality, high rates of absenteeism and turnover, and demand for higher wages to compensate for unappealing jobs. One response to such problems is through advanced applications of new technology. In automobile manufacturing, for example, robots now do many different kinds of work previously accomplished with human labor.

Job Enlargement and Job Rotation

In job simplification the number or variety of different tasks performed is limited. Although this makes the tasks easier to master, the repetitiveness can reduce motivation. This result has prompted alternative job design approaches that try to make jobs more interesting by adding breadth to the variety of tasks performed.

■ **Job enlargement** increases task variety by adding new tasks of similar difficulty to a job.

Job enlargement increases task variety by combining into one job two or more tasks that were previously assigned to separate workers. Sometimes called *horizontal loading*, this approach increases *job breadth* by having the worker perform more and different tasks, but all at the same level of responsibility and challenge.

Job rotation, another horizontal-loading approach, increases task variety by periodically shifting workers among jobs involving different tasks. Again, the responsibility level of the tasks stays the same. The rotation can be arranged according to almost any time schedule, such as hourly, daily, or weekly schedules. An important benefit of job rotation is training. It allows workers to become more familiar with different tasks and increases the flexibility with which they can be moved from one job to another.

■ **Job rotation** increases task variety by shifting workers among jobs involving tasks of similar difficulty.

Job Enrichment

A third job design alternative traces back to Frederick Herzberg's two-factor theory of motivation as described in Chapter 5. This theory would suggest that high levels of motivation should not be expected from jobs designed on the basis of simplification, enlargement, or rotation.[4] "Why," asks Herzberg, "should a worker become motivated when one or more 'meaningless' tasks are added to previously existing ones or when work assignments are rotated among equally 'meaningless' tasks?" Instead of pursuing one of these job design strategies, therefore, Herzberg recommends an alternative approach: building high-content jobs.

In Herzberg's model, **job enrichment** is the practice of enhancing job content by building into it more motivating factors such as responsibility, achievement, recognition, and personal growth. This job-design strategy differs markedly from strategies previously discussed in that it adds to job content the planning and evaluating duties that would otherwise be reserved for managers.

■ **Job enrichment** increases job content by giving workers more responsibility for planning and evaluating duties.

The content changes made possible by job enrichment (see OB Savvy 6.1) involve what Herzberg calls *vertical loading* to increase *job depth*. Enriched jobs, he states, help to satisfy the higher-order needs that people bring with them to work and will, therefore, increase their motivation to achieve high levels of job performance.

Despite the inherent appeal of Herzberg's ideas on job enrichment, two common questions raise words of caution. *Is job enrichment expensive?* Job enrichment can be very costly, particularly when it requires major changes in workflows, facilities, or technology. *Will workers demand higher pay when moving into enriched jobs?* Herzberg argues that if employees are being paid a truly competitive wage or salary, then the intrinsic rewards of performing enriched tasks will be adequate compensation. Other researchers are more skeptical, advising that pay must be carefully considered.[5]

OB SAVVY 6.1

Job Enrichment Advice from Frederick Herzberg

- Allow workers to plan.
- Allow workers to control.
- Maximize job freedom.
- Increase task difficulty.
- Help workers become task experts.
- Provide performance feedback.
- Increase performance accountability.
- Provide complete units of work.

Designing Jobs to Increase Motivation

OB scholars have been reluctant to recommend job enrichment as a universal solution to all job performance and satisfaction problems given concerns about increased costs and potential effects on workers. Also, individual differences must be considered in answering this additional question: "Is job enrichment for everyone?" A diagnostic approach developed by Richard Hackman and Greg Oldham offers a broader, contingency-based framework for job design to increase motivation.[6] Their "job characteristics" model provides a data-based approach for creating job designs with good person-job fit that maximize the potential for motivation and performance.

Job Characteristics Model

■ The **job characteristics model** identifies five core job characteristics—skill variety, task identity, task significance, autonomy, and feedback.

Figure 6.2 presents the **job characteristics model** and the five core job characteristics considered particularly important to job design. The higher a job scores on each characteristic, the more it is considered to be enriched. The core job characteristics are

- *Skill variety*—the degree to which a job includes a variety of different activities and involves the use of a number of different skills and talents
- *Task identity*—the degree to which the job requires completion of a "whole" and identifiable piece of work, one that involves doing a job from beginning to end with a visible outcome
- *Task significance*—the degree to which the job is important and involves a meaningful contribution to the organization or society in general
- *Autonomy*—the degree to which the job gives the employee substantial freedom, independence, and discretion in scheduling the work and determining the procedures used in carrying it out
- *Job feedback*—the degree to which carrying out the work activities provides direct and clear information to the employee regarding how well the job has been done.

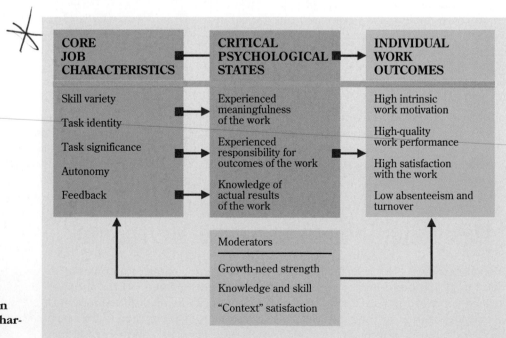

Figure 6.2   Job-design implications of job characteristics theory.

Hackman and Oldham recommend measuring the current status of each job on each core characteristic.[7] These characteristics can then be changed systematically to enrich the job and increase its motivational potential. This assessment can be accomplished using an instrument called the Job Diagnostic Survey (JDS), which is included in the *OB Skills Workbook* as part of the experiential exercise "Job Design." Scores on the JDS are combined to create a **motivating potential score**, or MPS, which indicates the degree to which the job is capable of motivating people. In their terms

MPS = Skill variety + Task identity + Task significance − Autonomy − Feedback

A job's MPS can be raised by combining tasks to create larger jobs, opening feedback channels to enable workers to know how well they are doing, establishing client relationships to experience such feedback directly from customers, and employing vertical loading to create more planning and controlling responsibilities.

When the core characteristics are enriched in these ways and the MPS for a job is raised as high as possible, the redesigned job can be expected to positively influence three critical psychological states for the individual: (1) experienced meaningfulness of the work, (2) experienced responsibility for the outcomes of the work, and (3) knowledge of actual results of the work. The positive psychological states, in turn, can be expected to create more positive work outcomes with respect to individual motivation, performance, and satisfaction.

Individual Difference Moderators The job characteristics model recognizes that the five core job characteristics do not affect all people in the same way. Rather than accept Herzberg's implication that enriched jobs should be good for everyone, this approach allows for individual differences. It accepts the idea that jobs should be designed to arrive at the best match between core characteristics and individual needs and talents. Specifically, the model suggests that enriched jobs will lead to positive outcomes only for those persons who are a good match for them. When the fit between the person and an enriched job is poor, positive outcomes are less likely, and problems may well result.

Looking back, Figure 6.2 highlights three individual difference moderators that can influence individual preferences in how their jobs are designed. The first moderator is *growth-need strength*—the degree to which a person desires the opportunity for self-direction, learning, and personal accomplishment at work. It is similar to Abraham Maslow's esteem and self-actualization needs and Alderfer's growth needs, as discussed in Chapter 5. When applied here, the expectation is that people high in growth-need strengths at work will respond positively to enriched jobs, whereas people low in growth-need strengths will find enriched jobs to be sources of anxiety.

The second moderator is *knowledge and skill*. People whose capabilities fit the demands of enriched jobs are predicted to feel good about them and perform well. Those who are inadequate or who feel inadequate in this regard are likely to experience difficulties.

The third moderator is *context satisfaction*, or the extent to which an employee is satisfied with aspects of the work setting such as salary levels, quality of supervision, relationships with co-workers, and working conditions. In general, people who are more satisfied with job context are more likely than dissatisfied ones to support and do well with job enrichment.

Research Results Considerable research has been done on the job characteristics model in a variety of work settings, including banks, dentist offices, corrections

■ The **motivating potential score** describes the extent to which the core characteristics of a job create motivating conditions.

Job Sharing Duo

Fifteen years of employment and an unusual story: Sharon Cercone and Linda Gladziszewski share a job. At last check, that job was as a compensation consultant at a Pittsburgh financial services company. Their boss says: "I think of them as a single individual." The two women alternate work days, allowing each other time for personal responsibilities; they communicate regularly through e-mail and keep notes on a common database. Part of their success with job sharing is attributed to managing their boss's expectations; deal with them as one person and let the two divide the work according to their individual strengths and weaknesses.

Leaders on Leadership

SPANX QUEEN LEADS FROM THE BOTTOM LINE

Her story begins this way: "Like so many women, I bought clothes that looked amazing in a magazine or on the hanger, but in reality . . ."

The words are Sara Blakely's, and her concerns led to product innovation, entrepreneurship, and ultimately, a business whose 2006 retail sales surpassed $150 million—Spanx. With $5,000 of her own money and a new idea for "body shaping" underwear, she cut the feet out of a pair of panty hose and never looked back. Her idea led from a spare room in her Atlanta apartment to an international operation that employs over 50 people. But it wasn't always easy.

Blakely's first attempts to convince manufacturers to try her product met with resistance. She didn't give up. After a mill made the first Spanx, she persuaded Neimann-Marcus to sell them and sent Oprah Winfrey samples. After Winfrey voted Spanx "one of her favorite things," sales and the firm took off. After about a year of fast-paced growth, Blakely turned operations over to a chief executive officer. This left her free to pursue creative efforts, new products, and brand development. She says that she recognized her limits and "was eager to delegate my weaknesses." It worked. She won the national Entrepreneur of the Year Award in 2002 and was voted Georgia's Woman of the Year in 2005. Her motivation to succeed extends beyond product and business goals alone. She has since started the Sara Blakely Foundation with the express purpose of "supporting and empowering women around the world."[8]

Question: Sara Blakely turned a personal need into a substantial business opportunity. But once the entrepreneurship is over and the new product is off and running, what's the motivation that creates staying power?

departments, telephone companies, and manufacturing firms, as well as in government agencies. Experts generally agree that the model and its diagnostic approach are useful, but not yet perfect, guides to job design.[9]

On average, job characteristics do affect performance but not nearly as much as they do satisfaction. The research also emphasizes the importance of growth-need strength as a moderator of the job design–job performance–job satisfaction relationships. Positive job characteristics affect performance more strongly for high-growth-need than for low-growth-need individuals. The relationship is about the same with job satisfaction. It is also clear that job enrichment can fail when job requirements are increased beyond the level of individual capabilities or interests. Finally, employee perceptions of job characteristics often differ from measures taken by managers and consultants. These perceptions are important and must be considered. After all, they will largely determine whether workers view a job as high or low in the core characteristics and, consequently, will affect work outcomes.

Social Information Processing

A note of caution on this strict diagnostic approach to job design is raised by Gerald Salancik and Jeffrey Pfeffer. They question whether or not jobs have stable and objective characteristics to which individuals respond predictably and consistently.[10] Instead, they view job design from the perspective of **social information processing theory**. This theory argues that individual needs, task perceptions, and reactions are a result of socially constructed realities. Social information in organizations influences the way people perceive their jobs and respond to them. The same holds true, for example, in the classroom.

Suppose that several of your friends tell you that the instructor for a course is bad, the content is boring, and the requirements involve too much work. You may then think that the critical characteristics of the class are the instructor, the content, and the workload, and that they are all bad. All of this may substantially influence the way you perceive your instructor and the course, and the way you deal with the class—regardless of the actual characteristics.

Research on social information processing indicates that both social information and core characteristics are important. Although social information processing influences task perceptions and attitudes, the job characteristics discussed earlier are also important. Indeed, how someone perceives job characteristics is likely to be influenced both by the objective characteristics themselves and by the social information present in the workplace.

■ The **social information processing theory** asserts that individual needs and task perceptions result from socially constructed realities.

Time Zone Warriors

Practical Questions and Answers

There are many issues with using job enrichment as a useful job design alternative. The following three questions and their answers help in summarizing some of the most important points and managerial implications.

Should everyone's job be enriched? The answer is clearly no. The logic of individual differences suggests that not everyone will want an enriched job. Individuals most likely to have positive reactions to job enrichment are those who need achievement, who exhibit a strong work ethic, or who are seeking higher-order growth-need satisfaction at work. Job enrichment also appears to be most advantageous when the job context is positive and when workers have the abilities needed to do the enriched job. Furthermore, costs, technological constraints, and workgroup or union opposition may make it difficult to enrich some jobs.[11]

Can job enrichment apply to groups? The answer is yes. The application of job-design strategies at the group level is growing in many types of settings. Part 3 discusses creative workgroup designs, including cross-functional work teams and self-managing teams.

What is the impact of culture on job enrichment? The answer is that it can be substantial. Research conducted in Belgium, Israel, Japan, the Netherlands, the United States, and Germany found unique aspects of what constitutes work in each country.[12] Work was seen as a social requirement most strongly in Belgium and Japan and least so in Germany. Work was regarded as something done for money in all countries but Belgium. In most cases, however, work was regarded as having both an economic and a societal contribution component. These results, as well as differences in such national cultural dimensions as power distance and individualism, reinforce a contingency approach to job enrichment and further suggest that cultural differences should be given consideration in job design.

It's hard to maintain your schedule, let alone practice flextime, when you have global responsibilities. For Lisa Ray, sales director of a North Carolina high-tech firm, one can say that "the sun never sets on her job." She frequently has to both travel and telephone across country borders and time zones. One of her business days started in North Carolina at 6 a.m. At 5 p.m. Ray flew to Chicago for a dinner meeting. At 10 p.m. she handled a conference call with a customer in Asia. When that call was finished, she spent an hour on e-mail. About 4 a.m. the next morning she was already awake to make telephone calls to Europe. By the end of the second day, she reported being "time zoned" and "not quite 100%" in her work.

Technology and Job Design

Sociotechnical systems integrate people and technology into high-performance work settings.

The concept of **sociotechnical systems** is used in organizational behavior to indicate the importance of integrating people and technology to create high-performance work systems.[13] As computers and information technologies continue to dominate the modern workplace, this concept is essential to new developments in job designs.

Automation and Robotics

As mentioned earlier, highly simplified jobs often cause problems because they offer little intrinsic motivation for the worker. Such tasks have been defined so narrowly that they lack challenge and lead to boredom when someone has to repeat them over and over again.

Given the technologies now available, one way to tackle this problem is through complete **automation**, using a machine to do work previously accomplished by a human. This approach increasingly involves the use of robots, which are becoming ever more versatile and reliable. In addition, robot prices are falling as the cost of human labor rises. Japan presently leads the world in robot use; the United States lags far behind, but its robot use is growing rapidly.[14]

Automation allows machines to do work previously accomplished by people.

Flexible manufacturing systems use adaptive technology and integrated job designs to easily shift production among alternative products.

Flexible Manufacturing Systems

In **flexible manufacturing systems**, adaptive computer-based technologies and integrated job designs are used to shift work easily and quickly among alternative products. This approach is increasingly common, for example, in companies supporting the automobile industry with machined metal products, including cylinder heads and gear boxes.[15]

A cellular manufacturing system, for example, might contain a number of automated production machines that cut, shape, drill, and fasten together various metal components. The machines can be quickly changed from manufacturing one product to another.[16] Workers in flexible manufacturing cells perform few routine assembly-line tasks. Rather, they ensure that the operations are handled correctly and deal with the changeover from one product configuration to another. They develop expertise across a wide range of functions, and the jobs have great potential for enriched core job characteristics.

Electronic Offices

Electronic office technology was the key when U.S. Healthcare, a large, private practice health maintenance organization (HMO), became interested in improving the quality of its health care services. The company installed large electronic bulletin boards that monitored progress toward a range of performance goals, put in robots to deliver the paper mail, and emphasized e-mail and computerized answering services. Essentially, the company tried to automate as many tasks as possible to free people for more challenging work. Similarly, Mutual Benefit Life completely reorganized the way it serviced insurance application forms—once handled by as many as 19 people across 5 departments. Mutual created a new case manager position responsible for processing applications from their inception until policies were issued.[17]

Continuing developments in electronic offices offer job enrichment possibilities for those workers equipped to handle the technology. But those jobs can be stressful and difficult for those who do not have the necessary education or skills.[18] Also, people who work continuously with computers are sometimes prone to experience physical ailments associated with repetitious keyboarding and mouse movements. Clearly, the technologies of the new workplace must be carefully integrated with the human factor.

Workflow and Process Reengineering

Another approach for improving job designs and performance is based on **process reengineering**—the analysis, streamlining, and reconfiguration of actions and tasks required to reach a work goal.[19] The process design approach systematically breaks down each action and task into specific components and subtasks, analyzes each for relevance and simplicity, and then does everything possible to reconfigure the process to eliminate wasted time, effort, and resources. The typical activities in such *process value analysis* are

1. Identify the core processes.
2. Map the core processes in respect to workflows.
3. Evaluate all tasks for the core processes.
4. Search for ways to eliminate unnecessary tasks or work.
5. Search for ways to eliminate delays, errors, and misunderstandings.
6. Search for efficiencies in how work is shared and transferred among people and departments.

> ▪ **Process reengineering** analyzes, streamlines, and reconfigures actions and tasks to achieve work goals.

An example of this approach might be to examine the various steps required to gain approval for a purchase order to buy a new computer. The process reengineering approach looks at every step in the process, from searching for items and vendors to obtaining bids, completing necessary forms, securing required signatures and approvals, actually placing the order, and so on to the point at which the new computer arrives, is checked in, is placed into an equipment inventory, and then is finally delivered to the workplace. In all this, one simple question drives the reengineering: What is necessary, and what else can be eliminated?

Alternative Work Arrangements

The chapter opening example of Best Buy highlighted a trend toward alternative ways of scheduling time that is becoming increasingly common in the workplace. These new arrangements are essentially reshaping the traditional 40-hour week, with its 9-to-5 schedules and work done at the company or place of business. Virtually all such plans are designed to influence employee satisfaction and to help employees balance the demands of their work and non-work lives.[20] They are becoming more and more important in fast-changing societies where demands for "work-life balance" and more "family-friendly" employers are growing ever more apparent.[21] For example, dual-career families with children, part-time students, older workers (retired or near retirement age), and single parents are all candidates for alternative work arrangements.

If there is any doubt regarding the ethical and moral consequences of workplace practices, a study by economists Alan Krueger and Alexandre Mas of the Princeton University Industrial Relations Section deserves attention. They suggest that labor strife at the Bridgestone/Firestone plant in Decatur, Illinois, could have contributed to the production of defective tires linked to deaths in a number of Ford Explorer road accidents. This plant, now closed, is shown by the authors to have produced tires more likely to fail during a period of labor-management strife. Managers everywhere should take notice. While circumstantial, this study helps support arguments calling for healthy and positive work environments. Ethical and socially responsible management that pays attention to the human factor, in other words, is important in order to integrate motivation with appropriate work design.[22]

Compressed Work Weeks

■■■ A **compressed work week** allows a full-time job to be completed in fewer than five full workdays.

A **compressed work week** is any scheduling of work that allows a full-time job to be completed in fewer than the standard five days. The most common form of compressed work week is the "4/40," or 40 hours of work accomplished in four 10-hour days.

This approach has many possible benefits. For the worker, additional time off is a major feature of this schedule. The individual often appreciates increased leisure time, three-day weekends, free weekdays to pursue personal business, and lower commuting costs. The organization can benefit, too, in terms of lower employee absenteeism and improved recruiting of new employees. But there are also potential disadvantages. Individuals can experience increased fatigue from the extended workday and family adjustment problems. The organization can experience work scheduling problems and customer complaints because of breaks in work coverage. Some organizations may face occasional union opposition and laws requiring payment of overtime for work exceeding eight hours of individual labor in any one day. Overall reactions to compressed work weeks are likely to be most favorable among employees who are allowed to participate in the decision to adopt the new work week, who have their jobs enriched as a result of the new schedule, and who have the strong higher-order needs identified in Maslow's hierarchy.[23]

Flexible Working Hours

■■■ **Flexible working hours** give employees some daily choice in scheduling arrival and departure times from work.

Another innovative work schedule, **flexible working hours**, or flextime, gives individuals a daily choice in the timing of their work commitments. One such schedule requires employees to work four hours of "core" time but leaves them free to choose their remaining four hours of work from among flexible time blocks. One person, for example, may start early and leave early, whereas another may start later and leave later. This flexible work schedule is becoming increasingly popular and is a valuable alternative for structuring work to accommodate individual interests and needs.

WAYS TO BEAT THE MOMMY DRAIN

It's no secret that more and more employers are turning to flexibility in work schedules to better accommodate today's workers. Among them, Accenture and Booz Allen Hamilton are taking special steps to make sure they can attract and retain talented working mothers. Here is a selection of ways top employers are counteracting the "Mommy drain," and responding to Daddy's needs as well.[24]

- Offer increased pay and extended time for maternity leave.
- Offer increased pay and extended time for parental leave.
- Allow employee pay set-asides to buy more time for maternal and parental leave.
- Create alternative and challenging jobs that require less travel.
- Make sure pay for performance plans do not discriminate against those on maternal or parental leave.
- Set up mentoring and networking systems to support working parents.
- Make sure new mothers feel they are wanted back at work.
- Keep in contact with employees on maternity and parental leaves.

Flextime increases individual autonomy in work scheduling and offers many opportunities and benefits (see OB Savvy 6.2). It is a way for dual-career couples to handle children's schedules as well as their own; it is a way to meet the demands of caring for elderly parents or ill family members; it is even a way to better attend to such personal affairs as medical and dental appointments, home emergencies, banking needs, and so on. Proponents of this scheduling strategy argue that the discretion it allows workers in scheduling their own hours of work encourages them to develop positive attitudes and to increase commitment to the organization.

A majority of American workplaces have had flextime programs for some years, and the number keeps growing.[25] An Aetna manager, commenting on the firm's flexible working hours program, said: "We're not doing flexible work scheduling to be nice, but because it makes business sense."[26]

OB SAVVY 6.2

Flextime Benefits

For organizations:
- Less absenteeism, tardiness, turnover
- More commitment
- Higher performance

For workers:
- Shorter commuting time
- More leisure time
- More job satisfaction
- Greater sense of responsibility

Job Sharing

In **job sharing**, one full-time job is assigned to two or more persons who then divide the work according to agreed-upon hours. Often, each person works half a day, but job sharing can also be done on a weekly or monthly basis. Although it is practiced by only a relatively small percentage of employers, human resource experts believe that job sharing is a valuable alternative work arrangement.[27]

Organizations benefit from job sharing when they can attract talented people who would otherwise be unable to work. An example is the qualified teacher who also is a parent. This person may be able to work only half a day. Through job sharing, two such persons can be employed to teach one class. Some job

Job sharing allows one full-time job to be divided among two or more persons.

sharers report less burnout and claim that they feel recharged each time they report for work. The tricky part of this arrangement is finding two people who will work well with each other.

When middle managers Sue Mannix and Charlotte Schutzman worked together at Bell Atlantic, for example, they faithfully coordinated each other's absences, with Schutzman working Mondays, Tuesdays, and Wednesday mornings, and Mannix working the rest of the workweek.[28] Job sharing should not be confused with a more controversial arrangement called *work sharing*. This occurs when workers agree to cut back on the number of hours they work in order to protect against layoffs. Workers may agree to voluntarily reduce 20 percent of hours worked and pay received, rather than have the employer cut 20 percent of the workforce during difficult economic times. Legal restrictions prohibit this practice in some settings.

Telecommuting

Telecommuting is work at home or in remote locations using computer and telecommunications linkages with the office.

Technology is influencing yet another alternative work arrangement that is becoming increasingly visible in many employment sectors ranging from higher education to government, and from manufacturing to services. **Telecommuting** is work done at home or in a remote location via the use of computers and advanced telecommunications linkages with a central office or other employment locations.

At IBM, Canada, an arrangement called *flexiplace* means working most of the time from a home office and coming into IBM corporate offices only for special meetings. In a practice known as *hoteling,* temporary offices are reserved for these workers during the times they visit the main office. Worldwide, some 20 percent of IBM's employees spend two or more days a week working at home or visiting customers.[29]

The notion of telecommuting is more and more associated with the *virtual office,* where the individual works literally "from the road" and while traveling from place to place or from customer to customer by car or airplane. In all cases, the worker remains linked electronically with the home office.[30] The number of workers who are telecommuting is growing daily, with organizations such as AT&T and Cisco Systems reporting that more than 50 percent of their workers telecommute at least part of the time.[31] IBM embraces virtual work not only as a means of helping employees with work-life balance issues, but also for bottom-line impact. The firm estimates that $100+ million are saved each year as some 42% of employees telecommute.

Telecommuting offers the individual the potential advantages of flexibility, the comforts of home, and the choice of locations consistent with the individual's lifestyle. In terms of advantages to the organization, this alternative often produces cost savings and efficiency as well as employee satisfaction. On the negative side, telecommuters sometimes complain about isolation from co-workers, decreased identification with the work team, and technical difficulties with the computer linkages essential to their work arrangement. Yet overall, the practice continues to grow, with more organizations now offering special training in the *virtual management* of telecommuters.

Research Insight
Telecommuting Found to Have a Complex Impact on Work-Family Conflicts

According to Timothy D. Golden, John F. Veiga, and Zeki Simsek, the literature on telecommuting and work-life conflict is equivocal. In some cases it suggests that the alternative work schedule reduces work-life conflict; in other cases the indication is that it increases such conflict. Using a sample of 454 professionals, the researchers conducted a survey to more closely examine the dynamics of telecommuting and work-family conflicts.

In this study the researchers expected that more telecommuting would be associated with lower reported work-to-family conflict, or with less interference of work on family matters. This is because of the flexibility of telecommuting in allowing people to deal emotionally and directly with family responsibilities. Data confirmed this hypothesis. A second hypothesis was that more telecommuting would be associated with greater reported family-to-work conflict, or with more interference of family on work matters. This is the result of the increased strains of knowing that telecommuting allowed people to give more time and emotional energy to family matters. Data also confirmed this hypothesis.

Also included in the study was an attempt to understand how moderator variables, such as household size, influence the prior relationships. One moderating hypothesis was that any negative relationship between telecommuting and work-to-family conflict would decrease more slowly with increasing household size. This was not supported. Although the data showed the expected direction,

they were not statistically significant. Another moderating hypothesis was that any positive relationship with family-to-work conflict would increase at a faster rate with increasing household size. This hypothesis was supported. Study findings also showed that job autonomy and scheduling flexibility positively moderated the relationship between telecommuting and work-to-family conflict.

The researchers concluded that more needs to be learned about telecommuting trade-offs as participants attempt to balance work and family responsibilities. They call for more research and ask for caution in terms of viewing telecommuting as a "panacea" for work-life balance issues in the workplace.[32]

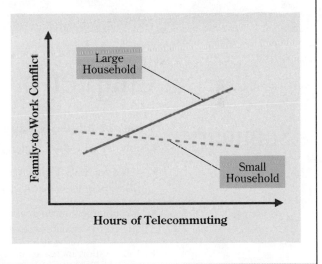

Part-Time Work

Part-time work has become an increasingly prominent and controversial work arrangement. When performing **temporary part-time work**, an employee is classified as "temporary" and works less than the standard 40-hour work week.

Temporary part-time work is temporary work for fewer hours than the standard week.

■■ **Permanent part-time work** is permanent work for fewer hours than the standard week.

When performing **permanent part-time work**, the employee is considered a "permanent" member of the workforce but contributes fewer hours than the standard 40-hour work week.

Usually, temporary part-timers are easily released and hired as needs dictate. Accordingly, many organizations use part-time work to hold down labor costs and to help smooth out peaks and valleys in the business cycle. Employers may also use part-time work to better manage what may be called "retention quality." These workers are highly skilled individuals who are committed to their careers; they want to continue to develop professionally, but they can only work part time. Part-time nurses, among others, fall in this category.[33]

The part-time work schedule can be a benefit to people who want to supplement other jobs or who want something less than a full work week for a variety of personal reasons. For someone who is holding two jobs, including at least one part-time position, the added burdens can be stressful and may affect performance in either one or both work settings. Furthermore, part-timers often fail to qualify for fringe benefits, such as health care, life insurance, and pensions, and they may be paid less than their full-time counterparts. Nevertheless, part-time work schedules are of growing practical importance because of the organizational advantages they offer.

Chapter 6   Study Guide

Summary

What are job-design approaches?

■ Job design is the creation of tasks and work settings for specific jobs.

■ Job design by scientific management or job simplification standardizes work and employs people in clearly defined and specialized tasks.

■ Job enlargement increases task variety by combining two or more tasks previously assigned to separate workers.

■ Job rotation increases task variety by periodically rotating workers among jobs involving different tasks.

■ Job enrichment builds bigger and more responsible jobs by adding planning and evaluating duties.

What are the keys to designing motivating jobs?

■ Job characteristics theory offers a diagnostic approach to job enrichment based on analysis of five core job characteristics: skill variety, task identity, task significance, autonomy, and feedback.

■ Job characteristics theory does not assume that everyone wants an enriched job; it indicates that job enrichment will be more successful for persons with high growth needs, requisite job skills, and context satisfaction.

■ The social information processing theory points out that information from co-workers and others in the workplace influences a worker's perceptions of and responses to a job.

■ Not everyone's job should be enriched; job enrichment can be done for groups as well as individuals; cultural factors may influence job enrichment success.

How are technology and jobs related?

■ Well-planned sociotechnical systems integrate people and technology for high performance.

■ Robotics and complete automation are increasingly used to replace people in order to perform jobs that are highly simplified and repetitive.

■ Workers in flexible manufacturing cells use the latest technology to produce high-quality products with short cycle times.

■ The nature of office work is being changed by computer workstation technologies, networks, and various forms of electronic communication.

■ Workflow and business process reengineering analyzes all steps in work sequences to streamline activities and tasks, save costs, and improve performance.

What alternative work arrangements are used today?

■ Today's complex society is giving rise to a number of alternative work arrangements designed to balance the personal demands on workers with job responsibilities and opportunities.

■ The compressed work week allows a full-time work week to be completed in fewer than five days, typically offering four 10-hour days of work and three days free.

■ Flexible working hours allow employees some daily choice in timing between work and non-work activities.

■ Job sharing occurs when two or more people divide one full-time job according to agreements among themselves and the employer.

■ Telecommuting involves work at home or at a remote location while communicating with the home office as needed via computer and related technologies.

■ Part-time work requires less than a 40-hour work week and can be done on a schedule classifying the worker as temporary or permanent.

Key Terms

Automation (p. 138)
Compressed work week (p. 140)
Flexible manufacturing systems (p. 138)
Flexible working hours (p. 140)
Job characteristics model (p. 134)
Job design (p. 130)
Job enlargement (p. 132)
Job enrichment (p. 133)
Job rotation (p. 133)
Job sharing (p. 141)
Job simplification (p. 132)
Motivating potential score (p. 135)
Permanent part-time work (p. 144)
Process reengineering (p. 139)
Social information processing theory (p. 137)
Sociotechnical systems (p. 138)
Telecommuting (p. 142)
Temporary part-time work (p. 143)

Self-Test 6

Multiple Choice

1. Job simplification is closely associated with _____ as originally developed by Frederick Taylor. (a) vertical loading (b) horizontal loading (c) scientific management (d) self-efficacy

2. Job _____ increases job _____ by combining into one job several tasks of similar difficulty. (a) rotation; depth (b) enlargement; depth (c) rotation; breadth (d) enlargement; breadth

3. If a manager redesigns a job through vertical loading, she would most likely _____. (a) bring tasks from earlier in the workflow into the job (b) bring tasks from later in the workflow into the job (c) bring higher level or managerial responsibilities into the job (d) raise the standards for high performance

4. In the job characteristics model, _____ indicates the degree to which an individual is able to make decisions affecting his or her work. (a) task variety (b) task identity (c) task significance (d) autonomy

5. In the job characteristics model, a person will be most likely to find an enriched job motivating if they _____. (a) receive stock options (b) have ability and support (c) experience vertical loading (d) are satisfied with the job context

6. When a job allows a person to do a complete unit of work, for example process an insurance claim from point of receipt from the customer to the point of final resolution with the customer, it would be considered high on which core characteristic? (a) task identity (b) task significance (c) task autonomy (d) feedback

7. An alternative to the diagnostic approach to job design is the _____ view which argues that task perceptions are a result of socially constructed realities. (a) sociotechnical systems (b) process reengineering (c) motivating potential (d) social information processing

8. The notion of a _____ is one example of how job enrichment can be applied to groups. (a) quality circle (b) self-managing team (c) cellular manufacturing (d) horizontal load

9. The potential impact of culture on job enrichment _____. (a) is too minimal to be of any importance (b) can be substantial and is therefore an important consideration (c) is only relevant in cultures that strongly social information processing (d) doesn't apply in cultures where pay scales are very low

10. The basic logic of sociotechnical systems is that _____. (a) people must be integrated with technology (b) technology is more important than people (c) people are more important than technology (d) technology alienates people

11. Flexible manufacturing systems _____. (a) are especially useful for health care organizations (b) break components down very specifically to reconfigure processes (c) are emphasized by Frederick Taylor (d) emphasize what is necessary and what can be eliminated

12. The "4/40" is a type of _____ work arrangement. (a) compressed workweek (b) "allow workers to change machine configurations to make different products" (c) job sharing (d) permanent part-time

13. The flexible working hours schedule allows workers to choose _____. (a) days of week to work (b) total hours to work per week (c) location of work (d) starting and ending times for workdays

14. When workers agree to cut back on the number of hours worked to avoid possible lay offs, this arrangement is known as _____. (a) job sharing (b) work sharing (c) job streamlining (d) work reduction

15. Telecommuting _____. (a) is similar to part-time work (b) involves flexible manufacturing (c) involves job sharing (d) is one kind of virtual office setup

Short Response

16. How can job enrichment be created by building job depth?
17. What role does growth-need strength play in the job characteristics model?
18. What are the potential advantages and disadvantages of a compressed work week?
19. What is the difference between job sharing and work sharing?

Applications Essay

20. You have just been called in as a consultant to recommend a program to create a motivational work setting in a department that sells men's and women's clothing. Use relevant job design and technology ideas from this chapter. Make any necessary assumptions and discuss your recommendations.

These learning activities from *The OB Skills Workbook* are suggested for Chapter 6.

OB in Action

CASE	EXPERIENTIAL EXERCISES	SELF-ASSESSMENTS
■ 6. Hovey and Bread	■ 3. My Best Job	■ 7. Two-Factor Profile
	■ 13. Tinker Toys	■ 8. Are You Cosmopolitan?
	■ 14. Job Design Preferences	
	■ 15. My Fantasy Job	

Plus—special learning experiences from *The Jossey-Bass/Pfeiffer Classroom Collection*

Rewards and Performance Management

Chapter at a Glance

The old adage "what gets measured happens" rings very true. Chapter 7 addresses motivation and rewards in a context of performance management. As you read Chapter 7, *keep in mind these study topics*.

MOTIVATION AND REWARDS

PERFORMANCE MANAGEMENT

PERFORMANCE APPRAISAL

CHAPTER 7 STUDY GUIDE

What gets measured happens

Would you buy into this vision: high quality products and minimum impact on the environment? Some 1,275 employees at the outdoor clothing supplier Patagonia Inc. do. Says one MBA who turned down a job with a global giant to start as a stock handler at one of the firm's California stores: "I wanted to work for a company that's driven by values." And those values driving Patagonia begin with the founder, Yvon Choutinard. "Most people want to do good things but don't. At Patagonia," he says, "it's an essential part of your life." The firm's stated mission is: "Build the best product, do no unnecessary harm, use business to inspire, and implement solutions to the environmental crisis." And Choutinard understands that it all happens through people.

Stop into its headquarters in Ventura, California, and you will find on-site day care and full medical benefits for all employees—full-time and part-time alike. In return, Choutinard expects the best: hard work and high performance achieved through creativity and collaboration. And he refuses to grow the firm too fast, preferring to keep things manageable so that values and vision are well served.

At a time when polls report that many Americans are losing or feeling less passion for their jobs because of high stress, bad bosses, and unmotivating jobs, Patagonia offers something different. Although employees are well paid and get the latest in bonus packages, the firm doesn't focus on money as the top reward. Its most popular perk is the "green sabbatical"—time off, with pay, to work for environmental causes. Says one of those who succeeded in landing a job where there are 900 resumes for every open position: "It's easy to go to work when you get paid to do what you love to do."[1]

> "It's easy to go to work when you get paid to do what you love to do."

Motivation and Rewards

The motivation theories and job design approaches discussed in the last two chapters all deal, in one way or another, with the rewards people get from their work and how these rewards impact performance. Now it is time to discuss how these multiple ideas and perspectives can be linked together in a context of performance management.

An Integrated Model of Motivation

Figure 7.1 outlines an integrated model of motivation, one that ties together much of the previous discussion regarding the basic relationship of effort, performance, and rewards. In the figure, job performance and satisfaction are separate, but potentially interdependent, work results. Performance is influenced most directly by individual attributes such as ability and experience; organizational support such as resources and technology; and effort, or the willingness of someone to work hard at what they are doing. It is in respect to effort that an individual's level of

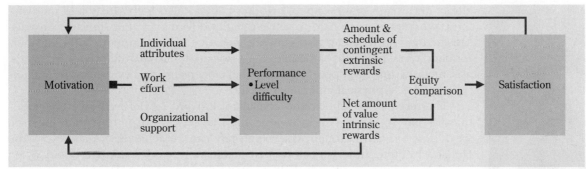

Figure 7.1   An integrated model of individual motivation to work.

motivation is of key importance. Motivation influences work effort, and the key to motivation is the ability to create a work setting that positively supports individual needs and goals.

Whether or not a work setting proves motivational for a given individual depends on the availability of rewards and their perceived value. Note the importance of performance contingency and immediacy in determining how rewards affect future performance. Note also that content theories are useful in the model as guides to understanding individual attributes and identifying the needs that give motivational value to the possible rewards. When the individual experiences valued rewards for work performance, motivation should be directly and positively affected. Motivation should also occur when job satisfactions result from rewards that are perceived to be equitable. When felt negative inequity results, satisfaction will be low, and motivation will be reduced.

Intrinsic and Extrinsic Rewards

The typical reward systems of organizations emphasize a mix of intrinsic and extrinsic rewards. Intrinsic rewards are positively valued work outcomes that the individual receives directly as a result of task performance; they do not require the participation of another person or source. It was intrinsic rewards that were largely at issue in the concept of job enrichment discussed in the last chapter. The expectation is that high "content" jobs, in terms of two-factor theory, or jobs high in "core characteristics" will create many intrinsic rewards. A feeling of achievement after completing a particularly challenging task in a job designed with a good person-job fit is an example.

Extrinsic rewards are positively valued work outcomes that are given to an individual or group by some other person or source in the work setting. They might include things like sincere praise for a job well done or symbolic tokens of accomplishment such as "employee-of-the-month" awards. Importantly too, anything dealing with compensation, or the pay and benefits one receives at work, is an extrinsic reward. And, like all extrinsic rewards, pay and benefits have to be well managed in all aspects of the integrated model for their motivational value to prove positive in terms of performance impact.

Pay for Performance

Pay is not only important as an extrinsic reward; it is an especially complex one. When pay functions well as a reward in the integrated model, it can help an organization

The nonprofit research firm Catalyst reports that the number of women holding top leadership positions in Fortune 500 firms' senior executive offices fell from 16.4 percent in 2005 to 15.6 percent in 2006. The number of female members on boards of directors showed little change from 2005, at 14.6 percent in 2006. The wage gap between hourly female and male workers also is trending down. In the mid 1990s, U.S. Labor Department data showed women earning 75.7 cents an hour per dollar earned by men, up from 65 cents in 1980. But in 2005 that figure had declined to 74.7 cents.

Merit pay is a compensation system that bases an individual's salary or wage increase on a measure of the person's performance accomplishments during a specified time period.

attract and retain highly capable workers. It can also help satisfy and motivate these workers to work hard to achieve high performance. But similarly, any dissatisfaction with pay can also generate negative effects on motivation and performance. Pay problems sometimes are associated with bad attitudes, grievances, absenteeism, turnover, poor organizational citizenship, and even adverse impacts on employees' physical and mental health.

The research of scholar and consultant Edward Lawler generally concludes that for pay to serve as a motivator, high levels of job performance must be viewed as the path through which high pay can be achieved.[2] A survey by the Hudson Institute, however, shows that this is more easily said than done. When asked if employees who do better get paid more, a sample of managers responded with 48 percent agreement; only 31 percent of non-managers indicated agreement. And when asked if their last pay raise had been based on performance, 46 percent of managers and 29 percent of non-managers said yes.[3]

Merit Pay   It is most common to talk about pay for performance in respect to **merit pay**, a compensation system that directly ties an individual's salary or wage increase to measures of performance accomplishments during a specified time period. Although research supports the logic and theoretical benefits of merit pay, it also indicates that the implementation of merit pay plans is not as universal or as easy as might be expected. In fact, surveys over the past 30 or so years have found that as many as 80 percent of respondents felt that they were not rewarded for a job well done.[4]

To work well, a merit pay plan should create a belief among employees that the way to achieve high pay is to perform at high levels. This means that the merit system should be based on realistic and accurate measures of individual work performance. It also means that the merit system is able to clearly discriminate between high and low performers in the amount of pay increases awarded. Finally, it is also important that any "merit" aspects of a pay increase are not confused with across-the-board "cost-of-living" adjustments.

Merit pay plans are just one attempt to enhance the positive value of pay as a work reward. But they are subject to criticisms. For example, merit pay plans may cause problems when they emphasize individual achievements and fail to recognize the high degree of task interdependence that is common in many organizations today. Also, merit pay systems must be consistent with overall organization strategies and environmental challenges if they are to be effective. For example, a firm facing a tight labor market with a limited supply of highly skilled individuals might benefit more from a pay system that emphasizes employee retention rather than strict performance results.[5] With these points in mind, it is appropriate to examine a variety of additional and creative pay practices.[6]

Gain-Sharing Plans   Another way to link pay with performance accomplishments is through **gain sharing**. Such a plan gives workers the opportunity to earn more by receiving shares of any productivity gains that they help to create. The Scanlon Plan is probably the oldest and best-known gain-sharing plan. Others you may hear about are the Lincoln Electric Plan, the Rucker Plan,™ or IMPROSHARE™.

Gain-sharing plans involve a specific measurement of productivity combined with a calculation of a bonus designed to offer workers a mutual share of any increase in total organizational productivity. The presence of the pay-for-performance incentives and a greater sense of personal responsibility for making performance contributions to the organization is expected to increase the motivation to work

Gain sharing is a pay system that links pay and performance by giving workers the opportunity to share in productivity gains through increased earnings.

ETHICS IN OB

PAYING CEOS FOR FAILURES

The models and theories indicate that rewards influence work behavior and job performance. Does the principle hold at the CEO level? One might wonder what is going on in some board of directors meetings when CEOs who perform poorly are given large paychecks, and even bonuses. When Home Depot's board released CEO Robert Nardelli, the payoff was a $210 million severance package—the firm's shares declined 8 percent during his time at the top; the ex-CEO of Pfizer, Hank McKinnell, received $213 million—Pfizer shares declined 40 percent during his tenure. Some experts are voicing complaints, and rightly so, you might suggest. They indicate that CEO compensation contracts are often not well conceived in respect to pay-for-performance linkages: too many CEOs get paid for being present in the job, instead of being paid for how well their firm performs while they are at the helm.[7]

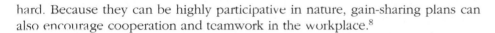

The "golden parachutes" written into the hiring contracts of new CEOs are not likely to go away. But is this practice correct?

hard. Because they can be highly participative in nature, gain-sharing plans can also encourage cooperation and teamwork in the workplace.[8]

Profit-Sharing Plans   **Profit sharing** is somewhat similar to gain sharing, but the two approaches to pay are not identical. Both approaches reward individuals according to some measure of organizational performance. Unlike in a gain-sharing approach, however, profit-sharing plans do not reward employees for specific productivity gains. Profit-sharing plans reward employees based on overall organizational profits: the more profits made, the more money that is available for distribution through profit sharing.[9] One of the criticisms in respect to pay-for-performance linkages is that organizational profits are not always a direct result of employees' efforts, or lack thereof. Poor profits in a time period may, for example, reflect things such as general economic conditions, over which employees have no control.

> ▬ **Profit-sharing plans** reward employees based on the entire organization's performance.

Employee Stock Ownership Plans   Another form of pay for performance is found in **employee stock ownership plans or ESOPs**. Companies may give stock to employees, or allow stock to be purchased by them at a price below market value. The incentive value of the stock awards or purchases is based on the notion that the "employee owners" will be motivated to work hard so that the organization will perform well, and its stock price will rise. As owners of stock, employees benefit from the gains. Of course, as is true with all stock investments, the company's stock prices can fall as well as rise.[10] When the technology bubble burst a few years ago, many people who had taken large parts of their compensation as stock or had invested heavily in their employer's stock through retirement plans were hurt substantially. In other words, there is risk to the potential reward of employee stock ownership, and that risk must be considered in respect to the motivational value of such pay systems.

> ▬ **ESOPs** allow employees to own stock in their employer's business and benefit from future increase in the stock price.

Bonuses   The awarding of cash bonuses, or extra pay for performance that meets certain benchmarks or is above expectations, has been a common practice for many employers. It is especially common in the higher executive ranks. Top managers in some industries earn annual bonuses of 50 percent or more of their base salaries. One of the trends now emerging is the attempt to extend such opportunities to employees at lower levels in organizations, and in both managerial and non-managerial jobs.

Lump-Sum Increases and Payments   While most pay plans distribute pay increases incrementally, typically as an adjustment to the weekly or monthly pay check, for example, an interesting alternative is the **lump-sum increase**. This type of program allows someone to elect the option of receiving all of an annual increase in one or more lump-sum payments. The full increase may be taken at the beginning of the year and then used immediately, or it may be taken at selected times during the year—such as the start of the holiday season. In either case, the expectation is that the raise has more motivational value for the individual because it arrives as a larger amount and can be used with more spectacular or demonstrable effect, such as funding a vacation or buying new furniture for the employee's home.

■■■ **Lump-sum increases** are part of a pay system in which people elect to receive their wage or salary increase in one or more lump-sum payments.

A related, but more controversial, option is the lump-sum payment. The lump-sum payment is an attempt by employers to hold labor costs in line while still giving workers more money if corporate earnings allow. It involves giving workers a one-time lump-sum payment, often based on a gain-sharing formula, instead of a yearly percentage wage or salary increase. In this way, a person's base pay remains fixed, whereas overall monetary compensation varies according to the bonus added to this figure by the annual lump-sum payment. American labor unions are generally resistant to lump sum payments because employees' base pay does not increase, and management determines the size of the bonuses. However, surveys generally show that about two-thirds of respondents have favorable reactions and think that the plans have a positive effect on performance.[11]

Pay for Skills

An alternative to pay for performance is to pay people according to the skills they possess and continue to develop. **Skill-based pay** rewards people for acquiring and developing job-relevant skills. Pay systems of this sort pay people for the mix and depth of skills they possess, not for the particular job assignment they hold. An example is the cross-functional team approach at Monsanto-Benevia, where each team member has developed quality, safety, administrative, maintenance, coaching, and team leadership skills. In most cases, these skills involve the use of high-tech, automated equipment. Workers are paid for this "breadth" of capability as well as for their willingness to use any of the skills needed by the company.

■■■ **Skill-based pay** is a system that rewards people for acquiring and developing job-relevant skills in number and variety relevant to the organization's needs.

Skill-based pay is one of the fastest-growing pay innovations in the United States. Among the better-known firms using this plan is Polaroid.[12] Besides flexibility, some advantages of skill-based pay are employee cross-training—workers learn to do one another's jobs; fewer supervisors—workers can provide more of these functions themselves; and more individual control over compensation—workers know in advance what is required to receive a pay raise. One disadvantage is possible higher pay and training costs that are not offset by greater productivity. Another is the possible difficulty of deciding on appropriate monetary values for each skill.[13]

Pay as Benefits

An employee's total compensation package includes not only direct pay but also any fringe benefits that are paid by the organization. These fringe benefits often add an equivalent of 10 to 40 percent to a person's salary. It is argued that organizations need to allow for individual differences when developing such benefit programs. Otherwise, the motivational value of this indirect form of pay incentive is lost.

One approach is to let individuals choose their total pay package by selecting benefits, up to a certain dollar amount, from a range of options made available by the organization. These **flexible benefit plans** allow workers to select benefits according to needs. A single worker, for example, may prefer quite a different combination of insurance and retirement contributions than would a married person.[14]

■ **Flexible benefit plans** are pay systems that allow workers to select benefits according to their individual needs.

Performance Management

The effort → performance → reward relationship is center stage in the integrated model of motivation. And it underlies the logic of any performance-based pay system. However, it also identifies an important managerial challenge and responsibility: accurately measuring performance and then correctly using those measurements in making pay and other human resource management decisions. If pay is to be based on performance as well as satisfy the demands of the integrated model of motivation in respect to equity considerations in particular, then performance must be measured in ways that are accurate and respected by everyone involved. Simply put, when the performance measurement fails, the motivational value of any pay or reward systems will fail as well.

Performance Measurement Process

The process of managing performance measurement and the various human resource management decisions and actions based on such measurement is called **performance management**. As described in Figure 7.2, performance management involves this sequence of typical steps: (1) identify and set clear and measurable performance goals, (2) take performance measurements to monitor goal progress, (3) provide feedback and coaching on performance results, and (4) use performance assessment for human resource management decisions such as promotions, transfers, terminations, pay raises, training, and career development.

■ **Performance management** is the process of managing performance measurement and the associated human resource management decisions.

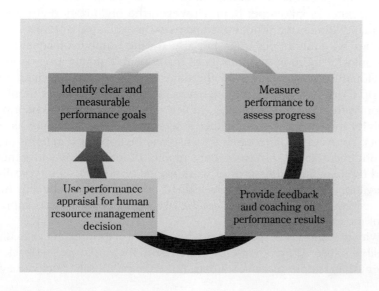

Figure 7.2 Essentials of the performance management process.

Microsoft Sheds Pounds

In five years some 2,152 Microsoft employees at the firm have lost 61,100 pounds in weight. At the age of 44 Strom Armstrong weighed 295 pounds with high blood pressure to boot; within a year he was down to 179 and was eating just 2000 calories a day. Microsoft's benefit program pays 80 percent of the cost of weight reduction programs for employees, including personal trainers, special counseling, support groups, and medical advice. It's a nice benefit that makes financial sense. Estimates are that obesity increases corporate medical claims by 20 percent.

Output measures of performance assess actual work results.

Activity measures of performance assess work efforts or inputs.

Purposes of Performance Measurement

As indicated in the figure, the foundation for any performance management system is performance measurement. On the one hand, measurement serves an evaluation purpose; on the other, it serves a counseling or developmental purpose. Both have uses and implications in a variety of human resource management decisions.

From an evaluative perspective, performance measurement lets people know where they stand relative to objectives and standards. As such, the performance appraisal is an input to decisions that allocate rewards and otherwise administer the organization's human resource management systems. Such decisions might involve factors such as promotions, transfers, and terminations, as well as pay increases.

From a counseling perspective, performance measurement facilitates decisions relating to planning for and gaining commitment to the continued training and personal development of workers. In this case the measurement provides a basis for feedback that lets people know where they stand in terms of the organization's expectations, individual strengths and weaknesses, and possible training alternatives that can be used for developmental purposes.

Performance Measurement Criteria and Standards

The chapter subtitle underscores both the opportunity and the risk in performance management. If "what gets measured happens," organizations had better be measuring the right things in the right ways. This is basic human resource management fundamentals, but worth repeating here. Any and all performance measurements should be based on clear job performance criteria, be accurate in assessing performance, provide a basis for differentiating between high and low performance, and be insightful in terms of feedback that can lead to improved levels of performance in the future.

Output measures of performance assess actual work results. For example, a final-stage assembler may have a goal of 15 completed computer monitors per hour. The number of monitors is easily measurable, and the organization can set standards concerning how many computer monitors should be completed per hour. Here, the performance dimension of interest is a quantitative one: 15 completed computer monitors per hour. However, the organization also may introduce a quality dimension. The individual may be evaluated in terms not only of the number of monitors per hour, but also on the number of units that pass a quality control inspection per hour. Both quantity and quality are important, and the individual cannot trade one for the other. Assembling 20 monitors per hour will not do if only 10 pass inspection; having a larger proportion of monitors pass inspection with only 10 monitors assembled per hour would also be a problem.

Activity measures of performance assess work efforts or inputs, as opposed to outputs. For example, a research scientist may be appraised in terms of her use of scientific methods to solve problems, quality of interactions with other scientists, and the like. Such measures of work inputs or activities are typically based on observation. By contrast, output measures are often obtained directly from production records. Activity measures can be used on their own or as supplements to output measures.

Activity measures are alternatives when output measures are difficult or just not possible to use. They can also be more useful for employee feedback and development than output measures alone. For example, a salesperson may sell 20

Leaders on Leadership

FORD MAKEOVER BEGINS IN THE "WAR ROOM"

When Alan Mulally took over as CEO of Ford Motor Company, the firm was in dire straits—declining share price, huge financial losses, and major downsizing underway. He came in as an industry outsider: his last job was as a senior executive at Boeing. But he also came with confidence: his 87-year-old mother calls him her "fix-it man." And, he came in running. One of Mulally's first moves was to send an e-mail to all Ford employees. In it he was humble, candid, and determined. "I came into this with my eyes wide open," he said, adding: "We have some very big decisions to make about what kind of business we need to become." But he was quick to point out his belief in people and to identify himself with the challenges to come. "People are the reason I'm so excited about being here," he said, while telling his audience that "we need to work together as never before to achieve our objectives."

Positive change at Ford under Mulally's leadership began in what he called the "war room," a place where he and the top executives meet to review performance measurement outcomes. They converse and discuss surrounded by charts, data, and documents pasted to the walls. It's a place where everyone is expected to be honest, reveal the guts of their operations, and share commitments to doing better in the future. When one executive posted poor results, Mulally applauded—much to everyone's surprise. "Data will set you free," he stated. "You can't manage a secret." He was building a new culture.[15]

Mulally was honest and open about Ford's problems. He also had a clear management approach and a plan of action. But is this enough for a leader to be successful when moving from years of experience in one industry to a top job in an entirely new one?

insurance policies a month when the quota is 25. However, activities such as number of sales calls per day or number of community volunteer events attended per week (where some potential clients are likely to be found) can provide more specific information than simply the percentage of monthly quota output measures. Where jobs lend themselves to systematic analysis, important activities can be inferred from the job analysis.

Performance Appraisal

The formal procedure for measuring and documenting a person's work performance is called **performance appraisal**. As might be expected, there are a variety of alternative performance appraisal methods, and they each have strengths and weaknesses that make them more appropriate for use in some situations than others.[16]

■ A **performance appraisal** is a process of systematically evaluating performance and providing feedback on which performance adjustments need to be made.

Performance Appraisal Methods

Comparative methods of performance appraisal seek to identify an employee's relative standing among those being rated; that is, comparative methods can establish that Bill performs better than Mary, who performs better than Leslie, or who performs better than Tom on a certain performance dimension. Comparative methods can indicate that one person is better than another on a given dimension, but not how much better. These methods also fail to indicate whether the person receiving the better rating is "good enough" in an absolute sense. It may well be that Bill is merely the best of a bad lot. Three comparative performance appraisal methods are (1) ranking, (2) paired comparison, and (3) forced distribution.

Absolute methods of performance appraisal specify precise measurement standards. For example, tardiness might be evaluated on a scale ranging from "never tardy" to "always tardy." Three of the more common absolute rating procedures are (1) graphic rating scales, (2) critical incident diaries, and (3) behaviorally anchored rating scales.

Ranking is a comparative technique of performance appraisal that involves the rank ordering of each individual from best to worst on each performance dimension.

Ranking   **Ranking** is the simplest of all the comparative techniques. It consists of merely rank ordering each individual from best to worst on each performance dimension being considered. For example, in evaluating work quality, a manager compares Smith, Jones, and Brown. The manager then ranks Brown number 1, Smith number 2, and Jones number 3. The ranking method, although relatively simple to use, can become burdensome when there are many people to consider.

Paired comparison is a comparative method of performance appraisal whereby each person is directly compared with every other person.

Paired Comparison   In a **paired comparison** method, each person is directly compared with every other person being rated. The frequency of endorsement across all pairs determines each person's final ranking. Every possible paired comparison within a group of ratees is considered, as shown below (italics indicate the person rated better in each pair):

Bill vs. Mary	*Mary* vs. Leslie	*Leslie* vs. Tom
Bill vs. Leslie	*Mary* vs. Tom	
Bill vs. Tom		

Number of times Bill is better   = 3
Number of times Mary is better   = 2
Number of times Leslie is better   = 1
Number of times Tom is better   = 0

The best performer in this example is Bill, followed by Mary, then Leslie, and then, last of all, Tom. When there are many people to compare, the paired comparison approach can be even more tedious than the ranking method.

Forced distribution is a method of performance appraisal that uses a small number of performance categories, such as "very good," "good," "adequate," "poor," and "very poor," and forces a certain proportion of people into each.

Forced Distribution   **Forced distribution** uses a small number of performance categories, such as "very good," "good," "adequate," "poor," and "very poor." Each rater is instructed to rate a specific proportion of employees in each of these categories. For example, 10 percent of employees must be rated as very good, 20 percent must be rated as good, and so on. This method forces the rater to use all of the categories and to avoid rating everyone as outstanding, poor, average, or the like. It can be a problem if most of the people are truly superior performers or if most of the people perform about the same.

MASTERING MANAGEMENT

LEGAL FOUNDATIONS PROTECTING AGAINST JOB DISCRIMINATION

Job discrimination occurs when someone is denied employment, a job assignment, or a career advancement opportunity because of reasons that are not related to job performance. Job discrimination, in this sense, is the enemy of good human resource management, and everyone should be familiar with basic legal protections for workers under American law.

- Equal Pay Act of 1963—requires equal pay for men and women performing equal work in an organization.
- Title VII of the Civil Rights Act of 1964 (as amended)—prohibits discrimination in employment based on race, color, religion, sex, or national origin.
- Age Discrimination in Employment Act of 1967—prohibits discrimination against persons over the age of 40, and restricts mandatory retirement.
- Pregnancy Discrimination Act of 1978—prohibits employment discrimination against pregnant workers.
- Americans with Disabilities Act of 1990—prohibits discrimination against a qualified individual on the basis of disability.
- Family and Medical Leave Act of 1993—allows employees job guarantees for up to 12 weeks of unpaid leave for childbirth, adoption, or family illness.

Graphic Rating Scales   **Graphic rating scales** list a variety of dimensions that are thought to be related to high-performance outcomes for a given job that the individual is accordingly expected to exhibit, including cooperation, initiative, and attendance. The scales allow the manager to assign the individual scores on each dimension. An example is shown in Figure 7.3. These ratings are sometimes given point values and combined into numerical ratings of performance.

The primary appeal of graphic rating scales is their ease of use. They are efficient in the use of time and other resources, and they can be applied to a wide range of jobs. Unfortunately, because of generality, they may not be linked to job analysis or to other specific aspects of a given job. This difficulty can be dealt with by ensuring that only relevant dimensions of work based on sound job analysis procedures are rated. However, there is a trade-off: the more the scales are linked to job analyses, the less general they are when comparing people on different jobs.

Critical Incident Diary   Sometimes **critical incident diaries** are used to record examples of a person's work behavior that led to either unusual success or failure in a given performance aspect. These incidents are typically recorded in a diary-type log that is kept daily or weekly under predetermined dimensions. In a sales job, for example, following up sales calls and communicating necessary customer information might be two of the dimensions recorded in a critical incident diary. Descriptive paragraphs can then be used to summarize each salesperson's performance for each dimension as activities are observed.

The critical incident approach is excellent for employee development and feedback. Since the method consists of qualitative statements rather than quantitative information, however, it is difficult to use for evaluative decisions. As a result, the critical incident technique is sometimes combined with one of the other methods.

▪ **A graphic rating scale** is a scale that lists a variety of dimensions thought to be related to high-performance outcomes in a given job and that the individual is expected to exhibit.

▪ A **critical incident diary** is a method of performance appraisal that records incidents of unusual success or failure for a given performance aspect.

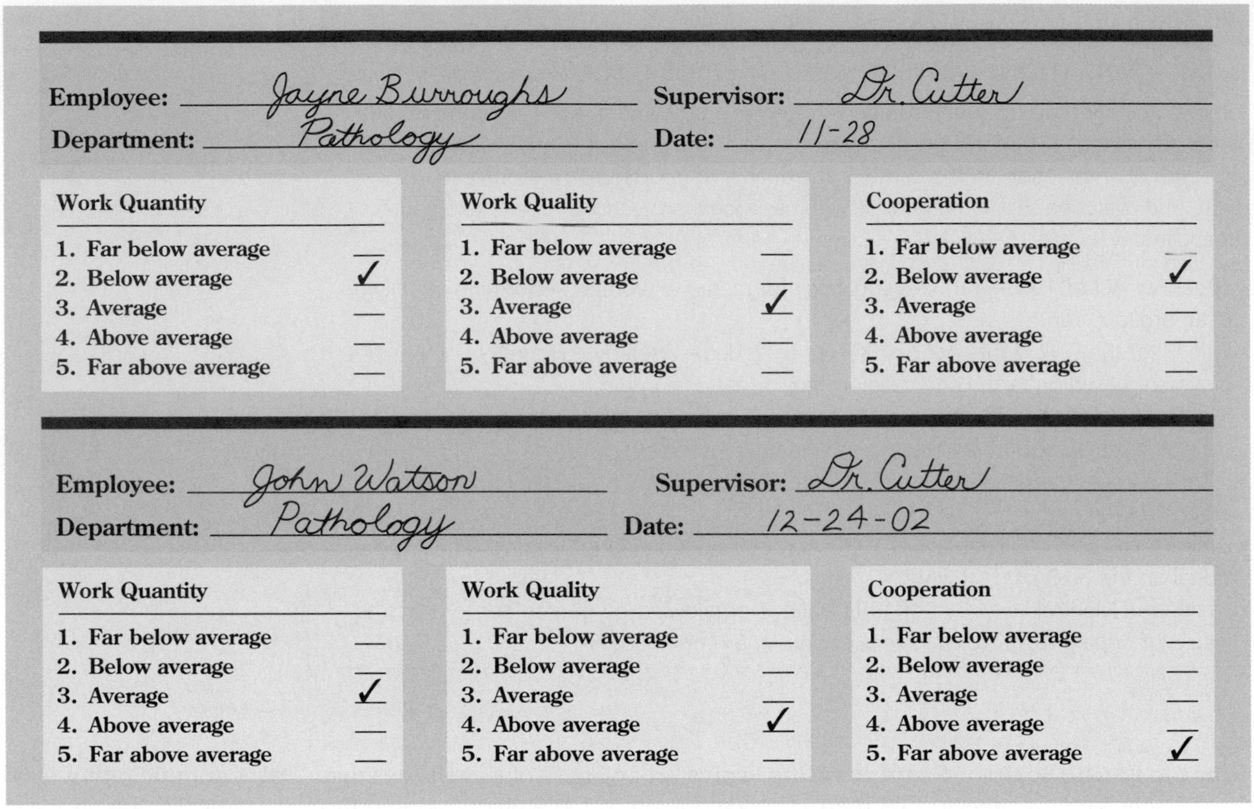

Employee: Jayne Burroughs Supervisor: Dr. Cutter
Department: Pathology Date: 11-28

Work Quantity		Work Quality		Cooperation	
1. Far below average		1. Far below average		1. Far below average	
2. Below average	✓	2. Below average		2. Below average	✓
3. Average		3. Average	✓	3. Average	
4. Above average		4. Above average		4. Above average	
5. Far above average		5. Far above average		5. Far above average	

Employee: John Watson Supervisor: Dr. Cutter
Department: Pathology Date: 12-24-02

Work Quantity		Work Quality		Cooperation	
1. Far below average		1. Far below average		1. Far below average	
2. Below average		2. Below average		2. Below average	
3. Average	✓	3. Average		3. Average	
4. Above average		4. Above average	✓	4. Above average	
5. Far above average		5. Far above average		5. Far above average	✓

Figure 7.3 **Sixth-month performance reviews using graphic rating scale.**

A **behaviorally anchored rating scale (BARS)** is a performance appraisal approach that describes observable job behaviors, each of which is evaluated to determine good versus bad performance.

Behaviorally Anchored Rating Scales The **behaviorally anchored rating scale (BARS)** is a performance appraisal approach that has received increased attention. The procedure for developing this type of scale starts with the careful collection of descriptions of observable job behaviors. These are typically provided by managers and personnel specialists and include descriptions of superior and inferior performance. Once a large sample of behavioral descriptions has been collected, each behavior is evaluated to determine the extent to which it describes good versus bad performance. The final step is to develop a rating scale in which the anchors are specific critical behaviors, each reflecting a different degree of performance effectiveness.

A sample BARS is shown in Figure 7.4 for a retail department manager. Note the specificity of the behaviors and the scale values for each. Similar behaviorally anchored scales would be developed for other dimensions of the job. The BARS approach is detailed and complex. It requires lots of time and effort to develop. But the BARS also provides specific behavioral information that is useful for counseling and feedback, especially when combined with the quantitative scales that are useful for evaluative comparative purposes.

Initial results of the use of BARS suggested that they were less susceptible to common errors than were more traditional scales. More recent evidence suggests that the scales may not be as superior as originally thought, especially if an equivalent amount of developmental effort is put into other types of measures.[17] A

Figure 7.4 Sample dimension from a behaviorally anchored rating scale.

Supervising Sales Personnel

Gives sales personnel a clear idea of their job duties and responsibilities; exercises tact and consideration in working with subordinates; handles work scheduling efficiently and equitably; supplements formal training with his or her own "coaching"; keeps informed of what the salespeople are doing on the job; and follows company policy in agreements with subordinates.

Effective   9   Could be expected to conduct full day's sales clinic with two new sales personnel and thereby develop them into top salespeople in the department.

8   Could be expected to give his or her sales personnel confidence and strong sense of responsibility by delegating many important tasks.

7   Could be expected never to fail to conduct weekly training meetings with his or her people at a scheduled hour and to convey to them exactly what is expected.

6   Could be expected to exhibit courtesy and respect toward his or her sales personnel.

5   Could be expected to remind sales personnel to wait on customers instead of conversing with one another.

4   Could be expected to be rather critical of store standards in front of his or her own people, thereby risking their development of poor attitudes.

3   Could be expected to tell an individual to come in anyway even though he or she called in to say he or she was ill.

2   Could be expected to go back on a promise to an individual who he or she had told could transfer back into previous department if he or she did not like the new one.

Ineffective   1   Could be expected to make promises to an individual about his or her salary being based on department sales even when he or she knew such a practice was against company policy.

somewhat simpler variation of behaviorally anchored scales is the Behavioral Observation Scale (BOS), which uses a five-point frequency scale (ranging from "almost always" to "almost never") for each separate statement of behavior.

Who Does the Performance Appraisal?

Performance appraisals traditionally have been conducted by an individual's immediate supervisor. The presumption is that the supervisor is both responsible for the subordinate's performance and best positioned to evaluate it. In many cases, however, others may be able to better perform at least some aspects of the appraisal.

Self and Peer Evaluations   It is very common now to include a **self-evaluation**, where the individual rates himself or herself, in any performance appraisal process. This is often considered a very useful starting point for a performance review discussion with one's boss, for example. It is also becoming more common to include

■ In a **self-evaluation** the individual rates his or her own performance.

■ In a **peer evaluation** other members of a work team or persons doing similar jobs rate the individual as a co-worker.

peer evaluations, where persons in the work team or those doing similar jobs rate the individual as a co-worker in the process. In workplaces where jobs are highly linked and interdependent, this type of approach helps incorporate a broader perspective on an employee's performance—namely, how well an employee's work fits with and supports that done by others.

360° Evaluation   To obtain as much appraisal information as possible, as many as one-quarter of U.S. organizations are now using not only the evaluations of bosses, peers, and subordinates, but also self-ratings, customer ratings, and ratings by others with whom the ratee deals outside the immediate work unit. Such a comprehensive approach is called a **360° evaluation**.[18] The number of appraisals typically ranges from 5 to 10 per person under evaluation. Firms such as Alcoa and UPS now use 360° evaluations. They are made to order for the new, flatter, team-oriented organizations that emphasize total quality or high-performance management, whereby input from many sources is crucial.

■ **360° evaluation** is a comprehensive approach that uses self-ratings, customer ratings, and ratings by others outside the work unit.

Computer technology now facilitates the collection and analysis of 360° evaluations. A typical example has the subordinate rates himself or herself on the importance of a given job function to the subordinate's performance, and on how well the subordinate thinks he or she is performing the function. The supervisor performs a similar evaluation of the employee. A computer program then highlights those areas on which there is the most disagreement, setting up the basis for further discussions with the supervisor.

OB SAVVY 7.1

Suggestions for a Group Performance Evaluation System

- Link the team's results to organizational goals.
- Start with the team's customers and the team work process needed to satisfy those needs: customer requirements, delivery and quality, waste and cycle time.
- Evaluate team and each individual member's performance.
- Train the team to develop its own measures.

Group Evaluation   As indicated earlier, the growing trend is toward group or team performance evaluations. Such an evaluation process is consistent with self-managed teams and high-performance organizations. Frequently, this emphasis is accompanied by a group-based compensation system such as discussed later in this chapter. Traditional, individually oriented appraisal systems often are no longer appropriate and need to be replaced with a group system such as suggested in OB Savvy 7.1.

Measurement Errors in Performance Appraisal

To be meaningful, an appraisal system must be reliable—provide consistent results each time it is used—and also must be valid—actually measure people on relevant job content. A number of measurement errors can threaten the reliability or validity of performance appraisals.[19]

■ A **halo error** results when one person rates another person on several different dimensions and gives a similar rating for each one.

Halo Errors   A **halo error** results when one person rates another person on several different dimensions and gives a similar rating for each dimension. For example, a sales representative considered to be a "go-getter" and thus rated high on "dynamism" also would be rated high on dependability, tact, and whatever other performance dimensions were used. The rater fails to discriminate between the person's strong and weak points; a "halo" carries over from one dimension to the next. This effect can create a problem when each performance dimension is considered an important and relatively independent aspect of the job. A variation is the single criterion error, in which only one of several important performance aspects is considered at all.

Leniency/Strictness Errors   Just as some professors are known as "easy A's," some managers tend to give relatively high ratings to virtually everyone under their supervision. This is known as a **leniency error**. Sometimes the opposite occurs: some raters tend to give everyone a low rating. This is called a **strictness error**. The problem in both instances is the inadequate discrimination between good and poor performers. Leniency is likely to be a problem when peers assess one another, especially if they are asked to provide feedback to each other, because it is easier to discuss high ratings than low ones.

Central Tendency Errors   **Central tendency errors** occur when managers lump everyone together around the average, or middle, category. This tendency gives the impression that there are no very good or very poor performers on the dimensions being rated. No true performance discrimination is made. Both leniency and central tendency errors are examples of raters who exhibit **low-differentiation errors**. These raters simply restrict themselves to only a small part of the rating scale.

Recency Errors   A different kind of error, known as a **recency error**, occurs when a rater allows recent events to influence a performance rating over earlier events. Take, for example, the case of an employee who is usually on time but shows up one hour late for work the day before his or her performance rating. The employee is rated low on "promptness" because the one incident of tardiness overshadows his or her usual promptness.

Personal Bias Errors   Raters sometimes allow specific biases to enter into performance evaluations. When this happens, **personal bias errors** occur. For example, a rater may intentionally give higher ratings to white employees than to nonwhite employees. In this case, the performance appraisal reflects a racial bias. Bias toward members of other demographic categories—such as that of age, gender, or disability—also can occur, based on stereotypes the rater may have. Such bias appears to have been widespread at Monarch Paper Company, when a former vice president was demoted to a warehouse-maintenance job for not accepting an early retirement offer. A federal jury judged the firm guilty of age bias.[20] This

A **leniency error** is the tendency to give relatively high ratings to virtually everyone.

A **strictness error** occurs when a rater tends to give everyone a low rating.

A **central tendency error** occurs when raters lump everyone's performance ratings around the average, or middle, category.

A **low-differentiation error** occurs when raters restrict themselves to a small part of the rating scale.

A **recency error** is a biased rating that develops by allowing the individual's most recent behavior to speak for his or her overall performance on a particular dimension.

A **personal bias error** occurs when a rater allows specific biases, such as racial, age, or gender, to enter into performance appraisal.

OB SAVVY 7.2
How to Reduce Performance Appraisal Errors

1. Train raters to understand the evaluation process rationale and recognize sources of measurement error.
2. Make sure raters observe ratees on an ongoing, regular basis, and that they do not try to limit evaluations to designated evaluation periods.
3. Do not have one rater rate too many ratees; ability to identify performance differences drops and fatigue sets in when large numbers are involved.
4. Make sure performance dimensions and standards are stated clearly; avoid terms such as "average" because different raters react differently to such terms.

Research Insight
Racial Bias May Exist in Supervisor Ratings of Workers

That is a conclusion of a research study by Joseph M. Stauffer and M. Ronald Buckley reported in a recent *Journal of Applied Psychology*. The authors point out that it is important to have performance criteria and supervisory ratings that are free of bias. They cite a meta-analysis by Kraiger and Ford (1985) that showed White raters tended to rate White employees more favorably than Black employees, while Black raters rated Blacks more favorably than Whites. They also cite a later study by Sackett and DuBois (1991) that disputed the finding that raters tended to favor members of their own racial groups.

In their study, Stauffer and Buckley reanalyzed the Sackett and DuBois data to pursue in more depth the possible interactions between rater and ratee race. The data included samples of military and civilian workers, each of whom was rated by Black and White supervisors. Their findings are that in both samples White supervisors gave significantly higher ratings to White workers than they did to Black workers, while Black supervisors also tended to favor White workers in their ratings.

Stauffer and Buckley advise caution in interpreting these results as meaning that the rating differences are the result of racial prejudice, saying the data aren't sufficient to address this issue. The researchers call for additional studies designed to further examine both the existence of bias in supervisory ratings and the causes of such bias. In terms of workplace implications, however, the authors are quite definitive: "If you are a White ratee then it doesn't matter if your supervisor is Black or White. If you are a Black ratee, then it is important whether your supervisor is Black or White."[20A]

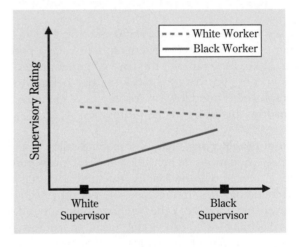

example shows that raters must reflect carefully on their personal biases and guard against their interference with performance-based ratings of subordinates.

Cultural Bias Errors   Managers must be aware of the cultural backgrounds that they bring with them to the task of performance appraisal. They should be careful to avoid criticizing employees for cultural differences, such as time orientation or ideas of appropriate power distance, unless these differences adversely affect performance on a regular basis.

Steps for Improving Performance Appraisals

As is true of most other issues in organizational behavior, managers must recognize certain trade-offs in setting up and implementing any performance appraisal system. In addition to the pros and cons already mentioned for each method, some specific issues to keep in mind in order to reduce errors and improve appraisals are highlighted in OB Savvy 7.2.[21]

The use of appraisals is fundamental to the performance management process. However, experience and research point to difficulties in practice. By way of a final reminder, the appraisal measures and methods must meet legal standards and be based on an analysis of job requirements as reflected in performance standards. Appraisal is appropriate only when performance standards are clearly understood by employees. Clearly defined individual dimensions should be used rather than global measures. Appraisal dimensions should be behaviorally based and supported by observable evidence. If rating scales are used, abstract trait names, such as "loyalty," should be avoided unless they can be defined in terms of observable behaviors. Rating scale anchors should be brief and logically consistent. The system must be validated and psychometrically sound, as must the ratings given by individual evaluators. And, an appeal mechanism should be in place in the event the evaluator and the person whose performance is being rated disagree.

Chapter 7   Study Guide

Summary

What is the link between motivation and rewards?

- The integrated model of motivation brings together insights from content, process, and learning theories around the basic effort → performance → reward linkage.
- Reward systems emphasize a mix of intrinsic rewards—such as a sense of achievement from completing a challenging task—and extrinsic rewards—such as receiving a pay increase.
- Pay for performance systems take a variety of forms, including merit pay, gain-sharing and profit-sharing plans, lump-sum increases, and employee stock ownership.
- Pay for skills is an increasingly common practice; flexible benefits plans are also increasingly common as the role of benefits as part of an employee's total compensation package gains in motivational importance.

What is performance management?

- Performance management is the process of managing performance measurement and the variety of human resource decisions associated with such measurement.
- Performance measurement serves both an evaluative purpose and a counseling purpose, with the latter providing feedback for personal development and future performance improvement.
- Performance measurement can be done using output measures of performance accomplishment and/or activity measures of performance efforts.

What are common performance appraisal alternatives?

- The ranking, paired comparison, and forced-distribution approaches are examples of comparative performance appraisal methods.

- The graphic rating scale, critical incident diary, and behaviorally anchored rating scale are examples of absolute performance appraisal methods.

- It is increasingly common not only for the supervisor to complete a performance appraisal, but also for self-appraisals and peer appraisals to be made.

- The concept of 360° evaluations involves the full circle of contacts a person may have in job performance—from bosses, to peers, to subordinates, to customers, and more—in the appraisal process.

- Measurement errors are common in performance appraisal; they include halo errors, central tendency errors, recency errors, personal bias errors, and cultural bias errors.

- Foundation steps in improving performance appraisals include making sure that they are based on solid job analysis, and that they fully satisfy all legal requirements and expectations.

Key Terms

Activity measures (p. 156)
Behaviorally anchored
    rating scale (BARS)
    (p. 160)
Central tendency error
    (p. 163)
Critical incident diary
    (p. 159)
ESOPs (p. 153)
Flexible benefit plans (p. 155)
Forced distribution (p. 158)
Gain sharing (p. 152)

Graphic rating scale (p. 159)
Halo error (p. 162)
Leniency error (p. 163)
Low-differentiation
    error (p. 163)
Lump-sum increases (p. 154)
Merit pay (p. 152)
Output measures (p. 156)
Paired comparison (p. 158)
Peer evaluation (p. 162)
Performance appraisal
    (p. 157)

Performance management
    (p. 155)
Personal bias error (p. 163)
Profit-sharing plans (p. 153)
Ranking (p. 158)
Recency error (p. 163)
Self-evaluation (p. 161)
Skill-based pay (p. 154)
Strictness error (p. 163)
360° evaluation (p. 162)

Self-Test 7

Multiple Choice

1. In the integrated model of motivation, what predicts effort? _____ (a) rewards (b) organizational support (c) ability (d) motivation

2. In the integrated model of motivation, a reward has motivating value only if _____. (a) it involves money (b) it is perceived as fair and equitable (c) it is intrinsic (d) it is extrinsic

3. Pay is generally considered a/an _____ reward, while a sense of personal growth experienced from working at a task is an example of a/an _____ reward. (a) extrinsic, skill-based (b) skill-based, intrinsic (c) extrinsic, intrinsic (d) absolute, comparative

4. Merit pay _____. (a) rewards people for increased job-related skills (b) is a form of gain sharing (c) is similar to a lump-sum pay increase (d) is pay for performance

5. If someone improves productivity by developing a new work process and receives a portion of the productivity savings as a monetary reward, this is an example of a/an _____ plan. (a) profit-sharing (b) gain-sharing (c) ESOP (d) pay-for-skills

6. In a flexible benefit plan, _____. (a) workers select benefits according to needs (b) there are high benefits early in a career and lower ones later (c) there are low benefits early in a career and higher ones later (d) rewards can be split between salary and non-salary payouts

7. The foundation element in any performance management system is _____.
(a) performance measurement (b) pay for performance (c) ESOP (d) paired comparisons

8. Performance measurement has two broad purposes in human resource management: evaluation and _____. (a) reward allocation (b) counseling (c) discipline (d) benefits calculations

9. Documenting the extent to which a researcher uses scientific methods to solve problems is a form of _____ measure of performance. (a) activity (b) absolute (c) relative (d) output

10. Ranking is a/an _____ approach to performance appraisal. (a) comparative (b) absolute (c) activity (d) merit

11. The critical incident diary is a/an _____ approach to performance appraisal. (a) comparative (b) absolute (c) activity (d) merit

12. If a performance appraisal method fails to accurately measure a person's performance on actual job content, it lacks _____. (a) performance contingency (b) leniency (c) validity (d) strictness

13. A written record that describes in detail various examples of a person's positive and negative work behaviors is most likely part of which performance appraisal method? _____ (a) forced distribution (b) critical incident diary (c) paired comparison (d) graphic rating scale

14. When a team leader evaluates the performance of all team members as "average," the possibility for _____ error in the performance appraisal is quite high. (a) personal bias (b) recency (c) halo (d) central tendency

15. One of the recommendations for improving performance appraisals is to _____. (a) do them only once a year (b) never discuss them directly with the person being rated (c) do not write anything down that is negative (d) make sure there is an appeal process

Short Response

16. Why would an ESOP have motivational value for the employee of a business firm?

17. Explain how a 360° evaluation works as a performance appraisal approach.

18. What are the weaknesses of a standard graphic rating scale for performance appraisal?

19. Explain the difference between halo errors and recency errors in performance appraisal.

Applications Essay

20. Assume you belong to a student organization on campus. Discuss in detail how the reward and performance management concepts in this chapter could be applied with advantage at the local and/or national level of the organization.

These learning activities from the *OB Skills Workbook* are suggested for Chapter 7.

OB in Action

CASE	EXPERIENTIAL EXERCISES	SELF-ASSESSMENTS
■ 7. Perfect Pizzeria	■ 17. Annual Pay Raises	■ 5. Personal Values
	■ 30. Upward Appraisal	■ 8. Are You Cosmopolitan?
	■ 31. 360° Feedback	

Plus—special learning experiences from *The Jossey-Bass/Pfeiffer Classroom Collection*

How Groups Work

Synergy is the goal

Chapter at a Glance

Groups that achieve synergy bring out the best in performance, creativity, and enthusiasm. This chapter will help you to understand the foundations of group behavior in organizations. As you read, *keep in mind these study topics.*

The new workplace places great value on change and adaptation. Organizations are continually under pressure to find new ways of operating in the quest for higher productivity, total quality and service, customer satisfaction, and better quality of working life. Among the many current trends and developments, none are more important than the various attempts to tap more creatively into the full potential of groups as critical organizational resources.

When you use an Apple computer or see an ad for one of its new products, an iPhone for example, it's important to remember the story of the original MacIntosh. A team created it. The brainchild of Apple's co-founder Steve Jobs, the MacIntosh team was composed of high-achieving members who were excited and turned on to a highly challenging task. They worked all hours and at an unrelenting pace. Housed in a separate building flying the Jolly Roger, the MacIntosh team

> "To meet competitive demands . . . the best organizations mobilize groups and teams."

combined youthful enthusiasm with great expertise and commitment to an exciting goal. The result was a benchmark computer produced in record time. Product innovation continues to be a hallmark of Apple Computer Inc. And that is what groups in organizations should be all about.[1]

There is no doubt that an organization's success depends in significant part on the performance of its internal networks of formal and informal groups. Groups are increasingly becoming focal points as organizations seek the advantages of smaller size, flatter structures, cross-functional integration, and more flexible operations. In order to meet competitive demands in challenging environments, the best organizations mobilize groups and teams in many capacities in the quest to reach their full potential as high-performance systems. Groups, in this sense, are an important component of the human resources and intellectual capital of organizations.

Groups in Organizations

There is no doubt that groups can be great resources for organizations, helping to accomplish things that are far beyond the efforts of any individual. But it takes the right membership, lots of commitments, and great leadership to achieve these results consistently. The pathways to such success all begin with a basic understanding of how groups work.

What Is an Effective Group?

■ **Groups** involve two or more people working together regularly to achieve common goals.

A **group** is a collection of two or more people who work with one another regularly to achieve common goals. In a true group, members (1) are mutually dependent on one another to achieve common goals and (2) interact regularly with one another to pursue those goals over a sustained period of time.[2] Groups are

170

important resources that are good for both organizations and their members. They help organizations accomplish important tasks. They also help to maintain a high-quality workforce by satisfying needs of their members. Consultant and management scholar Harold J. Leavitt is a well-known advocate for the power and usefulness of groups.[3] He describes "hot groups," ones such as the original MacIntosh team, that thrive in conditions of crisis and competition and whose creativity and innovativeness generate extraordinary returns.[4]

An **effective group** is one that achieves high levels of task performance, member satisfaction, and team viability. With regard to task performance, an effective group achieves its performance goals in the standard sense of quantity, quality, and timeliness of work results. For a formal workgroup, such as a manufacturing team, this may mean meeting daily production targets. For a temporary group, such as a new policy task force, this may involve meeting a deadline for submitting a new organizational policy to the company president. With regard to member satisfaction, an effective group is one whose members believe that their participation and experiences are positive and meet important personal needs. They are satisfied with their tasks, accomplishments, and interpersonal relationships. With regard to team viability, the members of an effective group are sufficiently satisfied to continue working well together on an ongoing basis and/or to look forward to working together again at some future point in time. Such a group has all-important long-term performance potential.

■■ **Effective groups** achieve high levels of task performance, member satisfaction, and team viability.

Synergy and Group Accomplishments

When groups are effective, they help organizations accomplish important tasks. In particular, they offer the potential for **synergy**—the creation of a whole that is greater than the sum of its parts. When synergy occurs, groups accomplish more than the total of their members' individual capabilities. Group synergy, as suggested in the chapter subtitle, is the goal; it is essential for organizations to become competitive and achieve long-term high performance in today's dynamic times.

■■ **Synergy** is the creation of a whole greater than the sum of its parts.

OB Savvy 8.1 lists several benefits that groups can bring to organizations. In three specific situations, groups often have performance advantages over individuals acting alone.[5] First, when there is no clear "expert" for a particular task or problem, groups seem to make better judgments than does the average individual alone. Second, groups are typically more successful than individuals when problems are complex, requiring a division of labor and the sharing of information. Third, because of their tendencies to make riskier decisions, groups can be more creative and innovative than individuals.

Groups are important settings where people learn from one another and share job skills and knowledge. The learning environment and the pool of experience within a group can be used to solve difficult and unique problems. This is especially helpful to newcomers, who often need help in their jobs. When group members support and help each other in acquiring and improving job competencies, they may even make up for deficiencies in organizational training systems.

OB SAVVY 8.1

WHY GROUPS ARE GOOD FOR ORGANIZATIONS

1. Groups are good for people.
2. Groups can improve creativity.
3. Groups can make better decisions.
4. Groups can increase commitments to action.
5. Groups help control their members.
6. Groups help offset large organization size.

Groups are also important sources of need satisfaction for their members. Opportunities for social interaction within a group can provide individuals with a sense of security through work assistance and technical advice. Group members can also provide emotional support for one another in times of special crisis or pressure. And the many contributions individuals make to groups can help members experience self-esteem and personal involvement.

At the same time that they have enormous performance potential, however, groups can also have problems. One concern is **social loafing**, also known as the Ringlemann effect. It is the tendency of people to work less hard in a group than they would individually.[6] Max Ringlemann, a German psychologist, pinpointed the phenomenon by asking people to pull on a rope as hard as they could, first alone and then in a group.[7] He found that average productivity dropped as more people joined the rope-pulling task. He suggested that people may not work as hard in groups because (1) their individual contributions are less noticeable in the group context, and (2) they prefer to see others carry the workload.

■■ **Social loafing** occurs when people work less hard in groups than they would individually.

You may have encountered this phenomenon in your work and study groups, and been perplexed in terms of how to best handle it. Some of the recommended ways for dealing with social loafing or preventing its occurrence include the following:

How to handle social loafing

- Define roles and tasks to maximize individual interests.
- Raise accountability by making individual performance expectations clear and identifiable.
- Tie individual rewards to their performance contributions to the group.

■■ **Social facilitation** is the tendency for one's behavior to be influenced by the presence of others in a group.

An important aspect of group work is **social facilitation**—the tendency for one's behavior to be influenced by the presence of others in a group or social setting.[8] In general, social facilitation theory indicates that working in the presence of others creates an emotional arousal or excitement that stimulates behavior and therefore affects performance. Arousal tends to work positively when one is proficient with the task. Here, the excitement leads to extra effort at doing something that already comes quite naturally. An example is the play of a world-class athlete in front of an enthusiastic hometown crowd. On the other hand, the effect of social facilitation can be negative when the task is not well learned. You may know this best in the context of public speaking. When asked to speak in front of a class or larger audience, you may well stumble as you try hard to talk in public about an unfamiliar topic.

Formal Groups

■■ **Formal groups** are officially designated for specific organizational purposes.

There are many ways organizations use groups to good advantage. Some exist as **formal groups** that are officially designated to serve specific organizational purposes. An example is the work unit headed by a manager and consisting of one or more direct reports. The organization creates such a group to perform a specific task, which typically involves the use of resources to create a product such as a report, decision, service, or commodity. The head of a formal group is responsible for the group's performance accomplishments, but all members contribute the required work. Also, the head of the group plays a key linchpin role that ties the group horizontally and vertically to the rest of the organization.[9]

Many formal groups are permanent and ongoing. Such permanent work groups appear on organization charts as departments (e.g., market research department), divisions (e.g., consumer products division), or teams (e.g., product-

ETHICS IN OB

MBA CHEATS

Tough headline and scary message, but all true. A study reported by Rutgers University professor Donald McCabe found that 56 percent of MBA students reported cheating by plagiarizing, downloading essays from the Web, and more. He believes the actual figure may be higher, and that some respondents held back confessions for fear of losing their anonymity. Another study, by University of Arkansas professor Tim West and colleagues, surveyed students who had cheated on an accounting test by finding answers online. When asked why, student responses ranged from being unsure that what they did was cheating, to blaming West for giving a test that had answers available on the Web, to rationalizing that "everyone cheats" and "this is how business operates."[10]

Question: Really? Is this the way business operates? Just because "everyone" may be doing something does that make it okay for us to do it as well? Berkshire Hathaway chairman Warren Buffett says: "The five most dangerous words in the English language are 'Everyone else is doing it.'" What do you think?

assembly team). Such groups can vary in size from very small departments or teams of just a few people to large divisions employing a hundred or more people. As permanent work groups, they are each officially created to perform a specific function on an ongoing basis. They continue to exist until a decision is made to change or reconfigure the organization for some reason.

Other formal groups are temporary and short lived. These temporary work groups are created to solve specific problems or perform defined tasks, and then disband once the purpose has been accomplished. Examples are the many temporary committees and task forces that are important components of any organization.[11] Indeed, today's organizations tend to make more use of cross-functional teams or task forces for special problem-solving efforts. The president of a company, for example, might convene a task force to examine the possibility of implementing flexible work hours for nonmanagerial employees. Usually, such temporary groups appoint chairpersons or heads who are held accountable for results, much as is the manager of a work unit. Another common form is the project team that is formed, often across functions, to complete a specific task with a well-defined end point. Examples include installing a new e-mail system and introducing a new product modification.

Information technology has brought a new type of group into the workplace. This is the **virtual group**, a group whose members convene and work together electronically via computers.[12] In this electronic age, virtual groups are increasingly common in organizations. Facilitated by ever-more-functional team-oriented software, or groupware, members of virtual groups can do the same things as members of face-to-face groups. They can share information, make decisions, and complete tasks. The important role of virtual groups or teams in the high-performance workplace is discussed in the next chapter.

■■■ Members of **virtual groups** work together via computer networks.

Informal Groups

Informal groups are unofficial and emerge to serve special interests.

Informal groups emerge without being officially designated by the organization. They form spontaneously through personal relationships or special interests, not by any specific organizational endorsement. Friendship groups, for example, consist of persons with natural affinities for one another. They tend to work together, sit together, take breaks together, and even do things together outside of the workplace. Interest groups consist of persons who share common interests. These may be job-related interests, such as an intense desire to learn more about computers, or non-work interests, such as community service, sports, or religion.

Informal groups often help people get their jobs done. Through their networks of interpersonal relationships, they have the potential to speed up the workflow as people assist each other in ways that formal lines of authority fail to provide. They also help individuals satisfy needs that are thwarted or otherwise left unmet in a formal group. In these and related ways, informal groups can provide their members with social satisfactions, security, and a sense of belonging.

Stages of Group Development

Whether a formal work unit, a temporary task force, or a virtual team, the group itself passes through a series of life cycle stages.[13] Depending on the stage the group has reached, the leader and members can face very different challenges. Figure 8.1 describes five stages of group development: (1) forming, (2) storming, (3) norming, (4) performing, and (5) adjourning.[14]

Forming Stage

In the forming stage of group development, a primary concern is the initial entry of members to a group. During this stage, individuals ask a number of questions as they begin to identify with other group members and with the group itself. Their concerns may include "What can the group offer me?" "What will I be asked to contribute?"

Figure 8.1   Five stages of group development.

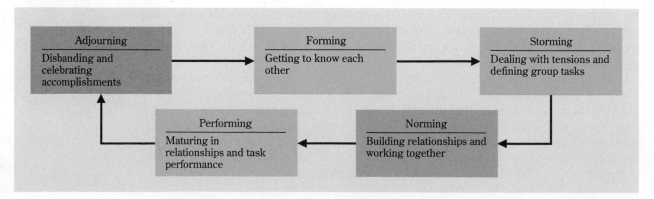

"Can my needs be met at the same time I contribute to the group?" Members are interested in getting to know each other and discovering what is considered acceptable behavior, in determining the real task of the group, and in defining group rules.

Storming Stage

The storming stage of group development is a period of high emotionality and tension among the group members. During this stage, hostility and infighting may occur, and the group typically experiences many changes. Coalitions or cliques may form as individuals compete to impose their preferences on the group and to achieve a desired status position. Outside demands such as premature performance expectations may create uncomfortable pressures. In the process, membership expectations tend to be clarified and attention shifts toward obstacles standing in the way of group goals. Individuals begin to understand one another's interpersonal styles, and efforts are made to find ways to accomplish group goals while also satisfying individual needs.

Norming Stage

The norming stage of group development, sometimes called initial integration, is the point at which the group really begins to come together as a coordinated unit. The turmoil of the storming stage gives way to a precarious balancing of forces. With the pleasures of a new sense of harmony, group members will strive to maintain positive balance. Holding the group together may become more important to some than successfully working on the group's tasks. Minority viewpoints, deviations from group directions, and criticisms may be discouraged as group members experience a preliminary sense of closeness. Some members may mistakenly perceive this stage as one of ultimate maturity. In fact, a premature sense of accomplishment at this point needs to be carefully managed as a stepping stone to the next-higher level of group development.

Performing Stage

The performing stage of group development, sometimes called total integration, marks the emergence of a mature, organized, and well-functioning group. The group is now able to deal with complex tasks and handle internal disagreements in creative ways. The structure is stable, and members are motivated by group goals and are generally satisfied. The primary challenges are continued efforts to improve relationships and performance. Group members should be able to adapt successfully as opportunities and demands change over time. A group that has achieved the level of total integration typically scores high on the criteria of group maturity as shown in Figure 8.2.

Adjourning Stage

A well-integrated group is able to disband, if required, when its work is accomplished. The adjourning stage of group development is especially important for the many temporary groups that are increasingly common in the new workplace, including task forces, committees, project teams, and the like. Members of these groups must be able to convene quickly, do their jobs on a tight schedule, and then adjourn—often to reconvene later if needed. Their willingness to disband when the job is done and to work well together in future responsibilities, group or otherwise, is an important long-term test of group success.

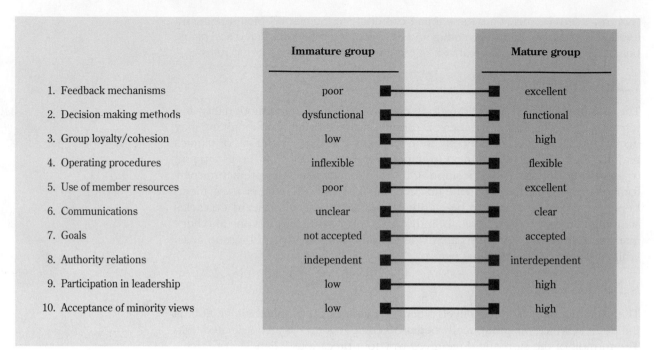

	Immature group	Mature group
1. Feedback mechanisms	poor	excellent
2. Decision making methods	dysfunctional	functional
3. Group loyalty/cohesion	low	high
4. Operating procedures	inflexible	flexible
5. Use of member resources	poor	excellent
6. Communications	unclear	clear
7. Goals	not accepted	accepted
8. Authority relations	independent	interdependent
9. Participation in leadership	low	high
10. Acceptance of minority views	low	high

Figure 8.2   Ten criteria for measuring the maturity of a group.

Foundations of Group Performance

To best understand the foundations of group performance, the open systems model shown in Figure 8.3 is helpful. This figure shows how groups, like organizations, pursue effectiveness by interacting with their environments to transform resource inputs into task outputs.[15]

Group Inputs

The inputs are the initial "givens" in any group situation. They are the foundations for all subsequent action. As a general rule of thumb, one can expect that the stronger the input foundations, the better the chances for long-term group effectiveness. Key

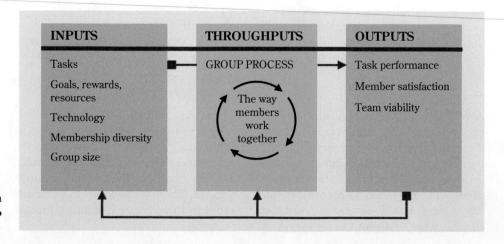

Figure 8.3   The work group as an open system transforming inputs into outputs.

group inputs include the nature of the task, goals, rewards, resources, technology, membership characteristics, diversity, and group size.

Tasks   The tasks they are asked to perform can place different demands on groups, with varying implications for group effectiveness. The technical demands of a group's task include its routineness, difficulty, and information requirements. The social demands of a task involve relationships, ego involvement, controversies over ends and means, and the like. Tasks that are complex in technical demands require unique solutions and more information processing; those that are complex in social demands involve difficulties reaching agreement on goals or methods for accomplishing them. Naturally, group effectiveness is harder to achieve when the task is highly complex.[16] To deal well with complexity, group members must apply and distribute their efforts broadly, and actively cooperate to achieve desired results. When their efforts lead to success at mastering complex tasks, however, group members tend to experience high levels of satisfaction with the group and its accomplishments.

Goals, Rewards, and Resources   Appropriate goals, well-designed reward systems, and adequate resources are all essential to support long-term performance accomplishments. A group's performance, just as an individual's performance, can suffer when goals are unclear, insufficiently challenging, or arbitrarily imposed. It can also suffer if goals and rewards are focused too much on individual-level instead of group-level accomplishments. And it can suffer if adequate budgets, the right facilities, effective work methods and procedures, and the best technologies are not available. By contrast, having the right goals, rewards, and resources can be a strong launching pad for group success.

Technology   Technology provides the means to get work accomplished. It is always necessary to have the right technology available for the task at hand. The nature of the workflow technology can also influence the way group members interact with one another while performing their tasks. It is one thing to be part of a group that crafts products to specific customer requests; it is quite another to be part of a group whose members staff one section of a machine-paced assembly line. The former technology permits greater interaction among group members. It will probably create a closer-knit group with a stronger sense of identity than one formed around one small segment of an assembly line.

Membership Characteristics   To achieve success, a group must have the right skills and competencies available for task performance and problem solving. Although talents alone cannot guarantee desired results, they establish an important baseline of performance potential. It is difficult to overcome the performance limits that result when the input competencies are insufficient to the task at hand.

In homogeneous groups, members are very similar to one another and typically find it quite easy to work together. But the homogeneity may cause performance limitations if their collective skills, experiences, and perspectives are not a good match for complex tasks. In heterogeneous groups, by contrast, members vary in age, gender, race, ethnicity, experience, culture, and the like. This variety brings together a wide pool of talent and viewpoints that is a good resource for problem solving. But heterogeneity may also create difficulties as diverse members struggle to define problems, share information, and handle interpersonal conflicts. These difficulties may be especially pronounced in the short run or early stages of group development. Once members learn how to work together, however, the advantages of membership diversity can be turned into enhanced performance potential.[17]

■■■ The **diversity-consensus dilemma** is the tendency for diversity in groups to create process difficulties even as it offers improved potential for problem solving.

■■■ **FIRO-B theory** examines differences in how people relate to one another based on their needs to express and receive feelings of inclusion, control, and affection.

■■■ **Status congruence** involves consistency between a person's status within and outside a group.

Along these same lines, researchers identify what is called the **diversity-consensus dilemma**. This is the tendency for the existence of diversity among group members to make it harder for them to work together, even though the diversity itself expands the skills and perspectives available for problem solving.[18] The challenge to group effectiveness in a culturally mixed multinational team, for example, is to take advantage of the diversity without suffering process disadvantages.[19]

The blend of personalities among the membership is also important in a group or team. The **FIRO-B theory** (with FIRO standing for "fundamental interpersonal orientation") identifies differences in how people relate to one another in groups based on their needs to express and receive feelings of inclusion, control, and affection.[20] Developed by William Schultz, the theory suggests that groups whose members have compatible needs are likely to be more effective than groups whose members are more incompatible. Symptoms of incompatibilities in a group include withdrawn members, open hostilities, struggles over control, and domination of the group by a few members. Schultz states the management implications of the FIRO-B theory this way: "If at the outset we can choose a group of people who can work together harmoniously, we shall go far toward avoiding situations where a group's efforts are wasted in interpersonal conflicts."[21]

Another source of diversity within group membership is status—a person's relative rank, prestige, or standing in a group. Status within a group can be based on any number of factors, including age, work seniority, occupation, education, performance, or standing in other groups. **Status congruence** occurs when a person's position within the group is equivalent in status to positions the individual holds outside the group. Problems are to be expected when status incongruence is present. In high-power-distance cultures such as Malaysia, for example, the chair of a committee is expected to be the highest-ranking member of the group. When present, such status congruity helps members feel comfortable in proceeding with their work. If the senior member is not appointed to head the committee, members are likely to feel uncomfortable and have difficulty working as a group. Similar problems might occur, for example, when a young college graduate is appointed to chair a project group composed of senior and more-experienced workers.

Group Size   The size of a group, as measured by the number of its members, can have an impact on group effectiveness. As a group becomes larger, more people are available to divide up the work and accomplish needed tasks. This can boost performance and member satisfaction, but only up to a point. As a group continues to grow in size, communication and coordination

problems often set in. Satisfaction may dip, and turnover, absenteeism, and social loafing may increase. Even logistical matters, such as finding time and locations for meetings, become more difficult for larger groups and can hurt performance.[22]

A good size for problem-solving groups is between five and seven members. Chances are that a group with fewer than five may be too small to adequately share responsibilities. With more than seven, individuals may find it harder to participate and offer ideas. Larger groups are also more prone to possible domination by aggressive members and have tendencies to split into coalitions or subgroups.[23] Groups with an odd number of members find it easier to use majority-vote rules to resolve disagreements. When speed is required, this form of conflict management is useful, and odd-numbered groups may be preferred. But when careful deliberations are required and the emphasis is more on consensus, such as in jury duty or very complex problem solving, even-numbered groups may be more effective unless an irreconcilable deadlock occurs.[24]

Group and Intergroup Dynamics

The effectiveness of any group requires more than having the right inputs. To achieve effectiveness, group members must work well together to turn the available inputs into the desired outputs. And when we speak about people "working together" in groups, the basic issues involve **group dynamics**—the forces operating in groups that affect the way members relate to and work with one another. In the open systems model, group dynamics are the processes through which inputs are transformed into outputs.

> **Group dynamics** are the forces operating in groups that affect the ways members work together.

What Goes on within Groups   George Homans described a classic model of group dynamics involving two sets of behaviors: required and emergent. In a workgroup, required behaviors are those formally defined and expected by the organization.[25] For example, they may include such behaviors as punctuality, respect for customers, and assistance to co-workers. Emergent behaviors are those that group members display in addition to what the organization asks of them. They derive not from outside expectations but from personal initiative.

Emergent behaviors in groups often include things that people do beyond formal job requirements and that help get the job done in the best ways possible. Rarely can required behaviors be specified so perfectly that they meet all the demands that arise in a work situation. This makes emergent behaviors essential. An example might be someone taking the time to send an e-mail message to an absent member to keep her informed about what happened during a group meeting. The concept of empowerment, often discussed in this book as essential to the high-performance workplace, relies strongly on unlocking this positive aspect of emergent behaviors.

Homans's model of group dynamics also describes member relationships in terms of activities, interactions, and sentiments, all of which have their required and emergent forms. Activities are the things people do or the actions they take in groups while working on tasks. Interactions are interpersonal communications and contacts. Sentiments are the feelings, attitudes, beliefs, or values held by group members. You might think of it this way in the context of a typical student work group: members of the group have different attitudes as they interact with one another to accomplish various task- and non-task-related activities.

Research Insight
Membership, Interactions, and Evaluation Structure Influence Social Loafing in Groups

"Why do individuals reduce their efforts or withhold inputs when in team contexts?" This question, asked by researchers Kenneth H. Price, David A. Harrison, and Joanne H. Gavin, is a perplexing one. It leads one into the area of social loafing theory, which the authors say has most often been examined in the laboratory. They designed a study of natural teams consisting of students working together in course study groups for a semester. Of specific interest were hypotheses linking the presence of individual evaluation, perceived dispensability, and perceived fairness of group processes with the presence or absence of social loafing.

Price and colleagues studied 144 groups with a total of 515 students in 13 undergraduate and graduate university courses. Participants completed a questionnaire before group work started and again at the end. The final questionnaire included a section asking respondents to rate the extent to which each other group member "loafed by not doing his or her share of the tasks, by leaving work for others to do, by goofing off, and by having other things to do when asked to help out"—in other words, the extent to which each group member engaged in social loafing.

Findings for this sample of students revealed that social loafing was not significantly related to the use of evaluation structures that identified individual contributions, was negatively related

to perceived fairness of group processes, and was positively related to perceived dispensability of one's contributions. In addition, the relationship between social loafing and perceived dispensability strengthened with greater identifiability of individual contributions. Task-relevant ability was negatively associated with perceived dispensability; the presence of relational differences among members was positively associated with perceived dispensability and negatively associated with perceived fairness of group processes.

The researchers suggest that this is the first study to show a link between decision making, organizational justice, and social loafing in groups. They also point out that the link found between relational differences and both perceived dispensability and fairness have implications regarding diversity management within groups.[25A]

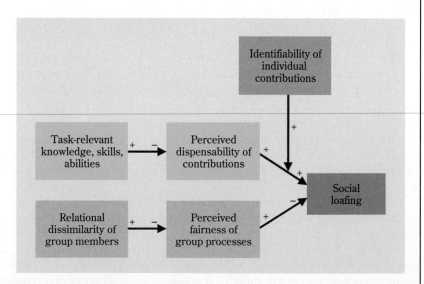

Leaders on Leadership

It's an act; it's a circus; it's a team. And that team is high talent, highly intricate, and high performing. Just ask Guy Laliberté,

founder, majority owner, and CEO of Cirque du Soleil. According to him, Cirque du Soleil isn't just acrobatics in motion; it's a complex organization whose success "depends on its capacity to balance creativity and business." In both respects he is an acknowledged success.

Cirque du Soleil was successful right from the start, but that quickly produced Laliberté's first team leadership challenge. The original members wanted to reinvest and improve the show; he wanted to invest in starting new troupes to perform in more locations. He proposed: "We'll use the profit to start the next troupe, and then reinvest in the show you're working on, and then you can do another new show. Let's build an armada."

And so they did. Cirque now has 13 troupes traveling around the world. Performers share 10 percent of the annual profits. Members of the top management team who commit to 10 or more years with the organization are given a percentage ownership in the company.

The group's Web site proclaims that it all began with a dream: "A group of young entertainers got together to amuse audiences, see the world, and have fun doing it." Dreams, yes; talent, too. Part of Cirque's success, says Laliberté, is the result of his abilities to hire the right people and create a corporate culture that maintains itself through members making sure that everyone lives up to each others' expectations. [26]

Question: Cirque du Soleil is unique, but there is a clear leadership message. What other nontraditional examples can you identify that provide team leadership insights?

What Goes on between Groups   The term **intergroup dynamics** refers to the dynamics that take place between two or more groups. Organizations ideally operate as cooperative systems in which the various components support one another. In the real world, however, competition and intergroup problems often develop within an organization and have mixed consequences.

On the negative side, such as when manufacturing and sales units don't get along, intergroup dynamics may divert energies as members focus more on their animosities toward the other group than on the performance of important tasks.[27] On the positive side, competition among groups can stimulate them to work harder, become more focused on key tasks, develop more internal loyalty and satisfaction, or achieve a higher level of creativity in problem solving. This effect is demonstrated at virtually any intercollegiate athletic event, and it is common in work settings as well. Japanese companies, for example, often use competitive themes to motivate their workforces. At Sony, workers once rallied around the slogan "beat Matsushita whatsoever."[28]

Organizations and their managers go to great lengths to avoid the negative and achieve the positive aspects of intergroup dynamics. Groups engaged in destructive

■ **Intergroup dynamics** are relationships between groups cooperating and competing with one another.

competition, for example, can be refocused on a common enemy or a common goal. Direct negotiations can be held among the groups, and members can be trained to work more cooperatively. It is important to avoid win-lose reward systems in which one group must lose something in order for the other to gain. Rewards can be refocused on contributions to the total organization and on how much groups help one another. In addition, cooperation tends to increase as interaction between groups increases.

Group Communication Networks

Figure 8.4 depicts three interaction patterns and communication networks that are common within organizations.[29] Having the right interaction pattern and communication network can make a big difference in the way groups function and in the performance results they achieve. Members of interacting groups work closely together on tasks in which close coordination of activities takes place. Information flows to everyone. This creates a **decentralized communication network** in which all group members communicate directly and share information with one another. Sometimes these structures are also referred to as all-channel or star communication networks.[30] They work best for groups trying to accomplish complex and nonroutine tasks. They also tend to create high levels of member satisfaction.

Members of co-acting groups work on tasks independently, linked together through some form of central coordination. Groups operating in this fashion divide up the work, and individuals working alone then complete most of it. Each individual's activities are coordinated, and the results are pooled by one person who acts as a central control point. Information flows among the members through the person in charge, who collects and redistributes information and task contributions. This creates a **centralized communication network**, with the

In **decentralized communication networks** members communicate directly with one another.

Centralized communication networks link group members through a central control point.

PATTERN	DIAGRAM	CHARACTERISTICS
Interacting Group Decentralized communication network		High interdependency around a common task Best at complex tasks
Co-acting Group Centralized communication network		Independent individual efforts on behalf of common task Best at simple tasks
Counteracting Group Restricted communication network		Subgroups in disagreement with one another Slow task accomplishment

Figure 8.4   Interaction patterns and communication networks in groups.

central person serving as the "hub." Sometimes these are called wheel or chain communication networks. They work best in groups when tasks are routine and/or easily subdivided. In co-acting groups it is usually the central or hub person who experiences the most satisfaction since he or she is most involved in and informed about all aspects of the group's work.

Counteracting groups exist when subgroups disagree on some aspect of workplace operations. The subgroups may experience issue-specific disagreements, such as a temporary debate over the best means to achieve a goal, or the disagreements may be of longer-term duration, such as labor–management disputes. In either case the resulting interaction pattern involves a **restricted communication network** in which polarized subgroups contest each others' positions and sometimes maintain antagonistic relations with one another. As would be expected, limited and biased communication between the counteracting groups often creates problems.

Restricted communication networks link subgroups that disagree with one another's positions.

Decision Making in Groups

One of the most important activities in any group is decision making, the process of choosing among alternative courses of action. Obviously, the quality and timeliness of decisions made and the processes through which they are arrived at can have an important impact on group effectiveness.

How Groups Make Decisions

Edgar Schein, a noted scholar and consultant, has worked extensively with groups to analyze and improve their decision-making processes.[31] He observes that groups may make decisions through any of the following six methods: lack of response, authority rule, minority rule, majority rule, consensus, or unanimity.

In decision by lack of response, one idea after another is suggested without any discussion taking place. When the group finally accepts an idea, all others have been bypassed and discarded by simple lack of response rather than by critical evaluation.

In decision by authority rule, the chairperson, manager, or leader makes a decision for the group. This can be done with or without discussion and is very time efficient. Whether the decision is a good one or a bad one depends on whether the authority figure has the necessary information and on how well other group members accept this approach.

In decision by minority rule, two or three people are able to dominate, or "railroad," the group into making a decision with which they agree. This is often done by providing a suggestion and then forcing quick agreement by challenging the group with such statements as: "Does anyone object? . . . No? Well, let's go ahead then."

One of the most common ways that groups make decisions, especially when early signs of disagreement set in, is decision by majority rule. Formal voting may take place, or members may be polled to find the majority viewpoint. This method parallels the democratic political system and is often used without awareness of its potential problems. The very process of voting can create coalitions. That is, some people will be "winners" and others will be "losers" when the final vote is tallied. Those in the minority—the "losers"—may feel left out or discarded without having had a fair say. As a result, they may be less enthusiastic about implementing the decision of the "winners." Lingering resentments may impair group effectiveness in the future.

Another decision alternative is *consensus*. Formally defined, **consensus** is a state of affairs whereby discussion leads to one alternative being favored by most members and the other members agreeing to support it. When a consensus is

Consensus is a group decision that has the expressed support of most members.

GUIDELINES FOR CONSENSUS DECISIONS

It's easy to say that consensus is good; it's a lot harder to strive for consensus as part of a group; it can be even harder to try to manage a group so that consensus is possible when tough decisions are needed. Here are some tips for personal behavior; these ideas will be of equal value to you as a leader with team members whom you hope to move toward consensus decisions.

1. Don't argue blindly; consider others' reactions to your points.
2. Be open and flexible, but don't change your mind just to reach quick agreement.
3. Avoid voting, coin tossing, and bargaining to avoid or reduce conflict.
4. Act in ways that encourage everyone's involvement in the decision process.
5. Allow disagreements to surface so that information and opinions can be deliberated.
6. Don't focus on winning versus losing; seek alternatives acceptable to all.
7. Discuss assumptions, listen carefully, and encourage participation by everyone.

Teamwork makes great zoo

The San Diego Zoo is known for showing its animals in natural settings with appropriate bioclimatic zones. Each zone is managed by its own team, typically consisting of 7 to 10 employees. Although team members are experts, their jobs blend and merge, making it difficult sometimes to tell who does what. Gone is the "it's-not-my-job" syndrome. If something needs to be done, it is the job of the entire team.

reached, even those who may have opposed the chosen course of action know that they have been listened to and have had a fair chance to influence the outcome. Consensus does not require unanimity. What it does require is the opportunity for any dissenting members to feel that they have been able to speak and that their voices have been heard.[32]

A decision by unanimity may be the ideal state of affairs. Here, all group members agree totally on the course of action to be taken. This is a "logically perfect" group decision method that is extremely difficult to attain in actual practice. One reason that groups sometimes turn to authority decisions, majority voting, or even minority decisions is the difficulty of managing the group process to achieve consensus or unanimity.[33]

Assets and Liabilities of Group Decision Making

The best groups do not limit themselves to just one decision-making method, using it over and over again regardless of circumstances. Instead, they operate in contingency fashion by changing decision methods to best fit the problem and situation at hand. An important leadership skill is helping a group choose the "right" decision method—one providing for a timely and quality decision to which the members are highly committed.

The choice among individual and group decision methods should be an informed one. When making such choices you should be aware of these potential assets and liabilities of group decision making.[34]

Potential advantages of group decision making

1. *Information*—more knowledge and expertise is available to solve the problem.
2. *Alternatives*—a greater number of alternatives are examined, avoiding tunnel vision.
3. *Understanding and acceptance*—the final decision is better understood and accepted by all group members.
4. *Commitment*—there is more commitment among all group members to make the final decision work.

Potential disadvantages of group decision making

1. *Social pressure to conform*—individuals may feel compelled to go along with the apparent wishes of the group.
2. *Minority domination*—the group's decision may be forced, or "railroaded through," by one individual or a small coalition.
3. *Time delays*—with more people involved in the dialogue and discussion, group decisions usually take longer to make than individual decisions.

Groupthink

An important potential problem when groups make decisions was identified by social psychologist Irving Janis and called **groupthink**—the tendency of members in highly cohesive groups to lose their critical evaluative capabilities.[35] Janis believes that because highly cohesive groups demand conformity, their members tend to become unwilling to criticize others' ideas and suggestions. Desires to hold the group together and to avoid unpleasant disagreements lead to an overemphasis on agreement and underemphasis on critical discussion. The result, all too often, can be a poor decision.

> ■ **Groupthink** is the tendency of cohesive group members to lose their critical evaluative capabilities.

Janis suggests that groupthink played a role in the lack of preparedness by U.S. forces at Pearl Harbor before the United States' entry into World War II. It has also been linked to flawed U.S. decision making during the Vietnam War, to events leading up to the space shuttle disasters and, most recently, to failures in American intelligence agencies on the status of weapons of mass destruction in Iraq.

There is no doubt that groupthink is a serious threat to the quality of decision making in groups. Leaders and members alike should be alert to the symptoms of groupthink and be quick to take any necessary action to prevent its occurrence.[36] For example, President Kennedy chose to absent himself from certain strategy discussions by his cabinet during the Cuban Missile Crisis. Reportedly, this facilitated discussion and helped improve decision making as the crisis was successfully resolved. OB Savvy 8.2 identifies steps that can be taken to avoid groupthink.

> **OB SAVVY 8.2**
> ### How to Avoid Groupthink
>
> • Assign the role of critical evaluator to each group member.
> • Have the leader avoid seeming partial to one course of action.
> • Create subgroups that each work on the same problem.
> • Have group members discuss issues with outsiders and report back.
> • Invite outside experts to observe and react to group processes.
> • Assign someone to be a "devil's advocate" at each meeting.
> • Write alternative scenarios for the intentions of competing groups.
> • Hold "second-chance" meetings after consensus is apparently achieved.

How to Improve Group Decisions

In order to take full advantage of the group as a decision-making resource, care should be exercised to manage process losses that are caused by problems with group dynamics.[37] Such process losses often occur when meetings are unstructured in their approach to a task or problem. In these settings the risk of social pressures to conform, domination, time pressures, and even highly emotional debates may detract from the purpose at hand. They are also settings in which special group decision techniques may be used to advantage.[38]

Brainstorming   In **brainstorming**, group members actively generate as many ideas and alternatives as possible, and they do so relatively quickly and without

> ■ **Brainstorming** involves generating ideas through "freewheeling" and without criticism.

inhibitions. You are probably familiar with the rules that typically govern the brain-storming process.

First, all criticism is ruled out. No one is allowed to judge or evaluate any ideas until the idea generation process has been completed. Second, "freewheel-ing" is welcomed. The emphasis is on creativity and imagination; the wilder or more radical the ideas, the better. Third, quantity is wanted. The emphasis is also on the number of ideas; the greater the number, the more likely a superior idea will appear. Fourth, "piggy-backing" is good. Everyone is encouraged to suggest how others' ideas can be turned into new ideas or how two or more ideas can be joined into still another new idea.

Nominal Group Technique   In any group there will be times when the opin-ions of members differ so much that antagonistic arguments will develop during discussions. At other times the group will be so large that open discussion and brainstorming are awkward to manage. In such cases a form of structured group decision making called the **nominal group technique** may be helpful.[39]

> ■ The **nominal group technique** involves struc-tured rules for generating and prioritizing ideas.

A nominal group puts people in small groups of six to seven members and asks everyone to respond individually and in writing to a "nominal question" such as "What should be done to improve the effectiveness of this work team?" Everyone is encouraged to list as many alternatives or ideas as they can. Next, participants are asked to read aloud their responses to the nominal question in round-robin fashion. The recorder writes each response on large newsprint as it is offered. No criticism is allowed. The recorder asks for any questions that may clarify items on the newsprint. This is again done in round-robin fashion, and no evaluation is allowed. The goal is simply to make sure that everyone present fully understands each response. A struc-tured voting procedure is then used to prioritize responses to the nominal question. The nominal group procedure allows ideas to be evaluated without risking the in-hibitions, hostilities, and distortions that may occur in an open meeting.

Delphi Technique   The Rand Corporation developed a third group-decision ap-proach, the **Delphi technique**, for situations when group members are unable to meet face to face. In this procedure, a series of questionnaires are distributed to a panel of decision makers, who submit initial responses to a decision coordinator. The coordi-nator summarizes the solutions and sends the summary back to the panel members, along with a follow-up questionnaire. Panel members again send in their responses, and the process is repeated until a consensus is reached and a clear decision emerges.

> ■ The **Delphi technique** involves generating deci-sion-making alternatives through a series of survey questionnaires.

Computer-Mediated Decision Making   Today's information and computer tech-nologies enable group decision making to take place across great distances with the help of group decision support systems.[40] The growing use of electronic brainstorming is one example of the trend toward virtual meetings. Assisted by special software, par-ticipants use personal computers to enter ideas at will, either through simultaneous in-teraction or over a period of time. The software compiles and disseminates the results.

IBM uses online brainstorming as part of a program called Innovation Jam. It links IBM employees, customers, and consultants in an "open source" approach. Says CEO Samuel J. Palmisano: "A technology company takes its most valued se-crets, opens them up to the world and says, O.K., world, you tell us what to do with them."[41] Both the nominal group and Delphi techniques also lend themselves to computer mediation. Electronic approaches to group decision making can of-fer several advantages, including the benefits of anonymity, greater number of ideas generated, efficiency of recording and storing for later use, and ability to handle large groups with geographically dispersed members.

Chapter 8   Study Guide

What is the nature of groups in organizations?

- A group is a collection of people who interact with one another regularly to attain common goals.
- Groups can help organizations by helping their members improve task performance and experience more satisfaction from their work.
- Organizations can be viewed as interlocking networks of groups whose managers serve as leaders in one group and subordinates in another.
- Synergy occurs when groups are able to accomplish more than their members could by acting individually.
- Formal groups such as work units and task forces are designated by the organization to serve an official purpose; informal groups are unofficial and emerge spontaneously because of special interests.

What are the stages of group development?

- Groups pass through various stages in their life cycles, and each stage poses somewhat distinct management problems.
- In the forming stage, groups have problems managing individual entry; in the storming stage, groups have problems managing expectations and status; in the norming or initial integration stage, groups have problems managing member relations and task efforts; in the performing or total integration stage, groups have problems managing continuous improvement and self-renewal; in the adjourning stage, groups have problems managing task completion and the process of disbanding.

What are the foundations of group performance?

- An effective group achieves high levels of task accomplishment, member satisfaction, and viability to perform successfully over the long term.
- As open systems, groups interact with their environments to obtain resources that are transformed into outputs.
- Group input factors, including goals, rewards, resources, technology, the task, membership characteristics, and group size establish the core foundations for effectiveness.
- Group dynamics are the way members work together to use inputs; they include the interactions, activities, and sentiments of group members, as well as on the required and emergent ways in which members work together.
- Intergroup dynamics are the forces that operate between two or more groups.
- Interacting groups with decentralized networks tend to perform well on complex tasks; co-acting groups with centralized networks may do well at simple tasks.
- Restricted communication networks are common in counteracting groups with subgroup disagreements.

How do groups make decisions?

- Groups can make decisions by lack of response, authority rule, minority rule, majority rule, consensus, and unanimity.

■ The potential assets of group decision making include having more information and generating more understanding and commitment.

■ The potential liabilities of group decision making include increased social pressures to conform and greater time requirements.

■ Groupthink is the tendency of some groups to lose critical evaluative capabilities.

■ Creativity in group decision making can be improved by brainstorming, the nominal group technique, and the Delphi technique, including computer-mediated applications.

Key Terms

Brainstorming (p. 185)
Centralized communication
    networks (p. 182)
Consensus (p. 183)
Decentralized communication
    networks (p. 182)
Delphi technique (p. 186)
Diversity-consensus
    dilemma (p. 178)

Effective groups (p. 171)
FIRO-B theory (p. 178)
Formal groups (p. 172)
Group dynamics (p. 179)
Groups (p. 170)
Groupthink (p. 185)
Informal groups (p. 174)
Intergroup dynamics
    (p. 181)

Nominal group technique
    (p. 186)
Restricted communication
    networks (p. 183)
Social facilitation (p. 172)
Social loafing (p. 172)
Status congruence (p. 178)
Synergy (p. 171)
Virtual groups (p. 173)

Self-Test 8

Multiple Choice

1. The FIRO-B theory deals with _____ in groups. (a) membership compatibilities (b) social loafing (c) dominating members (d) conformity

2. It is during the _____ stage of group development that members begin to come together as a coordinated unit. (a) storming (b) norming (c) performing (d) total integration

3. An effective group is defined as one that achieves high levels of task performance, member satisfaction, and _____. (a) coordination (b) harmony (c) creativity (d) team viability

4. Task characteristics, reward systems, and group size are all _____ that can make a difference in group effectiveness. (a) group processes (b) group dynamics (c) group inputs (d) human resource maintenance factors

5. The best size for a problem-solving group is usually _____ members. (a) no more than 3 or 4 (b) 5 to 7 (c) 8 to 10 (d) around 12 to 13

6. When two groups are in competition with one another, _____ may be expected within each group. (a) more in-group loyalty (b) less reliance on the leader (c) poor task focus (d) more conflict

7. A co-acting group is most likely to use a(n) _____ communication network. (a) interacting (b) decentralized (c) centralized (d) restricted

8. A complex problem is best dealt with by a group using a(n) _____ communication network. (a) all-channel (b) wheel (c) chain (d) linear

9. The tendency of groups to lose their critical evaluative capabilities during decision making is a phenomenon called _____. (a) groupthink (b) the slippage effect (c) decision congruence (d) group consensus

10. When a decision requires a high degree of commitment for its implementation, a(n) _____ decision is generally preferred. (a) authority (b) majority-vote (c) group-consensus (d) railroading

11. The Ringlemann effect describes (a) the tendency of groups to make risky decisions (b) social loafing. (c) social facilitation. (d) the satisfaction of members' social needs

12. Members of a multinational task force in a large international business should probably be aware that _____ might initially slow the progress of the group in meeting its task objectives. (a) synergy (b) groupthink (c) the diversity-consensus dilemma (d) intergroup dynamics

13. When a group member engages in social loafing, one of the recommended strategies for dealing with this situation is to _____. (a) forget about it (b) ask another member to force this person to work harder (c) give the person extra rewards and hope he or she will feel guilty (d) better define member roles to improve individual accountability

14. When a person holds a prestigious position outside of a group—for example, is a vice president—but is considered just another member of an employee involvement group that a lower-level supervisor has been appointed to head, the person might experience _____. (a) role underload (b) role overload (c) status incongruence (d) the diversity-consensus dilemma

15. If a group is susceptible to groupthink, which strategy is a recommended way to avoid its occurrence? _____ (a) Be sure the leader makes his or her opinions clear. (b) Isolate the group from outside influences. (c) Appoint one member to be a "devil's advocate" at each meeting. (d) Don't let subgroups form to work independently on the problem.

Short Response

16. In what ways are groups good for organizations?
17. What types of formal groups are found in organizations today?
18. What is the difference between required and emergent behaviors in group dynamics?
19. How can intergroup competition be bad for organizations?

Applications Essay

20. Alejandro Puron recently encountered a dilemma in working with his diversity task force. One of the team members claimed that a task force must always be unanimous in its recommendations. "Otherwise," she said, "we will not have a true consensus." Alejandro, the current task force leader, disagrees. He believes that unanimity is desirable but not always necessary to achieve consensus. You are a management consultant specializing in using groups in organizations. Alejandro calls you for advice. What would you tell him and why?

These learning activities from *The OB Skills Workbook* are suggested for Chapter 8.

OB in Action

CASE	EXPERIENTIAL EXERCISES	SELF-ASSESSMENT
■ 8. The Forgotten Group Member	■ 18. Serving on the Boundary	■ 9. Group Effectiveness
	■ 19. *Eggs*periential Exercise	■ 17. Decision-Making Biases

Plus—special learning experiences from *The Jossey-Bass/Pfeiffer Classroom Collection*

Chapter 9

Teamwork and Team Performance

Chapter at a Glance

Teams put creativity to work. This chapter introduces highly motivated and successful teams and teamwork as benchmarks of successful organizations today. As you read Chapter 9, *keep in mind these study topics.*

TEAMS AND TEAMWORK

  Types of Teams

  The Nature of Teamwork

  Diversity and Team Performance

TEAM BUILDING

  How Team Building Works

  Approaches to Team Building

IMPROVING TEAM PROCESSES

  Entry of New Members

  Task and Maintenance Leadership

  Roles and Role Dynamics

  Positive Norms

  Team Cohesiveness

TEAMS IN THE HIGH-PERFORMANCE WORKPLACE

  Problem-Solving Teams

  Cross-Functional Teams

  Virtual Teams

  Self-Managing Teams

CHAPTER 9 STUDY GUIDE

Teams are worth the work

The world of collegiate athletics is a good place to study teamwork, both the upsides and the downsides. And when talking about the positive side, the lessons from Sasho Cirovski as head coach of the University of Maryland's men's soccer team are worth a look. He has been through the ups and the downs, and he believes he has learned a lot in the process.

After a series of winning seasons, Cirovski's "Terps" struggled to win. Cirovski attributed it to a lack of team leadership. He had appointed his two best players to be the leaders, but their impact wasn't showing up on the field. He says: "I was recruiting talent, I wasn't doing a good job of recruiting leaders." With that realization he turned to the business world and asked his brother, Vancho, a human resources vice president at Cardinal Health. His brother suggested survey-

> ## "I was recruiting talent, I wasn't doing a good job of recruiting leaders."

ing team members to find out who they most relied on for advice and motivation. The goal was to find the natural team leaders, not just the most visible star players. The focus shifted to finding players who, as leaders, would be supported by the whole team. The survey revealed that one of the players was a huge positive influence—a sophomore whom Cirovski had not thought about; the player was "off the radar," so to speak.

Cirovski moved quickly with the data in hand. He appointed Scotty Buete to be the third team captain, telling him: "Everyone is looking for you to lead." And lead Buete did. Cirovski says: "Scotty was the glue, and I didn't see it." From that point on the Terps were back in contention. And as a side benefit, Cirovski's survey also identified two other younger players with strong leadership potential.[1]

Teams and Teamwork

When we think of the word "team," a variety of popular sporting teams usually comes to mind; just pick your sport. The word team is also popular in organizations, and workgroups can also be considered teams if they meet the demands of this definition. A **team** is a small group of people with complementary skills who work actively together to achieve a common purpose for which they hold themselves collectively accountable.[2]

Management scholar Jay Conger calls the team-based organization the management system of the future, the business world's response to the need for speed in an ever-more-competitive environment.[3] He cites the example of an American jet engine manufacturer that switched to cross-functional teams instead of staying with traditional functional work units. The firm cut the time required to design and produce new engines by 50 percent. Conger says: "Cross-functional teams are speed machines."[4] Clearly, we need to know more about such teams and the processes of teamwork in organizations.

■ **Teams** are groups of people who work actively together to achieve a purpose for which they are all accountable.

Types of Teams

A major challenge in any organization is to turn the formal groups discussed in the last chapter into true high-performance teams. And in work settings, teams must function well in all of the following settings.[5]

First, there are teams that recommend things. Established to study specific problems and recommend solutions to them, these teams typically work with a target completion date and disband once the purpose has been fulfilled. They are temporary groups including task forces, ad hoc committees, project teams, and the like. Members of these teams must be able to learn quickly how to work well together, accomplish the assigned task, and make good action recommendations for follow-up work by other people.

Second, there are teams that run things. Such management teams consist of people with the formal responsibility for leading other groups. These teams may exist at all levels of responsibility, from the individual work unit composed of a team leader and team members to the top-management team composed of a CEO and other senior executives. Teams can add value to work processes at any level and offer special opportunities for dealing with complex problems and uncertain situations. Key issues addressed by top-management teams include, for example, identifying overall organizational purposes, goals, and values; crafting strategies based on goals; and persuading others to support them.[6]

Third, there are teams that make or do things. These are functional groups and work units that perform ongoing tasks, such as marketing or manufacturing. Members of these teams must have effective long-term working relationships with one another, solid operating systems, and the external support needed to achieve effectiveness over a sustained period of time. They also need energy to keep up the pace and meet the day-to-day challenges of sustained high performance.

The Nature of Teamwork

Whatever their major purposes or tasks, all teams need members who believe in team goals and are motivated to work actively with others to accomplish them. Indeed, an essential criterion of a true team is that the members feel "collectively accountable" for what they accomplish.[7] This sense of collective accountability sets the stage for real **teamwork**, with team members actively working together in such a way that all their respective skills are effectively used to achieve a common purpose.[8] A commitment to teamwork is found in the willingness of every member to "listen and respond constructively to views expressed by others, give others the benefit of the doubt, provide support, and recognize the interests and achievements of others."[9] Although such teamwork is essential for any high-performance team, developing and sustaining it are challenging leadership tasks (see OB Savvy 9.1). The fact is that it takes a lot more work to build a well-functioning team than simply assigning members to the same group and then expecting them to do a great job.[10]

Teamwork occurs when group members work together in ways that use their skills effectively to accomplish a purpose.

OB SAVVY 9.1

How to Create a High-Performing Team

- Communicate high-performance standards.
- Set the tone in the first team meeting.
- Create a sense of urgency.
- Make sure members have the right skills.
- Establish clear rules for team behavior.
- As a leader, model expected behaviors.
- Find ways to create early "successes."
- Continually introduce new information.
- Have members spend time together.
- Give positive feedback.

Members of high-performance teams have the right mix of skills, including technical skills, problem-solving and decision-making skills, and interpersonal skills. A high-performance team has strong core values that help guide team members' attitudes and behaviors in directions consistent with the team's purpose. Such values act as an internal control system for a group or team that can substitute for outside direction and supervisory attention.

High-performance teams also are able to turn a general sense of purpose into specific performance objectives. Whereas a shared sense of purpose gives general direction to a team, commitment to targeted performance results makes this purpose truly meaningful. Specific objectives provide a clear focus for solving problems and resolving conflicts. They also set standards for measuring results and obtaining performance feedback. And they help group members understand the need for collective versus purely individual efforts.

Diversity and Team Performance

In order to create and maintain high-performance teams, all the various elements of group effectiveness discussed in Chapter 8 must be addressed and successfully managed. As previously noted, membership diversity is an important group input and it sometimes poses simultaneous problems and opportunities.[11]

When teams are relatively homogeneous—that is, when members are similar in respect to such things as age, gender, race, experience, ethnicity, and culture—there are certain potential benefits for group dynamics. It will probably be easier for members to quickly build social relationships and engage in the interactions needed for teamwork. On the other hand, homogeneous membership may limit the group in terms of ideas, viewpoints, and creativity.

When teams are more heterogeneous—with members diverse in demography, experiences, lifestyles, cultures, and more—they also have potential benefits. Membership diversity offers a rich pool of information, talent, and varied perspectives that can help improve team problem solving and increase creativity. These assets are especially valuable to teams working on complex and very demanding tasks, but they must be tapped for the team to realize the performance benefits.

Research indicates that team diversity can be a source of performance difficulties, especially early in the team's life or in the initial stages of development. Problems may occur as interpersonal stresses and conflicts that emerge from the heterogeneity. Working through these dynamics can slow group development and impede relationship building, information sharing, and problem solving.[12] But once such difficulties are resolved, as suggested in Figure 9.1, heterogeneous teams are well positioned to take full advantage of the performance advantages of membership diversity.[13] Although it may take a bit more time and effort to create teamwork from foundations of diversity, longer-term gains in creativity and performance can make it all worthwhile.

Figure 9.1   Diversity and team performance relationship.

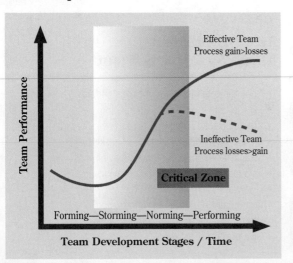

Team Performance

Effective Team
Process gain>losses

Ineffective Team
Process losses>gain

Critical Zone

Forming—Storming—Norming—Performing

Team Development Stages / Time

Team Building

Teamwork doesn't always happen naturally in a group. It is something that team members and leaders must continuously work hard to achieve. In the sports world, for example, coaches and managers focus on teamwork when building new teams at the start of each season; however, even experienced teams can run into problems as a season progresses. Members slack off or become disgruntled; some have performance "slumps"; some are traded to other teams. Even world-champion teams have losing streaks, and the most talented players can lose motivation at times, quibble among themselves, and end up contributing little to team success. When these things happen, the owners, managers, and players are apt to examine their problems, take corrective action to rebuild the team, and restore the teamwork needed to achieve high-performance results.[14]

Workgroups and teams have similar difficulties. When newly formed, they must master challenges as members come together and begin the process of growing and working together as they pass though the various stages of group development. Even when they are mature, most work teams encounter problems of insufficient teamwork at different points in time. This is why a process known as **team building** is so important. This is a sequence of planned activities designed to gather and analyze data on the functioning of a group and to initiate changes designed to improve teamwork and increase group effectiveness.[15]

When done well and at the right times, team building is an effective way to deal with actual teamwork difficulties, or to help prevent them from occurring in the first place.

Team building is a collaborative way to gather and analyze data to improve teamwork.

How Team Building Works

The action steps and process of continuous improvement typical of most team-building approaches are highlighted in Figure 9.2. The process begins when someone notices that a problem with team effectiveness exists or may develop.

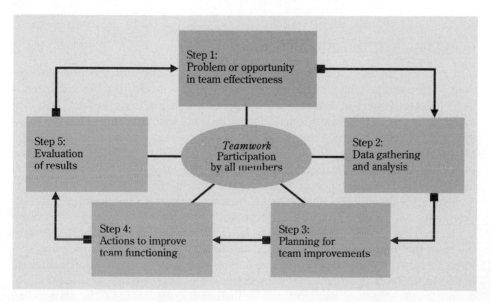

Figure 9.2   The team-building process.

MASTERING MANAGEMENT

WAYS TO HARNESS TEAM DIVERSITY

Jeanne Brett, Kristan Behfar, and Mary C. Kern have studied cross-cultural teams in full recognition that they can "often generate frustrating management dilemmas." At the same time that cultural diversity offers great potential in terms of perspectives, talents, and viewpoints, there is no doubt that obstacles exist, too. Here are four of their recommended strategies for better managing cross-cultural teams:[16]

1. Adaptation—everyone should admit openly to and assume personal responsibility for cultural gaps, and take concrete steps to work around them.

2. Structural intervention—the team can be reshaped and reorganized to reduce cultural frictions, such as creating small working groups that mix cultures.

3. Managerial intervention—setting norms right from the beginning can help ensure that the right processes are used to deal with cultural challenges.

4. Exit—a team member that is disruptive, uncooperative, and/or unwilling to learn/adapt to the culturally diverse setting can be removed from the team.

Members then work together to gather data relating to the problem, analyze these data, plan for improvements, and implement the action plans. The entire team-building process is highly collaborative. Everyone is expected to participate actively as group operations are evaluated and decisions are made on what needs to be done to improve the team's functioning in the future.

Team building is participatory, and it is data based. Whether the data are gathered by questionnaire, interview, nominal group meeting, or other creative methods, the goal is to get good answers to such questions as "How well are we doing in terms of task accomplishment?" "How satisfied are we as individuals with the group and the way it operates?" There are a variety of ways for such questions to be asked and answered in a collaborative and motivating manner.

Approaches to Team Building

In the formal retreat approach, team building takes place during an off-site "retreat." The agenda, which may cover from one to several days, is designed to engage team members in a variety of assessment and planning tasks. These are initiated by a review of team functioning using data gathered through survey, interviews, or other means. Formal retreats are often held with the assistance of a consultant, who is either hired from the outside or made available from in-house staff. Team-building retreats offer opportunities for intense and concentrated efforts to examine group accomplishments and operations.

Not all team building is done at a formal retreat or with the assistance of outside consultants. In a continuous improvement approach, the manager, team leader, or group members themselves take responsibility for regularly engaging in the team-building process. This method can be as simple as periodic meetings that implement the team-building steps; it can also include self-managed formal retreats. In all cases, the team members commit themselves to continuously monitoring group development and accomplishments and making the day-to-day

Nucor's inspiring boss

Dan DiMarco, CEO of Nucor Steel, is riding high with his company's success. But that has not gone to his head. In fact he is humble, preferring to dodge compliments rather than gather them in. He would rather praise Nucor's 11,600 workers, all of whom he calls his "teammates." DiMarco goes so far as to list everyone's names on the covers of the firm's annual reports. And about Nucor's success, he says: "What I get paid for is not looking at yesterday, but looking at the future."

changes needed to ensure team effectiveness. Such continuous improvement of teamwork is essential to the themes of total quality and total service management so important to organizations today.

The outdoor experience approach is an increasingly popular team-building activity that may be done on its own or in combination with other approaches. It places group members in a variety of physically challenging situations that must be mastered through teamwork, not through individual work. By having to work together in the face of difficult obstacles, team members are supposed to experience increased self-confidence, more respect for others' capabilities, and a greater commitment to teamwork. A popular sponsor of team building through outdoor experience is the Outward Bound Leadership School, but many others exist. For a group that has never participated in team building before, an outdoor experience can be an exciting way to begin; for groups familiar with team building, it can be a way of further enriching the experience.

Improving Team Processes

As more and more jobs are turned over to teams, and as more and more traditional supervisors are asked to function as team leaders, special problems relating to team processes may arise. Team leaders and members alike must be prepared to deal positively with such issues as introducing new members, handling disagreements on goals and responsibilities, resolving delays and disputes when making decisions, reducing friction, and dealing with interpersonal conflicts. Given the complex nature of group dynamics, team building in a sense is never done. Something is always happening that creates the need for further leadership efforts to help improve team processes.

Entry of New Members

Special difficulties are likely to occur when members first get together in a new group or work team, or when new members join an existing one. Problems arise as new members try to understand what is expected of them while dealing with the anxiety and discomfort of a new social setting. New members, for example, may worry about

Participation—"Will I be allowed to participate?"

Goals—"Do I share the same goals as others?"

Control—"Will I be able to influence what takes place?"

Relationships—"How close do people get?"

Processes—"Are conflicts likely to be upsetting?"

Edgar Schein points out that people may try to cope with individual entry problems in self-serving ways that may hinder group operations.[17] He identifies three behavior profiles that are common in such situations. The tough battler is frustrated by a lack of identity in the new group and may act aggressively or reject authority. This person wants answers to this question: "Who am I in this group?" The friendly helper is insecure, suffering uncertainties of intimacy and control. This person may show extraordinary support for others, behave in a dependent way, and seek alliances in subgroups or cliques. The friendly helper needs to know whether he or she will be liked. The objective thinker is anxious about how personal needs will be met in the group. This person may act in a passive, reflective, and even single-minded manner while struggling with the fit between individual goals and group directions.

Task and Maintenance Leadership

Research in social psychology suggests that teams have both "task needs" and "maintenance needs," and that both must be met for teams to be successful.[18] Even though anyone who is formally appointed as team leader should help fulfill these needs, all members should also contribute helpful activities. This sharing of responsibilities for contributions that move a group forward, called **distributed leadership**, is an important characteristic of any high-performance team.

Figure 9.3 describes group **task activities** as the various things members do that directly contribute to the performance of important group tasks. They include initiating discussion, sharing information, asking information of others, clarifying something that has been said, and summarizing the status of a deliberation.[19] A team will have difficulty accomplishing its objectives when task activities are not well performed. In an effective team, by contrast, members pitch in to contribute important task leadership as needed.

Maintenance activities support the social and interpersonal relationships among group members. They help a team stay intact and healthy as an ongoing and well-functioning social system. A team member can contribute maintenance leadership by encouraging the participation of others, trying to harmonize differences of opinion, praising the contributions of others, and agreeing to go along with a popular course of action. When maintenance leadership is poor, members become dissatisfied with one another, the value of their group membership diminishes, and emotional conflicts may drain energies otherwise needed for task performance. In an effective group, by contrast, maintenance activities support the relationships needed for team members to work well together over time.

In addition to helping meet a group's task and maintenance needs, however, team members share additional responsibility for avoiding disruptive behaviors that harm the group process. They include being overly aggressive toward other members, withdrawing and refusing to cooperate with others, horsing around when there is work to be done, using the group as a forum for self-confession, talking too much about irrelevant matters, and trying to compete for attention and recognition

■ Distributed leadership is the sharing of responsibility for meeting group task and maintenance needs.

■ Task activities directly contribute to the performance of important tasks.

■ Maintenance activities support the emotional life of the team as an ongoing social system.

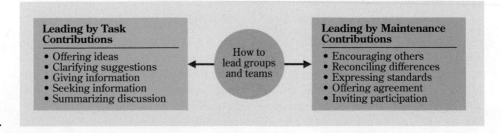

Figure 9.3   Task and maintenance leadership in group team dynamics.

Leading by Task Contributions
- Offering ideas
- Clarifying suggestions
- Giving information
- Seeking information
- Summarizing discussion

How to lead groups and teams

Leading by Maintenance Contributions
- Encouraging others
- Reconciling differences
- Expressing standards
- Offering agreement
- Inviting participation

Roles and Role Dynamics

In groups and teams, new and old members alike need to know what others expect of them and what they can expect from others. A **role** is a set of expectations associated with a job or position on a team. When team members are unclear about their roles or experience conflicting role demands, performance problems can occur. Although this is a common problem, it can be managed through awareness of role dynamics and their causes.

Role ambiguity occurs when a person is uncertain about his or her role. To do any job well, people need to know what is expected of them. In new group or team situations, role ambiguities may create problems as members find that their work efforts are wasted or unappreciated by others. Even in mature groups and teams, the failure of members to share expectations and listen to one another may, at times, create a similar lack of understanding. Being asked to do too much or too little as a team member can also create problems.

Role overload occurs when too much is expected, and the individual feels overwhelmed with work; **role underload** occurs when too little is expected, and the individual feels underused. Members of any group typically benefit from having clear and realistic expectations regarding their expected tasks and responsibilities.

Role conflict occurs when a person is unable to meet the expectations of others. The individual understands what needs to be done but for some reason cannot comply. The resulting tension can reduce satisfaction and affect both an individual's performance and relationships with other group members. There are four common forms of role conflict: (1) Intrasender role conflict occurs when the same person sends conflicting expectations. (2) Intersender role conflict occurs when different people signal conflicting and mutually exclusive expectations. (3) Person-role conflict occurs when one's personal values and needs come into conflict with role expectations. (4) Inter-role conflict occurs when the expectations of two or more roles held by the same individual become incompatible, such as the conflict between work and family demands.

■ A **role** is a set of expectations for a team member or person in a job.

■ **Role ambiguity** occurs when someone is uncertain about what is expected of him or her.

■ **Role overload** occurs when too much work is expected of the individual.

■ **Role underload** occurs when too little work is expected of the individual.

■ **Role conflict** occurs when someone is unable to respond to role expectations that conflict with one another.

Positive Norms

The **norms** of a group or team represent ideas or beliefs about how members are expected to behave. They can be considered as "rules" or "standards" of conduct.[20] Norms help clarify the expectations associated with a person's membership in a group. They allow members to structure their own behavior and to predict what others will do. They help members gain a common sense of direction, and they reinforce a desired group or team culture. When someone violates a group norm, other members typically respond in ways that are aimed at enforcing the norm. These responses may include direct criticisms, reprimands, expulsion, and social ostracism. Managers, task force heads, committee chairs, and team leaders should help their groups adopt positive norms that support organizational goals (see OB Savvy 9.2).

A key norm in any team setting is the performance norm that conveys expectations about how hard group members should work. Other norms are important, too. In order for a task force or a committee to operate effectively, for example, norms regarding

■ **Norms** are rules or standards for the behavior of group members.

OB SAVVY 9.2

Seven Steps to Positive Norms

1. Act as a positive role model.
2. Hold meetings to agree on goals.
3. Select members who can and will perform.
4. Provide support and training for members.
5. Reinforce and reward desired behaviors.
6. Hold meetings for performance feedback.
7. Hold meetings to plan for improvements.

Research Insight
Demographic Faultlines Pose Implications for Managing Teams in Organizations

Membership in organizations is becoming more diverse, and teams are becoming more important. According to researchers Dora Lau and Keith Murnighan, these trends raise some important research issues. They suggest that strong "faultlines" occur in groups when demographic diversity results in the formation of two or more subgroups whose members are similar to and strongly identify with one another within the subgroup. Examples include teams with subgroups forming around age, gender, race, ethnic, occupational, or tenure differences. When strong faultlines are present, members are expected to identify more strongly with their subgroups than with the team as a whole. Lau and Murnighan predict that this will affect what happens with the team in terms of conflict, politics, and performance.

Using subjects from 10 organizational behavior classes at a university, the researchers randomly assigned students to case-work groups based on sex and ethnicity in order to create different conditions of faultline strengths. After working on their cases, group members com-

pleted questionnaires about group processes and outcomes. Results showed, as predicted, that in strong faultline groups, members evaluated those in their subgroups more favorably than did members of weak faultline groups. Members of weak faultline groups also experienced less conflict, more psychological safety, and more satisfaction than did those in strong faultline groups. More communication across faultlines had a positive effect on outcomes for weak faultline groups but not for strong faultline groups. [20A]

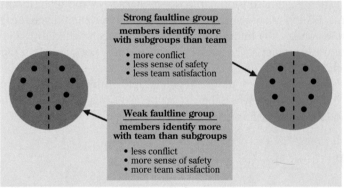

Strong faultline group
members identify more with subgroups than team
- more conflict
- less sense of safety
- less team satisfaction

Weak faultline group
members identify more with team than subgroups
- less conflict
- more sense of safety
- more team satisfaction

attendance at meetings, punctuality, preparedness, criticism, and social behavior are needed. Groups also commonly have norms regarding how to deal with supervisors, colleagues, and customers, as well as norms establishing guidelines for honesty and ethical behaviors.

Norms are often evident in the everyday conversations of people at work. The following examples show the types of norms that operate with positive and negative implications for groups and organizations.[21]

- *Ethics norms*—"We try to make ethical decisions, and we expect others to do the same" (positive); "Don't worry about inflating your expense account; everyone does it here" (negative).

- *Organizational and personal pride norms*—"It's a tradition around here for people to stand up for the company when others criticize it unfairly" (positive); "In our company, they are always trying to take advantage of us" (negative).

ETHICS IN OB

COACH'S DECISIONS SET MODEL FOR FOOTBALL PROGRAM

Don't take those high steps in the end zone if you want to play football at Ohio State. That's the message of head coach Jim Tressel. Doing a great job on the field is one thing, and celebrating accomplishments as a team is fine as well. But step out too high, as Antonio Smith did in a recent game against Penn State, and you will feel the coach's wrath. Says Tressel: "We talk a lot about handing the ball to the official and find the other 10 guys that made it possible and celebrate with them." This is part of Tressel's drive to move a program beset with past behavior problems on and off the field into a different realm. To address problems of players' misbehavior, he called the senior players together and gave them the task of making sure team-mates acted properly at all times. The school's athletic director says that Tressel did the right thing by "putting the accountability in the locker room . . . so players police themselves." This approach is classic Tressel: creating a team that he describes as caring "for one another from top to bottom, side to side and all be pulling the oars in the same direction." [22]

When there's bad behavior by members of a team or organization, who is responsible—the individuals involved, the team members, or the manager? Does Tressel's approach to self-policing on the foot-ball team have carry-over lessons for the world of work?

- *High-achievement norms*—"On our team, people always try to work hard" (positive); "There's no point in trying harder on our team; nobody else does" (negative).
- *Support and helpfulness norms*—"People on this committee are good listen-ers and actively seek out the ideas and opinions of others" (positive); "On this committee it's dog eat-dog and save your own skin" (negative).
- *Improvement and change norms*—"In our department people are always look-ing for better ways of doing things" (positive); "Around here, people hang on to the old ways even after they have outlived their usefulness" (negative).

Team Cohesiveness

The **cohesiveness** of a group or team is the degree to which members are attracted to and motivated to remain part of it.[23] Persons in a highly cohesive group value their membership and strive to maintain positive relationships with other group members. In this sense, cohesive groups and teams are good for their members. In contrast to less-cohesive groups, members of highly cohesive ones tend to be more energetic when working on group activities, less likely to be absent, and more likely to be happy about performance success and sad about failures. Cohesive groups generally have low turnover and satisfy a broad range of individual needs, often providing a source of loyalty, security, and esteem for their members.

Cohesiveness tends to be high when team members are similar in age, atti-tudes, needs, and backgrounds. It also tends to be high in groups of small size, where members respect one another's competencies, agree on common goals,

Cohesiveness is the degree to which members are attracted to a group and motivated to remain a part of it.

and work on interdependent tasks. Cohesiveness tends to increase when groups are physically isolated from others and when they experience performance success or crisis.

Conformity to Norms   Even though cohesive groups are good for their members, they may or may not be good for the organization. This will depend on the match of cohesiveness with performance norms. Figure 9.4 shows the performance implications of a basic rule of conformity in group dynamics: the more cohesive the group, the greater the conformity of members to group norms. When the performance norms are positive in a highly cohesive workgroup or team, the resulting conformity to the norm should have a positive effect on task performance as well as on member satisfaction. This is a best-case situation for everyone.

When the performance norms are negative in a highly cohesive group, however, the same power of conformity creates a worst-case situation for the organization. Although team members are highly motivated to support group norms, the organization suffers from poor performance results. In between these two extremes are mixed-case situations, in which a lack of cohesion fails to rally strong conformity to the norm. With its strength reduced, the outcome of the norm is somewhat unpredictable, and performance will most likely fall on the moderate or low side.

How to Influence Cohesiveness   Team leaders and managers must be aware of the steps they can take to build cohesiveness, such as in a group that has positive norms but suffers from low cohesiveness. They must also be ready to deal with situations when cohesiveness adds to the problems of negative and hard-to-change performance norms. Figure 9.5 shows how group cohesiveness can be increased or decreased by making changes in group goals, membership composition, interactions, size, rewards, competition, location, and duration.

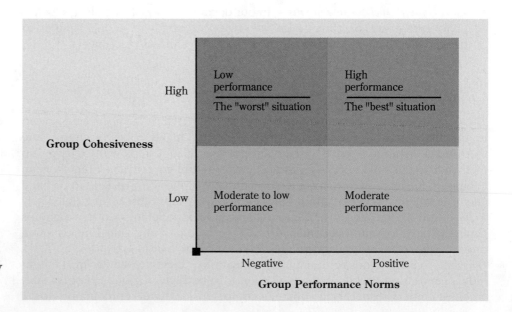

Figure 9.4   How cohesiveness and conformity to norms affect group performance.

Figure 9.5 **Ways to increase and decrease group cohesiveness.**

How to Decrease Cohesion	TARGETS	How to Increase Cohesion
Build agreement	Goals	Get agreement
Increase heterogeneity	Membership	Increase homogeneity
Restrict within team	Interactions	Enhance within team
Make team bigger	Size	Make team smaller
Focus within team	Competition	Focus on other teams
Reward individual results	Rewards	Reward team results
Open up to other teams	Location	Isolate from other teams
Disband the team	Duration	Keep team together

Teams in the High-Performance Workplace

When it was time to reengineer its order-to-delivery process to eliminate a noncompetitive and costly 26-day cycle time, Hewlett-Packard turned to a team. In just nine months, they had slashed the time to eight days, improved service, and cut costs. How did they do it? Team leader Julie Anderson said: "We took things away: no supervisors, no hierarchy, no titles, no job descriptions . . . the idea was to create a sense of personal ownership." Said a team member: "No individual is going to have the best idea, that's not the way it works—the best ideas come from the collective intelligence of the team."[24]

This isn't an isolated example. Organizations everywhere in the new workplace are finding creative ways of using teams to solve problems and make changes to improve performance. The catchwords of these new approaches to teamwork are empowerment, participation, and involvement, and the setting is increasingly described as a reorganization that looks and acts much more lateral or horizontal than vertical.[25]

Problem-Solving Teams

One way organizations can use teams is in creative problem solving. The term **employee involvement team** applies to a wide variety of teams whose members meet regularly to collectively examine important workplace issues. They discuss ways to enhance quality, better satisfy customers, raise productivity, and improve the quality of work life. In this way, employee involvement teams mobilize the full extent of workers' know-how and gain the commitment needed to fully implement solutions. An example is what some organizations call a **quality circle**. This is a small group of persons who meet periodically to discuss and develop solutions for problems relating to quality and productivity.[26]

■ Members of **employee involvement teams** meet regularly to examine work-related problems and opportunities.

■ Members of a **quality circle** meet regularly to find ways for continuous improvement of quality operations.

Cross-Functional Teams

■■■ **Cross-functional teams** bring together persons from different functions to work on a common task.

■■■ The **functional silos problem**, or functional chimneys problem, occurs when people fail to communicate across functions.

In today's organizations, teams are mainstays of efforts to achieve more horizontal integration and better lateral relations. The **cross-functional team**, consisting of members representing different functional departments or work units, plays an important role in this regard. Traditionally, many organizations have suffered from what is often called the **functional silos problem**. Sometimes also called the functional chimneys problem, this occurs when members of functional units stay focused on matters internal to their function and minimize their interactions with members dealing with other functions. In this sense, the functional departments or work units create artificial boundaries, or "silos," that discourage rather than encourage more integrative thinking and active coordination with other parts of the organization.

The new emphasis on team-based organizations, discussed often in this book, is designed to help break down this problem and improve lateral communication. [27] Members of cross-functional teams can solve problems with a positive combination of functional expertise and integrative or total systems thinking. They do so with the great advantages of better information and more speed.[28] Boeing, for example, used this concept to great advantage in designing and bringing to market the 777 passenger jet. A complex network of cross-functional teams brought together design engineers, mechanics, pilots, suppliers, and even customers to manage the "design/build" processes.

Virtual Teams

■■■ A **virtual team** convenes and operates with members linked together via networked computers and information technologies.

It used to be that teamwork was confined in concept and practice to those circumstances in which members could meet face to face. The advent of new technologies and sophisticated computer programs known as groupware has changed all that. **Virtual teams**, introduced in the last chapter as ones whose members meet at least part of the time electronically and with computer support, are a fact of life in many organizations today.[29] The real world of work in businesses and other organizations involves a variety of electronic communications that allow people, often separated by vast geographic distances, to work together through computer mediation, often separated by vast geographical space.[30]

Virtual teams, permanent or temporary, offer a number of potential advantages to their members and organizations. They bring cost effectiveness and speed to teamwork when members are not co-located or cannot easily meet face to face. They also bring the power of the computer to bear on typical team needs for information processing and decision making.[31] But there are potential difficulties and downsides to virtual teamwork as well.

When the computer is the go-between among virtual team members, group dynamics can be different from those of face-to-face settings. Although technology

Leaders on Leadership

PIZZAS GUIDE TEAMS AND TEAMWORK AT AMAZON.COM

Amazon.com's founder and CEO Jeff Bezos is creative in so many ways that analysts struggle to keep up with what he might do next. While some admire his ideas and constant willingness to pursue new high-tech ventures, others wish he would just stick to business—running the Amazon.com online store.

Interested? Check out the latest Bezos move. There's Elastic Compute Cloud, provid-

ing computing power to entrepreneurs and tech whizzes striving to make their marks along with the developers of YouTube, MySpace and others. The service is inexpensive and part of Bezos's goal of feeding innovation by making Amazon's technological capabilities accessible to outsiders. Recognizing that Amazon uses only about 10 percent of its available computing power at any given time, he wants to leverage the power by selling it to others. *Business Week* says that "Amazon is starting to rent out just about everything it uses to run its own business."

And in the Amazon house itself, there's a premium on talent, creativity,

and teamwork. In fact, one of Bezos's guideline for his firm's product development teams is this: no team should ever be larger than two pizzas can feed. That's part of a broader set of management principles he follows to stimulate innovation: measure everything, keep teams small, don't be afraid of weird ideas, open up to outsiders, and watch customers not competitors. About his approach, Bezos says: "We are willing to go down a bunch of dark passageways, and occasionally we find something that really works."

Speaking of passageways, there's Bezos's latest venture, Blue Origin, a vast step outside of the Amazon umbrella. It is his attempt to join the race to bring suborbital space travel into being. The story of this idea has yet to be written.[32]

Why does Jeff Bezos place such emphasis on keeping product development teams no larger than what two pizzas can feed? Is the size of a team really that important to its success?

Virtual teams harness global talent

Virtual teams are "in" at Texas Instruments, where physical distance does not stop people from working together. On any given day you can find talented engineers in Bangalore, India, laboring on complex chip designs with their counterparts in Texas. They go back and forth, taking advantage of the near half-day time differences. Says a TI group vice president: "Problems that used to take three years now take a year."

■ **Self-managing teams**, or self-directed work teams, are small groups empowered to make the decisions needed to manage themselves.

■ **Multiskilling** occurs when team members are trained in skills needed to perform different jobs.

makes communication possible among people separated by great distance, the team members may have very little, if any, direct "personal" contact. Virtual teams may suffer from less social rapport and less direct interaction among members. Whereas computer mediation may have the advantage of focusing interaction and decision making on facts and objective information rather than on emotional considerations, it may also increase risks as group decisions are made in a limited social context.

Just as with any form of teamwork, virtual teams rely on the efforts and contributions of their members as well as on organizational support to achieve effectiveness. And as suggested in the chapter subtitle, teamwork in any form always takes work. The same stages of development, the same input considerations, and the same process requirements are likely to apply with a virtual team as with any team. Where possible, the advantages of face-to-face and virtual teamwork should be combined for maximum benefit. The computer technology should also be appropriate to the task, and team members should be well trained in using it.[33] Also, researchers note that virtual teams may work best when the tasks are more structured, and the work is less interdependent.[34] An example might be a software development team with members from India and the United States who work together virtually across time zones and physical distance while basically building step-by-step upon one another's accomplishments.

Self-Managing Teams

A high-involvement work-group design that is becoming increasingly well established is known as the **self-managing team**. Sometimes called self-directed work teams, these are small groups empowered to make the decisions needed to manage themselves on a day-to-day basis.[35] Although there are different variations of this theme, Figure 9.6 shows that members of a true self-managing work team make decisions about scheduling work, allocating tasks, training for job skills, evaluating performance, selecting new team members, and controlling the quality of work. Members are collectively held accountable for the team's overall performance results.

How Self-Managing Teams Work   Self-managing teams, also called self-directed teams or empowered teams, are permanent and formal elements in the organizational structure.[36] They replace the traditional work group headed by a supervisor. What differentiates self-managing teams from the more traditional work group is that the team members assume duties otherwise performed by a manager or first-line supervisor. The team members, not a supervisor, perform and are collectively accountable for such activities as planning, work scheduling, performance evaluation, and quality control.

A self-managing team should probably include between 5 and 15 members. The teams must be large enough to provide a good mix of skills and resources but small enough to function efficiently. Members must have substantial discretion in determining work pace and in distributing tasks. This is made possible, in part, by **multiskilling**, whereby team members are trained in performing more than one job on the team. In self-managing teams, each person is expected to perform many different jobs—even all of the team's jobs—as needed. The more skills someone masters, the higher the base pay. Team members themselves conduct the job training and certify one another as having mastered the required skills.

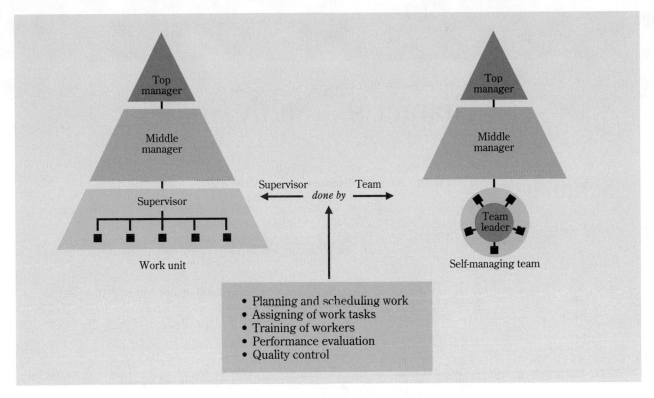

Figure 9.6   Organizational and management implications of self-managing teams.

Operational Implications of Self-Managing Teams   The expected benefits of self-managing teams include productivity and quality improvements, production flexibility and faster response to technological change, reduced absenteeism and turnover, and improved work attitudes and quality of work life. But these results are not guaranteed. Just as with all organizational changes, the shift to self-managing teams can encounter difficulties. Structural changes in job classifications and management levels will have consequent implications for supervisors and others used to more traditional ways. Simply put, with a self-managing team there is no larger a need for the formal first-line supervisor. The possible extent of this change is shown in Figure 9.6, where the first level of supervisory management in the traditional organization has been eliminated and replaced by self-managing teams. Note also that the supervisor's tasks are reallocated to the team.

For persons used to more traditional work, the new team-based work arrangements can be challenging. Managers must learn to deal with teams rather than individual workers; for any supervisors displaced by self-managing teams, the implications are even more personal and threatening. Given this situation, a question must be asked: Should all organizations operate with self-managing teams? The best answer is no. Self-managing teams are probably not right for all organizations, work situations, and people. They have great potential, but they also require a proper setting and support. At a minimum, the essence of any self-managing team—high involvement, participation, and empowerment—must be consistent with the values and culture of the organization.

Chapter 9   Study Guide

Summary

What is the nature of teams and teamwork?

- A team is a small group of people working together to achieve a common purpose for which they hold themselves collectively accountable.

- High-performance teams have core values, clear performance objectives, the right mix of skills, and creativity.

- Teamwork occurs when members of a team work together so that their skills are used effectively to accomplish common goals.

What is team building?

- Team building is a data-based approach to analyzing group performance and taking steps to improve performance in the future.

- Team building is participative and engages all group members in collaborative problem solving and action.

How does team building improve group performance?

- Individual entry problems are common when new teams are formed and when new members join existing teams.

- Task leadership involves initiating and summarizing, and making direct contributions to the group's task agenda; maintenance leadership involves gate keeping and encouraging, as well as helping to support the social fabric of the group over time.

- Role difficulties occur when expectations for group members are unclear, overwhelming, underwhelming, or conflicting.

- Norms, as rules or standards for what is considered appropriate behavior by group members, can have a significant impact on group processes and outcomes.

- Members of highly cohesive groups value their membership and are very loyal to the group; they also tend to conform to group norms.

How do teams contribute to the high-performance workplace?

- An employee involvement team is one whose members meet regularly to address important work-related problems and opportunities.

- Members of a quality circle, a type of employee involvement group, meet regularly to deal with issues of quality improvement in work processes.

- Cross-functional teams bring together members from different functions; members of virtual teams meet and work together via computer interface.

- Self-managing teams are small work groups that operate with empowerment and essentially manage themselves on a day-to-day basis.

- Members of self-managing teams typically plan, complete, and evaluate their own work; train and evaluate one another in job tasks; and share tasks and responsibilities.

- Self-managing teams have structural and management implications for organizations because they largely eliminate first-line supervisors.

Key Terms

Cohesiveness (p. 201)
Cross-functional teams (p. 204)
Distributed leadership (p. 198)
Employee involvement teams (p. 203)
Functional silos problem (p. 204)

Maintenance activities (p. 198)
Multiskilling (p. 206)
Norms (p. 199)
Quality circle (p. 203)
Role (p. 199)
Role ambiguity (p. 199)
Role conflict (p. 199)
Role overload (p. 199)

Role underload (p. 199)
Self-managing teams (p. 206)
Task activities (p. 198)
Team building (p. 195)
Teams (p. 192)
Teamwork (p. 193)
Virtual team (p. 204)

Self-Test 9

Multiple Choice

1. One of the essential criteria of a true team is _____. (a) large size (b) homogeneous membership (c) isolation from outside influences (d) sense of collective accountability

2. The team-building process can best be described as participative, data based, and _____. (a) action oriented (b) leader centered (c) ineffective (d) short-term

3. When a new team member is anxious about questions such as "Will I be able to influence what takes place?" the underlying issue is one of _____. (a) relationships (b) goals (c) processes (d) control

4. A person facing an ethical dilemma involving differences between personal values and the expectations of the team is experiencing _____ conflict. (a) person-role (b) intrasender role (c) intersender role (d) interrole

5. The statement "On our team, people always try to do their best" is an example of a(n) _____ norm. (a) support and helpfulness (b) high-achievement (c) organizational pride (d) organizational improvement

6. Highly cohesive teams tend to _____. (a) be bad for organizations (b) be good for their members (c) have more social loafing among members (d) have greater membership turnover

7. To increase team cohesiveness, one would _____. (a) make the group bigger (b) increase membership diversity (c) isolate the group from others (d) relax performance pressures

8. Self-managing teams _____. (a) reduce the number of different job tasks members need to master (b) largely eliminate the need for a traditional supervisor (c) rely heavily on outside training to maintain job skills (d) add another management layer to overhead costs

9. Which statement about self-managing teams is correct? _____ (a) They can improve performance but not satisfaction. (b) They should have limited decision-making authority. (c) They should operate without any team leaders. (d) They should let members plan their own work schedules.

10. A team member who does a good job at summarizing discussion, offering new ideas, and clarifying points made by others is providing leadership by contributing _____ activities to the group process. (a) required (b) disruptive (c) task (d) maintenance

11. The critical zone that often determines performance success of failure in diverse teams typically occurs in the storming or _____ stage of team development. (a) forming (b) norming (c) performing (d) conforming

12. In the team-building process _____ analyze(s) and develop(s) action plans in response to data on group functioning. (a) all of the members (b) the team leader (c) higher management (d) an outside consultant

13. When someone is being aggressive, makes inappropriate jokes, or talks about irrelevant matters in a group meeting, these are all examples of _____. (a) dysfunctional behaviors (b) maintenance activities (c) task activities (d) role dynamics

14. If you heard from an employee of a local bank that "it's a tradition here for us to stand up and defend the bank when someone criticizes it," you could assume that the bank employees had strong _____ norms. (a) support and helpfulness (b) organizational and personal pride (c) ethical and social responsibility (d) improvement and change

15. What can be predicted when you know that a work group is highly cohesive? _____ (a) high-performance results (b) high member satisfaction (c) positive performance norms (d) status congruity

Short Response

16. Describe the steps in a typical team-building process.

17. How can a team leader help build positive group norms?

18. How do cohesiveness and conformity to norms influence group performance?

19. What are members of self-managing teams typically expected to do?

Applications Essay

20. While surfing the Internet, you encounter this note posted in your favorite discussion group: "Help! I have just been assigned to head a new product design team at my company. The division manager has high expectations for the team and me, but I have been a technical design engineer for four years since graduating from college. I have never 'managed' anyone, let alone led a team. The manager keeps talking about her confidence that I will create a 'high-performance team.' Does anyone out there have any tips to help me master this challenge? Help! [signed] Galahad.' As a good citizen of the Internet, you decide to answer. What message will you send out?

These learning activities from *The OB Skills Workbook* are suggested for Chapter 9.

OB in Action

CASE	EXPERIENTIAL EXERCISES	SELF-ASSESSMENT
■ 9. NASCAR's Racing Teams	■ 20. Scavenger Hunt— Team Building	■ 9. Group Effective- ness
	■ 21. Work Team Dynamics	■ 13. Empowering Others
	■ 22. Identifying Group Norms	
	■ 23. Workgroup Cul- ture	
	■ 24. The Hot Seat	

Plus—special learning experiences from *The Jossey-Bass/Pfeiffer Classroom Collection*

Chapter 10

Power and Politics

Chapter at a Glance

Since individuals join organizations for their own reasons and to meet their own goals, they vie for their own interests in a hierarchical setting. Thus, analyses of power and politics are a key to understanding the behavior of individuals within organizations. As you read Chapter 10, *keep in mind these study topics*.

POWER AND INFLUENCE

Interdependence, Legitimacy, and Power

Obedience

Acceptance of Authority and the Zone of Indifference

SOURCES OF POWER AND INFLUENCE

Position Power

Personal Power

Building Influence

EMPOWERMENT

Keys to Empowerment

Power as an Expanding Pie

Beyond Empowerment to Valuing Employees as a Strategy

ORGANIZATIONAL POLITICS

The Traditions of Organizational Politics

The Politics of Self-Protection

Politics and Governance

CHAPTER 10 STUDY GUIDE

Build capacity to get things done

John Chambers, President and CEO of Cisco Systems ends many of his messages with "good leading and good managing." Cisco, the leading provider of network gear for the Internet, is back from the devastating tech bust at the turn of the century and looking to the future in a different way. Chambers cut fast and deep after the bust, disposing of some $2 billion in antiquated inventory, and immediately refocused the firm on building for the future.

"In today's environment, it's all about getting back to the basics . . ."

Chambers's immediate focus for Cisco is this: "In today's environment, its all about getting back to the basics in terms of focusing on the areas that a company can influence and control: cash generation, available market share gains, productivity increases, profitability, and technology innovation. These factors determine who will survive in this challenging economy." The future, according to Chambers, will not be centered on labor or capital in isolation, but rather will stress interaction. Rich network connections will lead to dramatic increases in productivity in the same way the development of airline networks eventually led to e-tickets. Rather than reducing the importance of employees, Chambers suggests an emphasis on interactions will favor those who can add value and content to networks.[1]

Power and Influence

What does John Chambers's emphasis on interactions have to do with power and politics? Plenty. The basis for both power and politics is the degree of interconnectedness among individuals.[2] As individuals pursue their own goals in a firm, they must also deal with the interests of others. There are never enough resources—money, people, time, or authority—to get all things done for all. Managers may see a power gap.[3] As discussed throughout this chapter, the power gap and its associated political dynamics have at least two sides. On the one hand, power and politics represent the seamy side of organizational life. Organizations are not democracies composed of individuals with equal influence. Some people have a lot more clout than others. There are winners and losers in the battles for resources and rewards. On the other hand, power and politics are important organizational tools that managers must use to get the job done. Many more organizational members can "win" when managers isolate the instances where individual and organizational interests are compatible.

In OB, **power** is defined as the ability to get someone to do something you want done or the ability to make things happen in the way you want them to. The essence of power is control over the behavior of others.[4] Without a direct or indirect connection it is not possible to alter the behavior of others.

While power is the force used to make things happen in an intended way, **influence** is what an individual has when he or she exercises power, and it is

Power is the ability to get someone else to do something you want done, or the ability to make things happen or get things done the way you want.

Influence is a behavioral response to the exercise of power.

214

expressed by others' behavioral response to that exercise of power. Chapters 11 and 12 will examine leadership as a key power mechanism to make things happen. This chapter discusses other aspects that form the context for leadership influence.

Interdependence, Legitimacy, and Power

Consistent with the opening about John Chambers and Cisco, it is important to reiterate that the foundation for power rests on interdependence. The fate of every member of an organization is, in part, determined by the actions of all other members. All members of an organization are, to some degree, interdependent. It is clear, however, that an individual is connected much more with the individuals in his or her work group, those in related groups, and his or her direct bosses. In today's modern organization the pattern of interdependence, and thus the base for power and politics, rests on a system of authority and control.[5] Organizations have societal backing to seek legitimate goals in legitimate ways.

The unstated underpinning of legitimacy in most organizations is an implicit technical and moral order. As noted later in this chapter, from home to school to work to retirement, individuals in U.S. society are taught to obey "higher authority." In U.S. firms, higher authority means those close to the top of the corporate pyramid. In other societies, higher authority does not have a bureaucratic or organizational reference but consists of those with moral authority, including tribal chiefs, religious leaders, and the like. In firms, the legitimacy of those at the top increasingly derives from their positions as representatives for various constituencies. This is a technical or instrumental role. For instance, senior managers may justify their lofty positions by suggesting they represent stockholders. The importance of stockholders is, in turn, a foundation for the capitalism economic system. Some senior executives also evoke ethics and social causes in their roles as authority figures, and many firms recognize that ethics is important as a legitimated foundation for institutional power. Social contribution and ethics provide the moral foundation of legitimacy. Take a look at Leaders on Leadership 10.1 and the information about Edward Zore, president of Northwestern Mutual. Yet, all of this justification and foundation would not be enough to get individuals to comply with orders if we were not prone to obedience.

Obedience

The mythology of American independence and unbridled individualism is so strong that it is important to spend some time explaining how most people are really quite obedient. The seminal studies of Stanley Milgram on obedience provide significant evidence for this assertion.[6]

Milgram designed experiments to determine the extent to which people obey the commands of an authority figure even if they believe they are endangering the life of another person. Subjects from a wide variety of occupations, ranging in age from 20 to 50, were paid a nominal fee for participation in the project. The subjects were falsely told that the purpose of the study was to determine the effects of punishment on learning. The subjects were to be the "teachers." The "learner," a confederate of Milgram's, was strapped to a chair in an adjoining room, an electrode attached to his wrist. The "experimenter," another confederate of Milgram's, was dressed in a laboratory coat. Appearing impassive and somewhat stern, the "experimenter" instructed the "teacher" to read a series of word pairs to the learner and then to reread the first word along with four other terms. The learner was supposed to indicate which of the

Leaders on Leadership

EDWARD J. ZORE, THE SIXTEENTH PRESIDENT OF NORTHWESTERN MUTUAL

In 2006, Northwestern Mutual was named the twenty-fifth recipient of the prestigious Baird award for management excellence. Northwestern Mutual is the largest direct provider of individual life insurance, with assets of more than $137 billion. It is the only company that has been ranked at the top of its industry on the list of most admired companies in America every year since the survey began. Zore does not "maximize stockholder wealth" since the customers actually own the firm. In a mutual, no stock options go to the executives. Instead, dividend proceeds are given back to the customers. It is refreshing in an era of questionable executive actions to hear a leading manager say: "Our mutuality is about fairness. It's about upholding strong principles." The Baird award is given only to executives whose firms demonstrate superior performance on behalf of customers, employees, shareholders, and the communities in which they operate.[6A]

Question: How does the Baird award alter Zore's potential for influence?

four terms was in the original pair by pressing a switch that caused a light to flash on a response panel in front of the "teacher."

The "teacher" was instructed to administer a shock to the "learner" each time a wrong answer was given. This shock was to be increased one level of intensity each time the learner made a mistake. The "teacher" controlled switches that ostensibly administered the electric shocks. In reality, there was no electric current in the apparatus. The "learners" purposely "erred" often and responded to each shock level in progressively distressing ways. If a "teacher" proved unwilling to administer a shock, the experimenter used the following sequential prods to get him or her to perform as requested: (1) "Please continue," (2) "The experiment requires that you continue," (3) "It is absolutely essential that you continue," and (4) "You have no choice; you must go on." Only when the "teacher" refused to go on after the fourth prod would the experiment be stopped.

So what happened? Some 65 percent of the "teachers" actually administered an almost lethal shock to the "learners." Shocked by his results, Milgram tried a wide variety of variations, all with similar if less dramatic results. He concluded that there is the tendency for individuals to comply and be obedient—to switch off and merely do exactly what they are told to do.

Acceptance of Authority and the Zone of Indifference

Obedience is not the only reason for compliance in organizations. A famous management scholar, Chester Barnard, suggested that it also stems from the "consent of the governed."[7]

Acceptance of Authority   In everyday organizational life, Barnard argued, subordinates accepted or followed a managerial directive only if four circumstances were met: First, the subordinate can and must understand the directive. Second, the subordinate must feel mentally and physically capable of carrying out the directive. Third, the subordinate must believe that the directive is not inconsistent with the purpose of the organization. Fourth, the subordinate must believe that the directive is not inconsistent with his or her personal interests. The requirements for understanding and capability are clear. Note the way in which the organizational purpose and personal interest requirements are stated: the subordinate does not need to understand how the proposed action will help the organization; rather, he or she only needs to believe that the requested action is not inconsistent with the purpose of the firm. Barnard found the issue of personal interest to be a bit more complicated. He built his analysis on the notion of a psychological contract between the individual and the firm.

Zone of Indifference   Most people seek a balance between what they put into an organization (contributions) and what they get from an organization in return (inducements). Within the boundaries of the psychological contract, therefore, employees will agree to do many things in and for the organization because they think they should. In exchange for certain inducements, subordinates recognize the authority of the organization and its managers to direct their behavior in certain ways. Based on his acceptance view of authority, Chester Barnard calls this area in which directions are obeyed the "zone of indifference."[8]

A zone of indifference is the range of authoritative requests to which a subordinate is willing to respond without subjecting the directives to critical evaluation or judgment. Directives falling within the zone are obeyed routinely. Requests or orders falling outside the zone of indifference are not considered legitimate under the terms of the psychological contract. Such "extraordinary" directives may or may not be obeyed. This link between the zone of indifference and the psychological contract is shown in Figure 10.1.

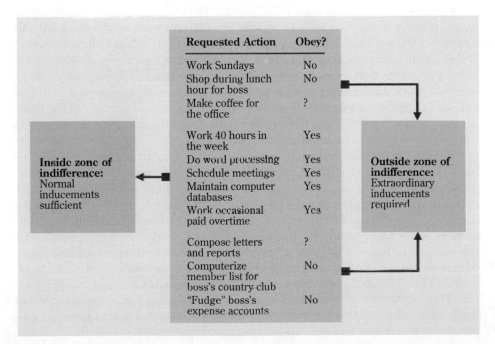

Requested Action	Obey?
Work Sundays	No
Shop during lunch hour for boss	No
Make coffee for the office	?
Work 40 hours in the week	Yes
Do word processing	Yes
Schedule meetings	Yes
Maintain computer databases	Yes
Work occasional paid overtime	Yes
Compose letters and reports	?
Computerize member list for boss's country club	No
"Fudge" boss's expense accounts	No

Inside zone of indifference: Normal inducements sufficient

Outside zone of indifference: Extraordinary inducements required

Figure 10.1   Hypothetical psychological contract for a secretary.

The zone of indifference is not fixed. There may be times when a boss would like a subordinate to do things falling outside the zone. In this case the manager must enlarge the zone to accommodate additional behaviors. We have chosen to highlight a number of ethical issues—issues that are at or may be beyond the typical zone of indifference. Research on ethical managerial behavior shows that supervisors can become sources of pressure for subordinates to do such things as support incorrect viewpoints, sign false documents, overlook the supervisor's wrongdoing, and do business with the supervisor's friends.[9] Most individuals will face such ethical dilemmas during their careers. Firm answers to these issues do not exist since they are cases of individual judgment. Saying no or "refusing to keep quiet" can be difficult and potentially costly. In addition, an individual might do some things for one boss but not for another. In different terms, the boss has two sources of power: position power and personal power.[10]

Sources of Power and Influence

Within each organization a manager's power is in large part determined by his or her position and personal power and by his or her ability to build upon combinations of these sources.

Position Power

One important source of power available to a manager stems solely from his or her position in the organization. Specifically, position power stems from roots associated with the position. There are six important aspects of position power: legitimate, reward, coercive, process, information, and representative power.[11]

Legitimate power or formal authority is the extent to which a manager can use the "right of command" to control other people.

Based on our discussion of obedience and the acceptance theory of authority, it is easy to understand **legitimate power**, or formal hierarchical authority. It stems from the extent to which a manager can use subordinates' internalized values or beliefs that the boss has a "right of command" to control their behavior. For example, the boss may have the formal authority to approve or deny such employee requests as job transfers, equipment purchases, personal time off, or overtime work. Legitimate power represents a special kind of power a manager has because subordinates believe it is legitimate for a person occupying the managerial position as their boss to have the right to command. If this legitimacy is lost, authority will not be accepted by subordinates.

Reward power is the extent to which a manager can use extrinsic and intrinsic rewards to control other people.

Reward power is the extent to which a manager can use extrinsic and intrinsic rewards to control other people. Examples of such rewards include money, promotions, compliments, or enriched jobs. Although all managers have some access to rewards, success in accessing and using rewards to achieve influence varies according to the skills of the manager. Power can also be founded on punishment instead of reward. For example, a manager may threaten to withhold a pay raise or to transfer, demote, or even recommend the firing of a subordinate who does not act as desired. Such **coercive power** is the extent to which a manager can deny desired rewards or administer punishments to control other people. The availability of coercive power also varies from one organization and manager to another. The presence of unions and organizational policies on employee treatment can weaken this power base considerably.

Coercive power is the extent to which a manager can deny desired rewards or administer punishment to control other people.

Process power is the control over methods of production and analysis. The source of this power is the placing of the individual in a position to influence how inputs are transformed into outputs for the firm, a department in the firm, or even a small group. Firms often establish process specialists who work with managers to ensure that production is accomplished efficiently and effectively. Closely related to this power is control of the analytical processes used to make choices. For example, many organizations have individuals with specialties in financial analysis. They may review proposals for investments from other parts of the firm. Their power derives not from the calculation itself, but from their ability to determine the analytical procedures used to judge the proposals.

Process power may be separated from legitimate hierarchical power simply because of the complexity of the firm's operations. A manager may have the formal hierarchical authority to decide but may be required to use the analytical schemes of others and/or to consult on effective implementation with process specialists. The issue of position power can get quite complex very quickly in sophisticated operations. This leads to another related aspect of position power—the role of access to and control of information.

Information power is the access to and/or the control of information. It is one of the most important aspects of legitimacy. The "right to know" and use information can be, and often is, conferred on a position holder. Thus, information power may complement legitimate hierarchical power. Information power may also be granted to specialists and managers who are in the middle of the firms' information systems. For example, the chief information officer of the firm may not only control all the computers, but this person may also have access to almost any information desired. Managers jealously guard the formal "right to know" because it means they are in a position to influence events, not merely react to them. For example, most chief executive officers believe they have the right to know about everything in "their" firm. Deeper in the organization, managers often protect information from others based on the notion that outsiders would not understand it. For instance, engineering drawings are not typically allowed outside an engineering department. In other instances, information is to be protected from outsiders. Marketing plans may be labeled "top secret." In most instances the nominal reason for controlling information is to protect the firm. The real reason is often to allow information holders to increase their power.

Representative power is the formal right conferred by the firm to speak as a representative for a potentially important group composed of individuals across departments or outside the firm. In most complex organizations there are a wide variety of different constituencies that may have an important impact on their firm's operations and/or its success. They include such groups as investors, customers, alliance partners, and unions. Astute executives often hire individuals to act as representatives of and to these constituencies to ensure that their influence is felt but does not dominate. So, for instance, investor relations managers are expected to deal with mundane inquiries from small investors, anticipate questions from financial analysts, and represent the sentiment of investors to senior management. To continue the example, the investor relations manager may be asked to anticipate the questions of investors and guide the type of responses senior management may make. The influence of the investor relations manager is in part based on the assignment to represent the interests of this important group.

Process power is the control over methods of production and analysis.

Information power is the access to and/or the control of information.

Representative power is the formal right conferred by the firm to speak for and to a potentially important group.

Expert power is the ability to control another's behavior because of the possession of knowledge, experience, or judgment that the other person does not have but needs.

Rational persuasion is the ability to control another's behavior because, through the individual's efforts, the person accepts the desirability of an offered goal and a reasonable way of achieving it.

OB SAVVY 10.1

Developing Trust to Build Personal Power

One key to ethically developing power is to build trust. To build trust, a manager should, at a minimum:
• Always honor implied and explicit social contracts.
• Seek to prevent, avoid, and rectify harm to others.
• Respect the unique needs of others.

Referent power is the ability to control another's behavior because of the individual's desire to identify with the power source.

Coalition power is the ability to control another's behavior indirectly because the individual owes an obligation to you or another as part of a larger collective interest.

Personal Power

Personal power resides in the individual and is independent of that individual's position. Personal power is important in many well-managed firms. Four bases of personal power are expertise, rational persuasion, reference, and coalitions.[12]

Expert power is the ability to control another person's behavior through the possession of knowledge, experience, or judgment that the other person does not have but needs. A subordinate obeys a supervisor possessing expert power because the boss ordinarily knows more about what is to be done or how it is to be done than does the subordinate. Expert power is relative, not absolute.

Rational persuasion is the ability to control another's behavior because, through the individual's efforts, the person accepts the desirability of an offered goal and a reasonable way of achieving it. Much of what a supervisor does day to day involves rational persuasion up, down, and across the organization. Rational persuasion involves both explaining the desirability of expected outcomes and showing how specific actions will achieve these outcomes. Relational persuasion rests on trust. OB Savvy 10.1 shows some basics in building trust as a key to build personal power.

Referent power is the ability to control another's behavior because the person wants to identify with the power source. In this case, a subordinate obeys the boss because he or she wants to behave, perceive, or believe as the boss does. This obedience may occur, for example, because the subordinate likes the boss personally and therefore tries to do things the way the boss wants them done. In a sense the subordinate attempts to avoid doing anything that would interfere with the pleasing boss-subordinate relationship. A person's referent power can be enhanced when the individual taps into the moral order or shows a clearer long-term path to a morally desirable end. In common language, individuals with the ability to tap into these more esoteric aspects of corporate life have "charisma" and "the vision thing." Followership is not based on what the subordinate will get for specific actions or specific levels of performance, but on what the individual represents—a path toward a loftier future.

Coalition Power is the ability to control another's behavior indirectly because the individual owes an obligation to you or to another as part of a larger collective interest. Coalitions are often built around issues of common interest.[13] To build a coalition, individuals negotiate trade-offs to arrive at a common position. Individuals may also horse trade across issues, granting support to one another. These trade-offs and trades represent informational obligations of support. To maintain the coalition the individual may be asked to support your position on an issue and act in accordance with your desires. If the other person does, you have a reciprocal obligation to support that person on his or her issue. These reciprocal obligations can extend to a network of individuals as well. A network of mutual support provides a powerful collective front that protects members and accomplishes shared interests.

Building Influence

A considerable portion of any manager's time is directed toward what is called power-oriented behavior. Power-oriented behavior is action directed primarily at developing or using relationships in which other people are to some degree willing to defer to one's wishes.[14] Figure 10.2 shows three basic dimensions of power and influence with which a manager will become involved in this regard: downward, upward, and lateral. Also shown in the figure are some preliminary ideas for achieving success along each of these dimensions.

The effective manager is one who succeeds in building and maintaining high levels of both position and personal power over time. Only then is sufficient power of the right types available when the manager needs to exercise influence on downward, lateral, and upward dimensions.

Building Position Power   Position power can be enhanced when a manager is able to demonstrate to others that the manager's work unit is highly relevant to organizational goals and is able to respond to urgent organizational needs. To increase centrality and criticality in the organization, managers may seek to acquire a more central role in the workflow by having information filtered through them, making at least part of their job responsibilities unique, and expanding their networks of communication contacts.

A manager may also attempt to increase task relevance. There are many ways to do this. The manager may attempt to become an internal coordinator within the firm or an external representative. When the firm is in a dynamic setting of

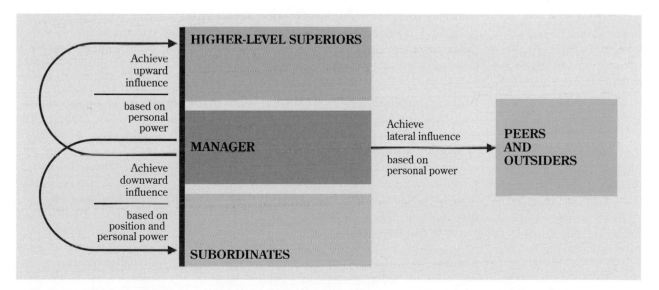

Figure 10.2   Three dimensions of managerial power and influence.

changing technology, the executive may also move to provide unique services and information to other units. A manager may shift the emphasis on his or her group's activities toward emerging issues central to the organization's top priorities. Effectively initiating new ideas and new projects may not be possible unless a manager also delegates more routine activities and expands both the task variety and task novelty for subordinates. Of course, not all attempts to build influence may be positive. For example, some managers are known to have defined tasks so they are difficult to evaluate by creating ambiguous job descriptions or developing a unique language for their work.

Building Personal Power   Personal power arises from the personal characteristics of the manager. Three personal characteristics—expertise, political savvy, and likability—have special potential for enhancing personal power in an organization. The most obvious is building expertise. Additional expertise may be gained by advanced training and education, participation in professional associations, and involvement in the early stages of projects.

A somewhat less obvious way to increase personal power is to learn political savvy—better ways to negotiate, persuade individuals, and understand the goals and means individuals are most willing to accept. The novice believes that most individuals are very much the same, see the same goals, and will accept much the same paths toward these goals. The more astute individual recognizes important individual differences. The most experienced managers are adept at using this awareness to build coalitions and develop a network of reciprocal obligations.

A manager's reference power is increased by characteristics that enhance his or her likeability and that create personal attraction in relationships with other people. These include pleasant personality characteristics, agreeable behavior patterns, and attractive personal appearance.

Using Information and Influence Techniques   From a purely analytical standpoint, most sources of power can be traced to position power or personal power. However, many of the influential actions and behaviors are combinations of these two powers.

Increasing Visibility and Control over Information   Most managers attempt to increase the visibility of their job performance by (1) expanding the number of contacts they have with senior people, (2) making oral presentations of written work, (3) participating in problem-solving task forces, (4) sending out notices of accomplishment, and (5) generally seeking additional opportunities to increase personal name recognition.[14] Most managers also recognize that, between superiors and subordinates, access to or control over information is an important element.

A boss may appear to expand his or her expert power over a subordinate by not allowing the subordinate access to critical information. Although the denial may appear to enhance the boss's expert power, it actually may reduce the subordinate's effectiveness. In a similar manner, a supervisor may also control access to key organizational decision makers. An individual's ability to contact key persons informally can offset some of this disadvantage. Furthermore, astute senior executives routinely develop "back channels" to lower-level individuals deep within the firm to offset the tendency of bosses to control information and access. Expert power is often relational and embedded within the organizational context. Many important decisions are made outside formal channels and are substantially influenced by key individuals with the requisite knowledge. By developing and using coalitions and networks, an individual may build on his or her expert power. Through coalitions and networks, an individual may alter the flow of information and the context for analysis. By developing coalitions and networks, executives also expand their access to information and their opportunities for participation.

Controlling Decision Premises   Executives also attempt to control, or at least influence, decision premises. A decision premise is a basis for defining the problem and for selecting among alternatives. By defining a problem in a manner that fits the executive's expertise, it is natural for that executive to be in charge of solving it. Thus, the executive subtly shifts his or her position power. Executives who want to increase their power often make their goals and needs clear and bargain effectively to show that their preferred goals and needs are best. They do not show their power base directly but instead provide clear "rational persuasion" for their preferences. So the astute executive does not threaten or attempt to invoke sanctions to build power. Instead, he or she combines personal power with the position of the unit to enhance total power. As the organizational context changes, different personal sources of power may become more important alone and in combination with the individual's position power. So there is an art to building power.

Perfecting Influence Techniques   Using position and personal power well to achieve the desired influence over other people is a challenge for most managers. Practically speaking, there are many useful ways of exercising relational influence. The most common techniques involve the following:[15]

> *Reason* Using facts and data to support a logical argument.
>
> *Friendliness* Using flattery, goodwill, and favorable impressions.
>
> *Coalition* Using relationships with other people for support.
>
> *Bargaining* Using the exchange of benefits as a basis for negotiation.
>
> *Assertiveness* Using a direct and forceful personal approach.
>
> *Higher authority* Gaining higher-level support for one's requests.
>
> *Sanctions* Using organizationally derived rewards and punishments.

Research on these strategies suggests that reason is the most popular technique overall.[16] In addition, friendliness, assertiveness, bargaining, and higher authority are used more frequently to influence subordinates than to influence supervisors. This pattern of influence attempts is consistent with the earlier observation that downward influence generally includes mobilization of both position and personal power sources, whereas upward influence is more likely to draw on personal power.

ETHICS IN OB

USING POWER ETHICALLY

Cavanagh, Moberg, and Velasquez argue that a person's behavior must satisfy the following criteria to be considered ethical:

1. The behavior must result in optimizing the satisfaction of people both inside and outside the organization to produce the greatest good for the greatest number.

2. The behavior must respect the rights of all affected parties, including the human rights of free consent, free speech, freedom of conscience, privacy, and due process.

3. The behavior must respect the rules of justice by treating people equitably and fairly, as opposed to arbitrarily.

There are, of course, exceptions in certain situations. These special cases must satisfy the criterion of overwhelming factors, in which the special nature of the situation results in (1) conflicts among criteria (e.g., a behavior results in some good and some bad being done), (2) conflicts within criteria (e.g., a behavior uses questionable means to achieve a positive end), or (3) incapacity to employ the criteria (e.g., a person's behavior is based on inaccurate or incomplete information).[16A]

> *Question: Which organizational political behaviors would be considered ethical under these standards?*

Little research is available on the subject of upward influence in organizations. This is unfortunate, since truly effective managers are able to influence their bosses as well as their subordinates. One study reports that both supervisors and subordinates view reason, or the logical presentation of ideas, as the most frequently used strategy of upward influence.[17] When queried on reasons for success and failure, however, the two groups show both similarities and differences in their viewpoints. The perceived causes of success in upward influence are similar for both supervisors and subordinates and involve the favorable content of the influence attempt, the favorable manner of its presentation, and the competence of the subordinate.[18] The two groups disagree on the causes of failure, however. Subordinates attribute failure in upward influence to the close mindedness of the supervisor, unfavorable content of the influence attempt, and unfavorable interpersonal relationships with the supervisor. In contrast, supervisors attribute failure to the unfavorable content of the attempt, the unfavorable manner in which it was presented, and the subordinate's lack of competence.

Knowing what can be done to build power is not the same as using power ethically. Ethics in OB provides some guidelines OB scholars have proposed for ethical actions.

Empowerment

Empowerment is the process by which managers help others acquire and use the power needed to make decisions affecting themselves and their work. More than ever before, managers in progressive organizations are expected to be good at (and highly comfortable with) empowering the people with whom they work. Rather than considering power to be something to be held only at higher levels in the traditional organizational pyramid, this view considers power to be something that can be shared by everyone working in flatter and more collegial structures.[19]

The concept of empowerment is one of the sweeping changes being witnessed in today's corporations. Corporate staff numbers are being cut back, layers of management are being eliminated, and the number of employees is being reduced as the volume of work increases. What is left is a leaner and trimmer organization staffed by fewer managers who must share more power as they go about their daily tasks. Indeed, empowerment is a key foundation of the increasingly popular self-managing work teams and other creative worker involvement groups.

■ **Empowerment** is the process by which managers help others acquire and use the power needed to make decisions affecting themselves and their work.

Keys to Empowerment

One of the bases for empowerment is a radically different view of power itself. So far, the discussion has focused on power that is exerted over other individuals. In this traditional view, power is relational in terms of individuals. In contrast, the concept of empowerment emphasizes the ability to make things happen. Power is still relational, but in terms of problems and opportunities, not just in terms of individuals. Cutting through all the corporate rhetoric on empowerment is quite difficult, since the term has become quite fashionable in management circles. Each individual empowerment attempt needs to be examined in light of how power in the organization has been or will be changed.

Changing Position Power   When an organization attempts to move power down the hierarchy, it must also alter the existing pattern of position power. Changing this pattern raises some important questions: Can "empowered" individuals give rewards and sanctions based on task accomplishment? Has their new right to act been legitimized with formal authority? All too often, attempts at empowerment disrupt well-established patterns of position power and threaten middle- and lower-level managers. As one supervisor said: "All this empowerment stuff sounds great for top management. They don't have to run around trying to get the necessary clearances to implement the suggestions from my group. They never gave me the authority to make the changes, only the new job of asking for permission."

Expanding the Zone of Indifference   When embarking on an empowerment program, management needs to recognize the current zone of indifference and systematically move to expand it. All too often management assumes that its directive for empowerment will be followed because management sees empowerment as a better way to manage. Management needs to show precisely how empowerment will benefit the individuals involved and provide the inducement needed to expand the zone of indifference.

Power as an Expanding Pie

Along with empowerment, employees need to be trained to expand their power and their new influence potential. This is the most difficult task for managers and can be a difficult challenge for employees, for it often changes the dynamic between supervisors and subordinates. The key is to change the concept of power within the organization from a view that stresses power over others to one that emphasizes the use of power to get things done. Under the new definition of power, all employees can be more powerful.

A clearer definition of roles and responsibilities may help managers empower others. For instance, senior managers may choose to concentrate on long-term, large-scale adjustments to a variety of challenging and strategic forces in the external environment. If top management tends to concentrate on the long term and downplay quarterly mileposts, others throughout the organization must be ready and willing to make critical operating decisions to maintain current profitability. By providing opportunities for creative problem solving coupled with the discretion to act, real empowerment increases the total power available in an organization. In other words, the top levels do not have to give up power in order for the lower levels to gain it. Note that senior managers must give up the illusion of control—the false belief that they can direct the actions of employees five or six levels of management below them.

The same basic arguments hold true in any manager-subordinate relationship. Empowerment means that all managers need to emphasize different ways of exercising influence. Appeals to higher authority and sanctions need to be replaced by appeals to reason. Friendliness must replace coercion, and bargaining must replace orders for compliance. Given the all too familiar history of an emphasis on coercion and compliance within firms, special support may be needed for individuals so that they become comfortable in developing their own power over events and activities.

What executives fear, and all too often find, is that employees passively resist empowerment by seeking directives they can obey or reject. The fault lies with the executives and the middle managers who need to rethink what they mean by power and their use of traditional position- and personal-power sources. The key is to lead, not push; reward, not sanction; build, not destroy; and expand, not shrink. To expand the zone of indifference also calls for expanding the inducements for thinking and acting, not just for obeying.

Beyond Empowerment to Valuing Others

A number of OB scholars argue that U.S. firms need to move beyond just empowering employees as well as change how they view employees in order to sustain a competitive advantage in an increasingly global economy.[20] While no one firm may have all the characteristics, Jeffery Pfeffer suggests that firms place employees at the center of their strategy.

(a) Develop employment security for a selectively recruited workforce.
(b) Pay high wages with incentive pay and the potential for employee ownership.
(c) Encourage information sharing and participation with an emphasis on self-managed teams.
(d) Emphasize training and skill development with cross use of talent and cross training.
(e) Pursue egalitarianism (at least symbolically) with little pay compression across units and extensive internal promotion.

Of course, such an approach also calls for taking a long-term view, coupled with a systematic emphasis on measuring what works and what does not, as well as having a supporting managerial philosophy. This is a long list. However, it appears consistent with the chapter opening by John Chambers of Cisco and his emphasis on people and interconnections.

Organizational Politics

Any study of power and influence inevitably leads to the subject of "politics." For many, this word may conjure up thoughts of illicit deals, favors, and special personal relationships. Perhaps this image of shrewd, often dishonest, practices of obtaining one's way is reinforced by Machiavelli's classic fifteenth-century work *The Prince,* which outlines how to obtain and hold power through political action. To Machiavelli the ends justified the means. It is important, however, to adopt a perspective that allows politics in organizations to function in a much broader capacity.[21]

The Traditions of Organizational Politics

There are two quite different traditions in the analysis of organizational politics. One tradition builds on Machiavelli's philosophy and defines politics in terms of self-interest and the use of nonsanctioned means. In this tradition, **organizational politics** may be formally defined as the management of influence to obtain ends not sanctioned by the organization or to obtain sanctioned ends through nonsanctioned means.[22] Managers are often considered political when they seek their own goals, or when they use means that are not currently authorized by the organization or that push legal limits. Where there is uncertainty or ambiguity, it is often extremely difficult to tell whether a manager is being political in this self-serving sense.[23] For instance, was John Meriwether a great innovator when he established Long Term Capital Management (LTCM) as a hedge fund to bet on interest-rate spreads?[24] Before its dramatic demise the firm included 2 Nobel laureates and some 25 PhDs. Or was he the consummate insider because he got the

> ■ **Organizational politics** is the management of influence to obtain ends not sanctioned by the organization or to obtain sanctioned ends through nonsanctioned means; it is also the art of creative compromise among competing interests.

MASTERING MANAGEMENT

HONE YOUR POLITICAL SKILLS

Want to become a better corporate politician? Gerald Ferris, Sherry Davidson and Pamela Perrewe suggest you build your political skills.

One, hone your social astuteness by becoming aware of others' concerns in order to improve your understanding of why they act the way they do.

Two, work on your interpersonal influence and on how to communicate and develop friendly relationships.

Three, sharpen your network ability by finding others both inside and outside the firm who have a shared set of interests.

Four, perfect your apparent sincerity so that others see you as a person that genuinely cares for others.[23A]

U.S. Federal Reserve to orchestrate a bailout when it looked as if he would either go broke or lose control to a rich investor? Or, as often happens in the world of corporate politics, could both of these statements be partially true?

The second tradition treats politics as a necessary function resulting from differences in the self-interests of individuals. Here, organizational politics is viewed as the art of creative compromise among competing interests. In the case of John Meriwether and LTCM, when it went bankrupt, the country's financial leaders were concerned that this event could cause a panic in the global financial markets and hurt everyone. So the Federal Reserve stepped in. That Meriwether did not lose everything was merely a by-product of saving the whole financial system.

In a heterogeneous society individuals will disagree as to whose self-interests are most valuable and whose concerns should therefore be bounded by collective interests. Politics arises because individuals need to develop compromises, avoid confrontation, and live together. The same holds true in organizations, where individuals join, work, and stay together because their self-interests are served. Furthermore, it is important to remember that the goals of the organization and the acceptable means of achieving them are established by organizationally powerful individuals in negotiation with others. Thus, organizational politics is also the use of power to develop socially acceptable ends and means that balance individual and collective interests.

Regardless of which perspective you take, you can improve your corporate political skills. Check out the ideas highlighted in Mastering Management.

Political Interpretation   The two different traditions of organizational politics are reflected in the ways executives describe their effects on managers and their organizations. In one survey, some 53 percent of those interviewed indicated that organizational politics enhanced the achievement of organizational goals and survival.[25] Yet some 44 percent suggested that it distracted individuals from organizational goals. In this same survey 60 percent of respondents suggested that organizational politics was good for career advancement; 39 percent reported that it led to a loss of power, position, and credibility.

Organizational politics is not automatically good or bad. It can serve a number of important functions, including overcoming personnel inadequacies, coping with change, and substituting for formal authority.

Even in the best-managed firms, mismatches arise among managers who are learning, burned out, lacking in needed training and skills, overqualified, or lacking the resources needed to accomplish their assigned duties. Organizational politics provides a mechanism for circumventing these inadequacies and getting the job done. Organizational politics can facilitate adaptation to changes in the environment and technology of an organization.

Organizational politics can help identify problems and move ambitious, problem-solving managers into the breach. It is quicker than restructuring. It allows the firm to meet unanticipated problems with people and re-

---

OB SAVVY 10.2

Political Skill as an Antidote to Stress

- Ever wonder why executives under tremendous daily stress do not burn out? Some argue it is their political skill that saves them. Which specific political skills? Think of these:
- The ability to use practical intelligence (as opposed to analytical or creative intelligence)
- The ability to be calculating and shrewd about social connections
- The ability to inspire trust and confidence
- The ability to deal with individuals having a wide variety of backgrounds, styles, and personalities

sources quickly, before small headaches become major problems. Finally, when a person's formal authority breaks down or fails to apply to a particular situation, political actions can be used to prevent a loss of influence. Managers may use political behavior to maintain operations and to achieve task continuity in circumstances when the failure of formal authority may otherwise cause problems. As shown in OB Savvy 10.2, political skill has even been linked to reductions in executive stress.

Political Forecasting   Managers may gain a better understanding of how political behavior can be used to forecast future actions by placing themselves in the positions of other persons involved in critical decisions or events. Each action and decision can be seen as having benefits for and costs to all parties concerned. Where the costs exceed the benefits, the manager may act to protect his or her position. Figure 10.3 shows a sample payoff table for two managers, Lee and Leslie, in a problem situation involving a decision as to whether or not to allocate resources to a special project. If both managers authorize the resources, the project gets completed on time, and their company keeps a valuable client. Unfortunately, if they do this, both Lee and Leslie overspend their budgets. Taken on its own, a budget overrun would be bad for the managers' performance records. Assume that the overruns are acceptable only if the client is kept. Thus, if both managers act, both they and the company win, as depicted in the upper-left block of the figure. Obviously, this is the most desirable outcome for all parties concerned.

Assume that Leslie acts, but Lee does not. In this case the company loses the client, Leslie overspends the budget in a futile effort, and Lee ends up within budget. While the company and Leslie lose, Lee wins. This scenario is illustrated in the lower-left block of the figure. The upper-right block shows the reverse situation, where Lee acts but Leslie does not. In this case, Leslie wins, while the company and Lee lose. Finally, if both Lee and Leslie fail to act, each stays within the budget and therefore gains, but the company loses the client.

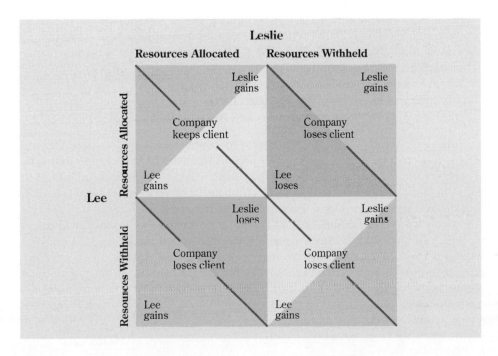

Figure 10.3   Political payoff matrix for the allocation of resources on a sample project.

Little Caesars

Marian Ilitch, co-founder of Little Caesars Pizza, has helped put her stamp on the corporate philosophy of Little Caesars by making it one of the best places for working women. The firm, headquartered in downtown Detroit, also has a long and distinguished record of supporting local charities. Marian Ilitch recently made a million-dollar contribution to establish a hospice in Detroit.

The company clearly wants both Lee and Leslie to act. But will they? Would you take the risk of overspending the budget, knowing that your colleague may refuse? The question of trust is critical here, but building trust among co-managers and other workers takes time and can be difficult. The involvement of higher-level managers may be needed to set the stage better. Yet in many organizations both Lee and Leslie would fail to act because the "climate" or "culture" too often encourages people to maximize their self-interest at minimal risk.

Subunit Power   To be effective in political action, managers should also understand the politics of subunit relations.[26] Line units are typically more powerful than are staff groups, and units toward the top of the hierarchy are often more powerful than are those toward the bottom. More subtle relationships are found among units at or near the same level in a firm. Political action links managers more formally to one another as representatives of their work units. Five of the more typical lateral, intergroup relations in which you may engage as a manager are workflow, service, advisory, auditing, and approval.[27] Workflow linkages involve contacts with units that precede or follow in a sequential production chain. Service ties involve contacts with units established to help with problems. For instance, an assembly-line manager may develop a service link by asking the maintenance manager to fix an important piece of equipment on a priority basis. In contrast, advisory connections involve formal staff units having special expertise, such as when a manager seeks the advice of the personnel department on evaluating subordinates. Auditing linkages involve units that have the right to evaluate the actions of others after action has been taken, whereas approval linkages involve units whose approval must be obtained before action may be taken. In general, units gain power as more of their relations with others are of the approval and auditing types. Workflow relations are more powerful than are advisory associations, and both are more powerful than are service relations.

The Politics of Self-Protection

While organizational politics may be helpful to the organization as a whole, it is probably more commonly known and better understood in terms of self-protection.[28] Whether or not management likes it, all employees recognize that in any organization they must watch out for themselves first. In too many organizations, if the employee doesn't protect himself or herself, no one else will. Individuals can employ three common strategies to protect themselves. They can (1) avoid action and risk taking, (2) redirect accountability and responsibility, or (3) defend their turf.

Avoidance   Avoidance is quite common in controversial areas where the employee must risk being wrong or where actions may yield a sanction. Perhaps the most common reaction is to "work to the rules." That is, employees are protected when they adhere strictly to all the rules, policies, and procedures and do not allow deviations or exceptions. Perhaps one of the most frustrating but effective techniques is to "play dumb." We all do this at some time or another. When was the last time you said: "Officer, I didn't know the speed limit was 35. I couldn't have been going 52." Although working to the rules and playing dumb are common techniques, experienced employees often practice somewhat more subtle techniques of self-protection, including depersonalization and stalling.

Depersonalization involves treating individuals, such as customers, clients, or subordinates, as numbers, things, or objects. Senior managers don't fire long-term employees; the organization is merely "downsized" or "delayered." Routine stalling involves slowing down the pace of work to expand the task so that the individuals look as if they are working hard. With creative stalling the employees may spend the time supporting the organization's ideology, position, or program while delaying implementation of changes they consider undesirable.

Redirecting Responsibility   Politically sensitive individuals will always protect themselves from accepting blame for the negative consequences of their actions. Again, a variety of well-worn techniques may be used for redirecting responsibility. "Passing the buck" is a common method employees and managers use. The trick here is to define the task in such a way that it becomes someone else's formal responsibility. The ingenious ways in which individuals can redefine an issue to avoid action and to transfer responsibility are often amazing. Both employees and managers may avoid responsibility by "buffing," or rigorous documentation. Here, individuals take action only when all the paperwork is in place, and it is clear that they are merely following procedure. Closely related to rigorous documentation is the "blind memo," or blind e-mail, which explains an objection to an action implemented by the individual. Here, the required action is taken, but the blind memo or e-mail is prepared should the action come into question. Politicians are particularly good at this technique. They will meet with a lobbyist and then send a memo to the files confirming the meeting. Any relationship between what was discussed in the meeting and the memo is accidental.

As the last example suggests, a convenient method some managers use to avoid responsibility is merely to rewrite history. If a program is successful, the manager claims to have been an early supporter. If a program fails, the manager was the one who expressed serious reservations in the first place. Although a memo in the files is often nice to have to show one's early support or objections, some executives do not even bother with such niceties. They merely start a meeting by recapping what has happened in such a way that makes them look good.

For the devious, there are three other techniques for redirecting responsibility. One technique is to blame the problem on someone or some group that has difficulty defending itself. Fired employees, outsiders, and opponents are often targets of such scapegoating. Closely related to scapegoating is blaming the problem on uncontrollable events. All of us have a natural tendency to do this.[29] The devious manager goes far beyond this natural tendency. A perennial

ETHICS IN OB

AVOIDING COMMON RATIONALIZATIONS FOR UNETHICAL BEHAVIOR

Choosing to be ethical often involves considerable personal sacrifice, and it involves avoiding common rationalizations. When confronting unethical actions, be sure you are not justifying unethical actions by suggesting that

(1) the behavior is not really illegal and so could be moral;

(2) the action appears to be in the firm's best interests;

(3) the action is unlikely ever to be detected; or

(4) it appears that the action demonstrates loyalty to the boss, the firm, or short-term stockholder interests.

Whereas these rationalizations may appear compelling at the moment of action, each deserves close scrutiny.

favorite is, "Given the unexpected severe decline in the overall economy, firm profitability was only somewhat below reasonable expectations." Meaning, the firm lost a bundle. Should these techniques fail, there is always another possibility: when facing apparent defeat, the manager can escalate commitment to a losing course of action. That is, when all appears lost, assert confidence in the original action, blame the problems on not spending enough money to implement the plan fully, and embark on actions that call for increased effort. The manager's hope is that he or she will be promoted, have a new job with another firm, or be retired by the time the negative consequences are recognized. This approach is called "skating fast over thin ice."[30]

Defending Turf   Defending turf is a time-honored tradition in most large organizations. As noted earlier in the chapter, managers seeking to improve their power attempt to expand the jobs their groups perform. Defending turf also results from the coalitional nature of organizations. That is, the organization may be seen as a collection of competing interests held by various departments and groups. As each group attempts to expand its influence, it starts to encroach on the activities of other groups. Turf protection is common in organizations, from the very lowest position to the executive suite.

When you see these actions by others, the question of ethical behavior should immediately come to mind. Check Ethics in OB to make sure you are not using organizational politics to justify unethical behavior.

Politics and Governance

From the era of robber barons such as Jay Gould in the 1890s, Americans have been fascinated with the politics of the chief executive suite. Recent accounts of alleged and proven criminal actions emanating from the executive suites of WorldCom, Enron, Global Crossings, and Tyco have encouraged the media spotlight to penetrate the mysterious veil shrouding politics at the top of organizations.[31] An analytical view of executive suite dynamics may lift some of the mystery.

■ **Agency theory** suggests that public corporations can function effectively even though their managers are self-interested and do not automatically bear the full consequences of their managerial actions.

Agency Theory   An essential power problem in today's modern corporation arises from the separation of owners and managers. A body of work called **agency theory** suggests that public corporations can function effectively even though their managers are self-interested and do not automatically bear the full consequences of their managerial actions. The theory argues that (1) all the interests of society are served by protecting stockholder interests, (2) stockholders have a clear interest in greater returns, and (3) managers are self-interested and unwilling to sacrifice these self-interests for others (particularly stockholders) and thus must be controlled. The term *agency theory* stems from the notion that managers are "agents" of the owners.

So what types of controls should be instituted? There are several types. One type of control involves making sure that what is good for stockholders is good for management. Incentives in the pay plan for executives may be adjusted to align the interests of management and stockholders. For example, executives may get most of their pay based on the stock price of the firm through stock options. A second type of control involves the establishment of a strong, independent board of directors, since the board is to represent the stockholders. While this may

Research Insight
When CEO Stock Options Are under Water

To align the interests of stockholders and the CEO, many advocates of agency theory suggest that CEOs should be given stock options. Here is how they work. If the current stock price is $100, the board of directors might reward the CEO with 10,000 options to buy the stock at $110, hoping that the CEO will be such a great leader that the stock price will rise well above $110. This is an option to buy, and no one would exercise an option to buy at $110 when the price is $100. In the colorful language of stock options, when the option "strike price" is less than the current price, the option is under water. Well, what happens if the stock price drops to, say, $50? The gap is huge. Will the board change the option price? Recent research by Pollock, Fischer, and Wade suggests that the board might cut the CEO a better deal. The chances that the CEO will benefit increase when (1) there is a larger gap between the option price and the current price and (2) the CEO is also chairperson of the board of directors. These results could be expected. What was not expected was the following: the greater the number of board members selected by the CEO and the more staggered their terms, the less likely the board is to give the CEO a favorable reevaluation. Why? Pollock, Fischer, and Wade speculate that giving the CEO a revised set of options is such a visible action that it would be broadcast to investors and the public. A weaker board dominated by the CEO could be afraid of losing legitimacy. By not revaluating the options, the board is sending a signal that they are not as weak as they appear. Like many other studies regarding power and politics, there are many surprises. The bottom line? The authors conclude that stock options are not a good way to align CEO and stockholder interests.[32]

sound unusual, it is not uncommon for a CEO to pick a majority of the board members and to place many top managers on the board. A third way is for stockholders with a large stake in the firm to take an active role on the board. For instance, mutual fund managers have been encouraged to become more active in monitoring management. And there is, of course, the so-called market for corporate control. For instance, poorly performing executives can be replaced by outsiders.[33] The problem with the simple application of all of these control mechanisms is that they do not appear to work very well even for stockholders and clearly, some suggest, not for others either.[34] See a recent example from the OB literature in OB Research Insight.

The recent storm of controversy over CEO pay illustrates using a simple application of agency theory to control executives. Traditionally, U.S. CEOs made about 25 to 30 times the pay of the average worker. This was similar to CEO pay scales in Europe and Japan. Today, many U.S. CEOs are making 300 times the average pay of workers.[35] How did they get so rich? Executive compensation specialists have derived plans that link executive pay to short-term increases in the firm's stock price. As one might expect, executives have become so interested in short-term stock price increases they may have downplayed other goals and other interests.[36] When a CEO downsizes, outsources jobs abroad, embarks on a merger campaign, or cuts such benefits as worker health care, short-term profits may jump dramatically and lift the stock price. Although the long-term health of the firm may be put in jeopardy, few U.S. CEOs seem able to resist the temptation. It is little wonder that there is renewed interest in how U.S. firms are governed. Rather than proposing some quick fix based on a limited theory of the firm, it is better to come to a broader understanding of some of the different views on the politics of the executive suite.

Resource Dependencies   Executive behavior can sometimes be explained in terms of **resource dependencies**—the firm's need for resources that are controlled by others.[37] Essentially, the resource dependence of an organization increases as (1) needed resources become more scarce, (2) outsiders have more control over needed resources, and (3) there are fewer substitutes for a particular type of resource controlled by a limited number of outsiders. Thus, one political role of the chief executive is to develop workable compromises among the competing resource dependencies facing the organization—compromises that enhance the executive's power. To create such compromises, executives need to diagnose the relative power of outsiders and to craft strategies that respond differently to various external resource suppliers. For larger organizations, many strategies may center on altering the firm's degree of resource dependence. Through mergers and acquisitions, a firm may bring key resources within its control. By changing the "rules of the game," a firm may also find protection from particularly powerful outsiders. For instance, before being absorbed by another firm, Netscape sought relief from the onslaught of Microsoft by appealing to the U.S. government. Markets may also be protected by trade barriers, or labor unions may be put in check by "right to work" laws. Even so, there are limits on the ability of even our largest and most powerful organizations to control all important external contingencies.

International competition has narrowed the range of options for chief executives: they can no longer ignore the rest of the world. Some may need to fundamentally redefine how they expect to conduct business. For instance, in the past U.S. firms could often go it alone without the assistance of foreign corporations. Now, chief executives are increasingly leading them in the direction of more joint ventures and strategic alliances with foreign partners from around the globe. Such "combinations" provide access to scarce resources and technologies among partners, as well as new markets and shared production costs.[38]

Organizational Governance   With some knowledge of agency theory and resource dependencies it is much easier to understand the notion of **organizational governance**. Organizational governance refers to the pattern of authority, influence, and acceptable managerial behavior established at the top of the organization. This system establishes what is important, how issues will be defined, who should and should not be involved in key choices, and the boundaries for acceptable implementation. Students of organizational governance suggest that a "dominant coalition" comprised of powerful organizational actors is a key to understanding a firm's governance.[39] Although one expects many top officers within the organization to be members of this coalition, the

■ **Resource dependencies** is the firm's need for resources that are controlled by others.

■ **Organizational governance** is the pattern of authority, influence, and acceptable managerial behavior established at the top of the organization.

dominant coalition occasionally includes outsiders with access to key resources. Thus, an analysis of organizational governance builds on the resource dependence perspective by highlighting the effective control of key resources by members of a dominant coalition. It also recognizes the relative power of key constituencies, such as the power of stockholders stressed in agency theory. This view of the executive suite recognizes that the daily practice of organizational governance is the development and resolution of issues. Through the governance system, the dominant coalition attempts to define reality. By accepting or rejecting proposals from subordinates, by directing questions toward the interests of powerful outsiders, and by selecting individuals who appear to espouse particular values and qualities, the pattern of governance is slowly established within the organization. Furthermore, this pattern rests, at least in part, on highly political foundations.

Although organizational governance was an internal and rather private matter in the past, it is now becoming more public and openly controversial. Some argue that senior managers don't represent shareholder interests well enough, as noted in the discussion of agency theory. Others are concerned that managers give too little attention to broader constituencies. We think managers should recognize the basis for their power and legitimacy.

Chapter 10   Study Guide

Summary

What are power and influence in an organization?

- Power is the ability to get someone else to do what you want him or her to do.

- Power vested in managerial positions derives from three sources: rewards, punishments, and legitimacy (formal authority).

- Influence is what you have when you exercise power.

- Position power is formal authority based on the manager's position in the hierarchy.

- Personal power is based on one's expertise and referent capabilities.

- Managers can pursue various ways of acquiring both position and personal power.

- Managers can also become skilled at using various techniques—such as reason, friendliness, ingratiation, and bargaining—to influence superiors, peers, and subordinates.

How are power, obedience, and formal authority intertwined in an organization?

- Individuals are socialized to accept power (the potential to control the behavior of others) and formal authority (the potential to exert such control through the legitimacy of a managerial position).

- The Milgram experiments illustrate that people have a tendency to obey directives coming from others who appear powerful and authoritative.

- Power and authority work only if the individual "accepts" them as legitimate.

- The zone of indifference defines the boundaries within which people in organizations let others influence their behavior.

What is empowerment?

- Empowerment is the process through which managers help others acquire and use the power needed to make decisions that affect them and their work.

- Clear delegation of authority, integrated planning, and the involvement of senior management are all important to implementing empowerment.

- Empowerment emphasizes power as the ability to get things done rather than the ability to get others to do what you want.

What is organizational politics?

- Politics involves the use of power to obtain ends not officially sanctioned; it also involves the use of power to find ways of balancing individual and collective interests in otherwise difficult circumstances.

- For the manager, politics often occurs in decision situations when the interests of another manager or individual must be reconciled with one's own.

- For managers, politics also involves subunits that jockey for power and advantageous positions vis-à-vis one another.

- The politics of self-protection involves efforts to avoid accountability, redirect responsibility, and defend one's turf.

- Although some suggest that executives are agents of the owners, politics also comes into play as resource dependencies with external environmental elements must be strategically managed.

- Organizational governance is the pattern of authority, influence, and acceptable managerial behavior established at the top of the organization.

- CEOs and managers can develop an ethical organizational governance system that is free from rationalizations.

Key Terms

Multiple Choice

Self-Test 10

1. Three bases of position power are _____. (a) reward, expertise, and coercive power (b) legitimate, experience, and judgment power (c) knowledge, experience, and judgment power (d) reward, coercive, and knowledge power

2. _____ is the ability to control another's behavior because, through the individual's efforts, the other person accepts the desirability of an offered goal and a reasonable way of achieving it. (a) Rational persuasion (b) Legitimate power (c) Coercive power (d) Charismatic power

3. A worker who behaves in a certain manner to ensure an effective boss-subordinate relationship shows _____ power. (a) expert (b) reward (c) approval (d) referent

4. One guideline for implementing a successful empowerment strategy is that _____. (a) delegation of authority should be left ambiguous and open to individual interpretation (b) planning should be separated according to the level of empowerment (c) it can be assumed that any empowering directives from management will be automatically followed (d) the authority delegated to lower levels should be clear and precise

5. The major lesson of the Milgram experiments is that _____. (a) individuals are very independent and unwilling to obey (b) individuals are willing to obey as long as it does not hurt another person (c) individuals will obey an authority figure even if it does appear to hurt someone else (d) individuals will always obey an authority figure

6. The range of authoritative requests to which a subordinate is willing to respond without subjecting the directives to critical evaluation or judgment is called the _____. (a) psychological contract (b) zone of indifference (c) Milgram experiments (d) functional level of organizational politics

7. The three basic power relationships that ensure success are _____. (a) upward, downward, and lateral (b) upward, downward, and oblique (c) downward, lateral, and oblique (d) downward, lateral, and external

8. In which dimension of power and influence would a manager find the use of both position power and personal power most advantageous? _____ (a) upward (b) lateral (c) downward (d) workflow

9. Reason, coalition, bargaining, and assertiveness are strategies for _____. (a) enhancing personal power (b) enhancing position power (c) exercising referent power (d) exercising influence

10. Negotiating the interpretation of a union contract is an example of
_____. (a) organizational politics (b) lateral relations (c) an approval relationship (d) an auditing linkage

11. _____ is the ability to control another's behavior because of the possession of knowledge, experience, or judgment that the other person does not have but needs. (a) Coercive power (b) Expert power (c) Information power (d) Representative power

12. _____ is the range of authoritative requests to which a subordinate is willing to respond without subjecting the directives to critical evaluation or judgment. (a) A zone of indifference (b) Legitimate authority (c) Power (d) Politics

13. The process by which managers help others acquire and use the power needed to make decisions affecting themselves and their work is called _____. (a) politics (b) managerial philosophy (c) authority (d) empowerment

14. The pattern of authority, influence, and acceptable managerial behavior established at the top of the organization is called _____. (a) organizational governance (b) agency linkage (c) power (d) politics

15. _____ suggests that public corporations can function effectively even though their managers are self-interested and do not automatically bear the full consequences of their managerial actions. (a) Power theory (b) Managerial philosophy (c) Virtual theory (d) Agency theory

Short Response

16. Explain how the various bases of position and personal power do or do not apply to the classroom relationship between instructor and student. What sources of power do students have over their instructors?

17. Identify and explain at least three guidelines for the acquisition of (a) position power and (b) personal power by managers.

18. Identify and explain at least four strategies of managerial influence. Give examples of how each strategy may or may not work when exercising influence (a) downward and (b) upward in organizations.

19. Define organizational politics and give an example of how it operates in both functional and dysfunctional ways.

Applications Essay

20. What explanations for mergers and acquisitions would you offer if it were found that they rarely produce positive financial gains for the shareholders?

These learning activities from *The OB Skills Workbook* are suggested for Chapter 10.

OB in Action

CASE	EXPERIENTIAL EXERCISES	SELF-ASSESSMENTS
■ 10. Faculty Empower-ment	■ 25. Interview a Leader ■ 28. My Best Manager: Revisited ■ 42. Power Circles	■ 13. Empowering Others ■ 14. Machiavellianism

Plus—special learning experiences from *The Jossey-Bass/Pfeiffer Classroom Collection*

Chapter 11

Leadership Theories

Leaders move things forward

Chapter at a Glance

Let's start by recalling the Chapter 1 discussion of managers and management activities, roles, networks, functions skills, and competencies. Then we ask: How are leaders and leadership linked to all of this? As you read Chapter 11, *keep in mind these study topics.*

LEADERSHIP FOUNDATIONS

Managers versus Leaders

Trait Theories

Behavioral Theories

Cross Cultural Implictions

SITUATIONAL CONTINGENCY LEADERSHIP

Fiedler's Leadership Contingency Theory

House's Path-Goal Theory of Leadership

Hersey and Blanchard's Situational Leadership Theory

Graen's Leader-Member Exchange Theory

Substitutes for Leadership Theory

IMPLICIT LEADERSHIP

Leadership as Attribution

Leadership Prototypes

INSPIRATIONAL LEADERSHIP PERSPECTIVES

Charismatic Leadership

Transformational and Transactional Leadership

Charismatic and Transformational Leadership Issues

CHAPTER 11 STUDY GUIDE

In 2001 Ed Mahoney was on his second trip to Guatemala City after retiring from a career in hotel and restaurant management. There, amid the stench of decayed food, he saw a fetid ravine swarming with vultures and several dozen human scavengers intercepting garbage trucks. This second trip was part of his commitment to volunteer at a day care center for a year, made after meeting Hanley Denning, the American founder of Safe Passage, an organization serving the children of the families scavenging Guatemala City's dump.

> **"You don't need too much to live on. Living in Guatemala makes you understand what is important in life."**

After this second trip he was so struck by the families' plight that he eventually hired on permanently as Safe Passage's finance manager. Since then, the number of children Safe Passage has served has increased from 185 to 550. At the same time, Mahoney's own material needs have diminished, and one of his enduring accomplishments has been his impact on opening a home for abused and neglected children. He is seen as an empathetic leader who 'leads well by doing good.' "You don't need too much to live on. Living in Guatemala makes you understand what is important in life," he says.[1]

Leadership Foundations

Managers versus Leaders

Often it is assumed that anyone in a managerial role is a leader. Currently, however, controversy has arisen over this assumption. We can all think of examples where managers do not perform much, if any, leadership as well as examples where leadership is performed by people who are not in managerial roles. As part of this controversy, one set of authors has even argued that not to clearly recognize this difference is a violation of "truth in advertising" since many studies labeled "leadership" may actually be about "management".[2]

A key way of differentiating between the two is to argue that the role of *management* is to promote stability or to enable the organization to run smoothly, whereas the role of *leadership* is to promote adaptive or useful changes.[3] Persons in managerial positions could be involved with both management and leadership activities, or they could emphasize one activity at the expense of the other. Both management and leadership are needed, however, and if managers do not assume responsibility for both, then they should ensure that someone else handles the neglected activity. The point is that when we discuss leadership, we do not assume it is identical to management.

For our purposes, we treat **leadership** as the process of influencing others to understand and agree about what needs to be done and how to do it, and the process of facilitating individual and collective efforts to accomplish shared objectives.[4]

The broader influence notions, of which leadership is a part, are dealt with in Chapter 13. Leadership appears in two forms: (1) *formal leadership*, which is exerted by persons appointed to or elected to positions of formal authority in organizations, and (2) *informal leadership*, which is exerted by persons who become influential because they have special skills that meet the resource needs of others. Although both types are important in organizations, this chapter will emphasize formal leadership.

The leadership literature is vast—thousands of studies at last count—and consists of numerous approaches.[5]

We have grouped these approaches into two chapters: Leadership Theories Chapter 11, and Emerging Leadership Perspectives, Chapter 12. This chapter focuses on trait and behavioral theory perspectives, attributional and symbolic leadership perspectives, and transformational and charismatic leadership approaches. Chapter 12 continues with emerging perspectives as Full-Range Leadership Theory; Project GLOBE (the Global Leadership and Organizational Behavior Effectiveness project); strategic leadership; authentic, spiritual and servant, and ethical leadership; shared or distributed leadership; and change leadership. Many of the perspectives in each chapter include several models. While each of these models may be useful to you in a given work setting, we invite you to mix and match them as necessary in your setting, just as we did earlier with the motivational models discussed in Chapter 6. Working with different models is a trial-and-error process, but it is a good way to bring together the contributions from each model in a combination that meets your needs, be they leadership, managerial, or other.

Trait Theories

Trait perspectives assume that traits play a central role in differentiating between leaders and nonleaders (leaders must have the "right stuff"[6]) or in predicting leader or organizational outcomes. The *great person-trait approach* reflects this leader/nonleader difference and is the earliest approach in studying leadership, having been introduced more than a century ago. What traits differentiated "great persons" from the masses? (For example, how did Catherine the Great differ from her subjects?[7]) Later studies examined both leader/nonleader differences and trait predictions of outcomes. For various reasons, including inadequate theorizing and trait measurement, the studies were not successful enough to provide consistent findings.

More recent work has yielded more promising results. A number of traits have been found that help identify important leadership strengths (see Figure 11.1). As it turns out, most of these traits also tend to predict leadership outcomes.[8]

Leaders tend to be energetic and to operate on an even keel. They crave power not as an end in itself but as a means to achieving a vision or desired goals. Leaders are also very ambitious and have a high need for achievement. At the same time, they have to be emotionally mature enough to recognize their own

Leadership is the process of influencing others to understand and agree about what needs to be done and how to do it, and the process of facilitating individual and collective efforts to accomplish shared objectives.

Trait perspectives assume that traits play a central role in differentiating between leaders and nonleaders or in predicting leader or organizational outcomes.

Figure 11.1   Traits with positive implications for successful leadership.

Energy and adjustment or stress tolerance: Physical vitality and emotional resilience

Prosocial power motivation: A high need for power exercised primarily for the benefit of others

Achievement orientation: Need for achievement, desire to excel, drive to success, willingness to assume responsibility, concern for task objectives

Emotional maturity: Well-adjusted, does not suffer from severe psychological disorders

Self-confidence: General confidence in self and in the ability to perform the job of a leader

Integrity: Behavior consistent with espoused values; honest, ethical, trustworthy

Perseverance or tenacity: Ability to overcome obstacles; strength of will

Cognitive ability, intelligence, social intelligence: Ability to gather, integrate, and interpret information; intelligence, understanding of social setting

Task-relevant knowledge: Knowledge about the company, industry, and technical aspects

Flexibility: Ability to respond appropriately to changes in the setting

---

strengths and weaknesses, and they are oriented toward self-improvement. Furthermore, as developed in Chapter 12, to be trusted they must have authenticity; without trust, they cannot hope to maintain the loyalty of their followers. Leaders also must not be easily discouraged. They need to stick to a chosen course of action and to push toward goal accomplishment. At the same time, they must be cognitively sharp enough to deal well with the large amount of information they receive. However, they do not need to be brilliant; they just need to show above-average intelligence. In addition, leaders must have a good understanding of their social setting. Finally, they must possess extensive specific knowledge concerning their industry, firm, and job.

Behavioral Theories

The **behavioral perspective** assumes that leadership is central to performance and other outcomes.

Similar to the trait perspective covered above, the **behavioral perspective** assumes that leadership is central to performance and other outcomes. In this case, however, instead of underlying traits, behaviors are considered. Two classic research programs—at the University of Michigan and at the Ohio State University— provide useful insights into leadership behaviors.

Michigan Studies   In the late 1940s, researchers at the University of Michigan introduced a research program on leadership behavior. They sought to identify the leadership pattern that results in effective performance. From interviews of high- and low-performing groups in different organizations, the researchers derived two basic forms of leader behaviors: employee centered and production centered. Employee-centered supervisors are those who place strong emphasis on their subordinates' welfare. In contrast, production-centered supervisors are more concerned with getting the work done. In general, employee-centered supervisors were found to have more productive workgroups than did the production-centered supervisors.[9]

ETHICS IN OB

COLLEGE ATHLETICS AND CORRUPTION

Do you "strongly agree," "agree," are "neutral" about, "disagree," or "strongly disagree" with this proposition: During a volleyball game, player A hits the ball over the net. The ball barely grazes off player B's fingers and lands out of bounds. However, the referee does not see player B touch the ball. Because the referee is responsible for calling rule violations, player B is not obligated to report the violation.

At an increasing rate, athletes are answering "strongly agree." In other words, winning is more important than fair play.

The above is one example of work conducted by Sharon Stoll, a University of Idaho faculty member and administrator, to see if athletes are as morally developed as the normal population. In a 20-year study of some 80,000 high school, college, and professional athletes, the athletes' responses on moral reasoning are worse than those of nonathletes. From the time male athletes enter big time sports, their moral reasoning does not improve and sometimes declines. The same has also recently become true of female athletes.

As a part of a leadership role in this problem, Stoll has developed an educational program as a component of "Winning with Character." The universities of Georgia and Maryland, among other athletic programs, hold weekly group discussions with athletes about problem areas.[9A]

Question: Would you expect the ethical response differences between athletes and nonathletes? What kinds of details might you suggest be included in the weekly group discussions?

These behaviors may be viewed on a continuum, with employee-centered supervisors at one end and production-centered supervisors at the other. Sometimes, the more general terms *human-relations oriented* and *task oriented* are used to describe these alternative leader behaviors.

Ohio State Studies　At about the same time as the Michigan studies, an important leadership research program was started at the Ohio State University. A questionnaire was administered in both industrial and military settings to measure subordinates' perceptions of their superiors' leadership behavior. The researchers identified two dimensions similar to those found in the Michigan studies: **consideration** and **initiating structure**.[10] A highly considerate leader is sensitive to people's feelings and, much like the employee-centered leader, tries to make things pleasant for his or her followers. In contrast, a leader high in initiating structure is more concerned with defining task requirements and other aspects of the work agenda; he or she might be seen as similar to a production-centered supervisor. These dimensions are related to what people sometimes refer to as socioemotional and task leadership, respectively.

At first, the Ohio State researchers believed that a leader high in consideration, or socioemotional warmth, would have more highly satisfied or better-performing subordinates. Later results indicated that leaders should be high in both consideration and initiating structure, however. This dual emphasis is reflected in the leadership grid approach.[11]

■ A leader high in **consideration** is sensitive to people's feelings and tries to make things pleasant for the followers.

■ A leader high in **initiating structure** is concerned with spelling out the task requirements and clarifying other aspects of the work agenda.

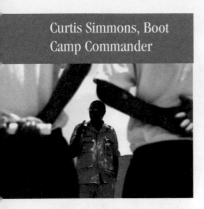

Boot camp commandant Curtis Simmons has the only boot camp among 14 youth commission facilities, or reform schools, in Texas. The camp does the same thing as other youth facilities but has a military stress to it. On this day he has just announced that he is getting two Play Stations. "We're going to play Madden," says Simmons. To play, cadets will have to remain in good standing. For Simmons the military-style program is designed to teach resocialization, not rehabilitation. "If you come from a neighborhood where everybody steals cars, and you don't steal cars, you're the crazy one, according to Simmons. If you are rehabilitated, you steal cars."

■■■ **Leadership grid** is an approach that uses a nine-position grid that places concern for production on the horizontal axis and concern for people on the vertical axis.

The Leadership Grid   Robert Blake and Jane Mouton have developed the leadership grid approach based on extensions of the Ohio State dimensions. **Ladership grid** results are plotted on a nine-position grid that places concern for production on the horizontal axis and concern for people on the vertical axis, where 1 is minimum concern and 9 is maximum concern. As an example, those with a 1/9 style—low concern for production and high concern for people—are termed "country club management." They do not emphasize task accomplishment but stress the attitudes, feelings, and social needs of people.

Similarly, leaders with a 1/1 style—low concern for both production and people—are termed "impoverished," while a 5/5 style is labeled "middle of the road." A 9/1 leader—high concern for production and low concern for people—has a "task management" style. Finally, a 9/9 leader, high on both dimensions, is considered to have a "team management" style, ideal in Blake and Mouton's framework.

Cross-Cultural Implications

It is important to consider how well the kinds of behavioral dimensions discussed earlier transfer internationally. Some work in the United States, Britain, Hong Kong, and Japan shows that the behaviors must be carried out in different ways in alternative cultures. For instance, British leaders are seen as considerate if they show subordinates how to use equipment, whereas in Japan the highly considerate leader helps subordinates with personal problems.[12]

Situational Contingency Leadership

The trait and behavioral perspectives assume that leadership, by itself, would have a strong impact on outcomes. Another development in leadership thinking has recognized, however, that leader traits and behaviors can act in conjunction with *situational contingencies*—other important aspects of the leadership situation—to predict outcomes.

House and Aditya argue that the effects of traits are enhanced by their relevance to the leader's situational contingencies.[13] For example, achievement motivation should be most effective for challenging tasks that require initiative and the assumption of personal responsibility for success. Leader flexibility should be most predictive in unstable environments or when leaders lead different people over time. Prosocial power motivation is likely to be most important in complex organizations where decision implementation requires lots of persuasion and social influence. "Strong" or "weak" situations also make a difference. An example of a strong situation is a highly formal organization with lots of rules, procedures, and so forth. Here, traits will have less impact than in a weaker, more unstructured situation (e.g., I can't show my dynamism as much when the organization restricts me). Traits sometimes have a direct relationship to outcomes or to leaders versus nonleaders. They may also make themselves felt by influencing leader behaviors (e.g., a leader high in energy engages in directive, take-charge behaviors).[14]

Fiedler's Leadership Contingency Theory

Fred Fiedler's work began the situational contingency era in the mid-1960s.[15] His theory holds that group effectiveness depends on an appropriate match between a leader's style (essentially a trait measure) and the demands of the situation. Specifically, Fiedler considers **situational control**—the extent to which a leader can determine what his or her group is going to do as well as the outcomes of the group's actions and decisions.

Fiedler uses an instrument called the **least preferred co-worker (LPC) scale** to measure a person's leadership style. Respondents are asked to describe the person with whom they have been able to work least well—their least preferred co-worker, or LPC—using a series of adjectives such as the following two:

Unfriendly ___ ___ ___ ___ ___ ___ ___ ___ Friendly
          1   2   3   4   5   6   7   8

Pleasant ___ ___ ___ ___ ___ ___ ___ ___ Unpleasant
          1   2   3   4   5   6   7   8

Fiedler argues that high-LPC leaders (those describing their LPC very positively) have a relationship-motivated style, whereas low-LPC leaders have a task-motivated style. He considers this task or relationship motivation to be a trait that leads to either directive or nondirective behavior, depending on the amount of situational control that the leader has. Here, a task-motivated leader tends to be nondirective in high- and low-control situations and directive in those in between. A relationship-motivated leader tends to be the opposite.

Figure 11.2 shows the task-motivated leader as having greater group effectiveness under high and low situational control and the relationship motivated leader as having a more effective group in those in-between situations. The figure also shows that Fiedler measures the range of control with the following three variables arranged in the situational combinations indicated:

- *Leader-member relations* (good/poor)—membership support for the leader
- *Task structure* (high/low)—spelling out the leader's task goals, procedures, and guidelines in the group
- *Position power* (strong/weak)—the leader's task expertise and reward or punishment authority

Consider an experienced and well-trained supervisor of a group manufacturing a part for a personal computer. The leader is highly supported by his group members and can grant raises and make hiring and firing decisions. This supervisor has very high situational control and is operating in situation 1 in Figure 11.2. Those leaders operating in situations 2 and 3 would have high situational control, though lower than our production supervisor. For these high-control situations a task-oriented leader behaving directively would have the most effective group.

Now consider the chair of a student council committee of volunteers (the chair's position power is weak) who are unhappy about this person being the chair and who have the low-structured task of organizing a Parents' Day program to improve university-parent relations. This low-control situation 8 calls for a task-motivated leader who needs to behave directively to keep the group together and focus on the ambiguous task; in fact, the situation demands it.

■ **Situational control** is the extent to which leaders can determine what their groups are going to do and what the outcomes of their actions and decisions are going to be.

■ The **least-preferred co-worker (LPC) scale** is a measure of a person's leadership style based on a description of the person with whom respondents have been able to work least well.

Fiedler's three situational control variables

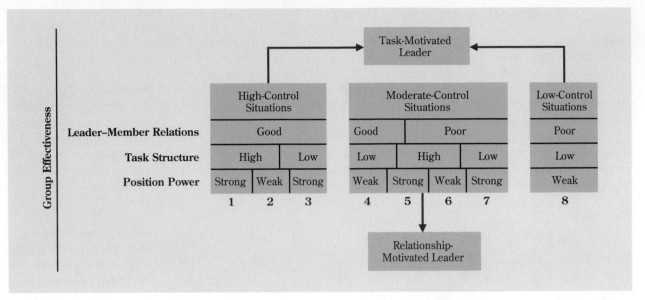

Figure 11.2   Summary of Fiedler's situational variables and their preferred leadership styles.

Finally, consider a well-liked academic department chair with tenured faculty. This is a situation 4 moderate-control situation with good leader-member relations, low task structure, and weak position power, calling for a relationship-motivated leader. The leader should emphasize nondirective and considerate relationships with the faculty.

Fiedler's Cognitive Resource Theory   Fiedler eventually moved beyond his contingency theory by developing a cognitive resource theory.[16] Cognitive resources are abilities or competencies. According to this approach, whether a leader should use directive or nondirective behavior depends on the following situational contingencies: (1) the leader's or subordinate group members' ability or competency, (2) stress, (3) experience, and (4) group support of the leader. Basically, cognitive resource theory is most useful because it directs us to leader or subordinate group-member ability, an aspect not typically considered in other leadership approaches.

The theory views directiveness as most helpful for performance when the leader is competent, relaxed, and supported. In this case, the group is ready, and directiveness is the clearest means of communication. When the leader feels stressed, he or she is diverted. In this case, experience is more important than ability. If support is low, then the group is less receptive, and the leader has less impact. Group-member ability becomes most important when the leader is nondirective and receives strong support from group members. If support is weak, then task difficulty or other factors have more impact than either the leader or the subordinates.

Evaluation and Application   The roots of Fiedler's contingency approach date back to the 1960s and have elicited both positive and negative reactions. The biggest controversy concerns exactly what Fiedler's LPC instrument measures.

Some question Fiedler's behavioral interpretation, whereby the specific behaviors of high- and low-LPC leaders change depending on the amount of situational control. Furthermore, the approach makes the most accurate predictions in situations 1 and 8 and 4 and 5; results are less consistent in the other situations.[17] Tests of cognitive resource theory have shown mixed results.[18]

In terms of application Fiedler has developed **leader match training**, which Sears, Roebuck and other organizations have used. Leaders are trained to diagnose the situation to match their high and low LPC scores with situational control, as measured by leader-member relations, task structure, and leader position power, following the general ideas shown in Figure 11.2. In cases with no match, the training shows how each of these situational control variables can be changed to obtain a match. Alternatively, another way of getting a match is through leader selection or placement based on LPC scores.[19] For example, a high-LPC leader would be selected for a position with high situational control, as in our earlier example of the manufacturing supervisor. As in the case of Fiedler's contingency theory, a number of studies have been designed to test leader match. Although they are not uniformly supportive, more than a dozen such tests have found increases in group effectiveness following the training.[20]

We conclude that although there are still unanswered questions concerning Fiedler's contingency theory, especially concerning the meaning of LPC, the theory and the leader match program have relatively strong support.[21] The approach and training program are also especially useful in encouraging situational contingency thinking.

House's Path-Goal Theory of Leadership

Another well-known approach to situational contingencies is one developed by Robert House based on the earlier work of others.[22] House's **path-goal theory of leadership** has its roots in the expectancy model of motivation discussed in Chapter 6. The term "path-goal" is used because of its emphasis on how a leader influences subordinates' perceptions of both work goals and personal goals, and the links, or paths, found between these two sets of goals.

The theory assumes that a leader's key function is to adjust his or her behaviors to complement situational contingencies, such as those found in the work setting. House argues that when the leader is able to compensate for things lacking in the setting, subordinates are likely to be satisfied with the leader. For example, the leader could help remove job ambiguity or show how good performance could lead to more pay. Performance should improve as the paths by which (1) effort leads to performance—expectancy—and (2) performance leads to valued rewards—instrumentality—become clarified.

House's approach is summarized in Figure 11.3. The figure shows four types of leader behavior (directive, supportive, achievement oriented, and participative) and two categories of situational contingency variables (subordinate attributes and work-setting attributes). The leader behaviors are adjusted to complement the situational contingency variables in order to influence subordinate satisfaction, acceptance of the leader, and motivation for task performance.

Directive leadership has to do with spelling out the what and how of subordinates' tasks; it is much like the initiating structure mentioned earlier. **Supportive leadership** focuses on subordinate needs and well-being and on

In leader match training, leaders are trained to diagnose the situation to match their high and low LPC scores with situational control.

Path-goal theory of leadership assumes that a leader's key function is to adjust his or her behaviors to complement situational contingencies.

Directive leadership spells out the what and how of subordinates' tasks.

Supportive leadership focuses on subordinate needs, well-being, and promotion of a friendly work climate.

Figure 11.3   Summary of major path-goal relationships in House's leadership approach.

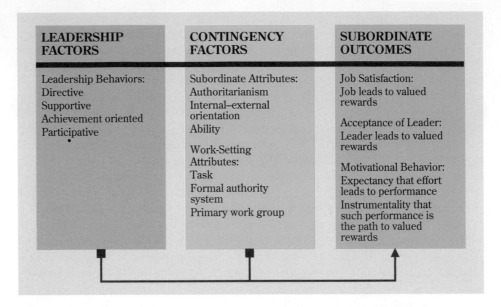

LEADERSHIP FACTORS	CONTINGENCY FACTORS	SUBORDINATE OUTCOMES
Leadership Behaviors: Directive Supportive Achievement oriented Participative	Subordinate Attributes: Authoritarianism Internal–external orientation Ability Work-Setting Attributes: Task Formal authority system Primary work group	Job Satisfaction: Job leads to valued rewards Acceptance of Leader: Leader leads to valued rewards Motivational Behavior: Expectancy that effort leads to performance Instrumentality that such performance is the path to valued rewards

▪ **Achievement-oriented leadership** emphasizes setting challenging goals, stressing excellence in performance, and showing confidence in people's ability to achieve high standards of performance.

▪ **Participative leadership** focuses on consulting with subordinates and seeking and taking their suggestions into account before making decisions.

promoting a friendly work climate; it is similar to consideration. **Achievement-oriented leadership** emphasizes setting challenging goals, stressing excellence in performance, and showing confidence in the group members' ability to achieve high standards of performance. **Participative leadership** focuses on consulting with subordinates, and seeking and taking their suggestions into account before making decisions.

Important subordinate characteristics are *authoritarianism* (close-mindedness, rigidity), *internal-external orientation* (i.e., locus of control), and *ability*. The key work-setting factors are the nature of the subordinates' tasks (task structure), the *formal authority system,* and the *primary workgroup*.

Predictions from Path-Goal Theory   Directive leadership is predicted to have a positive impact on subordinates when the task is ambiguous; it is predicted to have just the opposite effect for clear tasks. In addition, the theory predicts that when ambiguous tasks are being performed by highly authoritarian and close-minded subordinates, even more directive leadership is called for.

Supportive leadership is predicted to increase the satisfaction of subordinates who work on highly repetitive tasks or on tasks considered to be unpleasant, stressful, or frustrating; the leader's supportive behavior helps compensate for these adverse conditions. For example, many would consider traditional assembly-line auto worker jobs to be highly repetitive, perhaps even unpleasant and frustrating. A supportive supervisor could help make these jobs more pleasant. Achievement-oriented leadership is predicted to encourage subordinates to strive for higher performance standards and to have more confidence in their ability to meet challenging goals. For subordinates in ambiguous, nonrepetitive jobs, achievement-oriented leadership should increase their expectations that effort leads to desired performance.

Participative leadership is predicted to promote satisfaction on nonrepetitive tasks that allow for the ego involvement of subordinates. For example, on a challenging research project, participation allows employees to feel good about dealing with the challenge of the project on their own. On repetitive tasks, open-minded or nonauthoritarian subordinates will also be satisfied with a participative leader. On a task where employees screw nuts on bolts hour after hour, for example, those who are nonauthoritarian will appreciate having a leader who allows them to get involved in ways that may help break the monotony.

Evaluation and Application   House's path-goal approach has been with us for more than 30 years. Early work provided some support for the theory in general and for the particular predictions discussed earlier.[23] However, current assessments by well-known scholars have pointed out that many aspects have not been tested adequately, and there is very little recent research concerning the theory.[24] House himself a few years ago revised and extended path-goal theory into the theory of work-unit leadership. It's beyond our scope to discuss details of this new theory, but as a base the new theory expands the list of leader behaviors beyond those in path-goal theory, including aspects of both leadership theory and emerging perspectives leadership.[25] It remains to be seen how much research it will generate.

In terms of application there is enough support for the original path-goal theory to suggest two possibilities. First, training could be used to change leadership behavior to fit the situational contingencies. Second, the leader could be taught to diagnose the situation and to learn how to try to change the contingencies, as in leader match.

Hersey and Blanchard's Situational Leadership Theory

Like other situational contingency approaches, the **situational leadership model** developed by Paul Hersey and Kenneth Blanchard posits that there is no single best way to lead.[26] Hersey and Blanchard focus on the situational contingency of maturity, or "readiness," of followers, in particular. Readiness is the extent to which people have the ability and willingness to accomplish a specific task. Hersey and Blanchard argue that "situational" leadership requires adjusting the leader's emphasis on task behaviors—for instance, giving guidance and direction—and relationship behaviors—for example, providing socioemotional support—according to the readiness of followers to perform their tasks. Figure 11.4 identifies four leadership styles: delegating, participating, selling, and telling. Each emphasizes a different combination of task and relationship behaviors by the leader. The figure also suggests the following situational matches as the best choice of leadership style for followers at each of four readiness levels.

> A "telling" style (S1) is best for low follower readiness (R1). The direction provided by this style defines roles for people who are unable and unwilling to take responsibility themselves; it eliminates any insecurity about the task that must be done.
>
> A "selling" style (S2) is best for low-to-moderate follower readiness (R2). This style offers both task direction and support for people who are unable but willing to take task responsibility; it involves combining a directive approach with explanation and reinforcement in order to maintain enthusiasm.

Tailoring Education to the Child

Kathy Rollo is the principal of Murfee Elementary in Lubbock, Texas. She absolutely loves her job. "I know every child in the building and I really work hard to make sure I know what they need—what their strengths and weaknesses are," says Rollo. "I think our goal must be that we have to find whatever it takes to make every single child successful. There is no one-size-fits-all. Every child is different, and we have to figure out how that child learns and what that child needs to be successful, and do it," she argues. Others around her in the school system marvel at her dynamic leadership and the intensity of her interest in the students at her school.

■ **Situational leadership model** focuses on the situational contingency of maturity or "readiness" of followers.

Figure 11.4   Hersey and Blanchard model of situational leadership.

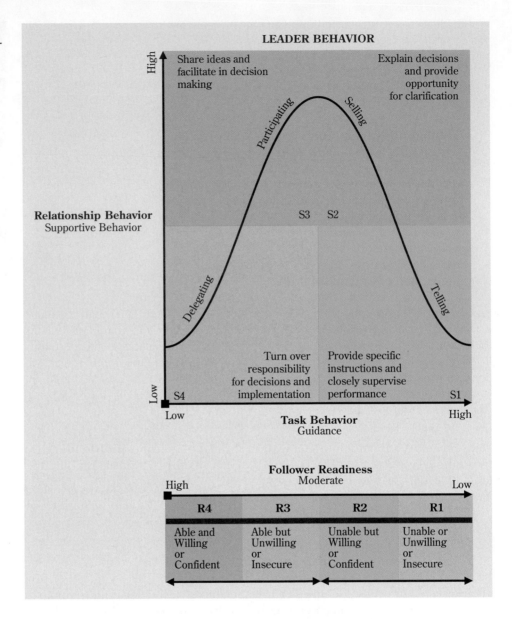

A *"participating" style (S3) is best for moderate-to-high follower readiness (R3)*. Able but unwilling followers require supportive behavior in order to increase their motivation; by allowing followers to share in decision making, this style helps enhance the desire to perform a task.

A *"delegating" style (S4) is best for high readiness (R4)*. This style provides little in terms of direction and support for the task at hand; it allows able and willing followers to take responsibility for what needs to be done.

This situational leadership approach requires the leader to develop the capability to diagnose the demands of situations and then to choose and implement the appropriate leadership response. The model gives specific attention to followers and their feelings about the task at hand and suggests that an effective leader focus especially on emerging changes in the level of readiness of the people involved in the work.

In spite of its considerable history and incorporation into training programs by a large number of firms, the situational leadership approach has received very little systematic research attention.[27]

Graen's Leader-Member Exchange Theory

Still another situational contingency perspective on which we focus is Graen's **leader-member exchange (LMX) theory**. This perspective emphasizes the quality of the working relationship between leaders and followers. An LMX scale assesses the degree to which leaders and followers have mutual respect for one another's capabilities, feel a deepening sense of mutual trust, and have a strong sense of obligation to one another. Taken together, these dimensions tend to influence the extent to which followers will be a part of the leader's "in-group" or "out-group".[28]

In-group followers tend to function as assistants, lieutenants, or advisers and to have higher-quality personalized exchanges with the leader than do out-group followers. The out-group followers tend to emphasize more formalized job requirements, and a relatively low level of mutual influence exists between leaders and out-group followers. The more personalized in-group exchanges typically involve a leader's emphasis on assignments to interesting tasks, delegation of important responsibilities, information sharing, and participation in the leader's decisions, as well as special benefits, such as personal support and approval and favorable work schedules.

Research suggests that high-quality LMX is associated with increased follower satisfaction and productivity, decreased turnover, increased salaries, and faster promotion rates. These findings are encouraging, and the approach continues to receive increasing emphasis in the literature, including work in Japan. Of course,

▪ **Leader-member exchange (LMX) theory** emphasizes the quality of the working relationship between leaders and followers.

MASTERING MANGEMENT

BUILDING HIGH-QUALITY EXCHANGE RELATIONSHIPS WITH EMPLOYEES

As we have argued in this chapter, the better your leader-member exchange relationship with your followers, the better for both of you in terms of possible employee satisfaction, productivity, decreased turnover, and faster promotion. Here are some tips to help.

- Meet separately with your employees in a testing phase to help each of you evaluate each other's motives, attitudes, and potential resources to be exchanged, and establish mutual role expectations.
- For those where the test meeting is most promising, work toward refining the original exchange relationship and developing mutual trust, loyalty, and respect for these "in-group" members.
- Some of these relationships will advance to a third ("mature") stage where exchange based on self-interest is transformed into mutual commitment to the vision, mission, and objectives of the work unit.
- Reward these second and third stage "in-group members" with greater status, influence, and benefits in return for extra attention from them, and remain responsive to their needs with strong reliance on persuasion and consultation.
- Follow up with day-to-day observations and discussions and work toward increasing the number of in-group members.[29A]

many questions remain, such as: What happens in the event of too much disparity in the treatment of in-group and out-group members? Will out-group members become resentful and sabotage team efforts? In addition, more needs to be learned about how the in-group/out-group exchange starts in the first place and how these relations change over time.[29]

Substitutes for Leadership Theory

A final situational contingency approach which we examine is leadership substitutes.[30] Scholars using it have developed a perspective that sometimes hierarchical leadership makes essentially no difference. These researchers contend that certain individual, job, and organization variables can serve as substitutes for leadership or neutralize a leader's impact on subordinates. Some examples of these variables are shown in Figure 11.5.

■■ **Substitutes for leadership** make a leader's influence either unnecessary or redundant in that they replace a leader's influence.

Substitutes for leadership make a leader's influence either unnecessary or redundant in that they replace a leader's influence. For example, in Figure 11.5 it will be unnecessary and perhaps not even possible for a leader to provide the kind of task-oriented direction already available from an experienced, talented, and well-trained subordinate. In contrast, neutralizers prevent a leader from behaving in a certain way or nullify the effects of a leader's actions. If a leader has little formal authority or is physically separated, for example, his or her leadership may be nullified even though task supportiveness may still be needed.

Figure 11.5   Some examples of leadership substitutes and neutralizers.

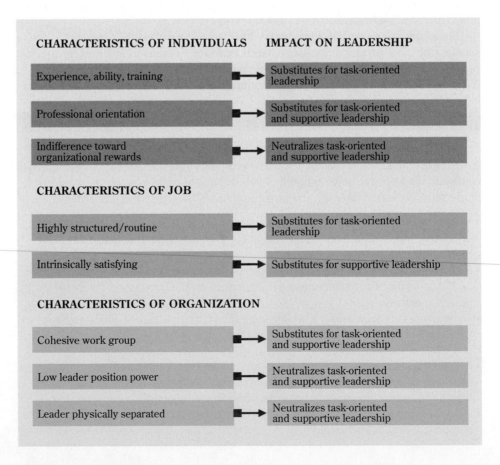

CHARACTERISTICS OF INDIVIDUALS   IMPACT ON LEADERSHIP

Experience, ability, training	→	Substitutes for task-oriented leadership
Professional orientation	→	Substitutes for task-oriented and supportive leadership
Indifference toward organizational rewards	→	Neutralizes task-oriented and supportive leadership

CHARACTERISTICS OF JOB

| Highly structured/routine | → | Substitutes for task-oriented leadership |
| Intrinsically satisfying | → | Substitutes for supportive leadership |

CHARACTERISTICS OF ORGANIZATION

Cohesive work group	→	Substitutes for task-oriented and supportive leadership
Low leader position power	→	Neutralizes task-oriented and supportive leadership
Leader physically separated	→	Neutralizes task-oriented and supportive leadership

Some research comparing Mexican and U.S. workers, as well as workers in Japan, suggests both similarities and differences between various substitutes in the countries examined. More generally, a review of 17 studies in the United States as well as other countries found mixed results for the substitutes theory. Among other things, the authors argued that the kinds of characteristics and leader behaviors should be broadened and that the approach appeared to be especially important for self-directed work teams.[31] With regard to these work teams, for example, in place of a hierarchical leader specifying standards and ways of achieving goals (task-oriented behaviors), the team might set its own standards and substitute those for the leader's.

A related perspective has been argued by Jeffrey Pfeffer, who looked at what happened when leaders at the top of the organization were changed. Pfeffer is among those contending that even CEOs of large corporations have little leadership impact on profits and effectiveness compared to environmental and industry forces, such as cutbacks in the federal defense budget. Pfeffer goes even further by arguing that these leaders are typically accountable to so many groups of people for the resources they use that their leadership impact is greatly constrained. Pfeffer contends that in light of such forces and constraints (similar in many respects to leadership substitutes), much of the impact a top leader does have is little more than symbolic; leaders and others develop explanations to legitimize the actions they take.[32]

Such symbolic treatment of leadership occurs particularly when performance is either extremely high or extremely low or when the situation is such that many people could have been responsible for the performance. The late James Meindl and his colleagues call this phenomenon the **romance of leadership**, whereby people attribute romantic, almost magical, qualities to leadership.[33] Consider the firing of a baseball manager or football coach whose team does not perform well. Neither the owner nor anyone else is really sure why this occurred. But the owner can't fire all the players, so a new team manager is brought in to symbolize "a change in leadership" that is "sure to turn the team around."

Romance of leadership is where people attribute romantic, almost magical, qualities to leadership.

Implicit Leadership

It is but a small step to move from the symbolic leadership extension of leadership substitutes to implicit leadership. In the mid 1970's a couple of researchers argued that "leadership factors are in the mind of the respondent. It remains to be established whether or not they are more than that."[34] This general notion is described here in two forms. The first one is labeled *leadership as attribution* and the second is termed *leadership prototypes*.

Leadership as Attribution

Recall from Chapter 4 that attribution theory focuses on people trying to understand causes, assess responsibilities, and to evaluate personal qualities, as all of these are involved with certain events. Attribution theory is particularly important in understanding leadership.

For openers, think about a work group or student group that you see as performing really well. Now assume that you are asked to describe the leader on one of the leadership scales discussed earlier in the chapter. If you are like many others, the group's high performance probably encouraged you to describe the leader favorably; in other words you attributed good things to the leader based on the group's performance. Similarly, recall that leaders themselves make attributions about subordinate performance and react differently depending on those attributions. For example, if leaders attribute an employee's poor performance to lack of effort, they may issue a reprimand, whereas if they attribute the poor performance to an external factor, such as work overload, they will probably try to fix the problem. A great deal of evidence supports these attributional views of subordinates and leaders.[35]

The above subordinate attributions concerning leadership have led some researchers to develop an **inference-based** attribution model that emphasizes leadership effectiveness as inferred by followers based on perceived group or organizational performance outcomes.[36] In other words, if the group or organization is performing well, they tend to attribute good leadership to the person in charge. If not, they attribute poor leadership to the person.

■■ Inference-based emphasizes leadership effectiveness as inferred by perceived group/ organizational performance outcomes.

Leadership Prototypes

Leadership prototypes are the second form of leadership considered to be in the mind of the beholder. Here, research argues that people have a mental image of the characteristics that make a "good" leader or that a "real" leader would possess to be considered effective in a given situation. Leadership prototypes are an alternative way to the inference-based approach to assess leadership and are termed *recognition based* (you know one when you see his or her characteristics profile). Though alternatives, sometimes the inference and recognition based views work together.[37]

■■ Recognition-based is leadership effectiveness based on how well a person fits characteristics of a good or effective leader.

These **recognition-based** prototypes usually consist of a mix of specific and more general characteristics. For example, a prototype of a bank president would differ in many ways from that of a high-ranking military officer. However, you could expect some core characteristics reflecting leaders in our society in general—for example, integrity and self efficacy.[38]

You also would expect differences in prototypes by country and by national culture. An early, small-scale study contrasted typical business leader prototypes between Japan and the United States.[39]

- Japan: responsible, educated, trustworthy, intelligent, disciplined
- United States: determined, goal oriented, verbally skilled, industrious, persistent.

More in-depth insights on such prototypes, as related to culture, are provided by the broad-scale Project GLOBE study to be discussed in the integrative approaches emphasized in Chapter 12. Additionally, an interesting twist to prototypes and culture is provided by a recent conceptual study.[40] This view argues in research, such as that by Hofstede discussed earlier, that the basic national culture dimensions reflected in the various societies may influence the likelihood of people in various countries tending to emphasize either the recognition-based or the inference-based approach in perceiving effective leaders.

In one example, from the Hofstede dimensions used by the above study, it is argued that the less power-distant the culture, the more the subordinates or followers will emphasize an inference-based process to perceive leadership. The reasoning is that in low-power-distance societies, the relative equality means that people tend to be perceptive concerning who is responsible for job outcomes and are comfortable inferring leadership from that person.

Along with predicted cultural influence toward inference- or recognition-based emphases, an important question is the across-time stability within groups of the dimensions identified in recognition-based inferences or leadership prototypes. In one study it was found that the dimensions were reasonably stable across different kinds of groups. However, across time, the dimensions changed toward more sensitivity, intelligence, dedication, and dynamism and less tyranny and masculinity. The researchers argue that in-depth understanding of effective leadership necessitates training approaches sensitive to what we have called implicit leadership or leadership prototypes.[41]

Inspirational Leadership Perspectives

The focus on leadership attributions and symbolic aspects moves us away from earlier views on leadership and into more inspirational charismatic and transformational leadership approaches and various aspects of vision related to them.

Charismatic Leadership

Robert House and his associates have done a lot of work based on extensions of an earlier charismatic theory House developed (not to be confused with House's path-goal theory or its extension discussed earlier in the chapter).[42] Of special interest is the fact that House's theory uses both trait and behavior combinations.

House's **charismatic leaders** are leaders who, by force of their personal abilities, are capable of having a profound and extraordinary effect on followers. These leaders are high in need for power and have high feelings of self-efficacy and conviction in the moral rightness of their beliefs. That is, the need for power motivates these people to want to be leaders. This need is then reinforced by their conviction of the moral rightness of their beliefs. The feeling of self-efficacy, in turn, makes these people believe they are capable of being leaders. These traits then influence such charismatic behaviors as role modeling, image building, articulating goals (focusing on simple and dramatic goals), emphasizing high expectations, showing confidence, and arousing follower motives.

Some of the more interesting and important work based on aspects of House's charismatic theory involves a study of U.S. presidents.[43] The research showed that behavioral charisma was substantially related to presidential performance and that the kind of personality traits described in House's theory, along with response to crisis among other things, predicted behavioral charisma for the sample of presidents. Related work by others also shows that voters who saw Bill Clinton as charismatic followed through by voting for him.[44] Finally, the Research Insight shows presidential use of metaphors enhances perceptions of charisma.

House and his colleagues summarize other work that partially supports the theory. Some of the more interesting related work has shown that negative, or "dark-side," charismatic leaders emphasize personalized power—focus on themselves—whereas positive, or "bright-side," charismatics emphasize socialized

Charismatic leaders are those leaders who, by force of their personal abilities, are capable of having a profound and extraordinary effect on followers.

power that tends to empower their followers. This helps explain differences between such dark-side leaders as Adolf Hitler and David Koresh, and a bright-side leader such as Martin Luther King Jr.[45]

Jay Conger and Rabindra Kanungo have developed a three-stage charismatic leadership model.[46] In the initial stage the leader critically evaluates the status quo. Deficiencies in the status quo lead to formulations of future goals. Before developing these goals the leader assesses available resources and constraints that stand in the way of the goals. The leader also assesses follower abilities, needs, and satisfaction levels. In the second stage the leader formulates and articulates the goals along with an idealized future vision. Here, the leader emphasizes articulation and impression-management skills. Then, in the third stage, the leader shows how these goals and the vision can be achieved. The leader emphasizes innovative and unusual means to achieve the vision. Martin Luther King Jr. illustrated these three stages in his nonviolent civil rights approach, thereby changing race relations in this country.

Conger and Kanungo have argued that if leaders use behaviors such as vision articulation, environmental sensitivity, and unconventional behavior, rather than maintaining the status quo, followers will tend to attribute charismatic leadership to them. Such leaders are also seen as behaving quite differently from those labeled "noncharismatic."[47]

Finally, an especially important question about charismatic leadership is whether it is described in the same way for close-up or at-a-distance leaders. Boas Shamir examined this issue in Israel.[48] He found that descriptions of distant charismatics (e.g., former Israeli prime minister Golda Meir) and close-up charismatics (e.g., a specific teacher) were generally more different than they were similar. Figure 11.6 shows the high points of his findings. Clearly, leaders with whom followers have close contact and those with whom they seldom, if ever, have direct contact are both described as charismatic but possess quite different traits and behaviors.

Transformational and Transactional Leadership

Building on notions originated by James MacGregor Burns, as well as on ideas from House's work, Bernard Bass has developed an approach that focuses on both transformational and transactional leadership.[49]

■ **Transactional leadership** involves leader-follower exchanges necessary for achieving routine performance agreed upon between leaders and followers.

Transactional leadership involves leader-follower exchanges necessary for achieving routine performance agreed upon between leaders and followers. These exchanges involve four dimensions:

(1) *Contingent rewards*—various kinds of rewards in exchange for mutually agreed-upon goal accomplishment;

(2) *Active management by exception*—watching for deviations from rules and standards and taking corrective action;

(3) *Passive management by exception*—intervening only if standards not met; and

(4) Laissez-faire—abdicating responsibilities and avoiding decisions.

■ **Transformational leadership** occurs when leaders broaden and elevate followers' interests and stir followers to look beyond their own interests to the good of others.

Transformational leadership goes beyond this routine accomplishment, however. For Bass, **transformational leadership** occurs when leaders broaden and elevate their followers' interests, when they generate awareness and acceptance of the group's purposes and mission, and when they stir their followers to look beyond their own self-interests to the good of others.

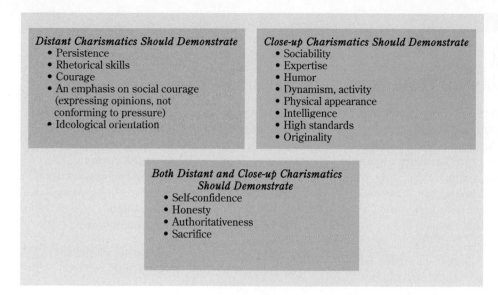

Dimensions of Transformational Leadership   Transformational leadership has four dimensions: *Charisma*, inspiration, intellectual stimulation, and individualized consideration. Charisma provides vision and a sense of mission, and it instills pride along with follower respect and trust. For example Steve Jobs, who founded Apple Computer, showed charisma by emphasizing the importance of creating the Macintosh as a radical new computer and has since followed up with products such as the iPod. Inspiration communicates high expectations, uses symbols to focus efforts, and expresses important purposes in simple ways. As an example, in the movie *Patton*, George C. Scott stood on a stage in front of his troops with a wall-sized American flag in the background and ivory-handled revolvers in holsters at his side. *Intellectual stimulation* promotes intelligence, rationality, and careful problem solving. For instance, your boss encourages you to look at a very difficult problem in a new way. *Individualized consideration* provides personal attention, treats each employee individually, and coaches and advises. For example, your boss drops by and makes remarks reinforcing your worth as a person.

Bass concludes that transformational leadership is likely to be strongest at the top-management level, where there is the greatest opportunity for proposing and communicating a vision. However, for him, it is not *restricted* to the top level; it is found throughout the organization. Furthermore, transformational leadership operates *in combination with* transactional leadership. Transactional leadership is similar to most of the leadership approaches mentioned earlier. Leaders need both transformational and transactional leadership in order to be successful, just as they need to display both leadership and management abilities.[50]

Evaluation and Application   Reviews have summarized a large number of studies using Bass's transformational approach. These reviews report significant favorable relationships between Bass's leadership dimensions and various aspects of performance and satisfaction, as well as extra effort, burnout and stress, and predispositions to act as innovation champions on the part of followers. The

Research Insight
Effects of Metaphor on Leadership and Charisma

This research examined the process by which charismatic leaders inspire and motivate followers. More specifically, the researchers examined the use of metaphors as a tool to clarify meaning, to inspire, and to provide motivation to followers. Speeches of United States presidents were used to provide metaphors suggesting how political leaders inspire their constituents at a distance.

The hypotheses were:

• Charismatic presidents – individuals who are articulate and who possess rhetorical skills – will use more metaphors than will non-charismatic presidents.

• Metaphoric use will be higher for inspiring passages of a speech than for the speech overall.

The researchers used thirty-six speeches from presidents who had given inaugural addresses. To control for length, the researchers divided the number of identified metaphors by the number of words in the speeches and termed these metaphor density scores. To investigate the second hypothe-sis, speech booklets were administered to students in two upper division political science courses. The students were asked to underline or highlight those passages they found to be the most inspiring. Each presidential speech was evaluated by between four and seven raters. The number of inspiring words indicated by the students was counted.

The findings for each hypothesis were:

	Overall Metaphor Density	Inspiring Passages Metaphor Density
Charismatics	.0059	.0112
Non-charismatics	.0030	.0059

The relationships for charismatics and non-charismatics are statistically significantly different from each other at the .05 or .01 level.

Based on the findings, it is concluded that charismatic presidents tend to use more metaphors than non-charismatics and that more inspiring passages tend to include higher metaphorical usage.[50A]

strongest relationships tend to be associated with charisma or inspirational leadership, although in most cases the other dimensions are also important. These findings are consistent with those reported elsewhere.[51] They broaden leadership outcomes beyond those cited in many leadership studies.

Charismatic and Transformational Leadership Issues

We now examine some charismatic and transformational leadership issues. First: *Can people be trained in charismatic/transformational leadership?* According to research in this area, the answer is yes. Bass and his colleagues have put a lot of work into such training efforts. For example, they have created a workshop where leaders are given initial feedback on their scores on Bass's measures. The leaders then devise improvement programs to strengthen their weaknesses and work with the trainers to develop their leadership skills. Bass as well as Bass and Avolio report findings that demonstrate the beneficial effects of this training. They also report the effectiveness of team training and programs tailored to individual firms' needs.[52] Similarly, Conger and Kanungo propose training to develop the kinds of behaviors summarized in their model, as suggested in OB Savvy 11.1.[53]

Leaders on Leadership

A LEADER OUT OF NOWHERE

Oksana Parylo, a second-year Ukrainian graduate student, is the first international student president of the Student Alumni Council (SAC) of the Southern Illinois University Alumni Asso-

ciation. However, her winning the election came as a surprise. She was not the most vocal organization member. Her quietness didn't seem to make her suitable for a leadership role. She was active in various activities, but she was very quiet.

However, when she gave her campaign speech, her audience was speechless—she was clearly a leader-in-waiting. In making the decision to run, she assumed that as an international student she might have communication problems. However, she did remember serving in similar leadership positions in her homeland. She recognized that the United States was a different country and culture, but she concluded that leadership skills could be used anywhere.

International students comprise 20 percent of SAC's composition. She says she was comfortable in SAC right away. "It was a great atmosphere." She had a smooth process in adjusting to the United States, to SAC, and to the university.

She has outlined goals for SAC as part of her presidency. A key goal is increasing membership. She also wants to enhance SAC's Web site. She plans to continue to build on SAC's Homecoming celebration efforts and generally to enhance SAC's visibility. She also plans to try to strengthen SAC's welcoming environment, which is already quite strong. She is "striving to uphold the standards that have been established before me."[51A]

Question: How is it that a quiet person such as Parylo can impress people enough to move into an important leadership role such as the one to which she has been elected?

Approaches with special emphasis on vision often emphasize training. Kouzas and Posner report results of a week-long training program at AT&T. The program involved training leaders on five dimensions oriented around developing, communicating, and reinforcing a shared vision. According to Kouzas and Posner, leaders showed an average 15 percent increase in these visionary behaviors 10 months after participating in the program.[54] Similarly, Sashkin and Sashkin have developed a leadership approach that emphasizes various aspects of vision and organizational culture change. They discuss a number of ways to train leaders to be more visionary and to enhance culture change.[55] All of these leadership training programs involve a heavy hands-on workshop emphasis so that leaders do more than just read about vision.

A second issue involves this question: *is charismatic/ transformational leadership always good?* As pointed out earlier, dark-side charismatics, such as Adolf Hitler, can have negative effects on followers. Similarly, charismatic/transformational

OB SAVVY 11.1

Emphasizing Your Charismatic Leadership Skills

- *Be sensitive to the most appropriate contexts for charisma*—Emphasize critical evaluation and problem detection.
- *Vision*—Use creative thinking to learn and think about profound change.
- *Communication*—Use oral and written linguistic aspects.
- *Impression management*—Use modeling, appearance, body language, and verbal skills.
- *Empowering*—Communicate high-performance expectations, improve decision-making participation, loosen up bureaucratic constraints, set meaningful goals, and establish appropriate reward systems.[55A]

leadership is not always helpful. Sometimes emphasis on a vision diverts energy from more important day-to-day activities. It is also important to note that such leadership by itself is not sufficient. That leadership needs to be used in conjunction with the leadership theories in this chapter. Finally, charismatic/transformational leadership is important not only at the top. A number of experts argue that it applies at all levels of organizational leadership.

Chapter 11   Study Guide

Summary

What are leadership foundations?

- Leadership is the process of influencing others to understand and agree about what needs to be done and how to do it, and the process of facilitating individual and collective efforts to accomplish shared objectives.

- Leadership and management differ in that management is designed to promote stability or to make the organization run smoothly, whereas the role of leadership is to promote adaptive change.

- Trait or great-person approaches argue that leader traits have a major impact on differentiating between leaders and nonleaders or predicting leadership outcomes.

- Traits are considered relatively innate and hard to change.

- Similar to trait approaches, behavioral theories argue that leader behaviors have a major impact on outcomes.

- The Michigan and Ohio State approaches are particularly important leader behavior theories.

- Leader behavior theories are especially suitable for leadership training.

What are situational contingency approaches to leadership?

- Leader situational contingency approaches argue that leadership, in combination with various situational contingency variables, can have a major impact on outcomes.
- The effects of traits are enhanced to the extent of their relevance to the situational contingencies faced by the leader.
- Strong or weak situational contingencies influence the impact of leadership traits.
- Fiedler's contingency theory, House's path-goal theory, Hersey and Blanchard's situational leadership theory, Graen's leader-member exchange theory, and Kerr and Jermier's substitutes for leadership theory are particularly important specific situational contingency approaches.
- Sometimes, as in the case of the substitutes for leadership approach, the role of situational contingencies replaces that of leadership, so that leadership has little or no impact in itself.

What are implicit leadership approaches to leadership?

- Attribution theory extends traditional leadership approaches by recognizing that substantive effects cannot always be objectively identified and measured.
- Leaders form attributions about why their employees perform well or poorly and respond accordingly as do employees concerning leaders.
- Leaders and followers often infer that there is good leadership when their group performs well. This is an inferential perspective.
- Leaders and followers often have in mind a good leader prototype; compare the leader against such a prototype; and conclude that the closer the fit, the better the leadership. This is a representational perspective.
- Some contend that leadership makes no real difference and is largely symbolic; others, following the "romance of leadership" notion, embrace this symbolic emphasis and attribute almost magical qualities to leadership.

What are inspirational perspectives to leadership?

- Charismatic and transformational leadership helps move followers to achieve goals that transcend their own self-interests and help transform the organization.
- Particularly important among such approaches are Bass's transformational theory and House's and Conger and Kanungo's charismatic perspectives.
- Transformational approaches are broader than charismatic ones and sometimes include charisma as one of their dimensions.
- Transformational/charismatic leadership, in general, are important because they go beyond traditional leadership in facilitating change in the increasingly fast-moving workplace.
- In terms of charismatic/transformational leadership training, Bass and his colleagues, Conger and Kanungo, and Kouzos and Posner, among others, have developed such training programs.
- Charismatic/transformational leadership are not always good, as shown by the example of Adolf Hitler.
- Charismatic/transformational leadership are not always helpful since even if good, they may divert energy away from other kinds of leadership.
- Charismatic/transformational leadership are important throughout the organization, as well as the top.

Key Terms

Achievement-oriented
  leadership (p. 250)
Behavioral perspective
  (p. 244)
Charismatic leaders
  (p. 257)
Consideration (p. 245)
Directive leadership
  (p. 249)
Inference-based (p. 256)
Initiating structure (p. 245)
Leader match training
  (p. 249)

Leader-member exchange
  (LMX) theory (p. 253)
Leadership (p. 243)
Leadership grid (p. 246)
Least-preferred co-worker
  (LPC) scale (p. 247)
Participative leadership
  (p. 250)
Path-goal theory of
  leadership (p. 249)
Recognition-based (p. 256)
Romance of leadership
  (p. 255)

Situational control (p. 247)
Situational leadership
  model (p. 251)
Substitutes for leadership
  (p. 254)
Supportive leadership
  (p. 249)
Trait perspectives (p. 243)
Transactional leadership
  (p. 258)
Transformational leadership
  (p. 258)

Self-Test 11

Multiple Choice

1. "Leadership is central, and other variables are less important" best describes
   _____ theories. (a) trait and behavioral (b) attribution (c) situational contingency (d) substitutes for leadership

2. Leader trait and behavioral approaches assume that traits and behaviors are
   _____. (a) equally important with other variables (b) more important than
   other variables (c) caused by other variables (d) symbolic of leadership

3. In comparing leadership and management, _____. (a) leadership promotes
   stability and management promotes change (b) leadership promotes change and
   management promotes stability (c) leaders are born but managers are developed
   (d) the two are pretty much the same

4. The earliest theory of leadership stated that individuals become leaders because of
   _____. (a) the behavior of those they lead (b) the traits they possess (c) the
   particular situation in which they find themselves (d) being very tall

5. Which leadership theory argues that a leader's key function is to act in ways that
   complement the work setting? _____ (a) trait (b) behavioral (c) path-goal
   (d) multiple influence

6. A leadership prototype _____. (a) is useful primarily for selection and training (b) uses LPC as an important component (c) depicts the image of a model leader
   (d) emphasizes leadership development

7. Conger and Kanungo's model emphasizes all of the following except _____.
   (a) active management by exception (b) vision articulation (c) environmental sensitivity (d) unconventional behavior

8. For situational leadership theory, _____. (a) management is substituted for
   leadership (b) position power is very important (c) there is considerable empirical
   support (d) maturity or readiness of followers is emphasized

9. Transformational leadership _____. (a) is similar to transactional leadership
   (b) is particularly useful in combination with transactional leadership (c) is not related to charismatic leadership (d) has been studied for more than 100 years

10. In terms of the importance of leadership, it has been argued that _____.
    (a) leadership makes little or no difference (b) only charismatic leadership is impor-
    tant (c) charismatic leadership is more important than transformational leadership
    (d) leadership is important only in a situational contingencies context

11. In the romance of leadership, _____. (a) supervisors are encouraged to lead
    each other to the alter (b) leaders are encouraged to marry each other (c) leaders are
    given credit for difficult-to-explain happenings (d) leadership substitutes for tradi-
    tional romantic actions

12. Attributional theory _____. (a) is one important leadership direction (b) is
    no longer popular in studying leadership (c) helps explain Fiedler's model (d) helps
    explain situational leadership

13. Close-up and at-a-distance charismatic leaders _____. (a) use the same be-
    haviors (b) exhibit a number of different behaviors (c) are hard to distinguish
    (d) have similar impacts on individual performance

14. In terms of charismatic or transformational leadership, _____. (a) people
    can be trained (b) these characteristics are inborn (c) neither is as important as trans-
    actional leadership (d) both tend to become managerial in orientation

15. Leadership traits _____. (a) are largely passé (b) are excellent substitutes for
    behaviors (c) are now being combined with behaviors (d) are too rigid to be used in
    analyzing leadership

Short Response

16. Define "leadership" and contrast it with "management."
17. Discuss the role of leader trait and behavior approaches in leadership.
18. Discuss the role of situational contingency approaches in leadership.
19. Discuss implicit theories and leadership prototype.

Applications Essay

20. You have just been called in by your boss to respond to a point mentioned on televi-
    sion that leadership is not real and is only a figment of peoples' imaginations. Prepare
    a report for your boss analyzing this argument and what might be done about it.

These learning activities from *The OB Skills Workbook* are suggested for Chapter 11.

OB in Action

CASE	EXPERIENTIAL EXERCISES	SELF-ASSESSMENTS
■ 11. The new Vice President	■ 25. Interview a Leader ■ 26. Leadership Skills Inventories ■ 27. Leadership and Participation in Decision Making	■ 10. Least Preferred Co-Worker Scale ■ 11. Leadership Style ■ 12. "TT" Leadership Style

Plus—special learning experiences from *The Jossey-Bass/Pfeiffer Classroom Collection*

Chapter 12

Emerging Leadership Perspectives

Chapter at a Glance

In Chapter 11, we covered Contemporary Leadership Approaches. In this chapter we cover Emerging Leadership Perspectives. Some of these are quite new. Others are recent extensions of contemporary approaches. Together, though, these emerging perspectives capture work that is still in the relatively early stages of development, regardless of its linkage to contemporary approaches, which may or may not have been around for awhile. As you read Chapter 12, *keep in mind these study topics.*

INTEGRATIVE LEADERSHIP

Full-Range Leadership Theory (FRLT)

Shared Leadership

Cross-Cultural Leadership: Project GLOBE

Strategic Leadership

MORAL LEADERSHIP

Ethical Leadership

Authentic Leadership

Servant Leadership

Spiritual Leadership

CHANGE LEADERSHIP

Leaders as Change Agents

Phases of Planned Change

Planned Change Strategies

Resistance to Change

CHAPTER 12 STUDY GUIDE

Great leaders walk the talk

William L. Lennox Jr. is a lieutenant general and the superintendent of the U.S. Military Academy at West Point in New York. He was commissioned as a lieutenant in 1971 and has served in a wide variety of field assignments and staff positions. In addition to his West Point bachelor's degree, he has a master's and PhD from Princeton.

He is both the commanding officer of West Point and its president. He considers himself to be more of a symbol than a commander of people or a place. West Point symbolizes duty, honor, country, and his constituents have great expectations and let him know if they think it is moving away from these high standards. He takes very seriously the realization that he has to produce Army lieutenants who are capable of combat and of leading units immediately, and at the same time he must produce strategic leaders for the Army who will be needed 20 or 30 years in the future.

He evaluates the Academy's performance through cadet grades and performance in different areas; by surveying battalion commanders and junior officers of the newly commissioned officers; and by looking at such things as promotion rates, retention rates, and who is selected for command. He sees the biggest challenges as the immediate and long-term development of skills that will continue to change dramatically from those formerly needed. In addition, having strong values is more important than ever. When asked about a tradition of excellence and the criticism of elitism, he argues that excellence is the hallmark, and graduates ought to be able to succeed and do well on their own.

Without using the term, General Lennox believes in contingency leadership—different behaviors for different situations. He also believes the most important advice for senior executives is to think long term and prepare the next generation. As he says: "Skills and abilities change to meet new demands, but the values you develop in your youth will shape your entire life."[1]

> "Skills and abilities change to meet new demands, but the values you develop in your youth will shape your entire life."

Integrative Leadership

We start our discussion of these emerging leadership perspectives with integrative leadership. We call this integrative because of the broad scope of perspectives treated and the way they tie together. These approaches range from full-range leadership theory, which involves nine dimensions covering both transformational and transactional leadership, to shared leadership, cross-cultural leadership, and, finally, strategic leadership.

Full-Range Leadership Theory (FRLT)

Beyond the generally promising results of transformational leadership theory cited in Chapter 11 and some attempts to consider it along with transactional leadership, has been an attempt to systematically extend the approach into what is called **full-range leadership theory** or (FRLT).[2] Some consider this an approach that ultimately could serve as a general leadership model that would reduce or eliminate the numerous models now emphasized. The theory currently consists of nine factors: five transformational, three transactional, and one nontransactional factor. The five transformational dimensions are slight revisions of the four factors mentioned in Chapter 11. The charismatic dimension has been divided into socialized charisma–labeled "idealized influence (attributed)" and "idealized influence (behavior)," respectively.

The transactional leadership dimensions are the ones we earlier treated. However, laissez-faire is dealt with as a nonleadership dimension. In other words, there are transformational, transactional, and nontransactional laissez-faire components to the model.

The approach is built around revisions to Bass's Multifactor Leadership Questionnaire. It is designed to recognize what are called **contextual variables** that link observations to a set of relevant facts, events, or points of view, such as organizational characteristics, work functions, external environment factors, and demographic variables. So far, environmental risk, leader hierarchical level, and leader-follower gender have received some consideration.

Current empirical work is quite promising and suggests that the FRLT can serve as a baseline for pointing out the systematic treatment of context on leadership and vice versa. Such results can help drive future leadership development approaches, among other things.

Shared Leadership

Our previous treatment of leadership, mirroring the theories discussed, has tended to treat it as vertical influence. The white-hatted rider on a white horse is contacted, comes into town, saves the day, and says: "My work here is done."

More and more, however, those concerned with leadership are seeing it as *not* being restricted to the vertical influence of the lone figure in a white hat. Leadership is not restricted simply to the vertical influence of a single individual but extends to other people as well.

One name for this alternative conception is the label "shared leadership." **Shared leadership** is defined as a dynamic, interactive influence process among individuals in groups for which the objective is to lead one another to the achievement of group or organizational goals or both. This influence process often involves peer or lateral influence; at other times it involves upward or downward hierarchical influence. The key distinction between shared leadership and traditional models of leadership is that the influence process involves more than just downward influence on subordinates by an appointed or elective leader. Rather, leadership is broadly distributed among a set of individuals instead of centralized in the hands of a single individual who acts in the role of a superior.[3]

We can more specifically illustrate shared and vertical leadership in terms of self-directing work teams. Although discussed in earlier chapters, such discussion did not deal very much with leadership.

Full-range leadership theory (FRLT) involves nine dimensions covering both transformational and transactional leadership, especially emphasizing contextual variables.

Contextual variables link observations to a set of relevant facts, events, or points of view, such as organizational characteristics, work functions, external environment factors, and demographic variables.

Shared leadership is a dynamic, interactive influence process among individuals in groups for which the objective is to lead one another to the achievement of group or organizational goals or both.

Leadership in Self-Directing Work Teams   This type of leadership can come from outside or inside the team. Within a team, such leadership can be assigned to one person, rotated across team members, or even shared simultaneously as different needs arise across time.

Outside the team, the leaders can be traditional, formally designated vertical first-level supervisors, or foremen or an outside vertical leader of a self-managing team whose duties tend to be quite different from those of a traditional supervisor. Often these nontraditional leaders are called "coordinators" or "facilitators." A key part of their job is to provide resources to their unit and serve as a liaison with other units, all without the authority trappings of traditional supervisors. Here, team members tend to carry out traditional managerial/leadership functions internal to the team along with direct performance activities.

The activities or functions vary and could involve a designated team role or even be defined more generally as a process to facilitate shared team performance ("whatever it takes"). In the latter case, you are likely to see job rotation activities, along with skill-based pay, as discussed in Chapter 7, where workers are paid for the mix and depth of skills they possess as opposed to the skills of a given job assignment they might hold.

If we argue that a key contribution to team performance (regardless of who provides it) is to create and maintain conditions for that performance, then the following are important considerations.[4]

Efficient, Goal-Directed Effort   The key here is to coordinate the effort both inside and outside the team. Team leaders can play a crucial role here. It is harder than it looks because you need to coordinate individual efforts with those of the team, and team efforts with those of the organization or major subunit. Among other things, such coordination calls for shared visions and goals and the like.

Adequate Resources   Teams rely on their leaders to obtain enough equipment, supplies, and so on to carry out the team's goals. As mentioned earlier, these are often handled by the outside facilitator and almost always involve internal and external negotiations so the facilitator can then do his or her negotiating outside the team.

Competent, Motivated Performance   Team members also need the appropriate knowledge, skills, abilities, and motivation to perform collective tasks well. Here, leaders may be able to influence team composition so as to enhance shared efficacy and performance. We often see this demonstrated with short-term teams such as task forces. Sometimes student teams are selected with this very point in mind.

A Productive, Supportive Climate   Here, we are talking about high levels of cohesiveness, mutual trust, and cooperation among team members. Sometimes these kinds of aspects are part of a team's "interpersonal climate." Team leaders contribute to this climate by role-modeling and supporting relationships that build the high levels indicated above. Team leaders can also work to enhance shared beliefs about team efficacy and collective capability.

Commitment to Continuous Improvement and Adaptation   A really good team should be able to adapt to changing conditions. Again, both internal and external team leaders may play a role.

Self-Leadership Activities   These shared and vertical self-directing team activities tend to encourage self-leadership activities, which in turn can help individuals and the team. Self-leadership represents a portfolio of self-influence strategies that are believed to positively influence individual behavior, thought processes, and related activities. Often, self-leadership activities are divided into three broad categories: behavior-focused, natural-reward, and constructive-thought-pattern strategies.[5]

Behavior-focused strategies tend to increase self-awareness, leading to the handling of behaviors involving necessary but not always pleasant tasks. These strategies include *self-observation, self-goal setting, self-reward, self-correcting feedback*, and *practice*. Self-observation involves examining your own behavior to increase awareness of when and why you engage in certain behaviors. Such examination identifies behaviors that should be changed, enhanced, or eliminated. Poor performance could lead to informal self-notes documenting the occurrence of unproductive office behaviors. Such heightened awareness is a first step toward behavior change.

Self-rewards, in conjunction with the above, can be quite useful in moving behaviors toward goal attainment. Self-rewards can be real (e.g., a steak dinner) or imaginary (imagining a steak dinner). Also, such things as the rehearsal of desired behaviors before actual performance can prove quite useful.

Constructive thought patterns focus on the creation or alteration of cognitive thought processes. Self-analysis and improvement of belief systems, mental imagery of successful performance outcomes, and positive self-talk can all help. As a package these three activities can influence and control team members' own thoughts through the use of specific cognitive strategies designed to facilitate habitual ways of thinking that can positively affect performance. Where the three above activities occur, they tend to serve as partial substitutes for hierarchical leadership even though they may be encouraged in a shared, in contrast to a vertical, leadership setting.

To summarize, in leaving this section on shared and vertical leadership, a final thought is in order. While you no longer want to restrict your leadership simply to the white-hat style of vertical leadership, neither is shared leadership the *only* way to go. As we have seen, shared leadership appears in many forms. In addition it often is used in combination with vertical leadership. As with a number of the leadership approaches discussed in Chapter 11, various contingencies operate that influence the emphasis that should be devoted to each of the leadership perspectives.

Cross-Cultural Leadership: Project GLOBE

The GLOBE (*Global Leadership and Organizational Behavior Effectiveness Research Program*) is an ambitious program that involves about 17,000 managers from 951 organizations functioning in 62 societies throughout the world, 140 or so country co-investigators, plus a coordinating team and four research associates. The project is headed by Robert House and is an ongoing one, with several books and articles scheduled over the next few years. The summary here is based on the first in a series of books, *Culture, Leadership, and Organizations* edited by House and four co-editors, and on related work.[6]

The study used a multiple-measure approach with a strong emphasis on questionnaires built around the assumption that leadership variables and cultural variables can be meaningfully applied at societal and organizational levels. Middle managers in the telecommunications, food, and banking industries comprised the sample. Figure 12.1 shows a simplified version of the GLOBE theoretical model.

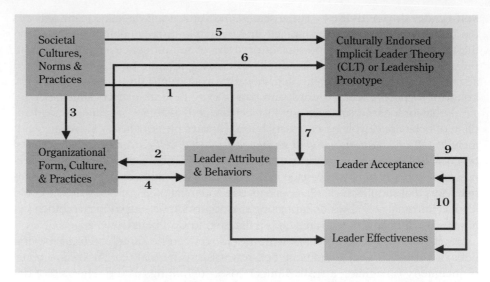

Figure 12.1   A simplified version of the original GLOBE theoretical model.
Source: See Robert J. House, Paul J. Hanges, Mansour Javidan, Peter W. Dorfman, and Vipin Gupta, eds., *Culture, Leadership, and Organizations* (Thousand Oaks, CA: Sage Publications, 2004).

1. Societal cultural norms of shared values and practices affect leaders' behavior. Founders and original organization members are immersed in their own societal culture. Also, are a reflection of prevailing organizational practices in their industries.
2. Leadership affects organizational form, culture, and practices: founders and subsequent leaders influence/maintain organizational culture.
3. Societal cultural values and practices also affect organizational culture and practices: societal culture has direct impact on organizational culture, and over time, organization cultures influence broader societal culture.
4. Organizational culture and practices also affect leaders' behavior: over time; founders and subsequent organizational leaders respond to organizational culture and alter their behaviors/leadership styles.
5&6. Societal culture/organizational culture practices influence the process by which people come to share implicit theories of leadership (CLT): over time, CLT profiles develop in each culture in response to societal and organizational culture/practices.
7. Leader acceptance is a function of the interaction between CLTs and leader attributes and behaviors: leader attributes/behaviors congruent with CLTs are more accepted than non-CLTs.
8. Leader effectiveness is a function of the interaction between strategic organizational contingencies (not shown) and leader attributes and behaviors. Leader attributes/behaviors that meet the requirements of strategic organizational contingencies will result in increased leader effectiveness.
9. Acceptance of the leader by followers facilitates leader effectiveness: leaders not accepted by organizational members will find it more difficult/arduous to influence these members than leaders who are accepted.
10. Leader effectiveness, over time, will increase leader acceptance: effective leaders will, over time, demonstrate effectiveness by being effective. Such demonstration will change some organizational members' behaviors toward the leader and result in increased leader effectiveness. Over time, followers not accepting the leader will leave voluntarily or involuntarily.

The central assumption behind the model is that the attributes and entities that differentiate a specified culture predict organizational practices, leader attributes, and behaviors that are most often carried out and are most effective in that culture. The specific assumptions comprising the model are numbered consecutively from 1 to 10 and are outlined in this simplified version.

Nine cultural dimensions used for both societal and organizational culture are briefly summarized in what follows, as are various aspects of leadership. Those suggested by Hofstede's earlier work are designated by an (H). The cultural dimensions are (1) *assertiveness:* assertive, confrontational, and aggressive in relationships; (2) *future orientation:* future-oriented behaviors such as delaying gratification and investing in the future (H); (3) *gender egalitarianism:* the collective minimizes gender inequality (H); (4) *uncertainty avoidance:* reliance on social norms, rules, etc., to alleviate future unpredictability (H); (5) *power distance:* expectation that power is equally distributed (H); (6) *institutional emphasis on collectivism vs. individualism:* organization/society rewards collective resources/action; (7) *in-group collectivism:* individuals express pride, loyalty, and similar attitudes in organizations/families; (8) *performance orientation:* the collective encourages/rewards group for performance improvement; (9) *humane orientation:* the collective encourages/rewards individuals for being fair, generous, kind, and the like.

There are six broad-based leadership dimensions encompassing 21 primary leadership dimensions and a larger number of leadership items and attributes: (1) *charismatic/value-based:* inspire, motivate, expect high performance outcomes; (2) *team-oriented:* team building and implementation of a common goal among team members; (3) *participative:* degree to which others are managed in making an implementation; (4) *humane-oriented:* support, consideration, compassion, and generosity; (5) *autonomous:* independent and individualistic leadership; (6) *self-protective:* ensuring safety and security of the individual, self-centered, and face saving.

The 62 countries used in the study were found to form 10 geographic clusters. Figure 12.2 shows where each country cluster averages (H, M, L) on each culturally endorsed implicit leadership dimension (CLT) when compared against the impact the CLT has for each leadership dimension. These CLTs are similar to what we termed "prototypes" in Chapter 11 and shows how many countries were included in each cluster. The heart of the figure presents summary comparisons among culture clusters to indicate which clusters are most likely to endorse or refute the importance of the six CLT leadership prototype dimensions. Among other things, Figure 12.2 shows a sharp contrast in CLTs between the Anglo cluster (of which the United States is a part) and the Middle East.

Finally, GLOBE sought understanding of which attributes of leadership are universally endorsed across all sampled countries as being related to either effective or ineffective leadership. Leadership that reflects integrity, charismatic-visionary, charismatic-inspirational, and team-oriented dimensions was universally endorsed as representing outstanding leadership. Leadership associated with irritability, egocentricity, noncooperativeness, malevolence, being a loner, dictatorial, and ruthless was identified as ineffective leadership.

Culturally contingent endorsement of leader characteristics involved being individualistic, being status conscious, and being a risk taker or exhibiting self-sacrificing behavior.

Representative Country and Number in Cluster	Societal Cluster	CLT Leadership Dimensions					
		Charismatic/ Value- Based	Team- Oriented	Partici- pative	Humane- Oriented	Autono- mous	Self- Protective
Russia-8	Eastern Europe	M	M	L	M	H	H
Argentina-4	Latin America	H	H	M	M	L	H
France-6	Latin Europe	H	M	M	L	L	M
China-6	Confucian Asia	M	H	L	H	M	H
Sweden-3	Nordic Europe	H	M	H	L	M	L
USA-7	Anglo	H	M	H	H	M	L
Nigeria-5	Sub-Sahara Africa	M	M	M	H	L	L
India-5	Southern Asia	H	H	L	H	M	H
Germany-4	Germanic Europe	H	L	H	M	H	L
Egypt-6	Middle East	L	L	L	M	M	H

Figure 12.2   Summary of Comparisons for CLT Leadership Dimensions

Source: Mansour Javidan, Peter W. Dorfman, Mary Sully de Luque, and Robert J. House, "In the Eye of the Beholder: Cross Cultural Lessons in Leadership from Project GLOBE," *Academy of Management Perspectives* 20.7 (2006), pp. 67–90.

Note: H=high rank; M=medium rank; L=low rank when compared against the impact the culturally endorsed implicit leadership theory (CLT) has for each leadership dimension.

Strategic Leadership

We now move to strategic leadership. There is not yet an overarching strategic leadership approach. Thus, we discuss three different perspectives, each of which considers strategic leadership in a somewhat different way. The first of these is termed multiple-level leadership. To this we add a top management teams (TMT) approach, and finally we focus on a strategic leadership approach developed by Boal and Hooijberg.

Multiple-Level Leadership   The multiple-level perspective[7] argues that there are three different organizational domains from the bottom to the top of the organization, typically made of no more than two managerial levels within a domain: (1) the *production domain* at the bottom of the organization; (2) the *organization domain* in the middle levels: and (3) the *systems domain* at the top. Each domain and level gets more complex than those beneath it in terms of its leadership and managerial requirements. But even the largest and most complex organizations can be designed to require no more than seven levels, from the lowest level to the highest top management level.

One way of expressing the increasing complexity is in terms of how long it takes to see the results of the key decisions required at a given domain and level. These roughly range from three months or so at the lowest level, which emphasizes hands-on work performance and practical judgment to solve ongoing problems, to 20 years or more at the top.

Since the problems become increasingly complex, you can expect that managers at each domain and level must demonstrate increasing cognitive and behavioral complexity in order to deal with increasing organizational complexity. One way of measuring a manager's cognitive complexity is in terms of how far into the future he or she can develop a vision. Notice that this measure is trait oriented, similar in some ways but different in others from intelligence. In other words, using an intelligence measure instead of a complexity measure will not do. Accompanying such vision should be increasing sophistication across a wide range of the kinds of leader behaviors described in Chapter 11 and in the present chapter. Thus, successful leaders at each domain and level are expected to think and act more complexly as they move up the organization.

This approach, or extensions of it, is now beginning to pick up momentum, although its underlying roots have been with us for many years. It is notable for emphasizing the impact of top leadership as it cascades deep within the organization. One example of such cascading, indirect leadership, is the leadership-at-a-distance discussed in Chapter 11. One way of thinking about such cascading is in terms of a *leadership of* emphasis at the top and much more of a *leadership in* emphasis as the cascading moves down the organization.

The systems domain *leadership of* at the top is normally responsible for creating complex systems, organizing acquisition of major resources, creating vision, developing strategy and policy, and identifying organizational design. These functions call for a much broader conception of leadership than does the lower-level *leadership in*. Of course, *leadership in* is also exercised in the systems and organization domains and involves the much more face-to-face approach stressed in that type of leadership. One example of *leadership of* is the indirect, cascading effects of an upper-domain decision concerning, say, leadership development programs to be implemented down the organization. Of course, upper-domain executives also exercise *leadership in* as well, as they interact with top management teams and their own direct reports. Indeed, the previously discussed shared leadership is an important consideration for these teams as it is for the top management teams to be discussed next.

Top-Management Teams   Top-management teams (TMTs) use demographic characteristics as proxies for harder-to-obtain psychological variables. Such variables as age, tenure, education, and functional background are used in this perspective. Researchers typically attempt to link such variables to various kinds of organizational outcomes, including sales growth, innovation, and executive turnover.[8]

Because of conflicting research findings, there has been recent work to enrich this approach. One such particularly important review argues that a given TMT is likely to face a variety of different situations over time. Demographic composition may be relatively stable but the tasks are dynamic and variable. Sometimes team members have similar information (symmetric) and interests, and sometimes not (asymmetric).

The researchers argue that group process must be handled differently and effectively for dynamic and less-dynamic tasks, and that group process can vary depending on dynamism along such lines as information, interests, power asymmetries, and selected combinations of these.

One example covering information asymmetry can be seen in a merger. Here, each team member is likely to have different unshared and distinct information about the strategy, organization, and finances of potential partner organizations. The researchers ultimately developed a process-oriented model to deal with predicted information, interests, and power asymmetries. They argue that such a model integrates insights from research on leadership, TMTs, small group process, and negotiation and has practical implications for how top-level executives can improve TMT effectiveness through appropriate process choices.

Boal and Hooijberg's Strategic Leadership Perspective   Let's start with a figure to help interpret the Boal and Hooijberg perspective.[9] Notice especially the charismatic, transformational, and vision leadership block discussed in Chapter 11. You should also recall the treatment of emotional intelligence (complexity) from an earlier chapter. We will briefly discuss these as they apply to Figure 12.3.

We start with the Emergent Theories and the Competing Values Framework (CVF).[10] CVF emphasizes flexibility versus control and internal focus versus external focus. The internal versus external focus dimension distinguishes between social actions, emphasizing such internal effectiveness measures as employee satisfaction and the like and focusing on external effectiveness measures such as market share and profitability. The control versus flexibility dimension contrasts social actions focused on goal clarity and efficiency and those emphasizing being adaptive to people and the external environment. As a whole, the two focus dimensions define four quadrants and eight leadership roles that address these distinct organizational demands.

Thus, CVF recognizes leaders often face competing requirements in meeting the competing demands of stakeholders. Top-level managers/leaders, for example, constantly need to balance demands from direct reports and other employees because doing so highlights executives' ability to change. Therefore, executives who have a large repertoire of leadership

Cognitive complexity is the underlying assumption that those high in cognitive complexity process information differently and perform certain tasks better than less cognitively complex people.

Absorptive capacity is the ability to learn.

Adaptive capacity refers to the ability to change.

Managerial wisdom is the ability to perceive variations in the environment and an understanding of the social actors and their relationships.

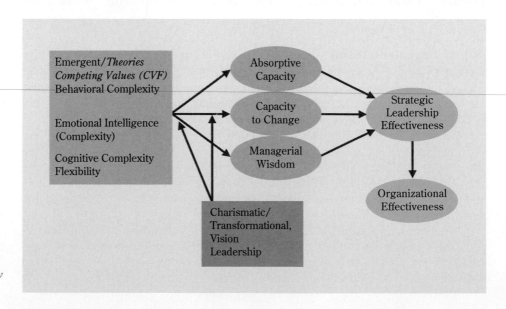

Figure 12.3 Boal and Hooijberg Perspective
Source: Kimberly B. Boal and Robert Hooijberg, "Strategic Leadership Research: Moving On", *The Leadership Quarterly* 11 (2009).

roles available and know when to apply these roles are more likely to be effective than leaders who have a small role repertoire and who indiscriminately apply these roles. This repertoire and selective application is termed *behavioral complexity.* To exhibit both repetitive and selective application, managers/leaders need cognitive and behavioral complexity as well as flexibility. Of course, they may understand and see the differences between their subordinates and superiors but not be able to behaviorally differentiate so as to satisfy the demands of each group. Recall from Chapter 3 that a similar term, emotional intelligence (Figure 12.3), calls for both discernment and appropriate action at the right time.

In terms of **cognitive complexity**, the underlying assumption is that those high in cognitive complexity process information differently and perform certain tasks better than less cognitively complex persons because they use more categories to discriminate. In other words, such complexity taps into *how* a person constructs meaning as opposed to *what* he or she thinks.

Figure 12.3 shows CVF, behavioral complexity, and emotional complexity and cognitive complexity as directly associated with *absorptive capacity, capacity to change,* and *managerial wisdom* as well as with *charismatic/transformational leadership*, and *vision*, the leadership dimensions we discussed in Chapter 11 and touched on above. In other words, the association between CVF and the above complexities and the capacities differs according to how well the charismatic/transformational and visionary leadership is carried out.

Finally, Boal and Hooijberg briefly discuss what they mean by each of the capacities and link them with strategic leadership effectiveness and ultimately with organizational effectiveness. **Absorptive capacity** is the ability to learn. It involves the capacity to recognize new information, assimilate it, and apply it toward new ends. It utilizes processes necessary to improve the organization-environment fit. Absorptive capacity of strategic leaders is of particular importance because those in such a position have a unique ability to change or reinforce organizational action patterns. Learning occurs through studying, through doing, and through using.

Adaptive capacity refers to the ability to change. Boal and Hooijberg argue that in the new, fast-changing competitive landscape, organizational success calls for strategic flexibility or for being able to respond quickly to competitive conditions.

Managerial wisdom involves the ability to perceive variation in the environment and an understanding of the social actors and their relationships. Thus, emotional intelligence is called for and the manager/leader must be able to take the right action at the right moment.

Let's look at an integrative example of an engineering company that used to have 100 percent of its contracts with the Department of Defense. As most people are aware, astute strategic leaders—those high in absorptive capacity, change, and managerial wisdom, as well as in the variables influencing these capacities—realized that a company reorientation was necessary given the decline in the defense budget; they had to reconceptualize the system within which their organization operated. Contract bidding procedures changed; the company no longer needed to comply with numerous government regulations in terms of its contracts, and executive leaders had to acquire new customers. These leaders tended to increase the three capacities noted above. Thus, they formulated different future visions and emphasized

Big Sports: Big Business

Gene Smith, the Ohio State University athletic director, heads up a medium-sized organization. In one year, the athletic department took in $104.7 million. The department includes more than 300 employees, 25 computer servers, and 36 varsity sports. Although folksy, Smith flips open his laptop to explain the niceties of his organization. Because of OSU's strategic location and flagship status, sports are particularly important. A key aspect of his job is protecting the program's integrity and steering athletes away from trouble. He does these with a nine-person NCAA rules compliance staff and a sensitivity for avoiding embarrassment.

Smith believes that athletics provides "teachable moments" and "character building." "Say you're the field goal kicker, there are 105,000 fans, and the score is 31–30. That's pressure," says Smith.

organizational transformation. They might even have appeared charismatic, if not visionary. Strategic leaders high in behavioral complexity (behavioral and cognitive complexity) and emotional intelligence (complexity) were likely to pick up on the trends more quickly than others and better prepare their organizations.

The Big Sports: Big Business marginal photo essay also provides fertile ground for you to apply the concepts of the Boal and Hooijberg perspective.

Moral Leadership

We now move from integrative leadership to moral leadership. All of us are currently aware of recent concerns with various moral leadership problems, such as those with Enron and those in various government, religious, and other organizations. As these problems have gained increasing attention, there has also been a stronger emphasis in the literature on such topics as ethical leadership, authentic leadership, servant leadership, and spiritual leadership. These are the topics covered in our treatment of moral leadership.

Ethical Leadership

We start with ethical leadership and then compare it with authentic, servant, and spiritual leadership; with the transformational leadership emphasized in Chapter 11; and with the FRLT perspective in this chapter. Figure 12.4 summarizes the similarities and differences among ethical, authentic, spiritual, and transformational leadership. A key similarity cutting across all these dimensions is role modeling, so important in social learning theory. Altruism, or concern for others, and in-

Figure 12.4 Similarities and differences between ethical, spiritual, authentic, and transformational theories of leadership

	Similarities with ethical leadership	Differences from ethical leadership
Authentic Leadership	Key similarities: – Concern for others (altruism) – Ethical decision making – Integrity – Role modeling	Key differences: – Ethical leaders emphasize moral management (more transactional) and "other" awareness – Authentic leaders emphasize authenticity and self-awareness
Spiritual Leadership	Key similarities: – Concern for others (altruism) – Integrity – Role modeling	Key differences: – Ethical leaders emphasize moral management – Spiritual leaders emphasize visioning, hope/faith; work as vocation
Transformational	Key similarities: – Concern for others (altruism) – Ethical decision making – Integrity – Role modeling	Key differences: – Ethical leaders emphasize ethical standards and moral management (more transactional) – Transformational leaders emphasize vision, values, and intellectual stimulation

Source: Michael E. Brown and Linda K. Trevino, "Ethical Leadership: A Review and Future Directions," *The Leadership Quarterly* 17.6 (December 2006), p. 598.

ETHICS IN OB

NICHOLAS NEGROPONTE WANTS TO SAVE THE WORLD

Nicholas Negroponte left MIT's Media Lab, which he founded and ran for two decades, to build a $100, super cheap laptop computer for poor children. His first models looked like little more than toys. In fact, one of them used a hand-cranked generator so an electric plug wouldn't be necessary. However, he soon replaced the crank with a fist-sized generator with a pull cord. Now the laptop is to the point where it is ready for production, and Taiwan's Quanta Computer will manufacture it.

An idea as radical as this attracts its share of critics, along with supporters such as Libya's Muammar Quaddafi and the leaders of such countries as Argentina, Brazil, and Nigeria. However, for now anyway, the critics have largely been quieted. The plan is to build millions of laptops within the next four years and ship some 50 million a year, hopefully by the end of 2008.

The major anticipated difficulty is obtaining reliable Internet access in remote regions. Negroponte is very aware of this. However, he argues that "it makes my day" when his project motivates others to get computers to poor kids faster, even if he cannot. Needless to say, the wide range of requirements to get the project up and running presents many leadership challenges.[10A]

> *Question: Keeping in mind the discussion in this chapter and in Chapter 11, what are these leadership challenges? How would you weave together whatever leadership approaches you think are relevant to deal with these challenges?*

tegrity are also important similarities. In terms of differences, authentic leaders stress authenticity and self-awareness and tend to be more transactional than do the other leadership aspects. Ethical leaders emphasize moral concerns, while spiritual leaders stress visioning, hope, and faith, as well as work as a vocation. Transformational leaders emphasize values, vision, and intellectual stimulation. Related literature specifies a number of ethical leadership propositions and suggests a number of topic areas particularly important for ethical leadership. In addition, some preliminary work has been done on measuring ethical leadership. Taken as a whole, it is obvious that any of these related approaches are important and ripe for systematic empirical and conceptual development. Even servant leadership would lend itself to further developments if those most strongly emphasizing it were so inclined.[11]

Authentic Leadership

Authentic leadership essentially argues "know thyself."[12] It involves both *owning* one's personal experiences (values, thoughts, emotions, and beliefs) and acting in accordance with one's true self (expressing what you really think and believe, and acting accordingly). Although no one is perfectly authentic, more authenticity is something to strive for. It reflects the unobstructed operation of one's true or core self day-to-day. It also underlies

NETWORKING FOR MORAL LEADERSHIP

Many employees are interested in philanthrophy that goes beyond just themselves and enables them to pool their money and time. For them you can emphasize moral leadership by encouraging the formation of giving circles that bring people together for charity. These are recent developments throughout the country that may arise informally or as a part of a formal voluntary organization such as the United Way. Here are some tips for establishing the circles.

• Decide on who is interested in setting up and participating in an organization that is interested in participating in a circle of members that will contribute a fixed amount of money and/or time toward a charitable cause at each meeting.
• Once the circle is established, provide a schedule of meeting locations and appetizers for each meeting.
• Assign an appropriate number of people (depending on size) to bring forward a cause for support.
• Educate members in activities to get more involved in philanthropic activities.
• Keep in touch with other volunteer organizations and giving circles.
• Decide on the scope of the charitable cause, whether broad, narrow, or variable.[12A]

virtually all other aspects of leadership, regardless of the particular theory or model involved.

Those high in authenticity are argued to have optimal self-esteem, or genuine, true, stable, and congruent self-esteem, as opposed to the fragile self-esteem based heavily on outside responses. Our Leaders on Leadership featuring Bill Walsh is a clear example. It also demonstrates Walsh's authentic relationships with followers and associates as well as his associated transparency, openness, trust, and emphasis on the development of his followers and associates. All these points draw on psychological well-being emphasized in the positive psychology literature.[13] Here, there is self-efficacy, which you will recall is an individual's belief about the likelihood of successfully completing a specific task; **optimism**, the expectation of positive outcomes; **hope**, the tendency to look for alternative pathways to reach a desired goal; and **resilience**, the ability to bounce back from failure and keep forging ahead. An increase in any one of these is seen as increasing the others. As you can see, these are important for a leader to demonstrate, and such demonstration is believed to positively influence his or her followers. The earlier-discussed modeling in social learning is quite relevant here. Indeed, some have termed the positive modeling behavior of followers as authentic followership to accompany the authentic leadership we discussed earlier.

Authentic leadership is now beginning to generate conceptual and empirical work, with more of the former than the latter. Therefore, it is difficult to go much further in the current discussion. However, there does appear to be enough interest so that the idea is more than a fad. Furthermore, as mentioned, it appears to bear a family resemblance to such concepts as servant leadership, spiritual leadership, and ethical leadership in general. We now turn to servant and spiritual leadership.

Optimism is the expectation of positive outcomes.

Hope is the tendency to look for alternative pathways to reach a desired goal.

Resilience is the ability to bounce back from failure and keep forging ahead.

Leaders on Leadership

AUTHENTIC LEADERSHIP

Bill Walsh, often considered to be a football genius, battled leukemia. A key question is what should be his legacy? For many, the legacy will be his genius on the field with his West Coast offense, his game management expertise, and expertise with Xs and Os.

However, his legacy runs deeper than this. Of the 32 present and recent past National Football League (NFL) head coaches, 4 played for him, 6 worked under him, and 20 worked under his disciples. He made a decision 18 years ago that, when asked, he wishes he could take back. He had had enormous success, winning three Super Bowls in eight years and was poised to win more. Indeed, his successor, George Seifert, won a fourth super Bowl the following year; he went on to three more National Football Conference title games in the next four years, and he won a fifth Super Bowl in January 1995. Walsh believed that, with the quarterbacks he had, he could have won many more. Thus, this is the one decision he wishes he had back: although he had been consulting and staying active in the field, he had not coached since he retired. However, at that time he was general manager and had other duties besides coaching, and he was suffering from burnout.

Throughout his career, Walsh made numerous decisions, many of them very hard and not very pleasant. Because of this, his impact had been so great that as news of his declining condition spread, his former players and associates rallied to support him. Joe Montana, a former quarterback, said: "I think there's a lot more feeling there than he ever imagined. He's seeing it now, though it's hard for it to have to come out this way." Even some of his former players, those with whom his relationships had become the most strained, expressed their affection. It looks as if his most important legacy will be that authenticity and relationships trump the number of Super Bowl rings.[13A]

Servant Leadership

Servant leadership was developed by Robert Greenleaf in 1964, who spelled out many of its ideas in articles and especially in books written in 1977 and 1978.[14] Essentially, he argued that the primary purpose of business should be to create a positive impact on its employees and its community. The leader is attuned to basic spiritual values and, in serving these, serves others including colleagues, the organization, and society. Viewed in this way servant leadership is not a special case of leadership but rather a special kind of service. Servant leadership helps others discover their inner spirit, earning and keeping their trust, and exhibits effective listening and service over self-interest. It is best demonstrated by those with a vision and a desire to serve others first, rather than by those seeking leadership roles. Servant leadership is usually seen as a philosophical movement, with 11 international Greenleaf Center offices throughout the world currently disseminating ideas and literature.

Servant leadership has not been systematically empirically tested, nor are its proponents interested in such testing. Regardless, its guiding philosophy is consistent with that of the other leadership family members discussed here.

Spiritual Leadership

Spiritual leadership can be seen as a field of inquiry within the broader setting of workplace spirituality.[15] Neither of these fields has a strong research base currently. Western religious theology and practice and leadership ethics and values provide much of the organizational base. In addition, the literature does not agree on whether spirituality and religion are the same. Where they are seen as different, organized religions provide rituals, routines, and ceremonies that can provide a vehicle for achieving spirituality. Of course, one could be religious by following religious rituals but lack spirituality, or one could reflect spirituality without being religious.

Even though we have argued that spiritual leadership does not yet have a strong research base, there has been some recent work with the beginnings of such a base. Not surprisingly, the work is termed Spiritual Leadership Theory or SLT. It is a causal leadership approach for organizational transformation designed to create an intrinsically motivated, learning organization. Spiritual leadership includes values, attitudes, and behaviors required to intrinsically motivate self and others to have a sense of spiritual survival through calling and membership. In other words, self and others experience meaning in their lives, believe they make a difference, and feel understood and appreciated. Such a sense of leader and follower survival tends to create value congruence across the strategic, empowered team and at the individual level; it ultimately encourages higher levels of organizational commitment, productivity, and employee well-being. Figure 12.4 summarizes the causal model.

Some key terms in Figure 12.5 are considered qualities of spiritual leadership: Vision—defines the destination and journey, reflects high ideals, encourages hope/faith; Altruistic love—trust/loyalty as well as forgiveness/acceptance/

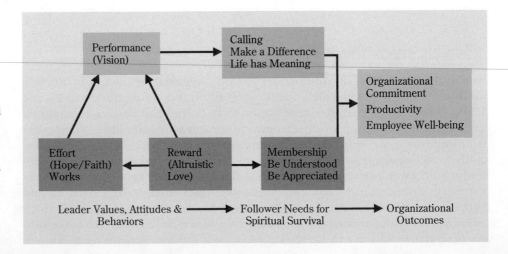

Figure 12.5 Causal model of spiritual leadership theory.
Source: Lewis W. Fry, Steve Vitucci, and Marie Cedillo, "Spiritual Leadership and Army Transformation: Theory, Measurement, and Establishing a Baseline," *The Leadership Quarterly* 16.5 (2005), p. 838.

gratitude, honesty, courage, humility from organization and followers; and Hope/Faith—endurance, perseverance, do what it takes, have stretch goals.

The model was tested in a U.S. Army attack squadron in Ft. Hood, Texas. Initial support was found for most of the relationships shown in Figure 12.5.

Change Leadership

A final emerging leadership perspective, joining integrative leadership and moral leadership, is change leadership. Change leadership helps deal with the idea of an organization that masters the challenges of change while still creating a satisfying, healthy, and effective workplace for its employees. As long ago as the year 2000, an article in the *Harvard Business Review* opened with the sentence: "The new economy has ushered in great business opportunities—and great turmoil."[16] The terms "turmoil" and "turbulence" are even more often used now than in 2000 to describe the current environment of business and management. The forces of globalization are full of problems and opportunities, and the new economy is constantly springing surprises on even the most experienced organizational executives. Flexibility, competence, and commitment are the rules of the day.

People in the new workplace must be comfortable dealing with adaptation and continuous change, along with greater productivity, willingness to learn from the successes of others, total quality, and continuous improvement.

To deal with all these concerns and more, we will examine leaders as change agents, phases of planned change, change strategies, and resistance to change.

Leaders as Change Agents

As previously argued, "change" is the watchword of the day for many, if not most, organizations. Some of this change may be described as *radical change*, or frame-breaking change.[17] This is **transformational change**, which results in a major overhaul of the organization or its component systems. Organizations experiencing transformational change undergo significant shifts in basic characteristics, including the overall purpose/mission, underlying values and beliefs, and supporting strategies and structures.[18] In today's business environments, transformational changes are often initiated by a critical event, such as a new CEO, a new ownership brought about by merger or takeover, or a dramatic failure in operating results. When it occurs in the life cycle of an organization, such radical change is intense and all encompassing.

Another common form of organizational change is **incremental change**, or frame-bending change. This type of change, being part of an organization's natural evolution, is frequent and less traumatic. Typical incremental changes include the introduction of new products, new technologies, and new systems and processes. Although the nature of the organization remains relatively the same, incremental change builds on the existing ways of operating to enhance or extend them in new directions. The capability of improving continuously through incremental change is an important asset in today's demanding environments.

The success of both radical and incremental change in organizations depends in part on **change agents** who lead and support the change processes. These are

Nathalie Sanchez

Nathalie Sanchez is knocking on the doors of farm workers left jobless after a freeze killed much of the California citrus crop. One of 10 students from Loyola Marymount University, she is spending a week of spring break on this servant leadership project. In the past she has traveled to the Dominican Republic for a fair trade coffee effort and to Guatemala for community development in a Mayan village.

Transformational change radically shifts the fundamental character of an organization.

Incremental change builds on the existing ways of operating to enhance or extend them in new directions.

Change agents are people who take action to change the behavior of people and systems.

Fred Smith of FedEx on Change

For Fred Smith, founder and CEO of FedEx, "change is shorthand for opportunity." He claims: "You'll get extinguished if you think you will not have to change." He further contends that you have to have a high degree of trust and outstanding communications capability.

Unplanned change occurs spontaneously and without a change agent's direction.

Planned change is intentional and occurs with a change agent's direction.

Performance gap is a discrepancy between the desired and actual state of affairs.

individuals and groups who take responsibility for changing the existing behavior patterns of another person or social system. Although change agents are sometimes hired as consultants from outside the organization, any manager or leader in today's dynamic times is expected to act in the capacity of change agent. Indeed, this responsibility is increasingly defined even more specifically as essential to the leadership role. Simply put, being an effective change agent means being really effective at "change leadership," such as demonstrated by Fred Smith, the founder and CEO of FedEx.

Planned and Unplanned Change   Not all change in organizations is the result of a change agent's direction. **Unplanned changes** occur spontaneously or randomly. They may be disruptive, such as a wildcat strike that ends in a plant closure, or beneficial, such as an interpersonal conflict that results in a new procedure designed to smooth the flow of work between two departments. When the forces of unplanned change begin to appear, the appropriate goal is to act quickly to minimize any negative consequences and maximize any possible benefits. In many cases, unplanned changes can be turned into good advantage.

In contrast, **planned change** is the result of specific efforts by a change agent. It is a direct response to someone's perception of a **performance gap**— a discrepancy between the desired and actual state of affairs. Performance gaps may represent problems to be resolved or opportunities to be explored. Most planned changes may be regarded as efforts intended to deal with performance gaps in ways that benefit an organization and its members. The processes of continuous improvement require constant vigilance to spot performance gaps—both problems and opportunities—and to take action to resolve them.

Forces and Targets for Change   The forces for change driving organizations of all types and sizes are ever-present in and around today's dynamic work settings. They are found in the *organization-environment relationship*, with mergers, strategic alliances, and divestitures among the examples of organizational attempts to redefine their relationships with challenging social and political environments. They are found in the *organizational life cycle*, with changes in culture and structure among the examples of how organizations must adapt as they evolve from birth through growth and toward maturity. They are found in the *political nature of organizations*, with changes in internal control structures, including benefits and reward systems that attempt to deal with shifting political currents.

Planned change based on any of these forces can be internally directed toward a wide variety of organizational components, most of which have already been discussed in this book. As shown in Figure 12.6, these targets include organizational purpose, strategy, structure, and people, as well as objectives, culture, tasks, and technology. When considering these targets, however, it must be recognized that they are highly intertwined in the workplace. Changes in any one are likely to require or involve changes in others. For example, a change in the basic *tasks*—what it is that people do—is almost inevitably accompanied by a change in *technology*—the way in which tasks are accomplished. Changes in tasks and technology usually require alterations in *structures*, including changes in the patterns of authority and communication as well as in the roles of workers. These technological and structural changes can, in turn, necessitate changes in the

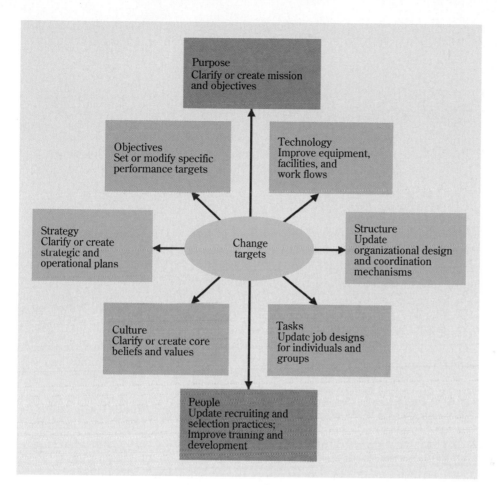

Figure 12.6 Organizational targets for planned change.

knowledge, skills, and behaviors of *people*—the members of the organization.[19] In all cases, of course, tendencies to accept easy-to-implement, but questionable, "quick fixes" to problems should be avoided.

Phases of Planned Change

Researchers suggest that the failure rate of organizational change attempts is as high as 70 percent.[20] The challenges of transformational change are especially large, but success can be enhanced by the OB Savvy 12.1 suggestions.[20A] One way to approach the task of improving the success rate of change initiatives is by understanding the underlying processes of social change in organizations. Psychologist Kurt Lewin recommends that any change effort be viewed in three phases—unfreezing, changing, and refreezing—all of which must be well handled for a change to be successful.[21] He also suggests that we may become easily preoccupied with the changing phase and neglect the importance of the unfreezing and refreezing

OB SAVVY 12.1

Increasing Transformational Change Effort Success

1. Develop a sense of urgency.
2. Have a powerful guiding coalition.
3. Have a compelling vision.
4. Communicate the vision.
5. Empower others to act.
6. Celebrate short-term wins.
7. Build on accomplishments.
8. Institutionalize results.

stages. Although the continuous nature of change means that these phases will often overlap in today's organizations, Lewin's understanding of the challenges of the change process remain very helpful.

■■■ **Unfreezing** is the stage at which a situation is prepared for change.

Unfreezing   In Lewin's model, **unfreezing** is the managerial responsibility of preparing a situation for change. It involves disconfirming existing attitudes and behaviors to create a felt need for something new. Environmental pressures, declining performance, recognition of a problem, or awareness that someone else has found a better way, among other things, facilitate the unfreezing stage. But many changes are never tried, or they fail simply because situations are not properly unfrozen to begin with.

Large systems seem particularly susceptible to what is sometimes called the *boiled frog phenomenon*.[22] This refers to the notion that a live frog will immediately jump out when placed in a pan of hot water. When placed in cold water that is then heated very slowly, however, the frog will stay in the water until the water boils the frog to death. Organizations, too, can fall victim to similar circumstances. When change agents fail to monitor their environments, recognize important trends, or sense the need to change, their organizations may slowly suffer and lose their competitive edge. Although the signals that change may be needed are available, they are not noticed or given any special attention—until it is too late. In contrast, people who are always on the alert and understand the importance of "unfreezing" in the change process lead the best organizations.

■■■ **Changing** is the stage in which specific actions are taken to create change.

Changing   The **changing** stage involves taking action to modify a situation by changing things, such as the people, tasks, structure, or technology of the organization. Lewin believes that many change agents are prone to an activity trap. They bypass the unfreezing stage and start changing things prematurely or too quickly. Although their intentions may be correct, the situation has not been properly prepared for change. This often leads to failure. Changing something is difficult enough in any situation, let alone having to do so without the proper foundations.

■■■ **Refreezing** is the stage in which changes are reinforced and stabilized.

Refreezing   The final stage in the planned change process is **refreezing**. Designed to maintain the momentum of a change and eventually institutionalize it as part of the normal routine, refreezing secures the full benefits of long-lasting change. Refreezing involves positively reinforcing desired outcomes and providing extra support when difficulties are encountered. It involves evaluating progress and results, and assessing the costs and benefits of the change. And it allows for modifications to be made in the change to increase its success over time. When all of this is not done and refreezing is neglected, changes are often abandoned after a short time or incompletely implemented.

Planned Change Strategies

Managers and other change agents use various means for mobilizing power, exerting influence over others, and getting people to support planned change efforts. As described in Figure 12.7, each of these strategies builds from the various bases of social power discussed in Chapter 12. Note in particular that each power source has somewhat different implications for the planned change process.[23]

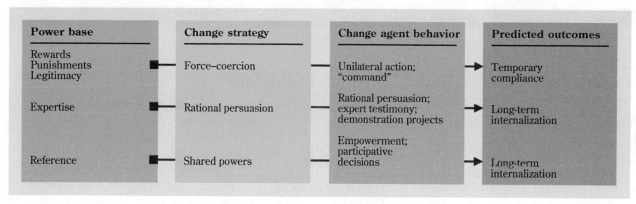

Figure 12.7   **Power bases, change strategies, and predicted change outcomes.**

Force-Coercion   A **force-coercion strategy** uses authority, rewards, or punishments as primary inducements to change. That is, the change agent acts unilaterally to "command" change through the formal authority of his or her position, to induce change via an offer of special rewards, or to bring about change via threats of punishment. People respond to this strategy mainly out of the fear of being punished if they do not comply with a change directive or out of the desire to gain a reward if they do. Compliance is usually temporary and continues only as long as the change agent and his or her legitimate authority are visible or as long as the opportunities for rewards and punishments remain obvious. Your actions as a change agent using the force-coercion strategy might match the following profile:

> *You believe that people who run things are basically motivated by self-interest and by what the situation offers in terms of potential personal gains or losses. Since you feel that people change only in response to such motives, you try to find out where their vested interests lie and then put the pressure on. If you have formal authority, you use it. If not, you resort to whatever possible rewards and punishments you have access to and do not hesitate to threaten others with these weapons. Once you find a weakness, you exploit it and are always wise to work "politically" by building supporting alliances wherever possible.*[24]

Rational Persuasion   Change agents using a **rational persuasion strategy** attempt to bring about change through the use of special knowledge, empirical support, or rational arguments. This strategy assumes that rational people will be guided by reason and self-interest in deciding whether or not to support a change. Expert power is mobilized to convince others that the change will leave them better off than before. It is sometimes referred to as an empirical-rational strategy of planned change. When successful, this strategy results in a longer-lasting, more naturalized change than does force-coercion. As a change agent taking the rational persuasion approach to a change situation, you might behave as follows:

> *You believe that people are inherently rational and are guided by reason in their actions and decision making. Once a specific course of action is demonstrated to be in a person's self-interest, you assume that reason and rationality will cause the person to adopt it. Thus, you approach*

■ **Force-coercion strategy** uses authority, rewards, and punishments to create change.

■ **Rational persuasion strategy** uses facts, special knowledge, and rational argument to create change.

Research Insight
Leadership and the Intricacies of Radical Change

Leaders and researchers have long been interested in learning more about the processes of organizational change. One area of special interest is the pace, sequencing, and nature of "radical change." Amis, Slack, and Hinings review the literature on change and note the importance of learning more about these issues in change leadership. They report an extensive study of changes in 36 Canadian Olympic NSOs over a 12-year period, one they describe as "probably the most turbulent in the history of Canadian amateur sport." The researchers found a pattern in the organizations that were most successful in their change transfor-

LESSONS OF RADICAL CHANGE

- Be cautious in trying to change rapidly
- Spend time building relationships among key change stakeholders
- Give priority to changing key elements first
- Be alert that resistance might be high in the most sensitive change areas

mations. The successful NSOs intermixed periods of change activity with ones of consolidation, where trust and working relationships were developed in support of change. These NSOs also followed a sequence that initiated change with a focus on "high-impact" organizational components, thus signaling to everyone its importance. They point out some of the difficulties of conducting research over such a long period of time with a set of organizations. They also call for more research to further investigate why and how pace, sequencing, and linearity affect the success of organizational changes.[24A]

change with the objective of communicating—through information and facts—the essential "desirability" of change from the perspective of the person whose behavior you seek to influence. If this logic is effectively communicated, you are sure of the person's adopting the proposed change.[25]

■■ **Shared-power strategy** uses participatory methods and emphasizes common values to create change.

Shared Power A **shared-power strategy** actively and sincerely involves the people who will be affected by a change in planning and making key decisions relating to this change. Sometimes called a normative-reeducative approach, this strategy tries to develop directions and support for change through involvement and empowerment. It builds essential foundations, such as personal values, group norms, and shared goals, so that support for a proposed change emerges naturally. Managers using normative-reeducative approaches draw on the power of personal reference and also share power by allowing others to participate in planning and implementing the change. Given this high level of involvement, the strategy is likely to result in a longer-lasting and internalized change. As a change agent who shares power and adopts a normative-reeducative approach to change, you are likely to fit this profile:

You believe that people have complex motivations. You feel that people behave as they do as a result of sociocultural norms and commitments to these norms. You also recognize that changes in these orientations involve changes in attitudes, values, skills, and significant relationships, not just changes in knowledge, information or intellectual rationales for action and practice. Thus, when seeking to change others, you are sensitive to the supporting or inhibiting effects of group pressures and norms. In working with people, you try to find out their side of things and to identify their feelings and expectations.[26]

Resistance to Change

In organizations, **resistance to change** is any attitude or behavior that indicates unwillingness to make or support a desired change. Change agents often view any such resistance as something that must be "overcome" in order for change to be successful. This is not always the case, however. It is helpful to view resistance to change as feedback that the change agent can use to facilitate gaining change objectives.[27] The essence of this constructive approach to resistance is to recognize that when people resist change, they are defending something important that appears to be threatened by the change attempt.

Resistance to change is an attitude or behavior that shows unwillingness to make or support a change.

Why People Resist Change   People have many reasons to resist change—fear of the unknown, insecurity, lack of a felt need to change, threat to vested interests, contrasting interpretations, and lack of resources, among other possibilities. A work team's members, for example, may resist the introduction of advanced workstation computers because they have never used the operating system and are apprehensive. They may wonder whether the new computers will eventually be used as justification for "getting rid" of some of them, or they may believe that they have been doing their jobs just fine and do not need the new computers to improve things. These and other viewpoints often create resistance to even the best and most well-intended planned changes.

Resistance to the Change Itself   Sometimes a change agent experiences resistance to the change itself. People may reject a change because they believe it is not worth their time, effort, or attention. To minimize resistance in such cases, the change agent should make sure that everyone who may be affected by a change knows specifically how it satisfies the following criteria.[28]

- *Benefit*—The change should have a clear relative advantage for the people being asked to change; it should be perceived as "a better way."
- *Compatibility*—The change should be as compatible as possible with the existing values and experiences of the people being asked to change.
- *Complexity*—The change should be no more complex than necessary; it must be as easy as possible for people to understand and use.
- *Triability*—The change should be something that people can try on a step-by-step basis and make adjustments as things progress.

Resistance to the Change Strategy   Change agents must also be prepared to deal with resistance to the change strategy. Someone who attempts to bring about change via force-coercion, for example, may create resistance among individuals who resent management of leadership by "command" or the use of threatened punishment. People may resist a rational persuasion strategy in which the data are suspect or the expertise of advocates is not clear. They may resist a shared-power strategy that appears manipulative and insincere.

Resistance to the Change Agent   Resistance to the change agent is directed at the person implementing the change and often involves personality and other differences. Change agents who are isolated and aloof from other persons in the change situation, who appear self-serving, or who have a high emotional involvement in the changes are especially prone to such problems. Research also indicates that change agents who differ from other persons in the change situation on such dimensions as age, education, and socioeconomic factors may encounter greater resistance to change.[29]

How to Deal with Resistance   An informed change agent has many options available for dealing positively with resistance to change, in any of its forms.[30] The first approach is through *education and communication*. The objective is to educate people about a change before it is implemented and to help them understand the logic of the change. Education and communication seem to work best when resistance is based on inaccurate or incomplete information. A second way is the use of *participation and involvement*. With the goal of allowing others to help design and implement the changes, this approach asks people to contribute ideas and advice or to work on task forces or committees that may be leading the change. This is especially useful when the change agent does not have all the information needed to successfully handle a problem situation.

Facilitation and support help to deal with resistance by providing help—both emotional and material—for people experiencing the hardships of change. A change agent using this approach actively listens to problems and complaints, provides training in the new ways, and helps others to overcome performance pressures. Facilitation and support are highly recommended when people are frustrated by work constraints and difficulties encountered in the change process. A *negotiation and agreement* approach offers incentives to actual or potential change resistors. Trade-offs are arranged to provide special benefits in exchange for assurances that the change will not be blocked. It is most useful when dealing with a person or group that will lose something of value as a result of the planned change.

Manipulation and co-optation make use of covert attempts to influence others, selectively providing information and consciously structuring events so that the desired change occurs. In some cases leaders of the resistance may be "bought off" with special side deals to gain their support. Manipulation and co-optation are common when other tactics do not work or are too expensive. Finally, *explicit or implicit coercion* employs the force of authority to get people to accept change. Often, resistors are threatened with a variety of undesirable consequences if they do not go along as planned. This may be done, for example, in crisis situations when speed is of the essence.

Figure 12.8 summarizes additional insights into how and when each of these methods may be used to deal with resistance to change. Regardless of the chosen strategy, it is always best to remember that the presence of resistance typically suggests that something can be done to achieve a better fit among the change, the situation, and the people affected. A good change agent deals with resistance to change by listening to feedback and acting accordingly.

Method	Use when	Advantages	Disadvantages
Education & communication	People lack information or have inaccurate information	Creates willingness to help with the change	Can be very time consuming
Participation & involvement	Other people have important information and/or power to resist	Adds information to change planning; builds commitment to the change	Can be very time consuming
Facilitation & support	Resistance traces to resource or adjustment problems	Satisfies directly specific resource or adjustment needs	Can be time consuming; can be expensive
Negotiation & agreement	A person or group will "lose" something because of the change	Helps avoid major resistance	Can be expensive; can cause others to seek similar "deals"
Manipulation & cooptation	Other methods don't work or are too expensive	Can be quick and inexpensive	Can create future problems if people sense manipulation
Explicit & implicit coercion	Speed is important and change agent has power	Quick; overpowers resistance	Risky if people get "mad"

Figure 12.8 Methods for dealing with resistance to change.

Chapter 12   Study Guide

What is integrative leadership?

Summary

- Integrative leadership ties together full-range leadership theory, shared leadership, cross-cultural leadership, and strategic leadership.

- Full-range leadership theory (FRLT) consists of nine factors, five transformational, three transactional, and one nontransactional factor. FRLT also recognizes contextual variables that link observations to a set of relevant facts, events, or points of view, such as organizational characteristics, work functions, external environment factors, and demographic variables.

- Shared leadership is a dynamic, interactive influence process among individuals in groups for which the objective is to lead one another to the achievement of group or organizational goals or both. The influence process often involves peer or lateral influence and at other times involves upward or downward hierarchical influence. Although broader than traditional vertical leadership, shared leadership may be used in combination with it.

- Cross-cultural leadership refers to Project GLOBE (Global Leadership and Organizational Effectiveness Research Program), which involves 62 societies, 951 organizations, and about 140 country co-investigators. It assumes that the attributes and entities that differentiate a specified culture predict organizational practices and leader attributes and behaviors that are most often carried out and most effective in that culture.

- Strategic leadership, as used here, consists of multiple-level leadership, top management teams, and Boal and Hooijberg's strategic leadership perspective.

- Multiple-level leadership consists of the production domain, organization domain, and systems domain as well as *leadership of* the whole organization and *leadership in* the organization.

- Top management teams use demographic characteristics in place of harder-to-obtain psychological variability.

- Boal and Hooijberg's theory uses emergent theories: cognitive complexity, emotional intelligence (complexity), and behavioral complexity as well as charismatic, transformational, and visionary leadership to influence absorptive capacity, capacity to change, and managerial wisdom, which in turn influence effectiveness.

What is moral leadership?

- Moral leadership consists of ethical leadership, authentic leadership, servant leadership, and spiritual leadership.

- Ethical leadership emphasizes moral concerns.

- Authentic leadership emphasizes *owning* one's personal experiences and acting in accordance with one's true or core self, which underlies virtually all other aspects of leadership.

- Servant leadership is where the leader is attuned to basic spiritual values and, in serving these, serves others including colleagues, the organization, and society.

- Spiritual leadership is a field of inquiry within the broader setting of workplace spirituality; it includes values, attitudes, and behaviors required to intrinsically motivate self and others to have a sense of spiritual survival through calling and membership.

What is change leadership?

- Change leadership helps deal with the idea of an organization that masters the challenges of both radical and incremental change while still creating a satisfying, healthy, and effective employee workplace. Change leadership deals with leaders as change agents, phases of planned change, change strategies, and resistance to change.

- Radical or transformational change results in a major overhaul of the organization or its component systems.

- Incremental or frame-bending change as part of an organization's natural evolution is frequent and less traumatic than radical change.

- Change agents are individuals and groups who take responsibility for changing the existing behavior pattern or social system; being a change agent is an integral part of a manager's leadership role.

- Planned change is a response to someone's perception of a performance gap—a discrepancy between the desired and actual state of affairs. It consists of unfreezing, changing, and refreezing phases.

- Planned change strategies consist of force–coercion, rational persuasion, and shared power.

- Resistance to change is any attitude or behavior that indicates unwillingness to make or support a desired change.

- Dealing with resistance to change involves education and communication, participation and involvement, facilitation and support, negotiation and agreement, manipulation and co-optation, and explicit or implicit agreement.

Key Terms

Absorptive capacity (p. 276)
Adaptive capacity (p. 276)
Change agents (p. 283)
Changing (p. 286)
Cognitive complexity
  (p. 276)
Contextual variables
  (p. 269)
Force-coercion strategy
  (p. 287)
Full-range leadership
  theory (FRLT) (p. 269)

Hope (p. 280)
Incremental change
  (p. 283)
Managerial wisdom
  (p. 276)
Optimisim (p. 280)
Performance gap (p. 284)
Planned change (p. 284)
Rational persuasion
  strategy (p. 287)
Refreezing (p. 286)
Resilience (p. 280)

Resistance to change
  (p. 289)
Shared leadership (p. 269)
Shared-power strategy
  (p. 288)
Transformational change
  (p. 283)
Unfreezing (p. 286)
Unplanned change (p. 284)

Self-Test 12

Multiple Choice

1. Full-range leadership is _____. (a) another name for transformational leadership (b) another name for transactional leadership (c) combines transactional and transformational leadership (d) is strongly supported by research findings

2. Shared leadership _____. (a) emphasizes vertical leadership (b) involves a white hat and a white horse (c) has almost totally replaced vertical leadership (d) is becoming more and more important in modern organizations

3. Project GLOBE _____. (a) considers both culture and leadership (b) is no longer a relevant program (c) was completed in 2004 (d) has nothing to do with cross-cultural leadership

4. The multiple-level strategic leadership approach _____. (a) emphasizes mostly *leadership of* (b) is an obsolete approach to leadership (c) is a face-to-face leadership approach (d) is the latest extension to Fiedler's work

5. Boal and Hooijberg _____. (a) have a very popular *leadership in* theory (b) have a theory with lots of research support (c) have a theory emphasizing three capacities (d) have a theory that is largely obsolete

6. Authentic leadership is _____. (a) virtually the same as ethical leadership (b) not a very widely discussed approach (c) not one that emphasizes knowing thyself (d) one that might serve as a base for numerous other leadership theories

7. Servant leadership is _____. (a) virtually the same as spiritual leadership (b) has much research support (c) has very little research support (d) is currently one of the more popular leadership approaches

8. Spiritual leadership is _____. (a) a kind of religion (b) beginning to develop a research stream (c) virtually the same as authentic leadership (d) ties together full-range leadership theory, shared leadership, cross-cultural leadership, and strategies leadership

9. Incremental change is _____. (a) more dramatic than radical change (b) less dramatic than radical change (c) is infrequently encountered (d) is usually very expensive

10. Full-range leadership theory _____. (a) has three levels and six domains (b) is an over-used approach (c) assumes decreasing complexity up the organization (d) is a promising broad range theory

11. Change leadership _____. (a) is very widely used (b) deals with leaders as change agents, phases of planned change, change strategies, and resistance to change (c) is practically unknown (d) is of recent origin

12. Performance gaps that create potential change situations include the existence of both problems to be resolved and _____. (a) costs to be avoided (b) people to be terminated (c) problems already resolved (d) opportunities to be explored

13. The presence or absence of a felt need for change is a critical issue in Lewin's _____ phase of planned change. (a) reflective (b) evaluative (c) unfreezing (d) changing

14. Which strategy relies mainly on empirical data and expert power? _____ (a) force–coercion (b) rational persuasion (c) shared power (d) authoritative command

15. Which change strategy is limited in effectiveness because it tends to create only temporary compliance? _____ (a) force–coercion (b) rational persuasion (c) shared power (d) normative reeducation

Short Response

16. Explain three ways in which shared leadership can be used in a self-directed work team.

17. Briefly compare and contrast the multiple-level leadership approach with the Boal and Hooijberg theory.

18. What should a manager do when forces for unplanned change appear?

19. What internal and external forces push for change in organizations?

Applications Essay

20. When Jorge Maldanado became general manager of the local civic recreation center, he realized that many changes would be necessary to make the facility a true community resource. Having the benefit of a new bond issue, the center had the funds for new equipment and expanded programming. All he needed to do now was get the staff committed to new initiatives. Unfortunately, his first efforts have been met with considerable resistance to change. A typical staff comment is, "Why do all these extras? Everything is fine as it is." How can Jorge use the strategies for dealing with resistance to change, as discussed in the chapter, to move the change process along?

OB in Action

These learning activities from *The OB Skills Workbook* are suggested for Chapter 12.

CASE	EXPERIENTIAL EXERCISES	SELF-ASSESSMENTS
■ 12. Motorola's Innovator-in-Chief	■ 7. Cultural cues	■ 2. A Twenty-First-Century manager ■ 4. Global Readiness Index

Plus—special learning experiences from *The Jossey-Bass/Pfeiffer Classroom Collection*

Decision Making

Chapter at a Glance

Organizations depend for their success on day-to-day decisions made by their members. The quality of these decisions influences both the long-term performance of an organization and its day-to-day "character"—in the eyes of employees, customers, and society at large. This chapter examines the many aspects of decision making in organizations. As you read Chapter 13, *keep in mind these study topics.*

CHAPTER 13 STUDY GUIDE

It's all about making the right choices

Today's challenging environments demand ever more rigor and creativity in the decision-making process. Consider the challenge to the managing partner at Plante Moran, William M. Hermann. In the aftermath of the accounting scandals at Arthur Andersen and Enron, firms that do both consulting and accounting are under new scrutiny. Fortunately for Bill Hermann, this consulting and accounting firm is unique, with an even more unique track record of accomplishment. Although it is comparatively small when compared to the industry giants, and it confines its practice to the middle of America (both in terms of location and size of its clients), it is highly respected. It leads accounting firms in the proportion of female partners.

And it is ranked as one of America's best places to work. The company's principle of decision making illustrates its uniqueness: "It is our intent to maintain timely yet thorough decision-making processes, with decisions made at the most appropriate level. We will strive to be effective by keeping a balance between participation and efficiency." This principle is but one of 15 guiding principles designed to help all staff associates and partners understand that this professional service firm believes it cannot long exist because of what it was, but only because of what it aspires to be. It must meet today's challenges with sound creative decisions offering real potential for the client.[1]

> "We will strive to be effective by keeping a balance between participation and efficiency."

The Decision-Making Process

Within an organization, managers must provide for decision making that encourages the free flow of new ideas and supports the efforts of people who want to make their ideas work as they reach for success. And just as with organizations themselves, the success of our individual careers depends on the quality of the decisions we make regarding our jobs and employment situations.

Steps in Decision Making

Formally defined, decision making is the process of choosing a course of action for dealing with a problem or opportunity.[2] The five basic steps involved in systematic decision making are

1. Recognize and define the problem or opportunity.
2. Identify and analyze alternative courses of action, and estimate their effects on the problem or opportunity.

3. Choose a preferred course of action.

4. Implement the preferred course of action.

5. Evaluate the results and follow up as necessary.

Cultural and Ethical Foundations of Decision Making

Decision making means making choices. Each aspect of the decision-making process is a linked choice. Although some may exclusively emphasize corporate goal attainment as the foundation for managerial choices, we think you should probe deeper. You should recognize that choices are embedded in cultural and ethical foundations.

Cultural Foundations of Decision Making   It is only reasonable to expect that as cultures vary, so, too, will choices concerning what is to be solved and how.[3] For example, there are historical cultural preferences for solving problems. The approach favored in this chapter emphasizes the North American view, stressing decisiveness, speed, and individual selection of alternatives. This view speaks more to choice and less to implementation. Yet, as we will see in this chapter, implementation can proceed almost separately from other aspects of the decision-making process.

Other cultures place less emphasis on individual choice than on developing implementations that work. They start with what is workable and better, rather than with a comparison of current conditions to some ideal or fixed goal.[4] If a change can improve the current situation, even if it is not apparently directed toward a problem identified by senior management, subordinate managers may work together to implement it. And then senior management may be informed of the success of the change. To emphasize the importance of smooth implementation over grand decision making, corporations may adopt systems similar to the Japanese *ringi* system. With a ringi system lower-level managers indicate their written approval of proposals prior to formal implementation. Written approval is an issue not of whether the change should be made, but whether it is feasible for the group to implement.[5]

The more important role of culture in decision making concerns not how problems are solved, but which concerns are elevated to the status of problems solvable within the firm. For instance, the very fact that a procedure is old may make it more suspect in the United States than in France.[6] In the United States far too many of our views may be dictated by Western bureaucratic thinking.[7] Not all cultures are as pluralistic, bluntly competitive, or impersonal as that of the United States. In other parts of the world, personal loyalties may drive decisions, and preserving harmony may be considered more important than achieving a bit more efficiency. In short, problems may be more person centered and socially defined than bureaucratically prescribed. While there is no clear common base for decision making across cultures, Nokia has an interesting way of approaching decision making in its global operations, as illustrated in Ethics in OB.

Ethical Foundations of Decision Making   While there is little question culture plays an important role in the decision-making process, we also suggest ethics should be considered as an important foundation. Recall the discussion of a framework for ethical decision making first introduced in Chapter 1.[8] An ethical dilemma was defined as a situation in which a person must decide whether or not

THE NOKIA WAY OF DECISION MAKING

Nokia, initially a Finnish Corporation, is the world's second largest mobile phone manufacturer and a leading supplier of digital and fixed networks. Its ability to maintain its leadership position in the fastest-growing telecommunications segments is based squarely on its employees and the way they make decisions. It is not just a Finnish way—it is a Nokia way. Their choice-making process is characterized by an emphasis on technology development and goal attainment, not bureaucracy, so that Nokia can quickly apply and refine the newest technologies. The decision-making process is embedded in four Nokia ethical values: customer satisfaction, respect for the individual, achievement, and continuous learning. Moreover, Nokia managers recognize that the application and emphasis on these values as well as their incorporation into the decision-making process will vary substantially across different cultures.[2A]

Question: Does Nokia's recognition of a varying emphasis on cultural values help in fostering ethical decisions?

to do something that, although personally or organizationally beneficial, may be considered unethical and perhaps illegal.

Often, ethical dilemmas are associated with risk and uncertainty and with non-routine problem situations. Just how decisions are handled under these circumstances, ones that will inevitably appear during your career, may well be the ultimate test of your personal ethical framework. As a manager you also have the responsibility to integrate ethical decision making into your part of the firm. When it comes to the ethics of decision making, the criteria individuals use to define problems and the values that underlie these criteria must be considered.[9] Moral conduct is involved in choosing problems, deciding who should be involved, estimating the impacts of alternatives, and selecting an alternative for implementation.

Moral conduct does not arise from after-the-fact embarrassment. As Stephen Fineman suggests: "If people are unable to anticipate shame or guilt before they act in particular ways, then moral codes are invalid. . . . Decisions may involve lying, deceit, fraud, evasion of negligence—disapproved of in many cultures. But ethical monitoring and control go beyond just the pragmatics of harm."[10] In other words, when you are the decision maker, decision making is not just a choice process followed by implementation for the good of the organization. It involves your values and your morality, whether or not you think it should. Thus, effectively implemented choices need not only solve a problem or capitalize on choices, but they also need to match your values and help others. It is little wonder, then, that decision making will likely be the biggest challenge of your organizational career.

We must also recognize that in settings where there is substantial change and where many new technologies prevail, a simple emphasis on a step-by-step view of the decision-making process may be flawed. To understand when and where to use the traditional or novel decision process calls for a further understanding of decision environments and the types of decisions to be made.

Decision Environments

Problem-solving and opportunity-seeking decisions in organizations are typically made under three different conditions or environments: certainty, risk, and uncertainty.[11]

Certain environments exist when information is sufficient to predict the results of each alternative in advance of implementation. When a person invests money in a savings account, for example, absolute certainty exists about the interest that will be earned on that money in a given period of time. Certainty is an ideal condition for managerial problem solving and decision making. The challenge is simply to locate the alternative that offers the best or ideal solution. Unfortunately, certainty is the exception instead of the rule in decision environments.

Risk environments exist when decision makers lack complete certainty regarding the outcomes of various courses of action but are aware of the probabilities associated with their occurrence. A probability, in turn, is the degree of likelihood of an event's occurrence. Probabilities can be assigned through objective statistical procedures or through personal intuition. For instance, managers can make statistical estimates of quality rejects in production runs, or a senior production manager can make similar estimates based on past experience. Risk is a common decision environment in today's organizations.

Uncertain environments exist when managers have so little information on hand that they cannot even assign probabilities to various alternatives and their possible outcomes. This is the most difficult of the three decision environments. Uncertainty forces decision makers to rely heavily on individual and group creativity to succeed in problem solving. It requires unique, novel, and often totally innovative alternatives to existing patterns of behavior. Responses to uncertainty are often heavily influenced by intuition, educated guesses, and hunches.

An uncertain decision environment may also be characterized as a rapidly changing organizational setting in terms of (1) external conditions, (2) the information technology requirements called for to analyze and make decisions, and (3) the personnel influencing problem and choice definitions. This has been called an **organized anarchy,** a firm or division in a firm in a transition characterized by rapid change and lack of a legitimate hierarchy and collegiality. Although this was once a unique setting, many high-tech firms and those with expanding global operations share many of the characteristics of an organized anarchy.[12] For instance, KPMG, one of the world's largest and most prestigious consulting firms, has a large practice in what the company calls "enterprise risk management" to help firms identify risks and manage them.[13]

Regardless of where they operate or the dominant culture of the managers, KPMG consultants know they must go far beyond the traditional risk mitigation notion of using controls to limit the exposure of a firm. They systematically ask managers to separately identify (1) strategic risks (threats to overall business success), (2) operational risks (threats inherent in the technologies used to reach business success), and (3) reputation risks (threats to a brand or to the firm's reputation). Although they also note the importance of threats from regulatory sources, KPMG consultants pay special attention to financial threats, challenges to information systems, and new initiatives from competitors, in addition to change in the competitive setting (e.g., recession, disasters). They want firms to focus on critical risks, develop a strategy for dealing with these critical risks, and define specific responsibilities for dealing with the identified risks. They coach execu-

Certain environments provide full information on the expected results for decision-making alternatives.

Risk environments provide probabilities regarding expected results for decision-making alternatives.

Uncertain environments provide no information to predict expected results for decision-making alternatives.

Organized anarchy is a firm or division of a firm in a transition characterized by rapid change and lack of a legitimate hierarchy.

tives to know their risk tolerances and to move toward viewing risks in the context of the firm's strategy. This allows leaders to recognize the risk environment in which they operate and incorporate this into their decision-making process. Further, by a systematic process, firms can more clearly identify which aspects of their environment and operations are risky and which are truly uncertain.

Types of Decisions

■ Programmed decisions simply implement solutions that have already been determined by past experience as appropriate for the problem at hand.

Routine and nonroutine problems in the modern workplace call for different types of decisions. Routine problems arise on a regular basis and can be addressed through standard responses, called **programmed decisions.** These decisions simply implement solutions that have already been determined by past experience as appropriate for the problem at hand. Examples of programmed decisions are reordering inventory automatically when stock falls below a predetermined level and issuing a written reprimand to someone who violates a certain personnel procedure.

Routine operations are at the heart of many corporations. Firms are finding that when they or their customers face programmed decisions, they can use new Web-based technologies to get speedier and better decisions. For example, REI (Recreational Equipment Inc.) tied their Web site to inventory-monitoring systems to quickly offer discounts on overstocked items.[14]

■ Nonprogrammed decisions are created to deal uniquely with a problem at hand.

Nonroutine problems are unique and new, often involving issues that have ever been encountered before. Because standard responses are not available, these circumstances call for creative problem solving. These **nonprogrammed decisions** are specifically crafted or tailored to the situation at hand. Higher-level managers generally spend a greater proportion of their decision-making time on nonroutine problems. An example is a senior marketing manager who has to respond to the introduction of a new product by a foreign competitor. Although past experience may help deal with this competitive threat, the immediate decision requires a creative solution based on the unique characteristics of the present market situation. Check the Mastering Management for some additional help.

■ Associative choices are decisions that can be loosely linked to nagging continual problems but that were not specifically developed to solve the problem.

For firms in or characterized by organized anarchy, we suggest there is a third class of decisions called associative choices. **Associative choices** are decisions that can be loosely linked to nagging continual problems but that are not specifically developed to solve the problem. Given the chaotic nature of the setting, the

---

MASTERING MANAGEMENT

AVOIDING COMMON MISTAKES IN DECISION MAKING

Paul Nutt is in expert in decision making. He suggests that many decision debacles involve faulty decision practices, premature commitments, and misallocation of resources. To avoid these mistakes he suggests

1. Spend time to uncover hidden ethical concerns.
2. Take care to manage the social and political forces that may block the decision.
3. Focus on clear objectives.
4. Explore a wide range of options.
5. Estimate risks.
6. Route out perverse incentive structures.[14A]

necessity of taking action as opposed to waiting, and the ability of employees to make nearly any "decision" work, a stream of associative choices may be used to improve the setting, even though the problems are not solved.

Decision-Making Models

The field of organizational behavior has historically emphasized two alternative approaches to decision making—classical and behavioral (Figure 13.1).[15] **Classical decision theory** models view the manager as acting in a world of complete certainty. **Behavioral decision theory** models accept the notion of bounded rationality and suggest that people act only in terms of what they perceive about a given situation.

Classical and Behavioral Decision Theory

Ideally, the manager faces a clearly defined problem, knows all possible action alternatives and their consequences, and then chooses the alternative that offers the best, or "optimum," solution to the problem. This optimizing style is an ideal way to make decisions. This classical approach is normative and prescriptive, and it is often used as a model for how managers should make decisions.

Information Technology in Extending Classical Decision Making. It is clear that artificial intelligence (AI), the study of how computers can be programmed to think like the human brain, will allow computers to displace many decision makers.[16] In the 1960's Nobel laureate and decision scientist Herbert Simon was convinced that computers would someday be more intelligent than humans. Today the applications of AI to organizational decision making are significant.

Most of us have access to decision-making support from expert systems that reason like human experts and follow "either–or" rules to make deductions. For

■ Classical decision theory views decision makers as acting in a world of complete certainty.

■ Behavioral decision theory views decision makers as acting only in terms of what they perceive about a given situation.

■ Artificial intelligence is the study of how computers can be programmed to think like the human brain.

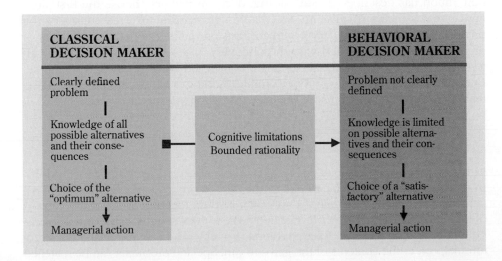

Figure 13.1 Decision making viewed from the classical and behavioral perspectives.

example, if you call an advertised 800 number to apply for a home equity loan, you will not get a human but a computer program that will take all the necessary information and provide confirmation of a loan.

Fuzzy logic that reasons beyond either–or choices and neural networks that reason inductively by simulating the brain's parallel processing capabilities are becoming operational realities that will move beyond simple programmed decisions. Uses for such systems may be found everywhere from hospitals, where they check on medical diagnoses, to investment houses, where they will analyze potential investment portfolios, to a wide and growing variety of other settings.[17] Behavioral scientists, however, are cautious about applying classical decision theory, even with AI extensions, to many decision situations. They recognize that the human mind is a wonderful creation, capable of infinite achievements. But they also recognize that human beings have cognitive limitations that restrict their information-processing capabilities. Information deficiencies and overload compromise the ability of decision makers to achieve complete certainty and otherwise operate according to the classical model. Human decision makers also operate with bounded rationality, whether this is in the choices of problems, the analysis of alternatives, or the development of AI systems themselves.

✶Bounded rationality is a shorthand term suggesting that, while individuals are reasoned and logical, humans have their limits. Individuals interpret and make sense of things within the context of their personal situations. They engage in decision making "within the box" of a simplified view of a more complex reality. This makes it difficult to realize the ideal of classical decision making. As a result, the classical model does not give a full and accurate description of how most decisions are made in organizations.[18]

Behavioral decision theory models accept the notion of bounded rationality and suggest that people act only in terms of what they perceive about a given situation. Because these perceptions are frequently imperfect, most organizational decision making does not take place in a world of complete certainty. Rather, the behavioral decision maker is viewed as acting most often under uncertain conditions and with limited information. Organizational decision makers face problems that are often ambiguous, and they have only partial knowledge of the available action alternatives and their consequences. This leads to a phenomenon that Herbert Simon has described as **satisficing**: decision makers choose the first alternative that appears to give an acceptable or a satisfactory resolution of the problem. As Simon states: "Most human decision making, whether individual or organizational, is concerned with the discovery and selection of satisfactory alternatives; only in exceptional cases is it concerned with the discovery and selection of optimal decisions."[19] For example, Sterling Bank decentralizes decision making to better serve its customers, even though the decentralized decisions will be satisficed.

Satisficing is choosing the first alternative that appears to give an acceptable or satisfactory resolution of the problem.

The Garbage Can Model

A third view of decision making stems from the so-called **garbage can model**.[20] In this view, the main components of the choice process—problems, solutions, participants, and choice situations—are all mixed up together in the "garbage can" of the organization. In many organizations where the setting is stable and the technology is well known and fixed, tradition, strategy, and the administrative structure help order the contents of the garbage can. Specific problems can be matched

Garbage can model views the main components of the choice process —problems, solutions, participants, and choice situations—as all mixed up together in the garbage can of the organization.

to specific solutions, an orderly process can be maintained, and the behavioral view of decision making may be appropriate. But when the setting is dynamic, the technology is changing, demands are conflicting, or the goals are unclear, things can get mixed up. More action than thinking can take place. Solutions emerge as "potential capabilities"—capabilities independent of problems or opportunities. Solutions often emerge not to solve specific problems but as lessons learned from the experience of other organizations. These new solutions/capabilities may be in the form of new employees, new technical experts, consultants, or reports on best practices. Many solutions may be implemented even if they cannot be tied to a specific problem. Solutions may also be implemented when no other solution has solved a persistent, chronic problem. Although implemented solutions change the organization, they are unlikely to solve persistent chronic problems.

The garbage can model highlights an important feature of decision making in many large organizations. Quite different individuals may do choice making and implementation. Often, the job of subordinates is to make the decisions of senior managers work. They must interpret the intentions of their bosses as well as solve local problems. Implementation becomes an opportunity to instill many changes related to the choices of more senior executives. So what is chosen gets implemented along with many other changes. The link between choice and implementation may become even weaker when senior managers are vague or do not vigorously follow up on implementation.

There is a final aspect of the garbage can view: many problems go unsolved. That is, all organizations have chronic, persistent deficiencies that never seem to get much better. In a garbage can view, this is because decision makers cannot agree to match these problems with solutions, make a choice, and implement the choice in a timely and consistent manner; nor do they know how to resolve chronic problems. It is only when a problem and a solution "bump into one another" under a decision maker willing to implement a choice that problems, solutions, and choice come together as expected under other views. Thus, one key job challenge for the astute manager is to make the appropriate linkages among problems and solutions.

Intuition, Judgment, and Creativity

Choices always bear the unique imprint of the individuals who make them, the politics within the organization, and the challenges facing the organization's decision makers. In reality, intuition, judgment, and creativity are just as critical to how decisions are made. A key element in decision making under risk and uncertainty is intuition.

Intuition

Intuition is the ability to know or recognize quickly and readily the possibilities of a given situation.[21] Intuition adds elements of personality and spontaneity to decision making. As a result, it offers the potential for creativity and innovation. In an earlier time scholars carried on a vigorous debate regarding how managers should plan and make decisions.[22] On one side of the issue were those who believed that planning could be accomplished in a systematic, step-by-step fashion. On the other

Decentralized Decision Making at Sterling Bank

Sterling Bank has grown from its initial start in 1974 to become one of the largest locally owned banks in Texas. A key to the bank's success was decentralizing decision making so that clients could get fast, accurate, high-quality service. Now clients can talk directly with a decision maker at each of the bank's 30 branches.

Intuition is the ability to know or recognize quickly the possibilities of a situation.

OB SAVVY 13.1

Ways to Improve Your Intuition

Relax
- Drop the problem for a while.
- Spend some quiet time by yourself.
- Try to clear your mind.

Use Common Mental Exercises
- Use images to guide your thinking.
- Let ideas run freely without a specific goal.

side were those who believed that the very nature of managerial work made this hard to achieve in actual practice. We now know that managers favor verbal communication. Thus, they are more likely to gather data and to make decisions in a relational or interactive way than in an isolated, systematic, step-by-step fashion.[23] Managers often deal with impressions. Thus, they are more likely to synthesize than to analyze data as they search for the "big picture" in order to redefine problems and link problems with a variety of solutions. Managers work fast, do a variety of things, and are frequently interrupted. Thus, they do not have a lot of quiet time alone to think, plan, or make decisions systematically. As OB Savvy suggests, managers may want to slow down a bit to improve their intuition.

Are managers correct when they favor the more intuitive and less systematic approach? The more chaotic environments and technologies of many of today's organizations press for this emphasis on intuition. Unfortunately, many business firms are better at implementing the common solutions of others than uniquely solving their own problems. Since managers do work in chaotic settings, this reality should be accepted, and decision makers should be confident in using their intuitive skills. However, they should combine analytical and intuitive approaches to create new and novel solutions to complex problems.

Judgmental Heuristics

Judgment, or the use of one's intellect, is important in all aspects of decision making. When we question the ethics of a decision, for example, we are questioning the judgment of the person making it. Research shows that people are prone to mistakes using biases that often interfere with the quality of decision making.[24] These can be traced to the use of **heuristics**: simplifying strategies or "rules of thumb" used to make decisions. Heuristics serve a useful purpose in making it easier to deal with uncertainty and the limited information common to problem situations. But they can also lead to systematic errors that affect the quality, and perhaps the ethical implications, of any decisions made. It is helpful to understand the common judgmental heuristics of availability, representativeness, and anchoring and adjustment.[25]

Heuristics are simplifying strategies or "rules of thumb" used to make decisions.

The Availability Heuristic   The **availability heuristic** involves assessing a current event based on past occurrences that are easily available in one's memory. An example is the product development specialist who bases a decision not to launch a new product on her recent failure with another product offering. In this case, the existence of a past product failure has negatively, and perhaps inappropriately, biased her judgment regarding how best to handle the new product.

The **availability heuristic** bases a decision on recent events relating to the situation at hand.

The Representativeness Heuristic   The **representativeness heuristic** involves assessing the likelihood that an event will occur based on its similarity to one's stereotypes of similar occurrences. An example is the team leader who selects a new member not because of any special qualities of the person, but only because the individual comes from a department known to have produced high performers in the past. In this case, it is the individual's current place of employment—not his or her job qualifications—that is the basis for the selection decision.

The **representativeness heuristic** bases a decision on similarities between the situation at hand and stereotypes of similar occurrences.

The Anchoring and Adjustment Heuristic   The **anchoring and adjustment heuristic** involves assessing an event by taking an initial value from historical precedent or an outside source, and then incrementally adjusting this value to make a current assessment. An example is the executive who makes salary increase recommendations for key personnel by simply adjusting their current base salaries by a percentage amount. In this case, the existing base salary becomes an "anchor" that drives subsequent salary increases. In some situations this anchor may be inappropriate, such as in the case of an individual whose market value has become substantially higher than is reflected by the base salary plus increment approach.

In addition to using the common judgmental heuristics, decision makers are also prone to more general biases in decision making. One bias is the **confirmation trap**, whereby the decision maker seeks confirmation for what is already thought to be true and neglects opportunities to acknowledge or find disconfirming information. A form of selective perception, this bias involves seeking only those cues in a situation that support a preexisting opinion. A second bias is the **hindsight trap**, whereby the decision maker overestimates the degree to which he or she could have predicted an event that has already taken place. One risk of hindsight is that it may foster feelings of inadequacy or insecurity in dealing with future decision situations.

Creativity

Creativity in decision making involves the development of unique and novel responses to problems and opportunities. In a dynamic environment full of nonroutine problems, creativity in crafting decisions often determines how well people and organizations do in response to complex challenges.[26] Creativity may also involve new ways to link ethical concerns to everyday product choices and then to environmental concerns, as is the case with Pella in Ethics in OB 13.2.

In the chapters on groups, we examined the group as an important resource for improving creativity in decision making. Indeed, making good use of such traditional techniques as brainstorming, nominal groups, and the Delphi method can greatly expand the creative potential of people and organizations. The addition of new computer-based group meeting and decision-making techniques extends this potential even further.

Stages of Creative Thinking   Creative thinking may unfold in a series of five stages. First is preparation.[27] Here people engage in the active learning and day-to-day sensing required to deal successfully with complex environments. The second stage is concentration, whereby actual problems are defined and framed so that alternatives can be considered for dealing with them. In the third stage, incubation, people look at the problems in diverse ways that permit the consideration of unusual alternatives, avoiding tendencies toward purely linear and systematic problem solving. The fourth stage is illumination, in which people respond to flashes of insight and recognize when all pieces to the puzzle suddenly fit into place. The fifth and final stage is certification, which proceeds with logical analysis to confirm that good problem-solving decisions have really been made.[28]

The **anchoring and adjustment heuristic** bases a decision on incremental adjustments to an initial value determined by historical precedent or some reference point.

The **confirmation trap** is the tendency to seek confirmation for what is already thought to be true and not search for disconfirming information.

The **hindsight trap** is a tendency to overestimate the degree to which an event that has already taken place could have been predicted.

Creativity generates unique and novel responses to problems.

ETHICS IN OB

PELLA: CREATIVELY LINKING ETHICS, ENVIRONMENTAL RESPONSIBILITY, AND OPERATIONS

Pella is one of the world's leading manufacturers of premium-quality windows and doors. Gary Christensen, president and CEO, encourages creativity to link ethics and environmental responsibility as he attempts to infuse both of them into all aspects of the firm's operations. One result: Pella now makes many of its windows from replenishable new-growth pine, recycled aluminum, and even some recycled glass. Although it is cheaper not to use these materials, Christensen encourages all Pella employees to make similar creative linkage choices.[29]

Question: Would you be willing to pay a bit more for a Pella window, knowing the company uses using environmentally responsible materials?

All these stages of creativity need support and encouragement in the organizational environment. However, creative thinking in decision making can be limited by a number of factors. Judgmental heuristics such as those just reviewed can limit the search for alternatives. When attractive options are left unconsidered, creativity can be limited. Cultural and environmental blocks can also limit creativity. This occurs when people are discouraged from considering alternatives viewed as inappropriate by cultural standards or inconsistent with prevailing norms.

Fostering Creativity   Perhaps the most important development in creativity research has been the recognition that group and organizational factors play an important role. To foster creativity, several scholars suggest that decision makers (1) diversify teams to include members with different backgrounds, training, and perspectives; (2) encourage analogical reasoning (applying a concept or idea from one domain to another); (3) stress periods of silent reflection; (4) record all ideas so that the same ones are not rediscovered; (5) establish high expectations for creativity; and (6) develop a physical space that encourages fun, divergent ideas.[30] It is important to recognize that when seeking high-quality creative decisions, more ideas can often produce better ones.[31]

There is also a series of studies suggesting that combining individual, group, and organizational conditions fosters creativity.[32] At the individual level, personality and individual cognitive skills (such as linguistic ability and the willingness to engage in divergent thinking as well as intelligence) are important. Further, individual creativity is higher when individuals are motivated by the task itself and derive satisfaction from task accomplishment. Creativity is further enhanced when the decision maker provides opportunities for creativity, eliminates as many constraints as possible, and provides rewards for creative effort.[33]

Above all, recent research suggests that creativity is a process involving the interaction of individuals.[34] The decision maker can stress engagement in the creative process and counsel individuals to share their ideas with others under a norm of constructive assistance. In this view, creativity is an ebb and flow of engagement among representatives from slightly different portions of the organization.[35] Decision makers should encourage subordinates to recognize ambiguity, contact others with different views, and be prepared to make considerable changes as they attempt to develop new meanings and interpretations of problems and causes as well as solutions. Often this will mean that subordinates will need to seek out individuals who are only loosely connected to their home departments.[36] The expansion of creative networks in order to change the views of individuals appears to be a key to the longer-term development of creativity.[37]

Computer support for creative group decision making, including Internet and intranet developments, has broken groups out of the confines of face-to-face interactions. With the software now available, problems can be defined and decisions can be made through virtual teamwork by people in geographically dispersed locations. We know that group-decision software can be especially useful for generating ideas, such as in electronic brainstorming. People working under electronically mediated conditions tend to stay focused on tasks and avoid the interpersonal conflicts and other problems common in face-to-face deliberations. On the negative side, decisions made by "electronic groups" carry some risks of being impersonal and perhaps less compelling in terms of commitments to implementation and follow-through.[38]

Managing the Decision-Making Process

As suggested by this discussion of creativity, people working at all levels, in all areas, and in all types and sizes of organizations are not supposed to simply make decisions. They must make good decisions—the right decisions in the right way at the right time.[39] Managing the decision-making process involves choices itself. Critical choices include which "problems" to work on, who to involve, how to involve them, and when to quit.

Choosing Problems to Address

Most people are too busy and have too many valuable things to do with their time to personally make decisions on every problem or opportunity that comes their way. The effective manager and team leader knows when to delegate decisions to others, how to set priorities, and when to abstain from acting altogether. Take a look at Terri Kelly of W. L. Gore & Associates and her unique approach to decision making in this unique firm.

When faced with the dilemma of whether or not to deal with a specific problem, asking and answering the following questions can sometimes help.[40]

Is the problem easy to deal with?   Small and less-significant problems should not get the same time and attention as bigger ones. Even if a mistake is made, the cost of a decision error on a small problem is also small. Might the problem resolve itself? Putting problems in rank order leaves the less significant for last. Surprisingly, many of these less important problems resolve themselves or are solved

Leaders on Leadership

TERRI KELLY, PRESIDENT AND CEO OF W. L. GORE

W. L. Gore and Associates is not like any other firm you know. There are no formal titles, but everyone knows who the leaders are. Almost everyone who works here evaluates everyone else. Yet, this is a huge firm, with revenues of almost $2 billion, with 26 sites and some 7,500 associates. You may know Gore for its GORE-TEX fabrics, but it makes a wide range of products, including NASA space suits based on their fluoropolymer expertise. The leader is Terri Kelly, and she has charged herself with maintaining Gore's record of innovation and its unique culture. Decision making? Said Kelly: "I spend a lot of time making sure we have the right people in the right roles. We need to empower divisions and push out responsibility."[41]

Question: Gore is now seeing new competition from Asian firms with lower costs and slightly lower-quality materials. Do you think Terri Kelly's innovative approach to decision making will continue?

by others before you get to them. One less problem to solve leaves decision-making time and energy for other uses.

Is this my decision to make?   Many problems can be handled by other persons. These should be delegated to people who are best prepared to deal with them; ideally, they should be delegated to people whose work they most affect.

Is this a solvable problem within the context of the organization?   The astute decision maker recognizes the difference between problems that realistically can be solved and those that are simply not solvable for all practical purposes.

Deciding Who Should Participate

A mistake commonly made by many new managers and team leaders is presuming that they must solve every problem by making every decision themselves.[42] In practice, good organizational decisions are made by individuals acting alone, by individuals consulting with others, and by groups of people working together. Several scholars argue that who participates and how decisions are to be made should reflect the issues at hand.

Paul Nutt, a leading authority on decision making in corporations, argues that half the decisions in organizations fail.[43] Why? A major reason is that the decision tactics managers most often use are those most prone to failure. Managers take too many shortcuts. Too often, they merely copy the choices of others and try to sell these to subordinates. While such copying appears practical and pragmatic, it fails to recognize unanticipated difficulties and delays. No two firms are alike, and subtle adjustments are typically needed to copy another's solution. Subordinates may believe the manager is just using his or her clout—not working for the best interests of all. Related to the overemphasis on immediate action is the tendency for managers to emphasize problems and solutions. The tactics related to success are underused. Managers need to focus on the outcomes they want, rather than the problems they see. Above all, managers need to use participation more.

To echo our discussion of the ringi system, we think it is critical that a choice be followed by effective implementation. Victor Vroom, Phillip Yetton, and Arthur Jago have developed a framework for helping managers choose the decision-making methods most appropriate for various problem situations to insure both better choices and implementation.[44]

Since making choices is complicated, their recommendations, charted in Figure 13.2, also appear complicated to many unfamiliar with decision trees. What these scholars have done is sequentially array the key factors that should guide your participation choices. The most important is the technical quality of the decision. If it is high, the figure starts you in one direction to consider other factors. If it is low, there are fewer factors to consider. Is this figure too complex and unrealistic? No, not really. Selecting the appropriate decision-making method for a problem is critical to effective implementation. Successful and experienced managers often consider the factors in the model. The figure is just a way to display the hard-won lessons of experience. So what attributes make a difference? As shown in the figure, the attributes are (1) the required quality of the decision, (2) the commitment needed from subordinates, (3) the amount of information the leader has, (4) the problem structure, (5) commitment probability—the chances subordinates would be committed if you made the choice, (6) goal congruence—the degree to which subordinates share the goals to be achieved by the choice, (7) subordinate conflict, and (8) subordinate information. For example, if the quality requirement is low and subordinates have high goal congruence, the model suggests you would make the choice. The analysis forces you to recognize how time, quality requirements, information availability, and subordinate acceptance issues can affect who should participate and how. It also reminds you that effective decision making can involve individual choices, working with others, and group decisions. The key to effectively managing participation in decision making is first knowing when to use each decision method and then knowing how to implement each of them well.

When individual decisions, also called **authority decisions**, are made, the manager or team leader uses information that he or she possesses and decides what to do without involving others. This decision method often reflects the prerogatives of a person's position of formal authority in the organization. For instance, in deciding a rotation for lunch hours in a retail store, the manager may post a schedule. In **consultative decisions**, by contrast, inputs on the problem are solicited from other persons. Based on this information and its interpretation, the decision maker arrives at a final choice. To continue the example, the manager may tell subordinates that a lunch schedule is needed and asks them when they would like to schedule their lunch and why before making the decision. In other cases, true **group decisions** can be made by both consulting with others and allowing them to help make the final choice. To complete the example, the manager may hold a meeting to get everyone's agreement on a lunch schedule or a system for deciding how to make the schedule. Vroom and his associates further clarify individual, consultative, and group decision options as follows:

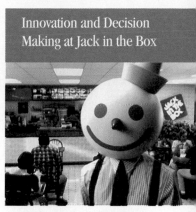

Innovation and Decision Making at Jack in the Box

Tired of the same old burger and fries? Check out Jack in the Box® restaurants. Jack in the Box has been a major innovator in the fast-food business. Its advertising features the company's fictional founder, Jack, and his irreverent commentary on most any topic relevant to the chain's primary audience—young men ages 18–34. Jack in the Box constantly explores new food trends, such as ethnic and regional foods aimed at adult tastes. From its award-winning ads to its broad selection of distinctive and innovative food products, the key to the company's success is senior management's support of creative decision making. They let ideas flow, and they encourage employees at all levels to look at the world in a different way.

■ **Authority decisions** are made by one individual using information he/she already possesses.

■ **Consultative decisions** are made by one individual after seeking input from or consulting with members of a group.

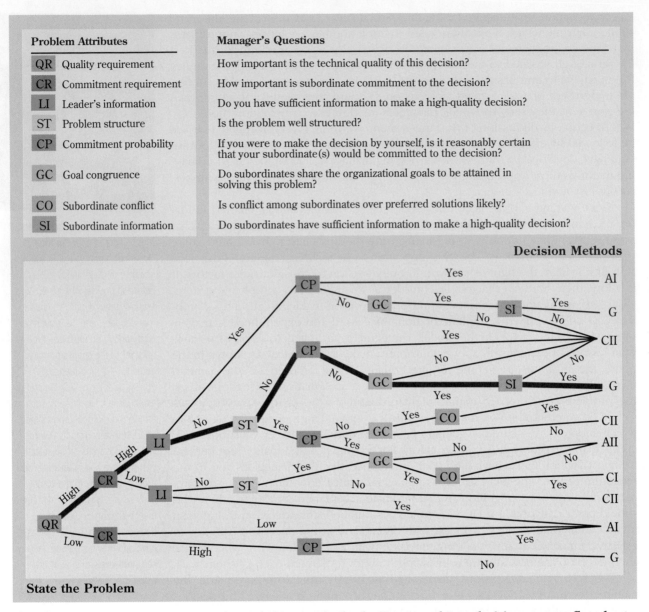

Problem Attributes

		Manager's Questions
QR	Quality requirement	How important is the technical quality of this decision?
CR	Commitment requirement	How important is subordinate commitment to the decision?
LI	Leader's information	Do you have sufficient information to make a high-quality decision?
ST	Problem structure	Is the problem well structured?
CP	Commitment probability	If you were to make the decision by yourself, is it reasonably certain that your subordinate(s) would be committed to the decision?
GC	Goal congruence	Do subordinates share the organizational goals to be attained in solving this problem?
CO	Subordinate conflict	Is conflict among subordinates over preferred solutions likely?
SI	Subordinate information	Do subordinates have sufficient information to make a high-quality decision?

Figure 13.2   Selecting alternative decision-making methods: the Vroom and Jago decision process flowchart.

▬ **Group decisions** are made by all members of the group.

- *AI (first variant on the authority decision):* The manager solves the problem or makes the decision alone, using information available at that time.
- *AII (second variant on the authority decision):* The manager obtains the necessary information from subordinate(s) or other group members and then decides on the problem's solution. The manager may or may not tell subordinates what the problem is before obtaining the information from them. The subordinates provide the necessary information but do not generate or evaluate alternatives.

- *CI (first variant on the consultative decision):* The manager shares the problem with relevant subordinates or other group members individually, getting their ideas and suggestions without bringing them together as a group. The manager then makes a decision that may or may not reflect the subordinates' input.

- *CII (second variant on the consultative decision):* The manager shares the problem with subordinates or other group members, collectively obtaining their ideas and suggestions. The manager then makes a decision that may or may not reflect the subordinates' input.

- *G (the group or consensus decision):* The manager shares the problem with the subordinates as a total group and engages the group in consensus seeking to arrive at a final decision.

In Figure 13.2 the problem attributes are sequentially depicted, and the various combinations of these attributes are linked to a recommendation. Try it by working through Figure 13.2 for an organizational problem with which you are familiar.

Knowing When to Quit

The organization's natural desire to continue on a selected course of action reinforces some natural tendencies among decision makers.[45] Once the agonizing process of making a choice is apparently completed, executives make public commitments to implementation, once implementation begins, managers are often reluctant to change their minds and admit a mistake. Instead of backing off, the tendency is to press on to victory. This is called **escalating commitment**—continuation and renewed efforts on a previously chosen course of action, even though it is not working. Escalating commitment is reflected in the popular adage, "If at first you don't succeed, try, try, again."

In beginning finance courses, students learn about the fallacy of sunk costs: money committed and spent is gone. The decision to continue is just that—a decision. It needs to be based on what investment is needed and the returns on that investment. This is one of the most difficult aspects of decision making to convey to executives simply because so many of these executives rose to their positions by turning apparently losing courses of action into winners.[46] The tendency to escalate commitments often outweighs the willingness to disengage from them. Decision makers may rationalize negative feedback as a temporary condition, protect their egos by not admitting that the original decision was a mistake, or characterize any negative results as a "learning experience" that can be overcome with added future effort.

The self-discipline required to admit mistakes and change direction, however, is sometimes difficult to achieve. Management itself may indirectly encourage this tendency as shown in the Research Insight. Escalating commitments are a form of decision entrapment that leads people to do things that the facts of a situation do not justify. We should be proactive in spotting "failures" and more open to reversing decisions or dropping plans that do not appear to be working.[47] But again, this is easier said than done. Good decision makers know when to call it quits. They are willing to reverse previous decisions and stop investing time and other resources in unsuccessful courses of action. The late W. C. Fields is said to have muttered: "If at first you don't succeed, try, try, again. Then quit."

Escalating commitment is the tendency to continue a previously chosen course of action even when feedback suggests that it is failing.

Research Insight
Unintended Support for Escalation of Commitment

In this chapter we have outlined the problem of escalating commitment. Some individuals escalate commitment to a losing course of action when it is clear to others they should quit. McNamara, Moon, and Bromiley asked whether monitoring by more senior management would help stop escalating commitment in a group of bank loan officers. At first glance their data seem to suggest that monitoring worked. When individual clients were put in higher-risk categories (poorer credit risks), loan officers on these accounts were monitored more closely. Undue overcommitment to these higher-risk individuals was apparently reduced.

On closer examination, however, the researchers found that loan officers were reluctant to admit that individual clients with deteriorating credit should be placed in a higher-risk category where the loan officer would be subject to greater monitoring. For this group of clients, there was overcommitment. The authors called this reluctance to recategorize "intervention avoidance." They argued that the question of escalation is more complex than traditionally recognized and may involve a host of organizational factors that indirectly influence the tendencies of individuals to make undesirable decision commitments.[48]

Chapter 13   Study Guide

Summary

What is the decision-making process in organizations?

- Decision making is a process of identifying problems and opportunities and choosing among alternative courses of action for dealing successfully with them.

- Culture counts; differences in culture alter by whom, how, when, and why decisions are made.

- Ethics is involved in each stage of the decision-making process, and effective decision making includes individual moral criteria and values.

- Organizational decisions are often made in risky and uncertain environments, where situations are ambiguous and information is limited.

- Routine and repetitive problems can be dealt with through programmed decisions; nonroutine or novel problems require nonprogrammed decisions that are crafted to fit the situation at hand.

What are the useful decision-making models?

- Classical, behavioral, and garbage can models are often useful views of decision making.

- According to classical decision theory, optimum decisions are made after fully analyzing all possible alternatives and their known consequences.

- According to behavioral decision theory, most organizational decisions are made with limited information and by satisficing—choosing the first acceptable or satisfactory solutions to problems.

- According to the garbage can model, the main components of the choice process—problems, solutions, participants, and choice situations—are all mixed up together in the garbage can of the organization.

- The pressures of time and the lack of information are two important decision-making realities.

How do intuition, judgment, and creativity affect decision making?

- Both systematic decision making and intuitive decision making are important in today's complex work environments.

- Intuition is the ability to quickly recognize the action possibilities for resolving a problem situation.

- The use of judgmental heuristics, or simplifying rules of thumb, is common in decision making but can lead to biased results.

- Common heuristics include availability decisions based on recent events, representativeness decisions based on similar events, and anchoring and adjustment decisions based on historical precedents.

- Creativity in finding unique and novel solutions to problems can be enhanced through both individual and group problem-solving strategies.

How do you manage the decision-making process?

- Good managers know that not every problem requires an immediate decision; they also know how and when to delegate decision-making responsibilities.

- A common mistake is for a manager or team leader to make all decisions alone; instead, a full range of individual, consultative, and group decision-making methods should be used.

- The Vroom-Yetton-Jago model offers a way of matching problems with appropriate decision methods based on quality requirements, information availability, and time constraints.

- Tendencies toward escalating commitment, continuing previously chosen courses of action even when they are not working, should be recognized in work settings.

Key Terms

Anchoring and adjustment
   heuristic (p. 307)
Artificial intelligence
   (p. 303)
Associative choices (p. 302)
Authority decisions (p. 311)
Availability heuristic
   (p. 306)
Behavioral decision theory
   (p. 303)
Certain environments (p. 301)
Classical decision theory
   (p. 303)

Confirmation trap (p. 307)
Consultative decisions
   (p. 311)
Creativity (p. 307)
Escalating commitment
   (p. 313)
Garbage can model
   (p. 304)
Group decisions (p. 312)
Heuristics (p. 306)
Hindsight trap (p. 307)
Intuition (p. 305)

Nonprogrammed decisions
   (p. 302)
Organized anarchy (p. 301)
Programmed decisions
   (p. 302)
Representativeness
   heuristic (p. 306)
Risk environments (p. 301)
Satisficing (p. 304)
Uncertain environments
   (p. 301)

Self-Test 13

Multiple Choice

1. After a preferred course of action has been implemented, the next step in the decision-making process is to _____. (a) recycle the process (b) look for additional problems or opportunities (c) evaluate results (d) document the reasons for the decision

2. In which environment does the decision maker deal with probabilities regarding possible courses of action and their consequences? _____ (a) certain (b) risk (c) organized anarchy (d) uncertain

3. In which characterization of the decision environment is associative choice most likely to occur? _____ (a) organized anarchy (b) certainty (c) risk (d) satisficing

4. A manager who must deal with limited information and substantial risk is most likely to make decisions based on _____. (a) optimizing (b) classical decision theory (c) behavioral decision theory (d) escalation

5. A team leader who makes a decision not to launch a new product because the last new product launch failed is falling prey to the _____ heuristic. (a) anchoring (b) availability (c) adjustment (d) representativeness

6. The five steps in the creativity process are preparation, _____, illumination, _____, and verification. (a) extension, evaluation (b) reduction, concentration (c) adaptation, extension (d) concentration, incubation

7. In Vroom's decision-making model, the choice among individual and group decision methods is based on criteria that include quality requirements, availability of information, and _____. (a) need for implementation commitments (b) size of the organization (c) number of people involved (d) position power of the leader

8. The saying "If at first you don't succeed, try, try again" is most associated with a decision-making tendency called _____. (a) groupthink (b) the confirmation trap (c) escalating commitment (d) associative choice

9. Among the applications of Artificial Intelligence, _____ attempt to have computers reason inductively to solve problems. (a) neural networks (b) expert systems (c) fuzzy logics (d) electronic brainstorms

10. Preferences for who makes decisions _____. (a) vary slightly across cultures (b) characterize individualistic cultures (c) are important only in high power distance cultures (d) vary substantially across cultures

11. Decisions that can be loosely linked to nagging continual problems but that were not specifically developed to solve the problem are called _____. (a) program decisions (b) associative choices (c) authority decisions (d) artificial intellegence

12. Which model views the main components of the choice process—problems, solutions, participants, and choice situations—as all mixed up together? (a) the garbage can model (b) the behavioral model (c) the turbulence model (d) the classical model

13. The _____ bases a decision on similarities between the situation at hand and stereotypes of similar occurrences. (a) representativeness heuristic (b) anchoring and adjustment heuristic (c) confirmation trap (d) hindsight trap

14. The _____ bases a decision on incremental adjustments to an initial value determined by historical precedent or some reference point. (a) representativeness heuristic (b) anchoring and adjustment heuristic (c) confirmation trap (d) hindsight trap

15. The _____ is the tendency to seek confirmation for what is already thought to be true and not to search for disconfirming information. (a) representativeness heuristic (b) anchoring and adjustment heuristic (c) confirmation trap (d) hindsight trap

Short Response

16. What are heuristics, and how can they affect individual decision making?

17. What are the main differences among individual, consultative, and group decisions?

18. What is escalating commitment, and why is it important to recognize it in decision making?

19. What questions might a manager or team leader ask to help determine which problems to deal with and in which priority?

Applications Essay

20. Your friends know you are taking OB courses and constantly show you Dilbert cartoons in which managers are implementing decisions that are unrelated to problems. What insight can you share with them to help them understand Dilbert better?

These learning activities from *The OB Skills Workbook* are suggested for Chapter 13.

OB in Action

CASE	EXPERIENTIAL EXERCISES	SELF-ASSESSMENTS
■ 13. Decisions, Decisions	■ 32. Role Analysis Negotiation	■ 16. Your Intuitive Ability
	■ 33. Lost at Sea	■ 17. Decision-Making Biases
	■ 34. Entering the Unknown	
	■ 36. The Ugli Orange	
	■ 38. Force-Field Analysis	

Plus—special learning experiences from *The Jossey-Bass/Pfeiffer Classroom Collection*

Chapter 14

Communication

Interact before you act

Chapter at a Glance

Interactions create the foundations for successful actions. This chapter examines the nature of interpersonal and organizational communication as pathways to effective interaction in organizations. As you read the chapter, *keep in mind these study topics.*

THE NATURE OF COMMUNICATION

The Communication Process

Feedback and Communication

Communication Channels

Communication Directions and Flows

INTERPERSONAL COMMUNICATION

Effective and Efficient Communication

Nonverbal Communication

Active Listening

Cross-Cultural Communication

COMMUNICATION BARRIERS

Physical Distractions

Semantic Problems

Mixed Messages

Absence of Feedback

Status Effects

ISSUES IN ORGANIZATIONAL COMMUNICATION

Electronic Communication

Workplace Privacy

Communication and Social Context

You may not realize it, but when you use a Lenovo to type an assignment, you're working on a Chinese-made computer. The Lenovo Group Ltd. bought IBM's personal computer division and is presently the third largest computer maker in the world. And who sits in the CEO slot? It's an American, Bill Amelio, who was hired away from a senior position at Dell.

In an interview with the *Wall Street Journal,* Amelio was asked if he considered Lenovo a Chinese company. His reply: "We're a global company. We rotate the headquarters between Beijing, Hong Kong, Singapore, Raleigh (North Carolina), and Paris." He says he does not even have time to think about jet lag, but he is fully aware of the challenges of managing and communicating across cultures. He points out that American and European executives tend to speak their minds and "make their voices heard." The Chinese, by contrast, are more prone to listening, and when they do speak, they choose their words carefully. "If a Chinese colleague is nodding silently," says Amelio, "it doesn't mean they're agreeing."

Amelio is well aware of the cross-cultural challenges of blending a worldwide team of talent. In an interview on CNN he said that trust, respect, and compromise are the key words. He also claims living and working in Asia has taught him a lot, and that he has gained new skills. "I work hard at listening a lot better," he says. "I tend to be somewhat impatient at times and it is much better to be patient . . . sometimes you have to kind of let things seep in for awhile."

Twenty-seven percent of Lenovo is owned by the Chinese government. One of Amelio's first tasks was to deal with a rumor, picked up by members of the U.S. Congress, that the firm's computers contained spy chips. He says without doubt that this was all politics and no substance. When asked if he speaks Mandarin, Amelio replies that he can say "hello" and "thank you." Not surprisingly, his goal is to attend an immersion language program.[1]

> ## "If a Chinese colleague is nodding silently . . . it doesn't mean they're agreeing."

The Nature of Communication

Communication is the glue that holds organizations together. It is the way we share information, ideas, goals, directions, expectations, feelings, and emotions in the context of coordinated action. But, how good are we as communicators . . . really? Respondents to a survey by the American Management Association, for example, gave their managers only a 63 percent success rating in respect to "communicating information and direction." In another survey respondents rated how skilled their managers were in "listening and asking questions." The managers averaged ratings of only 3.36 on a 5-point scale.[2] Obviously, there is a lot yet to be accomplished with respect to managerial and workplace communication.

The Communication Process

It is useful to describe **communication** as a process of sending and receiving messages with attached meanings. The key elements in the communication process are illustrated in Figure 14.1. They include a source, which encodes an intended meaning into a message, and a receiver, which decodes the message into a perceived meaning. The receiver may or may not give feedback to the source. Although this process may appear to be elementary, it is not quite as simple as it looks. **Noise** is the term used to describe any disturbance that disrupts communication effectiveness and interferes with the transference of messages within the communication process.

The information source is a person or group trying to communicate with someone else. The source seeks to communicate, in part, to change the attitudes, knowledge, or behavior of the receiver. A team leader, for example, may want to communicate with a division manager in order to explain why the team needs more time or resources to finish an assigned project. This involves encoding—the process of translating an idea or thought into a message consisting of verbal, written, or nonverbal symbols (such as gestures), or some combination of them. Messages are transmitted through various **communication channels**, such as face-to-face meetings, e-mail and online discussions, written letters or memoranda, and telephone communications or voice mail, among others. The choice of channel can have an important impact on the communication process. Some people are better at using certain channels over others, and specific channels are better able to handle some types of messages. In the case of the team leader communicating with the division manager, for example, it can make quite a difference whether the message is sent face to face, in a written memo, by voice mail, or by e-mail.

The communication process is not completed even though a message is sent. The receiver is the individual or group of individuals to whom a message is directed. In order for meaning to be assigned to any received message, its contents must be interpreted through decoding. This process of translation is complicated by

■■ **Communication** is the process of sending and receiving symbols with attached meanings.

■■ **Noise** is anything that interferes with the effectiveness of communication.

■■ **Communication channels** are the pathways through which messages are communicated.

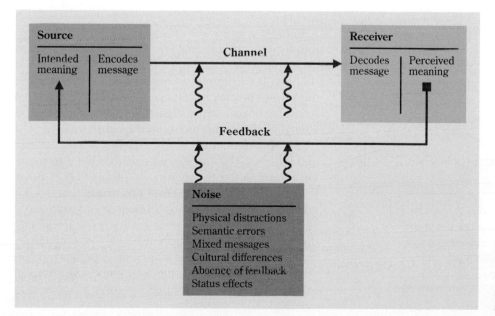

Figure 14.1   The communication process and possible sources of "noise."

many factors, including the knowledge and experience of the receiver and his or her relationship with the sender. A message may also be interpreted with the added influence of other points of view, such as those offered by friends, co-workers, or organizational superiors. Ultimately, the decoding may result in the receiver interpreting a message in a way that is different from that originally intended by the source.

Feedback and Communication

Feedback communicates how one feels about something another person has done or said.

Most receivers are well aware of the potential gap between the intended message of the source and the perceived meaning assigned to it by the recipient. One way in which these gaps are identified is **feedback**, the process through which the receiver communicates with the sender by returning another message. The exchange of information through feedback can be very helpful in improving the communication process, and the popular advice to always "keep the feedback channels open" is good to remember.

360-degree feedback provides performance feedback from peers, co-workers, and direct reports as well as from the supervisor.

In practice, giving feedback is often associated with one or more persons communicating an evaluation of what another person has said or done. An example is the process of **360-degree feedback** discussed in Chapter 7 as a setting in which not only a supervisor but also one's peers, co-workers, and direct reports provide feedback on performance. Just as in any feedback situation, all parties must engage in the 360° feedback situation carefully and with interpersonal skill.[3]

As pointed out in OB Savvy 14.1, there is an art to giving feedback so that the receiver accepts it and uses it constructively. Words that are intended to be polite and helpful can easily end up being perceived as unpleasant and even hostile. This risk is particularly evident in the performance appraisal process. A manager or team leader must be able to do more than just complete a written appraisal to document another person's performance for the record. To serve the person's developmental needs, feedback regarding the results of the appraisal—both the praise and the criticism—must be well communicated.

Communication Channels

Formal channels follow the official chain of command.

Informal channels do not follow the chain of command.

Information flows through both formal and informal communication channels in organizations. **Formal channels** follow the chain of command established by an organization's hierarchy of authority. For example, an organization chart indicates the proper routing for official messages passing from one level or part of the hierarchy to another. Because formal channels are recognized as authoritative, it is typical for communication of policies, procedures, and other official announcements to adhere to them. On the other hand, much "networking" takes place through the use of **informal channels** that do not adhere to the organization's hierarchy of authority.[4] They coexist with the formal channels but frequently diverge from them by skipping levels in the hierarchy or cutting across vertical chains of command. Informal channels help to create open communications in organizations and ensure that the right people are in contact with one another.[5]

OB SAVVY 14.1

How to Give Constructive Feedback

- Give it directly and in a spirit of mutual trust.
- Be specific, not general; use clear examples.
- Give it when receiver is most ready to accept.
- Be accurate; check its validity with others.
- Focus on things the receiver can control.
- Limit how much the receiver gets at one time.

A common informal communication channel is the **grapevine**, or network of friendships and acquaintances through which rumors and other unofficial information get passed from person to person. Grapevines have the advantage of being able to transmit information quickly and efficiently. Grapevines also help fulfill the needs of people involved in them. Being part of a grapevine can provide a sense of security that comes from "being in the know" when important things are going on. It also provides social satisfaction as information is exchanged interpersonally. The primary disadvantage of grapevines occurs when they transmit incorrect or untimely information. Rumors can be very dysfunctional, both to people and to organizations. One of the best ways to avoid rumors is to make sure that key persons in a grapevine get the right information to begin with.

Today, the traditional communication grapevine in organizations is often technology assisted. The most common form is probably the e-mail message, but as technology continues to evolve, so, too, does the grapevine. In more and more organizations people are communicating officially and unofficially by **blogs**—which are individual web sites that post personal accounts of events and situations as well as opinions and stories, and **wikis**—which are collaborative web sites to which individuals contribute material and edit material previously posted by others. As evidence of the power of technology in this regard, the U.S. military set strict regulations on blogs after becoming concerned about the messages being communicating by a proliferation of bloggers from personnel stationed in Iraq. On the other hand, reports indicate that by 2009 wikis will be used by at least 50% of organizations world-wide as a communications improvement tool.[6]

More than ever before, computer technology plays a major role in how information is shared and used in organizations. Research in the area of channel richness examines the capacity of communication media in a channel to convey information. It lends insight into how the technology used in various channel alternatives varies in implications for communication effectiveness.[7]

As indicated in Figure 14.2, the richest channels are face to face. Next are telephone, video conferences, and instant messaging, followed by e-mail, written memos, and letters. The leanest channels are posted notices and bulletins. When messages get more complex and open ended, richer channels are necessary to achieve effective communication. Leaner channels work well for more routine and straightforward messages, such as announcing the location of a previously scheduled meeting.

> ▰▰ **A grapevine** transfers information through networks of friendships and acquaintances.
>
> ▰▰ **Blogs** are individual web sites that communicate personal accounts of events and opinions.
>
> ▰▰ **Wikis** are collaborative web sites to which individuals contribute material and edit previous postings by others.
>
> ▰▰ **Channel richness** indicates the capacity of a channel to convey information.

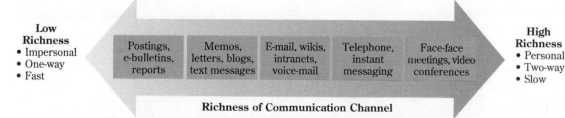

Low Richness
- Impersonal
- One-way
- Fast

| Postings, e-bulletins, reports | Memos, letters, blogs, text messages | E-mail, wikis, intranets, voice-mail | Telephone, instant messaging | Face-face meetings, video conferences |

High Richness
- Personal
- Two-way
- Slow

Richness of Communication Channel

Figure 14.2   Richness of communication channels.

Communication Directions and Flows

Communication among members of an organization, as well as between them and external customers, suppliers, distributors, alliance partners, and a host of outsiders, provides vital information for the enterprise. **Organizational communication** is the specific process through which information moves and is exchanged throughout an organization.[8] Information flows through both the formal and informal channels just described, and it flows downward, upward, and laterally.

■ Organizational communication is the many ways information moves through and is exchanged in organizations.

Within organizations, downward communication follows the chain of command from top to bottom. One of its major functions is to achieve influence through information. Lower-level personnel need to know what those in higher levels are doing and to be regularly reminded of key policies, strategies, objectives, and technical developments. Of special importance is feedback and information on performance results. Sharing such information helps minimize the spread of rumors and inaccuracies regarding higher-level intentions. It also helps create a sense of security and involvement among receivers, who believe they know the whole story. Unfortunately, a lack of adequate downward communication is often cited as a management failure. On the issue of corporate downsizing, for example, one sample showed that 64 percent of employees did not believe what management said, 61 percent felt uninformed about company plans, and 54 percent complained that decisions were not well explained.

The flow of messages from lower to higher organizational levels is upward communication. As shown in Figure 14.3, it serves several purposes. Upward communication keeps higher levels informed about what lower-level workers are doing, what their problems are, what suggestions they have for improvements, and how they feel about the organization and their jobs. The employee surveys used by Sun Microsystems and mentioned in the chapter opener are examples. Scott G. McNealy, CEO of Sun Microsystems, Inc., is well known for his unique vision of a high-tech future based on computer networking. He harnesses computing power at Sun

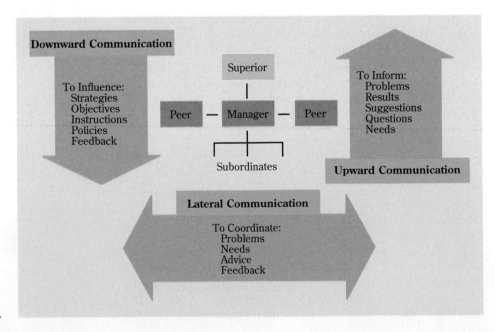

Figure 14.3 Directions for information flows in and around organizations.

to drive a comprehensive organizational communication program that includes e-mail questionnaires or polls to gather information on employee perceptions of such things as "performance inhibitors" that make it hard for them to do a good job. At Sun, top management recognizes that information and communication are keys to continued organizational development.[9] Even so, at Sun and elsewhere, status effects can potentially interfere with the effectiveness of upward communication.

The importance of lateral communication in the new workplace has been a recurrent theme in this book. Today's customer-sensitive organizations need timely and accurate feedback and product information. To serve customer needs they must get the right information—and get it fast enough—into the hands of workers. Furthermore, inside the organization, people must be willing and able to communicate across departmental or functional boundaries and to listen to one another's needs as "internal customers." New organization designs are emphasizing lateral communication in the form of cross-departmental committees, teams, or task forces as well as matrix structures. There is also growing attention to organizational ecology—the study of how building design may influence communication and productivity by improving lateral communications. Other developments include the innovations in information technology that continue to make it possible to move, share, and access information in new and timely ways. Wikis, for example, are a form of mass collaboration that is helping organizations operate in less hierarchical and more lateral fashions. Participation in a wiki allows people from different functions, locations, and positions to share information, brainstorm, discuss problems and their solutions, and otherwise build a knowledge base that is accessible throughout the organization and at any time.

Online Communities Are Big Businesses

What started as a hobby is turning into big business for some social networking entrepreneurs. Quentin English started with an e-mail list of 25 friends; now his site, quentinsfriends.com, links thousands of New Yorkers in an electronic marketplace. Erik Wachtmeister started aSmallWorld.net to keep in touch with a few global friends; it now links professionals worldwide. Andra Davidson created MothersClick.com as a site where new parents can share information. Perhaps there are some tips here for better communication within organizations. Has social networking arrived at your employer?

Interpersonal Communication

Our organizations are information rich and increasingly high tech. But even with the support provided by continuing developments in information technology, it is important to remember that people still drive organizational systems and performance. People who are willing and able to work together well and commit their mutual talents and energies to the tasks at hand are the foundations of any high-performance organization. And to create this foundation, people must excel in the processes of interpersonal communication.

Effective and Efficient Communication

When people communicate with one another, at least two important things are at issue. One is the accuracy of the communication—an issue of effectiveness; the other is its cost—an issue of efficiency.

Effective communication occurs when the intended meaning of the source and the perceived meaning of the receiver are virtually the same.[10] Although this should be the goal in any communication, it is not always achieved. Even now, we worry about whether or not you are interpreting these written words exactly as we intend. Our confidence would be higher if we were face-to-face in class together, and you could ask clarifying questions. Opportunities to offer feedback and ask questions are important ways of increasing the effectiveness of communication.

Efficient communication occurs at minimum cost in terms of resources expended. Time, for example, is an important resource. Picture your instructor

Effective communication is when the intended meaning equals the perceived meaning.

Efficient communication is low cost in its use of resources.

IT'S HARD TO COMMUNICATE WHEN YOU CAN'T READ

John Wood is a social entrepreneur. Once comfortably immersed in an executive career with Microsoft, his life changed on a vacation to the Himalayas of Nepal. Wood was shocked at the lack of schools. And he discovered a passion that determined what he calls the "second chapter" in his life: to provide the lifelong benefits of education to poor children. He quit his Microsoft job and started a nonprofit organization called Room to Read. So far the organization has built over 220 schools and 3,300 libraries in places like Cambodia, India, Nepal, Vietnam, and Laos.

Some 850 million people in the developing world can't read or write—one-seventh of the global population. Wood says: "I don't see how we are going to solve the world's problems without literacy." The Room to Read model is so efficient that it can build schools for as little as $6,000. *Time* magazine has honored Wood and his team as "Asian Heroes," and *Fast Company* magazine nominated his organization for a Social Capitalist Award.[11]

Question: How can Wood's commitment to better literacy apply in your local community? Do some organizations suffer because they have internal literacy problems and don't know it?

taking the time to communicate individually with each student in your class about the course subject matter. It would be virtually impossible to do so. Even if it were possible, it would be very costly in terms of time. People at work often choose not to visit one another personally to communicate messages. Instead, they rely on the efficiency of written memos, posted bulletins, group meetings, e-mail, or voice mail.

An efficient communication is not always effective. A change in policy posted by efficient e-mail may save time for the sender, but it may not achieve the desired interpretations and responses. Similarly, an effective communication may not be efficient. For a business manager to visit each employee and explain a new change in procedures may guarantee that everyone understands the change, but it may also be prohibitively expensive in terms of the required time expenditure.

Nonverbal Communication

▬ **Nonverbal communication** occurs through facial expressions, body motions, eye contact, and other physical gestures.

We all know that people communicate in ways other than the spoken or written word. Indeed, **nonverbal communication** that takes place through facial expressions, body position, eye contact, and other physical gestures is important both to understand and to master. It is the act of speaking without using words. Kinesics, the study of gestures and body postures, has achieved a rightful place in communication theory and research.[12]

The nonverbal side to communication can often hold the key to what someone is really thinking or meaning. It can also affect the impressions we make on others. Interviewers, for example, tend to respond more favorably to job candidates whose

Figure 14.4   **Furniture placement and nonverbal communication in the office.**

nonverbal cues, such as eye contact and erect posture, are positive than to those displaying negative nonverbal cues, such as looking down or slouching. The art of impression management during interviews and in other situations requires careful attention to both verbal and nonverbal aspects of communication, including one's dress, timeliness, and demeanor.

Nonverbal communication can also take place through the physical arrangement of space or workspace designs, such as that found in various office layouts. Proxemics, the study of the way space is used, is important to communication.[13] Figure 14.4 shows three different office arrangements and the messages they may communicate to visitors. Check the diagrams against the furniture arrangement in your office or that of your instructor or a person with whom you are familiar. What are you or they saying to visitors by the choice of furniture placement?[14]

Active Listening

The ability to listen well is a distinct asset to anyone whose job success depends on communicating with other people. After all, there are always two sides to the communication process: (1) sending a message, or "telling," and (2) receiving a message, or "listening." And as you know, too many of us emphasize the telling and neglect the listening.[15]

Everyone in the new workplace should develop good skills in **active listening**—the ability to help the source of a message say what he or she really means. The concept comes from the work of counselors and therapists, who are trained to help people express themselves and talk about things that are important to them.[16] Take a moment to review the guidelines for active listening shown in OB Savvy 14.2. Then read the conversations below. How would you feel as the group leader in each case?[17]

Active listening encourages people to say what they really mean.

> **OB SAVVY 14.2**
>
> ## Guidelines for Active Listening
>
> 1. Listen for content—try to hear exactly what is being said.
> 2. Listen for feelings—try to identify how the source feels about things.
> 3. Respond to feelings—let the source know that his or her feelings are recognized.
> 4. Note all cues—be sensitive to both verbal and nonverbal expressions.
> 5. Reflect back—repeat in your own words what you think you are hearing.

Example 1

Group leader: Hey, Sal, I don't get this work order. We can't handle this today. What do they think we are?

Branch manager: But that's the order. So get it out as soon as you can. We're under terrific pressure this week.

Group leader: Don't they know we're behind schedule already because of that software problem?

Branch manager: Look, I don't decide what goes on upstairs. I just have to see that the work gets out, and that's what I'm going to do.

Group leader: The team won't like this.

Branch manager: That's something you'll have to work out with them, not me.

Example 2

Group leader: Hey, Kelley, I don't get this work order. We can't handle this to-day. What do they think we are?

Branch manager: Sounds like you're pretty sore about it.

Group leader: I sure am. We're just about getting back to schedule while fighting that software breakdown. Now this comes along.

Branch manager: As if you didn't have enough work to do?

Group leader: Right, I don't know how to tell the team about this. They're under a real strain today. Seems like everything we do around here is rush, rush, rush.

Branch manager: I guess you feel like it's unfair to load anything more on them.

Group leader: Well, yes. But I know there must be plenty of pressure on every-body up the line. If that's the way it is, I'll get the word to them.

Branch manager: Thanks. If you'll give it a try, I'll do my best to hold with the schedule in the future.

The second example shows active listening skills on the part of the branch manager. She responded to the group leader's communication in a way that increased the flow of information. The manager learned more about the situation, while the group leader most likely felt better after having been able to really say what she thought—after being heard. Compare, by contrast, these outcomes with those in the first example where the manager lacked active listening skills.

Cross-Cultural Communication

We all know that outsourcing is big business these days. What we might not realize is that the success of international outsourcing often rests with the quality of cross-cultural communication. And all is not well. A recent study of large firms by

Accenture reports that 92 percent find that the biggest challenge in working with outsourcing providers is communication.[18] People must always exercise caution when they are involved in cross-cultural communication—whether between persons of different geographic or ethnic groupings within one country, or between persons of different national cultures.

A common problem in cross-cultural communication is **ethnocentrism**, the tendency to believe one's culture and its values are superior to those of others. It is often accompanied by an unwillingness to try to understand alternative points of view and to take the values they represent seriously. Another problem in cross-cultural communication arises from **parochialism**—assuming that the ways of your culture are the only ways of doing things. It is parochial for a traveling American businesswoman to insist that all of her business contacts speak English, whereas it is ethnocentric for her to think that anyone who dines with a spoon rather than a knife and fork lacks proper table manners.

> ▬ **Ethnocentrism** is the tendency to believe one's culture and its values are superior to those of others.
>
> ▬ **Parochialism** assumes the ways of your culture are the only ways of doing things.

The difficulties with cross-cultural communication are perhaps most obvious in respect to language differences. Advertising messages, for example, may work well in one country but encounter difficulty when translated into the language of another. Problems accompanied the introduction of Ford's European model, the "Ka," into Japan. (In Japanese, *ka* means "mosquito.") Gestures may also be used quite differently in the various cultures of the world. For example, crossed legs are quite acceptable in the United Kingdom but are rude in Saudi Arabia if the sole of the foot is directed toward someone. Pointing at someone to get their attention may be acceptable in Canada, but in Asia it is considered inappropriate and even offensive.[19]

The role of language in cross-cultural communication has additional and sometimes even more subtle sides. The anthropologist Edward T. Hall notes important differences in the ways different cultures use language, and he suggests that misunderstood communications are often caused by them.[20] Members of **low-context cultures** are very explicit in using the spoken and written word. In these cultures, such as those of Australia, Canada, and the United States, the message is largely conveyed by the words someone uses, and not particularly by the "context" in which they are spoken. In contrast, members of **high-context cultures** use words to convey only a limited part of the message. The rest must be inferred or interpreted from the context, which includes body language, the physical setting, and past relationships—all of which add meaning to what is being said. Many Asian and Middle Eastern cultures are considered high context, according to Hall, whereas most Western cultures are low context.

> ▬ In **low-context cultures** messages are expressed mainly by the spoken and written word.
>
> ▬ In **high-context cultures** words convey only part of a message, while the rest of the message must be inferred from body language and additional contextual cues.

International business experts advise that one of the best ways to gain understanding of cultural differences is to learn at least some of the language of the country that one is dealing with. Says one global manager: "Speaking and understanding the local language gives you more insight; you can avoid misunderstandings." A former American member of the board of a German multinational says: "Language proficiency gives a [non-German] board member a better grasp of what is going on . . . not just the facts and figures but also texture and nuance."[21] Although the prospect of learning another language may sound daunting, there is little doubt that it can be well worth the effort.[22]

Leaders on Leadership

PEPSI'S NEW CEO SPEAKS HINDI.

When Indra Nooyi was appointed CEO of PepsiCo, India celebrated, and the *Economic Times* proclaimed: "Nooyi has unfurled the Indian tricolor right on top of Pepsi's headquarters." Born in India and just 50 years old, her credits during a 12-year Pepsi career include acquisitions—Tropicana and Quaker Oats—and divestitures—selling off Pizza Hut and Kentucky Fried Chicken. A company press release reported that she was "driving critical cross-business initiatives." But Nooyi brings more than solid executive experience to the new role; she's a unique personality as well. She was part of an all-female rock band in college. Does it surprise you that she once broke spontaneously into the song "Day-O" after introducing Harry Belafonte as guest speaker at a Pepsi diversity event?

Nooyi is considered a transformational leader and a great strategist. And she knows how to communicate. When the company's board chairmanship was added to her CEO title, Nooyi said: "I'm incredibly honored by the board's confidence, and extraordinarily fortunate to follow in the footsteps of Steve Reinemund and all my illustrious predecessors." Her success story is one to watch.[23]

Question: When Nooyi praised her predecessors when taking over as board chairman, what was she trying to communicate? Will Nooyi's cross-cultural background be a leadership asset for Pepsi that Coke might find hard to match?

Communication Barriers

In all interpersonal communication, it is important to understand the sources of noise that can easily cause problems in the communication process. As shown earlier in Figure 14.1, potential noise comes from the cultural differences just discussed, as well as from physical distractions, semantic problems, mixed messages, absence of feedback, and status effects.

Physical Distractions

Any number of physical distractions can interfere with the effectiveness of a communication attempt. Some of these distractions are evident in the following conversation between an employee, George, and his manager.[24]

Okay, George, let's hear your problem (phone rings, boss picks it up, promises to deliver the report "just as soon as I can get it done"). Uh, now, where were we— oh, you're having a problem with marketing. They (the manager's secretary brings in some papers that need immediate signatures; he scribbles his name and the secretary leaves) . . . you say they're not cooperative? I tell you what, George, why don't you (phone rings again, lunch partner drops by) . . . uh, take a stab at handling it yourself. I've got to go now.

Besides what may have been poor intentions in the first place, George's manager allowed physical distractions to create information overload. As a result, the communication with George suffered. Setting priorities and planning can eliminate this mistake. If George has something to say, his manager should set aside adequate time for the meeting. In addition, interruptions such as telephone calls, drop-in visitors, and the like should be prevented. At a minimum, George's manager could start by closing the door to the office and instructing his secretary not to disturb them.

Semantic Problems

Semantic barriers to communication involve a poor choice or use of words and mixed messages. When in doubt regarding the clarity of your written or spoken messages, the popular **KISS principle** of communication is always worth remembering: "Keep it short and simple." Of course, that is often easier said than done. The following illustrations of the "bafflegab" that once tried to pass as actual "executive communication" are a case in point.[25]

■ **The KISS principle** stands for "keep it short and simple."

A. "We solicit any recommendations that you wish to make, and you may be assured that any such recommendations will be given our careful consideration."

B. "Consumer elements are continuing to stress the fundamental necessity of a stabilization of the price structure at a lower level than exists at the present time."

One has to wonder why these messages weren't stated more understandably: (A) "Send us your recommendations; they will be carefully considered." (B) "Consumers want lower prices."

Mixed Messages

Mixed messages occur when a person's words communicate one thing while his or her actions or body language communicate quite another. They are important to spot since nonverbal signals can add insight into what is really being said in face-to-face communication.[26] For instance, someone may voice cautious agreement during a business meeting at the same time that her facial expression shows stress, and she begins to lean back in her chair. The body language in this case may suggest the existence of important reservations, even though the words indicate agreement.

■ **Mixed messages** occur when words say one thing while nonverbal cues say something else.

Absence of Feedback

One-way communication flows from sender to receiver only, as in the case of a written memo or a voice-mail message. There is no direct and immediate feedback from the recipient. Two-way communication, by contrast, goes from sender to receiver and back again. It is characteristic of the normal interactive conversations in our daily experiences.

Research Insight
Workplace Identities and Office Décor

Research conducted by Kimberly D. Elsbach offers insight on how office décor can influence co-workers' perceptions of the officeholder's workplace identity—defined as "an individual's central and enduring status and distinctiveness categorizations in the workplace." Using a qualitative research design, Elsbach interviewed two samples of employees in corporate offices. She questioned them on how they interpreted variations in permanent office décor—things like furniture, photos, artifact decorations, art, personal mementos, and neatness. Findings showed that these types of "physical identity markers" are used to "cue

SAMPLE OFFICE DÉCOR IDENTITY MARKERS

Family photos—say family oriented, balanced, not work focused

Hobby photos, artifacts—say ambitious, outgoing, well rounded

Conversation pieces—say funny, off-beat, approachable

Awards, diplomas—say hard-working, successful, pretentious

Professional products—say "company person," functional expert

and/or affirm a person's workplace identity." Also, physical markers independent of the person—such as the apparent quality or expensiveness of office furniture—were found to relate more to perceived workplace status than to distinctiveness. The results help to confirm that such physical markers —office décor and things like personal dress— act along with behavioral markers as important influences on the ways people acquire identities at work. In respect to practical implications, Elsbach points out that employees working in certain settings may want to choose office décors that communicate a desired workplace identity.[26A]

Research indicates that two-way communication is more accurate and effective than is one-way communication, even though it is also more costly and time consuming. Because of their efficiency, however, one-way forms of communication—memos, letters, e-mail, voice mail, and the like—are frequently used in work settings. One-way messages are easy for the sender but often frustrating for the receiver, who may be left unsure of just what the sender means or wants done.

Status Effects

Status differences in organizations create potential communication barriers between persons of higher and lower ranks. On the one hand, given the authority of their positions, managers may be inclined to do a lot of "telling" but not much "listening." On the other hand, we know that communication is frequently biased when flowing upward in organizational hierarchies.[27] Subordinates may filter information and tell their superiors only what they think the bosses want to hear. Whether the reason is a fear of retribution for bringing bad news, an unwillingness to identify personal mistakes, or just a general desire to please, the result is the same: the higher-level decision maker may end up taking the wrong actions because of biased and inaccurate information supplied from below. This is sometimes called the **mum effect**, in reference to tendencies to sometimes keep "mum" from a desire to be polite and a reluctance to transmit bad news.[28]

The mum effect occurs when people are reluctant to communicate bad news.

To avoid such problems, managers and group leaders must develop trust in their work relationships with subordinates and team members, and take advantage of all opportunities for face-to-face communications. Management by wandering around, or **MBWA**, is now popularly acclaimed as one way to achieve this trust.[29] It simply means getting out of the office and talking regularly to people as they do their jobs. Managers who spend time walking around can greatly reduce the perceived "distance" between themselves and their subordinates. It helps create an atmosphere of open and free-flowing communication between the ranks. As a result, more and better information is available for decision making, and the relevance of decisions to the needs of operating workers increases. Of course, in today's electronic offices one can get out of the office and practice MBWA through online discussions, instant messaging, blogs, wikis, and more.

■■ **MBWA** involves getting out of the office to communicate directly with others.

Issues in Organizational Communication

One of the greatest changes in organizations and in everyday life in recent years has been the great explosion in new communication technologies. We have moved from the world of the telephone, mail, photocopying, and face-to-face meetings into one of voice mail, e-mail, instant messaging, blogs, wikis, video conferencing, computer-mediated conferencing, and more. Indeed, the ability to participate effectively in all aspects of the electronic office and workspace is well established as an essential career skill. The pace and extensiveness of these changes, along with the ever-present dynamics of social context, mean that everyone must keep themselves up to date with the issues and challenges of communication in organizations.

Electronic Communication

The impact of the new technologies is discussed throughout this book with respect to job design and the growth of telecommuting, organizational design and the growth of network organizations, and teamwork and the availability of software

No E-Mail Fridays

When Scott Dockter started sending e-mail to his assistant, just a few steps away, he recognized a problem. As CEO of PBD Worldwide Fulfillment Services, his response was an order: "No e-mail Fridays." He told the 275 employees of his firm to talk in person on Fridays and reduce e-mail exchanges the rest of the week. He believes the result is improved and faster decision making and problem solving, as well as better teamwork and client relations. One customer says: "You can't get to know someone through e-mail."

MASTERING MANAGEMENT

DON'T LET YOUR BLACKBERRY GET YOU DOWN

Look around in the airports, in meetings, on the street, or wherever: Blackberrys are taking over our time. And the sad fact is that it isn't just the amount of time spent dealing with that never-sleeping e-mail carrier that's the problem; the quality of the time is often in question. It's time to get better at managing your e-mail and, by default, managing your time. Here are some tips gleaned from corporate training.[30]

- Read e-mail items once, only once.
- Take action immediately to answer, move to folders, or delete.
- Regularly purge folders of outdated messages.
- Send group mail and use "reply to all" only when really necessary.
- Get off distribution lists that don't offer value to your work.
- Send short messages in the subject line, avoiding a full-text message.
- Put large files on Web sites, instead of sending as attachments.
- Don't send confidential, personal, or embarrassing messages by e-mail.
- Turn off the sound indicating arrival of a new e-mail.

for electronic meetings and decision making, among many other applications. Advances in information technology are allowing organizations to (1) distribute information much faster than before; (2) make more information available than ever before; (3) allow broader and more immediate access to this information; (4) encourage participation in the sharing and use of information; and (5) integrate systems and functions, and use information to link with environments in unprecedented ways.

The potential disadvantages of electronic communications must also be recognized: The technologies are largely impersonal; people interact with machines, not with one another. In addition, electronics removes nonverbal communications from the situation and thereby loses aspects that may otherwise add important context to an interaction. Studies now show that recipients are accurate less than 50 percent of the time in identifying the tone or intent of an e-mail.[31]

One of the problems in the electronic media lies in difficulties with understanding the emotional aspects of communication. In this respect, little smiley or frowning faces and other symbols often do not carry the message. Another problem is a failure in the electronic medium to control one's emotions, a skill considered essential in interpersonal communications. [32] Some argue, for example, that it is far easier to be blunt, overly critical, and insensitive when conveying messages electronically rather than face-to-face. The term **flaming** is sometimes used to describe rudeness in electronic communication. In this sense, the use of computer mediation may make people less inhibited and more impatient in what they say.

Flaming is expressing rudeness when using e-mail or other forms of electronic communication.

Another risk of the new communication technologies is information overload. In some cases, too much information may find its way into the communication networks and e-mail systems and basically overload the systems—both organizational and individual. Individual users may have difficulty sorting the useful from the trivial and may become impatient while doing so. Even the IT giant Intel experiences e-mail problems. An employee once commented: "We're so wrapped up in sending e-mail to each other, we don't have time to be dealing with the outside." Estimates are that close to 200 billion e-mails will be sent this year, and the number grows by about 20 percent annually.[33]

Workplace Privacy

Among the controversies in organizational communication today is the issue of privacy. An example is eavesdropping by employers on employee use of electronic messaging in corporate facilities. A study by the American Management Association found that electronic monitoring of employee performance increased by more than 45 percent in a year's time. You may be surprised to learn that the most frequently reported things bosses watch are the number of telephone calls and the time spent on telephone calls (39 percent), e-mail messages (27 percent), computer files (21 percent), telephone conversations (11 percent), and voice-mail messages (6 percent).[34]

Many organizations are developing internal policies regarding the privacy of employee communications, and the issue is gaining attention from legislators. A state law in Illinois now makes it legal for bosses to listen in on employees' telephone calls. But the law leaves the boundaries of appropriateness unclear. Such eavesdropping is common in some service areas such as airline reservations, where union concerns are sometimes expressed in the context of "big brother is watching you!" The privacy issue is likely to remain controversial as communication technologies continue to make it easier for employers to electronically monitor the performance and communications of their workers.

Communication and Social Context

There are lots of communication issues in the complex social settings of organizations today. One of continuing interest is the study of male and female communication styles. In *Talking 9 to 5* Deborah Tannen argues that men and women learn or are socialized into different styles; as a result, they often end up having difficulties communicating with one another.[35] She sees women as being more oriented toward relationship building in communication, for example, while men are more prone to seek status through communications.[36] Because people tend to surround themselves with those whose communication styles fit with their own, a further implication is that either women or men may dominate communications in situations where they are in the majority.[37]

More and more people are asking a question related to the prior discussion: "Are women better communicators than men?" A study by the consulting firm Lawrence A. Pfaff and Associates suggests they may well be.[38] The survey shows that supervisors rank female managers higher than male managers on communication, approachability, evaluations, and empowering others; the subordinates also rank women higher on these same items. A possible explanation is that early socialization and training better prepare women for the skills involved in communication and may make them more sensitive in interpersonal relationships. In contrast, men may be more socialized in ways that cause communication problems—such as aggression, competitiveness, and individualism.[39] In considering such possibilities, however, it is important to avoid gender stereotyping and to focus instead on the point of ultimate importance—how communication in organizations can be made most effective.[40]

In addition, our society also values the political correctness of communications in the workplace. The vocabulary of work is changing, and people are ever more on guard not to offend others by their choices of words. When you hear references to "people of color," the "physically challenged," and "seniors," for example, the intent is to communicate with respect for individual differences. The terminology we use and prefer today is often different from that heard in the past, and it will likely be different again in the future. People in organizations are aware of such issues, and many employers offer training to help their members understand and best deal with the importance of language that supports norms and cultures of inclusion, tolerance, and sensitivity to individual differences.

Chapter 14   Study Guide

What is the nature of communication in organizations?

Summary

- Communication is the process of sending and receiving messages with attached meanings.

- The communication process involves encoding an intended meaning into a message, sending the message through a channel, and receiving and decoding the message into perceived meaning.

- Noise is anything that interferes with the communication process.

- Feedback is a return message from the original recipient back to the sender.

- To be constructive, feedback must be direct, specific, and given at an appropriate time.

- Organizational communication is the specific process through which information moves and is exchanged within an organization.

- Organizations depend on complex flows of information—upward, downward, and laterally—to operate effectively.

What are the essentials of interpersonal communication?

- Communication is effective when both sender and receiver interpret a message in the same way.

- Communication is efficient when messages are transferred at a low cost.

- Nonverbal communication occurs through facial expressions, body position, eye contact, and other physical gestures.

- Active listening encourages a free and complete flow of communication from the sender to the receiver; it is nonjudgmental and encouraging.

- Communication in organizations uses a variety of formal and informal channels; the richness of the channel, or its capacity to convey information, must be adequate for the message.

- Parochialism and ethnocentrism contribute to the difficulties of experiencing truly effectual cross-cultural communication.

What are the barriers to effective communication?

- The possible barriers to communication include physical distractions, semantic problems, absence of feedback, and status effects.

- Mixed messages that give confused or conflicting verbal and nonverbal cues may interfere with communications.

- The absence of feedback can make it difficult to know whether or not an intended message has been accurately received.

- Status effects in organizations may result in restricted and filtered information exchanges between subordinates and their superiors.

What are current issues in organizational communication?

- As technologies continue to change the workplace, the emphasis on electronic communications and virtual workspaces brings many performance advantages.

- Potential disadvantages in the use of information technology include the loss of emotion and personality in the communication process.

- Researchers are interested in possible differences in communication styles between men and women and in the relative effectiveness of these styles for conditions in the new workplace.

- Current issues in organizational communication also include those of privacy and political correctness in workplace communications.

Key Terms

Active listening (p. 327)
Blogs (p. 323)
Channel richness (p. 323)
Communication (p. 321)
Communication channels
   (p. 321)
Effective communication
   (p. 325)
Efficient communication
   (p. 325)

Ethnocentrism (p. 329)
Feedback (p. 322)
Flaming (p. 334)
Formal channels (p. 322)
Grapevine (p. 323)
High-context culture (p. 329)
Informal channels (p. 322)
KISS principle (p. 331)
Low-context culture (p. 329)
MBWA (p. 333)

Mixed messages (p. 331)
Mum effect (p. 332)
Noise (p. 321)
Nonverbal communication
   (p. 326)
Organizational
   communication (p. 324)
Parochialism (p. 329)
Wikis (p. 323)
360-degree feedback (p. 322)

Multiple Choice

Self-Test 14

1. In _____ communication the cost is low, whereas in _____ communication the intended message is fully received. (a) effective; electronic (b) efficient; open (c) electronic; open (d) efficient; effective

2. When you give criticism to someone, the communication will be most effective when the criticism is _____. (a) general and nonspecific (b) given when the sender feels the need (c) tied to things the recipient can do something about (d) given all at once to get everything over with

3. Which communication is the best choice for sending a complex message? _____ (a) face to face (b) written memorandum (c) e-mail (d) telephone call

4. When someone's words convey one meaning but body posture conveys something else, a(n) _____ is occurring. (a) ethnocentric message (b) mixed message (c) semantic problem (d) status effect

5. Management by wandering around is a technique that can help overcome the limitations of _____ in the communication process. (a) status effects (b) semantics (c) physical distractions (d) proxemics

6. Which communication method has more two-way characteristics? _____ (a) e-mail (b) blog (c) voice mail (d) instant messaging

7. In _____, a variety of persons one works with, including peers and supervisor as well as direct reports, are involved in the process of performance evaluation. (a) 360° feedback (b) mixed messages (c) the Mum effect (d) a grapevine

8. Although new electronic communication technologies have the advantage of handling large amounts of information, they may also make communication among organizational members _____. (a) less accessible (b) less immediate (c) more informal (d) less personal

9. The study of gestures and body postures for their impact on communication is an issue of _____. (a) kinesics (b) proxemics (c) semantics (d) informal channels

10. In _____ communication the sender is likely to be most comfortable, whereas in _____ communication the receiver is likely to feel most informed. (a) one-way; two-way (b) top-down; bottom-up (c) bottom-up; top-down (d) two-way; one-way

11. A manager who spends a lot of time out of her office, walking around as well as talking with and listening to other people, could be described as using _____. (a) the KISS principle (b) MBWA (c) MBO (d) the grapevine

12. _____ is being used to improve horizontal linkages and support the lateral communication characteristic of the new workplaces. (a) Status effects (b) The MUM effect (c) Organizational ecology (d) Nonverbal communication

13. If someone is interested in proxemics as a means of improving communication with others, that person would likely pay a lot of attention to his or her _____. (a) office layout (b) status (c) active listening skills (d) 360-degree feedback

14. Among the rules for active listening is _____. (a) remain silent and communicate only nonverbally (b) confront emotions (c) don't let feelings become part of the process (d) reflect back what you think you are hearing

15. The impact of social context on communication among people in organizations is represented by concerns for _____. (a) the correctness of one's vocabulary (b) skill in the use of computer technology (c) privacy and electronic performance monitoring (d) flaming in an e-mail message

Short Response

16. Why is channel richness a useful concept for managers?
17. What place do informal communication channels have in organizations today?
18. Why is communication between lower and higher levels sometimes filtered?
19. Is there a gender difference in communication styles?

Applications Essay

20. "People in this organization don't talk to one another anymore. Everything is e-mail, e-mail, e-mail. If you are mad at someone, you can just say it and then hide behind your computer." With these words, Wesley expressed his frustrations with Delta General's operations. Xiaomei echoed his concerns, responding, "I agree, but surely the managing director should be able to improve organizational communication without losing the advantages of e-mail." As a consultant overhearing this conversation, how do you suggest the managing director respond to Xiaomei's challenge?

These learning activities from *The OB Skills Workbook* are suggested for Chapter 14.

OB in Action

CASE	EXPERIENTIAL EXERCISES	SELF-ASSESSMENTS
■ 14. The Poorly Informed Walrus	■ 29. Active Listening ■ 30. Upward Appraisal ■ 31. 360° Feedback	■ 12. "TT" Leadership Style ■ 13. Empowering Others

Plus—special learning experiences from *The Jossey-Bass/Pfeiffer Classroom Collection*

Conflict and Negotiation

Chapter at a Glance

Managerial work is interpersonal work, and the word "yes" when dealing with others can often open doors to success. Chapter 15 examines conflict and negotiation as key processes of organizational behavior. As you read, *keep in mind these study topics.*

CONFLICT IN ORGANIZATIONS
- Types of Conflict
- Levels of Conflict
- Functional and Dysfunctional Conflict
- Culture and Conflict

CONFLICT MANAGEMENT
- Stages of Conflict
- Causes of Conflict
- Indirect Conflict Management Approaches
- Direct Conflict Management Approaches

NEGOTIATION
- What Is Negotiation?
- Negotiation Goals and Outcomes
- Ethical Aspects of Negotiation
- Organizational Settings for Negotiation
- Culture and Negotiation

NEGOTIATION STRATEGIES
- Distributive Negotiation
- Integrative Negotiation
- How to Gain Integrative Agreements
- Common Negotiation Pitfalls
- Third-Party Roles in Negotiation

CHAPTER 15 STUDY GUIDE

"Yes" helps open doors

When Whitney Johns Martin needed investment capital to expand her consulting firm, it was very hard to find. As member of the board for the National Association of Women Business Owners, she took matters into her own hands and founded a venture capital fund, Capital Across America, specifically to serve female-owned businesses. The fund is described by Hoover's as targeting investments of $250,000 to $1.5 million "in businesses with at least three years of operating history, an average annual growth rate of 15%, and an eye on expanding operations."

More than 8 million business owners in the United States are women, and they employ one in four American corporate workers. But it is often hard for women to find investment capital. Men, who seemed more comfortable dealing with men, managed most of the venture capital funds that Martin dealt with when she was searching for investors.

> ## "Women often underestimate themselves and don't ask for enough during negotiations."

Martin believes that women and men have somewhat different approaches to business. According to her, women often underestimate themselves and don't ask for enough during negotiations. Men, she says by contrast, "shoot for the moon" and ask for more than they typically need. On the other hand, Martin finds that women have a great capacity to develop extensive networks and relationships with customers, suppliers, and others. These are all great business resources, and they can be especially helpful in rallying to deal with economic difficulties. As a final reminder in dealing with the venture capitalists, Martin tells women to remember the basics when entering the negotiation: "Have an excellent business plan."

Whitney Johns Martin is president of Whitney Johns and Company, founder and CEO of Capital Across America, and chair of the Nashville Branch of the Atlanta Federal Reserve Bank. She is a member of the National Women's Hall of Fame.[1]

Conflict in Organizations

Conflict occurs when parties disagree over substantive issues or when emotional antagonisms create friction between them.

Just as in the case of Whitney Johns Martin, the daily work of people in organizations is based intensely on communication and interpersonal relationships. We all, managers included, need skills to work well with others who don't always agree with us, and in situations that are often complicated and stressful.[2] **Conflict** occurs whenever disagreements exist in a social situation over issues of substance or whenever emotional antagonisms create frictions between individuals or groups.[3]

Managers and team leaders can spend considerable time dealing with conflicts, including those in which the manager or leader is directly involved as one of the principal actors.[4] In other situations the manager or leader may act as a mediator, or neutral third party, whose job it is to resolve conflicts between other people. But in all cases managers and team leaders have to be comfortable with conflict dynamics. This includes being able to recognize situations that have the potential for conflict, and then being able to deal with these situations in ways that will best serve the needs of both the organization and the people involved.[5]

Types of Conflict

Conflict as it is experienced in the daily workplace involves at least two basic forms. **Substantive conflict** is a fundamental disagreement over ends or goals to be pursued and the means for their accomplishment.[6] A dispute with one's boss over a plan of action to be followed, such as the marketing strategy for a new product, is an example of substantive conflict. When people work together every day, it is only normal that different viewpoints on a variety of substantive workplace issues will arise. At times people will disagree over such things as group and organizational goals, the allocation of resources, the distribution of rewards, policies and procedures, and task assignments. Dealing with such conflicts successfully is an everyday challenge for most managers.

In contrast, **emotional conflict** involves interpersonal difficulties that arise over feelings of anger, mistrust, dislike, fear, resentment, and the like.[7] This conflict is commonly known as a "clash of personalities." Emotional conflicts can drain the energies of people and distract them from important work priorities. They can emerge in a wide variety of settings and are common among co-workers as well as in superior-subordinate relationships. The latter form of emotional conflict is perhaps the most upsetting organizational conflict for any person to experience. Unfortunately, competitive pressures in today's business environment and the resulting emphasis on downsizing and restructuring have created more situations in which the decisions of a "tough" boss can create emotional conflict.

Substantive conflict involves fundamental disagreement over ends or goals to be pursued and the means for their accomplishment.

Emotional conflict involves interpersonal difficulties that arise over feelings of anger, mistrust, dislike, fear, resentment, and the like.

Leaders on Leadership

POVERTY AND LEADERSHIP MEET IN NOBEL PEACE PRIZE

Mohammad Yunus isn't shy about taking on governments, but he does so now with the credibility of a Nobel Peace Prize behind him. Yunus, an economist from Bangladesh who founded the Grameen Bank to provide small loans to help poor individuals start small businesses, is a leader of the campaign to end poverty. "Every single individual on earth has both the potential and the right to live a decent life," he says. The Nobel Prize award committee agrees, stating: "Across cultures and civilizations, Yunus and Grameen Bank have shown that even the poorest of the poor can work to bring about their own development." The Grameen Bank offers small loans in the $50–$150 range; they are unsecured, and often the borrowers are women. Yunus claims that the repayment rates run as high as 95 percent and that the resulting entrepeneurship assists families in breaking the cycle of poverty. One of Yunus's current goals is to convince more governments to support microfinance institutions like the Grameen Bank. He says that the Nobel Peace Prize has opened doors for him and his microfinance concepts. "Previously if we screamed," he says, "people didn't listen. Now, if we whisper, the whole world will hear."[8]

Question: Mohammad Yunus started with economic expertise and a commitment to poverty eradication. Although successful, it was the Nobel Peace Prize that really gave him leadership momentum on the world stage. What are the lessons here for gaining similar leadership momentum in any organization?

Levels of Conflict

When dealing personally with conflicts in the workplace, the relevant question becomes "How well prepared are you to encounter and deal successfully with conflicts of various types?" People at work may encounter conflict at the intrapersonal level (conflict within the individual), the interpersonal level (individual-to-individual conflict), the intergroup level (conflict among groups or teams), or the interorganizational level (conflict among organizations).

Some conflicts that affect behavior in organizations involve the individual alone. These **intrapersonal conflicts** often involve actual or perceived pressures from incompatible goals or expectations of the following types: *Approach-approach conflict* occurs when a person must choose between two positive and equally attractive alternatives. An example is when someone has to choose between a valued promotion in the organization or a desirable new job with another firm. *Avoidance-avoidance conflict* occurs when a person must choose between two negative and equally unattractive alternatives. An example is being asked either to accept a job transfer to another town in an undesirable location or to have one's employment with an organization terminated. *Approach-avoidance conflict* occurs when a person must decide to do something that has both positive and negative consequences. An example is being offered a higher-paying job whose responsibilities entail unwanted demands on one's personal time.

Interpersonal conflict occurs between two or more individuals who are in opposition to one another. It may be substantive or emotional or both. Two persons debating each other aggressively on the merits of hiring a specific job applicant is an example of a substantive interpersonal conflict. Two persons continually in disagreement over each other's choice of work attire is an example of an emotional interpersonal conflict. One of the places where interpersonal conflict often arises is in the performance evaluation process. When P. J. Smoot became learning and development leader at International Paper's Memphis, Tennessee, office, she realized that the traditional concept of the boss passing judgment on the subordinate just does not work. It is difficult to give performance reviews that end up motivating subordinates and improving their performance. Smoot reversed the traditional top-down process and initiated a new program that began the reviews from the bottom up—with the employee's self-evaluation. Smoot focused the manager's job on helping and guiding others to meet agreed-upon performance plans. Her advice: "Listen for understanding and then react honestly and constructively. Focus on the business goals, not the personality."[9]

Intergroup conflict that occurs among members of different teams or groups can also have substantive and/or emotional underpinnings. Intergroup conflict is quite common in organizations, and it can make the coordination and integration of task activities very difficult.[10] The classic example is conflict among functional groups or departments, such as marketing and manufacturing, in organizations. The growing use of cross-functional teams and task forces is one way of trying to minimize such conflicts and promote more creative and efficient team organizations.

Interorganizational conflict is most commonly thought of in terms of the competition and rivalry that characterizes firms operating in the same markets. A good example is the continuing battle between U.S. businesses and their global rivals. But interorganizational conflict is a much broader issue than that represented by market competition alone. Consider, for example, disagreements

■ **Intrapersonal conflict** occurs within the individual because of actual or perceived pressures from incompatible goals or expectations.

■ **Interpersonal conflict** occurs between two or more individuals in opposition to each other.

■ **Intergroup conflict** occurs among groups in an organization.

■ **Interorganizational conflict** occurs between organizations.

between unions and the organizations employing their members, between government regulatory agencies and the organizations subject to their surveillance, and between firms and those who supply them with raw materials.

Functional and Dysfunctional Conflict

Conflict in organizations can be upsetting both to the individuals directly involved and to others affected by its occurrence. It can be quite uncomfortable, for example, to work in an environment in which two co-workers are continually hostile toward each other. In OB, however, the two sides to conflict shown in Figure 15.1 are recognized: the functional or constructive side, and the dysfunctional or destructive side.

Functional conflict, also called *constructive conflict*, results in positive benefits to individuals, the group, or the organization. On the positive side, conflict can bring important problems to the surface so they can be addressed. It can cause decisions to be considered carefully and perhaps reconsidered to ensure that the right path of action is being followed. It can increase the amount of information used for decision making. And it can offer opportunities for creativity that can improve individual, team, or organizational performance. Indeed, an effective manager is able to stimulate constructive conflict in situations in which satisfaction with the status quo inhibits needed change and development.

Dysfunctional conflict, or *destructive conflict*, works to the disadvantage of an individual or a group. It diverts energies, hurts group cohesion, promotes interpersonal hostilities, and overall creates a negative environment for workers. This type of conflict occurs, for example, when two employees are unable to work together because of interpersonal differences (a destructive emotional conflict) or when the members of a committee fail to act because they cannot agree on group goals (a destructive substantive conflict). Destructive conflicts of these types can decrease work productivity and job satisfaction as well as contribute to absenteeism and job turnover. Managers must be alert to destructive conflicts and be quick to take action to prevent or eliminate them—or at least minimize their disadvantages.

■■■ **Functional conflict** results in positive benefits to the group.

■■■ **Dysfunctional conflict** works to the group's or organization's disadvantage.

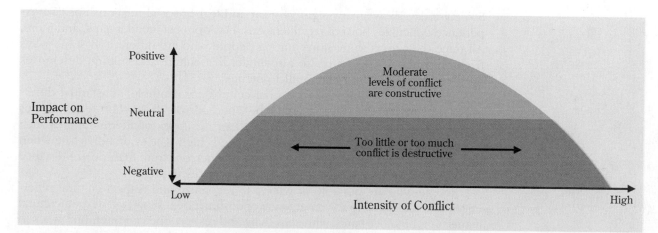

Figure 15.1 **The two faces of conflict: functional conflict and dysfunctional conflict.**

ETHICS IN OB

MANAGEMENT GURU BRINGS NEW LIFE TO LIBYA

Libya . . . leadership . . . training . . . entrepreneurship . . . reform. Is it possible to put these words together in a sentence that has a positive ending? It may sound far-fetched, but it makes perfect sense to Harvard's strategic management guru Michael Porter. Along with colleagues from the consulting firm Monitor Company, Porter has embarked on a program to help Libya move toward business revitalization and economic development. In doing so, he's working with Muammar al Qaddafi who, until recently, was a pariah on the world stage, and who remains in charge of a strong-arm government.

Qaddafi's Libya had been isolated, and his country was subjected to U.S. and U.N. economic sanctions until he announced that Libya was giving up its weapons of mass destruction program and reopening ties with Washington. Porter and his team have completed a leadership program for top business executives in Libya, worked closely with Qaddafi's son, Saif al Islam, who graduated from the London School of Economics, and helped institute a variety of government reforms. Porter says: "I didn't take this on because this is a big economy. It was very symbolic. If this can be successful, then other countries will be able to change." Symbolism, indeed. This example suggests it may be time to reinvigorate the great potential of collaboration and engagement, as opposed to confrontation and isolation, as pathways to solving global problems. And when it comes to international relations, isn't it interesting that the work of a management professor and consultant is helping to open Libya's doors to the world?[11]

> Question: Some might argue that Porter's efforts in Libya are ethically well intended but misdirected, helping only to support a totalitarian government. Others might see in his work there an example of how constructive engagement can trump destructive confrontation in helping to solve global problems. What about the events of everyday life? How often do you pass up possibilities for constructive engagement in daily affairs, both in your personal life and at work?

Culture and Conflict

Society today shows many signs of wear and tear in social relationships. We experience difficulties born of racial tensions, homophobia, gender gaps, and more. All trace their roots to tensions among people who are different in some ways from one another. They are also a reminder that culture and cultural differences must be considered for their conflict potential.

Among the dimensions of national culture, for example, substantial differences may be noted in time orientation. When persons from short-term cultures such as the United States try to work with persons from long-term cultures such as Japan, the likelihood of conflict developing is high. The same holds true when individualists work with collectivists and when persons from high-power-distance cultures work with those from low-power-distance cultures.[12]

People who are not able or willing to recognize and respect cultural differences can contribute to the emergence of dysfunctional situations in multicultural teams. On the other hand, with sensitivity and respect one can often find ways to work well across cultures and tap the performance advantages of both diversity and constructive conflict. Consider these comments from members of a joint European and American project team at Corning. "Something magical happens," says engineer John Thomas. "Europeans are very creative thinkers; they take time to really reflect on a problem to come up with the very best theoretical solution. Americans are more tactical and practical—we want to get down to developing a working solution as soon as possible." His partner at Fontainebleau in France says: "The French are more focused on ideas and concepts. If we get blocked in the execution of those ideas, we give up. Not the Americans. They pay more attention to details, processes, and time schedules. They make sure they are prepared and have involved everyone in the planning process so that they won't get blocked. But it's best if you mix the two approaches. In the end, you will achieve the best results."[13]

Conflict Management

Conflict can be addressed in many ways, but the important goal is to achieve or set the stage for true **conflict resolution**—a situation in which the underlying reasons for a given destructive conflict are eliminated. The process begins with a good understanding of causes and a recognition of the stage to which conflict has developed.

Conflict resolution occurs when the reasons for a conflict are eliminated.

Stages of Conflict

Most conflicts develop in stages, as shown in Figure 15.2. Managers should recognize that unresolved prior conflicts help set the stage for future conflicts of the same or related sort. Rather than trying to deny the existence of conflict or settle

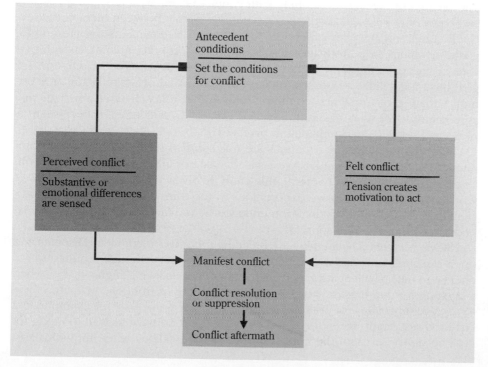

Figure 15.2   The stages of conflict.

on a temporary resolution, it is always best to deal with important conflicts so that they are completely resolved.[14] *Conflict antecedents* establish the conditions from which conflicts are likely to develop. When the antecedent conditions become the basis for substantive or emotional differences between people or groups, the stage of *perceived conflict* exists. Of course, this perception may be held by only one of the conflicting parties. It is important to distinguish between perceived and *felt conflict*. When conflict is felt, it is experienced as tension that motivates the person to take action to reduce feelings of discomfort. For conflict to be resolved, all parties should perceive the conflict and feel the need to do something about it.

When conflict is expressed openly in behavior, it is said to be manifest. Removing or correcting its antecedents may resolve a state of *manifest conflict*. Conflict can also be suppressed. With suppression, no change in antecedent conditions occurs; the manifest conflict behaviors are controlled. For example, one or both parties may choose to ignore the conflict in their dealings with one another. *Suppression* is a superficial and often temporary form of conflict resolution. Indeed, we have already noted that unresolved and suppressed conflicts fall into this category. Both may continue to fester and cause future conflicts over similar issues. In the short run, however, they may represent the best a manager can achieve until antecedent conditions can be changed.

Unresolved substantive conflicts can result in sustained emotional discomfort and escalate into dysfunctional emotional conflict between individuals. In contrast, truly resolved conflicts may establish conditions that reduce the potential for future conflicts or make it easier to deal with them. Thus, any manager should be sensitive to the influence of *conflict aftermath* on future conflict episodes.

Causes of Conflict

The process of dealing successfully with conflict begins with recognition of several types of conflict situations. *Vertical conflict* occurs between hierarchical levels. It commonly involves supervisor-subordinate disagreements over resources, goals, deadlines, or performance results. *Horizontal conflict* occurs between persons or groups at the same hierarchical level. These disputes commonly involve goal incompatibilities, resource scarcities, or purely interpersonal factors. A common variation of horizontal conflict is *line-staff conflict*. It often involves disagreements over who has authority and control over certain matters such as personnel selection and termination practices.

Also common to work situations are *role conflicts* that occur when the communication of task expectations proves inadequate or upsetting. As discussed with respect to teamwork in Chapter 9, this often involves unclear communication of work expectations, excessive expectations in the form of job overloads, insufficient expectations in the form of job underloads, and incompatibilities among expectations from different sources.

Workflow interdependencies are breeding grounds for conflicts. Disputes and open disagreements may erupt among people and units who are required to cooperate to meet challenging goals.[15] When interdependence is high—that is, when a person or group must rely on or ask for contributions from one or more others to achieve its goals—conflicts often occur. You will notice this, for example, in a fast-food restaurant, when the people serving the food have to wait too long for it to be delivered from the cooks. Conflict also escalates when individuals or groups lack adequate task direction or goals. *Domain ambiguities* involve misunderstandings over such things as customer jurisdiction or scope of authority.

Conflict is likely when individuals or groups are placed in ambiguous situations where it is difficult for them to understand just who is responsible for what. Actual or perceived *resource scarcity* can foster destructive competition. When resources are scarce, working relationships are likely to suffer. This is especially true in organizations that are experiencing downsizing or financial difficulties. As cutbacks occur, various individuals or groups try to position themselves to gain or retain maximum shares of the shrinking resource pool. They are also likely to try to resist resource redistribution or to employ countermeasures to defend their resources from redistribution to others.

Finally, *power or value asymmetries* in work relationships can create conflict. They exist when interdependent people or groups differ substantially from one another in status and influence or in values. Conflict resulting from asymmetry is prone to occur, for example, when a low-power person needs the help of a high-power person who does not respond, when people who hold dramatically different values are forced to work together on a task, or when a high-status person is required to interact with and perhaps be dependent on someone of lower status.

Indirect Conflict Management Approaches

Indirect conflict management approaches share the common quality of avoiding direct dealings with personalities. They include reduced interdependence, appeals to common goals, hierarchical referral, and alterations in the use of mythology and scripts.

Reduced Interdependence When workflow conflicts exist, managers can adjust the level of interdependency among units or individuals.[16] One simple option is *decoupling*, or taking action to eliminate or reduce the required contact between conflicting parties. In some cases the units' tasks can be adjusted to reduce the number of required points of coordination. The conflicting units can then be separated from one another, and each can be provided separate access to valued resources. Although decoupling may reduce conflict, it may also result in duplication and a poor allocation of valued resources.

Buffering is another approach that can be used when the inputs of one group are the outputs of another group. The classic buffering technique is to build an inventory, or buffer, between the two groups so that any output slowdown or excess is absorbed by the inventory and does not directly pressure the target group. Although it reduces conflict, this technique is increasingly out of favor because it increases inventory costs. This consequence is contrary to the elements of just-in-time delivery, which is now valued in operations management.

Conflict management can be facilitated by assigning people to serve as formal linking pins between groups that are prone to conflict.[17] Persons in *linking-pin roles*, such as project liaisons, are expected to understand the operations, members, needs, and norms of their host groups. They are supposed to use this knowledge to help the group work better with other groups in order to accomplish mutual tasks. Although expensive, this technique is often used when different specialized groups, such as engineering and sales, must closely coordinate their efforts on complex and long-term projects.

Boeing builds for white-collar and blue-collar togetherness

You may be surprised, but it wasn't always the case that the persons engineering our latest aircraft actually got to see them in production. All that has changed now at Boeing; new building designs have turned potential conflicts into collaboration. Vice President Carolyn Corvi was behind the push. She says: "For a long time I had the idea that it was wrong that the people who design airplanes didn't have a chance to see them unless they bought a ticket." Now Boeing's engineers, machinists, and managers meet and work together in conference rooms and cubicles with windowed walls facing the production floors.

Appeals to Common Goals   An *appeal to common goals* can focus the attention of potentially conflicting parties on one mutually desirable conclusion. By elevating the potential dispute to a common framework wherein the parties recognize their mutual interdependence in achieving common goals, petty disputes can be put in perspective. However, this can be difficult to achieve when prior performance is poor and individuals or groups disagree over how to improve performance. In this negative situation the manager needs to remember the attribution tendency of individuals to blame poor performance on others or on external conditions. In this case, conflict resolution begins by making sure that the parties take personal responsibility for improving the situation.

Hierarchical Referral   *Hierarchical referral* makes use of the chain of command for conflict resolution.[18] Here, problems are simply referred up the hierarchy for more senior managers to reconcile. Whereas hierarchical referral can be definitive in a given case, it also has limitations. If conflict is severe and recurring, the continual use of hierarchical referral may not result in true conflict resolution. Managers removed from day-to-day affairs may fail to diagnose the real causes of a conflict, and conflict resolution may be superficial. Busy managers may tend to consider most conflicts as results of poor interpersonal relations and may act quickly to replace a person with a perceived "personality" problem.

Altering Scripts and Myths   In some situations, conflict is superficially managed by scripts, or behavioral routines, that become part of the organization's culture.[19] The scripts become rituals that allow the conflicting parties to vent their frustrations and to recognize that they are mutually dependent on one another via the larger corporation. An example is a monthly meeting of "department heads," which is held presumably for purposes of coordination and problem solving but actually becomes just a polite forum for superficial agreement.[20] Managers in such cases know their scripts and accept the difficulty of truly resolving any major conflicts. By sticking with the script, expressing only low-key disagreement, and then quickly acting as if everything has been resolved, for instance, the managers publicly act as if problems are being addressed. Such scripts can be altered to allow and encourage active confrontation of issues and disagreements.

Direct Conflict Management Approaches

In Figure 15.3 the five approaches to conflict management are described from the perspective of their relative emphasis on cooperativeness and assertiveness in the relationship. Consultants and academics generally agree that true conflict resolution can occur only when the underlying substantive and emotional reasons for the conflict are identified and dealt with through a solution that allows all conflicting parties to "win."[21] This important issue of "who wins?" can be addressed from the perspective of each conflicting party.

Lose-Lose Conflict   *Lose-lose conflict* occurs when nobody really gets what he or she wants. The underlying reasons for the conflict remain unaffected, and a similar conflict is likely to occur in the future. Lose-lose conflicts often result when there is little or no assertiveness and conflict management takes the following forms. **Avoidance** is an extreme form of inattention; everyone simply pretends that the conflict does not really exist and hopes that it will go away.

■ **Avoidance** involves pretending a conflict does not really exist.

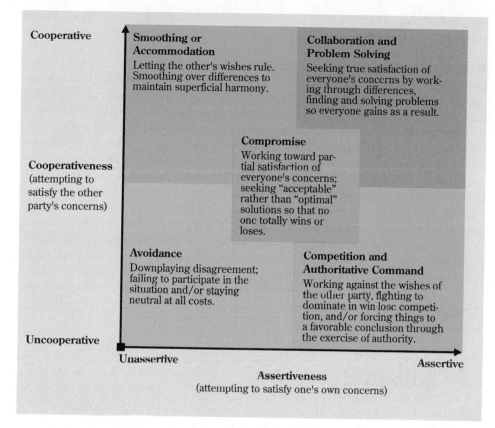

Figure 15.3 **Five ways to manage conflict.**

Cooperative

Smoothing or Accommodation
Letting the other's wishes rule. Smoothing over differences to maintain superficial harmony.

Collaboration and Problem Solving
Seeking true satisfaction of everyone's concerns by working through differences, finding and solving problems so everyone gains as a result.

Cooperativeness
(attempting to satisfy the other party's concerns)

Compromise
Working toward partial satisfaction of everyone's concerns; seeking "acceptable" rather than "optimal" solutions so that no one totally wins or loses.

Avoidance
Downplaying disagreement; failing to participate in the situation and/or staying neutral at all costs.

Competition and Authoritative Command
Working against the wishes of the other party, fighting to dominate in win-lose competition, and/or forcing things to a favorable conclusion through the exercise of authority.

Uncooperative

Unassertive   Assertive

Assertiveness
(attempting to satisfy one's own concerns)

▬▬ **Accommodation,** or **smoothing,** involves playing down differences and finding areas of agreement.

▬▬ **Compromise** occurs when each party gives up something of value to the other.

▬▬ **Competition** seeks victory by force, superior skill, or domination.

▬▬ **Authoritative command** uses formal authority to end conflict.

Accommodation, or **smoothing** as it is sometimes called, involves playing down differences among the conflicting parties and highlighting similarities and areas of agreement. This peaceful coexistence ignores the real essence of a given conflict and often creates frustration and resentment. **Compromise** occurs when each party gives up something of value to the other. As a result of no one getting their full desires, the antecedent conditions for future conflicts are established. See OB Savvy 15.1 for tips on when to use this and other conflict management styles.

Win-Lose Conflict In *win-lose conflict,* one party achieves its desires at the expense and to the exclusion of the other party's desires. This is a high-assertiveness and low-cooperativeness situation. It may result from outright **competition** in which one party achieves a victory through force, superior skill, or domination. It may also occur as a result of **authoritative command,** whereby a formal authority simply dictates a solution and specifies what is gained and what is lost by whom. Win-lose strategies fail to address the root causes of the conflict and tend to

OB SAVVY 15.1

When to Use Conflict Management Styles

- Collaboration and problem solving are preferred to gain true conflict resolution when time and cost permit.
- Avoidance may be used when an issue is trivial, when more important issues are pressing, or when people need to cool down temporarily and regain perspective.
- Authoritative command may be used when quick and decisive action is vital or when unpopular actions must be taken.
- Accommodation may be used when issues are more important to others than to yourself or when you want to build "credits" for use in later disagreements.
- Compromise may be used to arrive at temporary settlements of complex issues or to arrive at expedient solutions when time is limited.

suppress the desires of at least one of the conflicting parties. As a result, future conflicts over the same issues are likely to occur.

Win-Win Conflict *Win-win conflict* is achieved by a blend of both high cooperativeness and high assertiveness.[22] **Collaboration**, or **problem solving**, involves recognition by all conflicting parties that something is wrong and needs attention. It stresses gathering and evaluating information in solving disputes and making choices. Win-win conditions eliminate the reasons for continuing or resurrecting the conflict since nothing has been avoided or suppressed. All relevant issues are raised and openly discussed. The ultimate test for a win-win solution is whether or not the conflicting parties see that the solution (1) achieves each other's goals, (2) is acceptable to both parties, and (3) establishes a process whereby all parties involved see a responsibility to be open and honest about facts and feelings. When success is achieved, true conflict resolution has occurred.

Although collaboration and problem solving are generally favored as conflict resolution approaches, one limitation is the time and energy they require. It is also important to realize that both parties to the conflict need to be assertive and cooperative in order to develop a win-win joint solution. Finally, collaboration and problem solving may not be feasible if the firm's dominant culture does not place a value on cooperation.[23]

■ **Collaboration** involves recognition that something is wrong and needs attention through problem solving.

■ **Problem solving** uses information to resolve disputes.

Negotiation

Talk about conflict! Picture yourself trying to make a decision in the following situation: You have ordered a new state-of-the-art notebook computer for a staff member in your department. At about the same time another department ordered a different brand. Your boss indicates that only one brand will be ordered. Of course, you believe the one chosen by your department is the best. Or consider this one: You have been offered a new job in another location and want to take it but are disappointed with the salary. You remember from one of your college courses that compensation and benefits packages can sometimes be modified from the first offer—if the candidate approaches things right.[24] You are concerned about the costs of relocating and would like a signing bonus as well as a guarantee of an early salary review.

What Is Negotiation?

The preceding examples are just two of the many situations that involve managers and others in **negotiation**—the process of making joint decisions when the parties involved have different preferences.[25] Negotiation has special significance in work settings, where disagreements are likely to arise over such diverse matters as wage rates, task objectives, performance evaluations, job assignments, work schedules, work locations, and more.

■ **Negotiation** is the process of making joint decisions when the parties involved have different preferences.

Negotiation Goals and Outcomes

In negotiation two important goals must be considered: substance and relationship goals. *Substance goals* deal with outcomes that relate to the "content" issues under negotiation. The dollar amount of a wage agreement in a collective-bargaining situation is one example. Relationship goals deal with outcomes that relate to how well people involved in the negotiation and any constituencies they may represent are able to work with one another once the process is concluded. An example is the ability of union members and management representatives to work together effectively after a contract dispute has been settled.

Unfortunately, many negotiations result in damaged relationships because the negotiating parties become preoccupied with substance goals and self-interests. In contrast, effective negotiation occurs when substance issues are resolved and working relationships are maintained or even improved. It results in the recognition of overlapping interests and the appreciation that joint decisions are "for the better" of all parties. Three criteria for effective negotiation are described in OB Savvy 15.2.

Ethical Aspects of Negotiation

Managers and others involved in negotiations should strive for high ethical standards of conduct. This goal may be sidetracked by an overemphasis on self-interests. The motivation to behave ethically in negotiations is put to the test by each party's desire to "get more" than the other from the negotiation and/or by a belief that there are insufficient resources to satisfy all parties.[26] After the heat of negotiations dies down, the parties involved often try to rationalize or explain away questionable ethics as unavoidable, harmless, or justified. Such after-the-fact rationalizations may be offset by long-run negative consequences, such as not being able to achieve one's wishes again the next time. At the very least the unethical party may be the target of revenge tactics by those who were disadvantaged. Furthermore, once some people have behaved unethically in one situation, they may become entrapped by such behavior and prone to display it again in the future.[27]

Organizational Settings for Negotiation

Managers and team leaders should be prepared to participate in at least four major action settings for negotiations. In *two-party negotiation* the manager negotiates directly with one other person. In a *group negotiation* the manager is part of a team or group whose members are negotiating to arrive at a common decision. In an *intergroup negotiation* the manager is part of a group that is negotiating with another group to arrive at a decision regarding a problem or situation affecting both. And in a *constituency negotiation* the manager is involved in negotiation with other persons, with each party representing a broader constituency. A common example of *constituency negotiation* involves representatives of management and labor negotiating a collective bargaining agreement.

Culture and Negotiation

The existence of cultural differences in time orientation, individualism versus collectivism, and power distance can have a substantial impact on negotiation. For example, when American businesses try to negotiate quickly with their Chinese counterparts, they often do so with the goal of getting definitive agreements that will govern a working relationship. Culture is not always on their side. A typical Chinese

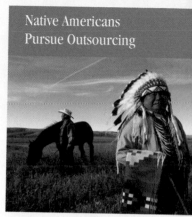

Native Americans Pursue Outsourcing

The goal was to gain yet another outsourcing client. But when Accenture's managing director, Randall L. Willis, was making his business pitch, he wasn't in a foreign country. He was on the Umatilla Indian reservation in Oregon. And his negotiation was successful. Tribal leaders agreed to give Accenture a five-year contract to manage Cayse Technologies, an outsourcing business owned by the Umatillas. It was a win-win for Accenture and the Confederated Tribes of the Umatilla Indian Reservation. Willis notes that more organizations want to outsource at home, not abroad. "Whether it's cost concerns or security," he says, "a number of industries would like to keep it in the U.S."

OB SAVVY 15.2

Criteria of an Effective Negotiation

1. *Quality*—The negotiation results offer a "quality" agreement that is wise and satisfactory to all sides.
2. *Harmony*—The negotiation is "harmonious" and fosters rather than inhibits good interpersonal relations.
3. *Efficiency*—The negotiation is "efficient" and no more time consuming or costly than absolutely necessary.

approach to negotiation might move much more slowly, require the development of good interpersonal relationships prior to reaching any agreement, display reluctance to commit everything to writing, and anticipate that any agreement reached will be subject to modification as future circumstances may require.[28] All this is quite the opposite of the typical expectations of negotiators used to the individualist and short-term American culture.

MASTERING MANAGEMENT

IT'S POSSIBLE TO GET A BETTER RAISE

We all do it—wish we'd asked for more when negotiating a starting salary or a pay raise. Why didn't we? And, even if we did, would it have made a difference? Chances are you'll go into a salary negotiation unprepared. And you may pay a price for that. There's quite a bit of advice around for how to negotiate pay raises. A compilation of thoughts and tips follows.[29]

- *Prepare, prepare, prepare*—do the research and find out what others make for a similar position inside and outside the organization, including everything from salary to benefits, bonuses, incentives, and job perks.
- *Document and communicate*—identify and communicate your value; put forth a set of accomplishments that show how you have saved or made money and created value for an employer, or how your skills and attributes will do so for a prospective one.
- *Advocate and ask*—be your own best advocate; in salary negotiation the rule is "Don't ask, don't get." But don't ask too soon; your boss or interviewer should be the first to bring up salary.

- *Stay focused on the goal*—the goal is to satisfy your interests to the maximum extent possible; this means everything from getting immediate satisfaction to being better positioned for future satisfaction.
- *View things from the other side*—test your requests against the employer's point of view; ask if you are being reasonable, convincing, and fair; ask how the boss could explain to higher levels and to your peers a decision to grant your request.
- *Don't overreact to bad news*—never "quit on the spot" if you don't get what you want; be willing to search for and consider alternative job offers.

Distributive negotiation focuses on positions staked out or declared by the parties involved, who are each trying to claim certain portions of the available pie.

Integrative negotiation focuses on the merits of the issues, and the parties involved try to enlarge the available pie rather than stake claims to certain portions of it.

Negotiation Strategies

Managers and other workers frequently negotiate with one another over access to scarce organizational resources. These resources may be money, time, people, facilities, equipment, and so on. In all such cases the general approach to, or strategy for, the negotiation can have a major influence on its outcomes. In **distributive negotiation** the focus is on "positions" staked out or declared by conflicting parties. Each party is trying to claim certain portions of the available "pie." In **integrative negotiation**, sometimes called *principled negotiation*, the focus is on the "merits" of the issues. Everyone involved tries to enlarge the available pie rather than stake claims to certain portions of it.[30]

Distributive Negotiation

In distributive bargaining approaches, the participants would each ask this question: "Who is going to get this resource?" This question, and the way in which it frames subsequent behavior, will have a major impact on the negotiation process and outcomes. A case of distributive negotiation usually unfolds in one of two directions, neither of which yields optimal results.

"Hard" distributive negotiation takes place when each party holds out to get its own way. This leads to competition, whereby each party seeks dominance over the other and tries to maximize self-interests. The hard approach may lead to a win-lose outcome in which one party dominates and gains. Or it can lead to an impasse.

"Soft" distributive negotiation, in contrast, takes place when one party is willing to make concessions to the other to get things over with. In this case one party tries to find ways to meet the other's desires. A soft approach leads to accommodation, in which one party gives in to the other, or to compromise, in which each party gives up something of value in order to reach agreement. In either case at least some latent dissatisfaction is likely to develop. Even when the soft approach results in compromise (e.g., splitting the difference between the initial positions equally), dissatisfaction may exist since each party is still deprived of what it originally wanted.

Figure 15.4 introduces the case of the graduating senior negotiating a job offer with a corporate recruiter.[31] The example illustrates the basic elements of classic two-party negotiation in distributive contexts. To begin, look at the situation from the graduate's perspective. She has told the recruiter that she would like a salary of $45,000; this is her initial offer. But she also has in mind a minimum reservation point of $35,000—the lowest salary that she will accept for this job. Thus she communicates a salary request of $45,000 but is willing to accept one as low as $35,000. The situation is somewhat the reverse from the recruiter's perspective. His initial offer to the graduate is $30,000, and his maximum reservation point is $40,000; this is the most he is prepared to pay.

The **bargaining zone** is defined as the range between one party's minimum reservation point and the other party's maximum reservation point. In Figure 15.4, the bargaining zone is $50,000–$55,000. This is a positive bargaining zone since the reservation points of the two parties overlap. Whenever a positive bargaining zone exists, bargaining has room to unfold. Had the graduate's minimum

> The **bargaining zone** is the zone between one party's minimum reservation point and the other party's maximum reservation point in a negotiating situation.

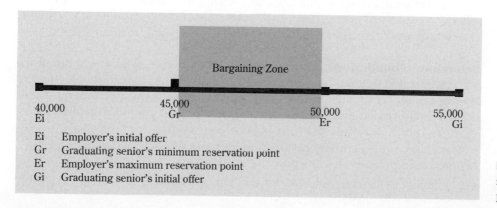

Ei	Employer's initial offer
Gr	Graduating senior's minimum reservation point
Er	Employer's maximum reservation point
Gi	Graduating senior's initial offer

Figure 15.4   The bargaining zone in classic two-party negotiation.

reservation point been greater than the recruiter's maximum reservation point (for example, $57,000), no room would have existed for bargaining. Classic two-party bargaining always involves the delicate tasks of first discovering the respective reservation points (one's own and the other's), and then working toward an agreement that lies somewhere within the resulting bargaining zone and is acceptable to each party.

Integrative Negotiation

In the integrative approach to negotiation, participants would ask: "How can the resource best be used?" Notice that this question is very different from the one described for distributive negotiation. It is much less confrontational, and it permits a broader range of alternatives to be considered in the process. From the outset there is much more of a "win-win" orientation. At one extreme, integrative negotiation may involve selective avoidance, in which both parties realize that there are more important things on which to focus their time and attention. The time, energy, and effort needed to negotiate may not be worth the rewards. Compromise can also play a role in the integrative approach, but it must have an enduring basis. This is most likely to occur when the compromise involves each party giving up something of perceived lesser personal value to gain something of greater value. For instance, in the classic two-party bargaining case over salary, both the graduate and the recruiter could expand the negotiation to include the starting date of the job. Since it will be a year before the candidate's first vacation, she may be willing to take a little less money if she can start a few weeks later. Finally, integrative negotiation may involve true collaboration. In this case, the negotiating parties engage in problem solving to arrive at a mutual agreement that maximizes benefits to each.

How to Gain Integrative Agreements

Underlying the integrative or principled approach is negotiation based on the merits of the situation. The foundations for gaining truly integrative agreements include supportive attitudes, constructive behaviors, and good information.[32]

Attitudinal Foundations   There are three attitudinal foundations of integrative agreements. First, each party must approach the negotiation with a *willingness to trust* the other party. This is a reason why ethics and maintaining relationships are so important in negotiations. Second, each party must convey a *willingness to share* information with the other party. Without shared information, effective problem solving is unlikely to occur. Third, each party must show a *willingness to ask concrete questions* of the other party. This further facilitates information sharing.

Behavioral Foundations   During a negotiation all behavior is important for both its actual impact and the impressions it leaves behind. Accordingly, the following behavioral foundations of integrative agreements must be carefully considered and included in any negotiator's repertoire of skills and capabilities:

- The ability to separate the people from the problem to avoid allowing emotional considerations to affect the negotiation
- The ability to focus on interests rather than positions

- The ability to avoid making premature judgments
- The ability to keep the acts of alternative creation separate from their evaluation
- The ability to judge possible agreements on an objective set of criteria or standards

Information Foundations The information foundations of integrative agreements are substantial. They involve each party becoming familiar with the BATNA, or "best alternative to a negotiated agreement." That is, each party must know what he or she will do if an agreement cannot be reached. This requires that both negotiating parties identify and understand their personal interests in the situation. They must know what is really important to them in the case at hand, and they must come to understand the relative importance of the other party's interests. As difficult as it may seem, each party must achieve an understanding of what the other party values, even to the point of determining its BATNA.

Common Negotiation Pitfalls

The negotiation process is admittedly complex on cultural and many other grounds. It is further characterized by all the possible confusions within interpersonal and group dynamics that sometimes get volatile. Accordingly, negotiators need to guard against some common negotiation pitfalls.[33]

The first pitfall is the tendency in negotiation to stake out your position based on the assumption that in order to gain your way, something must be subtracted from the gains of the other party. This *myth of the fixed pie* is a purely distributive approach to negotiation. The whole concept of integrative negotiation is based on the premise that the pie can sometimes be expanded or used to the maximum advantage of all parties, not just one.

Second, because parties to negotiations often begin by stating extreme demands, the possibility of *escalating commitment* is high. That is, once demands have been stated, people become committed to them and are reluctant to back down. Concerns for protecting one's ego and saving face may lead to the irrational escalation of a conflict. Self-discipline is needed to spot this tendency in one's own behavior as well as in the behavior of others.

Third, negotiators often develop *overconfidence* that their positions are the only correct ones. This can lead them to ignore the other party's needs. In some cases negotiators completely fail to see merits in the other party's position—merits that an outside observer would be sure to spot. Such overconfidence makes it harder to reach a positive common agreement.

Fourth, communication problems can cause difficulties during a negotiation. It has been said that "negotiation is the process of communicating back and forth for the purpose of reaching a joint decision."[34] This process can break down because of a *telling problem*—the parties don't really talk to each other, at least not in the sense of making themselves truly understood. It can also be damaged by a *hearing problem*—the parties are unable or unwilling to listen well enough to understand what the other is saying. Indeed, positive negotiation is most likely when each party engages in active listening and frequently asks questions to clarify what the other is saying. Each party occasionally needs to "stand in the other party's shoes" and to view the situation from the other's perspective.[35]

Behavioral foundations of integrative agreements

Research Insight
Words Affect Outcomes in Online Dispute Resolution

A study of dispute resolution among eBay buyers and sellers finds that using words that give "face" were more likely than words that attack "face" to result in the settlement of online disputes. Jeanne Brett, Marla Olekans, Ray Friedman, Nathan Goates, Cameron Anderson, and Cara Cherry Lisco studied real disputes being addressed through Square Trade, an online dispute resolution service to which eBay refers unhappy customers. The researchers note that a study by the National Consumer League reported that 41 percent of participants in online trading had problems, often associated with late deliveries. For purposes of the study a "dispute" was defined as a form of conflict in which one party to a transaction makes a claim that the other party rejects.

The researchers point out that most past research on dispute resolution has focused on situational and participant characteristics. In this case they adopted what they call a "language-based" approach based on the perspectives of face theory, essentially arguing that how participants use language to give and attack the face of the other party will have a major impact on results. For example, in filing a claim an unhappy buyer might use polite words that preserve the positive self-image or face of the seller, or they might use negative words that attack this sense of face. Examples of negative words are "*agitated, angry, apprehensive, despise, disgusted, frustrated, furious, and hate.*"

This study examined 386 eBay-generated disputes processed through Square Trade. Words used in the first social interchange between parties were analyzed. Results showed that expressing negative emotions and giving commands to the other party inhibited dispute resolution, whereas providing a causal explanation, offering suggestions, and communicating firmness all made dispute resolution more likely. An hypothesis that expressing positive emotions would increase the likelihood of dispute resolution was not supported. The study also showed that the longer a dispute played out, the less likely it was to be resolved.

In terms of practical implications the researchers specifically state: "Watch your language; avoid attacking the other's face either by showing your anger toward them, or expressing contempt; avoid signaling weakness; be firm in your claim. Provide causal accounts that take responsibility and give face." Finally, they note that these basic principles apply in other dispute resolution contexts, not just online.[35A]

Dispute resolution less likely when	Dispute resolution more likely when
• Negative emotions are expressed	• Causal explanation given
• Commands are issued	• Suggestion are offered
	• Communications are firm

Third-Party Roles in Negotiation

Alternative dispute resolution involves a neutral third party who helps others resolve negotiation impasses and disputes.

Negotiation may sometimes be accomplished through the intervention of third parties, such as when stalemates occur and matters appear not resolvable under current circumstances. In a process called **alternative dispute resolution**, a neutral third party works with persons involved in a negotiation to help them resolve impasses and settle disputes. There are two primary forms through which "ADR" is implemented.

In **arbitration**, such as the salary arbitration now common in professional sports, the neutral third party acts as a "judge" and has the power to issue a decision that is binding on all parties. This ruling takes place after the arbitrator listens to the positions advanced by the parties involved in a dispute. In **mediation**, the neutral third party tries to engage the parties in a negotiated solution through persuasion and rational argument. This is a common approach in labor–management negotiations, where trained mediators acceptable to both sides are called in to help resolve bargaining impasses. Unlike an arbitrator, the mediator is not able to dictate a solution.

In **arbitration** a neutral third party acts as judge with the power to issue a decision binding on all parties.

In **mediation** a neutral third party tries to engage the parties in a negotiated solution through persuasion and rational argument.

Chapter 15 Study Guide

Summary

What is conflict?

- Conflict appears as a disagreement over issues of substance or emotional antagonisms that create friction between individuals or groups.

- Conflict situations in organizations occur at intrapersonal, interpersonal, intergroup, and interorganizational levels.

- When kept within tolerable limits, conflict can be a source of creativity and performance enhancement; it becomes destructive when these limits are exceeded.

How can conflict be managed successfully?

- Most typically, conflict develops through a series of stages, beginning with antecedent conditions and progressing into manifest conflict.

- Unresolved prior conflicts set the stage for future conflicts of a similar nature.

- Indirect forms of conflict management include appeals to common goals, hierarchical referral, organizational redesign, and the use of mythology and scripts.

- Direct conflict management proceeds with different combinations of assertiveness and cooperativeness by conflicting parties.

- Win-win conflict resolution is preferred; it is achieved through collaboration and problem solving.

- Win-lose conflict resolution should be avoided; it is associated with competition and authoritative command.

What is negotiation?

- Negotiation occurs whenever two or more people with different preferences must make joint decisions.

- Managers may find themselves involved in various types of negotiation situations, including two-party, group, intergroup, and constituency negotiation.

- Effective negotiation occurs when issues of substance are resolved and human relationships are maintained, or even improved, in the process.

- Ethical conduct is important in successful negotiations.

What are the different strategies involved in negotiation?

- In distributive negotiation the focus of each party is on staking out positions in the attempt to claim desired portions of a "fixed pie."

- In integrative negotiation, sometimes called principled negotiation, the focus is on determining the merits of the issues and finding ways to satisfy one another's needs.

- The success of negotiations often depends on avoiding common pitfalls such as the myth of the fixed pie, escalating commitment, overconfidence, and both the telling and hearing problems.

- Third party roles in negotiation provide alternative dispute resolution through arbitration and mediation.

Key Terms

Accommodation, or smoothing (p. 351)
Alternative dispute resolution (p. 358)
Arbitration (p. 359)
Authoritative command (p. 351)
Avoidance (p. 350)
Bargaining zone (p. 355)
Collaboration (p. 352)
Competition (p. 351)

Compromise (p. 351)
Conflict (p. 342)
Conflict resolution (p. 347)
Distributive negotiation (p. 354)
Dysfunctional conflict (p. 345)
Emotional conflict (p. 343)
Functional conflict (p. 345)
Integrative negotiation (p. 354)

Intergroup conflict (p. 344)
Interorganizational conflict (p. 344)
Interpersonal conflict (p. 344)
Intrapersonal conflict (p. 344)
Mediation (p. 359)
Negotiation (p. 352)
Problem solving (p. 352)
Substantive conflict (p. 343)

Self-Test 15

Multiple Choice

1. A/an _____ conflict occurs in the form of a fundamental disagreement over ends or goals to be pursued and the means for accomplishment. (a) relationship (b) emotional (c) substantive (d) procedural

2. The indirect conflict management approach that uses chain of command for conflict resolution is known as _____. (a) hierarchical referral (b) avoidance (c) smoothing (d) appeal to common goals

3. Conflict that ends up being "functional" for the people and organization involved would most likely be _____. (a) of high intensity (b) of moderate intensity (c) of low intensity (d) nonexistent

4. One of the problems with the suppression of conflicts is that it _____. (a) creates winners and losers (b) is often a temporary solution that sets the stage for future conflict (c) works only with emotional conflicts (d) works only with substantive conflicts

5. When a manager asks people in conflict to remember the mission and purpose of the organization and to try to reconcile their differences in that context, she is using a conflict management approach known as _____. (a) reduced interdependence (b) buffering (c) resource expansion (d) appeal to common goals

6. The best time to use accommodation in conflict management is _____. (a) when quick and decisive action is vital (b) when you want to build "credit" for use in

later disagreements (c) when people need to cool down and gain perspective (d) when temporary settlement of complex issues is needed

7. Which is an indirect approach to managing conflict? _____ (a) buffering (b) win-lose (c) workflow interdependency (d) power asymmetry

8. A lose-lose conflict is likely when the conflict management approach focuses on _____. (a) linking pin roles (b) altering scripts (c) accommodation (d) problem-solving

9. Which approach to conflict management can be best described as both highly cooperative and highly assertive? _____ (a) competition (b) compromise (c) accommodation (d) collaboration

10. Both _____ goals should be considered in any negotiation. (a) performance and evaluation (b) task and substance (c) substance and relationship (d) task and performance

11. The three criteria for effective negotiation are _____. (a) harmony, efficiency, and quality (b) quality, efficiency, and effectiveness (c) ethical behavior, practicality, and cost-effectiveness (d) quality, practicality and productivity

12. Which statement is true? _____ (a) Principled negotiation leads to accommodation. (b) Hard distributive negotiation leads to collaboration. (c) Soft distributive negotiation leads to accommodation or compromise. (d) Hard distributive negotiation leads to win-win conflicts.

13. Another name for integrative negotiation is _____. (a) arbitration (b) mediation (c) principled negotiation (d) smoothing

14. When a person approaches a negotiation with the assumption that in order for him to gain his way, the other party must lose or give up something, which negotiation pitfall is being exhibited? _____ (a) myth of the fixed pie (b) escalating commitment (c) overconfidence (d) hearing problem

15. In the process of alternative dispute resolution known as _____, a neutral third party acts as a "judge" to determine how a conflict will be resolved. (a) mediation (b) arbitration (c) conciliation (d) collaboration

Short Response

16. List and discuss three conflict situations faced by managers.

17. List and discuss the major indirect conflict management approaches.

18. Under what conditions might a manager use avoidance or accommodation?

19. Compare and contrast distributive and integrative negotiation. Which is more desirable? Why?

Applications Essay

20. Discuss the common pitfalls you would expect to encounter in negotiating your salary for your first job, and explain how you would best try to deal with them.

These learning activities from *The OB Skills Workbook* are suggested for Chapter 15.

OB in Action

CASE	EXPERIENTIAL EXERCISES	SELF-ASSESSMENT
■ 15. The Missing Raise	■ 35. Vacation Puzzle ■ 36. The Ugli Orange ■ 37. Conflict Dialogues	■ 18. Conflict Management Styles

Plus—special learning experiences from *The Jossey-Bass/Pfeiffer Classroom Collection*

Chapter 16

Organizational Culture and Development

Chapter at a Glance

Organizations are more than a place to work; they are a place where individuals spend much of their adult lives. Thus, the culture of the organization is critical to its members. Here, we describe organizational culture, how it can be managed, and how a skilled manager can use organizational development. As you read Chapter 16, *keep in mind these study topics.*

ORGANIZATIONAL CULTURE

> Functions of Organizational Culture
>
> Subcultures and Countercultures
>
> National Culture and Corporate Culture

UNDERSTANDING ORGANIZATIONAL CULTURES

> Layers of Cultural Analysis
>
> Stories, Rites, Rituals, and Symbols
>
> Cultural Rules and Roles
>
> Shared Values, Meanings, and Organizational Myths

MANAGING ORGANIZATIONAL CULTURE

> Management Philosophy and Strategy
>
> Building, Reinforcing, and Changing Culture

ORGANIZATIONAL DEVELOPMENT

> Underlying Assumptions of OD
>
> OD Values and Principles
>
> Action-Research Foundations of OD
>
> OD Interventions

CHAPTER 16 STUDY GUIDE

How individuals work, live, and achieve together

Walk into the headquarters of R&R Partners, the Las Vegas–based advertising agency and lobbying firm, and it is immediately obvious that this is a fun place to work.[1] When visitors first enter the building, they are greeted overhead by lettering that reads, "R&R Partners Las Vegas Phoenix Reno Salt Lake City Washington DC. Just in case you had a late night, you're in the Las Vegas office." The handles to the doors are constructed out of the many advertising awards the agency has received. There is clearly an irreverent attitude at R&R. Yet underneath the fun atmosphere is a strong appreciation for the role that all the employees have in the success of the organization. Billy Vassiliadis, CEO, ensures that the organization's dedication to R&R is reflected in

> ## "Just in case you had a late night, you're in the Las Vegas office."

more than just words. R&R provides some of the best health care coverage in the industry, and it's not unusual for company-sponsored barbecues and happy hours to pop up on any given Friday. In fact, R&R was recently voted one of the top 10 places to work in Nevada. Within R&R there is a creative culture that permeates the entire organization: everyone is responsible for creating new ideas and campaigns. For instance, when new ideas are needed, everyone at R&R is invited into the agency's "war room" to brainstorm. These brainstorming sessions are called a SWARM. In a typical SWARM, an account team presents an issue. Everyone from the CEO to the receptionist is then invited to give his or her ideas.

Organizational Culture

To be successful in the advertising business, it is critical that companies have fresh and innovative ideas to market clients' goods and services. R&R Partners is a successful ad agency that is responsible for such edgy tag lines to lure tourists to Las Vegas as "What Happens in Vegas Stays in Vegas." To continue its success, R&R relies on its culture to provide the competitive edge.

■ **Organizational or corporate culture** is the system of shared actions, values, and beliefs that develops within an organization and guides the behavior of its members.

Organizational or corporate culture is the system of shared actions, values, and beliefs that develops within an organization and guides the behavior of its members.[2] In the business setting, this system is often referred to as the corporate culture. Just as no two individual personalities are the same, no two organizational cultures are identical. Today management scholars and consultants believe that cultural differences can have a major impact on the performance of organizations and the quality of work life experienced by their members. For instance, it appeared that Cantor Fitzgerald had died when most of its employees died on 9/11 with the collapse of the Twin Towers.[3] Such was not the case, as discussed in OB Savvy 16.1.

Functions of Organizational Culture

Through their collective experience, members of an organization solve two extremely important survival issues.[4] The first issue is one of external adaptation: What precisely needs to be accomplished, and how can it be done? The second is known as internal integration: How do members resolve the daily problems associated with living and working together?

External Adaptation   Issues of **External adaptation** deal with reaching goals: the tasks to be accomplished, methods to be used to achieve these goals, and the methods of coping with success and failure. Through their shared experiences, members may develop common views that help guide their day-to-day activities. Organizational members need to know the real mission of the organization, not just the pronouncements to key constituencies such as stockholders. From talking with one another, members will naturally develop an understanding of how they contribute to the mission via interaction. This view may emphasize the importance of human resources. On the other hand, employees may see themselves as cogs in a machine, or as costs to be reduced.

Closely related to the organization's mission and view of its contribution are the questions of responsibility, goals, and methods. For instance, at 3M employees believe that it is their responsibility to innovate and contribute creatively. They see these responsibilities reflected in how well the goals of developing new and improved products and processes are achieved.

Each collection of individuals in an organization also tends to (1) separate more important from less important external forces, (2) develop ways to measure their accomplishments, and (3) create explanations for why goals are not always met. At Dell, the retailer of computers and consumer electronics, for example, managers have moved away from judging their progress against specific targets to estimating the degree to which they are moving a development process forward. Instead of blaming a poor economy or upper-level managers for the firm's failure to reach a goal, Dell managers have set hard goals that are difficult to reach and have redoubled their efforts to improve participation and commitment.[5]

The final issues in external adaptation deal with two important, but often neglected, aspects of coping with external reality. First, individuals need to develop acceptable ways of telling outsiders just how good they really are. At 3M, for example, employees talk about the quality of their products and the many new, useful products they have brought to the market. Second, individuals must collectively know when to admit defeat. At 3M, the answer is easy for new projects: at the beginning of the development process, members establish "drop" points at which to quit the development effort and redirect it.[6]

In sum, external adaptation involves answering important instrumental or goal-related questions concerning coping with reality: What is the real mission? How do we contribute? What are our goals? How do we reach our goals? What external forces are important? How do we measure results? What do we do if we do not meet specific targets? How do we tell others how good we are? When do we quit?

Internal Integration   **Internal integration** deals with the creation of a collective identity and with finding ways of matching methods of working and living together.

OB SAVVY 16.1
The Power of Corporate Culture

When the terrorists plunged their captured airliners into the World Trade Center on September 11, 2001, the aftermath brought out the best in employees at Cantor. Because their main offices were located on floors 101–105 of the World Trade Center's north tower, some 700 of their 1,000 employees were never found. In the aftermath, Howard Lutnick, the senior surviving executive of Cantor, could not believe the response of the survivors. Immediately after the tragedy, employees demanded that they be allowed to return to work. Laboring continuously in borrowed offices, they used backup equipment and systems as well as their offices in Europe and Asia to restart their high-tech operation by the opening of the stock exchanges on September 17.[4A]

External adaptation deals with reaching goals: the tasks to be accomplished, the methods to be used to achieve those goals, and the methods of coping with success and failure.

Internal integration deals with the creation of a collective identity and with ways of working and living together.

Herman Miller

Herman Miller, the furniture manufacturer based in Zeeland, Michigan, consistently gains high marks from those rating corporate citizenship. Known for its employee-friendly culture, the company states on its Web site: "Our employees share a commitment to innovation and uncompromising participative management and environmental stewardship."

The process of internal integration often begins with the establishment of a unique identity; that is, each collection of individuals and each subculture within the organization develops some type of unique definition of itself. Through dialogue and interaction, members begin to characterize their world. They may see it as malleable or fixed, filled with opportunity or threatening. Real progress toward innovation can begin when group members collectively believe that they can change important parts of the world around them, and that what appears to be a threat is actually an opportunity for change.

Three important aspects of working together are (1) deciding who is a member and who is not, (2) developing an informal understanding of acceptable and unacceptable behavior, and (3) separating friends from enemies. These are important questions for managers as well. A key to effective total quality management, for instance, is that subgroups in the organization need to view their immediate supervisors as members of the group. The immediate supervisor is expected to represent the group to friendly higher managers. Of course, should management not be seen as friendly, the process of improving quality could quickly break down.

To work together effectively, individuals need to decide collectively how to allocate power, status, and authority. They need to establish a shared understanding of who will get rewards and sanctions for specific types of actions. Too often, managers fail to recognize these important aspects of internal integration. For example, a manager may fail to explain the basis for a promotion and to show why this reward, the status associated with it, and the power given to the newly promoted individual are consistent with commonly shared beliefs. Collections of individuals also need to work out acceptable ways to communicate and to develop guidelines for friendships. Although these aspects of internal integration may appear esoteric, they are vital. For example, to function effectively as a team, team members must recognize that some members will be closer than others; friendships are inevitable.[7]

Resolving the issues of internal integration helps individuals develop a shared identity and a collective commitment. It may well lead to longer-term stability and provide a lens for members to use to make sense of their part of the world. In sum, internal integration involves answers to important questions associated with living together: What is our unique identity? How do we view the world? Who is a member? How do we allocate power, status, and authority? How do we communicate? What is the basis for friendship? Answering these questions is important to organizational members because the organization is more than just a place to work.[8]

Subcultures and Countercultures

Although smaller firms often have a single dominant culture with a unitary set of shared actions, values, and beliefs, most larger organizations contain several subcultures as well as one or more countercultures.[9]

Subcultures are groups with unique patterns of values and philosophies that are consistent with the dominant culture of the larger organization or social system.

Subcultures **Subcultures** are groups of individuals with unique patterns of values and philosophies that are not inconsistent with the organization's dominant values and philosophy.[10] Interestingly, strong subcultures are often found in task forces, teams, and special project groups in organizations. The subculture emerges to bind individuals working intensely together to accomplish a specific task. For example, there are strong subcultures of stress engineers and liaison engineers in the Boeing Renton plant. These highly specialized groups must solve knotty technical issues to ensure that Boeing planes are safe. Although distinct, these groups of engineers share in the dominant values of Boeing.

Countercultures   In contrast, **countercultures** are groups where the patterns of values and philosophies outwardly reject those of the larger organization or social system.[11] When Steven Jobs reentered Apple computer as its CEO, he quickly formed a counterculture within Apple. Over the next 18 months, numerous clashes occurred as the followers of the former CEO, Gil Amelio, fought to maintain their place and the old culture. Jobs won and Apple won. His counterculture became dominant.[12]

Every large organization imports potentially important subcultural groupings when it hires employees from the larger society. In North America, for instance, subcultures and countercultures may naturally form based on ethnic, racial, gender, generational, or locational similarities. In Japanese organizations, subcultures often form based on the date of graduation from a university, gender, or geographic location. In European firms, ethnicity and language play an important part in developing subcultures, as does gender. In many less-developed nations, language, education, religion, or family social status are often grounds for forming societally popular subcultures and countercultures.

Within an organization mergers and acquisitions may produce adjustment problems. Employers and managers of an acquired firm may hold values and assumptions that are quite inconsistent with those of the acquiring firm. This is known as the "clash of corporate cultures."[13] As more firms globalize and use mergers and acquisitions to expand, they often must cope with importing subcultures and with the clash of corporate cultures. For instance, when Daimler Benz said it was merging with Chrysler Corporation, it was billed as a merger of equals. The new combined firm would have a global reach. The corporate culture clash came quickly, however, when Chrysler managers and employees realized that Daimler executives would control the new combination and forge it around the German partner.[14]

> **Countercultures** are groups where the patterns of values and philosophies outwardly reject those of the larger organization or social system.

National Culture and Corporate Culture

Corporate mergers across national boundaries often serve to highlight both corporate and national cultural differences, as in the case of Daimler Benz and Chrysler.[15] The difference between Sony's corporate emphasis on group achievements and Zenith's emphasis on individual engineering excellence, for example, can be traced to the Japanese emphasis on collective action versus the U.S. emphasis on individualism. National cultural values may also become embedded in the expectations of important organizational constituencies and in generally accepted solutions to problems.

When moving across national cultures, managers need to be sensitive to national cultural differences so that their actions do not violate common assumptions in the underlying national culture. To improve morale at General Electric's French subsidiary, Compagnie Générale de Radiologie, American managers invited all the European managers to a "get-acquainted" meeting near Paris. The Americans gave out colorful T-shirts with the GE slogan, "Go for One," a typical maneuver in many American training programs. The French resented the T-shirts.

One outspoken individual said: "It was like Hitler was back, forcing us to wear uniforms. It was humiliating." Firms often face problems in developing a common culture with strong ethical standards, as evidenced by the effort Flowserve makes to ensure an ethical corporate culture (see Ethics in OB).

Importing Societal Subgroups   Beyond the issues of becoming culturally sensitive, difficulties may also arise with importing groupings from the larger society. Some of these groupings are relevant to the organization, while other may be quite destructive. At the one extreme, senior managers can merely accept societal divisions and work within the confines of the larger culture. There are three primary difficulties with this approach. First, subordinated groups, such as members of a specific religion or ethnic group, are likely to form into a counterculture and to work more diligently to change their status than to better the firm. Second, the firm may find it extremely difficult to cope with broader cultural changes. For instance, in the United States the expected treatment of women, ethnic minorities, and the disabled has changed dramatically over the last 20 years. Firms that merely accept old customs and prejudices have experienced a greater loss of key personnel and increased communication difficulties, as well as greater interpersonal conflict, than have their more progressive counterparts. Third, firms that accept and build on natural divisions from the larger culture may find it extremely difficult to develop sound international operations. For example, many Japanese firms have had substantial difficulty adjusting to the equal treatment of women in their U.S. operations.[16]

Building Upon National Cultural Diversity   At the other extreme, managers can work to eradicate all naturally occurring national subcultures and countercultures. Firms are groping to develop what Taylor Cox calls the multicultural

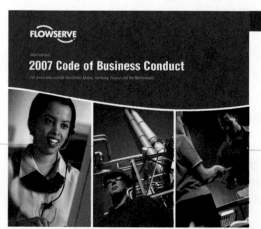

ETHICS IN OB

THE DILEMMA OF WHOSE ETHICS

It often goes unsaid that the culture of the organization should be ethical. Consider Flowserve. It is a recognized world leader in supplying pumps, valves, and seals to a wide variety of industries. It has over 14,000 employees in 56 countries. It has offices in the Americas, Australia, Eurasia, and the Middle East. Flowserve's solution for maintaining an ethical culture rests, in part, on a well-developed code of ethics as well as an emphasis on integrity and trust. In every location the company emphasizes Commitment, Creativity, Competence, Character, Confidence, and Collaboration. Since 2003 they have had a U.S. and international code of ethics. Flowserve managers incorporated national cultural and legal considerations into their international code. Employees can follow the well-developed and very specific code of ethics in their own language. Problems: Contact help at the ethics hotline. Select the appropriate language. The code of ethics shows exactly what you should consider in solving your problem.[16A]

Question: What is the appropriate balance among interests and values when attempting to create a unified organizational culture across national boundaries so that ethical standards respect and address national cultural and legal differences?

organization. The multicultural organization is a firm that values diversity but systematically works to block the transfer of societally based subcultures into the fabric of the organization.[17] Because Cox focuses on some problems unique to the United States, his prescription for change may not apply to organizations located in other countries with much more homogeneous populations.

Cox suggests a five-step program for developing the multicultural organization. First, the organization should develop pluralism with the objective of multibased socialization. To accomplish this objective, members of different naturally occurring groups need to school one another to increase knowledge and information and to eliminate stereotyping. Second, the firm should fully integrate its structure so that there is no direct relationship between a naturally occurring group and any particular job—for instance, there are no distinctly male or female jobs. Third, the firm must integrate the informal networks by eliminating barriers and increasing participation. That is, it must break down existing societally based informal groups. Fourth, the organization should break the linkage between naturally occurring group identity and the identity of the firm. In other words, the firm should not be just for the young, old, men, women, and so on. Fifth, the organization must actively work to eliminate interpersonal conflict based on either the group identity or the natural backlash of the largest societally based grouping.

Astute managers often modify the Cox approach with pragmatism. They recognize that some societally based groupings are relevant for achieving the firm's goals. The issue of generational groupings provides example. Strictly implementing Cox's recommendations would call for 20-year-olds to be represented proportionally in the senior management ranks; most corporations, however, want and need the judgment honed by experience for those roles.

Understanding Organizational Cultures

Not all aspects of organizational culture are readily apparent. Many aspects are deeply buried in the shared experience of organizational members. It may take years to understand some deeper aspects of the culture. This complexity has led some to explore different layers of analysis, ranging from easily observable to deeply hidden aspects of corporate culture.

Layers of Cultural Analysis

Figure 16.1 illustrates the observable aspects of culture, shared values, and underlying assumptions as three layers.[18] The deeper one gets, the more difficult it is to discover the culture, but the more important an aspect becomes.

The first level concerns observable culture, or "the way we do things around here." Important parts of an organization's culture emerge from the collective experience of its members. These emergent aspects of the culture help make it unique and may well provide a competitive advantage for the organization. Some of these aspects may be directly observed in day-to-day practices. Others may have to be discovered—for example, by asking members to tell stories of important incidents in the history of the organization. We often learn about the unique aspects of the organizational culture through descriptions of specific events. By observing employee actions, listening to stories, and asking members to interpret what is going on, one can begin to understand the organization's culture. The

Figure 16.1   Three levels of analysis in studying organizational culture.

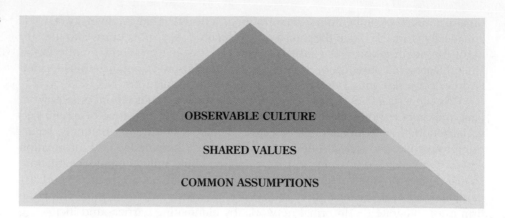

OBSERVABLE CULTURE

SHARED VALUES

COMMON ASSUMPTIONS

observable culture includes the unique stories, ceremonies, and corporate rituals that make up the history of the firm or a group within the firm.

The second layer recognizes that shared values can play a critical role in linking people together and can provide a powerful motivational mechanism for members of the culture. Many consultants suggest that organizations should develop a "dominant and coherent set of shared values."[19] The term "shared" in cultural analysis implies that the group is a whole. Every member may not agree with the shared values, but they have all been exposed to them and have often been told they are important. At R&R Partners, for example, creativity is part of everyone's vocabulary.

At the deepest layer of cultural analysis are common cultural assumptions; these are the taken-for-granted truths that collections of corporate members share as a result of their joint experience. It is often extremely difficult to isolate these patterns, but doing so helps explain why culture invades every aspect of organizational life.

Stories, Rites, Rituals, and Symbols

To begin understanding a corporate culture, it is often easiest to start with stories. Organizations are rich with stories of winners and losers, successes and failures. Perhaps one of the most important stories concerns the founding of the organization.[20] The founding story often contains the lessons learned from the heroic efforts of an embattled entrepreneur, whose vision may still guide the firm. The story of the founding may be so embellished that it becomes a **saga**—a heroic account of accomplishments.[21] Sagas are important because they are used to tell new members the real mission of the organization, how the organization operates, and how individuals can fit into the company. Rarely is the founding story totally accurate, and it often glosses over some of the more negative aspects of the founders. Such is the case with Monterey Pasta.[22]

On its Web site, Monterey Pasta says this of its history: "The Monterey Pasta Company was launched from a 400-square-foot storefront on Lighthouse Avenue in Monterey, California, in 1989. . . . The founders started their small fresh pasta company in response to the public's growing interest in healthy gourmet foods. Customers were increasingly excited about fresh pasta given its superior quality and nutritional value, as well as ease of preparation. . . . The company soon accepted its first major grocery account. . . . In 1993, the company completed its first public offering." The Web site fails to mention another interesting aspect of the firm: an

Sagas are embellished heroic accounts of the story of the founding of an organization.

unsuccessful venture into the restaurant business in the mid-1990s provided a significant distraction, and substantial losses were incurred before the company was refocused on its successful retail business. But why ruin a good founding story?

If you have job experience, you may well have heard stories concerning the following questions: How will the boss react to a mistake? Can someone move from the bottom to the top of the company? What will get me fired? These are common story topics in many organizations.[23] Often, the stories provide valuable hidden information about who is more equal than others, whether jobs are secure, and how things are really controlled. In essence, stories like these begin to suggest how organizational members view the world and live together.

Some of the most obvious aspects of organizational culture are rites and rituals.[24] **Rites** are standardized and recurring activities that are used at special times to influence the behaviors and understanding of organizational members; **rituals** are systems of rites. It is common, for example, for Japanese workers and managers to start their workdays together with group exercises and the singing of the "company song." Separately, the exercises and song are rites. Together, they form part of a ritual. In other settings, such as with Mary Kay Cosmetics, scheduled ceremonies reminiscent of the Miss America pageant (a ritual) are used regularly to spotlight positive work achievements and reinforce high-performance expectations with awards, including gold and diamond pins and fur stoles.

Rituals and rites may be unique to particular groups within the organization. Subcultures often arise from the type of technology deployed by the unit, the specific function being performed, and the specific collection of specialists in the unit. A unique language may well maintain the boundaries of the subculture. Often the language of a subculture, and its rituals and rites, emerge from the group as a form of jargon. In some cases the special language starts to move outside the firm and begins to enter the larger society. For instance, look at Microsoft Word's specialized language, with such terms as hyperlink, frames, and autoformat. It's a good thing the company also provides a Help button defining each term.

Another observable aspect of corporate culture centers on the symbols found in organizations. A **cultural symbol** is any object, act, or event that serves to transmit cultural meaning. Good examples are the corporate uniforms worn by UPS and FedEx delivery personnel. Although many such symbols are quite visible, their importance and meaning may not be.

> **Rites** are standardized and recurring activities used at special times to influence the behaviors and understanding of organizational members.

> **Rituals** are systems of rites.

> A **cultural symbol** is any object, act, or event that serves to transmit cultural meaning.

Cultural Rules and Roles

Organizational culture often specifies when various types of actions are appropriate and where individual members stand in the social system. These cultural rules and roles are part of the normative controls of the organization and emerge from its daily routines.[25] For instance, the timing, presentation, and methods of communicating authoritative directives are often quite specific to each organization. In one firm, meetings may be forums for dialogue and discussion, where managers set agendas and then let others offer new ideas, critically examine alternatives, and fully participate. The example of a SWARM at R&R Partners in the opening illustrates one form of cultural rules and roles. In another firm, the "rules" may be quite different. The manager could go into the meeting with fixed expectations. Private conservations prior to the meeting might be the place for any new ideas or critical examination. Here, the meeting is a forum for letting others know what is being done and for passing out orders on what to do in the future.

ETHICS IN AN ORGANIZATION'S CULTURE

Ethics Quality Inc. provides a quick test for you to see whether a firm has an ethical culture. Their Web test has 10 items, and the firm will also provide a more comprehensive survey for employees. The 10 items in their yes-or-no format are

1. Are you proud of your group's ethics?
2. Do the group's ethics work positively for everyone?
3. Is there cooperation in resolving problems and creating opportunities?
4. Is the group improving processes routinely?
5. Do improvements matter and/or last?
6. Is there serious resistance to change?
7. Is there sufficient trust and openness to solve problems?
8. Are there any damaging standards?
9. Does the leadership set good examples and reward good ethics?
10. Are bad ethics risking or hurting business results?

Question: Would these questions be useful in deciding where you took your first job?

Shared Values, Meanings, and Organizational Myths

To describe more fully the culture of an organization, it is necessary to go deeper than the observable aspects. To many researchers and managers, shared common values lie at the very heart of organizational culture.

Shared Values   Shared values help turn routine activities into valuable and important actions, tie the corporation to the important values of society, and possibly provide a distinctive source of competitive advantage. In organizations, what works for one person is often taught to new members as the correct way to think and feel. Important values are then attributed to these solutions to everyday problems. By linking values and actions, the organization taps into some of the strongest and deepest realms of the individual. The tasks a person performs are given not only meaning but value: what one does is not only workable but correct, right, and important. At LAM Research, for instance, the company is very clear about its core values, and they provide meaning for everyone's work.

Successful organizations share some common cultural characteristics.[26] Organizations with "strong cultures" possess a broadly and deeply shared value system. Unique, shared values can provide a strong corporate identity, enhance collective commitment, provide a stable social system, and reduce the need for formal and bureaucratic controls. For firms operating in very stable domestic environments, several consultants suggest they develop strong cultures.[27] What do these consultants mean? They want to see

A widely shared real understanding of what the firm stands for, often embodied in slogans;

A concern for individuals over rules, policies, procedures, and adherence to job duties;

A recognition of heroes, whose actions illustrate the company's shared philosophy and concerns;

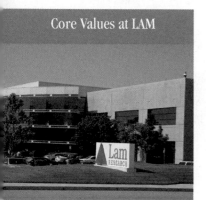

Core Values at LAM

LAM is a major supplier of wafer fabrication equipment and related services to the semiconductor industry. The company is very clear about its core values: achievement, honesty and integrity, innovation and continuous improvement, mutual trust and respect, open communication, ownership and accountability, teamwork, and think customer, then company, then individual.

A belief in ritual and ceremony as important to members as well as to building a common identity;

A well-understood sense of the informal rules and expectations so that employees and managers understand what is expected of them;

A belief that what employees and managers do is important, and that it is important to share information and ideas.

A strong culture can be a double-edged sword, however. A strong culture and value system can reinforce a singular view of the organization and its environment. If dramatic changes are needed, it may be difficult to change the organization. General Motors may have a "strong" culture, for example, but the firm faces enormous difficulty in its attempts to adapt its ways to a dynamic and highly competitive environment.

In many corporate cultures, one finds a series of common assumptions known to most everyone in the corporation: "We are different." "We are better at. . . ." "We have unrecognized talents." Cisco Systems provides an excellent example. Senior managers often share common assumptions, such as "We are good stewards," "We are competent managers," and "We are practical innovators." Like values, such assumptions become reflected in the organizational culture.

Shared Meanings   When observing the actions within a firm, it is important to keep in mind the three levels of analysis mentioned earlier. What you see as an outside observer may not be what organizational members experience because members may link actions to values and unstated assumptions.[28] For instance, in the aftermath of 9/11 many saw crane operators moving wreckage from an 18-acre pile of rubble into waiting trucks. Farther up the worksite, many saw steelworkers cutting beams while police seemed to stand around talking to a few firefighters. If you had probed the values and assumptions about what these individuals are doing, however, you would have gotten an entirely different picture. They were not just hauling away the remnants of the twin towers at the World Trade Center complex; they were rebuilding America. These workers had infused a larger shared meaning—or sense of broader purpose—into their tasks. Through interaction with one another, and as reinforced by the rest of their organizations and the larger society, their work had deeper meaning. In this deeper sense organizational culture is a "shared" set of meanings and perceptions. In most corporations these shared meanings and perceptions may not be as dramatic as those shared at Ground Zero, yet in most firms employees create and learn a deeper aspect of their organization's culture.

Organizational Myths   In many firms the management philosophy is supported by a series of organizational myths. **Organizational myths** are unproven and often unstated beliefs that are accepted uncritically. In a study of safety in nuclear power plants, senior managers were asked whether they felt there was a trade-off between safety and efficiency. The response was clear: a safe plant is an efficient plant. Yet most of these executives had seen data showing that measures of safety and efficiency were quite independent. To admit there was a trade-off raised the issue of making choices between efficiency and safety. All wanted to believe that to do one was to promote the other.[29]

While some may scoff at these organizational myths and want to see rational, hard-nosed analysis replace mythology, each firm needs a series of managerial

■ An **organizational myth** is an unproven and often unstated belief that is accepted uncritically.

myths.[30] Myths allow executives to redefine impossible problems into more manageable components. Myths can facilitate experimentation and creativity, and they allow managers to govern.

Managing Organizational Culture

Good managers are able to reinforce and support an existing strong culture; good managers are also able to help build resilient cultures in situations where they are absent. Two broad strategies for managing the corporate culture have received considerable attention in the OB literature. One strategy calls for managers to help modify observable culture, shared values, and common assumptions directly. As a unit manager you may be expected to build a strong culture. Check the Mastering Management on building a strong unit culture.

Later in the chapter we will discuss using organizational development to build the culture of the organization as well as groups within the organization.

MASTERING MANAGEMENT

DEVELOPING A STRONG UNIT CULTURE

To develop a strong culture for a unit you are managing, consider doing the following:

- Emphasize a shared real understanding of what the unit stands for.
- Stress a concern for members over rules and procedures.
- Talk about heroes of the past and their contributions.
- Develop rituals and ceremonies for the members.
- Reinforce informal rules and expectations consistent with shared values.
- Promote the sharing of ideas and information.

Management Philosophy and Strategy

The process of managing organizational culture calls for a clear understanding of the organizational subculture at the top and a firm recognition of what can and cannot be changed. The first step in managing an organizational culture is for management to recognize its own subculture. Key aspects of the top-management subculture are often referred to in the OB literature by the term management philosophy. A **management philosophy** links key goal-related strategic issues with key collaboration issues and comes up with a series of general ways by which the firm will manage its affairs.[31] A well-developed management philosophy is important because it links strategy to a more basic understanding of how the firm is to operate. Specifically, it (1) establishes generally understood boundaries for all members of the firm, (2) provides a consistent way of approaching new and novel situations, and (3) helps hold individuals together by assuring them of a known path toward success. In other words, it is the way in which top management addresses the questions of external adaptation. For instance, Cisco Systems has a clearly identified management philosophy linking the strategic concerns of growth, profitability, and customer service with observable aspects of culture and

■ **Management philosophy** is a philosophy that links key goal-related issues with key collaboration issues to come up with general ways by which the firm will manage its affairs.

selected desired underlying values. In the case of Cisco Systems' growth and profitability, customer service is linked to (1) empowering employees to generate the best ideas quickly and to implement them successfully, (2) hiring the best people because the ideas and intellectual assets of these colleagues drive success, and (3) developing and disseminating information to compete in the world of ideas. While elements of a management philosophy may be formally documented in a corporate plan or statement of business philosophy, it is the well-understood fundamentals these written documents signify that form the heart of a well-developed management philosophy.[32]

Building, Reinforcing, and Changing Culture

Managers can modify the visible aspects of culture, such as the language, stories, rites, rituals, and sagas. They can change the lessons to be drawn from common stories and even encourage other individuals to see the reality they see. Because of their positions, senior managers can interpret situations in new ways and can adjust the meanings attached to important corporate events. They can create new rites and rituals. Executives can back these initiatives with their words and actions. This takes time and enormous energy, but the long-run benefits can also be great. For example, consider the Center for Excellence developed by Chris Connor of Sherwin-Williams and his comments on the corporation's culture in Leaders on Leadership.[33]

Leaders on Leadership

Chris Connor is chairman and CEO of Sherwin-Williams. In 2004 he opened Sherwin-Williams Center of Excellence as a living archive of the firm's past accomplishments and dedication to excellence. It is a symbol of the corporate culture. How does Chris describe Sherwin-Williams's culture? "I love the culture of winning we've created at Sherwin-Williams. This is a company where individuals get promoted based on performance . . . We believe in providing training and developmental experiences for our employees . . . Sherwin-Williams believes in providing opportunity for people to build wealth—real wealth." His advice? "Look for a company that is committed to training and developing their most important asset: the people in their corporation. Make sure the company provides promotional opportunities quickly, based on hard work and performance . . ."[33A]

Question: What else would you like to know about Chris Connor and how he is managing the culture at Sherwin-Williams?

One of the key ways management influences the organizational culture is through the reward systems it establishes. In many larger U.S.-based firms the reward system matches the overall strategy of the firm and reinforces the culture emerging from day-to-day activities. Two patterns of reward systems, strategies, and corporate cultures are common. The first is a steady state strategy, matched with hierarchical rewards, which is consistent with what can be labeled a clan culture. Specifically, rewards emphasize and reinforce a culture characterized by long-term commitment, fraternal relationships, mutual interests, and collegiality; there is heavy pressure from peers to conform, and superiors act as mentors. Firms with this pattern exist in such industries as power generation, chemicals, mining, and pharmaceuticals. In contrast, the second pattern stresses evolution and change. Here the rewards emphasize and reinforce a more market culture. That is, rewards emphasize a contractual link between employee and employer, focused on short-term performance, and stress individual initiative; there is very little pressure from peers to conform, and supervisors act as resource allocators. Firms with this pattern often exist in the restaurant, consumer product, and industrial services industries.[34]

Beyond establishing reward systems, top managers can set the tone for a culture and for cultural change. Managers at Aetna Life and Casualty Insurance built on its humanistic traditions to provide basic skills to highly motivated but under-qualified individuals. Even in the highly cost-competitive steel industry, Nucor executives built on the basic entrepreneurial values of U.S. society to reduce the number of management levels by half.

Each of these examples illustrates how managers can help foster a culture that provides answers to important questions concerning external adaptation and internal integration. Recent work on the linkages between corporate culture and financial performance reaffirms the importance of an emphasis on helping employees adjust to the environment. It also suggests that this emphasis alone is not sufficient. Neither is an emphasis solely on stockholders or customers associated with long-term economic performance. Instead, managers must work to emphasize all three issues simultaneously. The need to provide a balanced emphasis can most easily be seen when executives violate ethical and legal standards, as in the case of misstating earnings described in Research Insights.

Early research on culture and cultural change often emphasized direct attempts by senior management to alter the values and assumptions of individuals by resocializing them—that is, trying to change their hearts so that their minds and actions would follow.[35] The goal was to establish a clear, consistent organization-wide consensus. More recent work suggests that this unified approach of working through values may not be either possible or desirable.[36]

Trying to change people's values from the top down without also changing how the organization operates and recognizing the importance of individuals does not work very well. Take another look at the example of Cisco Systems. Here managers realize that maintaining a dynamic, change-oriented culture is a mix of managerial actions, decisions about technology, and initiatives from all employees. The values are not set and imposed from someone on high. The shared values emerge, and they are not identical across all of Cisco's operating sites. For instance, subtle but important differences have emerged among the operations in Silicon Valley, North Carolina, and Australia.

It is also a mistake for managers to attempt to revitalize an organization by dictating major changes and ignoring shared values. Although things may

Research Insight
Loss of Reputation: The Real Consequences of "Cooking the Books"

Jonathan Karpoff, D. Scott Lee, and Gerald Martin investigated the consequences to firms caught inflating their earnings. The fines imposed by regulators and courts were, they found, only the tip of the penalty iceberg. The real costs to these firms far outdistanced the fines.

They studied larger firms cited by the Securities and Exchange Commission (SEC) for misstating earnings for over a 20-year period. They note that many politicians and even business leaders suggested that the fines levied for "cooking the books" appeared to be comparatively small, and thus this ethical and legal violation seemed to receive just a slap on the wrist. However, their analysis suggested that the real costs to these firms came from a loss of their reputations in the business community. Customers lost confidence, suppliers demanded greater assurances, and of course, the entire financial community undervalued the firms so that loan costs were higher, stock prices were lower, and scrutiny was more extensive.

How big is big? The fines averaged about $23 million a firm. The estimated financial cost from the loss of reputation was estimated at 7.5 times the average fine. That yields a loss of some $196 million.[36A]

change a bit on the surface, a deeper look often shows whole departments resisting change and many key people unwilling to learn new ways. Such responses may indicate that the managers responsible are insensitive to the effects of their proposed changes on shared values. They fail to ask whether the changes are contrary to the important values of participants within the firm, a challenge to historically important corporate-wide assumptions, and inconsistent with important common assumptions derived from the national culture outside the firm. Note the example of Steven Jobs at Apple earlier in this chapter. He did not make all the changes. Rather, he worked with others in many different levels of the firm to make changes in strategy, structure, products, and marketing to build on deep-seated common assumptions that long-term employees shared.

Organizational Development

To keep the culture fresh and competitive, the challenge today is to engage in a process of continuous self-assessment and planned change in order to stay abreast of problems and opportunities in a complex and demanding environment. **Organizational development (OD)** is a comprehensive approach to planned change that is designed to improve the overall effectiveness of organizations. Formally defined, OD is the application of behavioral science knowledge in a long-range effort to improve an organization's ability to cope with change in its external environment and to increase its internal problem-solving capabilities.[37] It is designed to work on issues of both external adaptation and internal integration.

Organizational development (OD) is the application of behavioral science knowledge in a long-range effort to improve an organization's ability to cope with change in its external environment and increase its problem-solving capabilities.

Importantly, OD seeks to achieve change in such a way that the organization's members become more active and confident in taking similar steps to maintain the culture and longer-run organizational effectiveness. A large part of any OD program's success in this regard rests with its assumptions, values, and action research foundations.

Underlying Assumptions of OD

The organizational development foundations for achieving change are rooted in underlying assumptions about individuals, groups, and organizations. At the individual level OD is guided by principles that reflect an underlying respect for people and their capabilities. It assumes that individual needs for growth and development are most likely to be satisfied in a supportive and challenging work environment. It also assumes that most people are capable of taking responsibility for their own actions and of making positive contributions to organizational performance.

At the group level OD is guided by principles that reflect a belief that groups can be good for both people and organizations. It assumes that groups help their members satisfy important individual needs and can be helpful in supporting organizational objectives. And it assumes that effective groups can be created by people working in collaboration to meet individual and organizational needs.

At the organizational level OD is guided by principles that show a respect for the complexity of an organization as a system of interdependent parts. It assumes that changes in one part of the organization will affect other parts as well. And it assumes that organizational structures and jobs can be designed to meet the needs of individuals and groups as well as the needs of the organization.

OD Values and Principles

Organizational development offers a systematic approach to planned change in organizations that addresses two main goals: outcome goals (mainly issues of external adaptation) and process goals (mainly issues of internal integration). Outcome goals include achieving improvements in task performance by improving external adaptation capabilities. In OD these goals focus on what is actually accomplished through individual and group efforts. Process goals include achieving improvements in such things as communication, interaction, and decision making among an organization's members. These goals focus on how well people work together, and they stress improving internal integration.

In pursuit of these goals, OD is intended to help organizations and their members by (1) creating an open problem-solving climate throughout an organization, (2) supplementing formal authority with that of knowledge and competence, (3) moving decision making to points where relevant information is available, (4) building trust and maximizing collaboration among individuals and groups, (5) increasing the sense of organizational "ownership" among members, and (6) allowing people to exercise self-direction and self-control at work.[38]

Action research is the process of systematically collecting data on an organization, feeding it back for action planning, and evaluating results by collecting and reflecting on more data.

Action-Research Foundations of OD

Organizational development practitioners refer to **action research** as the process of systematically collecting data on an organization, feeding it back to the members for action planning, and evaluating results by collecting and reflecting on more data after the planned actions have been taken. This is a data-based and collaborative approach to problem solving and organizational assessment. When used in the OD process, action research helps identify action directions that may enhance an organization's effectiveness. In a typical action-research sequence depicted in Figure 16.2, the sequence is initiated when someone senses a performance gap and decides to analyze the situation systematically for the problems and opportunities it represents. The process continues through the following steps: data gathering, data feedback, data analysis, and action planning. It continues to the point at which action is taken and results are evaluated. The evaluation or reassessment stage may or may not generate another performance gap. If it does, the action-research cycle begins anew.

OD Interventions

The action-research process should engage members of an organization in activities designed to accomplish the required diagnoses and to develop and implement plans for constructive change. Action research, data collection, and the diagnostic foundations should come together through the choice and use of OD "interventions." **Organizational development interventions** are activities initiated by the

▬ Organizational development interventions are activities initiated to support planned change and improve work effectiveness.

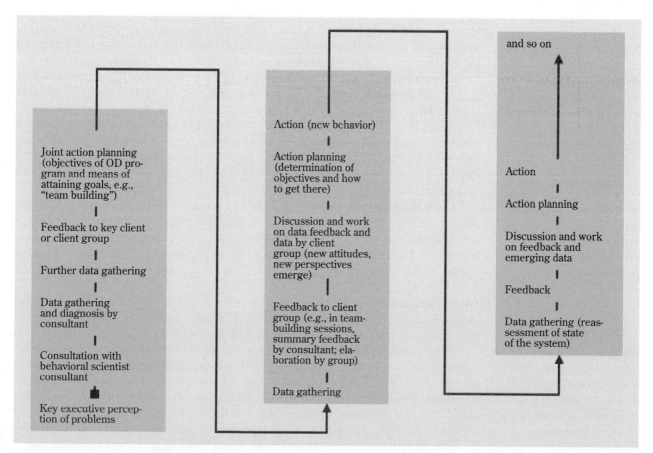

Figure 16.2   **An action-research model for organizational development.**

consultant to facilitate planned change and to assist the client in developing its own problem-solving capabilities. With less formality, many of these techniques are also now being used by managers to help them understand and improve their own operations.[39]

Organizationwide interventions   In OD an effective organization is one that achieves its major performance objectives while maintaining a high quality of work life for its members. OD interventions designed for system-wide application include several different types.

Survey feedback begins with the collection of data via questionnaire responses from organization members or a representative sample of such responses. The data are then presented, or fed back, to the members. Members subsequently engage in a collaborative process to interpret the data and develop action plans in response.

Confrontation meetings are designed to help determine quickly how an organization may be improved and to take initial actions to better the situation.[40] The intervention involves a one-day meeting conducted by an OD facilitator for a representative sample of organizational members, including top management. In a structured format, the consultant asks participants to make individual lists of what they think can be done to improve things. Then, through a series of small-group work sessions and the sharing of results, these ideas are refined into a tentative set of actions that top management then endorses for immediate implementation. The major trick is to get senior managers to propose changing their part of the firm. Confrontation meetings fail if all the proposed changes call for adjustments by subordinates without any alterations by the top managers.

Structural redesign involves realigning the structure of the organization or major subsystems to improve performance. It includes examining the best fit among structure, technology, and environment. In today's highly dynamic environments, in light of the increasing involvement of organizations in international operations and rapid changes in information technology, a structure can easily become out of date. Thus, structural redesign is an important OD intervention that can be used to help maintain the best fit between organizational structures and situational demands.

Collateral organization is designed to make creative problem solving possible by pulling a representative set of members out of the formal organization structure to engage in periodic small-group problem-solving sessions.[41] These collateral, or "parallel," structures are temporary and exist only to supplement the activities of the formal structure.

Group and intergroup interventions   OD interventions at the group level are designed to improve group effectiveness. The major interventions at this level are team building, process consultation, and intergroup team building.

Team building involves a manager or consultant engaging the members of a group in a series of activities designed to help them examine how the group functions and how it may function better. Similar to survey feedback at the organizational level, team building involves some form of data collection and feedback. The key elements, however, are a collaborative assessment of the data by all members of the group and the achievement of consensus regarding what may be done to improve group effectiveness. Team building is often done at "retreats,"

Survey feedback begins with the collection of data via questionnaires from organization members or a representative sample of them.

A **confrontation meeting** helps determine how an organization may be improved and start action toward improvement.

Structural redesign involves realigning the structure of the organization or major subsystem in order to improve performance.

Collateral organization involves a representative set of members in periodic small-group, problem-solving sessions.

Team building is designed to gather and analyze data on the functioning of a group and implement changes to increase its operating effectiveness.

or off-site meetings, where group members spend two to three days working intensely together on this reflection–analysis–planning process.

Process consultation involves structured activities that are facilitated by an OD practitioner and are designed to improve group functioning. Process consultation has a more specific focus than does team building, however: its attention is directed toward the key "processes" through which members of a group work with one another. The process consultant is concerned with helping a group function better on such things as norms, cohesiveness, decision-making methods, communication, conflict, and task and maintenance activities.

Intergroup team building is a special form of team building. It is designed to help two or more groups improve their working relationships with one another and, it is hoped, to experience improved group effectiveness as a result. Here, the OD practitioner engages the groups or their representatives in activities that increase awareness of how each group perceives the other. Given this understanding, collaborative problem solving can improve coordination between the groups and encourage more mutual support of one another as important components in the total organization.

Individual interventions   OD interventions may also occur at the individual level to support planned change in the whole organizational or for groups. The typical focus here is on role negotiations and job redesign.

Role negotiation is a means of clarifying what individuals expect to give and receive of one another in their working relationship. Because roles and personnel change over time, role negotiation can be an important way to maintain task understandings among individuals in an organization.

Job redesign is the process of creating long-term congruence between individual goals and organizational career opportunities. A good example is the Hackman and Oldham diagnostic approach to job enrichment discussed in Chapter 6.[42]

OD and continuous co-evolution   Today a new wave of successful high-tech firms exemplify the use of organizational development assumptions, values, and techniques without using the term OD. It is not that such firms as Herman Miller, Cisco, or R&R Partners are trying to force change on their employees. Rather, the managers in these systems take a very practical approach to managing culture. They realize that both external adaptation and internal integration are important for a variety of subcultures within their firms. They use OD intervention techniques to improve both. They do not dictate values or set common assumptions in isolation but rather with their fellow employees. They work with others to help nurture and guide the continual evolution of organizational culture from day to day.

▬ **Process consultation** helps a group improve on such things as norms, cohesiveness, decision-making methods, communication, conflict, and task and maintenance activities.

▬ **Intergroup team building** helps groups improve their working relationships with one another and experience improved group effectiveness.

▬ **Role negotiation** is a means of clarifying what individuals expect to give to and receive from one another in their working relationships.

▬ **Job redesign** is the process of creating long-term congruence between individual goals and organizational career opportunities.

Chapter 16   Study Guide

Summary

What is organizational culture?

- Organizational or corporate culture is the system of shared actions, values, and beliefs that develops within an organization and guides the behavior of its members.

- The functions of the corporate culture include responding to both external adaptation and internal integration issues.

- Most organizations contain a variety of subcultures, and a few have countercultures that can become the source of potentially harmful conflicts.

- The corporate culture also reflects the values and implicit assumptions of the larger national culture.

How do you understand an organizational culture?

- Organizational cultures may be analyzed in terms of observable actions, shared values, and common assumptions (the taken-for-granted truths).

- Observable aspects of culture include the stories, rites, rituals, and symbols that are shared by organization members.

- Cultural rules and roles specify when various types of actions are appropriate and where individual members stand in the social system.

- Shared meanings and understandings help everyone know how to act and expect others to act in various circumstances.

- Common assumptions are the taken-for-granted truths that are shared by collections of corporate members.

How can the organizational culture be managed?

- Executives may manage many aspects of the observable culture directly.

- Nurturing shared values among the membership is a major challenge for executives.

- Adjusting actions to common understandings limits the decision scope even of the CEO.

How can you use organizational development to improve the firm?

- All managers may use organizational development (OD) techniques in their attempts to manage, nurture, and guide cultural change.

- OD is a special application of knowledge gained from behavioral science to create a comprehensive effort designed to improve organizational effectiveness.

- With a strong commitment to collaborative efforts and human values, OD uses basic behavioral science principles with respect to individuals, groups, and organizations.

- OD has two main goals: outcome goals (mainly issues of external adaptation) and process goals (mainly issues of internal integration).

- Organizational development practitioners refer to action research as the process of systematically collecting data on an organization, groups, and individuals.

- Organization-wide interventions include survey feedback, confrontation meetings, structural redesign, and collateral organization.

- Group interventions include team building, process consultation, and intergroup team building.

- Individual interventions include role negotiation, job redesign, and career planning.

Key Terms

Action research (p. 378)
Collateral organization (p. 380)
Confrontation meeting (p. 380)
Countercultures (p. 367)
Cultural symbol (p. 371)
External adaptation (p. 365)
Intergroup team building (p. 381)
Internal integration (p. 365)

Job redesign (p. 381)
Management philosophy (p. 374)
Organizational development (p. 377)
Organizational development interventions (p. 379)
Organizational myth (p. 373)
Organizational or corporate culture (p. 364)

Process consultation (p. 381)
Rites (p. 371)
Rituals (p. 371)
Role negotiation (p. 381)
Sagas (p. 370)
Structural redesign (p. 380)
Subcultures (p. 366)
Survey feedback (p. 380)
Team building (p. 380)

Self-Test 16

Multiple Choice

1. Culture concerns all except _____. (a) the collective concepts shared by members of a firm (b) acquired capabilities (c) the personality of the leader (d) the beliefs of members

2. The three levels of cultural analysis highlighted in the text concern _____. (a) observable culture, shared values, and common assumptions (b) stories, rites, and rituals (c) symbols, myths, and stories (d) manifest culture, latent culture, and observable artifacts

3. External adaptation concerns _____. (a) the unproven beliefs of senior executives (b) the process of coping with outside forces (c) the vision of the founder (d) the processes working together

4. Internal integration concerns _____. (a) the process of deciding the collective identity and how members will live together (b) the totality of the daily life of members as they see and describe it (c) expressed unproven beliefs that are accepted uncritically and used to justify current actions (d) groups of individuals with a pattern of values that reject those of the larger society

5. When Japanese workers start each day with the company song, this is an example of a(n) _____. (a) symbol (b) myth (c) underlying assumption (d) ritual

6. _____ is a sense of broader purpose that workers infuse into their tasks as a result of interaction with one another. (a) A rite (b) A cultural symbol (c) A foundation myth (d) A shared meaning

7. The story of a corporate turnaround attributed to the efforts of a visionary manager is an example of _____. (a) a saga (b) a foundation myth (c) an internal integration (d) a latent cultural artifact

8. OD is designed primarily to improve _____. (a) the overall effectiveness of an organization (b) intergroup relations (c) synergy (d) the planned change process

9. The three stages in the OD process are _____. (a) data collection, intervention, and evaluation (b) diagnosis, intervention, and reinforcement (c) diagnosis, intervention, and evaluation (d) planning, implementing, and evaluating

10. OD is planned change plus _____. (a) evaluation (b) intervention (c) ability for self-renewal (d) reinforcement

11. A _____ is any object, act, or event that serves to transmit cultural meaning. (a) managerial philosophy (b) cultural symbol (c) ritual (d) saga

12. A _____ links key goal-related issues with key collaboration issues to come up with general ways by which the firm will manage its affairs. (a) managerial philosophy (b) cultural symbol (c) ritual (d) saga

13. _____ is the application of behavioral science knowledge in a long-range effort to improve an organization's ability to cope with change in its external environment and increase its problem-solving capabilities. (a) Process improvement (b) Organizational intervention (c) A benefit cycle (d) Organizational development (OD)

14. The patterns of values and philosophies that outwardly reject those of the larger organization or social system are called _____. (a) sagas (b) organizational development (c) rituals (d) countercultures

15. _____ involves realigning the structure of the organization or a major subsystem in order to improve performance. (a) Structural redesign (b) Organizational intervention (c) Process intervention (d) Career counseling

Short Response

16. Describe the five steps Taylor Cox suggests need to be developed to help generate a multicultural organization or pluralistic company culture.

17. List the three aspects that help individuals and groups work together effectively and illustrate them through practical examples.

18. Give an example of how cultural rules and roles affect the atmosphere in a college classroom. Provide specific examples from your own perspective.

19. What are the major elements of a strong corporate culture?

Applications Essay

20. Discuss the process of OD and provide an overview of its diagnostic foundations in a small business.

These learning activities from *The OB Skills Workbook* are suggested for Chapter 16.

OB in Action

CASE	EXPERIENTIAL EXERCISES	SELF-ASSESSMENTS
▪ 16. Never on Sunday	▪ 9. How We View Differences	▪ 8. Are You Cosmopolitan?
	▪ 23. Workgroup Culture	▪ 9. Group Effectiveness
	▪ 40. Fast-Food Technology	▪ 22. Which Culture Fits You?
	▪ 41. Alien Invasion	

Plus—special learning experiences from *The Jossey-Bass/Pfeiffer Classroom Collection*

Chapter 17

Organizational Goals and Structures

Chapter at a Glance

In Chapter 1 we said that organizations are collections of people working together to achieve common goals. In this chapter we discuss the goals of organizations and how firms can use the basic attributes of organizations to reach toward accomplishment.[1] As you read Chapter 17, *keep in mind these study topics.*

ORGANIZATIONAL GOALS

Societal Goals

Output Goals

Systems Goals

HIERARCHY AND CONTROL

All Organizations Have Hierarchies

Control as a Basic Feature

Centralization and Decentralization

ORGANIZING AND COORDINATING WORK

Traditional Departmental Structures

Coordination

BUREAUCRACIES AND COMMON FORMS OF BUREAUCRACY

Mechanistic Structure and the Machine Bureaucracy

Organic Structures and the Professional Bureaucracy

Hybrid Structures

CHAPTER 17 STUDY GUIDE

The key is to match structures to goals

Who says you can't manufacture and thrive in the United States? It is not Tim Solso, chairman and chief executive officer of Cummins Inc. Cummins, headquartered in Columbus, Indiana, is the world's leading producer of diesel engines. In 2001 Cummins was hemorrhaging cash and losing money. The fix was to reinforce its divisional structure, institute new process controls, and think globally. The divisional structure for Cummins has five major divisions: (1) Cummins Engines (a complete line of diesel and natural gas powered engines for light and heavy duty trucks, buses, and RVs), (2) Cummins Power Generation (power generating systems), (3) Components (with four units: heavy duty fuel, hydraulic and lube filtration; turbo technologies; emission solutions; and fuel systems), (4) Cummins Distribution (with distributors in 90 countries), and (5) Emerging Markets and Business (with operations mainly in China and India). To reduce costs and increase quality, Tim Solso adopted General Electric's Six Sigma approach based on the works of W. Edwards Deming.

And Solso moved some operations to India and China to provide a global platform for manufacturing.

In characterizing all the changes, Solso indicated, "The results? In 2005 international sales exceeded U.S. sales; 2006 set record profits over the 2005 record; the "new" Cummins is talking about a zero emissions diesel engine and early in 2007 announced an expansion of the Columbus diesel engine plant.[2]

> "We have reshaped the Company into what we are calling 'The New Cummins'—a company that is less cyclical, more diversified, more results oriented . . ."

Organizational Goals

The notion that organizations have goals is very familiar to us simply because our world is one of organizations. Most of us are born, go to school, work, and retire in organizations. Without organizations and their limited, goal-directed behavior, modern societies would simply cease to function. We would need to revert to older forms of social organization based on royalty, clans, and tribes. Organizational goals are so pervasive we rarely give them more than passing notice. Tim Solso, chairman and chief executive officer of Cummins Inc., knows the goals of his firm. He knows the type of social contribution it makes, whom it serves, and the myriad ways of improving its performance. He is aware that his organization's goals are multifaceted and sometimes conflict with one another. He is also aware that corporate goals are common to individuals within the firm only to the extent that an individual's interests can be partially served by the organization. And he understands that the pattern of goals selected and emphasized can help to motivate members and to gain support from outsiders. For instance, in the annual report Solso noted that Cummins Inc. was chosen as a top U.S. citizen by *Business Ethics,* identified in the Dow Jones Sustainability World Index, and included in the *Forbes* list of Best Big Companies in America. These accomplishments didn't just happen.[3]

No firm can be all things to all people. By selecting goals, firms also define what they are and what they will try to become. The choice of goals is based on the type of contribution the firm makes to the larger society and the types of outputs it seeks. Managers decide how to link conditions considered desirable for enhanced survival prospects with the firm's societal and output desires. From these apparently elementary choices executives can work with subordinates to develop ways of accomplishing the chosen targets. As the opening suggests, the goals of the firm should be internally consistent as well as consistent with the way in which the firm is organized—as is the case for Cummins Inc.

Societal Goals

Organizations do not operate in a social vacuum but reflect the needs and desires of the societies in which they operate. **Societal goals** reflect an organization's intended contributions to the broader society.[4] Organizations normally serve a specific societal function or an enduring need of the society. Astute top-level managers build on the professed societal contribution of the organization by relating specific organizational tasks and activities to higher purposes. By contributing to the larger society, organizations gain legitimacy, a social right to operate, and more discretion for their non-societal goals and operating practices. By claiming to provide specific types of societal contributions, an organization can also make legitimate claims on resources, individuals, markets, and products. For instance, would you not want more money to work for a tobacco firm than for a health food store? Tobacco firms are also very heavily taxed and under increasing pressure for regulation simply because their societal contribution is highly questionable.

Often, the social contribution of the firm is a part of its mission statement. **Mission statements** are simply written statements of organizational purpose. Weaving a mission statement together with an emphasis on implementation to provide direction and motivation is an executive order of the first magnitude. A good mission statement says whom the firm will serve and how it will go about accomplishing its societal purpose.[5]

We would expect to see the mission statement of a political party linked to generating and allocating power for the betterment of citizens. Mission statements for universities often profess to develop and disseminate knowledge. Since churches intend to instill values and protect the spiritual well-being of all, many do not have mission statements. Courts are expected to integrate the interests and activities of citizens. Finally, business firms are expected to provide economic sustenance and material well-being to society. Organizations that can effectively translate the positive character of their societal contributions into a favorable image have an advantage over firms that neglect this sense of purpose.

Executives who link their firm to a desirable mission can lay claim to important motivational tools that are based on a shared sense of noble purpose. Some executives and consultants talk of a "strategic vision" that links highly desirable and socially appealing goals to the contributions a firm intends to make.[6]

Societal goals are goals reflecting the intended contributions of an organization to the broader society.

Mission statements are written statements of organizational purpose.

Output Goals

Organizations need to refine their societal contributions in order to target their efforts toward a particular group.[7] In the United States, for example, it is generally expected that the primary beneficiary of business firms is the stockholder. Interestingly in Japan, in contrast, employees are much more important, and stockholders are considered on the same level of importance as banks and other financial institutions. Although each organization may have a primary beneficiary, its mission statement may also recognize the interests of many other parties. Thus, business mission statements often include goals regarding service to customers, the organization's obligations to employees, and its intention to support the community.

Output goals are the goals that define the type of business an organization is in.

As managers consider how they will accomplish their firm's mission, many begin with a clear statement of which business they are in.[8] This statement can form the basis for long-term planning and may help prevent huge organizations from diverting too many resources to peripheral areas. For some corporations, answering the question of which business they are in may yield a more detailed statement concerning their products and services. These product and service goals provide an important basis for judging the firm. **Output goals** define the type of business an organization is in and provide some substance to the more general aspects of mission statements. For instance, Cummins's output goals would center on its major divisions for engines, power generation, components, and distribution. These are the businesses Cummins has chosen.

Systems Goals

Fewer than 10 percent of the businesses founded in a typical year can be expected to survive until their twentieth birthdays.[9] The survival rate for public organizations is not much better. Even in organizations for which survival is not an immediate problem, managers seek specific types of conditions within their firms that minimize the risk of demise and promote survival. These conditions are positively stated as systems goals.

Systems goals are goals concerned with conditions within the organization that are expected to increase its survival potential.

Systems goals are concerned with the conditions within the organization that are expected to increase the organization's survival potential. The list of systems goals is almost endless since each manager and researcher links today's conditions to tomorrow's existence in a different way. For many organizations, however, the list includes growth, productivity, stability, harmony, flexibility, prestige, and human resource maintenance. In some busi-

---

MASTERING MANAGEMENT

SETTING THE MISSION

One key managerial skill is setting desirable, realistic, and achievable goals. This starts with a mission statement. It should be short, link highly desirable and socially appealing goals to the focus of the unit, and state the contributions intended. For example, Lobar Inc. is one of the few private Pennsylvania-based family-owned general contractors. The company's mission statement is quite clear: "To provide superior services at competitive prices while striving for excellence in customer relations and construction quality."

nesses, analysts consider market share and current profitability to be important systems goals. Other recent studies suggest that innovation and quality are also considered important.[10] In a very practical sense, systems goals represent short-term organizational characteristics that higher-level managers want to promote. Systems goals must often be balanced against one another. For instance, a productivity and efficiency drive, if taken too far, may reduce the flexibility of an organization. Sometimes the systems goals emphasized by the leaders may sound inconsistent with the overall image of the firm. For example, as shown in Leaders on Leadership, George A. Schaefer Jr. emphasizes delegation.

Different parts of the organization are often asked to pursue different types of systems goals. For example, higher-level managers may expect to see their production operations strive for efficiency while pressing for innovation from their R&D lab and promoting stability in their financial affairs. The relative importance of different systems goals can vary substantially across various types of organizations. Although we may expect the University of British Columbia or the University of New South Wales to emphasize prestige and innovation, few expect such businesses as Pepsi or Coke to subordinate growth and profitability to prestige.

Systems goals are important to a firm because they provide a road map that helps the firm link together various units of the organization to assure survival.

Leaders on Leadership

If you can't be the biggest, how about being Fifth Third? Fifth Third Bankcorp may be a strange name, and it is not the largest commercial bank in the United States, but it now has a loan and lease portfolio of almost $50 billion with 21,000 employees and 5.5 million customers served through 850 branches. George A. Schaefer Jr. is the president, CEO, and chief architect of this super-regional bank. Schaefer has continued to implement the fundamentals of sound organization as the bank has grown dramatically from its small Cincinnati base of operations to be a dominant presence in much of the Midwest and South. As Fifth Third acquired other banks, the acquired firms were allowed to maintain considerable autonomy. Each of the 16 affiliate banks has its own president and chief executive. Schaefer, who delegates extensively, is often reported to have said: "These people know their markets . . ." Since Schaefer does not like bureaucracy and red tape, operations are divided into Retail Banking, Commercial Banking, Investment Advisory Services, and Electronic Payment Processing. By continually stressing the basics, George Schaefer expects to see higher profit growth in the near future.[10A]

Question: How does maintaining autonomy in the regional operations facilitate a balance among organizational goals?

Well-defined systems goals are practical and easy to understand; they focus the manager's attention on what needs to be done. Accurately stated systems goals also offer managers flexibility in devising ways to meet important targets. They can be used to balance the demands, constraints, and opportunities facing the firm. In addition they can form a basis for dividing the work of the firm—a basis for developing a formal structure.

Hierarchy and Control

Successful organizations may develop a structure consistent with the pattern of goals established by senior management.[11] That is, decisions regarding what to accomplish must be matched with decisions on appropriate ways of organizing to reach these goals. The formal structure shows the planned configuration of positions, job duties, and lines of authority among different parts of the enterprise. The configuration selected provides the organization with specific strengths to reach toward some goals more than others. Traditionally, the formal structure of the firm has also been called the division of labor. Some still use this terminology to isolate decisions concerning formal structure from choices regarding the division of markets and/or technology. We will deal with environmental and technology issues in the next chapter after discussing structure as a foundation for managerial action. Here, we emphasize that the formal structure outlines the jobs to be done, the person(s) (in terms of position) who are to perform specific activities, and the ways the total tasks of the organization are to be accomplished. In other words, the formal structure is the skeleton of the firm.

All Organizations Have Hierarchies

■ **Vertical specialization** is a hierarchical division of labor that distributes formal authority.

In larger organizations, there is a clear separation of authority and duties by hierarchical rank. That is, firms are vertically specialized. This separation represents **vertical specialization**, a hierarchical division of labor that distributes formal authority and establishes where and how critical decisions are to be made. This division creates a hierarchy of authority—an arrangement of work positions in order of increasing authority.

In the United States, the distribution of formal authority is evident in the responsibilities typical of managers. Top managers or senior executives plan the overall strategy of the organization and plot its long-term future.[12] They also act as final judges for internal disputes and certify promotions, reorganizations, and the like. Middle managers guide the daily operations of the organization, help formulate policy, and translate top-management decisions into more specific guidelines for action. Lower-level managers supervise the actions of subordinates to ensure implementation of the strategies authorized by top management as well as compliance with the related policies established by middle management.

Managers in Japan often have different responsibilities than their counterparts in the typical U.S. firm. Japanese top managers do not develop and decide the overall strategy of the firm. Instead, they manage a process involving middle managers. The process involves extensive dialogue about actions the firm needs to

Journal of
Business
Ethics

Springer

ETHICS IN OB

INTEGRITY AS A FOUNDATION FOR ETHICS

One of the important keystones for promoting ethical behavior is integrity. Very simply, integrity is the match between an individual's statements and actions. Recently a group of OB researchers asked whether there was any link between managerial integrity and the satisfaction and commitment of subordinates—and whether there might be differences among nations. Across a dozen studies of different types of firms and different nations, the answer was the same: the greater the degree of managerial integrity, as judged by subordinates, the higher the satisfaction and commitment. So what has this to do with ethics? It is one of many studies documenting the important business case for firms to be ethical. If executives want key employees to stay, then it is smart as well as right to promote integrity.[12A]

Question: If it is both smart and right to promote integrity, why do managers say it is so difficult to maintain their integrity? How would changing circumstances make managerial integrity a challenge?

take. Lower-level managers are also expected to act as advocates for the ideas and suggestions of their subordinates. The strategy of the firm emerges from dialogue and discussion, and implementation proceeds according to the ideas and suggestions of lower managers and nonmanagers.

In many European firms the senior managers are highly trained in the core of the business. For example, it is not unusual for the head of a manufacturing firm to have a PhD in engineering. Thus, many European executives become more centrally involved in plotting the technical future of their firm. In contrast, few U.S. or Japanese executives have the necessary technical background to tackle this responsibility. Despite the differences in managerial responsibilities encountered in Japan, Europe, and North America, all organizations have vertical specialization. Further, recent research suggests that across nations employees want their manager's words and actions to be consistent (see Ethics in OB.)

The Organization Chart   Organization charts are diagrams that depict the formal structures of organizations. A typical chart shows the various positions, the position holders, and the lines of authority that link them to one another. `Figure 17.1 presents a partial organization chart for a large university. The total chart allows university employees to locate their positions in the structure and to identify the lines of authority linking them with others in the organization. For instance, in this figure the treasurer reports to the vice president of administration, who, in turn, reports to the president of the university.

While an organization chart may clearly indicate who reports to whom, it is also important to recognize that it does not show how work is done, who exercises the most power over specific issues, or how the firm will respond to its environment. An organization chart is just a beginning way to start understanding how a firm organizes its work. In firms facing constant change, the formal chart may be out of date quickly. However, organization charts can be important to the extent they accurately represent the "chain of command."

Organization charts are diagrams that depict the formal structures of organizations.

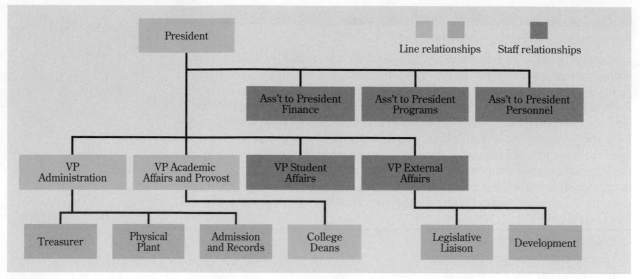

Figure 17.1   A partial organization chart for a state university.

The chain of command is a listing of who reports to whom up and down the firm and shows how executives, managers, and supervisors are hierarchically connected. Traditional management theory suggests that each individual should have one boss and each unit one leader. Under these circumstances, there is a "unity of command." Unity of command is considered necessary to avoid confusion, to assign accountability to specific individuals, and to provide clear channels of communication up and down the organization.

Span of Control   The number of individuals reporting to a supervisor is called the **span of control**. Narrower spans of control are expected when tasks are complex, when subordinates are inexperienced or poorly trained, or when tasks call for team effort. Unfortunately, narrow spans of control yield many organizational levels. The excessive number of levels is not only expensive, but it also makes the organization unresponsive to necessary change. Communications in such firms often become less effective because they are successively screened and modified so that subtle but important changes get ignored. Furthermore, with many levels, managers are removed from the action and become isolated.

■ **Span of control** refers to the number of individuals reporting to a supervisor.

New information technologies, discussed in the next chapter, now allow organizations to broaden the span of control, flatten their formal structures, and still maintain control of complex operations. At Nucor, for instance, senior managers pioneered the development of "minimills" for making steel and developed what they call "lean" management. At the same time, management has expanded the span of control with extensive employee education and training backed by sophisticated information systems. The result: Nucor has four levels of management from the bottom to the top.[13]

■ **Line units** are work-groups that conduct the major business of the organization.

Line and Staff Units   A very useful way to examine the vertical division of labor is to separate line and staff units. **Line units** and personnel conduct the major business of the organization. The production and marketing functions are two examples. In contrast, **staff units** and personnel assist the line units by providing specialized expertise and services, such as accounting and public relations. For example, the vice president of administration in a university (Figure 17.1) heads a staff unit, as does the vice president of student affairs. All academic departments are line units since they constitute the basic production function of the university.

Two additional useful distinctions are often made in firms regarding line and staff. One distinction is the nature of the relationship of a unit in the chain of command. A staff department, such as the office of the V.P. for External Affairs in Figure 17.1, may be divided into subordinate units, such as Legislative Liaison and Development (again see Figure 17.1). Although all units reporting to a higher level staff unit are considered staff from an organizational perspective, some subordinate staff units are charged with conducting the major business of the higher unit—they have a line relationship up the chain of command. In Figure 17.1 both Legislative Liaison and Development are staff units with a line relationship to the unit immediately above them in the chain of command—V.P. for External Affairs. Why the apparent confusion? It is a matter of history: the notion of line and staff originally come from the military, with its emphasis on command. In a military sense the V.P. for External Affairs is the commander of this staff effort—the individual responsible for this activity and the one held accountable.

A second useful distinction to be made for both line and staff units concerns the amount and types of contacts each maintains with outsiders to the organization. Some units are mainly internal in orientation; others are more external in focus. In general, internal line units (e.g., production) focus on transforming raw materials and information into products and services, whereas external line units (e.g., marketing) focus on maintaining linkages to suppliers, distributors, and customers. Internal staff units (e.g., accounting) assist the line units in performing their function. Normally, they specialize in specific technical or financial areas. External staff units (e.g., public relations) also assist the line units, but the focus of their actions is on linking the firm to its environment and buffering internal operations. To recapitulate, in the example in Figure 17.1, the Legislative Liaison unit is external staff with a line relationship to the office of the V.P. for External Affairs.

Staff units can be assigned predominantly to senior-, middle-, or lower-level managers. When staff responsibilities are assigned predominantly to senior management, the capability of senior management to develop alternatives and make decisions is expanded. When staff is at the top, senior executives can directly develop information and alternatives and check on the implementation of their decisions. Here, the degree of vertical specialization in the firm is comparatively lower because senior managers plan, decide, and control via their centralized staff. With new information technologies, fewer and fewer firms are placing most staff at the top. They are replacing internal staff with information systems and placing talented individuals further down the hierarchy. For instance, executives at Owens-Illinois have shifted staff from top management to middle management. When staff are moved to the middle of the organization, middle managers now have the specialized help necessary to expand their role.

Many firms are also beginning to ask whether certain staff should be a permanent part of the organization at all. Some are outsourcing many of their staff functions. Manufacturing firms are spinning off much of their accounting, personnel, and public relations activities to small, specialized firms.[14] Outsourcing by large firms has been a boon for smaller corporations.

> ■ **Staff units** are groups that assist the line units by performing specialized services for the organization.

Noble Drilling

Noble Drilling is one of the largest offshore drilling contractors in the world. It is a diversified service provider for the global oil and gas industry, with a fleet of some 50 offshore drilling units. The fleet is deployed in the North Sea, Brazil, West Africa, the Middle East, India, and Mexico. To give decision makers more flexibility, Noble Drilling has designed convertible platforms. The departmental structure used to match the diverse range of drilling equipment and service provided is based on the firm's products and services. With this departmental structure it can convert some of its fleet to drill in depths over 10,000 feet faster and more cheaply than others can build new capability.[1]

■■■ **Control** is the set of mechanisms used to keep actions and outputs within predetermined limits.

■■■ **Output controls** focus on desired targets and allow managers to use their own methods for reaching defined targets.

■■■ **Process controls** attempt to specify the manner in which tasks are to be accomplished.

For some time firms have used information technology to streamline operations and reduce staff in order to lower costs and raise productivity.[15] One way to facilitate these actions is to provide line managers and employees with information and managerial techniques designed to expand on their analytical and decision-making capabilities—that is, to replace internal staff.[16] We will return to this theme in the next chapter and pay special attention to information technology and its role in changing organizations. For now, let us turn our attention to those issues relating to control of the organization because the issue of control should not be separated from the division of labor.

Control as a Basic Feature

Vertical specialization, with its hierarchical division of labor that distributes formal authority, is only half the picture. Distributing formal authority calls for control. **Control** is the set of mechanisms used to keep action or outputs within predetermined limits. Control deals with setting standards, measuring results versus standards, and instituting corrective action. Effective control occurs before action actually begins. For instance, in setting standards, managers need to decide what will be measured and how accomplishment will be determined. While there are a wide variety of organizational controls, they may be roughly divided into output, process, and social controls. We will discuss social controls in the chapter on organizational culture; for now, we want to concentrate on the formal controls instituted by management.

Output Controls　Earlier in this chapter we suggested that systems goals could be used as a road map to tie together the various units of the organization toward achieving a practical objective. Developing targets or standards, measuring results against these targets, and taking corrective action are all steps involved in developing output controls.[17] **Output controls** focus on desired targets and allow managers to use their own methods to reach defined targets. Most modern organizations use output controls as part of an overall method of managing by exception.

Output controls are popular because they promote flexibility and creativity as well as facilitate dialogue concerning corrective action. Reliance on outcome controls separates what is to be accomplished from how it is to be accomplished. Thus, the discussion of goals is separated from the dialogue concerning methods. This separation can facilitate the movement of power down the organization: senior managers are reassured that individuals at all levels will be working toward the goals senior management believes are important, even as lower-level managers innovate and introduce new ways to accomplish these goals.

Process Controls　Few organizations run on outcome controls alone. Once a solution to a problem is found and successfully implemented, managers do not want the problem to recur, so they institute process controls. **Process controls** attempt to specify the manner in which tasks are accomplished. There are many types of process controls, but three have received considerable attention: (1) policies, procedures, and rules; (2) formalization and standardization; and (3) total quality management controls. Before we discuss each of these, check OB Savvy 17.1 for a note of caution.

Policies, Procedures, and Rules   Most organizations implement a variety of policies, procedures, and rules to help specify how goals are to be accomplished. Usually we think of a policy as a guideline for action that outlines important objectives and broadly indicates how an activity is to be performed. A policy allows for individual discretion and minor adjustments without direct clearance by a higher level manager. Procedures indicate the best method for performing a task, show which aspects of a task are the most important, or outline how an individual is to be rewarded.

Many firms link rules and procedures. Rules are more specific, rigid, and impersonal than policies. They typically describe in detail how a task or a series of tasks is to be performed, or they indicate what cannot be done. They are designed to apply to all individuals under specified conditions. For example, most car dealers have detailed instruction manuals for repairing a new car under warranty, and they must follow very strict procedures to obtain reimbursement from the manufacturer for warranty work.

Rules, procedures, and policies are often employed as substitutes for direct managerial supervision. Under the guidance of written rules and procedures, the organization can specifically direct the activities of many individuals. It can ensure virtually identical treatment even across distant work locations. For example, a McDonald's hamburger and fries taste much the same whether they are purchased in Hong Kong, Indianapolis, London, or Toronto simply because the ingredients and the cooking methods are defined in uniform written rules and procedures.

Formalization and Standardization   **Formalization** refers to the written documentation of rules, procedures, and policies that guide behavior and decision making. Beyond substituting for direct management supervision, formalization is often used to simplify jobs. Written instructions allow individuals with less training to perform comparatively sophisticated tasks. Written procedures may also be available to ensure that a proper sequence of tasks is executed, even if this sequence is performed only occasionally.

Most organizations have developed additional methods for dealing with recurring problems or situations. **Standardization** is the degree to which the range of allowable actions in a job or series of jobs is limited so that actions are performed in a uniform manner. It involves the creation of guidelines so that similar work activities are repeatedly performed in a similar fashion. Such standardized methods may come from years of experience in dealing with typical situations, or they may come from outside training. For instance, if you are late in paying your credit card bill, the bank will automatically send you a notification and start an internal process of monitoring your account.

Total Quality Management   The process controls discussed so far—policies, procedures, rules, formalization, and standardization—represent the lessons of

OB SAVVY 17.1

A Little Control Goes a Long Way

One of the key myths in management is the illusion of control. There are many variations of this, but one centers on the formal controls themselves. Many managers want to believe they can specify all the relevant goals for subordinates as well as precisely how these goals are to be accomplished. With too many output and process goals, subordinates have very little apparent flexibility. However, as the number of output and process controls escalates, so do the conflicts between the output and process controls. As a result, subordinates begin to pick and choose which controls they follow, and managers only have the illusion subordinates are reaching toward the goals managers specify in the way managers want.

Question: To what extent should managers specify both output and process goals?

Formalization is the written documentation of work rules, policies, and procedures.

Standardization is the degree to which the range of actions in a job or series of jobs is limited.

At Amgen it is high touch to get effective high tech

It does not get any higher tech than biotechnology, and Amgen is the world largest biotechnology company. But being high tech does not mean subordinating the employees to the technology. Rather, it means just the opposite. Effective high-tech managers often link the development and treatment of employees as an important system goal. As Kevin Scharer, Amgen's chairman and CEO says, "We have long been convinced that investing in our staff and nurturing a patient-focused values-based work environment is a key part of our ongoing success." To back this up Amgen offers a stock option program, fitness centers, and opportunities for career development in addition to the more traditional health and retirement benefits offered by many firms. And if you work at the corporate headquarters in Thousand Oaks, California, there is child care, car rental services, message services, and even a weekly farmers' market.
Question: What do you think Amgen expects in return for these additional benefits?

experience within an organization. That is, managers institute these process controls based on past experience, typically one at a time. Often there is no overall philosophy for using control to improve the overall operations of the company. Another way to institute process controls is to establish a total quality management process within the firm.

The late W. Edwards Deming is the modern-day founder of the total quality management movement.[18] When Deming's ideas were not generally accepted in the United States, he found an audience in Japan. Thus, to some managers, Deming's ideas appear in the form of the best Japanese business practices.

The heart of Deming's ideas is the institution of a process approach to continual improvement based on statistical analyses of the firm's operations. Around this core idea, Deming built a series of 14 points for managers to implement. As you look at these points, note the emphasis on both managers and employees working together and using statistical controls to continually improve. Deming's 14 points are

- Create a consistency of purpose in the company to
  a. innovate.
  b. put resources into research and education.
  c. put resources into maintaining equipment and new production aids.
- Learn a new philosophy of quality to improve every system.
- Require statistical evidence of process control and eliminate financial controls on production.
- Require statistical evidence of control in purchasing parts; this will mean dealing with fewer suppliers.
- Use statistical methods to isolate the sources of trouble.
- Institute modern on-the-job training.
- Improve supervision to develop inspired leaders.
- Drive out fear and instill learning.
- Break down barriers between departments.
- Eliminate numerical goals and slogans.
- Constantly revamp work methods.
- Institute massive training programs in statistical methods.
- Retrain people in new skills.
- Create a structure that will push every day on the above 13 points.

All levels of management are to be involved in the quality program. Managers are to improve supervision, train employees, retrain employees in new skills, and create a structure that pushes the quality program. Where the properties of the firm's outcomes are well defined, as in most manufacturing operations, Deming's system and emphasis on quality appears to work well when it is implemented in conjunction with empowerment and participative management.

Centralization and Decentralization

Different firms use very different mixes of vertical specialization, output controls, process controls, and managerial techniques to allocate the authority or discretion to act.[19] The farther up the hierarchy of authority the discretion to spend money, to hire people, and to make similar decisions is moved, the greater the degree of **centralization**. The more such decisions are delegated, or moved down the hierarchy of authority, the greater the degree of **decentralization**. Greater centralization is often adopted when the firm faces a single major threat to its survival. Thus, it is little wonder that armies tend to be centralized or that firms facing bankruptcy increase centralization.

Generally speaking, greater decentralization provides higher subordinate satisfaction and a quicker response to a diverse series of unrelated problems. Decentralization also assists in on-the-job training of subordinates for higher level positions. Decentralization is now a popular approach in many industries. For instance, Union Carbide is pushing responsibility down the chain of command, as are General Motors, Fifth Third Bank, and Hewlett-Packard. In each case the senior managers hope to improve both performance quality and organizational responsiveness. Closely related to decentralization is the notion of participation. Many people want to be involved in making decisions that affect their work. Participation results when a manager delegates some authority for such decision making to subordinates in order to include them in the choice process. Employees may want a say both in what the unit objectives should be and in how they may be achieved.[20]

Firms such as Intel Corporation, Eli Lilly, Texas Instruments, and Hoffman-LaRoche have also experimented by moving decisions down the chain of command and increasing participation. These firms found that just cutting the number of organizational levels was insufficient. They also needed to alter their controls regarding quality, stress constant improvement, and change other basic features of the organization. As these firms changed their degree of vertical specialization, they also changed the division of work among units or the firm's horizontal specialization.

> **Centralization** is the degree to which the authority to make decisions is restricted to higher levels of management.

> **Decentralization** is the degree to which the authority to make decisions is given to lower levels in an organization's hierarchy.

Organizing and Coordinating Work

Vertical specialization and control are not the complete picture either. Managers must also divide the total task into separate duties and group similar people and resources together.[21] Organizing work is formally known as horizontal specialization. **Horizontal specialization** is a division of labor that establishes specific work units or groups within an organization. This aspect of the organization is also often discussed under the title of departmentation. There are a variety of pure forms of departmentation. Whenever managers divide tasks and group similar type of skills and resources together, they must also be concerned with how each group's individual efforts will be integrated with others. Integration across the firm is the subject of coordination. As noted below, managers use a mix of personal and impersonal methods of coordination to tie the efforts of departments together.

> **Horizontal specialization** is a division of labor through the formation of work units or groups within an organization.

Traditional Departmental Structures

Since the pattern of departmentation is so visible and important in a firm, managers often refer to their pattern of departmentation as the departmental structure. While most firms use a mix of various types of departments, it is important to take a look at the traditional types and what they do and do not provide the firm.

Functional departmentation is grouping individuals by skill, knowledge, and action.

Functional Departments   Grouping individuals by skill, knowledge, and action yields a pattern of **functional departmentation**. Recall that Figure 17.1 shows the partial organization chart for a large university, in which each department has a technical specialty. Marketing, finance, production, and personnel are important functions in business. In many small firms this functional pattern dominates. Even large firms use this pattern in technically demanding areas. Figure 17.2 summarizes the advantages of the functional pattern. With all these advantages, it is not surprising that the functional form is extremely popular. It is used in most organizations, particularly toward the bottom of the hierarchy. The extensive use of functional departments also has some disadvantages, which are also summarized in Figure 17.2. Organizations that rely heavily on functional specialization may expect the following tendencies to emerge over time: an emphasis on quality from a technical standpoint, rigidity to change, and difficulty in coordinating the actions of different functional areas.

Divisional departmentation groups individuals and resources by products, territories, services, clients, or legal entities.

Divisional Departments   In **divisional departmentation** individuals and resources are grouped by products, territories, services, clients, or legal entities.[22] Figure 17.3 shows a divisional pattern of organization grouped around products, regions, and customers for three divisions of a conglomerate. This pattern is often used to meet diverse external threats and opportunities. The major advantages of the divisional pattern are its flexibility in meeting external demands, spotting external changes, integrating specialized individuals deep within the organization, and focusing on the delivery of specific products to specific customers. Among its disadvantages are duplication of effort by function, the tendency for divisional goals to be placed above corporate interests, and conflict among divisions. It is also not the structure most desired for training individuals in technical areas, and firms relying on this pattern may fall behind technically to competitors with a functional pattern.

Many larger, geographically dispersed organizations that sell to national and international markets may rely on departmentation by geography. The savings in time, effort, and travel can be substantial, and each territory can adjust to regional differences. Organizations that rely on a few major customers may organize their people and resources by client. Here, the idea is to focus attention on the needs

Major Advantages and Disadvantages of Functional Specialization	
Advantages	**Disadvantages**
1. Yields very clear task assignments, consistent with an individual's training.	1. May reinforce the narrow training of individuals.
2. Individuals within a department can easily build on one another's knowledge, training, and experience.	2. May yield narrow, boring, and routine jobs.
3. Provides an excellent training ground for new managers.	3. Communication across technical area is complex and difficult.
4. It is easy to explain.	4. "Top-management overload" with too much attention to cross-functional problems.
5. Takes advantage of employee technical quality.	5. Individuals may look up the organizational hierarchy for direction and reinforcement rather than focus attention on products, services, or clients.

Figure 17.2   Major advantages and disadvantages of functional specialization.

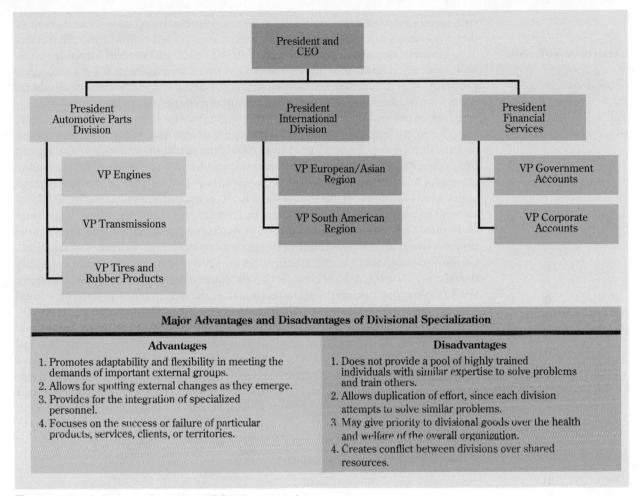

Figure 17.3 A divisional pattern of departmentation.

of the individual customer.[23] To the extent that customer needs are unique, departmentation by customer can also reduce confusion and increase synergy. Organizations expanding internationally may also form divisions to meet the demands of complex host country ownership requirements. For example, NEC, Sony, Nissan, and many other Japanese corporations have developed U.S. divisional subsidiaries to service their customers in the U.S. market. Some huge European-based corporations such as Philips and Nestlé have also adopted a divisional structure as part of their expansion to the United States. Similarly, most of the internationalized U.S.-based firms, such as IBM, GE, and DuPont, have incorporated the divisional structure as part of their internalization programs.

Matrix Structures A third unique form of departmentation was developed originally by the aerospace industry and is now becoming more popular; it is now called the matrix structure.[24] In aerospace efforts, projects are technically very complex, involving hundreds of subcontractors located throughout the world. Precise integration and controls are needed across many sophisticated functional specialties and corporations. This is often more than a functional or divisional

■ **Matrix departmenta-tion** is a combination of functional and divisional patterns wherein an individual is assigned to more than one type of unit.

structure can provide, for many firms do not want to trade the responsiveness of the divisional form for the technical emphasis provided by the functional form. Thus, **matrix departmentation** uses both the functional and divisional forms simultaneously. Figure 17.4 shows the basic matrix arrangement for an aerospace program. Note the functional departments on one side and the project efforts on the other. Workers and supervisors in the middle of the matrix have two bosses—one functional and one project.

The major advantages and disadvantages of the matrix form of departmentation are also summarized in Figure 17.4. The key disadvantage of the matrix method is the loss of unity of command. Individuals can be unsure as to what their jobs are, whom they report to for specific activities, and how various managers are to administer the effort. It can also be a very expensive method because it relies on individual managers to coordinate efforts deep within the firm. In Figure 17.4, note that the number of managers in a matrix structure almost doubles compared to the number in either a functional or a divisional structure. Despite these limitations the matrix structure provides a balance between functional and divisional concerns. Many problems can be resolved at the work level, where the balance among technical, cost, customer, and organizational concerns can be dealt with.

NBBJ, the world's third largest architectural practice, routinely uses a matrix structure. NBBJ projects range from the design of corporate offices and buildings to sports and entertainment complexes, research-and-development complexes, senior living systems, and even profits for academia. To meet these diverse challenges NBBJ uses a matrix structure to draw specialists from its global offices to complete major design projects. Its specialists may be found

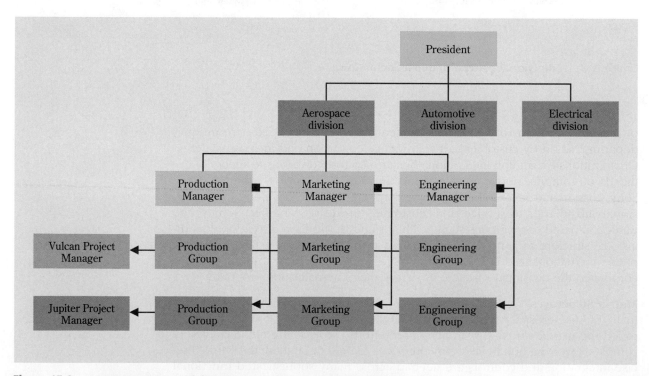

Figure 17.4   **A matrix pattern of departmentation in an aerospace division.**

in Columbus, Los Angeles, Raleigh, and San Francisco as well as in Oslo, Taipei, Tokyo, London, and New York, in addition to staff in its Seattle headquarters. NBBJ executives use senior contact staff in a local design studio to identify and focus on the specific needs of a client. They matrix across the global locations to supplement a local studio's staff with individuals whose unique skills are needed for a project.

Many organizations also use elements of the matrix structure without officially using the term matrix. For example, special project teams, coordinating committees, and task forces can be the beginnings of a matrix. These temporary structures can be used within a predominantly functional or divisional form without upsetting the unity of command or hiring additional managers.

Which form of departmentation should be used? As the matrix concept suggests, it is possible to departmentalize by two different methods at the same time. Actually, organizations often use a mixture of departmentation forms. It is often desirable to divide the effort (group people and resources) by two methods at the same time in order to balance the advantages and disadvantages of each. In the next chapter we will discuss several mixed forms. These mixed forms help firms use their division of labor to capitalize on environmental opportunities, capture the benefits of larger size, and realize the potential of new technologies in pursuit of strategic goals.

Coordination

Whatever is divided horizontally into departments must also be integrated.[25] **Coordination** is the set of mechanisms an organization uses to link the actions of its units into a consistent pattern. This linkage includes mechanisms to link managers with staff units, operating units with each other, and divisions with each other. Coordination is needed at all levels of management, not just across a few scattered units. Much of the coordination within a unit is handled by its manager. Smaller organizations may rely on their management hierarchy to provide the necessary consistency and integration. As the organization grows, however, managers become overloaded. The organization then needs to develop more efficient and effective ways of linking work units to one another.

Coordination is the set of mechanisms used in an organization to link the actions of its subunits into a consistent pattern.

Personal Methods of Coordination Personal methods of coordination produce synergy by promoting dialogue, discussion, innovation, creativity, and learning both within and across organizational units. Personal methods allow the organization to address the particular needs of distinct units and individuals simultaneously. There are a wide variety of personal methods of coordination.[26] Perhaps the most popular is direct contact between and among organizational members. As new information technologies have moved into practice, the potential for developing and maintaining effective contact networks has expanded. For example, many executives use cell phones, e-mail, and other computer-based links to supplement direct personal communication. Direct personal contact is also associated with the ever-present grapevine. Although the grapevine is notoriously inaccurate in its role as the corporate rumor mill, it is often both accurate enough and quick enough that managers cannot ignore it. Instead, managers need to work with and supplement the rumor mill with accurate information.

Managers are also often assigned to numerous committees to improve coordination across departments. Even though committees are generally expensive and have a very poor reputation, they can become an effective personal mechanism for mutual adjustment among unit heads. Committees can be effective in communicating complex qualitative information and in helping managers whose units must work together to adjust schedules, workloads, and work assignments to increase productivity. As more organizations develop flatter structures with greater delegation, they are finding that task forces can be quite useful. Whereas committees tend to be long lasting, task forces are typically formed with a more limited agenda. Individuals from different parts of the organization are assembled into a task force to identify and solve problems that cut across different departments.

No magic is involved in selecting the appropriate mix of personal coordination methods and tailoring them to the individual skills, abilities, and experience of subordinates. Managers need to know the individuals involved, their preferences, and the accepted approaches in different organizational units. As the Research Insights in OB 17.1 suggest, different personal methods can be tailored to match different individuals and the settings in which they operate. Personal methods are only one important part of coordination. The manager may also establish a series of impersonal mechanisms.

Research Insights
Coordination in Temporary Organizations

In today's world many individuals have jobs that take them to a number of different temporary settings, including a corporate task force, an alliance, or a special project. Coordinating the actions of the members in these temporary arrangements is often a problem. However, research by Beth Bechky offers some new insight. She studied the workers on a movie set, not the actors or producer but the crew—the folks who set up and run the equipment, shoot the movie, and make sure the sound is perfect. These individuals are generally "independent" contractors whose work must mesh quickly even though the crew has only been together a number of hours. How do they do it in the short-lived organization of a movie set? They negotiate their roles with each other. Each has his or her own specialization and assignment, but these must be coordinated with all others. While each recognizes others' career progression (some have more experience, and they are looked to for help), all recognize that the current assignment is one among the many they want in the future. Therefore, all are on their best behavior so they will be hired for the next movie. The more experienced crew members may provide enthusiastic thanks and be very polite when admonishing the less-experienced crew members. To enforce an emerging order and maintain coordination, all will use humor, polite ribbing, sarcastic comments, and teasing. Public display of anger is rare and frowned upon. With these mechanisms it only takes a few hours for the crew to emerge as an integrated unit.[26A]

Question: Why do you think a public display of anger is frowned upon?

Impersonal Methods of Coordination   Impersonal methods of coordination produce synergy by stressing consistency and standardization so that individual pieces fit together. Impersonal coordination methods are often refinements and extensions of process controls with an emphasis on formalization and standardization. Most larger organizations have written policies and procedures, such as schedules, budgets, and plans, which are designed to mesh the operations of several units into a whole by providing predictability and consistency.

Historically, firms used specialized departments to coordinate across units. However, this method is expensive and often results in considerably rigidity. The most highly developed form of impersonal coordination comes with the adoption of a matrix structure. As noted earlier, this form of departmentation is expressly designed to coordinate the efforts of diverse functional units. Many firms are using cross-functional task forces instead of maintaining specialized departments or implementing a matrix. These task forces are typically formed to solve a particular coordinate problem and then are disbanded upon successful implementation. The task force may call for new procedures, reassignment of tasks, and/or the institution of more personal methods to make sure departmental efforts mesh together.

The final example of impersonal coordination mechanisms is undergoing radical change in many modern organizations. Originally, management information systems were developed and designed so that senior managers could coordinate and control the operations of diverse subordinate units. These systems were intended to be computerized substitutes for schedules, budgets, and the like. In some firms the management information system still operates as a combined process control and impersonal coordination mechanism. In the hands of astute managers, however, the management information system becomes an electronic network, linking individuals throughout the organization. Using decentralized communication systems, supplemented with the phone, fax machine, and e-mail, once-centralized systems have evolved into a supplement to personal coordination.

In the United States there is an aversion to controls since the culture prizes individuality, democracy, and individual free will. Managers often institute controls under the umbrella of "coordination." Since some of the techniques used can be deployed for both, many managers suggest that all efforts at control and coordination are for coordination. It is extremely important to separate these two simply because the reactions to controls and coordination are quite different. The underlying logic of control involves setting targets, measuring performance, and taking corrective action to meet goals normally assigned by higher management. Thus, many employees see an increase in controls as a threat—based on a presumption that they have been doing something wrong. The logic of coordination is to get unit actions and interactions meshed together into a unified whole. While control involves the vertical exercise of formal authority involving targets, measures, and corrective action, coordination stresses cooperative problem solving. Most experienced employees recognize the difference between control and coordination regardless of what the boss calls it. Increasing controls rarely solves problems of coordination, and emphasizing coordination to solve control issues rarely works.

Bureaucracies and Common Forms of Bureaucracy

In the developed world, most firms are bureaucracies. In OB this term has a very special meaning beyond what might be its negative connotations. The famous German sociologist Max Weber suggested that organizations would thrive if they became bureaucracies by emphasizing legal authority, logic, and order.[27] **Bureaucracies** rely on a division of labor, hierarchical control, promotion by merit with career opportunities for employees, and administration by rule.

Weber argued that the rational and logical idea of bureaucracy was superior to building a firm based on charisma or cultural tradition. The "charismatic" ideal type of organization was overreliant on the talents of one individual and would likely fail when the leader left. Too much reliance on cultural traditions blocked innovation, stifled efficiency, and was often unfair. Since the bureaucracy prizes efficiency, order, and logic, Weber hoped that it could also be fair to employees and provide more freedom for individual expression than is usually allowed when tradition dominates or a dictator rules. Although far from perfect, Weber predicted that the bureaucracy, or some variation of this ideal form, would dominate modern society. And it has. Yet as noted in OB Savvy 17.2, in large firms this comes at some costs as well. While charismatic leadership and cultural traditions are still important today, it is the rational, legal, and efficiency aspects of the firm that characterize modern corporations.

The notion of a bureaucracy has evolved over time. We will discuss three popular basic types of bureaucracies: mechanistic, organic, and divisionalized. Some huge corporations are collections of very different firms called conglomerates. Each type is a different mix of the basic elements discussed in this chapter, and each mix yields firms with a slightly different blend of capabilities and natural tendencies. That is, each type of bureaucracy allows the firm to pursue some goals more easily than others.

■ **Bureaucracy** is an ideal form of organization, the characteristics of which were defined by the German sociologist Max Weber.

■ **Mechanistic type or machine bureaucracy** emphasizes vertical specialization and control through impersonal coordination and a heavy reliance on standardization, formalization, rules, policies, and procedures.

OB SAVVY 17.2

What to Expect in a Large Firm

Most large firms are bureaucracies; expect to see the following to some degree or another:

1. overspecialization with conflicts between highly specialized units
2. overreliance on the chain of command rather than bottom-up problem solving
3. reification of senior executives as rulers rather than as problem solvers for others
4. overemphasis on conformity
5. rules become ends in and of themselves

Question: Would you also expect to hear a lot about careers and career progression? Why?

Mechanistic Structure and the Machine Bureaucracy

The **mechanistic type** emphasizes vertical specialization and control.[28] Organizations of this type stress rules, policies, and procedures; specify techniques for decision making; and emphasize developing well-documented control systems backed by a strong middle management and supported by a centralized staff. There is often extensive use of the functional pattern of departmentation throughout the firm. Henry Mintzberg uses the term "machine bureaucracy" to describe an organization that is entirely structured in this manner.[29]

The mechanistic design results in a management emphasis on routine to produce efficiency. Firms often use this design in pursuing a strategy of becoming a low-cost leader. Until the implementation of new information systems, most large-scale firms in basic industries were machine bureaucracies. Included in this long list were all the auto firms, banks, insurance companies, steel mills, large retail establishments, and government offices. Efficiency was achieved through extensive vertical and horizontal specialization tied together by elaborate controls and impersonal coordination mechanisms.

There are, however, limits to the benefits of specialization backed by rigid controls. Employees do not like rigid designs, and so motivation becomes a problem. Unions further solidify narrow job descriptions by demanding fixed work rules and regulations to protect employees from the extensive vertical controls. Key employees may leave. In short, using a machine bureaucracy can hinder an organization's capacity to adjust to subtle external changes or new technologies. You are already familiar with this tendency toward stagnation—your high school was probably a machine bureaucracy with the assistant principal as the chief enforcement officer.

Organic Structures and the Professional Bureaucracy

The **organic type** is much less vertically oriented than its mechanistic counterpart; it emphasizes horizontal specialization. Procedures are minimal, and those that do exist are not as formalized. The organization relies on the judgments of experts and personal means of coordination. When controls are used, they tend to back up professional socialization, training, and individual reinforcement. Staff units tend to be placed toward the middle of the organization. Because this is a popular design in professional firms, Mintzberg calls it a "professional bureaucracy."[30]

Your university is probably a professional bureaucracy that looks like a broad, flat pyramid with a large bulge in the center for the professional staff. Power in this ideal type rests with knowledge. Furthermore, there often is an elaborate staff to "help" the line managers. Usually the staff has little formal power other than to block action. Control is enhanced by the standardization of professional skills and the adoption of professional routines, standards, and procedures. Other examples of organic types include most hospitals and social service agencies.

Although not as efficient as the machine bureaucracy, the professional bureaucracy is better for problem solving and for serving individual customer needs. Since lateral relations and coordination are emphasized, centralized direction by senior management is less intense. Thus, this type is good at detecting external changes and adjusting to new technologies, but at the expense of responding to central management direction.[31] For instance, many university deans and presidents talk about "herding cats" when it comes to managing faculty and students. Firms using this pattern find it easier to pursue product quality, quick response to customers, and innovation as strategies.

Hybrid Structures

Many very large firms have found neither the mechanistic nor the organic approach suitable for all their operations. Adopting a machine bureaucracy would overload senior management and produce too many levels of management. Adopting an organic type would mean losing control and becoming too inefficient. As a result, senior managers may opt for one of a number of hybrid types.

■ **Organic type or professional bureaucracy** emphasizes horizontal specialization, extensive use of personal coordination, and loose rules, policies, and procedures.

Land O'Lakes

Land O'Lakes is more than the butter company you know from the grocery store. It is a cooperative that sells dairy products and helps farmer members buy supplies. The cooperative is organized into divisions for (a) dairy operations, (b) feed, (c) seed, and (d) crop nutrients and crop protection products.

▬ **Conglomerates** are firms that own several different unrelated businesses.

We have already briefly introduced two of the more common hybrid types. One is an extension of the divisional pattern of departmentation, sometimes called a divisional firm. Here, the firm is composed of quasi-independent divisions so that different divisions can be more or less organic or mechanistic. While the divisions may be treated as separate businesses, they often share a similar mission and systems goals.[32] When adopting this hybrid type, each division can pursue a different strategy. Land O' Lakes, for instance, is a divisional cooperative.

A second hybrid is the true conglomerate. A **conglomerate** is a single corporation that contains a number of unrelated businesses. On the surface these firms look like divisionalized firms, but when the various businesses of the divisions are unrelated, the term conglomerate is used.[33] For instance, General Electric is a conglomerate that has divisions in quite unrelated businesses and industries ranging from producing light bulbs, to designing and servicing nuclear reactors, to building jet engines, and to operating the National Broadcasting Company. Many state and federal entities are also, by necessity, conglomerates. For instance, a state governor is the chief executive officer of those units concerned with higher education, welfare, prisons, highway construction and maintenance, police, and the like.

The conglomerate type also simultaneously illustrates three important points that will be the highlight of the next chapter: (1) All structures are combinations of the basic elements. (2) There is no one best structure—it all depends on a number of factors such as the size of the firm, its environment, its technology, and, of course, its strategy. (3) The firm does not stand alone but is part of a larger network of firms that competes against other networks.

Chapter 17   Study Guide

Summary

What are the different types of organizational goals?

- Societal goals: organizations make specific contributions to society and gain legitimacy from these contributions.

- A societal contribution focused on a primary beneficiary may be represented in the firm's mission statement.

- Output goals: as managers consider how they will accomplish their firm's mission, many begin with a very clear statement of which business they are in.

- Firms often specify output goals by detailing the types of specific products and services they offer.

- Systems goals: Corporations have systems goals to show the conditions managers believe will yield survival and success.

- Growth, productivity, stability, harmony, flexibility, prestige, and human resource maintenance are examples of systems goals.

What are the hierarchical aspects of organizations?

- The formal structure defines the intended configuration of positions, job duties, and lines of authority among different parts of the enterprise.

- The formal structure is also known as the firm's division of labor.

- Vertical specialization is the hierarchical division of labor that specifies where formal authority is located.

- Vertical specialization is used to allocate formal authority within the organization and may be seen on an organization chart.

- Typically, a chain of command exists to link lower-level workers with senior managers.

- The distinction between line and staff units also indicates how authority is distributed, with line units conducting the major business of the firm, and staff providing support.

- Managerial techniques, such as decision support and expert computer systems, are used to expand the analytical reach and decision-making capacity of managers and to minimize staff.

- Controls are sets of mechanisms the organization uses to keep action or outputs within predetermined levels.

- Output controls focus on desired targets and allow managers to use their own methods for reaching these targets.

- Process controls specify the manner in which tasks are to be accomplished through (1) policies, rules, and procedures; (2) formalization and standardization; and (3) total quality management processes.

- Firms are learning that decentralization often provides substantial benefits.

How is work organized and coordinated?

- Horizontal specialization is the division of labor that results in various work units and departments in the organization.

- Three main types or patterns of departmental structures exist: functional, divisional, and matrix. Each pattern of departmental structure has a mix of advantages and disadvantages.

- Organizations may successfully use any type, or a mixture, as long as the strengths of the structure match the needs of the organization.

- Coordination is the set of mechanisms an organization uses to link the actions of separate units into a consistent pattern.

- Personal methods of coordination produce synergy by promoting dialogue, discussion, innovation, creativity, and learning.

- Impersonal methods of control produce synergy by stressing consistency and standardization so that individual pieces fit together.

What are bureaucracies and what are the common structures?

- The bureaucracy is an ideal form based on legal authority, logic, and order that provides superior efficiency and effectiveness.

- Mechanistic, organic, and hybrids are common types of bureaucracies.

- Hybrid types include the divisionalized firm and the conglomerate. No one type is always superior to the others.

Key Terms

Bureaucracy (p. 406)
Centralization (p. 399)
Conglomerates (p. 408)
Control (p. 396)
Coordination (p. 403)
Decentralization (p. 399)
Divisional departmentation (p. 400)
Formalization (p. 397)
Functional departmentation (p. 400)

Horizontal specialization (p. 399)
Line units (p. 394)
Matrix departmentation (p. 402)
Mechanistic type or machine bureaucracy (p. 406)
Mission statements (p. 389)
Organic type or professional bureaucracy (p. 407)

Organization charts (p. 393)
Output controls (p. 396)
Output goals (p. 390)
Process controls (p. 396)
Societal goals (p. 389)
Span of control (p. 394)
Staff units (p. 395)
Standardization (p. 397)
Systems goals (p. 390)
Vertical specialization (p. 392)

Multiple Choice

1. The major types of goals for most organizations are _____. (a) societal, personal, and output (b) societal, output and systems (c) personal and impersonal (d) profits, corporate responsibility, and personal

2. The formal structures of organizations may be shown in a(n) _____. (a) environmental diagram (b) organization chart (c) horizontal diagram (d) matrix depiction

3. A major distinction between line and staff units concerns _____. (a) the amount of resources each is allowed to utilize (b) linkage of their jobs to the goals of the firm (c) the amount of education or training they possess (d) their use of computer information systems

4. The division of labor by grouping people and material resources deals with _____. (a) specialization (b) coordination (c) divisionalization (d) vertical specialization

5. Control involves all but _____. (a) measuring results (b) establishing goals (c) taking corrective action (d) selecting manpower

6. Grouping individuals and resources in the organization around products, services, clients, territories, or legal entities is an example of _____ specialization. (a) divisional (b) functional (c) matrix (d) mixed form

7. Grouping resources into departments by skill, knowledge, and action is the _____ pattern. (a) functional (b) divisional (c) vertical (d) means-end chains

8. A matrix structure _____. (a) reinforces unity of command (b) is inexpensive (c) is easy to explain to employees (d) gives some employees two bosses

9. _____ is the concern for proper communication enabling the units to understand one another's activities. (a) Control (b) Coordination (c) Specialization (d) Departmentation

10. Compared to the machine bureaucracy (mechanistic type), the professional bureaucracy (organic type) _____. (a) is more efficient for routine operations (b) has more vertical specialization and control (c) is larger (d) has a more horizontal specialization and coordination mechanism

True–False

11. Mission statements are written statements of organizational purpose.   T   F

12. A specific group, such as a political campaign, is an example of a primary beneficiary.   T   F

13. The configuration of positions, job duties, and lines of authority among the component parts of an organization is called its structure.   T   F

14. The hierarchy of authority is the process of breaking work into small components that serve the organization's purpose.   T   F

15. Specialization and coordination are two core issues in the concept of organizational structure.   T   F

Short Response

16. Compare and contrast output goals with systems goals.

17. Describe the types of controls that are typically used in organizations.

18. What are the major advantages and disadvantages of functional departmentation?

19. What are the major advantages and disadvantages of matrix departmentation?

Applications Essay

20. Describe some of the side effects of organizational controls in a large mechanistically structured organization, such as the United States Postal Service.

These learning activities from *The OB Skills Workbook* are suggested for Chapter 17.

OB in Action

CASE	EXPERIENTIAL EXERCISES	SELF-ASSESSMENTS
■ 17. First Community Financial	■ 13. Tinker Toys ■ 39. Organizations Alive ■ 40. Fast-Food Technology ■ 41. Alien Invasion	■ 2. A Twenty-First-Century Manager ■ 21. Organizational Design Preference

Plus—special learning experiences from *The Jossey-Bass/Pfeiffer Classroom Collection*

Chapter 18

Strategic Capabilities and Organizational Design

Chapter at a Glance

In this chapter we show how firms can use strategy and organizational design options to respond the demands of size, technology, and environment, and shape their competitive landscape to maintain dynamic capabilities. Keep in mind these study topics.

STRATEGY, INNOVATION, AND ORGANIZATIONAL LEARNING

Strategy

Innovation

Organizational Learning

Linking Strategy, Innovation, and Learning

ORGANIZATIONAL DESIGN

Organizational Design and Strategic Decisions

Organizational Design and Co-Evolution

DESIGNING FOR GREATER CAPABILITY

Size and Organizational Design

Technology and Organizational Design

Environment and Organizational Design

Using Networks and Alliances

PUTTING IT ALL TOGETHER

Building Dynamic Capabilities Across Borders

Building Your Skills into Dynamic Capabilities

CHAPTER 18 STUDY GUIDE

How to compete in the 21st century

You know General Mills for the big *G* on the morning cereal box, be it Cheerios, Wheaties, Lucky Charms, or Chex.[1] While this 75-year-old company traces its roots to the Minneapolis Milling Company, today the product mix also includes Progresso soups plus Green Giant canned and frozen vegetables. It has sales of over $12 billion, with a consistent string of yearly profits at or above the $1 billion mark. With well-known brands from the newly acquired Pillsbury (e.g., Betty Crocker) as well as Yoplait yogurt, you would think the CEO might emphasize steady expansion and protection of existing businesses. Not so: it is innovation that is emphasized at General Mills. As Stephen W. Sanger, president and CEO, has said: "If you want your market to grow at a faster pace than the population, you must constantly develop new approaches." So look for the big *G* on more easy-to-prepare foods, small packages for the smaller households in the United States organic products, and probably something you never thought of. Says Sanger: "We do not think of innovation as an R&D or marketing role, but as part of the company."

> "... you must constantly develop new approaches."

Strategy, Innovation, and Organizational Learning

What Is Strategy?

Strategy is the process of positioning the organization in the competitive environment and implementing actions to compete successfully. It is a pattern in a stream of decisions.

Strategy is the process of positioning the organization in the competitive environment and implementing actions to compete successfully. It is a pattern in a stream of decisions.[2] Choosing the types of contributions the firm intends to make to the larger society, precisely whom it will serve, and exactly what it will provide to others are conventional ways in which firms begin to make the pattern of decisions and corresponding implementations that define its strategy. The strategy process is ongoing. It should involve individuals at all levels of the firm to ensure that there is a recognizable, consistent pattern—yielding a superior capability over rivals—up and down the firm and across all its activities. This recognizable pattern involves the involvement of many facets to develop a sustainable, unique set of dynamic capabilities.

Obviously, a successful strategy does not evolve in a vacuum but is driven by the goals emphasized, the size, the nature of the technology used by the firm, and its setting as well as by the structure used to implement the strategy. In this chapter we will emphasize the development of dynamic capabilities of innovation and organizational learning as enduring features of a successful strategy by emphasizing innovation and learning. We emphasize these two dynamic capabilities simply because they are critical for firms competing in the 21st century.

What Is Innovation?

Perhaps the most important characteristics of a strategy that yields consistent sustained success are innovation and learning. The competitive world is constantly changing and evolving, so without innovation the firm falls behind, as illustrated in our opening description of General Mills. The best organizations don't stagnate; they consistently innovate to the extent that, as in the example of General Mills, innovation becomes a part of everyday operations.[3]

Innovation is the process of creating new ideas and putting them into practice.[4] It is the means by which creative ideas find their way into everyday practices, ideally practices that contribute to important aspects of the firm's strategy such as improved customer service or organizational productivity. **Product innovations** result in the introduction of new or improved goods or services to better meet customer needs. **Process innovations** result in the introduction of new and better work methods and operations.

The innovation continuum runs from exploration to exploitation.[5] That is, in the early stages of innovation, time, energy, and effort to explore potentials are necessary. Too much emphasis on exploration will yield a whole list of potential ideas for new products and processes, new clients and customers, and possible new markets, but with little payoff. It is important to stress exploitation to capture the economic value stemming from exploration.[6]

The innovation process is not complete until final application has been achieved. A new idea—even a great one—is not enough. In any organization the idea must pass through all stages of innovation and reach the point of final application before its value can be realized. The basic steps in a typical process of organizational innovation are shown in Figure 18.1. They include

1. *Idea creation*—to create an idea through spontaneous creativity, ingenuity, and information processing
2. *Initial experimentation*—to establish the idea's potential value and application
3. *Feasibility determination*—to identify anticipated costs and benefits

Innovation is the process of creating new ideas and putting them into practice.

Product innovations introduce new goods or services to better meet customer needs.

Process innovations introduce into operations new and better ways of doing things.

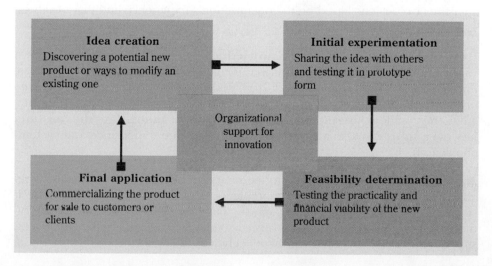

Figure 18.1   The innovation process: a case of new product development.

4. *Final application*—to produce and market a new product or service, or to implement a new approach to operations

Highly innovative firms and units often appear to be quite different from those that emphasize short-term efficiency. Highly innovative organizations recognize that innovation is an integral part of the overall strategy, and they have cultures that emphasize a commitment to innovation. This includes tolerance for mistakes and respect for well-intentioned ideas that just do not work. Highly innovative organizations have formal *structures* that support innovation, and we will show precisely what these are later in this chapter. These organizations also use decentralization and empowerment to overcome the limitations of great *size*. And they seek *environments* that both require and reward innovation. Finally, a focus on innovation, particularly process innovation, can be a critical component in maintaining long-term efficiency. Firms need to both explore and exploit to successfully compete.[7]

In highly innovative organizations special attention is given to the critical innovation roles of idea generators, information gatekeepers, product champions, and project leaders. Finally, innovative organizations benefit from *top-management support*. Senior managers provide good examples for others, eliminate obstacles to innovation, and try to get things done that make innovation easier.

Throughout the rest of the chapter we will highlight the links to innovation stemming from size, technology, and environment as well as formal structure to show how formal structure should be changed to make innovation a central feature of an organization or a department. Furthermore, to emphasize the importance of dynamic capabilities, we now discuss the companion to innovation: organizational learning.

Organizational Learning

■■■ **Organizational learning** is the process of knowledge acquisition, information distribution, information interpretation, and organizational retention.

Organizational learning is the process of acquiring knowledge and using information to adapt successfully to changing circumstances. For organizations to learn, they must engage in knowledge acquisition, information distribution, information interpretation, and organizational retention in adapting successfully to changing circumstances.[8] In simpler terms, organizational learning involves the adjustment of actions based on the organization's experience and that of others. The challenge is doing to learn and learning to do.

How Organizations Acquire Knowledge Firms obtain information in a variety of ways and at different rates during their histories. Perhaps the most important information is obtained from sources outside the firm at the time of its founding. During the firm's initial years, its managers copy, or mimic, what they believe are the successful practices of others.[9] As they mature, however, firms can also acquire knowledge through experience and systematic search.

■■■ **Mimicry** is the copying of the successful practices of others.

Mimicry **Mimicry** is important to the new firm because (1) it provides workable, if not ideal, solutions to many problems; (2) it reduces the number of decisions that need to be analyzed separately, allowing managers to concentrate on more critical issues; and (3) it establishes legitimacy or acceptance by employees, suppliers, and customers and narrows the choices calling for detailed explanation.

One of the key factors involved in examining mimicry is the extent to which managers attempt to isolate cause-effect relationships. Simply copying others without attempting to understand the issues involved often leads to failure. When mimicking others, managers need to adjust for the unique circumstances of their corporation. See OB Savvy 18.1 for tips about process benchmarking a form of mimicry.

Experience   A primary way to acquire knowledge is through experience. All organizations and managers can learn in this manner. Besides learning by doing, managers can also systematically embark on structured programs to capture the lessons to be learned from failure and success. For instance, a well-designed research and development program allows managers to learn as much through failure as through success.[10]

Learning by doing in an intelligent way is at the heart of many Japanese corporations, with their emphasis on statistical quality control, quality circles, and other such practices. Many firms have discovered that numerous small improvements can cumulatively add up to a major improvement in both quality and efficiency. The major problem with emphasizing learning by doing is the inability to forecast precisely what will change and how it will change. Managers need to believe that improvements can be made, listen to suggestions, and actually implement the changes. It is much more difficult to do than to say, however.[11]

Vicarious Learning   Vicarious learning involves capturing the lessons of others' experiences. Typically successful vicarious learning involves both scanning and grafting.[12]

Scanning involves looking outside the firm and bringing back useful solutions. At times these solutions may be applied to recognized problems. More often these solutions float around management until they are needed to solve a problem.[13] Astute managers can contribute to organizational learning by scanning external sources such as competitors, suppliers, industry consultants, customers, and leading firms. For instance, by reverse engineering the competitor's products (developing the engineering drawings and specifications from the existing product), an organization can quickly match all standard product features. By systematically exploring the proposed developments from suppliers, a firm may become a lead user and be among the first to capitalize on the developments of suppliers.

Grafting is the process of acquiring individuals, units, or firms to bring in useful knowledge. Almost all firms seek to hire experienced individuals from other firms simply because experienced individuals may bring with them a whole new series of solutions. Contracting out or outsourcing is the reserve of grafting and involves asking outsiders to perform a particular function. Whereas virtually all organizations contract out and outsource, the key question

---

OB SAVVY 18.1

Tips for Better Process Benchmarking

To effectively learn how to improve an administrative process from others, consider the following:

1. Carefully define the process to be investigated by comparing current operations with best practices either inside or outside the firm.
2. Organize a systematic effort by developing a plan, identifying who will be studied, who will conduct the study, where it will be done, and how it will be conducted.
3. After conducting the comparison between your current practices and best practices, prioritize the findings by ease of implementation and projected benefit, recognizing differences between the unit to be copied and your current unit.
4. Isolate applicability of the proposed changes: do they make sense and can they be applied?
5. Discuss implementation with all affected parties and monitor implementation for lessons learned.

Scanning is looking outside the firm and bringing back useful solutions to problems.

Grafting is the process of acquiring individuals, units, and/or firms to bring in useful knowledge to the organization.

for managers is often what to keep, as we will see in the analysis of alliances later in this chapter.

Information Distribution and Interpretation   Once information is obtained, managers must establish mechanisms to distribute relevant information to the individuals who may need it. A primary challenge in larger firms is to locate quickly who has the appropriate information and who needs specific types of information.

Although data collection is helpful, it is not enough. Data are not information; the information must be interpreted. Information within organizations is a collective understanding of the firm's goals and of how the data relate to one of the firm's stated or unstated objectives within the current setting. Unfortunately, the process of developing multiple interpretations is often thwarted by a number of common problems.[14]

Chief among the problems of interpretation are self-serving interpretations. Among managers, the ability to interpret events, conditions, and history to their own advantage is almost universal. Managers and employees alike often see what they have seen in the past or see what they want to see. Rarely do they see what is or can be.

Retention   Organizations contain a variety of mechanisms that can be used to retain useful information.[15] Seven important mechanisms are individuals, culture, transformation procedures, formal structures, ecology, external archives, and internal information technologies.

1. Individuals—The most important storehouses of information for organizations are employees. Organizations that retain a large and comparatively stable group of experienced individuals are expected to have a higher capacity to acquire, retain, and retrieve information. Collectively, these individuals hold memory via rich, vivid, and meaningful stories that outlive those who experienced the event.

2. Transformation mechanisms—Documents, rule books, written procedures, and even standard but unwritten methods of operation are all *transformation mechanisms* used to store accumulated information. In cases where operations are extremely complex but rarely needed, written sources of information are often invaluable.

3. Formal structure—The organization's *formal structure* and the positions in an organization are less obvious but equally important mechanisms for storing information. When an aircraft lands on the deck of a U.S. Navy aircraft carrier, there are typically dozens of individuals on the deck, apparently watching the aircraft land. Each person on the deck is there for a specific purpose. Each can often trace his or her position to a specific accident that would not have occurred had some individual originally been assigned that position.

4. Physical structures—Physical structures (or *ecology*, in the language of learning theorists) are potentially important mechanisms used to store information. For example, a traditional way of ordering parts and subcomponents in a factory is known as the "two-bin" system. One bin is always kept in reserve. Once an individual opens the reserve bin, he or she automatically orders replacements. In this way, the plant never runs out of components.

5. External archives—External archives can be tapped to provide valuable information about most larger organizations. Former employees, stock market analysts, suppliers, distributors, and the media can be important sources of valuable information. These external archives are important because they may provide a view of events quite different from that held within the organization.

6. IT Systems—Finally, internal information technology of a firm, or its IT system, can provide a powerful and individually tailored mechanism for storing information. All too often, however, managers are not using their IT systems strategically and are not tapping into them as mechanisms for retention.

Linking Strategy, Innovation, and Learning

As this quick overview of strategy, innovation, and learning suggests, there are many strategies, many ways to innovate, and many ways to learn. Historically, these three concepts have been discussed separately. Today, however, many OB scholars recognize that to compete successfully in the 21st-century global economy, individuals, units, and firms will need to be innovative and willing to learn. A firm based in a developed nation cannot successfully compete with firms based in developing counties just by being more efficient, any more than an individual in Western Europe or North America can "out efficiency" laborers from developing countries. There is just too much difference in the labor rates. Production technology is now spread out globally; transportation of goods is cheap, and the delivery of many services cuts across national boundaries. However, this does not mean firms in developed nations are doomed. Firms can know more about their local markets; they can carefully select what they produce, what services they provide, what they buy, and how they build capability. They must innovate and use their strategy to provide the necessary balance between exploration and exploitation of new ideas.[16] And they must be capable of sustained learning at the organizational level to capture the lessons learned from exploration and exploitation.[17]

It is important to emphasize that sustaining a competitive strategy with consistent innovation and learning involves more than just a commitment by individuals; it calls for a systematic adjustment of the organization's structure and processes to alterations in the size and scope of operations, the technology selected, and the environmental setting. The process involved in making these dynamic adjustments is known as organizational design.

Organizational Design

Organizational design is the process of choosing and implementing a structural configuration.[18] It goes beyond just indicating who reports to whom and what types of jobs are contained in each department. The design process takes the basic structural elements and molds them to the firm's desires, demands, constraints, and choices. The choice of an appropriate organizational design is contingent upon several factors, including the size of the firm, its operations and information technology, its environment, and, of course, the strategy it selects for growth and

Corning's Global Reach via Alliances

Corning's innovation-driven firm has engaged in developing a variety of advanced materials and technologies. Yet it does not commercialize new products alone. Instead, Corning relies on alliances with more than 50 affiliated companies in 16 countries.

■ **Organizational design** is the process of choosing and implementing a structural configuration for an organization.

survival. For example, IBM's senior management has selected a form of organization for each component of IBM that matches that component's contribution to the whole. The overall organizational design matches the technical challenges facing IBM, allows it to adjust to new developments, and helps it shape its competitive landscape. Above all, the design promotes the development of individual skills and abilities, but different designs stress different skills and abilities. As we discuss each major contingency factor, we will highlight the design option the firm's managers need to consider and link these options to aspects of innovation and learning.

Organizational Design and Strategic Decisions

To show the intricate intertwining of strategy and organizational design, it is important to reiterate and extend the dualistic notion of strategy.[19] Strategy is the positioning of a firm in its environment to provide it with the capability to succeed, and strategy is also a pattern in the stream of decisions. Below, we emphasize that what the firm intends to do must be backed up by capabilities for implementation in a setting that facilitates success.

In the past, executives were told that firms had available a limited number of economically determined generic strategies that were built upon the foundation of such factors as efficiency and innovation.[20] If the firm wanted efficiency, it should adopt the machine bureaucracy (many levels of management backed with extensive controls replete with written procedures). If it wanted innovation, it should adopt a more organic form (fewer levels of management with an emphasis on coordination). Today the world of corporations is much more complex, and executives have found much more sophisticated ways of competing.

Today many senior executives are emphasizing the skills and abilities that their firms need not only to compete but also to remain agile and dynamic in a rapidly changing world.[21] The structural configuration or organizational design of the firm should not only facilitate the types of accomplishment desired by senior management but should also allow for individuals to experiment, grow, and develop competencies so that the strategy of the firm can evolve.[22] Over time, the firm may develop specific administrative and technical skills as middle- and lower-level managers institute minor adjustments to solve specific problems. As they learn, so can their firms as long as the individual learning of employees can be transferred across and up the organization's hierarchy. As the skills of employees and managers develop, this development may be recognized by senior management and become a foundation for revisions to the overall strategy of the firm.

Organizational Design and Co-Evolution

With astute senior management the firm can co-evolve. That is, the firm can adjust to external changes even as it shapes some of the challenges facing it. Co-evolution is a process.[23] One aspect of this process is repositioning the firm in its setting as the setting itself changes. A shift in the environment may call for adjusting the firm's scale of operations. Senior management can also guide the process of positioning and repositioning in the environment. Co-evolution may call for changes in technology. For instance, a firm can introduce new products in new markets. It can change parts of its environment by joining with others to compete. However, senior management must also have the internal capabilities if it is to shape the firm's environment. The firm cannot introduce new products without extensive product development capabilities or rush into a new market it does not understand. Shaping capabilities via the organization's design is a dynamic aspect of co-evolution.

The second aspect of strategy we emphasized was a pattern in the stream of decisions. Take a look at Leaders on Leadership and what is emphasized by CEOs.

The organizational design can reinforce a focus and provide a setting for the continual development of employee skills. As the environment, strategy, and technology shift, we will see shifts in design and in the resulting capabilities. For example, IBM was once known as "big blue"—a button-down, white-shirt, blue-tie-and-black-shoe, second-to-market imitator with the bulk of its business centered on mainframe computers. IBM is now on the move in an entirely different way. As a result of innovation, it is now a major hub of e-commerce and is on the cutting edge as an integrator across systems, equipment, and service. To remain successful, IBM will continue to rely on the willingness of employees to take chances, refine their skills, and work together creatively.

Now it is time to see how an interplay of forces helps mold and shape the behavior in organizations and the development of competencies through a firm's organizational design. Even with co-evolution, managers must maintain a recognizable pattern of choices in the design that leads to accomplishing a broadly shared view of where the firm is going.

Leaders on Leadership

SAMUEL PALMISANO OF IBM

Samuel Palmisano is chairman and CEO of IBM. In 2004 he summarized the strategy for IBM simply by noting: "We have mobilized the entire IBM company and our expanding network of partners to make our e-business on demand strategy a reality." In a recent speech he suggested that the most successful leaders are choosing a new path forward—the path of innovation. Based on IBM interviews with some 750 CEOs and government leaders, Palmisano emphasized that the CEOs (1) saw innovation as the surest path to growth: two-thirds reported being inundated with change, new competitors, and commoditization, with innovation the only way out; (2) recognized that the primary focus of innovation needs to be on their business model, since innovation is not just for the product line but also for processes, management, and culture; (3) believed that innovation was cooperative, calling for teamwork inside and collaboration with other firms; and (4) reported they and their firms were not doing enough. Particularly important was the shortfall in using information to promote innovation and learning. As for IBM itself, Palmisano states: "We have committed the entire company to . . . leadership in innovation."[23A]

Question: How does Palmisano's emphasis on innovation provide others guidance to shape capabilities?

Designing for Greater Capability

To develop greater capabilities, managers must adjust the organizational design to take advantage of the size, technology, and environment of the firm even as they adjust the design to alter each of these. Firms need to grow, but must recognize the limitations of their current size. Firms need to advance their operations and information technology and still adjust their organizational design to current technological forces. Firms need to positively alter their environment, but they must also adjust to powerful environmental forces. A closer examination of size, technology, and environmental factors suggests a variety of design options managers can use to build capabilities over the long run.

Size and Organizational Design

The organizational design of the firm needs to be attuned to its size. For many reasons, large organizations cannot be just bigger versions of their smaller counterparts. As the number of individuals in a firm increases arithmetically, the number of possible interconnections among them increases geometrically. In other words, the direct interpersonal contact among all members in an organization must be managed. The design of small firms is directly influenced by its core operations technology, whereas larger firms have many core operations technologies in a wide variety of much more specialized units. In short, larger organizations are often more complex than smaller firms. While all larger firms are bureaucracies, smaller firms need not be. In larger firms, additional complexity calls for a more sophisticated organizational design. Such is not the case for the small firm.

Simple design is a configuration involving one or two ways of specializing individuals and units.

Small Size and the Simple Design The **simple design** is a configuration involving one or two ways of specializing individuals and units. That is, vertical specialization and control typically emphasize levels of supervision without elaborate formal mechanisms (e.g., rule books, policy manuals), and the majority of the control resides in the manager. Thus the simple design tends to minimize bureaucracy and rest more heavily on the leadership of the manager.

The simple design pattern is appropriate for many small firms, such as family businesses, retail stores, and small manufacturing firms.[24] The strengths of the simple design are simplicity, flexibility, and responsiveness to the desires of a central manager—in many cases, the owner. Because a simple design relies heavily on the manager's personal leadership, however, this configuration is only as effective as is the senior manager.

Take a look at an example simple design. B&A Travel is a comparatively small travel agency owed by Helen Druse. Reporting to Helen is part-time staff member Jane Bloom for accounting and finance. The operations arm is headed by Joan Wiland. Joan supervises 8 travel agents and keeps the dedicated computer system operating. Although each of the lead travel agents specializes in a geographical area, all but Sue Connely and Bart Merve take client requests for all types of trips. Sue is in charge of three major business accounts, and Bart heads a tour operation. Both of these agents report directly to Helen. Coordination is achieved through their dedicated intranet and Internet connections. Joan uses weekly meetings and a lot of personal contact by Helen and Joan to coordinate everyone. Control is enhanced by the computerized reservation system they all use. Helen makes sure each agent has a monthly sales target, and she routinely chats with important clients about their level of service. Helen realizes that developing participation from even the newest associate is an important tool in maintaining a "fun" atmosphere.

The Perils of Size and Age   As organizations age and begin to grow beyond the simple structure, they become more rigid, inflexible, and difficult to change.[25] Managerial scripts become routines, and both managers and employees begin to believe their prior success will continue into the future without an emphasis on innovation or learning. The organization or department becomes subject to routine scripts and common myths.

Managerial Scripts   A **managerial script** is a series of well-known routines for problem identification, alternative generation, and analysis common to managers within a firm.[26] Different organizations have different scripts, often based on what has worked in the past. In a way, the script is a ritual that reflects what the "memory banks" of the corporation hold. Managers become bound by what they have seen. The danger is that they may not be open to what actually is occurring. They may be unable to unlearn.

> A **managerial script** is a series of well-known routines for problem identification, alternative generation, and analysis common to managers within a firm.

The script may be elaborate enough to provide an apparently well-tested series of solutions based on the firm's experience. Older firms are rarely structured for learning; rather, they are structured for efficiency. That is, the organizational design emphasizes repetition, volume processing, and routine. In order to learn, the organization needs to be able to unlearn, switch routines to obtain information quickly, and provide various interpretations of events rather than just tap into external archives.

Few managers question a successful script. Consequently, they start solving today's problems with yesterday's solutions. Managers have been trained, both in the classroom and on the job, to initiate corrective action within the historically shared view of the world. That is, managers often initiate small, incremental improvements based on existing solutions instead of creating new approaches to identify the underlying problems.

Organizational Myths   An **organizational myth** is a commonly held cause-effect relationship or assertion that cannot be empirically supported.[27] Even though myths cannot be substantiated, both managers and workers may base their interpretations of problems and opportunities on these potentially faulty views. Three common myths often block the development of innovation and learning.

> An **organizational myth** is a commonly held cause-effect relationship or assertion that cannot be empirically supported.

The first common myth is the presumption that there *is a single unbiased organizational truth*. This myth is often expressed as "although others may be biased, I am able to define problems and develop solutions objectively." We are all subject to bias in varying degrees and in varying ways. The more complex the issue, the stronger the likelihood of many different supportable interpretations.

A second common myth is *the presumption of competence*. Managers at all levels are subject to believing that their part of the firm is okay and just needs minor improvements in implementation. As we have documented throughout this book, this is rarely the case. We are in the middle of a managerial revolution in which all managers need to reassess their general approach to managing organizational behavior in order to innovate and learn.

A third common myth is *the denial of trade-offs*. Most managers believe that their group, unit, or firm can avoid making undesirable trade-offs and simultaneously please nearly every constituency. Whereas the denial of trade-offs is common, it can be a dangerous myth in some firms. For instance, when complex, dangerous technologies are involved, safe operations may come at some sacrifice to efficiency. Yet some firms claim that "an efficient operation is a safe one" and aggressively move to improve efficiency. Although managers are stressing efficiency, they may fail to work on improving safety. The result may be a serious accident.[28]

As an organization grows and ages, these and other myths unique to their experience may well block innovation and organizational learning.

Technology and Organizational Design

Although the design for an organization should reflect its size, it must also be adjusted to fit technological opportunities and requirements.[29] That is, successful organizations are said to arrange their internal structures to meet the dictates of their dominant "operations technologies" or workflows and, more recently, information technology opportunities.[30] **Operations technology** is the combination of resources, knowledge, and techniques that creates a product or service output for an organization.[31] **Information technology** is the combination of machines, artifacts, procedures, and systems used to gather, store, analyze, and disseminate information so that it can be translated into knowledge.[32]

■■■ **Operations technology** is the combination of resources, knowledge, and techniques that creates a product or service output for an organization.

■■■ **Information technology** is the combination of machines, artifacts, procedures, and systems used to gather, store, analyze, and disseminate information so that it can be translated into knowledge.

Operations Technology and Organizational Design   As researchers in OB have charted the links between operations technology and organizational design, two common classifications for operations technology have received considerable attention: Thompson's and Woodward's.

Thompson's View of Technology   James D. Thompson classified technologies based on the degree to which the technology could be specified and the degree of interdependence among the work activities, with categories called intensive, mediating, and long linked.[33] Under *intensive technology* there is uncertainty as to how to produce desired outcomes. A group of specialists must be brought together interactively to use a variety of techniques to solve problems. Examples are found in a hospital emergency room or a research and development laboratory. Coordination and knowledge exchange are of critical importance with this kind of technology.

Mediating technology links parties that want to become interdependent. For example, banks link creditors and depositors as well as store money and information to facilitate such exchanges. Whereas all depositors and creditors are indirectly interdependent, the reliance is pooled through the bank. The degree of coordination among the individual tasks with pooled technology is substantially reduced, and information management becomes more important than coordinated knowledge application.

Under *long-linked technology*, also called mass production or industrial technology, the way to produce the desired outcomes is known. The task is broken down into a number of sequential steps. A classic example is the automobile assembly line. Control is critical, and coordination is restricted to making the sequential linkages work in harmony.

Woodward's View of Technology   Joan Woodward also divides technology into three categories: small-batch, mass production, and continuous-process manufacturing.[34] In units relying on *small-batch production*, a variety of custom prod-

ETHICS IN OB

AT MILLENNIUM CHEMICALS ETHICS IS A PART OF THEIR DESIGN AND STRATEGY

Millennium Chemicals is a major international chemical company providing commodity, industrial, and specialty chemicals in five continents. The company's goal is to develop safe, scientific solutions for customers not only in the form of chemical products but also in terms of problem-solving expertise, relevant information, and customer-tailored scientific services. Millennium is committed to building trust with all stakeholders, contributing to environmental protection, and maximizing health and safety in the workplace. This ethical commitment to customers, environment, and employees is not seen as an addition to the desire to create shareholder wealth, but as an integral part of the overall strategy of excellence.[34A]

Question: Do you believe that a company integrating ethics into its strategy and design can provide great returns to stockholders as well?

ucts are tailor-made to fit customer specifications, such as tailor-made suits. The machinery and equipment used are generally not very elaborate, but considerable craftsmanship is often needed. In *mass production*, the organization produces one or a few products through an assembly-line system. The work of one group is highly dependent on that of another, the equipment is typically sophisticated, and the workers are given very detailed instructions. Automobiles and refrigerators are produced in this way. Organizations using *continuous-process technology* produce a few products using considerable automation. Classic examples are automated chemical plants and oil refineries. Millennium Chemicals's operations are a good example of what Woodward called continuous-process manufacturing. As the Ethics in OB module suggests, innovative firms such as Millennium Chemicals are infusing ethics into day-to-day operations and making ethics a part of a recognizable pattern we have called strategy.

From her studies, Woodward concluded that the combination of structure and technology was critical to the success of the organization. When technology and organizational design were properly matched, a firm was more successful. Specifically, successful small-batch and continuous-process plants had flexible structures with small workgroups at the bottom; more rigidly structured plants were less successful. In contrast, successful mass-production operations were rigidly structured and had large work groups at the bottom. Since Woodward's studies, this technological imperative has been supported by various other investigations. Yet today we recognize that operations technology is just one factor involved in the success of an organization.[35]

Adhocracy as a Design Option for Innovation and Learning   The influence of operations technology is most clearly seen in small organizations and in specific departments within large ones. In some instances, managers and employees simply do not know the appropriate way to service a client or to produce a particular product. This is the extreme form of Thompson's intensive type of technology, and it may be found in some small-batch processes where a team of individuals must develop a unique product for a particular client.

■ **Adhocracy** is an organizational structure that emphasizes shared, decentralized decision making; extreme horizontal specialization; few levels of management; the virtual absence of formal controls; and few rules, policies, and procedures.

Henry Mintzberg suggests that at these technological extremes, the "adhocracy" may be an appropriate design.[36] An **adhocracy** is characterized by few rules, policies, and procedures; substantial decentralization; shared decision making among members; extreme horizontal specialization (as each member of the unit may be a distinct specialist); few levels of management; and virtually no formal controls. This design emphasizes innovation and learning.

The adhocracy is particularly useful when an aspect of the firm's operations technology presents two sticky problems: (1) the tasks facing the firm vary considerably and provide many exceptions, as in a management consulting firm, or (2) problems are difficult to define and resolve.[37] The adhocracy places a premium on professionalism and coordination in problem solving.[38] Large firms may use temporary task forces, form special committees, and even contract consulting firms to provide the creative problem identification and problem solving that the adhocracy promotes. For instance, Microsoft creates new autonomous departments to encourage talented employees to develop new software programs. Allied Chemical and 3M also set up quasi-autonomous groups to work through new ideas.

Information Technology and Organizational Design As stated earlier, *information technology* (IT) is the combination of machines, artifacts, procedures, and systems used to gather, store, analyze, and disseminate information so that it can be translated into knowledge.[39] Information technology, the Web, and the computer are not only virtually inseparable, but they have also fundamentally changed the organizational design of firms to capture new competencies.[40] While some even suggest that IT only refers to computer-based systems used in the management of the enterprise, we take a broader view.[41] With substantial collateral advances in telecommunication options, advances in the computer as a machine are much less profound than is IT in transforming how firms manage.

Most financial firms could not exist without IT because it is now the base for the industry. Early adopters created whole new segments of the industry with both major contributions to our economy and major new threats. For instance, IT is the foundation for multitrillion-dollar markets in international finance in which new exotic products are available that did not exist 20 years ago.

From an organizational standpoint IT can be used, among other things, as a partial substitute for some operations as well as some process controls and impersonal methods of coordination. It can also be used as a strategic capability as well as a capability for transforming information to knowledge for learning.

The Monster Reorganizes

TMP Worldwide is now Monster.com in recognition of the technology that is a key to its success. Monster.com is one of the best e-linkages for finding a new job. It recently reorganized its worldwide operations into regions to focus on Europe, Asia, and North America in an attempt to build more direct contacts with local firms and clients.

IT as a Substitute Old bureaucracies prospered and dominated other forms in part because they provided more efficient production through specialization and their approach to dealing with information. Where the organization used mediating technology or long-linked technology, the machine bureaucracy ran rampant. In these firms rules, policies, and procedures, as well as many other process controls, could be rigidly enforced based on very scant information.[42] Such was the case for the post office: postal clerks even had rules telling them how to hold their hands when sorting mail.

In many organizations the initial implementation of IT displaced the most routine, highly specified, and repetitive jobs.[43] A second wave of substitution replaced process controls and informal coordination mechanisms. That is, written rules, policies, and procedures could be replaced with a decision support system (DSS). In the case of a DSS, repetitive routine choices can be programmed into a computer-based system. For instance, if you apply for a credit card, a computer program will check your credit history and other financial information. If your application passes several preset tests, you will be issued a credit card.

IT to Add Capability   IT has also long been recognized for its potential to add capability.[44] For over 20 years scholars have talked of using IT to improve the efficiency, speed of responsiveness, and effectiveness of operations. Married to machines, IT became advanced manufacturing technology when computer-aided design (CAD) was combined with computer-aided manufacturing (CAM) to yield the automated manufacturing cell. More complex decision-support systems have provided middle- and lower-level managers with programs to aid in analyzing complex problems rather than just ratifying routine choices. Computer-generated reports now give even senior executives the opportunity to track the individual sales performance of the lowliest salesperson.

Instead of substituting for existing operations or process controls, IT now provides individuals deep within the organization the information they need to plan, make choices, coordinate with others, and control their own operations.

Connectivity is the watchword of today. Married to parallel developments in telecommunications, a whole world of electronic commerce, teleconferencing—with combinations of data, pictures, and sound—and cell phones has opened new opportunities for learning. For example, we now ask you to learn from the Internet connections and Web exercises at the end of each chapter.

IT systems can also empower individuals by expanding their jobs and making jobs both interesting and challenging. The emphasis on narrowly defined jobs replete with process controls imposed by middle management can be transformed to broadly envisioned, interesting jobs based on IT-embedded processes with output controls.

More than likely you will be involved with a "virtual" network of task forces and temporary teams to both define and solve problems. Here the members will only be connected electronically. Recent work on participants of the open-software movement (e.g., the ones refining and developing applications for Linux) suggests you will need to rethink what it means to "manage." Instead of telling others what to do, you will need to treat your colleagues as unpaid volunteers who expect to participate in governing the meetings and who are only tied to the effort by a commitment to identify and solve problems.[45] Mastering Management provides some guidelines to think about managing a project in a virtual environment.

MASTERING MANAGEMENT

MANAGING A VIRTUAL PROJECT

When you manage a "virtual" project,

1. Establish a set of mutually reinforcing motives for participation, including a share in success.
2. Stress self-governance and make sure there is a manageable number of high-quality contributors.
3. Outline a set of rules that members can adapt to their individual needs.
4. Encourage joint monitoring and sanctions of member behavior.
5. Stress shared values, norms, and behavior.
6. Develop effective work structures and processes such as by using project management software.
7. Emphasize the use of technology for communication and the norms for using it.[45a]

For the production segments of firms using long-linked technology such as in auto assembly plants and canneries, IT can be linked to total quality management (TQM) programs and embedded in the machinery. Data on operations can be transformed into knowledge of operations and systematically used to improve quality and efficiency. This has meant that firms have had to rethink their view of employees as brainless robots. To make TQM work with IT, all employees must plan, do, and control. As we discussed when we talked about job enrichment and job design in Chapter 8, combining IT and TQM with empowerment and participation is fundamental for success.[46]

The Virtual Organization and IT Opportunities   At the turn of the century e-business came on the scene.[47] It is morphing into the virtual organization just as on-site project teams have morphed into virtual project teams. Best we explain the e-business approach first and then show how some firms are moving to virtual organizations.

E-Business and IT   Whether it is business to business (B2B) or business to consumers (B2C), there is a whole new set of firms with information technology at the core of their operations. One of the more flamboyant early entrants into the B2C world is the now-familiar Amazon.com.[48] Opened in 1995 to sell books directly to customers via the Internet, it rapidly expanded to toys and games, health and beauty products, computers and video games, and cameras and photography. It is now a virtual general store. After years of losses Amazon.com posted a nice profit in 2003 and has continued to do so.

It is most interesting to examine the transformation in the design of this firm to illustrate the notion of co-evolution: the importance of innovation and the ability to learn with advanced IT. Initially, Amazon.com was organized as a simple structure. As it grew, it became more complex by adding divisions devoted to each of its separate product areas. To remain flexible and promote growth in both the volume of operations and the capabilities of employees, it did not develop an extensive bureaucracy. There are still very few levels of management. It built separate organizational components based on product categories (divisional structure) with minimal rules, policies, and procedures. In other words, the organizational design it adopted appeared relatively conventional.

What was not conventional was the use of IT for learning about customers and the use of IT for coordinating and tracking operations. Although its Web site was and is not the most technically advanced, you could and can easily order a book, track the delivery, and feel confident your order would arrive as promised. In recent years Amazon.com has used its IT prowess to develop strategic alliances with brick and mortar firms. It has used IT to change the competitive landscape.

The unfortunate downside of Amazon and its extensive use of the Web is an inherent clash between the values and ethics held by such firms and the value-free and ethics-free logic of the Internet. Look at one of the Web-based ethics issues facing Amazon.com in the Ethics in OB on page 431.

In comparison to Amazon.com, many other new dot-com firms have adopted a variation of the adhocracy as their design pattern. The thinking was that e-business is fundamentally different from the old bricks-and-mortar operations. Thus an entirely new structural configuration was needed to accommodate the development of new e-products and services. The managers of these firms forgot two important liabilities of the adhocracy as they grew. First, there are limits on the size of an effective adhocracy. Second, the actual delivery of their products and services did not require continual product innovation but rested more on being responsive to clients and maintaining efficiency. The design did not deliver what was needed: The companies had great Web sites, but they were grossly inefficient. Many died almost as quickly as they were formed.

The Emergence of the Virtual Organization   As IT has become widespread, firms are finding it can be the basis for a new way to compete. Some executives have started to develop what are called "virtual organizations."[49] A **virtual organization** is an ever-shifting constellation of firms, with a lead corporation that pools skills, resources, and experiences to thrive jointly. Members may come and go, as there are shifts in technology or alterations in environmental conditions. However, this ever-changing collection most likely has a relatively stable group of actors (usually independent firms) that normally includes customers, research centers, suppliers, and distributors all connected to each other. There is a lead organization that directs the constellation because this lead firm possesses a critical competence we all need. While this critical competence may be a key operations technology or access to customers, it always includes IT as a base for connecting the firms. It is also important to stress that key customers are an integral part of a virtual organization. Not only do customers purchase, but they also participate in the development of new products and services. Thus the virtual organization co-evolves by incorporating many types of firms.

The virtual organization works if it operates by some unique rules and is led in a most untypical way. First, the production system yielding the products and services customers desire needs to be a partner network among independent firms bound together by mutual trust and collective survival. As customer desires change, the proportion of work done by any member firm might change, and the

> A **virtual organization** is an ever-shifting constellation of firms, with a lead corporation that pools skills, resources, and experiences to thrive jointly.

ETHICS IN OB

ETHICS ISSUES WITH AMAZON.COM

In its code of ethics Amazon.com clearly states it ". . . will not tolerate any illegal discrimination." Yet, at least one unit of Amazon.com does appear to promote age discrimination. One of Amazon's wholly owned subsidiaries is IMDB. IMDB is a Web-based business with all the information a TV or Hollywood fan would want to know about almost every star, bit player, director, producer, or even those famous for being famous. What is the ethical problem? IMDB (Internet Movie Database) posts all kinds of information including the age of each female actor. It will not eliminate age information when requested. So? Hollywood pros use the site extensively. Casting directors are routinely using the age of female actors to deny jobs to those of "a certain age"—it's best you not be over 30. And who is responsible for promoting such age discrimination via IMDB? It is, of course, Jeff Bezos, founder and CEO of Amazon.com Books. They own it. He is the CEO.

Question: How does the CEO of a Web-based firm control the values of units that are adopting the value-free concepts of the Internet?

membership itself might change. In a similar fashion, the introduction of a new operations technology could shift the proportion of work among members or call for the introduction of new members. Second, this partner network needs to develop and maintain (1) an advanced information technology (rather than just face-to-face interaction), (2) trust and cross owning of problems and solutions, and (3) a common, shared culture. Developing these characteristics is a very tall order, but the virtual organization can be highly resilient, extremely competent, innovative, and reasonably efficient—characteristics that are usually trade-offs. The virtual organization can effectively compete on a global scale in very complex settings using advanced operations and information technologies.

The role of the lead firm is also quite unusual and actually makes a network of firms a virtual organization. The lead firm must take responsibility for the whole constellation and coordinate the actions and evolution of autonomous member firms. Executives in the lead firm need to have the vision to see how the network of participants will both effectively compete with a consistent-enough pattern of action to be recognizable and still rapidly adjust to technological and environmental changes. Executives should not only communicate this vision and inspire individuals in the independent member firms, but also treat members as if they were volunteers. To accomplish this across independent firms, the lead corporation and its members also need to rethink how they are internally organized and managed.

Environment and Organizational Design

As suggested by our discussion of the virtual organization, an effective organizational design also reflects powerful external forces as well as size and technological factors. Organizations, as open systems, need to receive inputs from the environment and, in turn, to sell outputs to their environment. Therefore, understanding the environment is important.[50]

The *general environment* is the set of cultural, economic, legal-political, and educational conditions found in the areas in which the organization operates. Firms expanding globally encounter multiple general environments.

The owners, suppliers, distributors, government agencies, and competitors with which an organization must interact to grow and survive constitute its *specific environment*. A firm typically has much more choice in the composition of its specific environment than its general environment. Although it is often convenient to separate the general and specific environmental influences on the firm, managers need to recognize the combined impact of both. Choosing some businesses, for instance, means entering global competition with advanced technologies.

Environmental Complexity   A basic concern that must be addressed in analyzing the environment of the organization is its complexity. A more complex environment provides an organization with more opportunities and more problems. **Environmental complexity** refers to the magnitude of the problems and opportunities in the organization's environment as evidenced by three main factors: the degree of richness, the degree of interdependence, and the degree of uncertainty stemming from both the general and the specific environment.

Environmental Richness   Overall, the environment is richer when the economy is growing, when individuals are improving their education, and when those on whom the organization relies are prospering. For businesses, a richer envi-

Environmental complexity is the magnitude of the problems and opportunities in the organization's environment as evidenced by the degrees of richness, interdependence, and uncertainty.

ronment means that economic conditions are improving, customers are spending more money, and suppliers (especially banks) are willing to invest in the organization's future. In a rich environment, more organizations survive, even if they have poorly functioning organizational designs. A richer environment is also filled with more opportunities and dynamism—the potential for change. The organizational design must allow the company to recognize these opportunities and capitalize on them.

The opposite of richness is decline. For business firms, a general recession is a good example of a leaner environment. Whereas corporate reactions vary, it is instructive to examine typical responses to decline. In the United States, firms have traditionally reacted to decline first by issuing layoffs to nonsupervisory workers and then by moving layoffs up the organizational ladder as the environment becomes leaner. Many European firms find it very difficult to cut full-time employees legally when the economy deteriorates. In sustained periods of decline, many firms have therefore turned to national governments for help. Much like U.S.-based firms, European-based firms view changes in organizational design as a last but increasingly necessary resort as they must now compete globally.

Environmental Interdependence   The link between external interdependence and organizational design is often subtle and indirect. The organization may co-opt powerful outsiders by including them. For instance, many large corporations have financial representatives from banks and insurance companies on their boards of directors. The organization may also adjust its overall design strategy to absorb or buffer the demands of a more powerful external element. Perhaps the most common adjustment is the development of a centralized staff department to handle an important external group. For instance, few large U.S. corporations lack some type of governmental relations group at the top. When service to a few large customers is considered critical, the organization's departmentation is likely to switch from a functional to a divisionalized form.[51]

Uncertainty and Volatility   Environmental uncertainty and volatility can be particularly damaging to large bureaucracies. In times of change, investments quickly become outmoded, and internal operations no longer work as expected. The obvious organizational design response to uncertainty and volatility is to opt for a more organic form. At the extremes, movement toward an adhocracy may be important. However, these pressures may run counter to those that come from large size and operations technology. In these cases it may be too hard or too time consuming for some organizations to make the design adjustments. Thus, the organization may continue to struggle while adjusting its design just a little bit at a time.

Using Networks and Alliances

In today's more complex global economy, organizational design must therefore go beyond the traditional boundaries of the firm.[52] Firms must learn to co-evolve by altering their environment. Two ways are becoming more popular: the management of networks and the development of alliances. Many North American firms are learning from their European and Japanese counterparts to develop networks of linkages to key firms upon which they rely. In Europe, for example, one finds *informal combines* or *cartels*. Here, competitors work cooperatively to share the market in order to decrease uncertainty and improve favorability for all. Except in rare cases these arrangements are often illegal in the United States.

In Japan the network of relationships among well-established firms in many industries is called a *keiretsu*. There are two common forms. The first is a bank-centered keiretsu, in which firms are linked to one another directly through cross-ownership and historical ties to one bank. The Mitsubishi group is a good example. In the second type, a vertical keiretsu, a key manufacturer is at the hub of a network of supplier firms or distributor firms. The manufacturer typically has both long-term supply contracts with members and cross-ownership ties. These arrangements help isolate Japanese firms from stockholders and provide a mechanism for sharing and developing technology. Toyota is an example of a firm at the center of a vertical keiretsu.

A very specialized form of network organization is evolving in U.S.-based firms as well. Here, the central firm specializes in core activities, such as design, assembly, and marketing, and works with a comparatively small number of participating suppliers on a long-term basis for both component development and manufacturing efficiency. The central firm is the hub of a network where others need it more than it needs any other member. While Nike was a leader in the development of these relationships, now it is difficult to find a large U.S. firm that does not outsource extensively. Executives seeking to find cheap sources of foreign labor often justify outsourcing from the U.S. firms. However, as a design option, managers should be examining how this alternative fits with the firm's strategy and technology as well. For instance, if the firm markets high-quality products matched with service, outsourcing may be inconsistent with the service requirements needed for success. Customers could move to firms that do not outsource service. This Research Insight provides some perspective on being in the center of a firm network. It is important, but not by itself.

More extreme variations of this network design such as the just-described virtual organization are also emerging to meet apparently conflicting environmental, size, and technological demands simultaneously. Firms are spinning off staff functions to reduce their overall size and take advantage of new IT options. For example, many call centers for computer questions and issues are outsourced to India. With too much outsourcing, the firm becomes too highly dependent upon others and loses the opportunity to be flexible and respond to new opportunities. It may lose valuable information. To continue the example, the use of foreign call centers cuts information flowing from customers to the core firm. With these new environmental challenges and technological opportunities, firms must choose and not just react blindly.

Interfirm alliances are announced cooperative agreements or joint ventures between two independent firms.

Another option is to develop **interfirm alliances**—announced cooperative agreements or joint ventures between two independent firms.[53] Often these agreements involve corporations that are headquartered in different nations. In high-tech areas, such as robotics, semiconductors, advanced materials (ceramics and carbon fibers), and advanced information systems, a single company often does not have all the knowledge necessary to bring new products to the market. Alliances are quite common in such high-technology industries. By creating international alliances, high-tech firms seek not only to develop technology but also to ensure that their solutions become standardized across regions of the world.

Developing and effectively managing an alliance is a managerial challenge of the first order. Firms are asked to cooperate rather than compete. The alliance's sponsors normally have different and unique strategies, cultures, and desires for the alliance itself. Both the alliance managers and sponsoring exec-

Research Insight
It Takes More Than Just Being in the Center of the Network to Get Innovation and Performance

Managers of units inside the organization are often searching for more innovation and a higher return on investment than is expected. Wepin Tsai looked at these two performance measures and tested three existing notions found in the current management literature. First, did units with a more central position in their corporate network perform better? Second, did units with more capable personnel (more experience with more new products) outperform others? Third, did both network position and capability make a combined difference? The answer: yes on all three. The big news was that it took both a central position in an extensive network and the capability to use this opportunity to get more innovation and greater than expected returns.[53A]

utives must be patient, flexible, and creative in pursuing the goals of the alliance and each sponsor. It is little wonder that many alliances are terminated prematurely.[54]

It is a myth, however, that all international alliances, particularly in high-tech areas, are short-lived. That is not always the case. The alliance between Warner-Lambert (best known as a U.S.-based pharmaceutical firm) and Japan's Sankyo (one of Japan's most successful pharmaceutical firms) dates to 1902 when Parke Davis, now a division of Warner-Lambert, selected Sankyo as a distributor for one of its drugs. As Warner-Lambert states in its annual report: "Our relationship has flourished like a great tree." The latest fruit from this relationship is Rezulin, a new medication to treat diabetes. First discovered by Sankyo, the drug was developed, perfected, and marketed by the alliance. It is one of the most successful new drugs in the United States. Maurice Renshaw, president of Parke-Davis, states: "We believe that when our business allies win, we win as well. "[55]

Putting It All Together

Based on a synthesis of successful management experiments by General Electric and their partners, a group of consultants and scholars put together a list of the changes firms need to consider if they are to compete globally in rapidly changing technical settings.[56] They used the buzz words of GE and labeled their package the "boundaryless organization."

Building Dynamic Capabilities Across Borders

The challenge to management in the 21st century is to eliminate barriers that block desired action vertically, horizontally, externally, and geographically. These barriers include (1) an overemphasis on vertical relations that can block communication up and down the firm; (2) an overemphasis on functions, product lines, or organizational units that blocks effective coordination; (3) maintaining rigid lines of demarcation between the firm and its partners that isolate it from others; and (4) reinforcing natural, cultural, national, and geographical borders that can limit globally coordinated action. The notion of a boundaryless organization is not about eliminating all boundaries; rather, the emphasis is to make boundaries much more permeable. We think the development of permeable boundaries with extensive coordination mechanisms will be a key characteristic of firms in the 21st century.[57]

There are several major factors associated with the inability to co-evolve dynamically and develop a cycle with positive benefits, but three are obvious from current research.[58] One is organizational inertia. It is very difficult to change organizations, and the larger the organization, the more inertia it often has. A second is hubris. Too few senior executives are willing to challenge their own actions or those of their firms because they see a history of success. They fail to recognize that yesterday's successful innovations are today's outmoded practices. A third is the issue of detachment. Executives often believe they can manage far-flung, diverse operations through analysis of reports and financial records. They lose touch and fail to make the needed adaptations required of all firms.

Inertia, hubris, and detachment are common maladies, but they are not the automatic fate of all corporations. Firms can successfully co-evolve. As we have repeatedly demonstrated, managers are trying to reinvent their firms every day. They hope to initiate a **benefit cycle**—a pattern of successful adjustment followed by further improvements.[59] General Mills, IBM, Cisco, and Microsoft are examples of firms experiencing benefit cycles. In such cycles the same problems do not keep reoccurring as the firm develops adequate mechanisms for learning. The firm has few major difficulties with the learning process, and managers continually attempt to improve knowledge acquisition, information distribution, information interpretation, and organizational memory.

■ **Benefit cycle** is a pattern of successful adjustment followed by further improvements.

Building Your Skills into Dynamic Capabilities

We know your future will be unlike the past. We think you can be a leader in the boundaryless revolution. How is it done? We think it is done through a systematic application of the concepts developed in this book to build your emerging skills into dynamic capabilities. You are almost finished, so it is time to look back at what you have learned. It is also a time to use this knowledge to look forward with the confidence to compete.

It is important to catalog the competencies needed and recognize what you do best and what you need from partners. In the boundaryless approach the firm is not alone but rather is part of a larger network, as we have discussed extensively in this chapter. You are not alone either. You will need to systematically examine the culture of any firm you join or choose as a partner. Is the culture actually consistent with the strategy of boundarylessness? In Chapter 16 we discussed the elements of culture, so you are well aware that any attempt to change basic values and underlying assumptions will be quite difficult. However, you learned it is important to reinforce innovation and learning up, across, and outward. The success of the boundaryless approach is based on what individuals in the middle and bottom of the organization create and on senior executive support. So pick your firm and your partners with care.

Of course, it is necessary for firms to have an appropriate basic structure in order to implement any strategy. You will want to make sure that in your chosen firm, the implementation pattern of vertical and horizontal specialization is consistent with what needs to be done. Check to make sure there are effective controls and coordination mechanisms in place. We discussed this extensively in Chapter 17 on goals and structures, so you now know what is needed.

To develop effective implementation it is important to attune accountability to make sure that who gets credit is consistent with what needs to be done. We covered this extensively in Chapter 7, so you are aware of the key issues in performance management and the development of rewards for the behavior being sought.

In moving into the global competition of the 21st century with a boundaryless strategy, particular attention must be paid to the organizational processes needed to learn, innovate, and continue to develop the critical technological and people skills necessary. The power dynamics within each unit of the firm need to be aligned to the new global, multinational arena of competition (see Chapter 10). The old politics of bureaucracy needs to be displaced with an emphasis on constructive negotiation (see Chapters 10 and 15). Decision making must identify the important issues as well as the right individuals to attempt to solve the right problems and address the right opportunities (see Chapter 13). All of this will call for a reassessment of actual work processes and job design (Chapter 6) to ensure that individuals can be motivated effectively to reach toward a bright future (see Chapter 5).

Of course, none of this can be done by a single individual. It will call for teams of individuals (see Chapter 8), and your future will most certainly involve building an effective team for higher performance (see Chapter 9). To effectively build a team will call upon you to recognize individual personality differences, team member emotions, and their values so that you can bring satisfaction and performance together in a meaningful experience (see Chapters 2 and 3). Of course, you recognize that right now this all sounds like mission impossible. But you have already started with a basic understanding of how to learn (remember Chapter 4).

We have left the final component for last because it is both the most important for you and the most difficult to understand. By reading this book and taking the course associated with it, you are on the way to becoming a leader. You may not believe it yourself, but the chances you will play an important role in the future of some firm are actually quite high. We spent two chapters on leadership to provide you with some basic leadership skills and information on how to use leadership for positive change (see Chapters 11 and 12). We know you will be much more skilled as you practice management. We know you will not stop learning. We know you will be involved in innovation. And we know you will compete globally.

We believe the future is yours. The future is yours to help shape with others. Believe it or not, you will be a leader. The question is where you will be leading others. We hope it is leading them to a better place.

Chapter 18   Study Guide

Summary

Why are strategy, innovation, and organizational learning important and linked?

- Strategy is the process of positioning the organization in the competitive environment and implementing actions to compete successfully. It is a pattern in a stream of decisions.

- Innovation is the process of creating new ideas and then implementing them in practical applications.

- Product innovations result in improved goods or services; process innovations result in improved work methods and operations.

- Steps in the innovation process normally include idea generation, initial experimentation, feasibility determination, and final application.

- Common features of highly innovative organizations include supportive strategies, cultures, structures, staffing, and senior leadership.

- Organizational learning is the process of acquiring knowledge and using information to adapt successfully to changing circumstances.

- For organizations to learn they must engage in knowledge acquisition, information distribution, information interpretation, and organizational retention in adapting successfully to changing circumstances.

- Firms use mimicry, experience, vicarious learning, scanning, and grafting to acquire information.

- Firms established mechanisms to convert information into knowledge.

- Chief among the problems of interpretation are self-serving interpretations.

- Firms retain information though individuals, transformation mechanisms, formal structure, physical structure, external archives, and their IT system.

- To compete successfully in the 21st-century global economy, individuals, units, and firms will need to be innovative and learn because of changes in the scope of operations, technology, and the environment.

What is organizational design, and how is it linked to strategy?

- Organizational design is the process of choosing and implementing a structural configuration for an organization.

- Organizational design is a way to implement the positioning of the firm in its environment.

- Organizational design provides a basis for a consistent stream of decisions.

- Strategy and organizational design are interrelated and must evolve along with changes in size, technology, and the environment.

How does the firm design for greater capability?

- The design of the organization needs to be adjusted to its size.

- Smaller firms often adopt a simple structure because it works, is cheap, and stresses the influence of the leader.

- With growth and aging firms become subject to routine managerial scripts and common myths.

- Operations technology and organizational design should be interrelated to ensure the firm produces the desired goods and/or services.

- Adhocracy is an organizational design used in technology-intense settings.

- Information technology is the combination of machines, artifacts, procedures, and systems used to gather, store, analyze, and disseminate information so that it can be translated into knowledge.

- IT provides an opportunity to change the design by substitution and the power to capture strategic advantages.

- IT forms the basis for the virtual organization.

- The environment is more complex when it is richer and more interdependent with higher volatility and greater uncertainty.

- The more complex the environment, the greater the demands on the organization, and firms should respond with more complex designs.

- Firms need not stand alone but can develop network relationships and alliances to cope with greater environmental complexity.

How do you put it all together to compete in the 21st century?

- To simultaneously cope with large size, sophisticated operations, IT technology, and a complex environment, a firm can work to minimize boundaries up and down the firm, across units, and among its partners.

- By honing the knowledge gained in this text you can develop the skills to compete successfully and become a leader in the 21st century.

Key Terms

Adhocracy (p. 428)
Benefit cycle (p. 436)
Environmental complexity (p. 432)
Grafting (p. 419)
Information technology (p. 426)
Innovation (p. 417)
Interfirm alliances (p. 434)
Managerial script (p. 425)

Mimicry (p. 418)
Operations technology (p. 426)
Organizational design (p. 421)
Organizational learning (p. 418)
Organizational myth (p. 425)

Process innovations (p. 417)
Product innovations (p. 417)
Scanning (p. 419)
Simple design (p. 424)
Strategy (p. 416)
Virtual organization (p. 431)

Self-Test 18

Multiple Choice

1. The design of the organization needs to be adjusted to all but _____.
   (a) the environment of the firm (b) the strategy of the firm (c) the size of the firm
   (d) the operations and information technology of the firm

2. _____ is the combination of resources, knowledge, and techniques that creates a product or service output for an organization. (a) Information technology
   (b) Strategy (c) Organizational learning (d) Operations technology

3. _____ is the combination of machines, artifacts, procedures, and systems used to gather, store, analyze, and disseminate information so that it can be translated into knowledge. (a) The specific environment (b) Strategy (c) Operations technology (d) Information technology

4. Which is an accurate statement about an adhocracy? _____ (a) The design facilitates information exchange and learning. (b) There are many rules and policies. (c) Use of IT is always minimal. (d) It handles routine problems efficiently

5. The set of cultural, economic, legal-political, and educational conditions in the areas in which a firm operates is called the _____. (a) task environment (b) specific environment (c) general environment

6. The segment of the environment that refers to the other organizations with which an organization must interact in order to obtain inputs and dispose of outputs is called _____. (a) the general environment (b) the strategic environment (c) the technological setting (d) the specific environment

7. _____ are announced cooperative agreements or joint ventures between two independent firms. (a) Mergers (b) Acquisitions (c) Interfirm alliances (d) Adhocracies

8. The process of acquiring knowledge, retaining knowledge within the organization, and distributing and interpreting information is called _____. (a) vicarious learning (b) experience (c) organizational learning (d) an organizational myth

9. Three methods of vicarious learning are _____. (a) scanning, grafting, and contracting out (b) grafting, contracting out, and mimicry (c) scanning, grafting, and mimicry (d) experience, mimicry, and scanning

10. Three important factors that block information interpretation are _____.
    (a) detachment, scanning, and common myths (b) self-serving interpretations, detachment, and common myths (c) contracting out, common myths, and detachment (d) common myths, managerial scripts, and self-serving interpretations

True–False

11. The organizational design for a small and a large firm are almost the same.   T   F

12. Organizations with well-defined and stable operations technologies have more opportunity to substitute managerial techniques for managerial judgment than do firms relying on more variable operations technologies.   T   F

13. Adhocracies tend to favor vertical specialization and control.   T   F

14. With extensive use of IT, more staff are typically added.   T   F

15. The general environment of organizations includes other organizations with which an organization must interact in order to obtain inputs and dispose of outputs.   T   F

Short Response

16. Explain why a large firm could not use a simple structure.

17. Explain the deployment of IT and its uses in organizations.

18. Describe the effect operations technology has on an organization from both Thompson's and Woodward's points of view.

19. What are the three primary determinants of environmental complexity?

Applications Essay

20. Why would Ford Motors want to shift to a matrix design organization for the design and development of cars and trucks but not do so in its manufacturing and assembly operations?

These learning activities from *The OB Skills Workbook* are suggested for Chapter 18.

OB in Action

CASE	EXPERIENTIAL EXERCISES	SELF-ASSESSMENTS
■ 18. Mission Management and Trust	■ 13. Tinker Toys ■ 39. Organizations Alive ■ 41. Alien Invasion	■ 2. A 21st-Century Manager ■ 9. Group Effectiveness ■ 21. Organizational Design Preferences

Plus—special learning experiences from *The Jossey-Bass/Pfeiffer Classroom Collection*

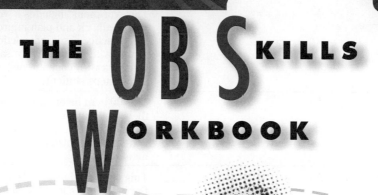

THE OB SKILLS WORKBOOK

Featuring
The Jossey-Bass/Pfeiffer
Classroom Collection

Pfeiffer
An Imprint of WILEY

JOSSEY-BASS
An Imprint of WILEY
Now you know.

SUGGESTED APPLICATIONS OF WORKBOOK MATERIALS

I. The Jossey-Bass/Pfeiffer Classroom Collection

Student Leadership Practices Inventory by Kouzes and Posner

Activity	Suggested Part	Overview
1. *Student Leadership Practices Inventory—Student Workbook*	All	This workbook includes a worksheet to help interpret feedback and plan improvement in each leadership practice assessed, sections on how to compare scores with the normative sample and how to share feedback with constituents, and more than 140 actual steps students can take to get results.
2. *Student Leadership Practices Inventory—Self*	All	This 30-item inventory will help students evaluate their performance and effectiveness as a leader. Results from the simple scoring process help students prepare plans for personal leadership development.
3. *Student Leadership Practices Inventory—Observer*	All	This version of the LPI is used by others to assess the individual's leadership tendencies, thus allowing for comparison with self-perceptions.

Experiential Exercises from The Pfeiffer Annual: Training

Activity	Suggested Part	Overview
1. *Sweet Tooth: Bonding Strangers into a Team*	Parts 1, 3, 4	Perception, teamwork, decision making, communication
2. *Interrogatories: Identifying Issues and Needs*	Parts 1, 3, 4	Current issues, group dynamics, communication
3. *Decode: Working with Different Instructions*	Parts 3, 4	Decision making, leadership, conflict, teamwork
4. *Choices: Learning Effective Conflict Management Strategies*	Parts 1, 2, 3, 4, 5	Conflict, negotiation, communication, decision making
5. *Internal/External Motivators: Encouraging Creativity*	Parts 2, 4, 5	Creativity, motivation, job design, decision making
6. *Quick Hitter: Fostering the Creative Spirit*	Parts 4, 5	Creativity, decision making, communication

 ## II. Cases for Critical Thinking

Case	Suggested Chapter	Cross-References and Integration
1. *Panera Bread Company*	1 Introducing Organizational Behavior	human resource management; organizational cultures; innovation; information technology; leadership
1a. *Management Training Dilemma*	Primer	ethics and decision makings; communication; conflict and negotiation

Case	Suggested Chapter	Cross-References and Integration
2. Crossing Borders	2 Values, Personality, and Individual Differences	diversity and individual differences; perception and attribution; performance management; job design; communication; conflict; decision making
3. SAS Institute	3 Emotions, Attitudes, and Job Satisfaction	organizaional cultures; globalization; innovation; motivation
4. MagRec, Inc.	4 Perception Attribution, and Learning	ethics and diversity; organizational structure, design, and culture; decision making; organizational change
5. It Isn't Fair	5 Motivation Theories	perception and attribution; performance management and rewards; communication; ethics and decision making
6. Hovey and Beard	6 Motivation and Job Design	organizational cultures; globalization; communication; decision making
7. Perfect Pizzeria	7 Rewards and Performance Management	organizational design; motivation; performance management and rewards
8. The Forgotten Group Member	8 How Groups Work	teamwork; motivation; diversity and individual differences; perception and attribution; performance management and rewards; communication; conflict; leadership
9. NASCAR's Racing Teams	9 Team Building and Team Performance	organizational cultures; leadership; motivation and reinforcement; communication
10. Faculty Empowerment and the Changing University Environment	10 Power and Politics	change; innovation and stress; job designs; communication; power and politics
11. The New Vice President	11 Leadership Theories	leadership; performance management and rewards; diversity and individual differences; communication; conflict and negotiation; power and influence
12. Motorola's Innovator in Chief	12 Emerging Leadership Perspectives	Innovation; conflict and negotiation; leadership; change and stress
13. Decisions, Decisions	13 Decision Making	organizational structure; organizational cultures; change and innovation; group dynamics and teamwork; diversity and individual differences
14. The Poorly Informed Walrus	14 Communication	diversity and individual differences; perception and attribution
15. The Missing Raise	15 Conflict and Negotiation	change; innovation and stress; job designs; communication; power and politics
16. Never on a Sunday	16 Organizational Culture and Development	ethics and diversity; organizational structure, design, and culture; decision making; organizational change
17. First Community Financial	17 Organizational Goals, and Structures	organizational structure, designs and culture; performance management and rewards
18. Mission Management and Trust	18 Strategic Capabilities and Organizational Design	organizational structure, designs and culture; performance management and rewards

Exercise	Suggested Chapter	Cross-References and Integration
1. My Best Manager	1 Introducing Organizational Behavior 3 Emotions, Attitudes, and Job Satisfaction	leadership
2. Graffiti Needs Assessment	1 Introducing Organizational Behavior	human resource management; communication
3. My Best Job	1 Introducing Organizational Behavior 6 Motivation and Job Design	motivation; job design; organizational cultures
4. What Do You Value in Work?	5 Motivation Theories	diversity and individual differences; performance management and rewards; motivation; job design; decision making
5. My Asset Base	3 Emotions, Attitudes, and Job Satisfaction	perception and attribution; diversity and individual differences; groups and teamwork; decision making
6. Expatriate Assignments	16 Organizational Culture and Development	perception and attribution; diversity and individual differences; decision making
7. Cultural Cues	12 Emerging Leadership Perspectives	perception and attribution; diversity and individual differences; decision making; communication; conflict; groups and teamwork
8. Prejudice in Our Lives	3 Emotions, Attitudes, and Job Satisfaction	perception and attribution; decision making; conflict; groups and teamwork
9. How We View Differences	4 Perception, Attribution, and Learning 16 Organizational Culture and Development	culture; international; diversity and individual differences; decision making; communication; conflict; groups and teamwork
10. Alligator River Story	4 Perception, Attribution, and Learning	diversity and individual differences; decision making; communication; conflict; groups and teamwork
11. Teamwork and Motivation	5 Motivation Theories	performance management and rewards; groups and teamwork
12. The Downside of Punishment	5 Motivation Theories	motivation; perception and attribution; performance management and rewards
13. Tinkertoys	6 Motivation and Job Design 17 Organizational Goals and Structures 18 Strategic Capabilities and Organizational Design	organizational structure; design and culture; groups and teamwork
14. Job Design Preferences	6 Motivation and Job Design	motivation; job design; organizational design; change
15. My Fantasy Job	6 Motivation and Job Design	motivation; individual differences; organizational design; change
16. Motivation by Job Enrichment	6 Motivation and Job Design	motivation; job design; perception; diversity and individual differences; change

Exercise	Suggested Chapter	Cross-References and Integration
17. *Annual Pay Raises*	5 Motivation Theories 7 Rewards and Performance Management	motivation; learning and reinforcement; perception and attribution; decision making; groups and teamwork
18. *Serving on the Boundary*	8 How Groups Work	intergroup dynamics; group dynamics; roles; communication; conflict; stress
19. *Eggsperiential Exercise*	8 How Groups Work	group dynamics and teamwork; diversity and individual differences; communication
20. *Scavenger Hunt—Team Building*	9 Teamwork and Team Performance	groups; leadership; diversity and individual differences; communication; leadership
21. *Work Team Dynamics*	9 Teamwork and Team Performance	groups; motivation; decision making; conflict; communication
22. *Identifying Group Norms*	9 Teamwork and Team Performance	groups; communication; perception and attribution
23. *Workgroup Culture*	9 Teamwork and Team Performance 16 Organizational Culture and Development	groups; communication; perception and attribution; job design; organizational culture
24. *The Hot Seat*	9 Teamwork and Team Performance	groups; communication; conflict and negotiation; power and politics
25. *Interview a Leader*	10 Power and Politics 11 Leadership Theories	performance management and rewards; groups and teamwork; new workplace; organizational change and stress
26. *Leadership Skills Inventories*	11 Leadership Theories	individual differences; perception and attribution; decision making
27. *Leadership and Participation in Decision Making*	11 Leadership Theories	decision making; communication; motivation, groups; teamwork
28. *My Best Manager: Revisited*	10 Power and Politics	diversity and individual differences; perception and attribution
29. *Active Listening*	14 Communication	group dynamics and teamwork; perception and attribution
30. *Upward Appraisal*	7 Rewards and Performance Management 14 Communication	perception and attribution; performance management and rewards
31. *360-Degree Feedback*	7 Rewards and Performance Management 14 Communication	communication; perception and attribution; performance management and rewards
32. *Role Analysis Negotiation*	13 Decision Making	communication; group dynamics and teamwork; perception and attribution; communication; decision making
33. *Lost at Sea*	13 Decision Making	communication; group dynamics and teamwork; conflict and negotiation
34. *Entering the Unknown*	13 Decision Making 15 Conflict and Negotiation	communication; group dynamics and teamwork; perception and attribution
35. *Vacation Puzzle*	15 Conflict and Negotiation	conflict and negotiation; communication; power; leadership
36. *The Ugli Orange*	13 Decision Making 15 Conflict and Negotiation	communication; decision making

Exercise	Suggested Chapter	Cross-References and Integration
37. Conflict Dialogues	15 Conflict and Negotiation	conflict; communication; feedback; perception; stress
38. Force-Field Analysis	13 Decision Making	decision making; organization structures, designs, cultures
39. Organizations Alive!	17 Organizational Goals and Structures 18 Strategic Capabilities and Design	organizational design and culture; performance management and rewards
40. Fast-Food Technology	16 Organizational Culture and Development 17 Organizational Goals and Structures	organizational design; organizational culture; job design
41. Alien Invasion	16 Organizational Culture and Development 17 Organizational Goals and Structures 18 Strategic Capabilities and Design	organizational structure and design; international; diversity and individual differences; perception and attribution
42. Power Circles Exercise	10 Power and Politics	influence; power; leadership; change management

 ## IV. Self-Assessment Inventories

Assessment	Suggested Chapter	Cross-References and Integration
See companion Web site for online versions of many assessment: www.wiley.com/college/schermerhorn		
1. Managerial Assumptions	1 Introducing Organizational Behavior	leadership
2. A Twenty-First-Century Manager	1 Introducing Organizational Behavior 12 Emerging Leadership Perspectives 17 Organizational Goals and Structures 18 Strategic Capabilities and Design	leadership; decision making; globalization
3. Turbulence Tolerance Test	1 Introducing Organizational Behavior 2 Values, Personality, and Individual Differences	perception; individual differences; organizational change and stress
4. Global Readiness Index	3 Emotions, Attitudes, and Job Satisfaction 12 Emerging Leadership Perspectives	diversity; culture; leading; perception; management skills; career readiness
5. Personal Values	3 Emotions, Attitudes, and Job Satisfaction 7 Rewards and Performance Management	perception; diversity and individual differences; leadership
6. Intolerance for Ambiguity	4 Perception, Attribution, and Learning	perception; leadership
7. Two-Factor Profile	5 Motivation Theories 6 Motivation and Job Design	job design; perception; culture; human resource management

Assessment	Suggested Chapter	Cross-References and Integration
8. Are You Cosmopolitan?	6 Motivation and Job Design 7 Rewards and Performance Management 16 Organizational Culture and Organizational Development	diversity and individual differences; organizational culture
9. Group Effectiveness	8 How Groups Work 9 Teamwork and Team Performance 16 Organizational Culture and Development 18 Strategic Capabilities and Design	organizational designs and cultures; leadership
10. Least Preferred Coworker Scale	11 Leadership Theories	diversity and individual differences; perception; group dynamics and teamwork
11. Leadership Style	11 Leadership Theories	diversity and individual differences; perception; group dynamics and teamwork
12. "TT" Leadership Style	11 Leadership Theories 14 Communication	diversity and individual differences; perception; group dynamics and teamwork
13. Empowering Others	9 Teamwork and Team Performance 10 Power and Politics 14 Communication	leadership; perception and attribution
14. Machiavellianism	10 Power and Politics	leadership; diversity and individual differences
15. Personal Power Profile	10 Power and Politics	leadership; diversity and individual differences
16. Your Intuitive Ability	13 Decision Making	diversity and individual differences
17. Decision-Making Biases	8 How Groups Work 13 Decision Making	teams and teamwork; communication; perception
18. Conflict Management Styles	15 Conflict and Negotiation	diversity and individual differences; communication
19. Your Personality Type	2 Values, Personality and Individual Differences	diversity and individual differences; job design
20. Time Management Profile	2 Values, Personality and Individual Differences	diversity and individual differences
21. Organizational Design Preference	17 Organizational Goals and Structures 18 Strategic Capabilities and Organizational Design	job design; diversity and individual differences
22. Which Culture Fits You?	16 Organizational Culture and Development	perception; diversity and individual differences

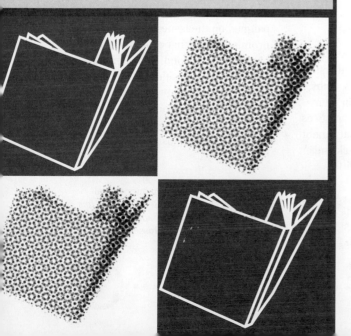

STUDENT LEADERSHIP PRACTICES INVENTORY
STUDENT WORKBOOK

James M. Kouzes
Barry Z. Posner, Ph.D.
Jossey-Bass Publishers • San Francisco

Jossey-Bass/Pfeiffer Classroom Collection

Printed in the United States of America.

Jossey-Bass books and products are available through most bookstores. To contact Jossey-Bass directly, call (888) 378-2537, fax to (800) 605-2665, or visit our website at www.josseybass.com.

Substantial discounts on bulk quantities of Jossey-Bass books are available to corporations, professional associations, and other organizations. For details and discount information, contact the special sales department at Jossey-Bass.

Printing 10 9 8 7 6 5 4 3 2

This book is printed on acid-free, recycled stock that meets or exceeds the minimum GPO and EPA requirements for recycled paper.

CONTENTS

People WHO BECOME
leaders
DON'T *always* **seek**
THE **challenges**
THEY **face.**
CHALLENGES
also SEEK **leaders.**

1
Leadership: What People Do When They're Leading

"*Leadership is everyone's business.*" That's the conclusion we have come to after nearly two decades of research into the behaviors and actions of people who are making a difference in their organizations, clubs, teams, classes, schools, campuses, communities, and even in their families. We found that leadership is an observable, learnable set of practices. Contrary to some myths, it is not a mystical and ethereal process that cannot be understood by ordinary people. Given the opportunity for feedback and practice, those with the desire and persistence to lead—to make a difference—can substantially improve their ability to do so.

The *Leadership Practices Inventory* (LPI) is part of an extensive research project into the everyday actions and behaviors of people, at all levels and across a variety of settings, as they are leading. Through our research we identified five practices that are common to all leadership experiences. In col-laboration with others, we extended our findings to student leaders and to school and college environments and created the student version of the LPI.[1] The LPI is a tool, not a test, designed to assess your current leadership skills. It will identify your areas of strength as well as areas of leadership that need to be further developed.

The *Student LPI* helps you discover the extent to which you (in your role as a leader of a student group or organization) engage in the following five leadership practices:

Challenging the Process. Leaders are pioneers—people who seek out new opportunities and are willing to change the status quo. They innovate, experiment, and explore ways to improve the organization. They treat mistakes as learning experiences. Leaders also stay prepared to meet whatever challenges may confront them. *Challenging the Process* involves

- Searching for opportunities
- Experimenting and taking risks

As an example of Challenging the Process, one student related how innovative thinking helped him win a student class election: "I challenged the process in more than one way. First, I wanted people to understand that elections are not necessarily popularity contests, so I campaigned on the issues and did not promise things that could not possibly be done. Second, I challenged the incumbent positions. They thought they would win easily because they were incumbents, but I showed them that no one has an inherent right to a position."

---

[1]For more information on our original work, see *The Leadership Challenge: How to Keep Getting Extraordinary Things Done in Organizations* (Jossey-Bass Publishers).

Challenging the Process for a student serving as treasurer of her sorority meant examining and abandoning some of her leadership beliefs: "I used to believe, 'If you want to do something right, do it yourself.' I found out the hard way that this is impossible to do. . . . One day I was ready to just give up the position because I could no longer handle all of the work. My adviser noticed that I was overwhelmed, and she turned to me and said three magic words: 'Use your committee.' The best piece of advice I would pass along about being an effective leader is that it is okay to experiment with letting others do the work."

Inspiring a Shared Vision.
Leaders look toward and beyond the horizon. They envision the future with a positive and hopeful outlook. Leaders are expressive and attract other people to their organization and teams through their genuineness. They communicate and show others how their interests can be met through commitment to a common purpose. *Inspiring a Shared Vision* involves

- Envisioning an uplifting future
- Enlisting others in a common vision

Describing his experience as president of his high school class, one student wrote: "It was our vision to get the class united and to be able to win the spirit trophy. . . . I told my officers that we could do anything we set our minds on. Believe in yourself and believe in your ability to accomplish things."

Enabling Others to Act.
Leaders infuse people with energy and confidence, developing relationships based on mutual trust. They stress collaborative goals. They actively involve others in planning, giving them discretion to make their own decisions. Leaders ensure that people feel strong and capable. *Enabling Others to Act* involves

- Fostering collaboration
- Strengthening people

It is not necessary to be in a traditional leadership position to put these principles into practice. Here is an example from a student who led his team as a team member, not from a traditional position of power: "I helped my team members feel strong and capable by encouraging everyone to practice with the same amount of intensity that they played games with. Our practices improved throughout the year, and by the end of the year had reached the point I was striving for: complete involvement among all players, helping each other to perform at our very best during practice times."

Modeling the Way.
Leaders are clear about their personal values and beliefs. They keep people and projects on course by behaving consistently with these values and modeling how they expect others to act. Leaders also plan projects and break them down into achievable steps, creating opportunities for small wins. By focusing on key priorities, they make it easier for others to achieve goals. *Modeling the Way* involves

- Setting the example
- Achieving small wins

Working in a business environment taught one student the importance of Modeling the Way. She writes: "I proved I was serious because I was the first one on the job and the last one to leave. I came prepared to work and make the tools available to my crew. I worked alongside them and in no way portrayed an attitude of superiority. Instead, we were in this together."

Encouraging the Heart.
Leaders encourage people to persist in their efforts by linking recognition with accomplishments and visibly recognizing contributions to the common vision. They express pride in the achievements of the group or organization, letting others know that their efforts are appreciated. Leaders also find ways to celebrate milestones. They nurture a team spirit, which enables people to sustain continued efforts. *Encouraging the Heart* involves

- Recognizing individual contributions
- Celebrating team accomplishments

While organizing and running a day camp, one student recognized volunteers and celebrated accomplishments through her actions. She explains: "We had a pizza party with the children on the last day of the day camp. Later, the volunteers were sent thank you notes and 'valuable volunteer awards' personally signed by the day campers. The pizza party, thank you notes, and awards served to encourage the hearts of the volunteers in the hopes that they might return for next year's day camp."

Somewhere,
sometime,
THE *leader within*
EACH OF **US**
MAY **get**
THE CALL
to STEP forward

2
Questions Frequently Asked About the *Student LPI*

Question 1: What are the right answers?

Answer: There are no universal right answers when it comes to leadership. Research indicates that the more frequently you are perceived as engaging in the behavior and actions identified in the *Student LPI,* the more likely it is that you will be perceived as an effective leader. The higher your scores on the Student LPI-Observer, the more others perceive you as (1) having personal credibility, (2) being effective in running meetings, (3) successfully representing your organization or group to nonmembers, (4) generating a sense of enthusiasm and cooperation, and (5) having a high-performing team. In addition, findings show a strong and positive relationship between the extent to which people report their leaders engaging in this set of five leadership practices and how motivated, committed, and productive they feel.

Question 2: How reliable and valid is the Student LPI?

Answer: The question of reliability can be answered in two ways. First, the *Student LPI* has shown sound psychometric properties. The scale for each leadership practice is internally reliable, meaning that the statements within each practice are highly correlated with one another. Second, results of multivariate analyses indicate that the statements within each leadership practice are more highly correlated (or associated) with one another than they are between the five leadership practices.

In terms of validity (or "So what difference do the scores make?"), the *Student LPI* has good face validity and predictive validity. This means, first, that the results make sense to people. Second, scores on the *Student LPI* significantly differentiate high-performing leaders from their less successful counterparts. Whether measured by the leader, his or her peers, or student personnel administrators, those student leaders who engage more frequently, rather than less frequently, in the five leadership practices are more effective.

Question 3: Should my perceptions of my leadership practices be consistent with the ratings other people give me?

Answer: Research indicates that trust in the leader is essential if other people (for example, fellow members of a group, team, or organization) are going to follow that person over time. People must experience the leader as believable, credible, and trustworthy. Trust—whether in a leader or any other person—is developed through consistency in behavior. Trust is further established when words and deeds are congruent.

This does not mean, however, that you will always be perceived in exactly the same way by every person in every situation. Some people may not see you as often as others do, and therefore they may rate you differently on the same behavior. Some people simply may not know you as well as others do. Also you may appropriately behave differently in different situations, such as in a crisis versus during more stable times. Others may have different expectations of you, and still others may perceive the rating descriptions (such as "once in a while" or "fairly often") differently.

Therefore, the key issue is not whether your self-ratings and the ratings from others are exactly the same, but whether people perceive consistency between what you say you do and what you actually do. The only way you can know the answer to this question is to solicit feedback. The Student LPI-Observer has been designed for this purpose.

Research indicates that people tend to see themselves more positively than others do. The Student LPI-Self norms are consistent with this general trend; scores on the Student LPI-Self tend to be somewhat higher than scores on the Student LPI-Observer. *Student LPI* scores also tend to be higher than LPI scores of experienced managers and executives in the private and public sector.

Question 4: Can I change my leadership practices?

Answer: It is certainly possible—even for experienced people—to learn new skills. You will increase your chances of changing your behavior if you receive feedback on what level you have achieved with a particular skill, observe a positive model of that skill, set some improvement goals for yourself, practice the skill, ask for updated feedback on your performance, and then set new goals. The practices that are assessed with the *Student LPI* fall into the category of learnable skills.

But some things can be changed only if there is a strong and genuine inner desire to make a difference. For example, enthusiasm for a cause is unlikely to be developed through education or job assignments; it must come from within.

Use the information from the *Student LPI* to better understand how you currently behave as a leader, both from your own perspective and from the perspective of others. Note where there are consistencies and inconsistencies. Understand which leadership behaviors and practices you feel comfortable engaging in and which you feel uncomfortable with. Determine which leadership behaviors and practices you can improve on, and take steps to improve your leadership skills and gain confidence in leading other people and groups. The following sections will help you to become more effective in leadership.

Perhaps NONE OF
us knows
OUR *true strength*
UNTIL **challenged**
TO **bring**
it **forth.**

3
Recording Your Scores

On pages W-14 through W-17 are grids for recording your *Student LPI* scores. The first grid (Challenging the Process) is for recording scores for items 1, 6, 11, 16, 21, and 26 from the Student LPI-Self and Student LPI-Observer. These are the items that relate to behaviors involved in Challenging the Process, such as searching for opportunities, experimenting, and taking risks. An abbreviated form of each item is printed beside the grid as a handy reference.

In the first column, which is headed "Self-Rating," write the scores that you gave yourself. If others were asked to complete the Student LPI-Observer and if the forms were returned to you, enter their scores in the columns (A, B, C, D, E, and so on) under the heading "Observers' Ratings." Simply transfer the numbers from page W-14 of each Student LPI-Observer to your scoring grids, using one column for each observer. For example, enter the first observer's scores in column A, the second observer's scores in column B, and so on. The grids provide space for the scores of as many as ten observers.

After all scores have been entered for Challenging the Process, total each column in the row marked "Totals." Then add all the totals for observers; do not include the "self" total. Write this grand total in the space marked "Total of All Observers' Scores." To obtain the average, divide the grand total by the number of people who completed the Student LPI-Observer. Write this average in the blank provided. The sample grid shows how the grid would look with scores for self and five observers entered.

	SELF-RATING	OBSERVERS' RATINGS										
		A	B	C	D	E	F	G	H	I	J	
1. Seeks challenge	5	4	2	4	4	2						
6. Keeps current	4	4	3	4	4	3						
11. Initiates experiment	3	3	2	2	2	1						
16. Looks for ways to improve	4	3	2	3	5	3						
21. Asks "What can we learn?"	2	3	2	3	3	2						TOTAL OF ALL OBSERVERS' SCORES
26. Lets others take risks	5	3	3	2	3	2						
TOTALS	23	20	14	18	21	13						86

TOTAL SELF-RATING: _____23_____   AVERAGE OF ALL OBSERVERS: ___17.2___

The other four grids should be completed in the same manner.

The second grid (Inspiring a Shared Vision) is for recording scores to the items that pertain to envisioning the future and enlisting the support of others. These include items 2, 7, 12, 17, 22, and 27.

The third grid (Enabling Others to Act) pertains to items 3, 8, 13, 18, 23, and 28, which involve fostering collaboration and strengthening others.

The fourth grid (Modeling the Way) pertains to items about setting an example and planning small wins.

These include items 4, 9, 14, 19, 24, and 29.

The fifth grid (Encouraging the Heart) pertains to items about recognizing contributions and celebrating accomplishments. These are items 5, 10, 15, 20, 25, and 30.

Grids for Recording *Student LPI* Scores

Scores should be recorded on the following grids in accordance with the instructions on page W-13. As you look at individual scores, remember the rating system that was used:

"1" means that you *rarely or seldom* engage in the behavior.

"2" means that you engage in the behavior *once in a while.*

"3" means that you *sometimes* engage in the behavior.

"4" means that you engage in the behavior *fairly often.*

"5" means that you engage in the behavior *very frequently.*

After you have recorded all your scores and calculated the totals and averages, turn to page W-17 and read the section on interpreting scores.

Challenging the Process

	SELF-RATING	OBSERVERS' RATINGS									
		A	B	C	D	E	F	G	H	I	J
1. Seeks challenge											
6. Keeps current											
11. Initiates experiment											
16. Looks for ways to improve											
21. Asks "What can we learn?"											
26. Lets others take risks											
TOTALS											

TOTAL OF ALL OBSERVERS' SCORES

TOTAL SELF-RATING: _____   AVERAGE OF ALL OBSERVERS: _____

Inspiring a Shared Vision

	SELF-RATING	OBSERVERS' RATINGS									
		A	B	C	D	E	F	G	H	I	J
2. Describes ideal capabilities											
7. Looks ahead and communicates future											
12. Upbeat and positive communicator											
17. Finds common ground											
22. Communicates purpose and meaning											
27. Enthusiastic about possibilities											
TOTALS											

TOTAL OF ALL OBSERVERS' SCORES

TOTAL SELF-RATING: _____   AVERAGE OF ALL OBSERVERS: _____

Enabling Others to Act

	SELF-RATING	OBSERVERS' RATINGS									
		A	B	C	D	E	F	G	H	I	J
3. Includes others in planning											
8. Treats others with respect											
13. Supports decisions of others											
18. Fosters cooperative relationships											
23. Provides freedom and choice											
28. Lets others lead											
TOTALS											

TOTAL OF ALL OBSERVERS' SCORES

TOTAL SELF-RATING: _____   AVERAGE OF ALL OBSERVERS: _____

Modeling the Way

	SELF-RATING	OBSERVERS' RATINGS									
		A	B	C	D	E	F	G	H	I	J
4. Shares beliefs about leading											
9. Breaks projects into steps											
14. Sets personal example											
19. Talks about guiding values											
24. Follows through on promises											
29. Sets clear goals and plans											
TOTALS											

TOTAL OF ALL OBSERVERS' SCORES

TOTAL SELF-RATING: _____   AVERAGE OF ALL OBSERVERS: _____

Encouraging the Heart

	SELF-RATING	OBSERVERS' RATINGS									
		A	B	C	D	E	F	G	H	I	J
5. Encourages other people											
10. Recognizes people's contributions											
15. Praises people for job well done											
20. Gives support and appreciation											
25. Finds ways to publicly celebrate											
30. Tells others about group's good work											
TOTALS											

TOTAL OF ALL OBSERVERS' SCORES

TOTAL SELF-RATING: _____   AVERAGE OF ALL OBSERVERS: _____

> THE unique ROLE
> OF leaders
> IS TO *take us*
> TO places
> WE'VE never
> *been* before.

4
Interpreting Your Scores

This section will help you to interpret your scores by looking at them in several ways and by making notes to yourself about what you can do to become a more effective leader.

Ranking Your Ratings

Refer to the previous chapter, "Recording Your Scores." On each grid, look at your scores in the blanks marked "Total Self-Rating." Each of these totals represents your responses to six statements about one of the five leadership practices. Each of your totals can range from a low of 6 to a high of 30.

In the blanks that follow, write "1" to the left of the leadership practice with the highest total self-rating, "2" by the next-highest total self-rating, and so on. This ranking represents the leadership practices with which you feel most comfortable, second-most comfortable, and so on. The practice you identify with a "5" is the practice with which you feel least comfortable.

Again refer to the previous chapter, but this time look at your scores in the blanks marked "Average of All Observers." The number in each blank is the average score given to you by the people you asked to complete the Student LPI-Observer. Like each of your total self-ratings, this number can range from 6 to 30.

In the blanks that follow, write "1" to the right of the leadership practice with the highest score, "2" by the next-highest score, and so on. This ranking represents the leadership practices that others feel you use most often, second-most often, and so on.

Self		Observers
_____	Challenging the Process	_____
_____	Inspiring a Shared Vision	_____
_____	Enabling Others to Act	_____
_____	Modeling the Way	_____
_____	Encouraging the Heart	_____

Comparing Your Self-Ratings to Observers' Ratings

To compare your Student LPI-Self and Student LPI-Observer assessments, refer to the "Chart for Graphing Your Scores" on the next page. On the chart, designate your scores on the five leadership practices (Challenging, Inspiring, Enabling, Modeling, and Encouraging) by marking each of these points with a capital "S" (for "Self"). Connect the five resulting "S scores" with a *solid line* and label the end of this line "Self" (see sample chart below).

If other people provided input through the Student LPI-Observer, designate the average observer scores (see the blanks labeled "Average of All Observers" on the scoring grids) by marking each of the points with a capital "O" (for "Observer"). Then connect the five resulting "O scores" with a *dashed line* and label the end of this line "Observer" (see sample chart). Completing this process will provide you with a graphic representation (one solid and one dashed line) illustrating the relationship between your self-perception and the observations of other people.

Chart for Graphing Your Scores

Percentile	Challenging the Process	Inspiring a Shared Vision	Enabling Others to Act	Modeling the Way	Encouraging the Heart
100%	30 29 28	30 29	30	30 29 28	30
	27	28	29		
				27	29
90%	26	27			
			28	26	28
	25	26			
80%		O 25			27
	24		S	25	
70%					26
	23	S	26	24	
60%			O	23 O	Self
	22	23			Observer
50%			25		24
	S	22			
40%		21		S	23
			24		
		20			22
30%	20			21	
		19	23	20	21
20%	19 O	18	22	19	20
	18	17	21		19
10%	17	16 15	20	18	18
	16 15	14	19 18	17 16	17 16

Chart for Graphing Your Scores

Percentile	Challenging the Process	Inspiring a Shared Vision	Enabling Others to Act	Modeling the Way	Encouraging the Heart
100%	30	30	30	30	30
	29	29		29	
	28			28	29
		28	29		
	27			27	
90%	26	27			28
			28	26	
	25	26			
80%					27
		25	27	25	
	24				
					26
70%					
		24		24	
	23		26		
					25
60%		23			
				23	
	22				
50%		22	25		24
	21			22	
40%		21			23
			24		
		20			22
30%	20			21	
			23		
		19		20	21
20%	19	18	22	19	20
	18	17	21	18	19
10%	17	16	20	17	18
	16	15	19	16	17
	15	14	18		16

Percentile Scores

Look again at the "Chart for Graphing Your Scores." The column to the far left represents the Student LPI-Self percentile rankings for more than 1,200 student leaders. A percentile ranking is determined by the percentage of people who score at or below a given number. For example, if your total self-rating for "Challenging" is at the 60th percentile line on the "Chart for Graphing Your Scores," this means that you assessed yourself higher than 60 percent of all people who have completed the *Student LPI;* you would be in the top 40 percent in this leadership practice. Studies indicate that a "high" score is one at or above the 70th percentile, a "low" score is one at or below the 30th percentile, and a score that falls between those ranges is considered "moderate."

Using these criteria, circle the "H" (for "High"), the "M" (for "Moderate"), or the "L" (for "Low") for each leadership practice on the "Range of Scores" table below. Compared to other student leaders around the country, where do your leadership practices tend to fall? (Given a "normal distribution," it is expected that most people's scores will fall within the moderate range.)

Range of Scores

In my perception				In others' perception			
Practice	**Rating**			**Practice**	**Rating**		
Challenging the Process	H	M	L	Challenging the Process	H	M	L
Inspiring a Shared Vision	H	M	L	Inspiring a Shared Vision	H	M	L
Enabling Others to Act	H	M	L	Enabling Others to Act	H	M	L
Modeling the Way	H	M	L	Modeling the Way	H	M	L
Encouraging the Heart	H	M	L	Encouraging the Heart	H	M	L

Exploring Specific Leadership Behaviors

Looking at your scoring grids, review each of the thirty items on the *Student LPI* by practice. One or two of the six behaviors within each leadership practice may be higher or lower than the rest. If so, on which specific items is there variation? What do these differences suggest? On which specific items is there agreement? Please write your thoughts in the following space.

Challenging the Process

_____

_____

_____

_____

Inspiring a Shared Vision

_____

_____

_____

_____

_____

_____

Enabling Others to Act

_____

_____

_____

_____

_____

_____

Modeling the Way

_____

_____

_____

_____

_____

_____

_____

_____

_____

_____

_____

Comparing Observers' Responses to One Another

Study the Student LPI-Observer scores for each of the five leadership practices. Do some respondents' scores differ significantly from others? If so, are the differences localized in the scores of one or two people? On which leadership practices do the respondents agree? On which practices do they disagree? If you try to behave basically the same with all the people who assessed you, how do you explain the difference in ratings? Please write your thoughts in the following space.

_____

_____

_____

_____

_____

_____

_____

_____

_____

_____

_____

Wanting TO LEAD AND
believing THAT
YOU *can lead* ARE THE
departure POINTS
ON THE PATH TO **leadership.**
LEADERSHIP IS AN ART—
A *performing* art—
AND THE **instrument**
IS THE **self.**

5
Summary and Action-Planning Worksheets

Take a few moments to summarize your *Student LPI* feedback by completing the following Strengths and Opportunities Summary Worksheet. Refer to the "Chart for Graphing Your Scores," the "Range of Scores" table, and any notes you have made.

After the summary worksheet you will find some suggestions for getting started on meeting the leadership challenge. With these suggestions in mind, review your *Student LPI* feedback and decide on the actions you will take to become an even more effective leader. Then complete the Action-Planning Worksheet to spell out the steps you will take. (One Action-Planning Worksheet is included in this workbook, but you may want to develop action plans for several practices or behaviors. You can make copies of the blank form before you fill it in or just use a separate sheet of paper for each leadership practice you plan to improve.)

Strengths and Opportunities Summary Worksheet

Strengths

Which of the leadership practices and behaviors are you most comfortable with? Why? Can you do more?

_____

_____

_____

_____

_____

_____

_____

Areas for Improvement

What can you do to use a practice more frequently? What will it take to feel more comfortable?

_____

_____

_____

_____

_____

_____

_____

The following are ten suggestions for getting started on meeting the leadership challenge.

Prescriptions for Meeting the Leadership Challenge

Challenge the Process
• Fix something
• Adopt the "great ideas" of others

Inspire a Shared Vision
• Let others know how you feel
• Recount your "personal best"

Enable Others to Act
• Always say "we"
• Make heroes of other people

Model the Way
• Lead by example
• Create opportunities for small wins

Encourage the Heart
• Write "thank you" notes
• Celebrate, and link your celebrations to your organization's values

Action-Planning Worksheet

1. What would you like to be better able to do?

_____

_____

_____

_____

_____

_____

_____

_____

_____

2. What specific actions will you take?

_____

_____

_____

_____

_____

_____

_____

_____

_____

_____

_____

_____

_____

3. What is the first action you will take? Who will be involved? When will you begin?

Action _____

_____

_____

People Involved

_____

_____

_____

_____

Target Date _____

4. Complete this sentence: "I will know I have improved in this leadership skill when . . ."

_____

_____

_____

_____

_____

5. When will you review your progress? _____

About the Authors

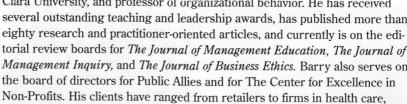

James M. Kouzes is chairman of TPG/Learning Systems, which makes leadership work through practical, performance-oriented learning programs. In 1993 *The Wall Street Journal* cited Jim as one of the twelve most requested "nonuniversity executive-education providers" to U.S. companies. His list of past and present clients includes AT&T, Boeing, Boy Scouts of America, Charles Schwab, Ciba-Geigy, Dell Computer, First Bank System, Honeywell, Johnson & Johnson, Levi Strauss & Co., Motorola, Pacific Bell, Stanford University, Xerox Corporation, and the YMCA.

Barry Z. Posner, PhD, is dean of the Leavey School of Business, Santa Clara University, and professor of organizational behavior. He has received several outstanding teaching and leadership awards, has published more than eighty research and practitioner-oriented articles, and currently is on the editorial review boards for *The Journal of Management Education, The Journal of Management Inquiry,* and *The Journal of Business Ethics.* Barry also serves on the board of directors for Public Allies and for The Center for Excellence in Non-Profits. His clients have ranged from retailers to firms in health care, high technology, financial services, manufacturing, and community service agencies.

Kouzes and Posner are coauthors of several best-selling and award-winning leadership books. *The Leadership Challenge: How to Keep Getting Extraordinary Things Done in Organizations* (2nd ed., 1995), with over 800,000 copies in print, has been reprinted in fifteen languages, has been featured in three video programs, and received a Critic's Choice award from the nation's newspaper book review editors. *Credibility: How Leaders Gain and Lose It, Why People Demand It* (1993) was chosen by *Industry Week* as one of the five best management books of the year. Their latest book is *Encouraging the Heart: A Leader's Guide to Rewarding and Recognizing Others* (1998).

STUDENT LEADERSHIP PRACTICES INVENTORY—SELF

Your Name: _____

Instructions

On the next two pages are thirty statements describing various leadership behaviors. Please read each statement carefully. Then rate *yourself* in terms of *how frequently* you engage in the behavior described. *This is not a test* (there are no right or wrong answers).

Consider each statement in the context of the student organization (for example, club, team, chapter, group, unit, hall, program, project) with which you are most involved. The rating scale provides five choices:

(1) If you RARELY or SELDOM do what is described in the statement, circle the number one (1).
(2) If you do what is described ONCE IN A WHILE, circle the number two (2).
(3) If you SOMETIMES do what is described, circle the number three (3).
(4) If you do what is described FAIRLY OFTEN, circle the number four (4).
(5) If you do what is described VERY FREQUENTLY or ALMOST ALWAYS, circle the number five (5).

Please respond to every statement.

In selecting the response, be realistic about the extent to which you *actually* engage in the behavior. Do *not* answer in terms of how you would like to see yourself or in terms of what you should be doing. Answer in terms of how you *typically* behave. The usefulness of the feedback from this inventory will depend on how honest you are with yourself about how frequently you actually engage in each of these behaviors.

For example, the first statement is "I look for opportunities that challenge my skills and abilities." If you believe you do this "once in a while," circle the number 2. If you believe you look for challenging opportunities "fairly often," circle the number 4.

When you have responded to all thirty statements, please turn to the response sheet on the back page and transfer your responses as instructed. Thank you.

STUDENT LEADERSHIP PRACTICES INVENTORY-SELF

How frequently do you typically engage in the following behaviors and actions? *Circle* the number that applies to each statement.

1 SELDOM OR RARELY	2 ONCE IN A WHILE	3 SOMETIMES	4 FAIRLY OFTEN	5 VERY FREQUENTLY

1. I look for opportunities that challenge my skills and abilities.	1	2	3	4	5
2. I describe to others in our organization what we should be capable of accomplishing.	1	2	3	4	5
3. I include others in planning the activities and programs of our organization.	1	2	3	4	5
4. I share my beliefs about how things can be run most effectively within our organization.	1	2	3	4	5
5. I encourage others as they work on activities and programs in our organization.	1	2	3	4	5
6. I keep current on events and activities that might affect our organization.	1	2	3	4	5
7. I look ahead and communicate about what I believe will affect us in the future.	1	2	3	4	5
8. I treat others with dignity and respect.	1	2	3	4	5
9. I break our organization's projects down into manageable steps.	1	2	3	4	5
10. I make sure that people in our organization are recognized for their contributions.	1	2	3	4	5
11. I take initiative in experimenting with the way we do things in our organization.	1	2	3	4	5
12. I am upbeat and positive when talking about what our organization is doing.	1	2	3	4	5
13. I support the decisions that other people in our organization make on their own.	1	2	3	4	5
14. I set a personal example of what I expect from other people.	1	2	3	4	5
15. I praise people for a job well done.	1	2	3	4	5
16. I look for ways to improve whatever project or task I am involved in.	1	2	3	4	5
17. I talk with others about how their own interests can be met by working toward a common goal.	1	2	3	4	5
18. I foster cooperative rather than competitive relationships among people I work with.	1	2	3	4	5
19. I talk about the values and principles that guide my actions.	1	2	3	4	5
20. I give people in our organization support and express appreciation for their contributions.	1	2	3	4	5
21. I ask, "What can we learn from this experience?" when things do not go as we expected.	1	2	3	4	5
22. I speak with conviction about the higher purpose and meaning of what we are doing.	1	2	3	4	5
23. I give others a great deal of freedom and choice in deciding how to do their work.	1	2	3	4	5
24. I follow through on the promises and commitments I make in this organization.	1	2	3	4	5
25. I find ways for us to celebrate our accomplishments publicly.	1	2	3	4	5
26. I let others experiment and take risks even when outcomes are uncertain.	1	2	3	4	5
27. I show my enthusiasm and excitement about what our organization is doing.	1	2	3	4	5
28. I provide opportunities for others to take on leadership responsibilities.	1	2	3	4	5
29. I make sure that we set goals and make specific plans for the projects we undertake.	1	2	3	4	5
30. I make it a point to tell others about the good work done by our organization.	1	2	3	4	5

Transferring the Scores

After you have responded to the thirty statements on the previous two pages, please transfer your responses to the blanks below. This will make it easier to record and score your responses. Notice that the numbers of the statements are listed *horizontally*. Make sure that the number you assigned to each statement is transferred to the appropriate blank. Fill in a response for every item.

1. _____	2. _____	3. _____	4. _____	5. _____
6. _____	7. _____	8. _____	9. _____	10. _____
11. _____	12. _____	13. _____	14. _____	15. _____
16. _____	17. _____	18. _____	19. _____	20. _____
21. _____	22. _____	23. _____	24. _____	25. _____
26. _____	27. _____	28. _____	29. _____	30. _____

Further Instructions

Please write your name here: _____

Please bring this form with you to the workshop (seminar or class) or return this form to:

_____

_____

_____

_____

If you are interested in feedback from other people, ask them to complete the Student LPI-Observer, which provides you with perspectives on your leadership behaviors as perceived by others.

Printed in the United States of America.

Jossey-Bass Publishers
350 Sansome Street
San Francisco, California 94104
(888) 378-2537
Fax (800) 605-2665

www.josseybass.com

Printing 10 9 8 7 6 5 4 3

This instrument is printed on acid-free, recycled stock that meets or exceeds the minimum GPO and EPA requirements for recycled paper.

ISBN: 0-7879-4426-2

STUDENT LEADERSHIP PRACTICES INVENTORY—OBSERVER

Name of Leader:_____

Instructions

On the next two pages are thirty descriptive statements about various leadership behaviors. Please read each statement carefully. Then rate *the person who asked you to complete this form* in terms of *how frequently* he or she typically engages in the described behavior. *This is not a test* (there are no right or wrong answers).

Consider each statement in the context of the student organization (for example, club, team, chapter, group, unit, hall, program, project) with which that person is most involved or with which you have had the greatest opportunity to observe him or her. The rating scale provides five choices:

(1) If this person RARELY or SELDOM does what is described in the statement, circle the number one (1).

(2) If this person does what is described ONCE IN A WHILE, circle the number two (2).

(3) If this person SOMETIMES does what is described, circle the number three (3).

(4) If this person does what is described FAIRLY OFTEN, circle the number four (4).

(5) If this person does what is described VERY FREQUENTLY or ALMOST ALWAYS, circle the number five (5).

Please respond to every statement.

In selecting the response, be realistic about the extent to which this person *actually* engages in the behavior. Do *not* answer in terms of how you would like to see this person behaving or in terms of what this person should be doing. Answer in terms of how he or she *typically behaves*. The usefulness of the feedback from this inventory will depend on how honest you are about how frequently you observe this person actually engaging in each of these behaviors.

For example, the first statement is, "He or she looks for opportunities that challenge his or her skills and abilities." If you believe this person does this "once in a while," circle the number 2. If you believe he or she looks for challenging opportunities "fairly often," circle the number 4.

When you have responded to all thirty statements, please turn to the response sheet on the back page and transfer your responses as instructed. Thank you.

STUDENT LEADERSHIP PRACTICES INVENTORY—OBSERVER

How frequently does this person typically engage in the following behaviors and actions? *Circle* the number that applies to each statement:

1 SELDOM OR RARELY	2 ONCE IN A WHILE	3 SOMETIMES	4 FAIRLY OFTEN	5 VERY FREQUENTLY

He or she:

1. looks for opportunities that challenge his or her skills and abilities.	1	2	3	4	5
2. describes to others in our organization what we should be capable of accomplishing.	1	2	3	4	5
3. includes others in planning the activities and programs of our organization.	1	2	3	4	5
4. shares his or her beliefs about how things can be run most effectively within our organization.	1	2	3	4	5
5. encourages others as they work on activities and programs in our organization.	1	2	3	4	5
6. keeps current on events and activities that might affect our organization.	1	2	3	4	5
7. looks ahead and communicates about what he or she believes will affect us in the future.	1	2	3	4	5
8. treats others with dignity and respect.	1	2	3	4	5
9. breaks our organization's projects down into manageable steps.	1	2	3	4	5
10. makes sure that people in our organization are recognized for their contributions.	1	2	3	4	5
11. takes initiative in experimenting with the way we do things in our organization.	1	2	3	4	5
12. is upbeat and positive when talking about what our organization is doing.	1	2	3	4	5
13. supports the decisions that other people in our organization make on their own.	1	2	3	4	5
14. sets a personal example of what he or she expects from other people.	1	2	3	4	5
15. praises people for a job well done.	1	2	3	4	5
16. looks for ways to improve whatever project or task he or she is involved in.	1	2	3	4	5
17. talks with others about how their own interests can be met by working toward a common goal.	1	2	3	4	5
18. fosters cooperative rather than competitive relationships among people he or she works with.	1	2	3	4	5
19. talks about the values and principles that guide his or her actions.	1	2	3	4	5
20. gives people in our organization support and expresses appreciation for their contributions.	1	2	3	4	5
21. asks "What can we learn from this experience?" when things do not go as we expected.	1	2	3	4	5
22. speaks with conviction about the higher purpose and meaning of what we are doing.	1	2	3	4	5
23. gives others a great deal of freedom and choice in deciding how to do their work.	1	2	3	4	5
24. follows through on the promises and commitments he or she makes in this organization.	1	2	3	4	5
25. finds ways for us to celebrate our accomplishments publicly.	1	2	3	4	5
26. lets others experiment and take risks even when outcomes are uncertain.	1	2	3	4	5
27. shows his or her enthusiasm and excitement about what our organization is doing.	1	2	3	4	5
28. provides opportunities for others to take on leadership responsibilities.	1	2	3	4	5
29. makes sure that we set goals and make specific plans for the projects we undertake.	1	2	3	4	5
30. makes it a point to tell others about the good work done by our organization.	1	2	3	4	5

Transferring the Scores

After you have responded to the thirty statements on the previous two pages, please transfer your responses to the blanks below. This will make it easier to record and score your responses. Notice that the numbers of the statements are listed *horizontally.* Make sure that the number you assigned to each statement is transferred to the appropriate blank. Fill in a response for every item.

1. _____   2. _____   3. _____   4. _____   5. _____

6. _____   7. _____   8. _____   9. _____   10. _____

11. _____   12. _____   13. _____   14. _____   15. _____

16. _____   17. _____   18. _____   19. _____   20. _____

21. _____   22. _____   23. _____   24. _____   25. _____

26. _____   27. _____   28. _____   29. _____   30. _____

Further Instructions

The above scores are for (name of person): _____

    Please bring this form with you to the workshop (seminar or class) or return this form to:

_____

_____

_____

_____

ISBN: 0-7879-4427-0

Printed in the United States of America.

Jossey-Bass Publishers
350 Sansome Street
San Francisco, California 94104
(888) 378-2537
Fax (800) 605-2665

www.josseybass.com

Printing 10 9 8 7 6 5 4 3 2 1

This instrument is printed on acid-free, recycled stock that meets or exceeds the minimum GPO and EPA requirements for recycled paper.

EXPERIENTIAL EXERCISES FROM THE PFEIFFER ANNUAL: TRAINING

1. Sweet Tooth: Bonding Strangers into a Team

R. A. Black, *The 2002 Annual: Volume 1, Training* © 2002 Jossey-Bass/Pfeiffer, a Wiley Imprint

EXPERIENTIAL EXERCISES FROM THE PFEIFFER ANNUAL: TRAINING

2. Interrogatories: Identifying Issues and Needs

C. Holton, *The 2002 Annual: Volume 1, Training* © 2002 Jossey-Bass/Pfeiffer, a Wiley Imprint

EXPERIENTIAL EXERCISES FROM THE PFEIFFER ANNUAL: TRAINING

3. Decode: Working with Different Instructions

S. Thiagarajan, *The 2003 Annual: Volume 1, Training* © 2003 Jossey-Bass/Pfeiffer, a Wiley Imprint

EXPERIENTIAL EXERCISES FROM THE PFEIFFER ANNUAL: TRAINING

4. Choices: Learning Effective Conflict Management Strategies

C. Kormanski, Sr. and C. Kormanski, Jr., *The 2003 Annual: Volume 1, Training* © 2003 Jossey-Bass/Pfeiffer, a Wiley Imprint

EXPERIENTIAL EXERCISES FROM THE PFEIFFER ANNUAL: TRAINING

5. Internal/External Motivators: Encouraging Creativity

E. A. Smith, *The 2003 Annual: Volume 1, Training* © 2003 Jossey-Bass/Pfeiffer, a Wiley Imprint

EXPERIENTIAL EXERCISES FROM THE PFEIFFER ANNUAL: TRAINING

6. Quick Hitter: Fostering the Creative Spirit

M. G. Hernandez and T. T. Coronas, *The 2003 Annual: Volume 1, Training* © 2003 Jossey-Bass/Pfeiffer, a Wiley Imprint

SWEET TOOTH: BONDING STRANGERS INTO A TEAM

Process Procedure:

The general idea is just to relax, have fun, and get to know one another while completing a task. Form groups of five. All groups in the room will be competing to see which one can first complete the items below with the name of a candy bar or sweet treat. The team that completes the most items correctly first will win a prize.

1. Pee Wee . . ., baseball player.
2. Dried up cows.
3. Kids' game minus toes.
4. Not bad and more than some.
5. Explosion in the sky.
6. Polka. . . .
7. Rhymes with Bert's, dirts, hurts.
8. Happy place to drink.
9. Drowning prevention device.
10. Belongs to a mechanic from Mayberry's cousin.
11. They're not "lesses"; they're. . . .
12. Two names for a purring pet.
13. Takes 114 licks to get to the center of these.
14. Sounds like asteroids.
15. A military weapon.
16. A young flavoring.
17. Top of mountains in winter.
18. To catch fish you need to. . . .
19. Sounds like riddles and fiddles.

Source: Robert Allan Black, The 2002 Annual Volume 1, Training/© 2002 John Wiley & Sons, Inc.

Questions for discussion:
- What lessons about effective teamwork can be learned from this activity?
- What caused each subgroup to be successful?
- What might be learned about effective teamwork from what happened during this activity?
- What might be done next time to increase the chances of success?

Variation
- Have the individual subgroups create their own lists of clues for the names of candies/candy bars/sweets. Collect the lists and make a grand list using one or two from each group's contribution. Then hold a competition among the total group.

INTERROGATORIES: IDENTIFYING ISSUES AND NEEDS

Procedure:

This activity is an opportunity to discover what issues and questions people have brought to the class. The instructor will select from the topic list below. Once a topic is raised, participants should ask any questions they have related to that topic. No one is to *answer* a question at this time. The goal is to come up with as many questions as possible in the time allowed. Feel free to build on a question already asked, or to share a completely different question.

Interrogatories Starter Topic List

- Class requirements
- Coaching
- Communication
- Customers
- Instant messaging
- Job demands
- Leadership
- Management
- Meetings
- Mission
- Performance appraisal
- Personality
- Priorities
- Project priorities
- Quality
- Rules
- Service
- Social activities
- Success
- Task uncertainty
- Teamwork
- Time
- Training
- Values
- Work styles

Source: Cher Holton, The 2002 Annual: Volume 1, Training/© 2002 John Wiley & Sons, Inc.

Questions for discussion:
- How did you feel about this process?
- What common themes did you hear?
- What questions would you most like to have answered?

DECODE: WORKING WITH DIFFERENT INSTRUCTIONS

Procedure:

1. You are probably familiar with codes and cryptograms from your childhood days. In a cryptogram, each letter in the message is replaced by another letter of the alphabet. For example, LET THE GAMES BEGIN! May become this cryptogram:

YZF FOZ JUKZH CZJVQ!

In the cryptogram Y replaces L, Z replaces E, F replaces T, and so on. Notice that the same letter substitutions are used throughout this cryptogram: Every E in the sentence is replaced by a Z, and every T is replaced by an F.

Here's some information to help you solve cryptograms:

Letter Frequency

The most commonly used letters of the English language are *e, t, a, i, o, n, s, h,* and *r.*

The letters that are most commonly found at the beginning of words are *t, a, o, d,* and *w.*

The letters that are most commonly found at the end of words are *e, s, d,* and *t.*

Word Frequency

One-letter words are either *a* or *I.*

The most common two-letter words are *to, of, in, it, is, as, at, be, we, he, so, on, an, or, do, if, up, by,* and *my.*

The most common three-letter words are *the, and, are, for, not, but, had, has, was, all, any, one, man, out, you, his, her,* and *can.*

The most common four-letter words are *that, with, have, this, will, your, from, they, want, been, good, much, some,* and *very.*

2. The goal of the activity is to learn to work together more effectively in teams. Form into groups of four to seven members each. Have members briefly share their knowledge of solving cryptogram puzzles.

3. In this exercise all groups will be asked to solve the same cryptogram. If a team correctly and completely solves the cryptogram within two minutes, it will earn two hundred points. If it takes more than two minutes but fewer than three minutes, the team will earn fifty points.

4. Before working on the cryptogram, each participant will receive an Instruction Sheet with hints on how to solve cryptograms. Participants can study this sheet for two minutes only. (The sheet will be collected after two minutes.) They may not mark up the Instruction Sheet but they may take notes on an index card or a blank piece of paper. The Instruction Sheets will be taken back after two minutes.

5. At any time a group can send one of its members to ask for help from the instructor. The instructor will decode any *one* of the words in the cryptogram selected by the group member.

6. After the points are tallied, the instructor will lead class discussion.

DECODE CRYPTOGRAM

ISV'B   JZZXYH BPJB BPH SVQE

,

‗ ‗ ‗ ‗ ‗ ‗ ‗ ‗ ‗ ‗ ‗ ‗ ‗ ‗ ‗ ‗ ‗ ‗ ‗ ‗

UJE BS UCV CZ BS FSYTHBII.

‗ ‗ ‗ ‗ ‗ ‗ ‗ ‗ ‗ ‗ ‗ ‗ ‗ ‗ ‗ ‗ ‗ ‗ ‗

ZSYHBCYHZ BPH AHZB UJE BS

‗ ‗ ‗ ‗ ‗ ‗ ‗ ‗ ‗ ‗ ‗ ‗ ‗ ‗ ‗ ‗ ‗ ‗ ‗ ‗

UCV CZ BS FSSTHWJBH UCBP

‗ ‗ ‗ ‗ ‗ ‗ ‗ ‗ ‗ ‗ ‗ ‗ ‗ ‗ ‗ ‗ ‗ ‗

SBPHWZ—Z. BPCJMJWJOJV

‗ ‗ ‗ ‗ ‗ ‗ ‗—‗. ‗ ‗ ‗ ‗ ‗ ‗ ‗ ‗ ‗

Source: Sivasailam "Thiagi" Thiagarajan, *The 2003 Annual: Volume 1, Training/© 2003 John Wiley & Sons, Inc.*

CHOICES: LEARNING EFFECTIVE CONFLICT MANAGEMENT STRATEGIES

Procedure: Form teams of three.

Assume you are a group of top managers who are responsible for an organization of seven departments. Working as a team, choose an appropriate strategy to intervene in the situations below when the conflict must be managed in some way. Your choices are *withdrawal, suppression, integration, compromise,* and *authority.* Refer to the list below for some characteristics of each strategy. Write your team's choice following each situation number. Engage in discussion led by the instructor.

CHOICES: STRATEGIES AND CONTINGENCIES

Withdrawal Strategy

Use When (Advantages)
- Choosing sides is to be avoided
- Critical information is missing
- The issue is outside the group
- Others are competent and delegation is appropriate
- You are powerless

Be Aware (Disadvantages)
- Legitimate action ceases
- Direct information stops
- Failure can be perceived
- Cannot be used in a crisis

Suppression (and Diffusion) Strategy

Use When (Advantages)
- A cooling down period is needed
- The issue is unimportant
- A relationship is important

Be Aware (Disadvantages)
- The issue may intensify
- You may appear weak and ineffective

Integration Strategy

Use When (Advantages)
- Group problem solving is needed
- New alternatives are helpful
- Group commitment is required
- Promoting openness and trust

Be Aware (Disadvantages)
- Group goals must be put first
- More time is required for dialogue
- It doesn't work with rigid, dull people

Compromise Strategy

Use When (Advantages)
- Power is equal
- Resources are limited
- A win-win settlement is desired

Be Aware (Disadvantages)
- Action (a third choice) can be weakened
- Inflation is encouraged
- A third party may be needed for negotiation

Authority Strategy

Use When (Advantages)
- A deadlock persists
- Others are incompetent
- Time is limited (crisis)
- An unpopular decision must be made
- Survival of the organization is critical

Be Aware (Disadvantages)
- Emotions intensify quickly
- Dependency is promoted
- Winners and losers are created

Source: Chuck Kormanski, Sr. and Chuck Kormanski, Jr., *The 2003 Annual: Volume 1, Training/*© *2003 John Wiley & Sons, Inc.*

Situation #1

Two employees of the support staff have requested the same two-week vacation period. They are the only two trained to carry out an essential task using a complex computer software program that cannot be mastered quickly. You have encouraged others to learn this process so there is more backup for the position, but heavy workloads have prevented this from occurring.

Situation #2

A sales manager has requested a raise because there are now two salespeople on commission earning higher salaries. The work performance of this individual currently does not merit a raise of the amount requested, mostly due to the person turning in critical reports late and missing a number of days of work. The person's sales group is one of the highest rated in the organization, but this may be the result of having superior individuals assigned to the team, rather than to the effectiveness of the manager.

Situation #3

It has become obvious that the copy machine located in a customer service area is being used for a variety of personal purposes, including reproducing obscene jokes. A few copies have sometimes been found lying on or near the machine at the close of the business day. You have mentioned the matter briefly in the organization's employee newsletter, but recently you have noticed an increase in the activity. Most of the office staff seems to be involved.

Situation #4

Three complaints have filtered upward to you from long-term employees concerning a newly hired individual. This person has a pierced nose and a visible tattoo. The work performance of the individual is adequate and the person does not have to see customers; however, the employees who have complained allege that the professional appearance of the office area has been compromised.

Situation #5

The organization has a flex-time schedule format that requires all employees to work the core hours of 10 a.m. to 3 p.m., Monday through Friday. Two department managers have complained that another department does not always maintain that policy. The manager of the department in question has responded by citing recent layoffs and additional work responsibilities as reasons for making exceptions to policy.

Situation #6

As a result of a recent downsizing, an office in a coveted location is now available. Three individuals have made a request to the department manager for the office. The manager has recommended that the office be given to one of the three. This individual has the highest performance rating, but was aided in obtaining employment with the company by the department manager, who is a good friend of the person's family. Colleagues prefer not to work with this individual, as there is seldom any evidence of teamwork.

Situation #7

Two department managers have requested a budget increase in the areas of travel and computer equipment. Each asks that your group support this request. The CEO, not your group, will make the final decision. You are aware that increasing funds for one department will result in a decrease for others, as the total budget figures for all of these categories are set.

Situation #8

Few of the management staff attended the Fourth of July picnic held at a department manager's country home last year. This particular manager, who has been a loyal team player for the past twenty-one years, has indicated that he/she plans to host the event again this year. Many of you have personally found the event to be boring, with little to do but talk and eat. Already a few of the other managers have suggested that the event be held at a different location with a new format or else be cancelled.

Situation #9

It has come to your attention that a manager and a subordinate in the same department are having a romantic affair openly in the building. Both are married to other people. They have been taking extended lunch periods, yet both remain beyond quitting time to complete their work. Colleagues have begun to complain that neither is readily available mid-day and that they do not return messages in a timely manner.

Situation #10

Two loyal department managers are concerned that a newly hired manager who is wheelchair-bound has been given too much in the way of accommodations beyond what is required by the Americans with Disabilities Act. They have requested similar changes to make their own work lives easier. Specifically, they cite office size and location on the building's main floor as points of contention.

INTERNAL/EXTERNAL MOTIVATORS: ENCOURAGING CREATIVITY

Procedure:

1. This interactive, experience-based activity is designed to increase participants' awareness of creativity and creative processes. Begin by thinking of a
   job that you now hold or have held. Then complete Questions 1 and 2 from
   the Internal/External Motivators Questionnaire (see below).
2. Form into groups. Share your questionnaire results and make a list of responses to Question 1.
3. Discuss and compare rankings of major work activities listed for Question
   2. Make a list with at least two responses from each participant.
4. Individually record your answers to Questions 3 and 4 below. Then share
   your answers and again list member responses within your group.
5. Individually, compare your responses to Questions 1 and 2 with your responses to Questions 3 and 4. Then answer Question 5. Again, share with
   the group and make a group list of answers to Question 5 for the recorder,
   who is to record these answers on the flip chart. (Ten minutes.)

Questions for Discussion:

- What was the most important part of this activity for you?
- What have you learned about motivation?
- What impact will having done this activity have for you back in the work-
  place?
- How will what you have learned change your leadership style or future par-
  ticipation in a group?
- What will you do differently based on what you have learned?

INTRINSIC/EXTRINSIC MOTIVATORS QUESTIONNAIRE

1. How could you do your job in a more creative manner? List some ways in
   the space below:

2. List four or five major work activities or jobs you perform on a regular basis
   in the left-hand boxes on the chart below. Use a seven-point scale that
   ranges from 1 (low) to 7 (high) to rate each work activity on three separate
   dimensions: (a) level of difficulty, (b) potential to motivate you, and (c) opportunity to add value to the organization.

Source: Elizabeth A. Smith, *The 2003 Annual: Volume 1, Training/*© 2003 John
Wiley & Sons, Inc.

Major Work Activity	Level of Difficulty	Potential to Motivate	Opportunity to Add Value
1.			
2.			
3.			
4.			
5.			

3. List five motivators or types of rewards that would encourage you to do your job in a more creative manner.

4. List three motivators or types of rewards from Question 3 above that you believe would *definitely increase your creativity*. Indicate whether these motivators are realistic or unrealistic in terms of your job or work setting. Indicate whether each is intrinsic or extrinsic.

Motivators	Realistic/ Unrealistic	Intrinsic	Extrinsic
1.			
2.			
3.			

5. List three types of work activities you like to perform and the motivators or rewards that would stimulate and reinforce your creativity.

Work Activity	Rewards That Reinforce Creativity
1.	
2.	
3.	

QUICK HITTER: FOSTERING THE CREATIVE SPIRIT

Part A Procedure:

1. Write the Roman numeral nine (IX) on a sheet of paper.
2. Add one line to make six. After you have one response, try for others.

Questions for discussion:

- What does solving this puzzle show us about seeing things differently?
- Why don't some people consider alternatives easily?
- What skills or behaviors would be useful for us to develop our ability to see different points of view?

Part B Procedure:

1. Rent the video or DVD of "Patch Adams." In this video Patch (Robin Williams) is studying to become a doctor, but he does not look, act, or think like a traditional doctor. For Patch, humor is the best medicine. He is always willing to do unusual things to make his patients laugh. Scenes from this video can be revealing to an OB class.
2. Show the first Patch Adams scene (five minutes)—this is in the psychiatric hospital where Patch has admitted himself after a failed suicide attempt. He meets Arthur in the hospital. Arthur is obsessed with showing people four fingers of his hand and asking them: "How many fingers can you see?" Everybody says four. The scene shows Patch visiting Arthur to find out the solution. Arthur's answer is: "If you only focus on the problem, you will never see the solution. Look further. You have to see what other people do not see."
3. Engage the class in discussion of these questions and more:
   - How does this film clip relate to Part A of this exercise?
   - What restricts our abilities to look beyond what we see?
   - How can we achieve the goal of seeing what others do not see?
4. Show the second Patch Adams scene (five minutes)—this is when Patch has left the hospital and is studying medicine. Patch and his new friend Truman are having breakfast. Truman is reflecting on the human mind and on the changing of behavioral patterns (the adoption of programmed answers) as a person grows older. Patch proposes to carry out the Hello Experiment. The objective of the experiment is "to change the programmed answer by changing the usual parameters."
5. Engage the class in discussion of these questions and more:
   - What is a programmed answer?
   - What is the link between our programmed answers and our abilities to exhibit creativity?
   - How can we "deprogram" ourselves?
6. Summarize the session with a wrap-up discussion of creativity, including barriers and ways to encourage it.

Source: Mila Gascó Hernández and Teresa Torres Coronas, *The 2003 Annual: Volume 1, Training/© 2003 John Wiley & Sons, Inc.*

CASES FOR CRITICAL THINKING

CASE 1
Panera Bread Company

Developed by Carol P. Harvey, Assumption College, and
John R. Schermerhorn, Jr., Ohio University

Panera Bread is in the business of satisfying customers
with fresh baked breads, gourmet soups, and efficient
service. The relatively new franchise has surpassed
all expectations for success. But how did a startup
food company get so big, so fast? By watching and carefully timing market trends.

Company History

Despite its abundance of restaurants, Panera Bread is a
relatively new company, having only been known as such
since 1997. Its roots go back to 1981, when Louis Kane
and Ron Shaich founded Au Bon Pain Company Inc., having merged Kane's three existing Au Bon Pain stores
with Shaich's Cookie Jar store. The chain of French-style
bakeries offered baguettes, coffee, and sandwiches
served on either French bread or croissants. It performed quite well on the East Coast, becoming the dominant operator in the bakery-café category, and it even
expanded internationally.

As part of its expansion, in 1993 Au Bon Pain purchased the Saint Louis Bread Company, a Missouri-based
chain of about 20 bakery-cafés. To experiment with a different restaurant format and new menu offerings, the
company renovated the Saint Louis Bread Company
stores and reimagined their identity, naming them Panera
Bread. Clearly, something worked: from 1993 to 1997 the
average unit volumes at these stores increased by 75%.

Executives at Au Bon Pain saw the potential for this
new restaurant concept and dedicated themselves—and
all of the company's financial resources—to building this
brand. In 1999 the company sold all of its business units
except for the Panera-concept stores. The reorganized
company was, not surprisingly, christened Panera Bread.

Since then the new brand has sought to distinguish
itself in the soup-and-sandwich restaurant category. Its
offerings have grown to include not only a variety of
soups and sandwiches, but also soufflès, salads, panini,
and a selection of pastries and sweets. Most of the menu
offerings somehow pay homage to the company name
and heritage—bread. Panera takes great pride in noting
that its loaves are hand made and baked fresh daily. To
conserve valuable real estate in the retail outlets, as well
as to cut the necessary training for new employees, many
bread doughs are manufactured off-site at one of the
company's 17 manufacturing plants. The dough is then

delivered by truck—over as many as 9.7 million miles per year—daily to the stores for shaping and baking.

At this point, there are nearly 950 Panera Bread outlets in 37 states. Franchise stores outnumber company-owned outlets approximately two to one.

Modern Tastes, Modern Trends

Panera's success has come partly from its ability to predict long-term trends and orient the company toward innovating to fulfill consumers. Its self-perception as a purveyor of artisan bread well predated the current national trend for fresh bread and the explosion of artisan bakeries throughout metropolitan America. In addition, proactively responding to unease in the marketplace about the role of trans fats in a healthy diet, Panera voluntarily removed trans fats from its menu. "Panera recognized that trans fat was a growing concern to our customers and the medical community. Therefore we made it a priority to eliminate it from our menu," said Tom Gumpel, Director of Bakery Development for Panera Bread.

According to Ron Shaich, chairman and CEO of Panera, "Real success never comes by simply responding to the day-to-day pressures; in fact, most of that is simply noise. The key to leading an organization is understanding the long-term trends at play and getting the organization ready to respond to it.

Value Creation and Customer Satisfaction

As a retail bakery-café, Panera Bread has taken the concept of "quick casual" dining one step further than its competition. Each loca-

tion features an earth-toned decor with a fireplace, comfortable couches, and current newspapers available to customers. Patrons order and pay at the counter and then wait for their names to be called to pick up their food. The menu features a wide variety of made-to-order sandwiches prepared with freshly baked artisan breads, desserts, crisp salads, homemade soups, and gourmet beverages.

Unlike the paper and plastic fast-food experience, here food is served in baskets or in china plates and cups, and customers eat with metal silverware. Diners are encouraged to linger or to read. At Panera Bread locations, book club and business meetings are welcomed. There is also a separate bakery counter where customers can purchase breads and pastries to take home. However, Ron Shaich says that Panera bakery-cafés "aren't just about the atmosphere. It isn't just about the food. It is the totality of it. This is where you go everyday to catch your breath and chill out."

Panera caught sight of the demand for free Wi-Fi early on, and now more than 700 of its stores offer customers a complimentary access. According to spokesperson Julie Somers, the decision to offer Wi-Fi began as a way to separate Panera from the competition and to exemplify the company's welcoming atmosphere.

"We are the kind of environment where all customers are welcome to hang out," Somers said. "They can get a quick bite or a cup of coffee, read the paper or use a computer, and stay as long as they like. And in the course of staying, people may have a cappuccino and a pastry or a soup." She went on to note that the chief corporate benefit

to offering Wi-Fi is that wireless customers tend to help fill out the slow time between main meal segments.

Executive Vice-President Neal Yanofsky concurred. "We just think it's one more reason to come visit our cafés," he said. And wireless users' tendency to linger is just fine with him. "It leads to food purchases," he concluded.

Staffing/Human Capital

Although Panera has an aggressive growth strategy that requires the organization to open many stores each year, becoming a franchise owner requires considerable financial investment and business experience. In addition to a net worth of $7.5 million and liquid assets of $3 million, each applicant must also have worked as a multi-unit restaurant operator. Unlike most franchises Panera does not allow an owner to open in only one location. Instead the owner must open 15 or more bakery-cafés in six years within a defined geographical area.

Managers and assistant managers receive competitive salaries and benefits and have the potential of a quarterly bonus. Job requirements vary by location but include outstanding interpersonal skills, formal education, and work experience in the food service industry. Under these full-time employees work many associates who perform counter service and food preparation duties. These workers, who are the customers' primary contact with Panera Bread, are usually paid slightly above the minimum wage, receive no tips, and preferably have some restaurant or fast food experience. Unless they are full-time employees, they do not receive benefits.

Profits Rise along with the Dough

Panera's attention to the monitoring of trends has paid off handsomely.[1] The company's stock has grown to create more than $1 billion in shareholder value. Since its founding, *Business Week* recognized Panera as one of its "100 Hot Growth Companies." The organization's future will depend on the company's ability to meet the needs of its stakeholders by continuing to create a satisfying customer experience, being responsive to changing business environments, and adapting to an increasingly diverse workforce.

Review Questions

1. What do you describe as Panera's purpose, mission, and strategy? Use the firm's Web site for further information and assistance.
2. How well has Ron Shaich utilized the open systems model of organizations in moving Panera Bread Company forward in its competitive environment?
3. What are the challenges to the management process posed by Panera's fast-paced growth? What problems do you see Shaich having to resolve to continue his record of success with the firm?
4. Visit a Panera store near you, or a competitor. Based on your customer experience, what are the strengths and weaknesses of this business going forward? ∎

CASE 1A
Management Training Dilemma

Developed by John R. Schermerhorn, Jr., Ohio University

Shane Alexander is the personnel director of the Central State Medical Center. One of her responsibilities is to oversee the hospital's supervisory training programs. Recently Shane attended a professional conference where a special "packaged" training program was advertised for sale. The package includes a set of videotaped lectures by a distinguished management consultant plus a workbook containing readings, exercises, cases, tests, and other instructional aids. The subjects covered in the program include motivation, group dynamics, communication skills, leadership effectiveness, performance appraisal, and the management of planned change.

In the past Shane felt that the hospital had not lived up to its supervisory training goals. One of the reasons for this was the high cost of hiring external consultants to do the actual instruction. This packaged program was designed, presumably, so that persons from within the hospital could act as session coordinators. The structure of the program provided through the videotapes and workbook agenda was supposed to substitute for a consultant's expertise. Because of this, Shane felt that use of the packaged program could substantially improve supervisory training in the hospital.

The cost of the program was $3,500 for an initial purchase of the videotapes plus 50 workbooks. Additional workbooks were then available at $8 per copy. Before purchasing the program, Shane needed the approval of the senior administrative staff.

At the next staff meeting Shane proposed purchasing the training program. She was surprised at the response. The hospital president was noncommittal; the vice-president was openly hostile; and the three associate administrators were varied in their enthusiasm. It was the vice-president's opinion that dominated the discussion. He argued that to invest in such a program on the assumption that it would lead to improved supervisory practices was unwise. "This is especially true in respect to the proposed program," he said. "How could such a package possibly substitute for the training skills of an expert consultant?"

Shane argued her case and was left with the following challenge. The administrators would allow $1,000 to be spent to rent the program with 30 workbooks. It would be up to Shane to demonstrate through a trial program that an eventual purchase would be worth while.

There were 160 supervisors in the hospital. The program was designed to be delivered in eight $2\frac{1}{2}$ hour sessions. It was preferred to schedule one session per week, with no more than 15 participants per session.

Shane knew that she would have to present very strong evidence to gain administrative support for the continued use of the program. Given the opportunity, she decided to implement a trial program in such a way that conclusive evidence on the value of the packaged training would be forthcoming.

Review Questions

1. If you were Shane, what type of research design would you use to test this program? Why?

2. How would the design actually be implemented in this hospital setting?
3. What would be your research hypothesis? What variables would you need to measure to provide data that could test this hypothesis? How would you gather these data?
4. Do you think the administrator's request for "proof before purchase" was reasonable? Why or why not? ■

CASE 2
Crossing Borders

Developed by Bernardo M. Ferdman, Alliant International University, and Plácida I. Gallegos, Organizational Constultant, San Diego, CA and The Kaleel Jamison Consulting Group, Inc.

This case study is based on the experiences of Angelica Garza, a woman of Mexican American heritage who worked for 10 years in the human resource (HR) function of a multinational medical products company. This maquiladora plant was in Tijuana, Baja California, a large city directly across the U.S.–Mexican border from San Diego, California. Maquiladoras are manufacturing plants owned by foreign capital in the regions of Mexico bordering the United States, which have been set up to take advantage of favorable laws and cheap labor.

The Tijuana plant was one of a number of operations for USMed. Six other U.S. facilities were located in the Northeast, the Midwest, and Florida. In addition to her work in the manufacturing plant, where Angelica spent most of her time, she was also responsible for human resources for the small, primarily administrative facility in Chula Vista, on the U.S. side of the border. Eventually, there were 34 Americans—12 on the Mexican side and 22 on the U.S. side—and approximately 1100 Mexican nationals on the payroll.

There was little connection between Angelica and the HR managers at the other USMed plants, either in the United States or abroad. Angelica reported that USMed had no overall policy or strategy for deal-

ing with human resources generally and diversity specifically.

The transition in Mexico was not a smooth one for Angelica. Nothing in her U.S. experience had prepared her for what she encountered in Mexico. Her Anglo colleagues had only vague knowledge about the operation in Tijuana, and they had little interest in understanding or relating to the Mexican workforce. Given her Hispanic upbringing in the United States, Angelica had some understanding of the culture and values of the Mexican employees. Her Spanish-speaking skills also enabled her to understand and relate to the workers. Although she had some understanding of the workers, however, the assumption on the part of U.S. management that her knowl-

edge and connection to the Mexican workers was seamless was false. There were many cultural differences between her and the Mexican employees that the Anglo managers were unaware of:

In retrospect now, I can look back and [I'm] just amazed at what I was involved in at the time. I mean, I didn't have a clue. One of the things you find is that [people assume that Mexican Americans are most suited to work with Mexicans.] I guess just because I was of Mexican-American descent, it was like I would just know how to mingle with this total[ly] different culture.

As a result, Angelica experienced a great deal of frustration and misunderstanding. Her attempts to intercede between the management in Mexico and that in the United States often led to her disenfranchisement from her American colleagues, who did not value or appreciate her ideas or suggestions. Further complicating her experience in Mexico was the mixed reactions she engendered from the Mexican nationals. Because of her American status, Angelica was misunderstood and sometimes resented by Mexican employees and, at the same time, she lacked support from the U.S. organization.

I found that the Mexican women who were there [two women in accounting who were Mexican nationals, and had been there for about 5 years] were resentful. My saving grace was that I was an American because the Mexican women there looked at the Americans as being like a step above or whatever. And there was resentment of me coming in and taking away jobs. They perceived it as: They weren't doing a good job and we were coming in and taking responsibilities away from them. So me being a woman coming in, I was scrutinized by the two women who had been there. I couldn't get information from them. They gave me the least information or help they could and would be critical of anything I did once I took it from them.

Source: This is an abridged version of a case appearing in the Field Guide of E. E. Kossek and S. Cobel, *Managing Diversity: Human Resource Strategies for Transforming the Workplace* (Oxford, England: Blackwell, 1996).

You know, I look back and it was probably pretty frightening for them [the Mexican nationals] too, because we all came in and we knew what we had to do; [USMed was] very straightforward about, you know, you fail to do this and you can lose your job and you've got to do that or you could lose your job, so getting them to follow these protocols and these operating procedures was very difficult. Change is difficult anyway, but getting them to follow some of those rules [was] real challenging.

Angelica understood the employees' approach to the work as stemming from local conditions and from Mexican cultural styles. The great expansion of maquiladoras brought a number of changes, including new expectations and different cultural styles on the part of the managers. At first, potential employees were unfamiliar with these new expectations; the employers needed to train the workers if they were to meet these expectations. This was happening in the context of the meeting of two cultures. In her role, Angelica saw herself as more American than Mexican, yet also as different from her Anglo colleagues. She saw herself as bringing American training, expectations, and styles:

Well, see I'm American. I mean I was an American manager, and that's where I was coming from. But I was forced to come up with systems that would eliminate future misunderstandings or problems. Being a Mexican American I thought it would be easier working in Mexico because I had some exposure to the culture, but it was a real culture shock for me. It was a different group of people socioeconomically. A lot of those people came from ranchitos, [from] out in the sticks, where there were no restrooms or showers. There weren't infrastructures in Tijuana at all. It's pretty

good now compared to what it was 10 years ago. We used to go to work through people's backyards and dirt roads. Dead dogs were marks for how to get there! And I think now, that if you go to Tijuana now—it's been 10 years of maquiladoras there—you can find more qualified Mexican managers or supervisors or clerical people. [Finding] bilingual secretaries and engineers [was like] getting needles in a haystack back then.

I found myself being the only woman in an old-boy-network environment, and that was pretty tough. And it was also tough working in the Mexican environment. Because the Mexican men that I would deal with would look down on me because I was a woman. Again, my saving grace was because I was an American woman. If I had been a Mexican national woman, then I would have really had probably more problems. [For example] I had to work a lot, real close with the Mexican accounting manager, who was a male. And he would come to me and tell me how I had screwed up my numbers, or you didn't do this right, and stuff like that. I would go over the numbers and it was just a difference in terms of how things were calculated. Specifically, calculating an annual salary. He would do it by using 365 days, when I would do it by 52 weeks and you'd take your daily rate, it was different, it would always be off a little bit. But, I reported them the way the Americans would be expecting to see them.

Review Questions

1. What competencies are appropriate to ensure greater effectiveness of U.S. employees operating in a maquiladora or other non-U.S. organization?
2. What are some of the costs of not understanding diversity? What could the organization have gained by approaching the plant with greater cultural understanding?
3. From the HR perspective, what were the unique challenges that Angelica faced at various points in her work for USMed?
4. Angelica worked in a plant outside the United States. What do her experiences and perspectives tell us that applies to domestic operations? ■

CASE 3
SAS Institute
....

Founded in 1976 by Dr. James Goodnight and Dr. John Sall, both professors at North Carolina State University, SAS Institute, Inc. provides business intelligence (BI) software and services at more than 40,000 customer sites worldwide, including 90 percent of the *Fortune* 500 companies. SAS, which stands for "statistical analysis software," is headquartered in Cary, North Carolina. It is the world's largest privately held software company, with more than 100 offices worldwide and approximately 10,000 employees.[1]

Fast Company describes the SAS Institute as a modern company that is like a kingdom in a fairy-tale land: "Although this company is thoroughly modern (endowed with advanced computers, the best child care, art on almost every wall, and athletic facilities that would make an NBA trainer drool), there is something fairy-tale-like about the place. The inhabitants are happy, productive, well rounded—in short, content in a way that's almost unheard-of today. They are loyal to the kingdom and to its king, who in turn is the model of a benevolent leader. The king—almost unbelievably—goes by the name Goodnight."

SAS is strongly committed to its employees. The company strives to hire talented people and goes to extraordinary lengths to keep their employees satisfied. James Goodnight, the CEO of SAS, says: "We've made a conscious effort to ensure that we're hiring and keeping the right talent to improve our products and better serve our customers. To attract and retain that talent, it's essential that we maintain our high standards in regards to employee relations."

SAS has been widely recognized for its work-life programs and its emphasis on employee satisfaction. The company's various honors include being recognized by *Working Mothers* magazine as one of "100 Best Companies for Working Mothers" and by *Fortune* magazine as one of the "100 Best Companies to Work for in America." The *Working Mothers* recognition has been received 13 times, and the *Fortune* recognition has occurred for six consecutive years.

SAS pays its employees competitively, targeted at the average for the software industry. It does not provide stock options like other companies in the industry. Instead of relying on high salaries and stock options to attract and retain workers

like many software companies do, SAS takes a very different approach. It focuses on providing meaningful and challenging work, and it encourages teamwork. SAS also provides a host of benefits that appeal to employees and help keep them satisfied. As one employee who took a 10 percent pay cut to join SAS said: "It's better to be happy than to have a little more money."

Employees are given the freedom, flexibility, responsibility, and resources to do their jobs, and they are also held accountable for results. Managers know what employees are doing and they work alongside them, writing computer code. "The company employs very few external contractors and very few part-time staff, so there is a strong sense of teamwork throughout the organization." SAS employees are clearly involved in their work. One employee, Kathy Passarella, notes: "When you walk down the halls here, it's rare that you hear people talking about anything but work."

The various employee benefits that SAS provides include an employee fitness and recreation center, an employee laundry service, a heavily subsidized employee cafeteria, live piano music in the employee cafeteria, subsidized on-site child care, and a free health center. All of these benefits are geared toward employees having a better work experience or a better balance between their work lives and their personal lives. The company's commitment to work-life balance is evident in SAS's 35-hour work week, which clearly recognizes the importance of employees' personal lives.

In reflecting on the company's generous benefits package, David Russo, SAS's head of human resources, says: "To some people, this looks like the Good Ship Lollipop, floating down the stream. It's not. It's part of a soundly

designed strategy." That strategy is intended "to make it impossible for people not to do their work."

While SAS goes to extraordinary lengths to ensure that employees are satisfied, the company expects and demands productivity and performance results in return. The owners of SAS want employees to be satisfied because they believe satisfied employees will be excellent performers and will provide exceptional service to the company's customers. "If you treat employees as if they make a difference to the company, they will make a difference to the company. . . . Satisfied employees create satisfied customers." This viewpoint might be described as a form of enlightened realism and enlightened self-interest on the part of the company. Satisfied employees make for satisfied customers, and satisfied customers make for an ongoing stream of revenue and profit for SAS.

SAS's leaders recognize both the benefits and costs associated with keeping employees satisfied. One of the most significant benefits for SAS is a very low annual turnover rate, which is less than 4 percent, as compared to approximately 25 percent for the industry as a whole. This low turnover saves the company about $70 million annually in employee replacement costs. On the cost side, of course, is the company's monetary outlay for the various programs. David Russo argues that the employee replacement cost saving more than pays for the company's generous benefits. "That's the beauty of it," says Russo. "There's no way I could spend all the money we save."

Perhaps of more concern on the "cost side" is the potential for employees failing to perform. In commenting on the company's performance expectations for employees, Goodnight says: "I like to be around happy people, but if they don't get that next release out, they're not going to be very happy." Pondering the likelihood that SAS employees would take advantage of the company's relaxed atmosphere, John Sall, co-owner of SAS, observes: "I can't imagine that playing Ping-Pong would be more interesting than work." David Russo adds some additional perspective: "If you're out sick for six months, you'll get cards and flowers, and people will come to cook dinner for you. If you're out sick for six Mondays in a row, you'll get fired. We expect adult behavior."

Clearly, human resource management at SAS is a two-way street. SAS has an HR strategy and related policies and practices that attract, motivate, and retain highly capable workers who make significant contributions to the ongoing success of the company. Goodnight and the other SAS leaders expect nothing less than superior performance from their employees, and they continue

to get it. The employees are loyal and committed to the company, and they are productive—so loyal, committed, and productive, in fact, that only a small percentage of employees ever leave once they have been hired at SAS.

Having quality employees who want to stay—isn't this the human resources goal that should challenge all companies?

Review Questions

1. What is the basic management philosophy that governs employee relationship management at SAS Institute?
2. How do the SAS human resources strategy, policies, and practices influence employees' emotions, attitudes, and job satisfaction?
3. What lessons can other employers learn from the SAS experience that would be transferable to other types of work settings, jobs, and employee characteristics? ■

it the second-largest supplier in North America. Financially, the company suffered heavily because of price erosions caused by Far East competition. Unlike all its competitors, the company resisted moving its manufacturing operations offshore. But the company accumulated losses to a point of bankruptcy. Finally MagRec entered a major international joint venture and received many new sales orders. Things looked good again. But . . .

Pat's Dilemma

When Fred Marsh promoted me to Sales Manager, I was in seventh heaven. Now, six months later, I feel I am in hell. This is the first time in my life that I am really on my own. I have been working with other people all my life. I tried my best and what I could not solve, I took upstairs. Now it's different because I am the boss (or am I?). Fred has taught me a lot. He was my mentor and gave me this job when he became vice president. I have always respected him and listened to his judgment. Now thinking back I wonder whether I should have listened to him at all on this problem.

It started one late Friday evening. I had planned to call my West Coast customer, Partco, to discuss certain contract clauses. I wanted to nail this one fast (Partco had just been acquired by Volks, Inc.). Partco was an old customer in fact, through good and bad it had always stayed with us. It was also a *major* customer. I was about to call Partco when Dinah Coates walked in clutching a file. I had worked with Dinah for three years. She was good. I knew that my call to Partco would have to wait. Dinah had been cleaning out old files and came across a report about design and manufacturing defects in Partco heads. The report had been written

---

CASE 4
MAGREC, Inc.
....

Developed by Mary McGarry, Empire State College and Barry R. Armandi, SUNY-Old Westbury

Background

MagRec, Incorporated was started by Mr. Leed, a brilliant engineer (he has several engineering patents) who was a group manager at Fairchild Republic. The company's product was magnetic recording heads, a crucial device used for reading, writing, and erasing data on tapes and disks.

Like any other startup, MagRec had a humble beginning. It struggled during the early years, facing cash-flow and technical problems. After a slow start, it grew rapidly and gained 35 percent of the tape head market, making

nine years ago. The cover memo read as follows:

To: Ken Smith, Director of Marketing
From: Rich Grillo, V.P. Operations
Sub: Partco Head Schedule

This is to inform you that due to pole-depth problems in design, the Partco heads (all 514 in test) have failed. They can't reliably meet the reading requirements. The problem is basically a design error in calculations. It can be corrected. However, the fix will take at least six months. Meanwhile Ron Scott in production informs me that the entire 5,000 heads (the year's production) have already been pole-slotted, thus they face the same problem.

Ken, I don't have to tell you how serious this is, but how can we OK and ship them to Partco knowing that they'll cause read error problems in the field? My engineering and manufacturing people realize this is the number one priority. By pushing the Systems Tech job back we will be back on track in less than six months. In the interim I can modify Global Widgets heads. This will enable us to at least continue shipping some product to Partco. As a possible alternate I would like to get six Partco drives. Michaels and his team feel that with quick and easy changes in the drives tape path they can get the head to work. If this is true we should be back on track within six to eight weeks.

A separate section of the report reads as follows:

Confidential
(Notes from meeting with Don Updyke and Rich Grillo)

Solution to Partco heads problem
All Partco heads can be reworked (.8 hrs. ea.—cost insignificant) to solve Partco's read problems by grinding an extra three-thousandths of an inch off the top of the head. This will reduce the over-all pole depth to a point where no read errors occur. The heads will fully meet specifications in all respects except one, namely life. Don estimates that due to the reduced chrome layer (used for wear) the heads' useful life will be 2500 hours instead of 6000 hours of actual usage.

Our experience is that no customer keeps accurate records to tell actual usage and life. Moreover, the cost is removed since Partco sells drives to MegaComputer, who sells systems to end-users. The user at the site hardly knows or rarely complains about extra costs such as the replacement of a head 12 to 18 months down the line instead of the normal 2 years. Besides, the service technicians always innovatively believe in and offer plausible explanations—such as the temperature must be higher than average—or they really must be using the computer a lot.

I have directed that the heads be reworked and shipped to Partco. I also instructed John to tell Partco that due to inclement weather this week's shipment will be combined with next week's shipment.

Dinah was flabbergasted. The company planned to sell products deliberately that it knew would not meet life requirements, she said, "risking our reputation as a quality supplier. Partco and others buy our heads thinking they are the best. Didn't we commit fraud through outright misrepresentation?"

Dinah insisted I had to do something. I told her I would look into the matter and get back to her by the end of next week.

Over the weekend I kept thinking about the Partco issue. We had no customer complaints. Partco had always been extremely pleased with our products and technical support. In fact, we were their sole suppliers. MegaComputer had us placed on the preferred, approved ship to stock, vendors list. It was a fact that other vendors were judged against our standards. MegaComputer's Quality Control never saw our product or checked it.

Monday morning I showed the report to Fred. He immediately recollected it and began to explain the situation to me.

MagRec had been under tremendous pressure and was growing rapidly at the time. "That year we had moved into a new 50,000 sq. ft. building and went from 50 or 60 employees to over 300. Our sales were increasing dramatically." Fred was heading Purchasing at the time and every week the requirements for raw materials would change. "We'd started using B.O.A.s (Broad Order Agreements, used as annual purchasing contracts) guaranteeing us the right to increase our numbers by 100 percent each quarter. The goal was to maintain the numbers. If we had lost Partco then, it could have had a domino effect and we could have ended up having no customers left to worry about."

Fred went on to explain that it had only been a short-term problem that was corrected within the year and no one ever knew it existed. He told me to forget it and to move the file into the back storage room. I conceded. I thought of all the possible hassles. The thing was ancient history anyway. Why should I be concerned about it? I wasn't even here when it happened.

The next Friday Dinah asked me what I had found out. I told her Fred's feelings on the matter and that I felt he had some pretty good arguments regarding the matter. Dinah became angry. She said I had changed since my promotion and that I was just as guilty as the crooks who'd cheated the customers by selling low-life heads as long-life heads. I told her to calm down. The decision was made years ago. No one got hurt and the heads weren't defective. They weren't causing any errors.

I felt bad but figured there wasn't much to do. The matter was closed as far as I was concerned, so I returned to my afternoon chores. Little was I to know the matter was not really closed.

That night Fred called me at 10:00. He wanted me to come over to the office right away. I quickly changed, wondering what the emergency was. I walked into Fred's office. The coffee was going. Charlie (Personnel Manager) was there. Rich Grillo (V.P. Operations) was sitting on the far side of Fred's conference table. I instinctively headed there for that was the designated smoking corner.

Ken (Director of Marketing) arrived 15 minutes later. We settled in. Fred began the meeting by thanking everyone for coming. He then told them about the discovery of the Partco file and filled them in on the background. The problem now was that Dinah had called Partco and gotten through to their new vice president, Tim Rand. Rand had called Fred at 8 P.M. at home and said he was personally taking the Red Eye to find out what this was all about. He would be here in the morning.

We spent a grueling night followed by an extremely tense few weeks. Partco had a team of people going through our tests, quality control, and manufacturing records. Our production slipped, and overall morale was affected.

Mr. Leed personally spent a week in California assuring Partco that this would never happen again. Though we weathered the storm, we had certain losses. We were never to be Partco's sole source again. We still retained 60 percent of

their business but had to agree to lower prices. The price reduction had a severe impact. Although Partco never disclosed to anyone what the issues were (since both companies had blanket nondisclosure agreements), word got around that Partco was paying a lower price. We were unable to explain to our other customers why Partco was paying this amount. Actually I felt the price word got out through Joe Byrne (an engineer who came to Partco from Systems Tech and told his colleagues back at Systems Tech that Partco really knew how to negotiate prices down). He was unaware, however, of the real issues. Faced with customers who perceived they were being treated inequitably, we experienced problems. Lowering prices meant incurring losses; not lowering them meant losing customers. The next two financial quarters saw sales dollars decline by 40 percent. As the sales manager, I felt pretty rotten presenting my figures to Fred.

With regard to Dinah, I now faced a monumental problem. The internal feeling was she should be avoided at all costs. Because of price erosions, we faced cutbacks. Employees blamed her for production layoffs. The internal friction kept mounting. Dinah's ability to interface effectively with her colleagues and other departments plummeted to a point where normal functioning was impossible.

Fred called me into his office two months after the Partco episode and suggested that I fire Dinah. He told me that he was worried about results. Although he had nothing personally against her, he felt that she must go because she was seriously affecting my department's overall performance. I defended Dinah by stating that the Partco matter would blow over and given time I could smooth things out. I

pointed out Dinah's accomplishments and stated I really wanted her to stay. Fred dropped the issue, but my problem persisted.

Things went from bad to worse. Finally, I decided to try to solve the problem myself. I had known Dinah well for many years and had a good relationship with her before the incident. I took her to lunch to address the issue. Over lunch, I acknowledged the stress the Partco situation had put on her and suggested that she move away for a while to the West Coast, where she could handle that area independently.

Dinah was hurt and asked why I didn't just fire her already. I responded by accusing her of causing the problem in the first place by going to Partco.

Dinah came back at me, calling me a lackey for having taken her story to Fred and having brought his management message back. She said I hadn't even attempted a solution and that I didn't have the guts to stand up for what was right. I was only interested in protecting my backside and keeping Fred happy. As her manager, I should have protected her and taken some of the heat off her back. Dinah refused to transfer or to quit. She told me to go ahead and fire her, and she walked out.

I sat in a daze as I watched Dinah leave the restaurant. What the heck went wrong? Had Dinah done the morally right thing? Was I right in defending MagRec's position? Should I have taken a stand with Fred? Should I have gone over Fred's head to Mr. Leed? Am I doing the right thing? Should I listen to Fred and fire Dinah? If not, how do I get my department back on track? What am I saying? If Dinah is right, shouldn't I be defending her rather than MagRec?

Review Questions

1. Place yourself in the role of the manager. What should you do now? After considering what happened, would you change any of your behaviors?
2. Do you think Dinah was right? Why or why not? If you were she and you had it to do all over again, would you do anything differently? If so, what and why?
3. Using cognitive dissonance theory, explain the actions of Pat, Dinah, and Fred. ■

CASE 5
It Isn't Fair
....

Developed by Barry R. Armandi, SUNY–Old Westbury

Mary Jones was in her senior year at Central University and interviewing for jobs. Mary was in the top 1 percent of her class, active in numerous extracurricular activities, and highly respected by her professors. After the interviews, Mary was offered positions with every company with which she interviewed. After much thought, she decided to take the offer from Universal Products, a multinational company. She felt that the salary was superb ($40,000), there were excellent benefits, and there was good potential for promotion.

Mary started work a few weeks after graduation and learned her job assignments and responsibilities thoroughly and quickly. Mary was asked on many occasions to work late because report deadlines were often moved forward. Without hesitation she said "Of course!" even though as an exempt employee she would receive no overtime.

Frequently she would take work home with her and use her personal computer to do further analyses. At other times she would come into the office on weekends to monitor the progress of her projects or just to catch up on the ever-growing mountain of correspondence.

On one occasion her manager asked her to take on a difficult assignment. It seemed that the company's Costa Rican manufacturing facility was having production problems. The quality of one of the products was highly questionable, and the reports on the matter were confusing. Mary was asked to be part of a team to investigate the quality and reporting problems. The team stayed in poor accommodations for the entire three weeks they were there. This was because of the plant's location near its resources, which happened to be in the heart of the jungle. Within the three-week period the team had located the source of the quality problem, corrected it, and altered the reporting documents and processes. The head of the team, a quality engineer, wrote a note to Mary's manager stating the following: "Just wanted to inform you of the superb job Mary Jones did down in Costa Rica. Her suggestions and insights into the reporting system were invaluable. Without her help we would have been down there for another three weeks, and I was getting tired of the mosquitoes. Thanks for sending her."

Universal Products, like most companies, has a yearly performance review system. Since Mary had been with the company for a little over one year, it was time for her review. Mary entered her manager's office nervous, since this was her first review ever and she didn't know what to expect. After closing the door and exchanging the usual pleasantries, her manager, Tom, got right to the point.

Tom: Well, Mary, as I told you last week this meeting would be for your annual review. As you are aware, your performance and compensation are tied together. Since the philosophy of the company is to reward those who perform, we take these reviews very sincerely. I have spent a great deal of time thinking about your performance over the past year, but before I begin I would like to know your impressions of the company, your assignments, and me as a manager.

Mary: Honestly, Tom, I have no complaints. The company and my job are everything I was led to believe. I enjoy working here. The staff are all very helpful. I like the team atmosphere, and my job is very challenging. I really feel appreciated and that I'm making a contribution. You have been very helpful and patient with me. You got me involved right from the start and listened to my opinions. You taught me a lot and I'm very grateful. All in all I'm happy being here.

Tom: Great, Mary, I was hoping that's the way you felt because from my vantage point, most of the people you worked with feel the same. But before I give you the qualitative side of the review, allow me to go through the quantitative appraisal first. As you know, the rankings go from 1 (lowest) to 5 (highest). Let's go down each category and I'll explain my reasoning for each.

Tom starts with category one (Quantity of Work) and ends with category ten (Teamwork). In each of the categories, Tom has either given

Mary a 5 or a 4. Indeed, only two categories have a 4 and Tom explains these are normal areas for improvement for most employees.

Tom: As you can see, Mary, I was very happy with your performance. You have received the highest rating I have ever given any of my subordinates. Your attitude, desire, and help are truly appreciated. The other people on the Costa Rican team gave you glowing reports, and speaking with the plant manager, she felt that you helped her understand the reporting system better than anyone else. Since your performance has been stellar, I'm delighted to give you a 10 percent increase effective immediately!

Mary: (mouth agape, and eyes wide) Tom, frankly I'm flabbergasted! I don't know what to say, but thank you very much. I hope I can continue to do as fine a job as I have this last year. Thanks once again.

After exchanging some parting remarks and some more thank-you's, Mary left Tom's office with a smile from ear to ear. She was floating on air! Not only did she feel the performance review process was uplifting, but her review was outstanding and so was her raise. She knew from other employees that the company was only giving out a 5 percent average increase. She figured that if she got that, or perhaps 6 or 7, she would be happy. But to get 10 percent . . . wow!! Imagine . . .

Sue: Hi, Mary! Lost in thought? My, you look great. Looks like you got some great news. What's up?

Susan Stevens was a recent hire, working for Tom. She had graduated from Central University also, but a year after Mary. Sue had excelled while at Central, graduating in the top 1 percent of her class. She had laudatory letters of recommendation from her professors and was into many after-school clubs and activities.

Mary: Oh, hi, Sue! Sorry, but I was just thinking about Universal and the opportunities here.

Sue: Yes, it truly is . . .

Mary: Sue, I just came from my performance review and let me tell you, the process isn't that bad. As a matter of fact I found it quite rewarding, if you get my drift. I got a wonderful review, and can't wait till next year's. What a great company!

Sue: You can say that again! I couldn't believe them hiring me right out of college at such a good salary. Between you and me, Mary, they started me at $45,000. Imagine that? Wow, was I impressed. I just couldn't believe that they would . . . Where are you going, Mary? Mary? What's that you say, "It isn't fair"? What do you mean? Mary? Mary . . .

Review Questions

1. Indicate Mary's attitudes before and after meeting Sue. If there was a change, why?
2. What do you think Mary will do now? Later?
3. What motivation theory applies best to this scenario? Explain. ■

CASE 6
Hovey and Beard Company

Source: Abridged and adapted from George Strauss and Alex Bavelas, "Group Dynamics and Intergroup Relations" (under the title "The Hovey and Beard Case"), in *Money and Motivation*, ed. William F. Whyte (New York: Harper & Row, 1955).

The Hovey and Beard Company manufactures a variety of wooden toys, including animals, pull toys, and the like.[1] The toys were manufactured by a transformation process that began in the wood room. There, toys were cut, sanded, and partially assembled. Then the toys were dipped into shellac and sent to the painting room.

In years past, the painting had been done by hand, with each employee working with a given toy until its painting was completed. The toys were predominantly two-colored, although a few required more colors. Now in response to increased demand for the toys, the painting operation was changed so that the painters sat in a line by an endless chain of hooks. These hooks moved continuously in front of the painters and passed into a long horizontal oven. Each painter sat in a booth designed to carry away fumes and to backstop excess paint. The painters would take a toy from a nearby tray, position it in a jig inside the painting cubicle, spray on the color according to a pattern, and then hang the toy on a passing hook. The rate at which the hooks moved was calculated by the engineers so that each painter, when fully trained, could hang a painted toy on each hook before it passed beyond reach.

The painters were paid on a group bonus plan. Since the operation was new to them, they received a learning bonus that decreased by regular amounts each month. The learning bonus was scheduled to vanish in six months, by which time it was expected that they would be on their own—that is, able to meet the production standard and earn a group bonus when they exceeded it.

By the second month of the training period, trouble developed. The painters learned more slowly than had been anticipated and it began to look as though their production would stabilize far below what was planned. Many of the hooks were going by empty. The painters complained that the hooks moved too fast and that the engineer had set the rates wrong. A few painters quit and had to be replaced with new ones. This further aggravated the learning problem. The team spirit that the management had expected to develop through the group bonus was not in evidence except as an expression of what the engineers called "resistance." One painter, whom the group regarded as its leader (and the management regarded as the ring-leader), was outspoken in taking the complaints of the group to the supervisor. These complaints were that the job was messy, the hooks moved too fast, the incentive pay was not correctly calculated, and it was too hot working so close to the drying oven.

A consultant was hired to work with the supervisor. She recommended that the painters be brought together for a general discussion of the working conditions. Although hesitant, the supervisor agreed to this plan.

The first meeting was held immediately after the shift was over at 4 P.M. It was attended by all eight painters. They voiced the same complaints again: the hooks went by too fast, the job was too dirty, and the room was hot and poorly ventilated. For some reason, it was this last item that seemed to bother them most. The supervisor promised to discuss the problems of ventilation and temperature with the engineers, and a second meeting was scheduled. In the next few days the supervisor had several talks with the engineers. They,

along with the plant superintendent, felt that this was really a trumped-up complaint and that the expense of corrective measures would be prohibitively high.

The supervisor came to the second meeting with some apprehensions. The painters, however, did not seem to be much put out. Rather, they had a proposal of their own to make. They felt that if several large fans were set up to circulate the air around their feet, they would be much more comfortable. After some discussion, the supervisor agreed to pursue the idea. The supervisor and the consultant discussed the idea of fans with the superintendent. Three large propeller-type fans were purchased and installed.

The painters were jubilant. For several days the fans were moved about in various positions until they were placed to the satisfaction of the group. The painters seemed completely satisfied with the results, and the relations between them and the supervisor improved visibly.

The supervisor, after this encouraging episode, decided that further meetings might also prove profitable. The painters were asked if they would like to meet and discuss other aspects of the work situation. They were eager to do this. Another meeting was held and the discussion quickly centered on the speed of the hooks. The painters maintained that the engineer had set them at an unreasonably fast speed and that they would never be able to fill enough of them to make a bonus.

The discussion reached a turning point when the group's leader explained that it wasn't that the painters couldn't work fast enough to keep up with the hooks but that they couldn't work at that pace all day long. The supervisor explored the point. The painters were unanimous in their opinion that they

could keep up with the belt for short periods if they wanted to. But they didn't want to because if they showed they could do this for short periods then they would be expected to do it all day long. The meeting ended with an unprecedented request by the painters: "Let us adjust the speed of the belt faster or slower depending on how we feel." The supervisor agreed to discuss this with the superintendent and the engineers.

The engineers reacted negatively to the suggestion. However, after several meetings it was granted that there was some latitude within which variations in the speed of the hooks would not affect the finished product. After considerable argument with the engineers, it was agreed to try out the painters' idea.

With misgivings, the supervisor had a control with a dial marked "low, medium, fast" installed at the booth of the group leader. The speed of the belt could now be adjusted anywhere between the lower and upper limits that the engineers had set.

The painters were delighted and spent many lunch hours deciding how the speed of the belt should be varied from hour to hour throughout the day. Within a week the pattern had settled down to one in which the first half hour of the shift was run on a medium speed (a dial setting slightly above the point marked "medium"). The next two and a half hours were run at high speed, and the half hour before lunch and the half hour after lunch were run at low speed. The rest of the afternoon was run at high speed with the exception of the last 45 minutes of the shift, which was run at medium.

The constant speed at which the engineers had originally set the belt was actually slightly below the "medium" mark on the control dial;

the average speed at which the painters were running the belt was on the high side of the dial. Few, if any, empty hooks entered the oven, and inspection showed no increase of rejects from the paint room.

Production increased, and within three weeks (some two months before the scheduled ending of the learning bonus) the painters were operating at 30 to 50 percent above the level that had been expected under the original arrangement. Naturally, their earnings were correspondingly higher than anticipated. They were collecting their base pay, earning a considerable piece-rate bonus, and still benefiting from the learning bonus. They were earning more now than many skilled workers in other parts of the plant.

Management was besieged by demands that the inequity between the earnings of the painters and those of other workers in the plant be taken care of. With growing irritation between the superintendent and the supervisor, the engineers and supervisor, and the superintendent and engineers, the situation came to a head when the superintendent revoked the learning bonus and returned the painting operation to its original status: the hooks moved again at their constant, time-studied, designated speed. Production dropped again and within a month all but two of the eight painters had quit. The supervisor stayed on for several months, but, feeling aggrieved, left for another job.

Review Questions

1. How does the painters' job score on the core job characteristics before and after the changes were made? How can the positive impact of the job redesign be explained?

2. Was the learning bonus handled properly in this case? How can its motivational impact be explained? What alternative approaches could have been taken with similar motivational results?

3. How do you explain the situation described in the last paragraph of the case? How could this outcome have been avoided by appropriate managerial actions? ∎

CASE 7
Perfect Pizzeria

Perfect Pizzeria in Southville, in deep southern Illinois, is the second-largest franchise of the chain in the United States. The headquarters is located in Phoenix, Arizona. Although the business is prospering, employee and managerial problems exist.

Each operation has one manager, an assistant manager, and from two to five night managers. The managers of each pizzeria work under an area supervisor. There are no systematic criteria for being a manager or becoming a manager trainee. The franchise has no formalized training period for the manager. No college education is required. The managers for whom the case observer worked during a four-year period were relatively young (ages 24 to 27) and only one had completed college. They came from the ranks of night managers or assistant managers, or both. The night managers were chosen for their ability to perform the duties of the regular employees. The assistant managers worked a two-hour shift during the luncheon period five days a week to gain knowledge about bookkeeping and management. Those becoming managers remained at that level unless they expressed interest in investing in the business.

The employees were mostly college students, with a few high school students performing the less challenging jobs. Since Perfect Pizzeria was located in an area with few job opportunities, it had a relatively easy task of filling its employee quotas. All the employees, with the exception of the manager, were employed part time and were paid the minimum wage.

The Perfect Pizzeria system is devised so that food and beverage costs and profits are computed according to a percentage. If the percentage of food unsold or damaged in any way is very low, the manager gets a bonus. If the percentage is high, the manager does not receive a bonus; rather, he or she receives only his or her normal salary.

There are many ways in which the percentage can fluctuate. Since the manager cannot be in the store 24 hours a day, some employees make up for their paychecks by helping themselves to the food. When a friend comes in to order a pizza, extra ingredients are put on the friend's pizza. Occasional nibbles by 18 to 20 employees throughout the day at the meal table also raise the percentage figure. An occasional bucket of sauce may be spilled or a pizza accidentally burned.

In the event of an employee mistake, the expense is supposed to come from the individual. Because of peer pressure, the night manager seldom writes up a bill for the erring employee. Instead, the establishment takes the loss and the error goes unnoticed until the end of the month when the inventory is taken. That's when the manager finds out that the percentage is high and that there will be no bonus.

In the present instance, the manager took retaliatory measures. Previously, each employee was entitled to a free pizza, salad, and all the soft drinks he or she could drink for every 6 hours of work. The manager raised this figure from 6 to 12 hours of work. However, the employees had received these 6-hour benefits for a long time. Therefore, they simply took advantage of the situation whenever the manager or the assistant was not in the building. Although the night manager theoretically had complete control of the operation in the evenings, he did not command the respect that the manager or assistant manager did. This was because he received the same pay as the regular employees, he could not reprimand other employees, and he was basically the same age or sometimes even younger than the other employees.

Thus, apathy grew within the pizzeria. There seemed to be a further separation between the manager and his workers, who started out as a closely knit group. The manager made no attempt to alleviate the problem, because he felt it would iron itself out. Either the employees that were dissatisfied would quit or they would be content to put up with the new regulations. As it turned out, there was a rash of employee dismissals. The manager had no problem filling the vacancies with new workers, but the loss of key personnel was costly to the business.

With the large turnover, the manager found that he had to spend more time in the building, supervising and sometimes taking the place of inexperienced workers. This was in direct violation of the franchise regulation, which stated that a manager would act as a supervisor and at no time take part in the actual food preparation. Employees were not placed under strict supervision with the manager working alongside them. The operation no longer worked smoothly because of differences between the remaining experienced workers and the manager concerning the way in which a particular function should be performed.

After a two-month period, the manager was again free to go back to his office and leave his subordinates in charge of the entire operation. During this two-month period, the percentage had returned to the previous low level, and the manager received a bonus each month. The manager felt that his problems had been resolved and that conditions would remain the same, since the new personnel had been properly trained.

It didn't take long for the new employees to become influenced by the other employees. Immediately after the manager had returned to his supervisory role, the percentage began to rise. This time the manager took a bolder step. He cut out any benefits that the employees had—no free pizzas, salads, or drinks. With the job market at an even lower ebb than usual, most employees were forced to stay. The appointment of a new area supervisor made it impossible for the manager to "work behind the counter," since the supervisor was centrally located in Southville.

The manager tried still another approach to alleviate the rising percentage problem and maintain his

bonus. He placed a notice on the bulletin board stating that if the percentage remained at a high level, a lie detector test would be given to all employees. All those found guilty of taking or purposefully wasting food or drinks would be immediately terminated. This did not have the desired effect on the employees, because they knew if they were all subjected to the test, all would be found guilty and the manager would have to dismiss all of them. This would leave him in a worse situation than ever.

Even before the following month's percentage was calculated, the manager knew it would be high. He had evidently received information from one of the night managers about the employees' feelings toward the notice. What he did not expect was that the percentage would reach an all-time high. That is the state of affairs at the present time.

Review Questions

1. Consider the situation where the manager changed the time period required to receive free food and drink from 6 to 12 hours of work. Try to apply each of the motivational approaches to explain what happened. Which of the approaches offers the most appropriate explanation? Why?
2. Repeat Question 1 for the situation where the manager worked beside the employees for a time and then later returned to his office.
3. Repeat Question 1 for the situation as it exists at the end of the case.
4. Establish and justify a motivational program based on one or a combination of motivation theories to deal with the situation as it exists at the end of the case. ∎

CASE 8
The Forgotten Group Member

Developed by Franklin Ramsoomair, Wilfred Laurier University

The Organizational Behavior course for the semester appeared to promise the opportunity to learn, enjoy, and practice some of the theories and principles in the textbook and class discussions. Christine Spencer was a devoted, hard-working student who had been maintaining an A–average to date. Although the skills and knowledge she had acquired through her courses were important, she was also very concerned about her grades. She felt that grades were paramount in giving her a competitive edge when looking for a job and, as a third-year student, she realized that she'd soon be doing just that.

Sunday afternoon. Two o'clock. Christine was working on an accounting assignment but didn't seem to be able to concentrate. Her courses were working out very well this semester, all but the OB. Much of the mark in that course was to be based on the quality of groupwork, and so she felt somewhat out of control. She recollected the events of the past five weeks. Professor Sandra Thiel had divided the class into groups of five people and had given them a major group assignment worth 30 percent of the final grade. The task was to analyze a seven-page case and to come up with a written analysis. In addition, Sandra had asked the groups to present the case in class, with the idea that the rest of the class members would be "members of the board of directors of the company" who would be listening to how the manager and her team dealt with the problem at hand.

Christine was elected "Team Coordinator" at the first group meeting. The other members of the group were Diane, Janet, Steve, and Mike. Diane was quiet and never volunteered suggestions, but when directly asked, she would come up with high-quality ideas. Mike was the clown. Christine remembered that she had suggested that the group should get together before every class to discuss the day's case. Mike had balked, saying "No way!! This is an 8:30 class, and I barely make it on time anyway! Besides, I'll miss my *Happy Harry* show on television!" The group couldn't help but laugh at his indignation. Steve was the businesslike individual, always wanting to ensure that group meetings were guided by an agenda and noting the tangible results achieved or not achieved at the end of every meeting. Janet was the reliable one who would always have more for the group than was expected of her. Christine saw herself as meticulous and organized and as a person who tried to give her best in whatever she did.

It was now week 5 into the semester, and Christine was deep in thought about the OB assignment. She had called everyone to arrange a meeting for a time that would suit them all, but she seemed to be running into a roadblock. Mike couldn't make it, saying that he was working that night as a member of the campus security force. In fact, he seemed to miss most meetings and would send in brief notes to Christine, which she was supposed to discuss for him at the group meetings. She wondered how to deal with this. She also remembered the inci-

dent last week. Just before class started, Diane, Janet, Steve, and she were joking with one another before class. They were laughing and enjoying themselves before Sandra came in. No one noticed that Mike had slipped in very quietly and had unobtrusively taken his seat.

She recalled the cafeteria incident. Two weeks ago, she had gone to the cafeteria to grab something to eat. She had rushed to her accounting class and had skipped breakfast. When she got her club sandwich and headed to the tables, she saw her OB group and joined them. The discussion was light and enjoyable as it always was when they met informally. Mike had come in. He'd approached their table. "You guys didn't say you were having a group meeting," he blurted. Christine was taken aback.

We just happened to run into each other. Why not join us?"

"Mike looked at them, with a noncommittal glance. "Yeah . . . right," he muttered, and walked away.

Sandra Thiel had frequently told them that if there were problems in the group, the members should make an effort to deal with them first. If the problems could not be resolved, she had said that they should come to her. Mike seemed so distant, despite the apparent camaraderie of the first meeting.

An hour had passed, bringing the time to 3 P.M., and Christine found herself biting the tip of her pencil. The written case analysis was due next week. All the others had done their designated sections, but Mike had just handed in some rough handwritten notes. He had called Christine the week before, telling her that in addition to his course and his job, he was having problems with his girlfriend. Christine empathized with him. Yet, this was a group project! Besides, the final mark would be peer evaluated. This meant that whatever mark Sandra gave them could be lowered or raised, depending on the group's opinion about the value of the contribution of each member. She was definitely worried. She knew that Mike had creative ideas that could help to raise the overall mark. She was also concerned for him. As she listened to the music in the background, she wondered what she should do.

Review Questions

1. How could an understanding of the stages of group development assist Christine in leadership situations such as this one?
2. What should Christine understand about individual membership in groups in order to build group processes that are supportive of her work group's performance?
3. Is Christine an effective group leader in this case? Why or why not? ∎

CASE 9
NASCAR'S Racing Teams
Developed by David S. Chappell, Ohio University, modified by Hal Babson, Columbus State Community College and John R. Schermerhorn, Jr, Ohio University

The most popular team sport, based on total spectator audience, is not basketball, baseball, football, or even soccer: it is stock car racing. The largest stock car racing group in the world is the National Association for Stock Car Auto Racing (NASCAR). The NASCAR Nextel Cup Series kicks off in February and runs through November. Along the way it serves as a marketing powerhouse.

Not only are over 12 million fans attracted to NASCAR's races, but another 250 million watch races on television. Drivers are involved in cable network shows as well as syndicated radio shows each week. NASCAR's official Web site, at www.nascar.com, ranks among the five most popular sites on the Internet. Companies such as the Coca-Cola Co. take advantage of NASCAR's popularity with merchandise, collectibles, apparel, accessories, toys, and other marketing tie-ins. The race cars themselves have been described by some as "200 mile-per-hour billboards."

You Win as a Team

Jeff Gordon is one of NASCAR's most successful and well-known drivers; he's been a sensation ever since he started racing go-carts and quarter-midget cars at the age of 5. But as the driver of a successful race car he represents just the most visible part of an incredibly complex racing organization—a high-performance system whose ultimate contribution takes place on race day. For several years a team known as the Rainbow Warriors handled Gordon's car. Their leader was crew chief Ray Evernham, recognized by many as one of the very best in the business. Posted

on the wall of his workshop was this sign:

Success is a ruthless competitor, for it flatters and nourishes our weaknesses and lulls us into complacency.

While Gordon represented the star attraction, many believed that it was Evernham who pulled the whole act together. He was responsible for a group of over 120 technicians and mechanics with an annual budget estimated between $10 and $12 million! And he had strong opinions as to what it takes to consistently finish first: painstaking preparation, egoless teamwork, and thoroughly original strategizing—principles that apply to any high-performance organization.

Evernham believed that teams needed to experiment with new methods and processes. When he assembled his Rainbow Warriors pit crew, none of them had Nextel/Winston Cup experience and none worked on the car in any other capacity. With the use of a pit crew coach, the Rainbow Warriors provide Gordon with an approximately one-second advantage with each pit stop, which, at a speed of 200 miles per hour, equates to 300 feet of race track.

"When you coach and support a superstar like Jeff Gordon, you give him the best equipment possible, you give him the information he needs, and then you get out of the way. But racing is a team sport. Everyone who races pretty much has the same car and the same equipment. What sets us apart is our people. I like to talk about our "team IQ"—because none of us is as smart as all of us.

"I think a lot about people, management, and psychology: Specifically, how can I motivate my guys and make them gel as a team? I surround them with ideas about teamwork. I read every leadership book I can get my hands on. One thing that I took from my reading is the idea of a 'circle of strength.' When the

Rainbow Warriors meet, we always put our chairs in a circle. That's a way of saying that we're stronger as a team than we are on our own."

Evernham backed up this belief in team by emphasizing team performance over individual performance. When the car won a race, everyone shared in the prize money. In addition, when Evernham earned money through personal-service activities such as speaking tours and autograph signings, he shared what he earned with the team. "I wouldn't be in a position to earn that income if it weren't for the team. Everyone should feel as if his signature is on the finished product."

High-performance teams do not happen by chance; rather, they are the result of good recruiting and meticulous attention to learning every detail of the job.

From NASCAR to Pit Crew U

It's not only the fans who have noticed what goes on in the NASCAR pit crews and racing teams. The next time you fly on United Airlines check out the ground crews. You might notice some similarities with the teams handling pit stops for NASCAR racers. In fact, there's a good chance the members of the ramp crews have been through what is being called "Pit Crew U."[1] United is among many organizations that are sending employees to Pit Instruction and Training in Mooresville, North Carolina. At the same facility where real racing crews train, United's ramp workers learn to work under pressure while meeting the goals of teamwork, safety, and job preparedness. The objective is to replace work practices that may sometimes result in aircraft delays and service inadequacies—things that a NASCAR team must avoid in order to stay competitive in races.

Is Pit Crew U the model of the future for building high-performance teams?

Review Questions

1. In what ways do Evernham's leadership tactics prove consistent with the ideas on teams and teamwork advanced in the text?
2. What are the potential strengths and weaknesses of the Pit Crew U model as an approach to high-performance team building in businesses and other types of organizations?
3. What can someone who takes over a highly successful team from a leader like Evernham do to maintain and even improve team success in the future? ∎

CASE 10
Faculty Empowerment and the Changing University Environment

Source: Developed by John Bowen, Columbus State Community College

In a typical university, the instructor enjoys a very high level of empowerment and opportunity for creativity in achieving course objectives. Within general limitations of the course description, instructors tend to have a good deal of flexibility in selecting course content, designing instructional activities, and selecting assignments. This allows them to tailor courses in varying ways to do what may seem to work best in a given situation. For example, an instructor teaching a course four times a year may design one section to cover course content in a somewhat different manner or with a slightly different focus due to the unique background and interests of the students. Since not all students learn or can be effectively evaluated in exactly the same way, an instructor normally is able to respond to varying situations by the way in which the text is used, the specific activities assigned, and choice of tests and other means of measuring student performance.

One of the settings in which instructor empowerment has been especially functional is the presence of adult learners (those working full-time and attending school part-time, or returning to school after substantial work experience). Often adult learners have quite different needs than the more traditional student. Course variations that include unique learning opportunities that tap their work experiences and that accommodate the nature of their work schedules are often necessary. Flexibility and responsiveness by the instructor is also important. A major news event may create intense student interest in a course-related topic, but it might not occur at the specific point in the course in which the topic was scheduled to be covered, and the level of interest might require more time being allocated to the discussion than was originally planned. Assignment schedules and requirements are also a challenge when dealing with adult learners. Not all have work schedules such that they have the same amount of work week after week, but instead they may have variations in workloads that may include substantial travel commitments.

Where instructors have a good deal of empowerment, quality of education is maintained through instructor selection and development and through oversight by department heads. The supervision often includes reviews of any changes in course plans, learning activities, exams, assignments, and syllabus. This is facilitated by reviews of student feedback and through personal observation of the instructor conducting a class.

Regardless of the extent to which such quality control measures may or may not work, competition among colleges and universities is beginning to have an impact on faculty empowerment. In the past, schools tended to focus on a given geographic area, certain fields of study, or a particular class of students. Thus, competitive pressures were often relatively minimal. Today competition in the education market is not just local or even national, but is becoming increasingly global. Accelerating the trend is the use of online classes that can enable students in distant locations to take classes over the Internet.

The need to compete for revenues and to contain costs has also produced pressure for universities to operate more like businesses. This has, in some cases, resulted in more standardization of courses and instructional methods, consequently reducing the traditional empowerment of instructors. As an example of what is being done, consider two universities: Upstate University and Downstate University. Upstate and Downstate share two commonalities: (1) each sees their primary target student market as the working adult and (2) each is increasing the use of standardization in instructional methods.

Upstate University focuses on the working adult: 82 percent of its 8200 students are employed and the average age is 32. It still holds traditional face-to-face classes on its main cam-pus and in nearby communities, but its programs now include standardized online courses (including a program for military personnel) in both masters and undergraduate degree programs. It has developed a "Balanced Learning Format" approach involving standardized quality, content, and delivery for its courses—both online and traditional courses.

Downstate University was started to provide a means through which poor but qualified students could work and pay for their education. The school offers both undergraduate and masters degree programs. Enrollment at the main campus is now approximately 2,000 students but it has over 19,000 other students attending around the nation and around the world. Those students attend classes online and at 37 other campuses in 20 states—most of those students are working adults.

Upstate has standardized its courses so that certain specific activities and points are to be covered in each class session. The instructor does not set the assignments (problems, text questions, etc.). Rather, the student taking the course can go online and see what is required for both the instructor and student. The amount of time to be devoted to particular discussion or activities must follow a given script for each class session or at least be within guidelines in which some flexibility may exist. As a result, all instructors covering a given class session will be following the same script—often saying and doing much the same thing. This approach largely limits creativity to the person or persons involved in developing and modifying the course. Any ideas to change the course would normally have to be approved by that developer. Changes are infrequent, however, perhaps because some instructors might be unwilling to contact the course developer and take the time to argue the need for a change.

Downstate is modifying its courses in ways that are similar to the approach taken at Upstate, although not identical. Standardized test banks are being used. Objective test questions are to be randomly selected from within the test banks and scored by computer, thus reducing subjective evaluation (and any possible favoritism) by individual instructors.

At both Upstate and Downstate, online instruction is playing an increasingly important role. The goal is to assure that all online interaction between students and instructors is proper and consistent with school policies. Online classes are conducted so that any communication must be either at the class Web site or through use of the school's own e-mail system. Thus the institution can monitor not only what goes on in the "electronic classroom" (the Web site for the course) but also in what might be comparable to the private chats which traditional students in the past had in the instructor's office. Furthermore, to the extent that a course is online and that all activity is completed using either the course Web site or the school's e-mail system, protection is provided to both students and instructors. There is always proof available that an assignment was or was not received on time; student complaints or grade challenges are much more verifiable.

From the perspective of administration at both universities, the approach to more standardization ensures uniformity of quality in instructional delivery across settings, students, and instructors. It also provides a benefit in regards to the recruitment of adjunct (part-time) instructors that are increasingly used. Since not all such instructors have the same level of creativity and experience, having a standardized course and common script for all to follow is presumed to help maintain quality of instruction across instructors and course sections. Many instructors—especially those who have taught in the past under empowered conditions, find the new developments at both Upstate and Downstate frustrating. They believe that their prerogatives and talents as professionals are not being fully respected.

Review Questions

1. Would you rather be a student in a class that has been standardized or one in which the instructor has a high degree of empowerment? Why?
2. What issues involving power and politics are involved in moving from a setting that encouraged faculty empowerment to one that required much more standardization of instruction? How would you deal with those issues if you were involved in university administration?
3. In the specific case of adult learners and use of multiple instructors, is it possible to reach a compromise between standardization and empowerment so that the benefits of standardization can be obtained while still allowing for the flexibility that comes with empowerment? How can this apply to courses taught online versus face-to-face? ■

CASE 11
The New Vice President

[*Note:* Please read only those parts identified by your instructor. Do not read ahead.]

Part A

When the new president at Mid-West U took over, it was only a short time before the incumbent vice president announced his resignation. Unfortunately, there was no one waiting in the wings, and a hiring freeze prevented a national search from commencing.

Many faculty leaders and former administrators suggested that the president appoint Jennifer Treeholm, the Associate Vice President for Academic Affairs, as interim. She was an extremely popular person on campus and had 10 years of experience in the role of associate vice president. She knew everyone and everything about the campus. Jennifer, they assured him, was the natural choice. Besides, Jennifer *deserved* the job. Her devotion to the school was unparalleled, and her energy knew no bounds. The new president, acting on advice from many campus leaders, appointed Jennifer interim vice president for a term of up to three years. He also agreed that she could be a candidate for the permanent position when the hiring freeze was lifted.

Jennifer and her friends were ecstatic. It was high time more women moved into important positions on campus. They went out for dinner to their every-Friday-night watering hole to celebrate and reflect on Jennifer's career.

Except for a brief stint outside of academe, Jennifer's entire career had been at Mid-West U. She started out teaching Introductory History, then, realizing she wanted to get on the tenure track, went back to school and earned her Ph.D. at Metropolitan U while continuing to teach at Mid-West. Upon completion of her degree, she was appointed as an assistant professor and eventually earned the rank of associate based on her popularity and excellent teaching.

Not only was Jennifer well liked, but she devoted her entire life, it seemed, to Mid-West, helping to form the first union, getting grants, writing skits for the faculty club's annual follies, and going out of her way to befriend everyone who needed support.

Eventually, Jennifer was elected president of the Faculty Senate. After serving for two years, she was offered the position of associate vice president. During her 10 years as associate vice president, she handled most of the academic complaints, oversaw several committees, wrote almost all of the letters and reports for the vice president, and was even known to run personal errands for the president. People just knew they could count on Jennifer.

Review Questions

1. At this point, what are your predictions about Jennifer as the interim vice president?

Source: Adapted from Donald D. Bowen et al., *Experiences in Management and Organizational Behavior.* 4th ed. (New York: Wiley, 1997).

2. What do you predict will be her management/leadership style?
3. What are her strengths? Her weaknesses? What is the basis for your assessment?

After you have discussed Part A, please read Part B.

Part B

Jennifer's appointment as interim vice president was met with great enthusiasm. Finally the school was getting someone who was "one of their own," a person who understood the culture, knew the faculty, and could get things done.

It was not long before the campus realized that things were not moving and that Jennifer, despite her long-standing popularity, had difficulty making tough decisions. Her desire to please people and to try to take care of everyone made it difficult for her to choose opposing alternatives. (To make matters worse, she had trouble planning, organizing, and managing her time.)

What was really a problem was that she did not understand her role as the number-two person at the top of the organization. The president expected her to support him and his decisions without question. Over time the president also expected her to implement some of his decisions—to do his dirty work. This became particularly problematic when it involved firing people or saying "no" to old faculty cronies. Jennifer also found herself uncomfortable with the other members of the president's senior staff. Although she was not the only woman (the general counsel, a very bright, analytical woman was part of the group), Jennifer found the behavior and decision-making style to be different from what she was used to.

Most of the men took their lead from the president and discussed very little in the meetings. Instead, they

would try to influence decisions privately. Often a decision arrived in a meeting as a "fait accompli." Jennifer felt excluded and wondered why, as vice president, she felt so powerless.

In time, she and the president spent less and less time together talking and discussing how to move the campus along. Although her relations with the men on the senior staff were cordial, she talked mostly to her female friends.

Jennifer's friends, especially her close-knit group of longtime female colleagues, all assured her that it was because she was "interim." "Just stay out of trouble," they told her. Of course this just added to her hesitancy when it came to making tough choices.

As the president's own image on campus shifted after his "honeymoon year," Jennifer decided to listen to her friends rather than follow the president's lead. After all, her reputation on campus was at stake.

Review Questions

1. What is the major problem facing Jennifer?
2. What would you do if you were in her position?
3. Would a man have the same experience as Jennifer?
4. Are any of your predictions about her management style holding up?

Part C

When the hiring freeze was lifted and Jennifer's position was able to be filled, the president insisted on a national search. Jennifer and her friends felt this was silly, given that she was going into her third year in the job. Nonetheless, she entered the search process.

After a year-long search, the Search Committee met with the president. The external candidates were not acceptable to the campus. Jennifer, they recommended, should

only be appointed on a permanent basis if she agreed to change her management style.

The president mulled over his dilemma, then decided to give Jennifer the benefit of the doubt and the opportunity. He appointed her permanent provost, while making the following private agreement with her.

1. She would organize her office and staff and begin delegating more work to others.
2. She would "play" her number-two position, backing the president and echoing his position on the university's vision statement.
3. She would provide greater direction for the Deans who report to her.

Jennifer agreed to take the position. She was now the university's first female vice president and presided over a council of 11 deans, three of whom were her best female friends. Once again, they sought out their every-Friday-night watering hole for an evening of dinner and celebration.

Review Questions

1. If you were Jennifer, would you have accepted the job?
2. What would you do as the new, permanent, vice president?
3. Will Jennifer change her management style? If so, in what ways?
4. What are your predictions for the future?

Part D

Although people had predicted that things would be better once Jennifer was permanently in the job, things in fact became more problematic. People now expected Jennifer to be able to take decisive action. She did not feel she could.

Every time an issue came up, she would spend weeks, sometimes months, trying to get a sense of the campus. Nothing moved once it hit her office. After a while, people began referring to the vice president's office as "the black hole" where things just went in and disappeared.

Her immediate staff were concerned and frustrated. Not only did she not delegate effectively, but her desire to make things better led her to try to do more and more herself.

The vice president's job also carried social obligations and requests. Here again, she tried to please everyone and often ran from one evening obligation to another, trying to show her support and concern for every constituency on campus. She was exhausted, overwhelmed, and knowing the mandate under which she was appointed, anxious about the president's evaluation of her behavior.

The greatest deterioration occurred within her Dean's Council. Several of the male Deans, weary of waiting for direction from Jennifer regarding where she was taking some of the academic proposals of the president, had started making decisions without Jennifer's approval.

"Loose cannons," was how she described a couple of them. "They don't listen. They just march out there on their own."

One of the big problems with two of the deans was that they just didn't take "no" for an answer when it came from Jennifer. Privately, each conceded that her "no" sounded like a "maybe." She always left room open to renegotiate.

Whatever the problem, and there were several by now, Jennifer's ability to lead was being questioned. Although her popularity was as high as ever, more and more people on campus were expressing their frustrations with what sometimes appeared as mixed signals from her and the president and sometimes was seen as virtually no direction. People wanted priorities. Instead, crisis management reigned.

Review Questions

1. If you were president, what would you do?
2. If you were Jennifer, what would you do?

Conclusion

Jennifer had a few "retreats" with her senior staff. Each time, she committed herself to delegate more, prioritize, and work on time management issues, but within 10 days or so, everything was back to business as usual.

The president decided to hire a person with extensive corporate experience to fill the vacant position of Vice President of Finance and Administration. The new man was an experienced team player who had survived mergers, been fired and bounced back, and had spent years in the number-two position in several companies. Within a few months he had earned the respect of the campus as well as the president and was in fact emerging as the person who really ran the place. Meanwhile, the president concentrated on external affairs and fund-raising.

Jennifer felt relieved. Her role felt clearer. She could devote herself to academic and faculty issues and she was out from under the pressure to play "hatchet man."

As she neared the magic age for early retirement, she began to talk more and more about what she wanted to do next. ∎

CASE 12
Motorola's Innovator-in-Chief

When he became CEO of Motorola in 2004, Ed Zander faced a unique situation. He was in charge of a company that was struggling for competitive success. Even though it was the birthplace of the popular Six Sigma approach to quality management, Motorola was struggling to bring compelling new products to market at a time when something new in communications was happening almost every day.

Zander was facing a difficult problem: a historically successful firm with an established culture that was in need of transformational change. He says: "I found it necessary to drive change at Motorola, as the status quo was obviously not delivering the desired results. . . . I hoped to make Motorola a company that was led more from the outside—that is, by customers."[1]

The results spoke for themselves; Zander brought innovation back at Motorola, as evidenced by the popularity of its RAZR mobile phone. One analyst remarked: "Zander instilled new business prac-tices, refocused the company's attention on customers, and shook up a stodgy corporate culture that had put the future of the venerable Chicago-area-based conglomerate in doubt."[2]

When asked to describe his leadership approach as Motorola's innovator-in-chief, Zander offered these comments during an interview with *BizEd Magazine*.[3]

"Companies that don't innovate don't survive, and leaders who don't innovate are replaced by those willing to take risks. The key to success is to drive innovation."

"To succeed, companies must set clear innovation goals, select the right ideas for development, and create an agile organization to drive ongoing innovation."

"So when a company reaches the height of its success, a good leader will shake things up by 'breaking' the business."

"Drive innovation by moving people around. Changing the company's organizational structure allows different people to interact and new, innovative ideas to take shape."

"Successful corporate leaders need to be willing to make big bets. Sometimes you will be right, other times you will be wrong. But you never win without being bold."

Review Questions

1. Is Zander providing a road map for transformational leadership that will work in almost any type of organization? Why or why not?
2. How can someone pursue Zander's leadership suggestions while meeting the conditions of authentic and servant leadership?
3. What role do the force-coercion, rational persuasion, and shared power change strategies play in leadership that is as committed to change and innovation as Zander was at Motorola?
4. What problems might a leader like Zander experience after having a high profile success such as the Razr?

CASE 13
Decisions, Decisions
∙∙∙∙∙∙∙∙∙∙∙∙∙∙∙∙∙∙∙∙∙∙∙∙∙∙∙∙∙∙

Developed by John R. Schermerhorn, Jr.

The Case of the Wedding Ring

Setting—A woman is preparing for a job interview.

Dilemma—She wants the job desperately and is worried that her marital status might adversely affect the interview.

Decision—Should she or should she not wear her diamond engagement ring?

Considerations—When queried for a column in *The Wall Street Journal*, some women claimed that they would try to hide their marital status during a job interview.[1] One says: "Although I will never remove my wedding band, I don't want anyone to look at my engagement ring and think, she doesn't need this job, what is she doing working?" Even the writer remembers that she considered removing her engagement ring some years back when applying for a job. "I had no idea about the office culture," she said. "I didn't want anyone making assumptions, however unreasonable, about my commitment to work."

Wellness or Invasive Coercion?

Setting—Scotts Miracle-Gro Company, Marysville, Ohio.

Dilemma—Corporate executives are concerned about rising health-care costs. CEO Jim Hagedorn backs an aggressive wellness program and anti-smoking campaign to improve health of employees and reduce health-care costs for the firm. Scott employees are asked to take extensive health-risk assessments; failure to do so increases their health insurance premiums by $40 a month. Employees found to have "moderate to high" health risks are assigned health coaches and given action plans; failure to comply adds another $67 per month. In states where the practice is legal, the firm will not hire a smoker and tests new employees for nicotine use. In response to complaints that the policy is intrusive, Hagedorn says: "If people understand the facts and still choose to smoke, it's suicidal. And we can't encourage suicidal behavior."

Decision—Is Hagedorn doing the right thing by leading Scott's human resource policies in this direction?

Considerations—Joe Pellegrini's life was probably saved by his employer. After urging from a Scott's health coach he saw his doctor about weight and cholesterol concerns. This led to a visit with a heart specialist who inserted two stents, correcting a 95% blockage. Scott Rodrigues' life was changed by his employer; he is suing Scott's for wrongful dismissal. A smoker, he claims that he was fired after failing a drug test for nicotine even though he wasn't informed about the test and had been told the company would help him stop smoking. CEO Hagedorn says: "This is an area where CEOs are afraid to go. A lot of people are watching to see how badly we get sued."[2]

Super Sales Woman Won't Ask for Raise

Setting—A woman is described as a "productive star" and "supersuccessful" member of an 18 person sales force.[3]

Dilemma—She finds out that both she and the other woman salesperson are being paid 20% less than the men. Her sister wants her to talk with her boss and ask for more pay. She says: "No, I'm satisfied with my present pay and I don't want to 'rock the boat'." The sister can't understand how and why she puts up with this situation, allowing herself to be paid less than a man for at least equal and quite possibly better performance.

Considerations—In the past ten years women have lost ground relative to men when it comes to pay; whereas they previously earned 75.7 cents for each dollar earned by a man, a decade later they are earning 74.7 cents. Some claim that one explanation for the wage gap and its growing size is that women tolerate the situation and allow it to continue, rather than confronting the gap in their personal circumstances and trying to change it.

Wal-Mart Goes Public with Annual Bonuses

Setting—Wal-Mart executives released to the public information on the annual bonuses paid to store employees.[4]

Dilemma—Wal-Mart's founder, Sam Walton, started the bonus program in 1986 as a way of linking employees with the firm's financial success. Historically Wal-Mart did not divulge the annual bonuses. Recently the firm has received considerable negative publicity regarding the wages paid to employees and the benefits they are eligible to receive. But a spokesperson indicated that going public with the bonuses was not a response to such criticism. A former human resource executive at the firm says: "This is just an example of how they really treat their people well and they're putting it out there to let the facts speak for themselves."

Considerations—Some 813,759 employees shared a bonus pool of $529.8 million. A current employee said she received "substantially over $1,000," and that this was higher than the prior year's bonus. Wal-Mart is planning to give the bonuses on a quarterly basis to link them more frequently with performance. One of the firm's critics, WakeUpWalMart.com, was critical, charging: "Wal-Mart values are so misplaced that it gives executives hundreds of millions in bonuses and the mere crumbs to associates."

Review Questions

1. Use the decision-making model presented in the chapter to map the decisions being made in these situations. Identify how, where, and why different decisions might be made.

2. What are the issues involved in these situations? How are they best addressed by the decision makers?

3. Find other decision-making examples that raise similar issues and quandaries. Share them with classmates and analyze the possible decisions. ■

CASE 14
The Poorly Informed Walrus

Developed by Barbara McCain, Oklahoma City University

"How's it going down there?" barked the big walrus from his perch on the highest rock near the shore. He waited for the good word.

Down below the smaller walruses conferred hastily among themselves. Things weren't going well at all, but none of them wanted to break the news to the Old Man. He was the biggest and wisest walrus in the herd, and he knew his business, but he had such a terrible temper that every walrus in the herd was terrified of his ferocious bark.

"What will we tell him?" whispered Basil, the second-ranking walrus. He well remembers how the Old Man had raved and ranted at him the last time the herd had caught less than its quota of herring, and he had no desire to go through that experience again. Nevertheless, the walrus noticed for several weeks that the water level in the nearby Arctic bay had been falling constant-

ly, and it had become necessary to travel much farther to catch the dwindling supply of herring. Someone should tell the Old Man; he would probably know what to do. But who? and how?

Finally Basil spoke up: "Things are going pretty well, Chief," he said. The thought of the receding water line made his heart grow heavy, but he went on: "As a matter of fact, the beach seems to be getting larger."

The Old Man grunted. "Fine, fine," he said. "That will give us a bit more elbow room." He closed his eyes and continued basking in the sun.

The next day brought more trouble. A new herd of walruses moved in down the beach and, with the supply of herring dwindling, this invasion could be dangerous. No one wanted to tell the Old Man, though only he could take the steps necessary to meet this new competition.

Reluctantly, Basil approached the big walrus, who was still sunning himself on the large rock. After some smalltalk, he said, "Oh, by the way, Chief, a new herd of walruses seems to have moved into our territory." The Old Man's eyes snapped open, and he filled his great lungs in preparation for a mighty bellow. But Basil added quickly, "Of course, we don't anticipate any trouble. They don't look like herring eaters to me. More likely interested in minnows. And as you know, we don't bother with minnows ourselves."

The Old Man let out the air with a long sigh. "Good, good," he said. "No point in our getting excited over nothing then, is there?"

Things didn't get any better in the weeks that followed. One day, peering down from the large rock, the Old Man noticed that part of the herd seemed to be missing. Summoning Basil, he grunted peevishly. "What's going on, Basil? Where is everyone?" Poor Basil didn't have the courage to tell the Old Man that many of the younger walruses were leaving every day to join the new herd. Clearing his throat nervously, he said, "Well

Chief, we've been tightening up things a bit. You know, getting rid of some of the dead wood. After all, a herd is only as good as the walruses in it."

"Run a tight ship, I always say," the Old Man grunted. "Glad to hear that all is going so well."

Before long, everyone but Basil had left to join the new herd, and Basil realized that the time had come to tell the Old Man the facts. Terrified but determined, he flopped up to the large rock. "Chief," he said, "I have bad news. The rest of the herd has left you." The old walrus was so astonished that he couldn't even work up a good bellow. "Left me?" he cried. "All of them? But why? How could this happen?"

Basil didn't have the heart to tell him, so he merely shrugged helplessly.

"I can't understand it," the old walrus said. "And just when everything was going so well."

Review Questions

1. What barriers to communication are evident in this fable?
2. What communication "lessons" does this fable offer to those who are serious about careers in the new workplace? ■

CASE 15
The Case of the Missing Raise

Prepared by John R. Schermerhorn, Jr., Ohio University

••

It was late February, and Marsha Lloyd had just completed an important long-distance telephone call with Professor Fred Massie, head of the Department of Management at Central University. During the conversation Marsha accepted an offer to move from her present position at Private University, located in the East, to Central in the Midwest as an Assistant Professor. Marsha and her husband John then shared the following thoughts.

Marsha: "Well, it's final."
John: "It's been a difficult decision, but I know it will work out for the best."
Marsha: "Yes, however, we are leaving many things we like here."
John: "I know, but remember, Professor Massie is someone you respect a great deal and he is offering you a challenge to come and introduce new courses at Central. Besides, he will surely be a pleasure to work for."
Marsha: "John we're young, eager and a little adventurous. There's no reason we shouldn't go."
John: "We're going dear."

Marsha Lloyd began the fall semester eagerly. The points discussed in her earlier conversations with Fred were now real challenges, and she was teaching new undergraduate and graduate courses in Central's curriculum. Overall, the transition to Central had been pleasant. The nine faculty members were warm in welcoming her, and Marsha felt it would be good working with them. She also felt comfortable with the performance standards that appeared to exist in the department. Although it was certainly not a "publish or perish" situation, Fred had indicated during the recruiting process that research and publications would be given increasing weight along with teaching and service in future departmental decisions. This was consistent with Marsha's personal belief that a professor should live up to each of these responsibilities. Although there was some conflict in evidence among the faculty over what weighting and standards should apply to these performance areas, she sensed some consensus that the multiple responsibilities should be respected.

It was April, and spring vacation time. Marsha was sitting at home reflecting upon her experiences to date at Central. She was pleased. Both she and John had adjusted very well to Midwestern life. Although there were things they both missed from their prior location, she was in an interesting new job and they found the rural environment of Central very satisfying. Marsha had also received positive student feedback on her fall semester courses, had presented two papers at a recent professional meeting, and had just been informed that two of her papers would be published by a journal. This was a good record and she felt satisfied. She had been working hard and it was paying off.

The spring semester had ended and Marsha was preoccupied. It was time, she thought, for an end-of-the-year performance review by Fred Massie. This anticipation had been stimulated, in part, by a recent meeting of the College faculty in which the Dean indicated that a 7% pay raise pool was now available for the coming year. He was encouraging department chairpersons to distribute this money differentially based on performance merit. Marsha had listened closely to the Dean and liked what she heard. She felt this meant that Central was really trying to establish a performance-oriented reward system. Such a system was consistent with her personal philosophy and, indeed, she taught such reasoning in her courses.

Throughout May, Marsha kept expecting to have a conversation with Fred Massie on these topics. One day, the following memo appeared in her faculty mailbox.

MEMORANDUM
TO: Fellow Faculty
FROM: Fred
RE: Raises for Next Year

The Dean has been most open about the finances of the College as evi-

denced by his detail and candor regarding the budget at the last faculty meeting. Consistent with that philosophy I want to provide a perspective on raises and clarify a point or two.

The actual dollars available to our department exclusive of the chairman total 7.03%. In allocating those funds I have attempted to reward people on the basis of their contribution to the life of the Department and the University, as well as professional growth and development. In addition, it was essential this year to adjust a couple of inequities which had developed over a period of time. The distribution of increments was the following:

5% or less	3	7 + %–9%	3
5 + %–7%	2	More than 9%	2

Marsha read the memo with mixed emotions. Initially, she was upset that Fred had obviously made the pay raise decisions without having spoken first with her about her performance. Still, she felt good because she was sure to be one of those receiving a 9 + % increase. "Now," she mused to herself, "it will be good to sit down with Fred and discuss not only this past year's efforts, but my plans for next year's as well."

Marsha was disappointed when Fred did not contact her for such a discussion. Furthermore, she found herself frequently involved in informal conversations with other faculty members who were speculating over who received the various pay increments.

One day Carla Block, a faculty colleague, came into Marsha's office and said she had asked Fred about her raise. She received a 7 + % increase, and also learned that the two 9 + % increases had been given to senior faculty members. Marsha was incredulous. "It can't be," she thought, "I was a top performer this past year. My teaching and publications records are strong, and I feel I've been a positive force in the

department." She felt Carla could be mistaken and waited to talk the matter out with Fred.

A few days later another colleague reported to Marsha the results of a similar conversation with Fred. This time Marsha exploded internally. She felt she deserved just reward.

The next day Marsha received a computerized notice on her pay increment from the Accounting Office. Her raise was 7.2%. That night, after airing her feelings with John, Marsha telephoned Fred at home and arranged to meet with him the next day.

Fred Massie knocked on the door to Marsha's office and entered. The greetings were cordial. Marsha began the conversation. "Fred, we've always been frank with one another and now I'm concerned about my raise," she said. "I thought I had a good year, but I understand that I've received just an average raise." Fred Massie was a person who talked openly, and Marsha could trust him. He responded to Marsha in this way.

Yes, Marsha, you are a top performer. I feel you have made great contributions to the Department. The two 9 + % raises went to correct "inequities" that had built up over a period of time for two senior people. I felt that since the money was available this year that I had a responsibility to make the adjustments. If we don't consider them, you received one of the three top raises, and I consider any percentage differences between these three very superficial. I suppose I could have been more discriminating at the lower end of the distribution, but I can't give zero increments. I know you had a good year. It's what I expected when I hired you. You haven't let me down. From your perspective I know you feel you earned an "A," and I agree. I gave you a "B +". I hope you understand why.

Marsha sympathized with Fred's logic and felt good having spoken with him.

Although she wasn't happy, she understood Fred's position. Her final comment to Fred was this. "You know, it's not the absolute dollar value of the raise that hurts. It's the sense of letdown. Recently, for example, I turned down an extensive consulting job that would have paid far more than the missing raise. I did so because I felt it would require too many days away from the office. I'm not sure my colleagues would make that choice."

In the course of a casual summer conversation, Carla mentioned to Marsha that she heard two of the faculty who had received 4 + % raises had complained to Fred and the Dean. After lodging the complaints they had received additional salary increments. "Oh great," Marsha responded to herself, "I thought I had put this thing to rest."

About three weeks later, Marsha, Fred, Carla, and another colleague were in a meeting with the Dean. Although the meeting was on a separate matter, something was said which implied that Carla had also received an additional pay increment. Marsha confronted the Dean and learned that this was the case. Carla had protested to Fred and the Dean, and they raised her pay on the justification that an historical salary inequity had been overlooked. Fred was visibly uncomfortable as a discussion ensued on how salary increments should be awarded and what had transpired in the department in this respect.

Fred eventually excused himself to attend another meeting. Marsha and the others continued to discuss the matter with the Dean and the conversation became increasingly heated. Finally, they each rose to terminate the meeting and Marsha felt compelled to say one more thing. "It's not that I'm not making enough money," she said to the Dean, "but I just don't feel I received my fair share, especially in terms of your own stated policy of

rewarding faculty on the basis of performance merit."

With that remark, Marsha left the meeting. As she walked down the hall to her office, she said to herself, "Next year there will be no turning down consulting jobs because of a misguided sense of departmental responsibility."

Review Questions

1. What is Marsha's conflict management style and how has it influenced events in this case?

What were Marsha's goals and what conflict management style would have worked best in helping her achieve them?

2. What is Fred's conflict management style and how has it influenced events in this case?

3. Once Marsha found out what her raise was to be, how could she have used the notion and elements of distributive negotiation to create a situation where Fred would make a raise adjustment that was favorable and motivating for her? ■

CASE 16
Never on a Sunday

Developed by Anne C. Cowden, California State University, Sacramento and John R. Schermerhorn, Jr., Ohio University

McCoy's Building Supply Centers of San Marcos, Texas, have been in continuous successful operation for over 70 years in an increasingly competitive retail business. McCoy's is one of the nation's largest family-owned and -managed building-supply companies, serving 10 million customers a year in a regional area currently covering New Mexico, Texas, Oklahoma, Arkansas, Mississippi, and Louisiana. McCoy's strategy has been to occupy a niche in the market of small and medium-sized cities.

McCoy's grounding principle is acquiring and selling the finest-quality products that can be found and providing quality service to customers. As an operations-oriented company. McCoy's has always managed without many layers of management. Managers are asked to concentrate on service-related issues in their stores: get the merchandise on the floor, price it, sell it, and help the customer carry it out. The majority of the administrative workload is handled through headquarters so that store employees can concentrate on customer service. The top management team (Emmett McCoy and his two sons, Brian and Mike, who serve as co-presidents) has established 11 teams of managers drawn from the different regions McCoy's stores cover. The teams meet regularly to discuss new products, better ways for product delivery, and a host of items integral to maintaining customer satisfaction. Team leadership is rotated among the managers.

McCoy's has a workforce of 70 percent full-time and 30 percent part-time employees. McCoy's philosophy values loyal, adaptable, skilled employees as the most essential element of its overall success. To operationalize this philosophy, the company offers extensive on-the-job training. The path to management involves starting at the store level and learning all facets of operations before advancing into a management program. All management trainees are required to relocate to a number of stores. Most promotions come from within. Managers are rarely recruited from the outside. This may begin to change as the business implements more technology requiring greater reliance on college-educated personnel.

Permeating all that McCoy's does is a strong religious belief, including a strong commitment to community. The firm has a long-standing reputation of fair dealing that is a source of pride for all employees.

Many McCoy family members are Evangelical Christians who believe in their faith through letting their "feet do it"—that is, showing their commitment to God through action, not just talk. Although their beliefs and values permeate the company's culture in countless ways, one very concrete way is reflected in the title of this case: Never on a Sunday. Even though it's a busy business day for retailers, all 103 McCoy's stores are closed on Sunday.

Atlanta, Georgia

Courteous service fuels growth at Chick-fil-A. But don't plan on stopping in for a chicken sandwich on a Sunday; all of the chain's 1250 stores are closed. It is a tradition started by 85-year-old founder Truett Cathy, who believes that employees deserve a day of rest. Known as someone who believes in placing "people before profits," Truett has built a successful and fast growing fast-food franchise.

Headquartered in Atlanta, where its first restaurant was opened, Chick-fil-A is wholly owned by Truett's family and is now headed by his son. It has a reputation as a great employer, processing about 10,000 inquiries each year for 100 open restaurant operator jobs. Chick-fil-A's turnover among restaurant operators is only 3%, compared to an industry average as high as 50%. It is also a relatively inexpensive franchise, costing $5,000, compared to the $50,000 that is typical of its competitors.

The president of the National Restaurant Association Educational Foundation says: "I don't think there's any chain that creates such a wonderful culture around the way they treat their people and the respect they have for their employees."

Truett asks his employees to always say "my pleasure" when thanked by a customer. He says: "It's important to keep people happy." The results seem to speak for themselves. Chick-fil-A is the twenty-fifth largest restaurant chain in the United States, and reached over $2 billion in sales in 2006.[1]

Review Questions

1. How have the personal beliefs of the McCoy and Cathy families influenced the organizational cultures of their firms?
2. What lessons for developing high-performance organizational cultures can these two cases provide for other firms that aren't family run?
3. What would be the challenges for a new leader who is interested in moving her organization in the direction of the McCoy or Chick-fil-A cultures? ■

CASE 17
First Community Financial

Developed by Marcus Osborn, RSR Partners

First Community Financial is a small business lender that specializes in asset-based lending and factoring for a primarily small-business clientele. First Community's business is generated by high-growth companies in diverse industries, whose capital needs will not be met by traditional banking institutions. First Community Financial will lend in amounts up to $1 million, so its focus is on small business. Since many of the loans that it administers are viewed by many banks as high-risk loans, it is important that the sales staff and loan processors have a solid working relationship. Since the loans and factoring deals that First Community finances are risky, the interest that it charges is at prime plus 6 percent or sometimes higher.

First Community is a credible player in the market because of its history and the human resource policies of the company. The company invests in its employees and works to assure that turnover is low. The goal of this strategy is to develop a consistent, professional team that has more expertise than its competitors.

Whereas Jim Adamany, president and CEO, has a strong history in the industry and is a recognized expert in asset-based lending and factoring, First Community has one of the youngest staff and management teams in the finance industry. In the banking industry, promotions are slow in coming, because many banks employ conservative personnel programs. First Community, however, has recruited young, ambitious people who are specifically looking to grow with the company. As the company grows, so will the responsibility and rewards for these young executives. In his early thirties, for example, Matt Vincent is a vice president; at only 28, Brian Zcray is director of marketing.

Since First Community has a diverse product line, it must compete in distinct markets. Its factoring products compete with small specialized factoring companies. Factoring is a way for businesses to improve their cash flow by selling their invoices at a discount. Factoring clients are traditionally the smallest clients finance companies must serve. Education about the nature of the product is crucial if the company is to be successful, since this is often a new approach to financing for many companies. First Community's sales staff is well trained in understanding its product lines and acts as the client's representative as they work through the approval process.

To assure the loans or factoring deals fit within the risk profile of the company, First Community must ask many complex financial questions. Many small businesses are intimidated by credit officers, so First Community handles all of these inquiries through the business development officers. The business development officers, in turn, must understand the needs of their credit officers, who are attempting to minimize risk to the company while

maintaining a friendly rapport with the client. By centralizing the client contract through educated sales representatives, First Community is able to ask the hard financial questions and still keep the clients interested in the process. A potential customer can be easily discouraged by a credit administrator's strong questioning about financial background. Utilizing the business development officers as an intermediary reduces the fear of many applicants about the credit approval process. Thus, a sales focus is maintained throughout the recruitment and loan application process.

Internally at First Community Financial there is a continual pressure between the business development staff and the credit committee. The business development staff is focused on bringing in new clients. Their compensation is in large part dependent on how many deals they can execute for the company. Like sales staff in any industry, they are aggressive and always look for new markets for business. The sales staff sells products from both the finance department and the factoring department, so they must interact with credit officers from each division. In each of these groups are credit administrators specifically responsible for ensuring that potential deals meet the lending criteria of the organization. While the business development officer's orientation is to bring in more and more deals, the credit administrator's primary goal is to limit bad loans.

The pressure develops when business development officers bring in potential loans that are rejected by the credit administrators. Since the business development officers have some experience understanding the credit risks of their clients, they often understand the policy reasoning for denying or approving a loan. The business development offi-

cers have additional concerns that their loans that have potential to be financed are approved because many of the referral sources of the sales staff will only refer deals to companies that are lending. If First Community fails to help many of a bank's referral clients, that source of business may dry up, as bankers refer deals to other lending institutions.

These structural differences are handled by focused attempts at improving communication. As noted before, the First Community staff experiences an extremely low turnover rate. This allows for the development of a cohesive team. With a cohesive staff, the opportunity to maintain frank and open communication helps bridge the different orientations of the sales staff and the administration divisions. A simple philosophy that the opinions of all staff are to be respected is continually implemented.

Since approving a loan is often a policy decision, the sales staff and the loan administrators can have an open forum to discuss whether a loan will be approved. CEO Jim Adamany approves all loans, but since he values the opinions of all of his staff, he provides them all an opportunity to communicate. Issues such as the loan history for an applicant's industry, current bank loan policies, and other factors can be openly discussed from multiple perspectives.

Review Questions

1. What coordinative mechanisms does First Community use to manage the potential conflict between its sales and finance/auditing functions?
2. What qualities should First Community emphasize in hiring new staff to ensure that its functional organizational structure will not yield too many problems?

3. What are the key types of information transfer that First Community needs to emphasize, and how is this transmitted throughout the firm?

4. Why might a small finance company have such a simple structure while a larger firm might find this structure inappropriate? ■

CASE 18
Mission Management and Trust
· ·

Developed by Marcus Osborn, RSR Partners

With more than 500 business and political leaders in attendance from across the state of Arizona, CEO Carmen Barmudez of Mission Management and Trust accepted the prestigious ATHENA Award. The ATHENA, which is presented by the Arizona Chamber of Commerce, is annually awarded to companies that have a demonstrated track record in promoting women's issues within their company and the community. The 50-pound bronze statue that was presented to Mission Management and Trust was particularly special for the company's leadership because it was a tangible demonstration of their commitment to the community and to women's issues.

Mission Management and Trust is a small, newly formed company of just eight employees that has already made great headway in an industry that is dominated by giant corporations. Mission Management and Trust opened its doors just two years ago, and it already manages over $45 million in assets. What makes Mission's development even more impressive is that Mission is the first minority- and women-owned trust company in the nation.

The trust management industry provides services to individuals, organizations, and companies who want their assets managed and protected by specialized outside firms. Mission Management provides personal service to its customers at a level of sophistication that is unusual for a firm of its small size. Understanding that the trust management business is highly competitive, Mission developed a unique strategy that highlighted socially conscious policies combined with good business relations.

When the company was formed, it was created with more than the goal of just making a profit. Founder Carmen Barmudez started Mission with three principal goals in mind. "1. To run a top-quality trust company; 2. To promote within the company and, by example, increase opportunities for women and minorities; and 3. To donate a portion of all revenue to charitable projects supported by clients and staff." As these statements demonstrate, Mission Management and Trust was created with a specific purpose that was focused not just on the business of trust management but on the responsibility of being a good corporate citizen.

Even with these lofty goals, Mission faced the problem of finding clients who not only wanted quality services but were not hindered by some of the potential sacrifices a socially conscious investment company might make. Many investors want a high rate of return for their trusts, and social policy is of a much lesser concern. This was not the market Mission wanted to address, so it had to be selective in developing a client base.

Mission needed to find clients that fit its social philosophy about investing and corporate responsibility. The ideal customers would be individuals and organizations that were committed to socially conscious policies and wanted an investment strategy that reflected this commitment. Mission found a perfect niche in the market with religious institutions. Churches and other civic organizations across the nation have trusts that they use to fund special projects and maintain operating expenses. They need effective service, but in many cases these organizations must be mindful of investing in companies and other projects that do not reflect their ideals. For example, a trust company that invests in companies in the highly profitable liquor and cigarette industries would not be consistent with the philosophy of many religious organizations. Mission services this niche by developing an organization that is structurally designed to make socially conscious decisions.

Mission has already begun to meet one of its principal goals, which is to donate a portion of its profits to charities. It donated $4500 to causes ranging from Catholic Community Services to the Jewish Community Center scholarship program. These donations not only fulfill a goal of the organization but assist in the socially conscious client recruitment. Mission's target client base will find Mission a much more attractive trust company because of its charity programs. A religious organization can be comforted with the reality that some of the dollars it spends on trust management will be recycled into causes it promotes itself. The Mission policy makes good social policy, but it also makes good marketing sense. Understanding your clients is crucial to developing a small business, and Mission has mastered this principle.

Mission makes the most of its commitment to charitable causes by keeping its clients informed about the trust's activities and, more importantly, its community activities. *The Mission Bell,* a regular publication of Mission Management and Trust, details news and issues about the trust industry, company activities, and, most importantly, how Mission's social responsibility philosophy is being implemented. The name *Mission Bell* is more consistent with a religious publication than a corporate investing sheet, but it is consistent with its clients' needs. The name of the publication and its content clarifies Mission's role and purpose. For example, the *Mission Bell* summer issue presented articles on new hires, breaking investment news, and an article about how Mission is working with other groups to support socially responsible corporate investing. Thus, the Mission philosophy is clearly defined in its marketing and communication strategies.

To be consistent with the goals of the organizations, Carmen Barmudez collected a small staff of highly experienced individuals whose backgrounds and principles fit Mission's ideals. She frequently comments that the best business decision she ever made was "giving preference to intelligent, talented, compatible people whose main attribute was extensive experience." Mission employees are not just experts in the field of finance but leaders in their communities. These dual qualifications fulfill three important requirements that are crucial for the company's success. First, community involvement creates an appreciation of the investment sensitivities that are required by the organizations that Mission services. Second, individuals who are involved in the community have well-developed contacts that can be useful in business recruitment. Finally, socially active employees are committed to the purpose of the organization and help unify the corporate culture within Mission.

Claire B. Moore, vice president of Mission Management and Trust, is a perfect example of how a corporate philosophy has been translated into practical personnel decisions. Claire was recruited because she had extensive banking experience, as demonstrated by her vice presi-

dent position in Bank of America (Arizona). Her professional qualifications are augmented by her extensive involvement in the community, which includes the University of Arizona Foundation Planned Giving Council, Tucson Symphony, and the Junior League, to name a few.

The Mission case is a clear example of how matching a philosophy with a market can bear solid results. Mission's commitment to its ideals is evident and reflected in all of its business practices. When human resources, investing, marketing, and strategic planning decisions are made with unified goals in mind, the chances are good that a strong, successful corporate culture will develop.

Review Questions

1. How do the mission elements of Mission Management differ from most firms?
2. Does donating to charity before the firm is fully established mean that Mission is not demonstrating financial prudence?
3. Could Mission's unique mission contribute to effective coordination as well as adjustment to the market?
4. Would Mission's unique mission still yield success with more traditional investors? ∎

eXPERIENTIAL eXERCISES

My Best Manager

Procedure

1. Make a list of the attributes that describe the best manager you ever worked for. If you have trouble identifying an actual manager, make a list of attributes you would like the manager in your next job to have.
2. Form a group of four or five persons and share your lists.
3. Create one list that combines all the unique attributes of the "best" managers represented in your group. Make sure that you have all attributes listed, but list each only once. Place a check mark next to those that were reported by two or more members. Have one of your members prepared to present the list in general class discussion.
4. After all groups have finished Step 3, spokespersons should report to the whole class. The instructor will make a running list of the "best" manager attributes as viewed by the class.
5. Feel free to ask questions and discuss the results.

Graffiti Needs Assessment: Involving Students in the First Class Session

Contributed by Barbara K. Goza, Visiting Associate Professor, University of California at Santa Cruz and Associate Professor, California State Polytechnic University, Pomona. From *Journal of Management Education*, 1993.

Procedure

1. Complete the following sentences with as many endings as possible.
   1. When I first came to this class, I thought . . .
   2. My greatest concern this term is . . .
   3. In 3 years I will be . . .
   4. The greatest challenge facing the world today is . . .
   5. Organizational behavior specialists do . . .
   6. Human resources are . . .
   7. Organizational research is . . .
   8. The most useful question I've been asked is . . .
   9. The most important phenomenon in organizations is . . .
   10. I learn the most when . . .
2. Your instructor will guide you in a class discussion about your responses. Pay careful attention to similarities and differences among various students' answers.

My Best Job

Procedure

1. Make a list of the top five things you expect from your first (or next) full-time job.
2. Exchange lists with a nearby partner. Assign probabilities (or odds) to each goal on your partner's list to indicate how likely you feel it is that the goal can be accomplished. (*Note:* Your instructor may ask that everyone use the same probabilities format.)
3. Discuss your evaluations with your partner. Try to delete superficial goals or modify them to become more substantial. Try to restate any unrealistic goals to make them more realistic. Help your partner do the same.
4. Form a group of four to six persons. Within the group, have everyone share what they now consider to be the most "realistic" goals on their lists. Elect a spokesperson to share a sample of these items with the entire class.
5. Discuss what group members have individually learned from the exercise. Await further class discussion led by your instructor.

What Do You Value in Work?

Procedure

1. The following nine items are from a survey conducted by Nicholas J. Beutell and O. C. Brenner ("Sex Differences in Work Values," *Journal of Vocational Behavior*, Vol.

28, pp. 29–41, 1986). Rank the nine items in terms of how important (9 = most important) they would be to you in a job.

How important is it to you to have a job that:
____ Is respected by other people?
____ Encourages continued development of knowledge and skills?
____ Provides job security?
____ Provides a feeling of accomplishment?
____ Provides the opportunity to earn a high income?
____ Is intellectually stimulating?
____ Rewards good performance with recognition?
____ Provides comfortable working conditions?
____ Permits advancement to high administrative responsibility?

2. Form into groups as designated by your instructor. Within each group, the *men in the group* will meet to develop a consensus ranking of the items as they think the *women* in the Beutell and Brenner survey ranked them. The reasons for the rankings should be shared and discussed so they are clear to everyone. The *women in the group* should not participate in this ranking task. They should listen to the discussion and be prepared to comment later in class discussion. A spokesperson for the men in the group should share the group's rankings with the class.

3. (*Optional*) Form into groups as designated by your instructor, but with each group consisting entirely of men or women. Each group should meet and decide which of the work values members of the *opposite* sex ranked first in the Beutell and Brenner survey. Do this again for the work value ranked last. The reasons should be discussed, along with reasons that each of the other values probably was not ranked first . . . or last. A spokesperson for each group should share group results with the rest of the class.

Source: Adapted from Roy J. Lewicki, Donald D. Bowen, Douglas T. Hall, and Francine S. Hall, *Experiences in Management and Organizational Behavior,* 3rd ed. (New York: John Wiley & Sons, Inc., 1988), pp. 23–26. Used by permission.

EXERCISE 5

My Asset Base

A business has an asset base or set of resources that it uses to produce a good or service of value to others. For a business, these are the assets or resources it uses to achieve results, including capital, land, patented products or processes, buildings and equipment, raw materials, and the human resources or employees, among others.

Each of us has an asset base that supports our ability to accomplish the things we set out to do. We refer to our personal assets as *talents, strengths,* or *abilities.* We probably inherit our talents from our parents, but we acquire many of our abilities and strengths through learning. One thing is certain: we feel very proud of the talents and abilities we have.

Procedure

1. Printed here is a T chart that you are to fill out. On the right-hand side of the T, list four or five of your accomplishments—*things you have done of which you are most proud.* Your accomplishments should only include those things for which you can take credit, those *things for which you are primarily responsible.* If you are proud of the sorority to which you belong, you may be justifiably proud, but don't list it unless you

can argue that the sorority's excellence is due primarily to your efforts. However, if you feel that having been invited to join the sorority is a major accomplishment for you, then you may include it.

When you have completed the right-hand side of the chart, fill in the left-hand side by listing *talents, strengths,* and *abilities* that you have that have enabled you to accomplish the outcomes listed on the right-hand side.

My Asset Base

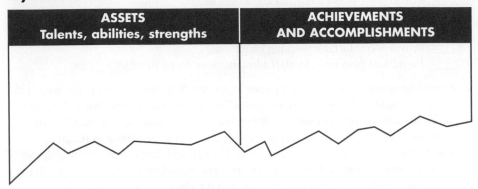

ASSETS Talents, abilities, strengths	ACHIEVEMENTS AND ACCOMPLISHMENTS

2. Share your lists with other team members. As each member shares his or her list, pay close attention to your own perceptions and feelings. Notice the effect this has on your attitudes toward the other team members.
3. Discuss these questions in your group:
   (a) How did your attitudes and feelings toward other members of the team change as you pursued the activity? What does this tell you about the process whereby we come to get to know and care about people?
   (b) How did you feel about the instructions the instructor provided? What did you expect to happen? Were your expectations accurate?

Source: Adapted from Donald D. Bowen et al., *Experiences in Management and Organizational Behavior,* 4th ed. (New York: John Wiley & Sons, Inc., 1997).

Expatriate Assignments

Contributed by Robert E. Ledman, Morehouse College

This exercise focuses on issues related to workers facing international assignments. It illustrates that those workers face a multitude of issues. It further demonstrates that managers who want employees to realize the maximum benefits of international assignments should be aware of, and prepared to deal with, those issues. Some

of the topics that are easily addressed with this exercise include the need for culture and language training for the employees and their families and the impact that international assignments may have on an employee's family and how that may affect an employee's willingness to seek such assignments.

Procedure

1. Form into "families" of four or five. Since many students today have only one parent at home, it is helpful if some groups do not have students to fill both

Source: Robert E. Ledman, Gannon University. Presented in the Experiential Exercise Track of the 1996 ABSEL Conference and published in the *Proceedings* of that conference.

parental roles in the exercise. Each student is assigned to play a family member and given a description of that person. Descriptions of family members are given below.

2. Enter into a 20-minute discussion to explore how a proposed overseas assignment will affect the family members. Your goal is to try to reach a decision about whether the assignment should be taken. You must also decide whether the entire family or only the family member being offered the assignment will relocate. The assignment is for a minimum of two years, with possible annual extensions resulting in a total of four years, and your family, or the member offered the assignment, will be provided, at company expense, one trip back to the states each year for a maximum period of 15 days. The member offered the assignment will not receive any additional housing or cost-of-living supplements described in the role assignment if he or she chooses to go overseas alone and can expect his or her living expenses to exceed substantially the living allowance being provided by the company. In your discussion, address the following questions:

   (a) What are the most important concerns your family has about relocating to a foreign country?

   (b) What information should you seek about the proposed host country to be able to make a more informed decision?

   (c) What can the member offered the assignment do to make the transition easier if he or she goes overseas alone? If the whole family relocates?

   (d) What should the member offered the assignment do to ensure that this proposed assignment will not create unnecessary stress for him or her and the rest of the family?

   (e) What lessons for managers of expatriate assignees are presented by the situation in this exercise?

Try to reach some "family" consensus. If a consensus is not possible, however, resolve any differences in the manner you think the family in the role descriptions would ultimately resolve any differences.

3. Share your answers with the rest of the class. Explain the rationale for your answers and answer questions from the remainder of the class.

4. (*Optional*) After each group has reported on a given question, the instructor may query the class about how their answers are consistent, or inconsistent, with common practices of managers as described in the available literature.

Descriptions of Family Members
Person Being Offered Overseas Assignment

This person is a middle- to upper-level executive who is on a fast track to senior management. He or she has been offered the opportunity to manage an overseas operation, with the assurance of a promotion to a vice presidency upon return to the states. The company will pay all relocation expenses, including selling costs for the family home and the costs associated with finding a new home upon return. The employer will also provide language training for the employee and cultural awareness training for the entire family. The employee will receive a living allowance equal to 20 percent of his or her salary. This should be adequate to provide the family a comparable standard of living to that which is possible on the employee's current salary.

Spouse of the Person Offered an Overseas Assignment (Optional)

This person is also a professional with highly transferable skills and experience for the domestic market. It is unknown how easily he or she may be able to find employment in the foreign country. This person's income, though less than his or her spouse's, is necessary if the couple is to continue paying for their child's college tuition and to prepare for the next child to enter college in two years. This person has spent 15 years developing a career, including completing a degree at night.

Oldest Child

This child is a second-semester junior in college and is on track to graduate in 16 months. Transferring at this time would probably mean adding at least one semester to complete the degree. He or she has been dating the same person for over a year; they have talked about getting married immediately after graduation, although they are not yet formally engaged.

Middle Child

This child is a junior in high school. He or she has already begun visiting college campuses in preparation for applying in the fall. This child is involved in a number of school activities; he or she is a photographer for the yearbook and plays a varsity sport. This child has a learning disability for which services are being provided by the school system.

Youngest Child

This child is a middle school student, age 13. He or she is actively involved in Scouting and takes piano lessons. This child has a history of medical conditions that have required regular visits to the family physician and specialists. This child has several very close friends who have attended the same school for several years.

Cultural Cues

Contributed by Susan Rawson Zacur and W. Alan Randolph, University of Baltimore

Introduction

In the business context, culture involves shared beliefs and expectations that govern the behavior of people. In this exercise, *foreign culture* refers to a set of beliefs and expectations different from those of the participant's home culture (which has been invented by the participants).

Procedure

1. (10–15 minutes) Divide into two groups, each with color-coded badges. For example, the blue group could receive blue Post-it notes and the yellow group could receive yellow Post-it notes. Print your first name in bold letters on the badge and wear it throughout the exercise.

   Work with your group members to invent your own cultural cues. Think about the kinds of behaviors and words that will signify to all members that they belong together in one culture. For each category provided below, identify and record at least one important attribute for your culture.

Cultural Cues:	Your Culture:
Facial expression:	_____
Eye contact (note: you must have some eye contact in order to observe others):	_____
Handshake:	_____
Body language (note: must be evident while standing):	_____
Key words or phrases:	_____

   Once you have identified desirable cultural aspects for your group, practice them. It is best to stand with your group and to engage one another in conversations involving two or three people at a time. Your aim in talking with one another is to learn as much as possible about each other—hobbies, interests, where you live, what your family is like, what courses you are taking, and so on, all the while practicing the behaviors and words identified above. It is not necessary for participants to answer questions of a personal nature truthfully. Invention is permissible because the conversation is only a means to the end of cultural observation. Your aim at this point is to become comfortable with the indicators of your particular culture. Practice until the indicators are second nature to you.

2. Now assume that you work for a business that has decided to explore the potential for doing business with companies in a different culture. You are to learn as much as possible about another culture. To do so, you will send from one to three representatives from your group on a "business trip" to the other culture. These representatives must, insofar as possible, behave in a manner that is consistent with your culture. At the same time, each representative must endeavor to learn as much as possible about the

Source: Adapted by Susan Rawson Zacur and W. Alan Randolph from *Journal of Management Education,* Vol. 17, No. 4 (November 1993), pp. 510–516.

people in the other culture, while keeping eyes and ears open to cultural attributes that will be useful in future negotiations with foreign businesses. (*Note:* At no time will it be considered ethical behavior for the representative to ask direct questions about the foreign culture's attributes. These must be gleaned from firsthand experience.)

While your representatives are away, you will receive one or more exchange visitors from the other culture, who will engage in conversation as they attempt to learn more about your organizational culture. You must strictly adhere to the cultural aspects of your own culture while you converse with the visitors.

3. (5–10 minutes) All travelers return to your home cultures. As a group, discuss and record what you have learned about the foreign culture based on the exchange of visitors. This information will serve as the basis for orienting the next representatives who will make a business trip.

4. (5–10 minutes) Select one to three different group members to make another trip to the other culture to check out the assumptions your group has made about the other culture. This "checking out" process will consist of actually practicing the other culture's cues to see whether they work.

5. (5–10 minutes) Once the traveler(s) have returned and reported on findings, as a group prepare to report to the class what you have learned about the other culture.

EXERCISE 8

Prejudice in Our Lives

Contributed by Susan Schor of Pace University and Annie McKee of The Wharton School, University of Pennsylvania with the assistance of Ariel Fishman of The Wharton School

Procedure

1. As a large class group, generate a list of groups that tend to be targets of prejudice and stereotypes in our culture—such groups can be based on gender, race, ethnicity, sexual orientation, region, religion, and so on. After generating a list, either as a class or in small groups, identify a few common positive and negative stereotypes associated with each group. Also consider relationships or patterns that exist between some of the lists. Discuss the implications for groups that have stereotypes that are valued in organizations versus groups whose stereotypes are viewed negatively in organizations.

2. As an individual, think about the lists you have now generated, and list those groups with which you identify. Write about an experience in which you were stereotyped as a member of a group. Ask yourself the following questions and write down your thoughts:

   (a) What group do I identify with?
   (b) What was the stereotype?
   (c) What happened? When and where did the incident occur? Who said what to whom?
   (d) What were my reactions? How did I feel? What did I think? What did I do?

   (e) What were the consequences? How did the incident affect myself and others?

3. Now, in small groups, discuss your experiences. Briefly describe the incident and focus on how the incident made you feel. Select one incident from the ones shared in your group to role-play for the class. Then, as a class, discuss your reactions to each role play. Identify the prejudice or stereotype portrayed, the feelings the situation evoked, and the consequences that might result from such a situation.

4. Think about the prejudices and stereotypes you hold about other people. Ask yourself, "What groups do I feel prejudice toward? What stereotypes do I hold about members of each of these groups?" How may such a prejudice have developed—did a family member or close friend or television influence you to stereotype a particular group in a certain way?

5. Now try to identify implications of prejudice in the workplace. How do prejudice and stereotypes affect workers, managers, relationships between people, and the organization as a whole? Consider how you might want to change erroneous beliefs as well as how you would encourage other people to change their own erroneous beliefs.

How We View Differences

Contributed by Barbara Walker

Introduction

Clearly, the workplace of the future will be much more diverse than it is today: more women, more people of color, more international representation, more diverse lifestyles and ability profiles, and the like. Managing a diverse workforce and working across a range of differences is quickly becoming a "core competency" for effective managers.

Furthermore, it is also becoming clear that diversity in a work team can significantly enhance the creativity and quality of the team's output. In today's turbulent business environment, utilizing employee diversity will give the manager and the organization a competitive edge in tapping all of the available human resources more effectively. This exercise is an initial step in the examination of how we work with people whom we see as different from us. It is fairly simple, straightforward, and safe, but its implications are profound.

Procedure

1. Read the following:

Imagine that you are traveling in a rental car in a city you have never visited before. You have a one-hour drive on an uncrowded highway before you reach your destination. You decide that you would like to spend the time listening to some of your favorite kind of music on the car radio.

The rental car has four selection buttons available, each with a preset station that plays a different type of music. One plays *country music,* one plays *rock,* one plays *classical,* and one plays *jazz.* Which type of music would you choose to listen to for the next hour as you drive along? (Assume you want to relax and just stick with one station; you don't want to bother switching around between stations.)

Source: Exercise developed by Barbara Walker, a pioneer on work on valuing differences. Adapted for this volume by Douglas T. Hall. Used by permission of Barbara Walker.

2. Form into groups based on the type of music that you have chosen. All who have chosen country will meet in an area designated by the instructor. Those who chose rock will meet in another area, and so on. In your groups, answer the following question. Appoint one member to be the spokesperson to report your answers back to the total group.

Question

For each of the other groups, what words would you use to describe people who like to listen to that type of music?

3. Have each spokesperson report the responses of her or his group to the question in Step 2. Follow with class discussion of these additional questions:
   (a) What do you think is the purpose or value of this exercise?
   (b) What did you notice about the words used to describe the other groups? Were there any *surprises* in this exercise for you?
   (c) Upon what sorts of data do you think these images were based?
   (d) What term do we normally use to describe these generalized perceptions of another group?
   (e) What could some of the consequences be?
   (f) How do the perceptual processes here relate to other kinds of intergroup differences, such as race, gender, culture, ability, ethnicity, health, age, nationality, and so on?
   (g) What does this exercise suggest about the ease with which intergroup stereotypes form?
   (h) What might be ways an organization might facilitate the valuing and utilizing of differences between people?

Alligator River Story

Source: From Sidney B. Simon, Howard Kirschenbaum, and Leland Howe, *Values Clarification, The Handbook,* rev. ed., copyright © 1991, Values Press, P.O. Box 450, Sunderland, MA. 01375.

The Alligator River Story

There lived a woman named Abigail who was in love with a man named Gregory. Gregory lived on the shore of a river. Abigail lived on the opposite shore of the same river. The river that separated the two lovers was teeming with dangerous alligators. Abigail wanted to cross the river to be with Gregory. Unfortunately, the bridge had been washed out by a heavy flood the previous week. So she went to ask Sinbad, a riverboat captain, to take her across. He said he would be glad to if she would consent to go to bed with him prior to the voyage. She promptly refused and went to a friend named Ivan to explain her plight. Ivan did not want to get involved at all in the situation. Abigail felt her only alternative was to accept Sinbad's terms. Sinbad fulfilled his promise to Abigail and delivered her into the arms of Gregory.

When Abigail told Gregory about her amorous escapade in order to cross the river, Gregory cast her aside with disdain. Heartsick and rejected, Abigail turned to Slug with her tail of woe. Slug, feeling compassion for Abigail, sought out Gregory and beat him brutally. Abigail was overjoyed at the sight of Gregory getting his due. As the sun set on the horizon, people heard Abigail laughing at Gregory.

Procedure

1. Read "The Alligator River Story."

2. After reading the story, rank the five characters in the story beginning with the one whom you consider the most offensive and end with the one whom you consider the least objectionable. That is, the character who seems to be the most reprehensible to you should be entered first in the list following the story, then the second most reprehensible, and so on, with the least reprehensible or objectionable being entered fifth. Of course, you will have your own reasons as to why you rank them in the order that you do. Very briefly note these too.

3. Form groups as assigned by your instructor (at least four persons per group with gender mixed).

4. Each group should:
   (a) Elect a spokesperson for the group
   (b) Compare how the group members have ranked the characters
   (c) Examine the reasons used by each of the members for their rankings
   (d) Seek consensus on a final group ranking

5. Following your group discussions, you will be asked to share your outcomes and reasons for agreement or nonagreement. A general class discussion will then be held.

Teamwork and Motivation

Contributed by Dr. Barbara McCain, Oklahoma City University

Procedure

1. Read this situation.

You are the *owner* of a small manufacturing corporation. Your company manufactures widgets—a commodity. Your widget is a clone of nationally known widgets. Your widget, "WooWoo," is less expensive and more readily available than the nationally known brand. Presently, the sales are high. However, there are many rejects, which increases your cost and delays the delivery. You have 50 employees in the following departments: sales, assembly, technology, and administration.

2. In groups, discuss methods to motivate all of the employees in the organization—rank them in terms of preference.

3. Design an organization motivation plan that encourages high job satisfaction, low turnover, high productivity, and high-quality work.

4. Is there anything special you can do about the minimum-wage service worker? How do you motivate this individual? On what motivation theory do you base your decision?

5. Report to the class your motivation plan. Record your ideas on the board and allow all groups to build on the first plan. Discuss additions and corrections as the discussion proceeds.

Individual Worker	Team Member
Talks	
Me oriented	
Department focused	
Competitive	
Logical	
Written messages	
Image	
Secrecy	
Short-term sighted	
Immediate results	
Critical	
Tenure	

Directions: Fill in the right-hand column with descriptive terms. These terms should suggest a change in behavior from individual work to teamwork.

EXERCISE 12

The Downside of Punishment

Contributed by Dr. Barbara McCain, Oklahoma City University

Procedure

There are numerous problems associated with using punishment or discipline to change behavior. Punishment creates negative effects in the workplace. To better understand this, work in your group to give an example of each of the following situations:

1. Punishment may not be applied to the person whose behavior you want to change.

2. Punishment applied over time may suppress the occurrence of socially desirable behaviors.

3. Punishment creates a dislike of the person who is implementing the punishment.

4. Punishment results in undesirable emotions such as anxiety and aggressiveness.

5. Punishment increases the desire to avoid punishment.

6. Punishing one behavior does not guarantee that the desired behavior will occur.

7. Punishment follow-up requires allocation of additional resources.

8. Punishment may create a communication barrier and inhibit the flow of information.

Source: Adapted from class notes: Dr. Larry Michaelson, Oklahoma University.

EXERCISE 13

Tinker Toys

Contributed by Bonnie McNeely, Murray State University

Materials Needed
Tinker Toy sets.

Procedure
1. Form groups as assigned by the instructor. The mission of each group or temporary organization is to build the tallest possible Tinker Toy tower. Each group should determine worker roles: at least four students will be builders, some will be consultants who offer suggestions, and the remaining students will be observers who remain silent and complete the observation sheet provided below.

2. Rules for the exercise:
   (a) Fifteen minutes allowed to plan the tower, but *only 60 seconds* to build.
   (b) No more than two Tinker Toy pieces can be put together during the planning.
   (c) All pieces must be put back in the box before the competition begins.
   (d) Completed tower must stand alone.

Observation Sheet
1. What planning activities were observed?

   Did the group members adhere to the rules?

2. What organizing activities were observed?

Source: Adapted from Bonnie McNeely, "Using the Tinker Toy Exercise to Teach the Four Functions of Management, *Journal of Management Education,* Vol. 18, No. 4 (November 1994), pp. 468–472.

Was the task divided into subtasks? Division of labor?

3. Was the group motivated to succeed? Why or why not?

4. Were any control techniques observed?

Was a timekeeper assigned?

Were backup plans discussed?

5. Did a clear leader emerge from the group?

What behaviors indicated that this person was the leader?

How did the leader establish credibility with the group?

6. Did any conflicts within the group appear?

Was there a power struggle for the leadership position?

EXERCISE 14

Job Design Preferences

Procedure

1. Use the left column to rank the following job characteristics in the order most important *to you* (1—highest to 10—lowest). Then use the right column to rank them in the order you think they are most important *to others*.

____	Variety of tasks	____
____	Performance feedback	____
____	Autonomy/freedom in work	____
____	Working on a team	____
____	Having responsibility	____
____	Making friends on the job	____
____	Doing all of a job, not part	____
____	Importance of job to others	____
____	Having resources to do well	____
____	Flexible work schedule	____

2. Form workgroups as assigned by your instructor. Share your rankings with other group members. Discuss where you have different individual preferences and where your impressions differ from the preferences of others. Are there any major patterns in your group—for either the "personal" or the "other" rankings? Develop group consensus rankings for each column. Designate a spokesperson to share the group rankings and results of any discussion with the rest of the class.

My Fantasy Job

Contributed by Lady Hanson, California State Polytechnic University, Pomona

Procedure

1. Think about a possible job that represents what you consider to be your ideal or "fantasy" job. For discussion purposes, try to envision it as a job you would hold within a year of finishing your current studies. Write down a brief description of that job in the space below. Start the description with the following words—*My fantasy job would be* . . .

2. Review the description of the Hackman/Oldham model of Job Characteristics Theory offered in the textbook. Note in particular the descriptions of the core characteristics. Consider how each of them could be maximized in your fantasy job. Indicate in the spaces that follow how specific parts of your fantasy job will fit into or relate to each of the core characteristics.

   (a) Skill variety: _____

   (b) Task identity: _____

   (c) Task significance: _____

   (d) Autonomy: _____

   (e) Job feedback: _____

3. Form into groups as assigned by your instructor. In the group have each person share his or her fantasy job and the descriptions of its core characteristics. Select one person from your group to tell the class as a whole about her or his fantasy job. Be prepared to participate in a general discussion regarding the core characteristics and how they may or may not relate to job performance and job satisfaction. Consider also the likelihood that the fantasy jobs of class members are really attainable—in other words: Can "fantasy" become fact?

Motivation by Job Enrichment

Contributed by Diana Page, University of West Florida

Procedure

1. Form groups of five to seven members. Each group is assigned one of the following categories:

(a) Bank teller
(b) Retail sales clerk
(c) Manager, fast-food service (e.g., McDonald's)
(d) Wait person
(e) Receptionist
(f) Restaurant manager
(g) Clerical worker (or bookkeeper)
(h) Janitor

2. As a group, develop a short description of job duties for the job your group has been assigned. The list should contain approximately four to six items.

3. Next, using job characteristics theory, enrich the job using the specific elements described in the theory. Develop a new list of job duties that incorporate any or all of the core job characteristics suggested by Richard Hackman and Greg Oldham, such as skill variety, task identity, and so on. Indicate for each of the new job duties which job characteristic(s) was/were used.

4. One member of each group should act as the spokesperson and will present the group's ideas to the class. Specifically describe one or two of the old job tasks. Describe the modified job tasks. Finally, relate the new job tasks the group has developed to specific job core characteristics such as skill variety, skill identity, and so on.

5. The group should also be prepared to discuss these and other follow-up questions:
(a) How would a manager go about enlarging but not enriching this job?
(b) Why was this job easy or hard?
(c) What are the possible constraints on actually accomplishing this enrichment in the workplace?
(d) What possible reasons are there that a worker would *not* like to have this newly enriched job?

EXERCISE 17

Annual Pay Raises

Procedure

1. Read the job descriptions below and decide on a percentage pay increase for each of the eight employees.

2. Make salary increase recommendations for each of the eight managers that you supervise. There are no formal company restrictions on the size of raises you give, but the total for everyone should not exceed the $10,900 (a 4 percent increase in the salary pool) that has been budgeted for this purpose. You have a variety of information on which to base the decisions, including a "productivity index" (PI), which Industrial Engineering computes as a quantitative measure of operating efficiency for each manager's work unit. This index ranges from a high of 10 to a low of 1. Indicate the percentage increase *you* would give each manager in the blank space next to each manager's name. Be prepared to explain why.

_____ *A. Alvarez* Alvarez is new this year and has a tough workgroup whose task is dirty and difficult. This is a hard position to fill, but you don't feel Alvarez is particularly good. The word around is that the other managers agree with you. PI = 3. Salary = $33,000.

_____ *B. J. Cook* Cook is single and a "swinger" who enjoys leisure time. Everyone laughs at the problems B.J. has getting the work out, and you feel it certainly is lacking. Cook has been in the job two years. PI = 3. Salary = $34,500.

_____ *Z. Davis*   In the position three years, Davis is one of your best people, even though some of the other managers don't agree. With a spouse who is independently wealthy, Davis doesn't need money but likes to work. PI = 7. Salary = $36,600.

_____ *M. Frame*   Frame has personal problems and is hurting financially. Others gossip about Frame's performance, but you are quite satisfied with this second-year employee. PI = 7. Salary = $34,700.

_____ *C. M. Liu*   Liu is just finishing a fine first year in a tough job. Highly respected by the others, Liu has a job offer in another company at a 15 percent increase in salary. You are impressed, and the word is that the money is important. PI = 9. Salary = $34,000.

_____ *B. Ratin*   Ratin is a first-year manager whom you and the others think is doing a good job. This is a bit surprising since Ratin turned out to be a "free spirit" who doesn't seem to care much about money or status. PI = 9. Salary = $33,800.

_____ *H. Smith*   Smith is a first-year manager recently divorced and with two children to support as a single parent. The others like Smith a lot, but your evaluation is not very high. Smith could certainly use extra money. PI = 5. Salary = $33,000.

_____ *G. White*   White is a big spender who always has the latest clothes and a new car. In the first year on what you would call an easy job, White doesn't seem to be doing very well. For some reason, though, the others talk about White as the "cream of the new crop." PI = 5. Salary = $33,000.

3. Convene in a group of four to seven persons and share your raise decision.

4. As a group, decide on a new set of raises and be prepared to report them to the rest of the class. Make sure that the group spokesperson can provide the rationale for each person's raise.

5. The instructor will call on each group to report its raise decisions. After discussion, an "expert's" decision will be given.

EXERCISE 18

Serving on the Boundary

Contributed by Joseph A. Raelin, Boston College

Procedure

The objective of this exercise is to experience what it is like being on the boundary of your team or organization and to experience the boundary person's divided loyalties.

1. As a full class, decide on a stake you are willing to wager on this exercise. Perhaps it will be 5¢ or 10¢ per person or even more.

2. Form into teams. Select or elect one member from your team to be an expert. The expert will be the person most competent in the field of international geography.

3. The experts will then form into a team of their own.

4. The teams, including the expert team, are going to be given a straightforward question to work on. Whichever team comes closest to deriving the correct answer will win the pool from the stakes already collected. The question is any one of the following as assigned by the instructor: (a) What is the airline distance between Beijing and Moscow (in miles)? (b) What is the highest point in Texas (in feet)? (c) What was the number of American battle deaths in the Revolutionary War?

5. Each team should now work on the question, including the expert team. However, after all the teams come up with a verdict, the experts will be allowed to return to their "home" team to inform the team of the expert team's deliberations.

6. The expert team members are now asked to reconvene as an expert team. They should determine their final answer to the question. Then, they are to face a decision. The instructor will announce that for a period of up to two minutes, any expert may either return to their home team (to sink or swim with the answer of the home team) or remain with the expert team. As long as two members remain in the expert team, it will be considered a group and may vie for the pool. Home teams, during the two-minute decision period, can do whatever they would like to do—within bounds of normal decorum—to try to persuade their expert member to return.

7. After the two minutes are up, teams will hand in their verdicts to the question, and the team team the closest answer (up or down) will be awarded the pool.

8. Class members should be prepared to discuss the following questions:
   (a) What did it feel like to be a boundary person (the expert)?
   (b) What could the teams have done to corral any of the boundary persons who chose not to return home?

EXERCISE 19

Eggsperiential Exercise

Contributed by Dr. Barbara McCain, Oklahoma City University

Materials Needed

1 raw egg per group

6 plastic straws per group

1 yard of plastic tape

1 large plastic jar

Procedure

1. Form into equal groups of five to seven people.
2. The task is to drop an egg from the chair onto the plastic without breaking the egg. Groups can evaluate the materials and plan their task for 10 minutes. During this period the materials may not be handled.
3. Groups have 10 minutes for construction.
4. One group member will drop the egg while standing on top of a chair in front of the class. One by one a representative from each group will drop their eggs.
5. Optional: Each group will name the egg.
6. Each group discusses their individual/group behav-

iors during this activity. Optional: This analysis may be summarized in written form. The following questions may be utilized in the analysis:
   (a) What kind of group is it? Explain.
   (b) Was the group cohesive? Explain.
   (c) How did the cohesiveness relate to performance? Explain.
   (d) Was there evidence of groupthink? Explain.
   (e) Were group norms established? Explain.
   (f) Was there evidence of conflict? Explain.
   (g) Was there any evidence of social loafing? Explain.

EXERCISE 20

Scavenger Hunt — Team Building

Contributed by Michael R. Manning and Paula J. Schmidt, New Mexico State University

Introduction

Think about what it means to be a part of a team—a successful team. What makes one team more successful than another? What does each team member need to do in order for their team to be successful? What are the characteristics of an effective team?

Procedure

1. Form teams as assigned by your instructor. Locate the items on the list below while following these important rules:

   a. Your team *must stay together at all times*—that is, you cannot go in separate directions.

   b. Your team must return to the classroom in the time allotted by the instructor.

   The team with the most items on the list will be declared the most successful team.

2. Next, reflect on your team's experience. What did each team member do? What was your team's strategy? What made your team effective? Make a list of the most important things your team did to be succesful. Nominate a spokesperson to summarize your team's discussion for the class. What items were similar between teams? That is, what helped each team to be effective?

Items for Scavenger Hunt

Each item is to be identified and brought back to the classroom.

1. A book with the word "team" in the title.
2. A joke about teams that you share with the class.

Source: Adapted from Michael R. Manning and Paula J. Schmidt, *Journal of Management Education,* Building Effective Teams: A Quick Exercise Based on a Scavenger Hunt (Thousand Oaks, CA: Sage Publications, 1995), pp. 392–398. Used by permission. Reference for list of items for scavenger hunt from C. E. Larson and F. M. Lafas, *Team Work: What Must Go Right/What Can Go Wrong* (Newbury Park, CA: Sage Publications, 1989).

3. A blade of grass from the university football field.
4. A souvenir from the state.
5. A picture of a team or group.
6. A newspaper article about a team.
7. A team song to be composed and performed for the class.
8. A leaf from an oak tree.
9. Stationery from the dean's office.
10. A cup of sand.
11. A pine cone.
12. A live reptile. (*Note:* Sometimes a team member has one for a pet or the students are ingenious enough to visit a local pet store.)
13. A definition of group "cohesion" that you share with the class.
14. A set of chopsticks.
15. Three cans of vegetables.
16. A branch of an elm tree.
17. Three unusual items.
18. A ball of cotton.
19. The ear from a prickly pear cactus.
20. A group name.

(*Note:* Items may be substituted as appropriate for your locale.)

EXERCISE 21

Work Team Dynamics

Introduction

Think about your course work team, a work team you are involved in for another course, or any other team suggested by the instructor. Indicate how often each of the following statements accurately reflects your experience in the team. Use this scale:

1 = Always   2 = Frequently   3 = Sometimes   4 = Never

____ 1. My ideas get a fair hearing.

____ 2. I am encouraged for innovative ideas and risk taking.

____ 3. Diverse opinions within the team are encouraged.

____ 4. I have all the responsibility I want.

_____ 5. There is a lot of favoritism shown in the team.

_____ 6. Members trust one another to do their assigned work.

_____ 7. The team sets high standards of performance excellence.

_____ 8. People share and change jobs a lot in the team.

_____ 9. You can make mistakes and learn from them on this team.

_____ 10. This team has good operating rules.

Procedure

Form groups as assigned by your instructor. Ideally, this will be the team you have just rated. Have all team members share their ratings, and make one master rating for the team as a whole. Circle the items on which there are the biggest differences of opinion. Discuss those items and try to find out why they exist. In general, the better a team scores on this instrument, the higher its creative potential. If everyone has rated the same team, make a list of the five most important things members can do to improve its operations in the future. Nominate a spokesperson to summarize the team discussion for the class as a whole.

_____

Source: Adapted from William Dyer, _Team Building,_ 2nd ed. (Reading, MA: Addison-Wesley, 1987), pp. 123–125.

EXERCISE 22 •

Identifying Group Norms

Procedure

1. Choose an organization you know quite a bit about.
2. Complete the questionnaire below, indicating your responses using one of the following:

> (a) Strongly agree or encourage it.
> (b) Agree with it or encourage it.
> (c) Consider it unimportant.
> (d) Disagree with or discourage it.
> (e) Strongly disagree with or discourage it.

_If_ an employee in this organization were to . . . _Most other employees would:_

1. Show genuine concern for the problems that face the organization and make suggestions about solving them . . .
2. Set very high personal standards of performance . . .   _____
3. Try to make the workgroup operate more like a team when dealing with issues or problems . . .   _____
4. Think of going to a supervisor with a problem . . .   _____
5. Evaluate expenditures in terms of the benefits they will provide for the organization . . .   _____

6. Express concern for the well-being of other members of the organization . . . ____

7. Keep a customer or client waiting while looking after matters of personal convenience . . . ____

8. Criticize a fellow employee who is trying to improve things in the work situation . . . ____

9. Actively look for ways to expand his or her knowledge to be able to do a better job . . . ____

10. Be perfectly honest in answering this questionnaire . . . ____

Scoring

A = +2, B = +1, C = 0, D = –1, E = –2

1. Organizational/Personal Pride
   Score ____
2. Performance/Excellence
   Score ____
3. Teamwork/Communication
   Score ____
4. Leadership/Supervision
   Score ____
5. Profitability/Cost-Effectiveness
   Score ____

6. Colleague/Associate Relations
   Score ____
7. Customer/Client Relations
   Score ____
8. Innovativeness/Creativity
   Score ____
9. Training/Development
   Score ____
10. Candor/Openness
    Score ____

EXERCISE 23

Workgroup Culture

Contributed by Conrad N. Jackson, MPC Inc.

Procedure

1. The bipolar scales on this instrument can be used to evaluate a group's process in a number of useful ways. Use it to measure where you see the group to be at present. To do this, *circle* the number that best represents *how you see the culture of the group.* You can also indicate how you think the group *should* function by using a different symbol, such as a square (□) or a caret (^), to indicate how you saw the group at some time in the past.

2. (a) If you are assessing your own group, have everyone fill in the instrument, summarize the scores, then discuss their bases (what members say and do that has led to these interpretations) and implications. This is often an extremely productive intervention to improve group or team functioning.

(b) If you are assessing another group, use the scores as the basis for your feedback. Be sure to provide specific feedback on behavior *you have observed* in addition to the subjective interpretations of your ratings on the scales in this instrument.

(c) The instrument can also be used to compare a group's self-assessment with the assessment provided by another group.

1. Trusting	1 : 2 : 3 : 4 : 5	Suspicious
2. Helping	1 : 2 : 3 : 4 : 5	Ignoring, blocking
3. Expressing feelings	1 : 2 : 3 : 4 : 5	Suppressing feelings
4. Risk taking	1 : 2 : 3 : 4 : 5	Cautious
5. Authenticity	1 : 2 : 3 : 4 : 5	Game playing
6. Confronting	1 : 2 : 3 : 4 : 5	Avoiding
7. Open	1 : 2 : 3 : 4 : 5	Hidden, diplomatic

Source: Adapted from Donald D. Bowen, et al., *Experiences in Management and Organizational Behavior,* 4th ed. (New York: John Wiley & Sons, Inc., 1997.)

The Hot Seat

Contributed by Barry R. Armandi, SUNY–Old Westbury

Procedure
1. Form into groups as assigned by your instructor.
2. Read the following situation.

A number of years ago, Professor Stevens was asked to attend a departmental meeting at a university. He had been on leave from the department, but a junior faculty member discreetly requested that he attend to protect the rights of the junior faculty. The Chair, or head of the department, was a typical Machiavellian, whose only concerns were self-serving. Professor Stevens had had a number of previous disagreements with the Chair. The heart of the disagreements centered around the Chair's abrupt and domineering style and his poor relations with the junior faculty, many of whom felt mistreated and scared.

The department was a conglomeration of different professorial types. Included in the mix were behavioralists, generalists,

computer scientists, and quantitative analysts. The department was embedded in the school of business, which had three other departments. There was much confusion and concern among the faculty, since this was a new organizational design. Many of the faculty were at odds with each other over the direction the school was now taking.

At the meeting, a number of proposals were to be presented that would seriously affect the performance and future of certain junior faculty, particularly those who were behavioral scientists. The Chair, a computer scientist, disliked the behaviorists, who he felt were "always analyzing the motives of people." Professor Stevens, who was a tenured full professor and a behaviorist, had an objective to protect the interests of the junior faculty and to counter the efforts of the Chair.

Including Professor Stevens, there were nine faculty present. The accompanying diagram below shows the seating

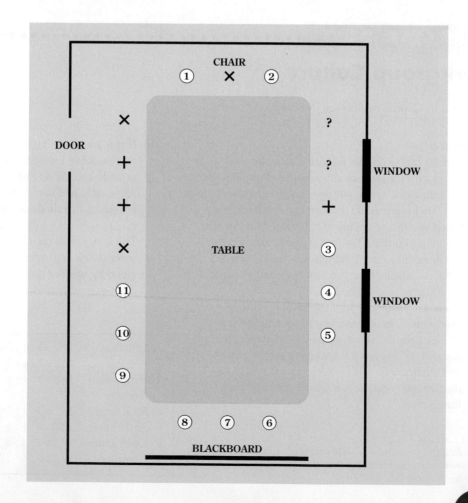

arrangement and the layout of the room. The ×s signify those faculty who were allies of the Chair. The +s are those opposed to the Chair and supportive of Professor Stevens, and the ?s were undecided and could be swayed either way. The circled numbers represent empty seats. Both ?s were behavioralists, and the + next to them was a quantitative analyst. Near the door, the first × was a generalist, the two +s were behavioralists, and the second × was a quantitative analyst. The diagram shows the seating of everyone but Professor Stevens, who was the last one to enter the room. Standing at the door, Professor Stevens

surveyed the room and within 10 seconds knew which seat was the most effective to achieve his objective.

3. Answer the following questions in your group.
   (a) Which seat did Professor Stevens select and why?
   (b) What is the likely pattern of communication and interaction in this group?
   (c) What can be done to get this group to work harmoniously?

EXERCISE 25

Interview a Leader

Contributed by Bonnie McNeely, Murray State University

Procedure
1. Make an appointment to interview a leader. It can be a leader working in a business or nonprofit organization, such as a government agency, school, and so on. Base the interview on the form provided here, but feel free to add your own questions.
2. Bring the results of your interview to class. Form into groups as assigned by your instructor. Share the responses from your interview with your group and compare answers. What issues were similar? Different? Were the stress levels of leaders working in nonprofit organizations as high as those working in for-profit firms? Were you surprised at the number of hours per week worked by leaders?
3. Be prepared to summarize the interviews done by your group as a formal written report if asked to do so by the instructor.

Interview Questionnaire

Student's Name _____ Date _____

1. Position in the organization (title):
2. Number of years in current position:
   Number of years of managerial experience:
3. Number of people directly supervised:
4. Average number of hours worked a week:
5. How did you get into leadership?
6. What is the most rewarding part of being a leader?
7. What is the most difficult part of your job?
8. What would you say are the *keys to success* for leaders?
9. What advice do you have for an aspiring leader?
10. What type of ethical issues have you faced as a leader?
11. If you were to enroll in a leadership seminar, what topics or issues would you want to learn more about?
12. (Student's question)
Gender: M____ F____ Years of formal education____
Level of job stress: Very high____ High____ Average____ Low____
Profit organization____ Nonprofit organization ____
Additional information/Comments:

_____

Source: Adapted from Bonnie McNeely, "Make Your Principles of Management Class Come Alive," *Journal of Management Education,* Vol. 18, No. 2 (May 1994), pp. 246–249.

Leadership Skills Inventories

Procedure

1. Look over the skills listed below and ask your instructor to clarify those you do not understand.
2. Complete each category by checking either the "Strong" or "Needs Development" category in relation to your own level with each skill.
3. After completing each category, briefly describe a situation in which each of the listed skills has been utilized.
4. Meet in your groups to share and discuss inventories. Prepare a report summarizing major development needs in your group.

Instrument

	Strong	Needs Development	Situation
Communication			
Conflict management			
Delegation			
Ethical behavior			
Listening			
Motivation			
Negotiation			
Performance appraisal and feedback			
Planning and goal setting			
Power and influence			
Presentation and persuasion			
Problem solving and decision making			
Stress management			
Team building			
Time management			

Leadership and Participation in Decision Making

Procedure

1. For the 10 situations described below, decide which of the three styles you would use for that unique situation. Place the letter A, P, or L on the line before each situation's number.

   A—authority; make the decision alone without additional inputs.
   P—consultative; make the decision based on group inputs.
   L—group; allow the group to which you belong to make the decision.

Decision Situations

_____ 1. You have developed a new work procedure that will increase productivity. Your boss likes the idea and wants you to try it within a few weeks. You view your employees as fairly capable and believe that they will be receptive to the change.

_____ 2. The industry of your product has new competition. Your organization's revenues have been dropping. You have been told to lay off three of your ten employees in two weeks. You have been the supervisor for over one year. Normally, your employees are very capable.

_____ 3. Your department has been facing a problem for several months. Many solutions have been tried and have failed. You finally thought of a solution, but you are not sure of the possible consequences of the change required or its acceptance by the highly capable employees.

_____ 4. Flextime has become popular in your organization. Some departments let each employee start and end work whenever they choose. However, because of the cooperative effort of your employees, they must all work the same eight hours. You are not sure of the level of interest in changing the hours. Your employees are a very capable group and like to make decisions.

_____ 5. The technology in your industry is changing faster than the members of your organization can keep up. Top management hired a consultant who has given the recommended decision. You have two weeks to make your decision. Your employees are capable, and they enjoy participating in the decision-making process.

_____ 6. Your boss called you on the telephone to tell you that someone has requested an order for your department's product with a very short delivery date. She asked that you call her back with the decision about taking the order in 15 minutes. Looking over the work schedule, you realize that it will be very difficult to deliver the order on time. Your employees will have to push hard to make it. They are cooperative, capable, and enjoy being involved in decision making.

_____ 7. A change has been handed down from top management. How you implement it is your decision. The change takes effect in one month. It will personally affect everyone in your department. The acceptance of the department members is critical to the success of the change. Your employees are usually not too interested in being involved in making decisions.

_____ 8. You believe that productivity in your department could be increased. You have thought of some ways that may work, but you're not sure of them. Your employees are very experienced; almost all of them have been in the department longer than you have.

_____ 9. Top management has decided to make a change that will affect all of your employees. You know that they will be upset because it will cause them hardship. One or two may even quit. The change goes into effect in 30 days. Your employees are very capable.

_____ 10. A customer has offered you a contract for your product with a quick delivery date. The offer is open for two days. Meeting the contract deadline would require employees to work nights and weekends for six weeks. You cannot require them to work overtime. Filling this profitable contract could help get you the raise you want and feel you deserve. However, if you take the contract and don't deliver on time, it will hurt your chances of getting a big raise. Your employees are very capable.

2. Form groups as assigned by your instructor. Share and compare your choices for each decision situation. Reconcile any differences and be prepared to defend your decision preferences in general class discussion.

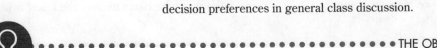

My Best Manager: Revisited

Contributed by J. Marcus Maier, Chapman University

Procedure

1. Refer to the list of qualities—or profiles—the class generated earlier in the course for the "Best Manager."
2. Looking first at your Typical Managers profile, suppose you took this list to 100 average people on the street (or at the local mall) and asked them whether ____ (Trait X, quality Y) was "more typical of men or of women in our culture." What do you think *most* of them would say? That ____ (X, Y etc.) is more typical of *women*? or of *men*? Or of neither/both?[1] Do this for every trait on your list(s). (5 minutes)
3. Now do the same for the qualities we generated in our Best Manager profile. (5 min.)
4. A straw vote is taken, one quality at a time, to determine the class's overall gender identification of each trait, focusing on the Typical Managers profile (10–15 min.). Then this is repeated for the Best Manager profile (10–15 min.).[2]
5. Discussion. What do you see in the data this group has generated? How might you interpret these results? (15–20 min.)

Source: Based on Maier's 1993 article, "The Gender Prism," *Journal of Management Education,* 17(3), 285–314. 1994 Fritz Roethlisberger Award Recipient for Best Paper (Updated, 1996).

[1] This gets the participants to move outside of their *own* conceptions to their awareness of *societal* definitions of masculinity and femininity.

[2] This is done by a rapid show of hands, looking for a clear majority vote. An "f" (for "feminine") is placed next to those qualities that a clear majority indicate are more typical of women, an "m" (for "masculine") next to those qualities a clear majority indicate would be more typical of men. (This procedure parallels the median-split method used in determining Bem Sex Role Inventory classifications.) If no clear majority emerges (i.e., if the vote is close), the trait or quality is classified as "both" (f/m). The designations "masculine" or "feminine" are used (rather than "men" or "women") to underscore the *socially constructed* nature of each dimension.

Active Listening

Contributed by Robert Ledman, Morehouse College

Procedure

1. Review active listening skills and behaviors as described in the textbook and in class.
2. Form into groups of three. Each group will have a listener, a talker, and an observer (if the number of students is not evenly divisible by three, two observers are used for one or two groups).
3. The "talkers" should talk about any subject they wish, but only *if* they are being actively listened to. Talkers should stop speaking as soon as they sense active listening has stopped.
4. The "listeners" should use a list of active listening skills and behaviors as their guide, and practice as many of them as possible to be sure the talker is kept

---

Source: Adapted from the presentation entitled "An Experiential Exercise to Teach Active Listening," presented at the Organizational Behavior Teaching Conference, Macomb, IL, 1995.

talking. Listeners should contribute nothing more than "active listening" to the communication.

5. The "observer" should note the behaviors and skills used by the listener and the effects they seemed to have on the communication process.

6. These roles are rotated until each student has played every role.

7. The instructor will lead a discussion of what the observers saw and what happened with the talkers and listeners. The discussion focuses on what behaviors from the posted list have been present, which have been absent, and how the communication has been affected by the listener's actions.

● ● ● ● ● ● ● EXERCISE 30 ●

Upward Appraisal

Procedure

1. Form workgroups as assigned by your instructor.
2. The instructor will leave the room.
3. Convene in your assigned workgroups for a period of 10 minutes. Create a list of comments, problems, issues, and concerns you would like to have communicated to the instructor in regard to the course experience to date. *Remember,* your interest in the exercise is twofold: (a) to communicate your feelings to the instructor and (b) to learn more about the process of giving and receiving feedback.
4. Select one person from the group to act as spokesperson in communicating the group's feelings to the instructor.
5. The spokespersons should briefly convene to decide on what physical arrangement of chairs, tables, and so forth is most appropriate to conduct the feedback session. The classroom should then be rearranged to fit the desired specifications.
6. While the spokespersons convene, persons in the remaining groups should discuss how they expect the forthcoming communications event to develop. Will it be a good experience for all parties concerned? Be prepared to critically observe the actual communication process.
7. The instructor should be invited to return, and the feedback session will begin. Observers should make notes so that they may make constructive comments at the conclusion of the exercise.
8. Once the feedback session is complete, the instructor will call on the observers for comments, ask the spokespersons for reactions, and open the session to discussion.

● ● ● ● ● ● ● EXERCISE 31 ●

360° Feedback

Contributed by Timothy J. Serey, Northern Kentucky University

Introduction

The time of performance reviews is often a time of genuine anxiety for many organizational members. On the one hand, it is an important organizational ritual and a key part of the Human Resource function. Organizations usually codify the process and provide a mechanism to appraise performance. On the other hand, it is rare for managers to feel comfortable with this process. Often, they feel discomfort over "playing God." One possible reason for this is that managers rarely receive formal training about how to provide feedback.

From the manager's point of view, if done properly, giving feedback is at the very heart of his or her job as "coach" and "teacher." It is an investment in the professional development of another person, rather than the punitive element we so often associate with hearing from "the boss." From the subordinate's perspective, most people want to know where they stand, but this is usually tempered by a fear of "getting it in the neck." In many organizations, it is rare to receive straight, non-sugar-coated feedback about where you stand.

Procedure

1. Review the section of the book dealing with feedback before you come to class. It is also helpful if individuals make notes about their perceptions and feelings about the course *before* they come to class.
2. Groups of students should discuss their experiences, both positive and negative, in this class. Each group should determine the dimensions of evaluating the class itself *and* the instructor. For example, students might select criteria that include the practicality of the course, the way the material is structured and presented (e.g., lecture or exercises), and the instructor's style (e.g., enthusiasm, fairness).
3. Groups select a member to represent them in a subgroup that next provides feedback to the instructor before the entire class.
4. The student audience then provides the subgroup with feedback about their effectiveness in this exercise. That is, the larger class provides feedback to the subgroup about the extent to which students actually put the principles of effective feedback into practice (e.g., descriptive, not evaluative; specific, not general).

Source: Adapted from Timothy J. Serey, *Journal of Management Education,* Vol. 17, No. 2 (May 1993). © 1993 by Sage Publications, Inc. Reprinted by permission of Sage Publications.

EXERCISE 32

Role Analysis Negotiation

Contributed by Paul Lyons, Frostburg State University

Introduction

A role is the set of various behaviors people expect from a person (or group) in a particular position. These role expectations occur in all types of organizations, such as one's place of work, school, family, clubs, and the like. Role ambiguity takes place when a person is confused about the expectations of the role. And sometimes, a role will have expectations that are contradictory—for example, being loyal to the company when the company is breaking the law.

The Role Analysis Technique, or RAT, is a method for improving the effectiveness of a team or group. RAT helps to clarify role expectations, and all organization members have responsibilities that translate to expectations. Determination of role requirements, by consensus—involving all concerned—will ultimately result in more effective and mutually satisfactory behavior. Participation and collaboration in the definition and analy-

Source: Adapted from Paul Lyons, "Developing Expectations with the Role Analysis Technique," *Journal of Management Education.* Vol. 17, No. 3 (August 1993), pp. 386–389. © Sage Publications.

sis of roles by group members should result in clarification regarding who is to do what as well as increase the level of commitment to the decisions made.

Procedure

Working alone, carefully read the course syllabus that your instructor has given you. Make a note of any questions you have about anything for which you need clarification or understanding. Pay particular attention to the performance requirements of the course. Make a list of any questions you have regarding what, specifically, is expected of you in order for you to be successful in the course. You will be sharing this information with others in small groups.

EXERCISE 33

Lost at Sea

Introduction

Consider this situation. You are adrift on a private yacht in the South Pacific when a fire of unknown origin destroys the yacht and most of its contents. You and a small group of survivors are now in a large raft with oars. Your location is unclear, but you estimate being about 1000 miles south–southwest of the nearest land. One person has just found in her pockets five $1 bills and a packet of matches. Everyone else's pockets are empty. The following items are available to you on the raft.

	A	B	C
Sextant	___	___	
Shaving mirror	___	___	
5 gallons of water	___	___	
Mosquito netting	___	___	
1 survival meal	___	___	
Maps of Pacific Ocean	___	___	
Floatable seat cushion	___	___	
2 gallons oil-gas mix	___	___	
Small transistor radio	___	___	
Shark repellent	___	___	
20 square feet black plastic	___	___	
1 quart of 20-proof rum	___	___	
15 feet of nylon rope	___	___	
24 chocolate bars	___	___	
Fishing kit	___	___	

Source: Adapted from "Lost at Sea: A Consensus-Seeking Task," in *The 1975 Handbook for Group Facilitators*. Used with permission of University Associates, Inc.

Procedure

1. *Working alone,* rank in Column A the 15 items in order of their importance to your survival ("1" is most important and "15" is least important).
2. *Working in an assigned group,* arrive at a "team" ranking of the 15 items and record this ranking in Column B. Appoint one person as group spokesperson to report your group rankings to the class.
3. *Do not write in Column C* until further instructions are provided by your instructor.

EXERCISE 34

Entering the Unknown

Contributed by Michael R. Manning, New Mexico State University; Conrad N. Jackson, MPC Inc., Huntsville, Alabama; and Paula S. Weber, New Mexico Highlands University

Procedure

1. Form into groups of four or five members. In each group spend a few minutes reflecting on members' typical entry behaviors in new situations and their behaviors when they are in comfortable settings.
2. According to the instructor's directions, students count off to form new groups of four or five members each.
3. The new groups spend the next 15–20 minutes getting to know each other. There is no right or wrong way to proceed, but all members should become more aware of their entry behaviors. They should act in ways that can help them realize a goal of achieving comfortable behaviors with their group.
4. Students review what has occurred in the new groups, giving specific attention to the following questions:
   (a) What topics did your group discuss (content)? Did these topics involve the "here and now" or were they focused on "there and then"?
   (b) What approach did you and your group members take to the task (process)? Did you try to initiate or follow? How? Did you ask questions? Listen? Respond to others? Did you bring up topics?
   (c) Were you more concerned with how you came across or with how others came across to you? Did you play it safe? Were you open? Did you share things even though it seemed uncomfortable or risky? How was humor used in your group? Did it add or detract?
   (d) How do you feel about the approach you took or the behaviors you exhibited? Was this hard or easy? Did others respond the way you had anticipated? Is there some behavior you would like to do more of, do better, or do less of?
   (e) Were your behaviors the ones you had intended (goals)?
5. Responses to these questions are next discussed by the class as a whole. (*Note:* Responses will tend to be mixed within a group, but between groups there should be more similarity.) This discussion helps individuals become aware of and understand their entry behaviors.
6. Optional individuals have identified their entry behaviors; each group can then spend 5–10 minutes discussing members' perceptions of each other:
   (a) What behaviors did they like or find particularly useful? What did they dislike?

(b) What were your reactions to others? What ways did they intend to come across? Did you see others in the way they had intended to come across?
(Alternatively, if there is concern about the personal nature of this discussion, ask the groups to discuss what they liked/didn't like without referring to specific individuals.)

EXERCISE 35

Vacation Puzzle

Contributed by Barbara G. McCain and Mary Khalili, Oklahoma City University

Procedure

Can you solve this puzzle? Give it a try and then compare your answers with those of classmates. Remember your communicative skills!

Puzzle

Khalili, McCain, Middleton, Porter, and Quintaro teach at Oklahoma City University. Each gets two weeks of vacation a year. Last year, each took his or her first week in the first five months of the year and his or her second week in the last five months. If each professor took each of his or her weeks in a different month from the other professors, in which months did each professor take his or her first and second week?

Here are the facts:

(a) McCain took her first week before Khalili, who took *hers* before Porter; for their second week, the order was reversed.
(b) The professor who vacationed in March also vacationed in September.
(c) Quintaro did not take her first week in March or April.
(d) Neither Quintaro nor the professor who took his or her first week in January took his or her second week in August or December.
(e) Middleton took her second week before McCain but after Quintaro.

Month	Professor
January	
February	
March	
April	
May	
June	
July	
August	
September	
October	
November	
December	

Source: Adapted to classroom activity by Dr. Mary Khalili.

The Ugli Orange

Introduction

In most work settings, people need other people to do their job, benefit the organization, and forward their career. Getting things done in organizations requires us to work together in cooperation, even though the ultimate objectives of those other people may be different from our own. Your task in the present exercise is learning how to achieve this cooperation more effectively.

Procedure

1. The class will be divided into pairs. One student in each pair will read and prepare the role of Dr. Roland, and one will play the role of Dr. Jones (role descriptions to be distributed by instructor). Students should read their respective role descriptions and prepare to meet with their counterpart (see Steps 2 and 3).
2. At this point the group leader will read a statement. The instructor will indicate that he or she is playing

---

Source: Adapted from Hall et al., *Experiences in Management and Organizational Behavior,* 3rd ed. (New York: John Wiley and Sons, Inc.), 1988. Originally developed by Robert J. House. Adapted by D. T. Hall and R. J. Lewicki, with suggested modifications by H. Kolodny and T. Ruble.

the role of Mr. Cardoza, who owns the commodity in question. The instructor will tell you
(a) How long you have to meet with the other
(b) What information the instructor will require at the end of your meeting
After the instructor has given you this information, you may meet with the other firm's representative and determine whether you have issues you can agree to.

3. Following the meetings (negotiations), the spokesperson for each pair will report any agreements reached to the entire class. The observer for any pair will report on negotiation dynamics and the process by which agreement was reached.
4. Questions to consider:
(a) Did you reach a solution? If so, what was critical to reaching that agreement?
(b) Did you and the other negotiator trust one another? Why or why not?
(c) Was there full disclosure by both sides in each group? How much information was shared?
(d) How creative and/or complex were the solutions? If solutions were very complex, why do you think this occurred?
(e) What was the impact of having an "audience" on your behavior? Did it make the problem harder or easier to solve?

Conflict Dialogues

Contributed by Edward G. Wertheim, Northeastern University

Procedure

1. Think of a conflict situation at work or at school and try to re-create a segment of the dialogue that gets to the heart of the conflict.
2. Write notes on the conflict dialogue using the following format

Introduction

- Background
- My goals and objectives

- My strategy
- Assumptions I am making

Dialogue (re-create part of the dialogue below and try to put what you were really thinking in parentheses).

Me:

Other:

Me:

Other, etc.

3. Share your situation with members of your group. Read the dialogue to them, perhaps asking someone to play the role of "other."
4. Discuss with the group:
   (a) The style of conflict resolution you used (confrontation, collaboration, avoidance, etc.)
   (b) The triggers to the conflict, that is, what really set you off and why
   (c) Whether or not you were effective
   (d) Possible ways of handling this differently
5. Choose one dialogue from within the group to share with the class. Be prepared to discuss your analysis and also possible alternative approaches and resolutions for the situation described.

EXERCISE 38

Force-Field Analysis

Procedure

1. Choose a situation in which you have high personal stakes (for example, how to get a better grade in course X; how to get a promotion; how to obtain a position).
2. Using a version of the Sample Force-Field Analysis Form on the next page, apply the technique to your situation.
   (a) Describe the situation as it now exists.
   (b) Describe the situation as you would like it to be.
   (c) Identify those "driving forces"—the factors that are presently helping to move things in the desired direction.
   (d) Identify those "restraining forces"—the factors that are presently holding things back from moving in the desired direction.
3. Try to be as specific as possible in terms of the above in relation to your situation. You should attempt to be exhaustive in your listing of these forces. List them all!
4. Now go back and classify the strength of each force as weak, medium, or strong. Do this for both the driving and the restraining forces.
5. At this point you should rank the forces regarding their ability to influence or control the situation.
6. In small groups share your analyses. Discuss the usefulness and drawbacks to using this method for personal situations and its application to organizations.
7. Be prepared to share the results of your group's discussion with the rest of the class.

Sample Force-Field Analysis Form

Current Situation:	Situation as You Would Like It to Be:
Driving Forces:	**Restraining Forces:**

EXERCISE 39

Organizations Alive!

Contributed by Bonnie L. McNeely, Murray State University

Procedure

1. Find a copy of the following items from actual organizations. These items can be obtained from the company where you now work, a parent's workplace, or the university. Universities have mission statements, codes of conduct for students and faculty, organizational charts, job descriptions, performance appraisal forms, and control devices. Some student organizations also have these documents. All the items do not have to come from the same organization. *Bring these items to class.*

   (a) Mission statement   (d) Job description
   (b) Code of ethics   (e) Performance appraisal form
   (c) Organizational chart   (f) Control device

2. Form groups in class as assigned by your instructor. Share your items with the group, as well as what you learned while collecting these items. For example, did you find that some firms have a mission, but it is not written down? Did you find that job descriptions existed, but they were not really used or had not been updated in years?

Source: Adapted from Bonnie L. McNeely, "Make Your Principles of Management Class Come Alive," *Journal of Management Education*, Vol. 18, No. 2 (May 1994), pp. 246–249.

EXERCISE 40

Fast-Food Technology

Contributed by D. T. Hall, Boston University, and F. S. Hall, University of New Hampshire

Introduction

A critical first step in improving or changing any organization is *diagnosing* or analyzing its present functioning.

Many change and organization development efforts fall short of their objectives because this important step was not taken or was conducted superficially. To illustrate this, imagine how you would feel if you went to your doctor complaining of stomach pains and he recommended surgery without conducting any tests, without obtaining any further information, and without a careful physical examination. You would probably switch doctors! Yet managers often attempt major changes with correspondingly little diagnostic work in advance. (It could be said that they undertake vast projects with half-vast ideas.)

In this exercise, you will be asked to conduct a group diagnosis of two different organizations in the fast-food business. The exercise will provide an opportunity to integrate much of the knowledge you have gained in other exercises and in studying other topics. Your task will be to describe the organizations as carefully as you can in terms of several key organizational concepts. Although the organizations are probably very familiar to you, try to step back and look at them as though you were seeing them for the first time.

Procedure

1. In groups of four or six people, your assignment is described below.

One experience most people in this country have shared is that of dining in the hamburger establishment known as McDonald's. In fact, someone has claimed that twenty-fifth-century archeologists may dig into the ruins of our present civilization and conclude that twentieth-century religion was devoted to the worship of golden arches.

Your group, Fastalk Consultants, is known as the shrewdest, most insightful, and most overpaid management consulting firm in the country. You have been hired by the president of McDonald's to make recommendations for improving the motivation and performance of personnel in their franchise operations. Let us assume that the key job activities in franchise operations are food preparation, order taking and dealing with customers, and routine cleanup operations.

Recently the president of McDonald's has come to suspect that his company's competitors—such as Burger King, Wendy's, Jack-in-the-Box, Dunkin' Donuts, various pizza establishments, and others—are making heavy inroads into McDonald's market. He has also hired a market research firm to investigate and compare the relative merits of the sandwiches, french fries, and drinks served in McDonald's and the competitor, and has asked the market research firm to assess the advertising campaigns of the two organizations. Hence, you will not need to be concerned with marketing issues, except as they may have an impact on employee behavior. The president wants *you* to look into the *organization* of the franchises to determine the strengths and weaknesses of each. Select a competitor that gives McDonald's a good "run for its money" in your area.

The president has established an unusual contract with you. *He wants you to make your recommendations based upon your observations as a customer.* He does not want you to do a complete diagnosis with interviews, surveys, or behind-the-scenes observations. He wants your report in two parts. Remember, the president wants concrete, specific, and practical recommendations. Avoid vague generalizations such as "improve communications" or "increase trust." Say very clearly *how* management can improve organizational performance. Substantiate your recommendations by reference to one or more theories of motivation, leadership, small groups, or job design.

Part I

Given his organization's goals of profitability, sales volume, fast and courteous service, and cleanliness, the president of McDonald's wants an analysis that will *compare and contrast McDonald's and the competitor* in terms of the following concepts:

Organizational goals
Organizational structure
Technology
Environment
Employee motivation
Communication
Leadership style
Policies/procedures/rules/standards
Job design
Organizational climate

Part II

Given the corporate goals listed under Part I, what specific actions might McDonald's management and franchise owners take in the following areas to achieve these goals (profitability, sales volume, fast and courteous service, and cleanliness)?

Job design and workflow
Organizational structure (at the individual restaurant level)
Employee incentives
Leadership
Employee selection

How do McDonald's and the competition differ in these aspects? Which company has the best approach?

2. Complete the assignment by going as a group to one McDonald's and one competitor's restaurant. If possible, have a meal in each place. To get a more valid comparison, visit a McDonald's and a competitor located in the same area. After observing each restaurant, meet with your group and prepare your 10-minute report to the executive committee.

3. In class, each group will present its report to the rest of the class, who will act as the executive committee. The group leader will appoint a timekeeper to be sure that each group sticks to its 10-minute time limit. Possible discussion questions include:

(a) What similarities are there between the two organizations?

(b) What differences are there between the organizations?

(c) Do you have any "hunches" about the reasons for the particular organizational characteristics you found? For example, can you try to explain why one organization might have a particular type of structure? Incentive system? Climate?

(d) Can you try to explain one set of characteristics in terms of some other characteristics you found? For example, do the goals account for structure? Does the environment explain the structure?

EXERCISE 41

Alien Invasion

Procedure

This is an exercise in organizational culture. You will be assigned to a team (if you are not already in one) and instructed to visit an organization by your instructor.

1. Visit the assigned site as a team working under conditions set forth in the "situation" below.
2. Take detailed notes on the cultural forms that you observe.
3. Prepare a presentation for the class that describes these forms and draw any inferences you can about the nature of the culture of the organization—its ideologies, values, and norms of behavior.
4. Be sure to explain the basis of your inferences in terms of the cultural forms observed.

You will have 20 minutes to report your findings, so plan your presentation carefully. Use visual aids to help your audience understand what you have found.

Situation

You are Martians who have just arrived on Earth in the first spaceship from your planet. Your superiors have ordered you to learn as much about Earthlings and the way they behave as you can without doing anything to make them aware that you are Martians. It is vital for the future plans of your superiors that you do nothing to disturb the Earthlings. Unfortunately, Martians communicate by emitting electromagnetic waves and are incapable of speech, so you cannot talk to the natives. Even if you did, it is reported by the usually reliable Bureau of Interplanetary Intelligence that Earthlings may become cannibalistic if annoyed. However, the crash course in Earth languages taught by the bureau has enabled you to read the language.

Remember, these instructions limit your data collection to observation and request that you *not* talk to the "natives." There are two reasons for this instruction. First, your objective is to learn what the organization does when it is simply going about its normal business and not responding to a group of students asking questions. Second, you are likely to be surprised at how much you can learn by simply observing if you put your mind to it. Many skilled managers employ this ability in sensing what is going on as they walk through their plant or office area.

Since you cannot talk to people, some of the cultural forms (legends, sagas, etc.) will be difficult to spot unless you are able to pick up copies of the organization's promotional literature (brochures, company reports, advertisements) during your visit. Do not be discouraged, because the visible forms such as artifacts, setting, symbols, and (sometimes) rituals can convey a great deal about the culture. Just keep your eyes, ears, and antennae open!

Source: Adapted from Donald D. Bowen et al., *Experiences in Management and Organizational Behavior,* 4th ed. (New York: John Wiley & Sons, Inc., 1997).

Power Circles

Contributed by Marian C. Schultz, University of West Florida

This exercise is designed to examine power and influence in the classroom setting. Specifically, it allows you to identify the combination of power bases used by your instructor in accomplishing his or her objectives for the course.

Procedure

1. Recall that the instructor's power includes the following major bases: (a) the authority that comes from the instructor's position (position power), (b) the knowledge, skill, and expertise of the instructor in the subject area (expert power), and (c) the regard in which you personally hold the instructor (referent power).

2. Indicate the configuration of power that is most evident in the way the instructor behaves in the course overall and according to the following "power circle." This circle can be filled in to represent the relative emphasis on the three power bases (e.g., 60 percent position, 30 percent expert, and 10 percent referent). Use the grid at the right to draw/fill in the circle to show the profile of instructor's power. The instructor will also complete a self-perceived power circle profile.

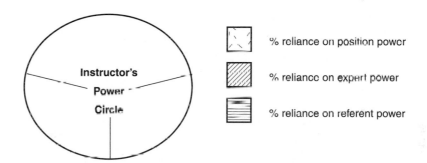

3. Consider also some possible special situations in which the instructor would have to use his or her power in the classroom context. Draw one power circle for each of the following situations, showing for each the power profile most likely to be used by the instructor to accomplish his or her goal.
   - Instructor wants to change the format of the final examination.
   - Instructor wants to add an additional group assignment to course requirements.
   - Instructor wants to have students attend a special two-hour guest lecture on a Saturday morning.
   - Instructor wants students to come to class better prepared for discussions of assigned material.

     The instructor will also complete a self-perceived power circle profile for each situation.

4. Share your power circles with those developed by members of your assigned group. Discuss the profiles and the reasons behind them in the group. Appoint one group member as spokesperson to share results in general class discussion. Discuss with the group the best way to communicate this feedback effectively to the instructor in the presence of all class members, and help prepare the spokesperson for the feedback session.

5. Have the instructor share his or her power profiles with the class. Ask the instructor to comment on any differences between the self-perceptions and the views of the class. Comment as a class on the potential significance to leaders and managers of differences in the way they perceive themselves and the ways they are perceived by others.

6. Discuss with the instructor and class how people may tend to favor one or more of the power bases (i.e., to develop a somewhat predictable power circle profile). Discuss as well how effective leaders and managers need to use power contingently, and modify their use of different power bases and power circle profiles to best fit the needs of specific influence situations.

SELF-ASSESSMENT INVENTORIES

Find online versions of many assessments at www.wiley.com/college/schermerhorn

Managerial Assumptions

Instructions
Read the following statements. Use the space to the left to write "Yes" if you agree with the statement, or "No" if you disagree with it. Force yourself to take a "yes" or "no" position for every statement.

1. Are good pay and a secure job enough to satisfy most workers?

2. Should a manager help and coach subordinates in their work?
3. Do most people like real responsibility in their jobs?
4. Are most people afraid to learn new things in their jobs?
5. Should managers let subordinates control the quality of their work?
6. Do most people dislike work?
7. Are most people creative?
8. Should a manager closely supervise and direct work of subordinates?

Source: Schermerhorn, John R., Jr., *Management*, 5th ed. (New York, John Wiley & Sons, Inc., 1996), p. 51. By permission.

9. Do most people tend to resist change?

10. Do most people work only as hard as they have to?

11. Should workers be allowed to set their own job goals?

12. Are most people happiest off the job?

13. Do most workers really care about the organization they work for?

14. Should a manager help subordinates advance and grow in their jobs?

Scoring

Count the number of "yes" responses to items 1, 4, 6, 8, 9, 10, 12; write that number here as [X = ____]. Count the number of "yes" responses to items 2, 3, 5, 7, 11, 13, 14; write that score here [Y = ____].

Interpretation

This assessment gives insight into your orientation toward Douglas McGregor's Theory X (your "X" score) and Theory Y (your "Y" score) assumptions. You should review the discussion of McGregor's thinking in Chapter 1 and consider further the ways in which you are likely to behave toward other people at work. Think, in particular, about the types of "self-fulfilling prophecies" you are likely to create.

ASSESSMENT 2

A Twenty-First-Century Manager

Instructions

Rate yourself on the following personal characteristics. Use this scale.

S	= Strong, I am very confident with this one.
G	= Good, but I still have room to grow.
W	= Weak, I really need work on this one.
?	= Unsure, I just don't know.

1. *Resistance to stress:* The ability to get work done even under stressful conditions.

2. *Tolerance for uncertainty:* The ability to get work done even under ambiguous and uncertain conditions.

3. *Social objectivity:* The ability to act free of racial, ethnic, gender, and other prejudices or biases.

4. *Inner work standards:* The ability to personally set and work to high-performance standards.

5. *Stamina:* The ability to sustain long work hours.

6. *Adaptability:* The ability to be flexible and adapt to changes.

7. *Self-confidence:* The ability to be consistently decisive and display one's personal presence.

8. *Self-objectivity:* The ability to evaluate personal strengths and weaknesses and to understand one's motives and skills relative to a job.

9. *Introspection:* The ability to learn from experience, awareness, and self-study.

Source: See *Outcome Management Project,* Phase I and Phase II Reports (St. Louis: American Assembly of Collegiate Schools of Business, 1986 & 1987).

10. *Entrepreneurism:* The ability to address problems and take advantage of opportunities for constructive change.

Scoring

Give yourself 1 point for each S, and 1/2 point for each G. Do not give yourself points for W and ? responses. Total your points and enter the result here [PMF = ____].

Interpretation

This assessment offers a self-described *profile of your management foundations* (*PMF*). Are you a perfect 10, or is your PMF score something less than that? There shouldn't be too many 10s around. Ask someone who knows you to assess you on this instrument. You may be surprised at the differences between your PMF score as self-described and your PMF score as described by someone else. Most of us, realistically speaking, must work hard to grow and develop continually in these and related management foundations. This list is a good starting point as you consider where and how to further pursue the development of your managerial skills and competencies. The items on the list are recommended by the American Assembly of Collegiate Schools of Business (AACSB) as skills and personal characteristics that should be nurtured in college and university students of business administration. Their success—and yours—as twenty-first-century managers may well rest on (1) an initial awareness of the importance of these basic management foundations and (2) a willingness to strive continually to strengthen them throughout your work career.

Turbulence Tolerance Test

Instructions

The following statements were made by a 37-year-old manager in a large, successful corporation. How would you like to have a job with these characteristics? Using the following scale, write your response to the left of each statement.

> 4 = I would enjoy this very much; it's completely acceptable.
>
> 3 = This would be enjoyable and acceptable most of the time.
>
> 2 = I'd have no reaction to this feature one way or another, or it would be about equally enjoyable and unpleasant.
>
> 1 = This feature would be somewhat unpleasant for me.
>
> 0 = This feature would be very unpleasant for me.

_____ 1. I regularly spend 30 to 40 percent of my time in meetings.

_____ 2. Eighteen months ago my job did not exist, and I have been essentially inventing it as I go along.

_____ 3. The responsibilities I either assume or am assigned consistently exceed the authority I have for discharging them.

_____ 4. At any given moment in my job, I have on average about a dozen phone calls to be returned.

_____ 5. There seems to be very little relation between the quality of my job performance and my actual pay and fringe benefits.

_____ 6. About 2 weeks a year of formal management training is needed in my job just to stay current.

_____ 7. Because we have very effective equal employment opportunity (EEO) in my company and because it is thoroughly multinational, my job consistently brings me into close working contact at a professional level with people of many races, ethnic groups and nationalities, and of both sexes.

_____ 8. There is no objective way to measure my effectiveness.

_____ 9. I report to three different bosses for different aspects of my job, and each has an equal say in my performance appraisal.

_____ 10. On average, about a third of my time is spent dealing with unexpected emergencies that force all scheduled work to be postponed.

_____ 11. When I have to have a meeting of the people who report to me, it takes my secretary most of a day to find a time when we are all available, and even then I have yet to have a meeting where everyone is present for the entire meeting.

_____ 12. The college degree I earned in preparation for this type of work is now obsolete, and I probably should go back for another degree.

_____ 13. My job requires that I absorb 100–200 pages of technical materials per week.

_____ 14. I am out of town overnight at least one night per week.

_____ 15. My department is so interdependent with several other departments in the company that all distinctions about which departments are responsible for which tasks are quite arbitrary.

Source: Peter B. Vail, _Managing as a Performance Art: New Ideas for a World of Chaotic Change_ (San Francisco: Jossey-Bass, 1989), pp. 8–9. Used by permission.

_____ 16. In about a year I will probably get a promotion to a job in another division that has most of these same characteristics.

_____ 17. During the period of my employment here, either the entire company or the division I worked in has been reorganized every year or so.

_____ 18. While there are several possible promotions I can see ahead of me, I have no real career path in an objective sense.

_____ 19. While there are several possible promotions I can see ahead of me, I think I have no realistic chance of getting to the top levels of the company.

_____ 20. While I have many ideas about how to make things work better, I have no direct influence on either the business policies or the personnel policies that govern my division.

_____ 21. My company has recently put in an "assessment center" where I and all other managers will be required to go through an extensive battery of psychological tests to assess our potential.

_____ 22. My company is a defendant in an antitrust suit, and if the case comes to trial, I will probably have to testify about some decisions that were made a few years ago.

_____ 23. Advanced computer and other electronic office technology is continually being introduced into my division, necessitating constant learning on my part.

_____ 24. The computer terminal and screen I have in my office can be monitored in my bosses' offices without my knowledge.

Scoring

Total your responses and divide the sum by 24; enter the score here [TTT = _____].

Interpretation

This instrument gives an impression of your tolerance for managing in turbulent times—something likely to characterize the world of work well into the future. In general, the higher your TTT score, the more comfortable you seem to be with turbulence and change—a positive sign. For comparison purposes, the average scores for some 500 MBA students and young managers was 1.5–1.6. The test's author suggests the TTT scores may be interpreted much like a grade point average in which 4.0 is a perfect A. On this basis, a 1.5 is below a C! How did you do?

••• ASSESSMENT 4 •••••••••••••••••••••••••••••••••••••

Global Readiness Index

Instructions

Rate yourself on each of the following items to establish a baseline measurement of your readiness to participate in the global work environment.

Rating Scale:

1 = Very Poor
2 = Poor
3 = Acceptable

Source: Developed from "Is Your Company Really Global," *Business Week* (December 1, 1997).

4 = Good
5 = Very Good

_____ 1. I understand my own culture in terms of its expectations, values, and influence on communication and relationships.

_____ 2. When someone presents me with a different point of view, I try to understand it rather than attack it.

_____ 3. I am comfortable dealing with situations where the available information is incomplete and the outcomes unpredictable.

_____ 4. I am open to new situations and am always

looking for new information and learning opportunities.

_____ 5. I have a good understanding of the attitudes and perceptions toward my culture as they are held by people from other cultures.

_____ 6. I am always gathering information about other countries and cultures and trying to learn from them.

_____ 7. I am well informed regarding the major differences in government, political systems, and economic policies around the world.

_____ 8. I work hard to increase my understanding of people from other cultures.

_____ 9. I am able to adjust my communication style to work effectively with people from different cultures.

_____ 10. I can recognize when cultural differences are influencing working relationships and adjust my attitudes and behavior accordingly.

Interpretation

To be successful in the twenty-first-century work environment, you must be comfortable with the global economy and the cultural diversity that it holds. This requires a *global mind-set* that is receptive to and respectful of cultural differences, *global knowledge* that includes the continuing quest to know and learn more about other nations and cultures, and *global work skills* that allow you to work effectively across cultures.

Scoring

The goal is to score as close to a perfect "5" as possible on each of the three dimensions of global readiness. Develop your scores as follows.

Items $(1 + 2 + 3 + 4)/4$
= _____ Global Mind-Set Score

Items $(5 + 6 + 7)/3$
= _____ Global Knowledge Score

Items $(8 + 9 + 10)/3$
= _____ Global Work Skills Score

ASSESSMENT 5

Personal Values

Instructions

Below are 16 items. Rate how important each one is to you on a scale of 0 (not important) to 100 (very important). Write the numbers 0–100 on the line to the left of each item.

Not important				Somewhat important				Very important		
0	10	20	30	40	50	60	70	80	90	100

_____ 1. An enjoyable, satisfying job.

_____ 2. A high-paying job.

_____ 3. A good marriage.

_____ 4. Meeting new people; social events.

_____ 5. Involvement in community activities.

_____ 6. My religion.

_____ 7. Exercising, playing sports.

_____ 8. Intellectual development.

_____ 9. A career with challenging opportunities.

_____ 10. Nice cars, clothes, home, etc.

_____ 11. Spending time with family.

_____ 12. Having several close friends.

_____ 13. Volunteer work for not-for-profit organizations, such as the cancer society.

Source: Robert N. Lussier, *Human Relations in Organizations,* 2nd ed. (Homewood, IL: Richard D. Irwin, 1993). By permission.

_____ 14. Meditation, quiet time to think, pray, etc.
_____ 15. A healthy, balanced diet.
_____ 16. Educational reading, TV, self-improvement programs, etc.

Scoring

Transfer the numbers for each of the 16 items to the appropriate column below, then add the two numbers in each column.

	Professional	Financial	Family	Social
	1. ____	2. ____	3. ____	4. ____
	9. ____	10. ____	11. ____	12. ____
Totals	____	____	____	____
	Community	**Spiritual**	**Physical**	**Intellectual**
	5. ____	6. ____	7. ____	8. ____
	13. ____	14. ____	15. ____	16. ____
Totals	____	____	____	____

Interpretation

The higher the total in any area, the higher the value you place on that particular area. The closer the numbers are in all eight areas, the more well-rounded you are. Think about the time and effort you put forth in your top three values. Is it sufficient to allow you to achieve the level of success you want in each area? If not, what can you do to change? Is there any area in which you feel you should have a higher value total? If yes, which, and what can you do to change?

ASSESSMENT 6

Intolerance for Ambiguity

Instructions

To determine your level of tolerance (intolerance) for ambiguity, respond to the following items. PLEASE RATE EVERY ITEM; DO NOT LEAVE ANY ITEM BLANK. Rate each item on the following seven-point scale:

1	2	3	4	5	6	7
strongly disagree	moderately disagree	slightly disagree		slightly agree	moderately agree	strongly agree

Rating

_____ 1. An expert who doesn't come up with a definite answer probably doesn't know too much.

_____ 2. There is really no such thing as a problem that can't be solved.

_____ 3. I would like to live in a foreign country for a while.

_____ 4. People who fit their lives to a schedule probably miss the joy of living.

_____ 5. A good job is one where what is to be done and how it is to be done are always clear.

Source: Based on Budner, S. Intolerance of Ambiguity as a Personality Variable, _Journal of Personality,_ Vol. 30, No. 1, (1962), pp. 29–50.

____ 6. In the long run it is possible to get more done by tackling small, simple problems rather than large, complicated ones.

____ 7. It is more fun to tackle a complicated problem than it is to solve a simple one.

____ 8. Often the most interesting and stimulating people are those who don't mind being different and original.

____ 9. What we are used to is always preferable to what is unfamiliar.

____ 10. A person who leads an even, regular life in which few surprises or unexpected happenings arise really has a lot to be grateful for.

____ 11. People who insist upon a yes or no answer just don't know how complicated things really are.

____ 12. Many of our most important decisions are based on insufficient information.

____ 13. I like parties where I know most of the people more than ones where most of the people are complete strangers.

____ 14. The sooner we all acquire ideals, the better.

____ 15. Teachers or supervisors who hand out vague assignments give a chance for one to show initiative and originality.

____ 16. A good teacher is one who makes you wonder about your way of looking at things.

____ Total

Scoring

The scale was developed by S. Budner. Budner reports test–retest correlations of .85 with a variety of samples (mostly students and health care workers). Data, however, are more than 30 years old, so mean shifts may have occurred. Maximum ranges are 16–112, and score ranges were from 25 to 79, with a grand mean of approximately 49.

The test was designed to measure several different components of possible reactions to perceived threat in situations which are new, complex, or insoluble. Half of the items have been reversed.

To obtain a score, first *reverse* the scale score for the eight "reverse" items, 3, 4, 7, 8, 11, 12, 15, and 16 (i.e., a rating of $1 = 7$, $2 = 6$, $3 = 5$, etc.), then add up the rating scores for all 16 items.

Interpretation

Empirically, low tolerance for ambiguity (high intolerance) has been positively correlated with:

- Conventionality of religious beliefs
- High attendance at religious services
- More intense religious beliefs
- More positive views of censorship
- Higher authoritarianism
- Lower Machiavellianism

The application of this concept to management in the 1990s is clear and relatively self-evident. The world of work and many organizations are full of ambiguity and change. Individuals with a *higher* tolerance for ambiguity are far more likely to be able to function effectively in organizations and contexts in which there is a high turbulence, a high rate of change, and less certainty about expectations, performance standards, what needs to be done, and so on. In contrast, individuals with a lower tolerance for ambiguity are far more likely to be unable to adapt or adjust quickly in turbulence, uncertainty, and change. These individuals are likely to become rigid, angry, stressed, and frustrated when there is a high level of uncertainty and ambiguity in the environment. High levels of tolerance for ambiguity, therefore, are associated with an ability to "roll with the punches" as organizations, environmental conditions, and demands change rapidly.

Two-Factor Profile

Instructions

On each of the following dimensions, distribute a total of 10 points between the two options. For example:

Summer weather   (7) ....(3) Winter weather

1. Very responsible job   (___) ....(___) Job security

2. Recognition for   (___) ....(___) Good relations
   work accomplishments   with co-workers

3. Advancement   (___) ....(___) A boss who knows
   opportunities at work   his/her job well

4. Opportunities to grow   (___) ....(___) Good working
   and learn on the job   conditions

5. A job that I can   (___) ....(___) Supportive rules,
   do well   policies of employer

6. A prestigious or   (___) ....(___) A high base wage
   high-status job   or salary

Scoring

Summarize your total scores for all items in the *left-hand column* and write it here:
MF = ___.
Summarize your total scores for all items in the *right-hand column* and write it here:
HF = ___.

Interpretation

The "MF" score indicates the relative importance that you place on motivating or satisfier factors in Herzberg's two-factor theory. This shows how important job content is to you. The "HF" score indicates the relative importance that you place on hygiene or dissatisfier factors in Herzberg's two-factor theory. This shows how important job context is to you.

Are You Cosmopolitan?

Instructions

Answer the questions below using a scale of 1 to 5: 1 representing "strongly disagree"; 2, "somewhat disagree"; 3, "neutral"; 4, "somewhat agree"; and 5, "strongly agree."

____ 1. You believe it is the right of the professional to make his or her own decisions about what is to be done on the job.

Source: Developed from Joseph A. Raelin, *The Clash of Cultures, Managers and Professionals* (Harvard Business School Press, 1986).

_____ 2. You believe a professional should stay in an individual staff role regardless of the income sacrifice.

_____ 3. You have no interest in moving up to a top administrative post.

_____ 4. You believe that professionals are better evaluated by professional colleagues than by management.

_____ 5. Your friends tend to be members of your profession.

_____ 6. You would rather be known or get credit for your work outside rather than inside the company.

_____ 7. You would feel better making a contribution to society than to your organization.

_____ 8. Managers have no right to place time and cost schedules on professional contributors.

Scoring and Interpretation

A "cosmopolitan" identifies with the career profession, and a "local" identifies with the employing organization. Total your scores. A score of 30–40 suggests a cosmopolitan work orientation, 10–20 a "local" orientation, and 20–30 a mixed orientation.

ASSESSMENT 9

Group Effectiveness

Instructions

For this assessment, select a specific group you work with or have worked with; it can be a college or work group. For each of the eight statements below, select how often each statement describes the group's behavior. Place the number 1, 2, 3, or 4 on the line next to each of the 8 numbers.

Usually	Frequently	Occasionally	Seldom
1	2	3	4

_____ 1. The members are loyal to one another and to the group leader.

_____ 2. The members and leader have a high degree of confidence and trust in each other.

_____ 3. Group values and goals express relevant values and needs of members.

_____ 4. Activities of the group occur in a supportive atmosphere.

_____ 5. The group is eager to help members develop to their full potential.

_____ 6. The group knows the value of constructive conformity and knows when to use it and for what purpose.

_____ 7. The members communicate all information relevant to the group's activity fully and frankly.

_____ 8. The members feel secure in making decisions that seem appropriate to them.

Scoring

_____ Total. Add up the eight numbers and place an X on the continuum below that represents the score.

Effective group   8 . . . 16 . . . 24 . . . 32   Ineffective group

Interpretation

The lower the score, the more effective the group. What can you do to help the group become more effective? What can the group do to become more effective?

Least Preferred Coworker Scale

Instructions

Think of all the different people with whom you have ever worked—in jobs, in social clubs, in student projects, or whatever. Next, think of the *one person* with whom you could work *least* well—that is, the person with whom you had the most difficulty getting a job done. This is the one person—a peer, boss, or subordinate—with whom you would least want to work. Describe this person by circling numbers at the appropriate points on each of the following pairs of bipolar adjectives. Work rapidly. There are no right or wrong answers.

Pleasant	8 7 6 5 4 3 2 1	Unpleasant
Friendly	8 7 6 5 4 3 2 1	Unfriendly
Rejecting	1 2 3 4 5 6 7 8	Accepting
Tense	1 2 3 4 5 6 7 8	Relaxed
Distant	1 2 3 4 5 6 7 8	Close
Cold	1 2 3 4 5 6 7 8	Warm
Supportive	8 7 6 5 4 3 2 1	Hostile
Boring	1 2 3 4 5 6 7 8	Interesting
Quarrelsome	1 2 3 4 5 6 7 8	Harmonious
Gloomy	1 2 3 4 5 6 7 8	Cheerful
Open	8 7 6 5 4 3 2 1	Guarded
Backbiting	1 2 3 4 5 6 7 8	Loyal
Untrustworthy	1 2 3 4 5 6 7 8	Trustworthy
Considerate	8 7 6 5 4 3 2 1	Inconsiderate
Nasty	1 2 3 4 5 6 7 8	Nice
Agreeable	8 7 6 5 4 3 2 1	Disagreeable
Insincere	1 2 3 4 5 6 7 8	Sincere
Kind	8 7 6 5 4 3 2 1	Unkind

Scoring

This is called the "least preferred coworker scale" (LPC). Compute your LPC score by totaling all the numbers you circled; enter that score here [LPC = ____].

Interpretation

The LPC scale is used by Fred Fiedler to identify a person's dominant leadership style. Fiedler believes that this style is a relatively fixed part of one's personality and is therefore difficult to change. This leads Fiedler to his contingency views, which suggest that the key to leadership success is finding (or creating) good "matches" between style and situation. If your score is 73 or above, Fiedler considers you a "relationship-motivated" leader; if your score is 64 and below, he considers you a "task-motivated" leader. If your score is between 65 and 72, Fiedler leaves it up to you to determine which leadership style is most like yours.

Source: Fred E. Fiedler and Martin M. Chemers. *Improving Leadership Effectiveness: The Leader Match Concept,* 2nd ed. (New York: John Wiley & Sons, Inc., 1984). Used by permission.

Leadership Style

Instructions

The following statements describe leadership acts. Indicate the way you would most likely act if you were leader of a workgroup, by circling whether you would most likely behave in this way:

> always (A); frequently (F); occasionally (O); seldom (S); or never (N)

A F O S N   1. Act as group spokesperson.
A F O S N   2. Encourage overtime work.
A F O S N   3. Allow members complete freedom in their work.
A F O S N   4. Encourage the use of uniform procedures.
A F O S N   5. Permit members to solve their own problems.
A F O S N   6. Stress being ahead of competing groups.
A F O S N   7. Speak as a representative of the group.
A F O S N   8. Push members for greater effort.
A F O S N   9. Try out ideas in the group.
A F O S N   10. Let the members work the way they think best.
A F O S N   11. Work hard for a personal promotion.
A F O S N   12. Tolerate postponement and uncertainty.
A F O S N   13. Speak for the group when visitors are present.
A F O S N   14. Keep the work moving at a rapid pace.
A F O S N   15. Turn members loose on a job.
A F O S N   16. Settle conflicts in the group.
A F O S N   17. Focus on work details.
A F O S N   18. Represent the group at outside meetings.
A F O S N   19. Avoid giving the members too much freedom.
A F O S N   20. Decide what should be done and how it should be done.
A F O S N   21. Push for increased production.
A F O S N   22. Give some members authority to act.
A F O S N   23. Expect things to turn out as predicted.
A F O S N   24. Allow the group to take initiative.
A F O S N   25. Assign group members to particular tasks.
A F O S N   26. Be willing to make changes.
A F O S N   27. Ask members to work harder.
A F O S N   28. Trust members to exercise good judgment.
A F O S N   29. Schedule the work to be done.
A F O S N   30. Refuse to explain my actions.
A F O S N   31. Persuade others that my ideas are best.
A F O S N   32. Permit the group to set its own pace.
A F O S N   33. Urge the group to beat its previous record.
A F O S N   34. Act without consulting the group.
A F O S N   35. Ask members to follow standard rules.

T _____   P _____

Scoring

1. Circle items 8, 12, 17, 18, 19, 30, 34, and 35.
2. Write the number 1 in front of a *circled item number* if you responded S (seldom) or N (never) to that item.

3. Write a number 1 in front of *item numbers not circled* if you responded A (always) or F (frequently).
4. Circle the number 1's which you have written in front of items 3, 5, 8, 10, 15, 18, 19, 22, 24, 26, 28, 30, 32, 34, and 35.
5. *Count the circled number 1's.* This is your score for leadership *concern for people.* Record the score in the blank following the letter P at the end of the questionnaire.
6. *Count the uncircled number 1's.* This is your score for leadership *concern for task.* Record this number in the blank following the letter T.

"TT" Leadership Style

Instructions

For each of the following 10 pairs of statements, divide 5 points between the two according to your beliefs, perceptions of yourself, or according to which of the two statements characterizes you better. The 5 points may be divided between the a and b statements in any one of the following ways: 5 for a, 0 for b; 4 for a, 1 for b; 3 for a, 2 for b; 1 for a, 4 for b; 0 for a, 5 for b, but not equally (2 ½) between the two. Weigh your choices between the two according to the one that characterizes you or your beliefs better.

1. (a) As leader I have a primary mission of maintaining stability.
   (b) As leader I have a primary mission of change.
2. (a) As leader I must cause events.
   (b) As leader I must facilitate events.
3. (a) I am concerned that my followers are rewarded equitably for their work.
   (b) I am concerned about what my followers want in life.
4. (a) My preference is to think long range: what might be.
   (b) My preference is to think short range: what is realistic.
5. (a) As a leader I spend considerable energy in managing separate but related goals.
   (b) As a leader I spend considerable energy in arousing hopes, expectations, and aspirations among my followers.

Source: Questionnaire by W. Warner Burke, Ph.D. Used by permission.

6. (a) Although not in a formal classroom sense, I believe that a significant part of my leadership is that of teacher.
   (b) I believe that a significant part of my leadership is that of facilitator.
7. (a) As leader I must engage with followers at an equal level of morality.
   (b) As leader I must represent a higher morality.
8. (a) I enjoy stimulating followers to want to do more.
   (b) I enjoy rewarding followers for a job well done.
9. (a) Leadership should be practical.
   (b) Leadership should be inspirational.
10. (a) What power I have to influence others comes primarily from my ability to get people to identify with me and my ideas.
    (b) What power I have to influence others comes primarily from my status and position.

Scoring

Circle your points for items 1b, 2a, 3b, 4a, 5b, 6a, 7b, 8a, 9b, 10a and add up the total points you allocated to these items; enter the score here [T = ____]. Next, add up the total points given to the uncircled items 1a, 2b, 3a, 4b, 5a, 6b, 7a, 8b, 9a, 10b; enter the score here [T = ____].

Interpretation

This instrument gives an impression of your tendencies toward "transformational" leadership (your **T** score) and "transactional" leadership (your T score). You may want to refer to the discussion of these concepts in Chapter 15. Today, a lot of attention is being given to the transformational aspects of leadership—those personal qualities that inspire a sense of vision and desire for extraordinary accomplishment in followers. The most successful leaders of the future will most likely be strong in both "T"s.

Empowering Others

Instructions

Think of times when you have been in charge of a group—this could be a full-time or part-time work situation, a student workgroup, or whatever. Complete the following questionnaire by recording how you feel about each statement according to this scale.

> 1 = Strongly disagree
>
> 2 = Disagree
>
> 3 = Neutral
>
> 4 = Agree
>
> 5 = Strongly agree

When in charge of a group I find:

____ 1. Most of the time other people are too inexperienced to do things, so I prefer to do them myself.

____ 2. It often takes more time to explain things to others than just to do them myself.

____ 3. Mistakes made by others are costly, so I don't assign much work to them.

Source: Questionnaire adapted from L. Steinmetz and R. Todd, *First Line Management,* 4th ed. (Homewood, IL: BPI/Irwin, 1986), pp. 64–67. Used by permission.

____ 4. Some things simply should not be delegated to others.

____ 5. I often get quicker action by doing a job myself.

____ 6. Many people are good only at very specific tasks, and thus can't be assigned additional responsibilities.

____ 7. Many people are too busy to take on additional work.

____ 8. Most people just aren't ready to handle additional responsibilities.

____ 9. In my position, I should be entitled to make my own decisions.

Scoring

Total your responses; enter the score here [____].

Interpretation

This instrument gives an impression of your *willingness to delegate.* Possible scores range from 9 to 45. The higher your score, the more willing you appear to be to delegate to others. Willingness to delegate is an important managerial characteristic. It is essential if you—as a manager—are to "empower" others and give them opportunities to assume responsibility and exercise self-control in their work. With the growing importance of empowerment in the new workplace, your willingness to delegate is well worth thinking about seriously.

Machiavellianism

Instructions

For each of the following statements, circle the number that most closely resembles your attitude.

Statement	Disagree A Lot	Disagree A Little	Neutral	Agree A Little	Agree A Lot
1. The best way to handle people is to tell them what they want to hear.	1	2	3	4	5
2. When you ask someone to do something for you, it is best to give the real reason for wanting it rather than reasons that might carry more weight.	1	2	3	4	5
3. Anyone who completely trusts someone else is asking for trouble.	1	2	3	4	5
4. It is hard to get ahead without cutting corners here and there.	1	2	3	4	5
5. It is safest to assume that all people have a vicious streak, and it will come out when they are given a chance.	1	2	3	4	5
6. One should take action only when it is morally right.	1	2	3	4	5
7. Most people are basically good and kind.	1	2	3	4	5
8. There is no excuse for lying to someone else.	1	2	3	4	5
9. Most people forget more easily the death of their father than the loss of their property.	1	2	3	4	5
10. Generally speaking, people won't work hard unless forced to do so.	1	2	3	4	5

Scoring and Interpretation

This assessment is designed to compute your Machiavellianism (Mach) score. Mach is a personality characteristic that taps people's power orientation. The high-Mach personality is pragmatic, maintains emotional distance from others, and believes that ends can justify means. To obtain your Mach score, add up the numbers you checked for questions 1, 3, 4, 5, 9, and 10. For the other four questions, reverse the numbers you have checked, so that 5 becomes 1; 4 is 2; and 1 is 5. Then total both sets of numbers to find your score. A random sample of adults found the national average to be 25. Students in business and management typically score higher.

The results of research using the Mach test have found: (1) men are generally more Machiavellian than women; (2) older adults tend to have lower Mach scores than younger adults; (3) there is no significant difference between high Machs and low Machs on measures of intelligence or ability; (4) Machiavellianism is not significantly related to demographic characteristics such as educational level or marital status; and (5) high Machs tend to be in professions that emphasize the control and manipulation of people—for example, managers, lawyers, psychiatrists, and behavioral scientists.

Source: From R. Christie and F. L. Geis, *Studies in Machiavellianism* (New York: Academic Press, 1970). By permission.

Personal Power Profile

Contributed by Marcus Maier, Chapman University

Instructions

Below is a list of statements that may be used in describing behaviors that supervisors (leaders) in work organizations can direct toward their subordinates (followers). First, carefully read each descriptive statement, thinking in terms of *how you prefer to influence others.* Mark the number that most closely represents how you feel. Use the following numbers for your answers.

> 5 = Strongly agree
>
> 4 = Agree
>
> 3 = Neither agree nor disagree
>
> 2 = Disagree
>
> 1 = Strongly disagree

To influence others, I would prefer to:	Strongly Disagree	Disagree	Neither Agree nor Disagree	Agree	Strongly Agree
1. Increase their pay level	1	2	3	4	5
2. Make them feel valued	1	2	3	4	5
3. Give undesirable job assignments	1	2	3	4	5
4. Make them feel like I approve of them	1	2	3	4	5
5. Make them feel that they have commitments to meet	1	2	3	4	5
6. Make them feel personally accepted	1	2	3	4	5
7. Make them feel important	1	2	3	4	5
8. Give them good technical suggestions	1	2	3	4	5
9. Make the work difficult for them	1	2	3	4	5
10. Share my experience and/or training	1	2	3	4	5
11. Make things unpleasant here	1	2	3	4	5
12. Make being at work distasteful	1	2	3	4	5
13. Influence their getting a pay increase	1	2	3	4	5
14. Make them feel like they should satisfy their job requirements	1	2	3	4	5
15. Provide them with sound job-related advice	1	2	3	4	5
16. Provide them with special benefits	1	2	3	4	5
17. Influence their getting a promotion	1	2	3	4	5
18. Give them the feeling that they have responsibilities to fulfill	1	2	3	4	5
19. Provide them with needed technical knowledge	1	2	3	4	5
20. Make them recognize that they have tasks to accomplish	1	2	3	4	5

Source. Modified version of T. R. Hinkon and C. A. Schriesheim, "Development and Application of New Scales to Measure the French and Raven (1959) Bases of Social Power," *Journal of Applied Psychology,* Vol. 74 (1989), pp. 561–567.

Scoring

Using the grid below, insert your scores from the 20 questions and proceed as follows: *Reward power*—sum your response to items 1, 13, 16, and 17 and divide by 4. *Coercive power*—sum your response to items 3, 9, 11, and 12 and divide by 4. *Legitimate power*—sum your response to questions 5, 14, 18, and 20 and divide by 4. *Referent power*—sum your response to questions 2, 4, 6, and 7 and divide by 4. *Expert power*—sum your response to questions 8, 10, 15, and 19 and divide by 4.

Reward	Coercive	Legitimate	Referent	Expert
1 ____	3 ____	5 ____	2 ____	8 ____
13 ____	9 ____	14 ____	4 ____	10 ____
16 ____	11 ____	18 ____	6 ____	15 ____
17 ____	12 ____	20 ____	7 ____	19 ____
Total ____	____	____	____	____
Divide by 4 ____	____	____	____	____

Interpretation

A high score (4 and greater) on any of the five dimensions of power implies that you prefer to influence others by employing that particular form of power. A low score (2 or less) implies that you prefer not to employ this particular form of power to influence others. This represents your power profile. Your overall power position is not reflected by the simple sum of the power derived from each of the five sources. Instead, some combinations of power are synergistic in nature—they are greater than the simple sum of their parts. For example, referent power tends to magnify the impact of other power sources because these other influence attempts are coming from a "respected" person. Reward power often increases the impact of referent power, because people generally tend to like those who give them things that they desire. Some power combinations tend to produce the opposite of synergistic effects, such that the total is less than the sum of the parts. Power dilution frequently accompanies the use of (or threatened use of) coercive power.

ASSESSMENT 16

Your Intuitive Ability

Instructions

Complete this survey as quickly as you can. Be honest with yourself. For each question, select the response that most appeals to you.

1. When working on a project, do you prefer to:
   (a) Be told what the problem is but be left free to decide how to solve it?
   (b) Get very clear instructions about how to go about solving the problem before you start?
2. When working on a project, do you prefer to work with colleagues who are:
   (a) Realistic?

Source: AIM Survey (El Paso, TX: ENFP Enterprises, 1989). Copyright © 1989 by Weston H. Agor. Used by permission.

   (b) Imaginative?
3. Do you most admire people who are:
   (a) Creative?
   (b) Careful?
4. Do the friends you choose tend to be:
   (a) Serious and hard working?
   (b) Exciting and often emotional?
5. When you ask a colleague for advice on a problem you have, do you:
   (a) Seldom or never get upset if he or she questions your basic assumptions?
   (b) Often get upset if he or she questions your basic assumptions?
6. When you start your day, do you:
   (a) Seldom make or follow a specific plan?
   (b) Usually first make a plan to follow?

7. When working with numbers do you find that you:
   (a) Seldom or never make factual errors?
   (b) Often make factual errors?
8. Do you find that you:
   (a) Seldom daydream during the day and really don't enjoy doing so when you do it?
   (b) Frequently daydream during the day and enjoy doing so?
9. When working on a problem, do you:
   (a) Prefer to follow the instructions or rules when they are given to you?
   (b) Often enjoy circumventing the instructions or rules when they are given to you?
10. When you are trying to put something together, do you prefer to have:
    (a) Step-by-step written instructions on how to assemble the item?
    (b) A picture of how the item is supposed to look once assembled?
11. Do you find that the person who irritates you *the most* is the one who appears to be:
    (a) Disorganized?
    (b) Organized?
12. When an expected crisis comes up that you have to deal with, do you:
    (a) Feel anxious about the situation?
    (b) Feel excited by the challenge of the situation?

Scoring

Total the number of "a" responses circled for questions 1, 3, 5, 6, 11; enter the score here [A = ____]. Total the number of "b" responses for questions 2, 4, 7, 8, 9, 10, 12; enter the score here [B = ____]. Add your "a" and "b" scores and enter the sum here [A + B = ____]. This is your *intuitive score*. The highest possible intuitive score is 12; the lowest is 0.

Interpretation

In his book *Intuition in Organizations* (Newbury Park, CA: Sage, 1989), pp. 10–11, Weston H. Agor states: "Traditional analytical techniques . . . are not as useful as they once were for guiding major decisions. . . . If you hope to be better prepared for tomorrow, then it only seems logical to pay some attention to the use and development of intuitive skills for decision making." Agor developed the prior survey to help people assess their tendencies to use intuition in decision making. Your score offers a general impression of your strength in this area. It may also suggest a need to further develop your skill and comfort with more intuitive decision approaches.

ASSESSMENT 17

Decision-Making Biases

Instructions

How good are you at avoiding potential decision-making biases? Test yourself by answering the following questions:

1. Which is riskier:
   (a) driving a car on a 400-mile trip?
   (b) flying on a 400-mile commercial airline flight?

2. Are there more words in the English language:
   (a) that begin with "r"?
   (b) that have "r" as the third letter?

3. Mark is finishing his MBA at a prestigious university. He is very interested in the arts and at one time considered a career as a musician. Is Mark more likely to take a job:
   (a) in the management of the arts?
   (b) with a management consulting firm?

4. You are about to hire a new central-region sales director for the fifth time this year. You predict that the next director should work out reasonably well since the last four were "lemons" and the odds favor hiring at least one good sales director in five tries. Is this thinking
   (a) correct?
   (b) incorrect?

5. A newly hired engineer for a computer firm in the Boston metropolitan area has 4 years' experience and good all-around qualifications. When asked to estimate the starting salary for this employee, a chemist with very little knowledge about the profession or industry guessed an annual salary of $35,000. What is your estimate?
   $____ per year

Source: Incidents from Max H. Bazerman, *Judgment in Managerial Decision Making,* 3rd ed. (New York: John Wiley & Sons, Inc., 1994), pp. 13–14. Used by permission.

Scoring

Your instructor will provide answers and explanations for the assessment questions.

Interpretation

Each of the preceding questions examines your tendency to use a different judgmental heuristic. In his book *Judgment in Managerial Decision Making,* 3rd ed. (New York: John Wiley & Sons, 1994), pp. 6–7, Max Bazerman calls these heuristics "simplifying strategies, or rules of thumb" used in making decisions. He states, "In general, heuristics are helpful, but their use can sometimes lead to severe errors. . . . If we can make managers aware of the potential adverse impacts of using heuristics, they can then decide when and where to use them." This assessment offers an initial insight into your use of such heuristics. An informed decision maker understands the heuristics, is able to recognize when they appear, and eliminates any that may inappropriately bias decision making.

Test yourself further. Before hearing from your instructor, go back and write next to each item the name of the judgmental heuristic (see Chapter 3 text discussion) that you think applies.

Then write down a situation that you have experienced and in which some decision-making bias may have occurred. Be prepared to share and discuss this incident with the class.

ASSESSMENT 18

Conflict Management Styles

Instructions

Think of how you behave in conflict situations in which your wishes differ from those of one or more persons. In the space to the left of each statement below, write the number from the following scale that indicates how likely you are to respond that way in a conflict situation.

| 1 = very unlikely | 2 = unlikely | 3 = likely | 4 = very likely |

____ **1.** I am usually firm in pursuing my goals.

____ **2.** I try to win my position.

____ **3.** I give up some points in exchange for others.

____ **4.** I feel that differences are not always worth worrying about.

____ **5.** I try to find a position that is intermediate between the other person's and mine.

____ **6.** In approaching negotiations, I try to be considerate of the other person's wishes.

____ **7.** I try to show the logic and benefits of my positions.

____ **8.** I always lean toward a direct discussion of the problem.

____ **9.** I try to find a fair combination of gains and losses for both of us.

____ **10.** I attempt to work through our differences immediately.

____ **11.** I try to avoid creating unpleasantness for myself.

____ **12.** I try to soothe the other person's feelings and preserve our relationships.

____ **13.** I attempt to get all concerns and issues immediately out in the open.

____ **14.** I sometimes avoid taking positions that would create controversy.

____ **15.** I try not to hurt others' feelings.

Scoring

Total your scores for items 1, 2, 7; enter that score here [*Competing* = ____]. Total your scores for items 8, 10, 13; enter that score here [*Collaborating* = ____]. Total your scores

---

Source: Adapted from Thomas-Kilmann, *Conflict Mode Instrument,* Copyright © 1974, Xicom, Inc., Tuxedo, NY 10987. Used by permission.

for items 3, 5, 9; enter that score here [*Compromising* = ____]. Total your scores for items 4, 11, 14; enter that score here. [*Avoiding* = ____]. Total your scores for items 6, 12, 15; enter that score here [*Accommodating* = ____].

Interpretation

Each of the scores above corresponds to one of the conflict management styles discussed in Chapter 15. Research indicates that each style has a role to play in management but that the best overall conflict management approach is collaboration; only it can lead to problem solving and true conflict resolution. You should consider any patterns that may be evident in your scores and think about how to best handle conflict situations in which you become involved.

ASSESSMENT 19

Your Personality Type

Instructions

How true is each statement for you?

	Not True at All		Not True or Untrue		Very True
1. I hate giving up before I'm absolutely sure that I'm licked.	1	2	3	4	5
2. Sometimes I feel that I should not be working so hard, but something drives me on.	1	2	3	4	5
3. I thrive on challenging situations. The more challenges I have, the better.	1	2	3	4	5
4. In comparison to most people I know, I'm very involved in my work.	1	2	3	4	5
5. It seems as if I need 30 hours a day to finish all the things I'm faced with.	1	2	3	4	5
6. In general, I approach my work more seriously than most people I know.	1	2	3	4	5
7. I guess there are some people who can be nonchalant about their work, but I'm not one of them.	1	2	3	4	5
8. My achievements are considered to be significantly higher than those of most people I know.	1	2	3	4	5
9. I've often been asked to be an officer of some group or groups.	1	2	3	4	5

Scoring

Add all your scores to create a total score = ____.

Interpretation

Type A personalities (hurried and competitive) tend to score 36 and above. Type B personalities (relaxed) tend to score 22 and below. Scores of 23–35 indicate a balance or mix of Type A and Type B.

Source: From *Job Demands and Worker Health* (HEW Publication No. [NIOSH] 75–160) (Washington, DC: US Department of Health, Education and Welfare, 1975), pp. 253–254.

Time Management Profile

Instructions

Complete the following questionnaire by indicating "Y" (yes) or "N" (no) for each item. Force yourself to respond "yes" or "no". Be frank and allow your responses to create an accurate picture of how you tend to respond to these kinds of situations.

____ 1. When confronted with several items of similar urgency and importance, I tend to do the easiest one first.

____ 2. I do the most important things during that part of the day when I know I perform best.

____ 3. Most of the time I don't do things someone else can do; I delegate this type of work to others.

____ 4. Even though meetings without a clear and useful purpose upset me, I put up with them.

____ 5. I skim documents before reading them and don't complete any that offer a low return on my time investment.

____ 6. I don't worry much if I don't accomplish at least one significant task each day.

____ 7. I save the most trivial tasks for that time of day when my creative energy is lowest.

____ 8. My workspace is neat and organized.

____ 9. My office door is always "open"; I never work in complete privacy.

____ 10. I schedule my time completely from start to finish every workday.

____ 11. I don't like "to do" lists, preferring to respond to daily events as they occur.

____ 12. I "block" a certain amount of time each day or week that is dedicated to high-priority activities.

Scoring

Count the number of "Y" responses to items 2, 3, 5, 7, 8, 12. [Enter that score here ____.] Count the number of "N" responses to items 1, 4, 6, 9, 10, 11. [Enter that score here ____.] Add together the two scores.

Interpretation

The higher the total score, the closer your behavior matches recommended time management guidelines. Reread those items where your response did not match the desired one. Why don't they match? Do you have reasons why your behavior in this instance should be different from the recommended time management guideline? Think about what you can do (and how easily it can be done) to adjust your behavior to be more consistent with these guidelines. For further reading, see Alan Lakein, *How to Control Your Time and Your Life* (New York: David McKay), and William Oncken, *Managing Management Time* (Englewood Cliffs, NJ: Prentice Hall, 1984).

Source: Suggested by a discussion in Robert E. Quinn, Sue R. Faerman, Michael P. Thompson, and Michael R. McGrath, *Becoming a Master Manager: A Contemporary Framework* (New York: John Wiley & Sons, Inc., 1990), pp. 75–76.

Organizational Design Preference

Instructions

To the left of each item, write the number from the following scale that shows the extent to which the statement accurately describes your views.

> 5 = strongly agree
>
> 4 = agree somewhat
>
> 3 = undecided
>
> 2 = disagree somewhat
>
> 1 = strongly disagree

I prefer to work in an organization where:

1. Goals are defined by those in higher levels.
2. Work methods and procedures are specified.
3. Top management makes important decisions.
4. My loyalty counts as much as my ability to do the job.

Source: John F. Veiga and John N. Yanouzas, *The Dynamics of Organization Theory: Gaining a Macro Perspective* (St. Paul, MN: West, 1979), pp. 158–160. Used by permission.

5. Clear lines of authority and responsibility are established.
6. Top management is decisive and firm.
7. My career is pretty well planned out for me.
8. I can specialize.
9. My length of service is almost as important as my level of performance.
10. Management is able to provide the information I need to do my job well.
11. A chain of command is well established.
12. Rules and procedures are adhered to equally by everyone.
13. People accept authority of a leader's position.
14. People are loyal to their boss.
15. People do as they have been instructed.
16. People clear things with their boss before going over his or her head.

Scoring

Total your scores for all questions. Enter the score here [____].

Interpretation

This assessment measures your preference for working in an organization designed along "organic" or "mechanistic" lines. The higher your score (above 64), the more comfortable you are with a mechanistic design; the lower your score (below 48), the more comfortable you are with an organic design. Scores between 48 and 64 can go either way. This organizational design preference represents an important issue in the new workplace. Indications are that today's organizations are taking on more and more organic characteristics. Presumably, those of us who work in them will need to be comfortable with such designs.

ASSESSMENT 22

Which Culture Fits You?

Instructions

Check one of the following organization "cultures" in which you feel most comfortable working.

1. A culture that values talent, entrepreneurial activity, and performance over commitment; one that offers large financial rewards and individual recognition.
2. A culture that stresses loyalty, working for the good of the group, and getting to know the right people; one that believes in "generalists" and step-by-step career progress.
3. A culture that offers little job security; one that operates with a survival mentality, stresses that every individual can make a difference, and focuses attention on "turnaround" opportunities.
4. A culture that values long-term relationships; one that emphasizes systematic career development, regular

Source: Developed from Carol Hymowitz, "Which Corporate Culture Fits You?" *Wall Street Journal* (July 17, 1989), p. B1.

training, and advancement based on gaining of functional expertise.

Scoring

These labels identify the four different cultures: 1 = "the baseball team," 2 = "the club," 3 = "the fortress," and 4 = "the academy."

Interpretation

To some extent, your future career success may depend on working for an organization in which there is a good fit between you and the prevailing corporate culture. This assessment can help you learn how to recognize various cultures, evaluate how well they can serve your needs, and recognize how they may change with time. A risk taker, for example, may be out of place in a "club" but fit right in with a "baseball team." Someone who wants to seek opportunities wherever they may occur may be out of place in an "academy" but fit right in with a "fortress."

Notes

Case 1 References

[1] Panera facts and quotes from www.panera.com; and Ron Shaich, speech at Annual Meeting 2006, Temple Israel (June 28, 2006).

Case 3 References

[1] Information and quotes from "About Our Company," www.sas.com/corporate/overview; Charles Fishman, "Sanity Inc.," *Fast Company* (January 1999), p. 84ff.; "SAS Marks 6th Straight Year on Fortune List of '100 Best Companies to Work For'," www.sas.com/news/preleases/010803/news1.html; "Company Work/Life," www.sas.com/corporate/worklife; "Keeping Employees Without Breaking the Bank," The Workforce Stability Institute, www.employee.org; "Investment in the Work Environment Helps Retain Staff," www.cscresearchservices.com.

Case 9 References

[1] Information from Susan Carey, "Racing to Improve," *The Wall Street Journal* (March 24, 2006).

Case 12 References

[1] Sharon Shinn, "The CEO of Accessibility," *BizEd* (March/April 2007), pp. 18–24.

[2] Jeffrey Bartash, "Zander Puts Mojo Back into Motorola, www.marketwatch.com (December 6, 2005).

[3] Shinn, op. cit.

Case 13 References

[1] Information from Sara Schaefer Munoz, "Is Hiding Your Wedding Band Necessary at a Job Interview?" *The Wall Street Journal* (March 15, 2007), p. D3.

[2] Information and quotes from "Get Healthy—Or Else," *Business Week* (February 26, 2007), cover story; and, "Wellness—or Orwellness?" *Business Week* (March 19, 2007), cover story.

[3] Information from "Anne Fisher, "Why Women Get Paid Less," *Fortune* (March 20, 2007), retrieved from www.fortune.com.

[4] Information from Marcus Kabel, "Wal-Mart Goes Public with Annual Bonuses," *The Columbus Dispatch* (March 23, 2007), pp. H1, H2.

Case 16 References

[1] Information from "Daniel Yee, "Chick-Fil-A Recipe Winning Customers," *The Columbus Dispatch* (September 9, 2006), p. D1.

Glossary

360° evaluation is a comprehensive approach that uses self-ratings, customer ratings, and ratings by others outside the work unit.

360-degree feedback provides performance feedback from peers, co-workers, and direct reports as well as from the supervisor.

Ability reflects a person's existing capacity to perform the various tasks needed for a given job.

Absorptive capacity is the ability to learn.

Accommodation, or smoothing, involves playing down differences and finding areas of agreement.

Achievement-oriented leadership emphasizes setting challenging goals, stressing excellence in performance, and showing confidence in people's ability to achieve high standards of performance.

Action research is the process of systematically collecting data on an organization, feeding it back for action planning, and evaluating results by collecting and reflecting on more data.

Active listening encourages people to say what they really mean.

Activity measures of performance assess work efforts or inputs.

Adaptive capacity refers to the ability to change.

Adhocracy is an organizational structure that emphasizes shared, decentralized decision making; extreme horizontal specialization; few levels of management; the virtual absence of formal controls; and few rules, policies, and procedures.

Affective component of an attitude is a specific feeling regarding the personal impact of the antecedents.

Affects is a generic term that covers a broad range of feelings that individuals express.

Agency theory suggests that public corporations can function effectively even though their managers are self-interested and do not automatically bear the full consequences of their managerial actions.

Alternative dispute resolution involves a neutral third party who helps others resolve negotiation impasses and disputes.

Anchoring and adjustment heuristic bases a decision on incremental adjustments to an initial value determined by historical precedent or some reference point.

Aptitude represents a person's capability of learning something.

Arbitration is when a neutral third party acts as judge with the power to issue a decision binding on all parties.

Artificial intelligence is the study of how computers can be programmed to think like the human brain.

Associative choices are decisions that can be loosely linked to nagging continual problems but that were not specifically developed to solve the problem.

Attitude is a predisposition to respond in a positive or negative way to someone or something in one's environment.

Attribution theory is the attempt to understand the cause of an event, assess responsibility for outcomes of the event, and assess the personal qualities of the people involved.

Authoritarianism is a tendency to adhere rigidly to conventional values and to obey recognized authority.

Authoritative command uses formal authority to end conflict.

Authority decisions   are made by one individual using information he/she already possesses.

Automation   allows machines to do work previously accomplished by people.

Availability heuristic   bases a decision on recent events relating to the situation at hand.

Avoidance   involves pretending a conflict does not really exist.

Bargaining zone   is the zone between one party's minimum reservation point and the other party's maximum reservation point in a negotiating situation.

Behavioral component   is an intention to behave in a certain way based on your specific feelings or attitudes.

Behavioral decision theory   views decision makers as acting only in terms of what they perceive about a given situation.

Behavioral perspective   assumes that leadership is central to performance and other outcomes.

Behaviorally anchored rating scale (BARS)   is a performance appraisal approach that describes observable job behaviors, each of which is evaluated to determine good versus bad performance.

Beliefs   represent ideas about someone or something and the conclusions people draw about them.

Benefit cycle   is a pattern of successful adjustment followed by further improvements.

Blogs   are individual web sites that communicate personal accounts of events and opinions.

Brainstorming   involves generating ideas through "freewheeling" and without criticism.

Bureaucracy   is an ideal form of organization, the characteristics of which were defined by the German sociologist Max Weber.

Case study   is an in-depth analysis of one or a small number of settings.

Causality   is the assumption that change in the independent variable has caused change in the dependent variable.

Central tendency error   occurs when raters lump everyone's performance ratings around the average, or middle, category.

Centralization   is the degree to which the authority to make decisions is restricted to higher levels of management.

Centralized communication networks   link group members through a central control point.

Certain environments   provide full information on the expected results for decision-making alternatives.

Change agents   are people who take action to change the behavior of people and systems.

Changing   is the stage in which specific actions are taken to create change.

Channel richness   indicates the capacity of a channel to convey information.

Charismatic leaders   are those leaders who, by force of their personal abilities, are capable of having a profound and extraordinary effect on followers.

Classical conditioning   is a form of learning through association that involves the manipulation of stimuli to influence behavior.

Classical decision theory   views decision makers as acting in a world of complete certainty.

Coalition power   is the ability to control another's behavior indirectly because the individual owes an obligation to you or another as part of a larger collective interest.

Coercive power   is the extent to which a manager can deny desired rewards or administer punishment to control other people.

Cognitive complexity   is the underlying assumption that those high in cognitive complexity process information differently and perform certain tasks better than less cognitively complex people.

Cognitive components   reflect the beliefs, opinions, knowledge, or information a person possesses and values of an attitude.

Cognitive dissonance   describes a state of inconsistency between an individual's attitude and behavior.

Cohesiveness is the degree to which members are attracted to a group and motivated to remain a part of it.

Collaboration   involves recognition that something is wrong and needs attention through problem solving.

Collateral organization   involves a representative set of members in periodic small-group, problem-solving sessions.

Communication channels   are the pathways through which messages are communicated.

Communication   is the process of sending and receiving symbols with attached meanings.

Competition seeks victory by force, superior skill, or domination.

Compressed work week allows a full-time job to be completed in fewer than five full workdays.

Compromise occurs when each party gives up something of value to the other.

Conceptual skill is the ability to analyze and solve complex problems.

Confirmation trap is the tendency to seek confirmation for what is already thought to be true and not search for disconfirming information.

Conflict occurs when parties disagree over substantive issues or when emotional antagonisms create friction between them.

Conflict resolution occurs when the reasons for a conflict are eliminated.

Confrontation meeting helps determine how an organization may be improved and start action toward improvement.

Conglomerates are firms that own several different unrelated businesses.

Consensus is a group decision that has the expressed support of most members.

Consideration is being sensitive to people's feelings and triyng to make things pleasant for the followers.

Constructive stress has a positive impact on both attitudes and performance.

Consultative decisions are made by one individual after seeking input from or consulting with members of a group.

Content theories profile different needs that may motivate individual behavior.

Contextual variables link observations to a set of relevant facts, events, or points of view, such as organizational characteristics, work functions, external environment factors, and demographic variables.

Contingency approach seeks ways to meet the needs of different management situations.

Continuous reinforcement is a reinforcement schedule that administers a reward each time a desired behavior occurs.

Contrast effects occur when an individual's characteristics are contrasted with those of others recently encountered, who rank higher or lower on the same characteristics.

Control is the set of mechanisms used to keep actions and outputs within predetermined limits.

Controlling monitors performance and takes any needed corrective action.

Coordination is the set of mechanisms used in an organization to link the actions of its subunits into a consistent pattern.

Countercultures are groups where the patterns of values and philosophies outwardly reject those of the larger organization or social system.

Creativity generates unique and novel responses to problems.

Critical incident diary is a method of performance appraisal that records incidents of unusual success or failure for a given performance aspect.

Cross-functional teams bring together persons from different functions to work on a common task.

Cultural symbol is any object, act, or event that serves to transmit cultural meaning.

Culture is the learned and shared way of thinking and acting among a group of people or society.

Decentralization is the degree to which the authority to make decisions is given to lower levels in an organization's hierarchy.

Decentralized communication networks members communicate directly with one another.

Deep acting is trying to modify your true inner feelings based on display rules.

Delphi technique involves generating decision-making alternatives through a series of survey questionnaires.

Demographic characteristics are the background variables (e.g., age, gender) that help shape what a person becomes over time.

Dependent variable is the event or occurrence expressed in a hypothesis that indicates what the researcher is interested in explaining.

Dependent variables are outcomes of practical value and interest.

Destructive stress has a negative impact on both attitudes and performance.

Developmental approaches are systematic models of ways in which personality develops across time.

Directive leadership spells out the what and how of subordinates' tasks.

Display rules govern the degree to which it is appropriate for people from different cultures to display their emotions similarly.

Distributed leadership is the sharing of responsibility for meeting group task and maintenance needs.

Distributive justice is the degree to which all people are treated the same under a policy.

Distributive negotiation focuses on positions staked out or declared by the parties involved, who are each trying to claim certain portions of the available pie.

Diversity-consensus dilemma is the tendency for diversity in groups to create process difficulties even as it offers improved potential for problem solving.

Divisional departmentation groups individuals and resources by products, territories, services, clients, or legal entities.

Dogmatism leads a person to see the world as a threatening place and to regard authority as absolute.

Dysfunctional conflict works to the group's or organization's disadvantage.

Effective communication is when the intended meaning equals the perceived meaning.

Effective groups achieve high levels of task performance, member satisfaction, and team viability.

Effective manager is one who helps others achieve high levels of both performance and satisfaction.

Efficient communication is low cost in its use of resources.

Emotional adjustment traits measure how much an individual experiences emotional distress or displays unacceptable acts.

Emotional conflict involves interpersonal difficulties that arise over feelings of anger, mistrust, dislike, fear, resentment, and the like.

Emotional contagion is when the customer catches the emotions of the salesperson.

Emotional dissonance is inconsistencies between emotions we feel and emotions we project.

Emotional intelligence is the ability to manage oneself and one's relationships effectively.

Emotional labor is a situation where a person displays organizationally desired emotions during interpersonal transactions at work.

Emotions are intense feelings directed at someone or something.

Employee assistance programs provide help for employees who are experiencing stressful personal problems.

Employee involvement teams meet regularly to examine work-related problems and opportunities.

Empowerment is the process by which managers help others acquire and use the power needed to make decisions affecting themselves and their work.

Environmental complexity is the magnitude of the problems and opportunities in the organization's environment as evidenced by the degrees of richness, interdependence, and uncertainty.

Equity theory posits that people will act to eliminate any felt inequity in the rewards received for their work in comparison with others.

ERG theory identifies existence, relatedness, and growth needs.

Escalating commitment is the tendency to continue a previously chosen course of action even when feedback suggests that it is failing.

ESOPs allow employees to own stock in their employer's business and benefit from future increase in the stock price.

Ethics mindfulness is an enriched awareness that causes one to consistently behave with ethical consciousness.

Ethnocentrism is the tendency to believe one's culture and its values are superior to those of others.

Existence needs are desires for physiological and material well-being.

Expectancy is the probability that work effort will be followed by performance accomplishment.

Expectancy theory argues that work motivation is determined by individual beliefs regarding effort/performance relationships and work outcomes.

Expert power is the ability to control another's behavior because of the possession of knowledge, experience, or judgment that the other person does not have but needs.

External adaptation deals with reaching goals: the tasks to be accomplished, the methods to be used to achieve those goals, and the methods of coping with success and failure.

Extinction is the withdrawal of the reinforcing consequences for a given behavior.

Feedback communicates how one feels about something another person has done or said.

Field experiment is a research study that is conducted in a realistic setting, whereby the researcher intervenes and manipulates one or more independent variables and controls the situation as carefully as the situation permits.

Field survey is a research design that relies on the use of some form of questionnaire for the primary purpose of describing and/or predicting some phenomenon.

FIRO-B theory examines differences in how people relate to one another based on their needs to express and receive feelings of inclusion, control, and affection.

Flaming is expressing rudeness when using e-mail or other forms of electronic communication.

Flexible benefit plans are pay systems that allow workers to select benefits according to their individual needs.

Flexible manufacturing systems use adaptive technology and integrated job designs to easily shift production among alternative products.

Flexible working hours give employees some daily choice in scheduling arrival and departure times from work.

Force-coercion strategy uses authority, rewards, and punishments to create change.

Forced distribution is a method of performance appraisal that uses a small number of performance categories, such as "very good," "good," "adequate," "poor," and "very poor," and forces a certain proportion of people into each.

Formal channels follow the official chain of command.

Formal groups are officially designated for specific organizational purposes.

Formalization is the written documentation of work rules, policies, and procedures.

Full-range leadership theory (FRLT) involves nine dimensions covering both transformational and transactional leadership, especially emphasizing contextual variables.

Functional conflict results in positive benefits to the group.

Functional departmentation is grouping individuals by skill, knowledge, and action.

Functional silos problem or functional chimneys problem, occurs when people fail to communicate across functions.

Fundamental attribution error is the tendency to underestimate the influence of situational factors and to overestimate the influence of personal factors in evaluating someone else's behavior.

Gain sharing is a pay system that links pay and performance by giving workers the opportunity to share in productivity gains through increased earnings.

Garbage can model views the main components of the choice process —problems, solutions, participants, and choice situations—as all mixed up together in the garbage can of the organization.

Grafting is the process of acquiring individuals, units, and/or firms to bring in useful knowledge to the organization.

Grapevine transfers information through networks of friendships and acquaintances.

Graphic rating scale is a scale that lists a variety of dimensions thought to be related to high-performance outcomes in a given job and that the individual is expected to exhibit.

Group decisions are made by all members of the group.

Group dynamics are the forces operating in groups that affect the ways members work together.

Groups involve two or more people working together regularly to achieve common goals.

Groupthink is the tendency of cohesive group members to lose their critical evaluative capabilities.

Growth needs are desires for continued personal growth and development.

Halo effect occurs when one attribute of a person or situation is used to develop an overall impression of the person or situation.

Halo error results when one person rates another person on several different dimensions and gives a similar rating for each one.

Heuristics are simplifying strategies or "rules of thumb" used to make decisions.

Hierarchy of needs theory offers a pyramid of physiological, safety, social, esteem, and self-actualization needs.

High-content cultures words convey only part of a message, while the rest of the message must be inferred from body language and additional contextual cues.

Higher-order needs   in Maslow's hierarchy are esteem and self-actualization.

Hindsight trap   is a tendency to overestimate the degree to which an event that has already taken place could have been predicted.

Hope   is the tendency to look for alternative pathways to reach a desired goal.

Horizontal specialization   is a division of labor through the formation of work units or groups within an organization.

Human skill   is the ability to work well with other people.

Hygiene factors   in the job context are sources of job dissatisfaction.

Inclusivity   is the degree to which an organization's culture respects and values diversity.

Incremental change   builds on the existing ways of operating to enhance or extend them in new directions.

Independent variable   is the event or occurrence that is presumed by a hypothesis to affect one or more other events or occurrences as dependent variables.

Independent variables   are presumed causes that influence dependent variables.

Individualism-collectivism   is the tendency of a culture's members to emphasize individual self-interests or group relationships.

Inference-based   emphasizes leadership effectiveness as inferred by perceived group/organizational performance outcomes.

Influence   is a behavioral response to the exercise of power.

Informal channels   do not follow the chain of command.

Informal groups   are unofficial and emerge to serve special interests.

Information power   is the access to and/or the control of information.

Information technology   is the combination of machines, artifacts, procedures, and systems used to gather, store, analyze, and disseminate information so that it can be translated into knowledge.

Initiating structure   is concerned with spelling out the task requirements and clarifying other aspects of the work agenda.

Innovation   is the process of creating new ideas and putting them into practice.

Instrumental values   reflect a person's beliefs about the means for achieving desired ends.

Instrumentality   is the probability that performance will lead to various work outcomes.

Integrative negotiation   focuses on the merits of the issues, and the parties involved try to enlarge the available pie rather than stake claims to certain portions of it.

Interactional justice   is the degree to which the people are treated with dignity and respect in decisions affecting them.

Interfirm alliances   are announced cooperative agreements or joint ventures between two independent firms.

Intergroup conflict   occurs among groups in an organization.

Intergroup dynamics   are relationships between groups cooperating and competing with one another.

Intergroup team building   helps groups improve their working relationships with one another and experience improved group effectiveness.

Intermittent reinforcement   is a reinforcement schedule that rewards behavior only periodically.

Internal integration   deals with the creation of a collective identity and with ways of working and living together.

Interorganizational conflict   occurs between organizations.

Interpersonal conflict   occurs between two or more individuals in opposition to each other.

Intervening variable   is an event or occurrence that provides the linkage through which an independent variable is presumed to affect a dependent variable.

Interview   involves face-to-face, telephone, or computer-assisted interactions to ask respondents questions of interest.

Intrapersonal conflict   occurs within the individual because of actual or perceived pressures from incompatible goals or expectations.

Intuition   is the ability to know or recognize quickly the possibilities of a situation.

Job burnout   shows itself as loss of interest in and satisfaction with a job because of stressful working conditions.

Job characteristics model   identifies five core job characteristics—skill variety, task identity, task significance, autonomy, and feedback.

Job design is the process of defining job tasks and the work arrangements to accomplish them.

Job enlargement increases task variety by adding new tasks of similar difficulty to a job.

Job enrichment increases job content by giving workers more responsibility for planning and evaluating duties.

Job redesign is the process of creating long-term congruence between individual goals and organizational career opportunities.

Job rotation increases task variety by shifting workers among jobs involving tasks of similar difficulty.

Job satisfaction is a positive feeling about one's work and work setting.

Job sharing allows one full-time job to be divided among two or more persons.

Job simplification standardizes tasks and employs people in very routine jobs.

KISS principle stands for "keep it short and simple."

Laboratory experiment is conducted in an artificial setting in which the researcher intervenes and manipulates one or more independent variables in a highly controlled situation.

Law of contingent reinforcement is the view that for a reward to have maximum reinforcing value, it must be delivered only if the desired behavior is exhibited.

Law of effect is the observation that behavior resulting in a pleasing outcome is likely to be repeated; behavior that results in an unpleasant outcome is not likely to be repeated.

Law of immediate reinforcement states that the more immediate the delivery of a reward after the occurrence of a desirable behavior, the greater the reinforcing effect on behavior.

Leader match training leaders are trained to diagnose the situation to match their high and low LPC scores with situational control.

Leader-member exchange (LMX) theory emphasizes the quality of the working relationship between leaders and followers.

Leadership is the process of influencing others to understand and agree about what needs to be done and how to do it, and the process of facilitating individual and collective efforts to accomplish shared objectives.

Leadership grid is an approach that uses a nine-position grid that places concern for production on the horizontal axis and concern for people on the vertical axis.

Leading creates enthusiasm to work hard to accomplish tasks successfully.

Learning is an enduring change in behavior that results from experience.

Least-preferred co-worker (LPC) scale is a measure of a person's leadership style based on a description of the person with whom respondents have been able to work least well.

Legitimate power or formal authority is the extent to which a manager can use the "right of command" to control other people.

Leniency error is the tendency to give relatively high ratings to virtually everyone.

Life stressors are things that arise in our personal lives to create stress.

Lifelong learning is continuous learning from everyday experiences.

Line units are workgroups that conduct the major business of the organization.

Locus of control is the extent to which a person feels able to control his or her own life and is concerned with a person's internal–external orientation.

Long-term/short-term orientation is the degree to which a culture emphasizes long-term or short-term thinking.

Low-context cultures messages are expressed mainly by the spoken and written word.

Low-differentiation error occurs when raters restrict themselves to a small part of the rating scale.

Lower-order needs in Maslow's hierarchy are physiological, safety, and social.

Lump-sum increases are part of a pay system in which people elect to receive their wage or salary increase in one or more lump-sum payments.

Maintenance activities support the emotional life of the team as an ongoing social system.

Management by objectives, or **MBO,** is a process of joint goal setting between a supervisor and a subordinate.

Management philosophy is a philosophy that links key goal-related issues with key collaboration issues to come up with general ways by which the firm will manage its affairs.

Managerial script is a series of well-known routines for problem identification, alternative generation, and analysis common to managers within a firm.

Managerial wisdom   is the ability to perceive variations in the environment and an understanding of the social actors and their relationships.

Managers   are responsible for supporting the work efforts of other people.

Masculinity-femininity   is the degree to which a society values assertiveness or relationships.

Matrix departmentation   is a combination of functional and divisional patterns wherein an individual is assigned to more than one type of unit.

MBWA   involves getting out of the office to communicate directly with others.

Mechanistic type or machine bureaucracy   emphasizes vertical specialization and control through impersonal coordination and a heavy reliance on standardization, formalization, rules, policies, and procedures.

Mediation   is when a neutral third party tries to engage the parties in a negotiated solution through persuasion and rational argument.

Merit pay   is a compensation system that bases an individual's salary or wage increase on a measure of the person's performance accomplishments during a specified time period.

Mimicry   is the copying of the successful practices of others.

Mission statements   are written statements of organizational purpose.

Mixed messages   occur when words say one thing while nonverbal cues say something else.

Models   are simplified views of reality that attempt to explain real-world phenomena.

Moderator variable   is an event or occurrence that, when systematically varied, changes the relationship between an independent variable and a dependent variable.

Moods   are less intense as compared with emotions, and they frequently lack a contextual stimulus.

Motivating potential score   describes the extent to which the core characteristics of a job create motivating conditions.

Motivation   refers to forces within an individual that account for the level, direction, and persistence of effort expended at work.

Motivator factors   in the job content are sources of job satisfaction.

Multiculturalism   refers to pluralism and respect for diversity in the workplace.

Multiskilling   occurs when team members are trained in skills needed to perform different jobs.

Mum effect   occurs when people are reluctant to communicate bad news.

Need for achievement (nAch)   is the desire to do better, solve problems, or master complex tasks.

Need for affiliation (nAff)   is the desire for friendly and warm relations with others.

Need for power (nPower)   is the desire to control others and influence their behavior.

Negative affectivity   are those who are "down" most of the time.

Negative reinforcement   is the withdrawal of negative consequences, which tends to increase the likelihood of repeating the behavior in a similar setting; it is also known as avoidance.

Negotiation   is the process of making joint decisions when the parties involved have different preferences.

Noise   is anything that interferes with the effectiveness of communication.

Nominal group technique   involves structured rules for generating and prioritizing ideas.

Nonprogrammed decisions   are created to deal uniquely with a problem at hand.

Nonreactive measures   are used to obtain data without disturbing the setting.

Nonverbal communication   occurs through facial expressions, body motions, eye contact, and other physical gestures.

Norms   are rules or standards for the behavior of group members.

Observation   involves watching an event, object, or person and recording what is seen.

Open systems   transform human and material resource inputs into finished goods and services.

Operant conditioning   is the process of controlling behavior by manipulating, or "operating" on, its consequences.

Operations technology   is the combination of resources, knowledge, and techniques that creates a product or service output for an organization.

Optimism   is the expectation of positive outcomes.

Organic type or professional bureaucracy   emphasizes horizontal specialization, extensive use of personal coordination, and loose rules, policies, and procedures.

Organization charts   are diagrams that depict the formal structures of organizations.

Organizational behavior   is the study of individuals and groups in organizations.

Organizational behavior modification (OB Mod) is the systematic reinforcement of desirable work behavior and the non-reinforcement or punishment of unwanted work behavior.

Organizational communication is the many ways information moves through and is exchanged in organizations.

Organizational culture is a shared set of beliefs and values within an organization.

Organizational design is the process of choosing and implementing a structural configuration for an organization.

Organizational development (OD) is the application of behavioral science knowledge in a long-range effort to improve an organization's ability to cope with change in its external environment and increase its problem-solving capabilities.

Organizational development interventions are activities initiated to support planned change and improve work effectiveness.

Organizational governance is the pattern of authority, influence, and acceptable managerial behavior established at the top of the organization.

Organizational justice is an issue of how fair and equitable people view workplace practices.

Organizational learning is the process of acquiring knowledge and using information to adapt successfully to changing circumstances.

Organizational learning is the process of knowledge acquisition, information distribution, information interpretation, and organizational retention.

Organizational myth is an unproven and often unstated belief that is accepted uncritically.

Organizational myth is a commonly held cause-effect relationship or assertion that cannot be empirically supported.

Organizational or corporate culture is the system of shared actions, values, and beliefs that develops within an organization and guides the behavior of its members.

Organizational politics is the management of influence to obtain ends not sanctioned by the organization or to obtain sanctioned ends through nonsanctioned means; it is also the art of creative compromise among competing interests.

Organizations are collections of people working together to achieve a common purpose.

Organized anarchy is a firm or division of a firm in a transition characterized by rapid change and lack of a legitimate hierarchy.

Organizing divides up tasks and arranges resources to accomplish them.

Output controls focus on desired targets and allow managers to use their own methods for reaching defined targets.

Output goals are the goals that define the type of business an organization is in.

Output measures of performance assess actual work results.

Paired comparison is a comparative method of performance appraisal whereby each person is directly compared with every other person.

Parochialism assumes the ways of your culture are the only ways of doing things.

Participative leadership focuses on consulting with subordinates and seeking and taking their suggestions into account before making decisions.

Path-goal theory of leadership assumes that a leader's key function is to adjust his or her behaviors to complement situational contingencies.

Peer evaluation other members of a work team or persons doing similar jobs rate the individual as a co-worker.

Perception is the process through which people receive, organize, and interpret information from their environment.

Performance appraisal is a process of systematically evaluating performance and providing feedback on which performance adjustments need to be made.

Performance gap is a discrepancy between the desired and actual state of affairs.

Performance management is the process of managing performance measurement and the associated human resource management decisions.

Permanent part-time work is permanent work for fewer hours than the standard week.

Personal bias error occurs when a rater allows specific biases, such as race, age, or gender, to enter into a performance appraisal.

Personal wellness involves maintaining physical and mental health to better deal with stress when it occurs.

Personality represents the overall profile, or combination of characteristics, that captures the unique nature of a person as that person reacts and interacts with others.

Personality dynamics are the ways in which an individual integrates and organizes social traits, values and motives, personal conceptions, and emotional adjustment.

Planned change   is intentional and occurs with a change agent's direction.

Planning   sets objectives and identifies the actions needed to achieve them.

Positive affectivity   are those who have a tendency to be perpetually positive.

Positive reinforcement   is the administration of positive consequences that tend to increase the likelihood of repeating the behavior in similar settings.

Power   is the ability to get someone else to do something you want done, or the ability to make things happen or get things done the way you want.

Power distance   is the willingness of a culture to accept status and power differences among its members.

Problem solving   uses information to resolve disputes.

Procedural justice   is the degree to which rules are always properly followed to implement policies.

Process consultation   helps a group improve on such things as norms, cohesiveness, decision-making methods, communication, conflict, and task and maintenance activities.

Process controls   attempt to specify the manner in which tasks are to be accomplished.

Process innovations   introduce into operations new and better ways of doing things.

Process power   is the control over methods of production and analysis.

Process reengineering   analyzes, streamlines, and reconfigures actions and tasks to achieve work goals.

Process theories   examine the thought processes that motivate individual behavior.

Product innovations   introduce new goods or services to better meet customer needs.

Profit-sharing plans   reward employees based on the entire organization's performance.

Programmed decisions   simply implement solutions that have already been determined by past experience as appropriate for the problem at hand.

Projection   is the assignment of personal attributes to other individuals.

Punishment   is the administration of negative consequences that tend to reduce the likelihood of repeating the behavior in similar settings.

Quality circle   meet regularly to find ways for continuous improvement of quality operations.

Questionnaires   ask respondents for their opinions, attitudes, perceptions, and/or descriptions of work-related matters.

Ranking   is a comparative technique of performance appraisal that involves the rank ordering of each individual from best to worst on each performance dimension.

Rational persuasion   is the ability to control another's behavior because, through the individual's efforts, the person accepts the desirability of an offered goal and a reasonable way of achieving it.

Rational persuasion strategy   uses facts, special knowledge, and rational argument to create change.

Recency error   is a biased rating that develops by allowing the individual's most recent behavior to speak for his or her overall performance on a particular dimension.

Recognition-based   is leadership effectiveness based on how well a person fits characteristics of a good or effective leader.

Referent power   is the ability to control another's behavior because of the individual's desire to identify with the power source.

Refreezing   is the stage in which changes are reinforced and stabilized.

Reinforcement   is the administration of a consequence as a result of behavior.

Relatedness needs   are desires for satisfying interpersonal relationships.

Reliability   is the consistency and stability of a score from a measurement scale.

Representative power   is the formal right conferred by the firm to speak for and to a potentially important group.

Representativeness heuristic   bases a decision on similarities between the situation at hand and stereotypes of similar occurrences.

Research design   is an overall plan or strategy for conducting research to test a hypothesis.

Resilience   is the ability to bounce back from failure and keep forging ahead.

Resistance to change   is an attitude or behavior that shows unwillingness to make or support a change.

Resource dependencies   is the firm's need for resources that are controlled by others.

Restricted communication networks link subgroups that disagree with one another's positions.

Reward power is the extent to which a manager can use extrinsic and intrinsic rewards to control other people.

Risk environments provide probabilities regarding expected results for decision-making alternatives.

Rites are standardized and recurring activities used at special times to influence the behaviors and understanding of organizational members.

Rituals are systems of rites.

Role is a set of expectations for a team member or person in a job.

Role ambiguity occurs when someone is uncertain about what is expected of him or her.

Role conflict occurs when someone is unable to respond to role expectations that conflict with one another.

Role negotiation is a means of clarifying what individuals expect to give to and receive from one another in their working relationships.

Role overload occurs when too much work is expected of the individual.

Role underload occurs when too little work is expected of the individual.

Romance of leadership is where people attribute romantic, almost magical, qualities to leadership.

Sagas are embellished heroic accounts of the story of the founding of an organization.

Satisficing is choosing the first alternative that appears to give an acceptable or satisfactory resolution of the problem.

Scanning is looking outside the firm and bringing back useful solutions to problems.

Schemas are cognitive frameworks that represent organized knowledge about a given concept or stimulus developed through experience.

Scientific method involves four steps: the research question or problem, hypothesis generation or formulation, the research design, and data gathering, analysis, and interpretation.

Selective perception is the tendency to single out for attention those aspects of a situation or person that reinforce or emerge and are consistent with existing beliefs, values, and needs.

Self-concept is the view individuals have of themselves as physical, social, and spiritual or moral beings.

Self-conscious emotions help individuals stay aware of and regulate their relationships with others.

Self-efficacy is the person's belief that he or she can perform adequately in a situation.

Self-evaluation is when the individual rates his or her own performance.

Self-fulfilling prophecy is the tendency to create or find in another situation or individual that which one has expected to find.

Self-managing teams, or self-directed work teams, are small groups empowered to make the decisions needed to manage themselves.

Self-monitoring reflects a person's ability to adjust his or her behavior to external situational (environmental) factors.

Self-serving bias is the tendency to deny personal responsibility for performance problems but accept personal responsibility for performance success.

Shaping is the creation of a new behavior by the positive reinforcement of successive approximations to the desired behavior.

Shared leadership is a dynamic, interactive influence process among individuals in groups for which the objective is to lead one another to the achievement of group or organizational goals or both.

Shared-power strategy uses participatory methods and emphasizes common values to create change.

Simple design is a configuration involving one or two ways of specializing individuals and units.

Situational control is the extent to which leaders can determine what their groups are going to do and what the outcomes of their actions and decisions are going to be.

Situational leadership model focuses on the situational contingency of maturity or "readiness" of followers.

Skill-based pay is a system that rewards people for acquiring and developing job-relevant skills in number and variety relevant to the organization's needs.

Social emotions refer to individuals' feelings based on information external to themselves.

Social facilitation is the tendency for one's behavior to be influenced by the presence of others in a group.

Social information processing theory asserts that individual needs and task perceptions result from socially constructed realities.

Social learning theory uses modeling or vicarious learning to acquire behavior through observing and imitating others by means of perception and attribution.

Social loafing occurs when people work less hard in groups than they would individually.

Social traits are surface-level traits that reflect the way a person appears to others when interacting in various social settings.

Societal goals are goals reflecting the intended contributions of an organization to the broader society.

Sociotechnical systems integrate people and technology into high-performance work settings.

Span of control refers to the number of individuals reporting to a supervisor.

Staff units are groups that assist the line units by performing specialized services for the organization.

Stakeholders are people and groups with an interest or "stake" in the performance of the organization.

Standardization is the degree to which the range of actions in a job or series of jobs is limited.

Status congruence involves consistency between a person's status within and outside a group.

Stereotyping occurs when one thinks of an individual as belonging to a group or category (e.g., elderly person), and the characteristics commonly associated with the group or category are assigned to the individual in question.

Stimulus is something that incites action.

Strategy guides organizations to operate in ways that outperform competitors.

Strategy is the process of positioning the organization in the competitive environment and implementing actions to compete successfully. It is a pattern in a stream of decisions.

Stress is tension from extraordinary demands, constraints, or opportunities.

Stress management takes an active approach to dealing with stress that is influencing behavior.

Stress prevention involves minimizing the potential for stress to occur.

Stressors are things that cause stress.

Strictness error occurs when a rater tends to give everyone a low rating.

Structural redesign involves realigning the structure of the organization or major subsystem in order to improve performance.

Subcultures are groups with unique patterns of values and philosophies that are consistent with the dominant culture of the larger organization or social system.

Substantive conflict involves fundamental disagreement over ends or goals to be pursued and the means for their accomplishment.

Substitutes for leadership make a leader's influence either unnecessary or redundant in that they replace a leader's influence.

Supportive leadership focuses on subordinate needs, well-being, and promotion of a friendly work climate.

Surface acting is hiding your inner feelings and forgoing emotional expressions as a response to display rules.

Survey feedback begins with the collection of data via questionnaires from organization members or a representative sample of them.

Synergy is the creation of a whole greater than the sum of its parts.

Systems goals are goals concerned with conditions within the organization that are expected to increase its survival potential.

Task activities directly contribute to the performance of important tasks.

Task performance is the quantity and quality of work produced.

Team building is a collaborative way to gather and analyze data to improve teamwork.

Team building is designed to gather and analyze data on the functioning of a group and implement changes to increase its operating effectiveness.

Teams are groups of people who work actively together to achieve a purpose for which they are all accountable.

Teamwork occurs when group members work together in ways that use their skills effectively to accomplish a purpose.

Technical skill is an ability to perform specialized tasks.

Telecommuting is work at home or in remote locations using computer and telecommunications linkages with the office.

Temporary part-time work is temporary work for fewer hours than the standard week.

Terminal values reflect a person's preferences concerning the "ends" to be achieved.

Theory is a set of systematically interrelated concepts, definitions, and hypotheses that are advanced to explain and predict phenomena.

Trait perspectives assume that traits play a central role in differentiating between leaders and non-leaders or in predicting leader or organizational outcomes.

Transactional leadership involves leader-follower exchanges necessary for achieving routine performance agreed upon between leaders and followers.

Transformational change radically shifts the fundamental character of an organization.

Transformational leadership occurs when leaders broaden and elevate followers' interests and stir followers to look beyond their own interests to the good of others.

Two-factor theory identifies job context as the source of job dissatisfaction and job content as the source of job satisfaction.

Type A orientations are characterized by impatience, desire for achievement, and a more competitive nature than Type B.

Type B orientations are characterized by an easygoing and less competitive nature than Type A.

Uncertain environments provide no information to predict expected results for decision-making alternatives.

Uncertainty avoidance is the cultural tendency to be uncomfortable with uncertainty and risk in everyday life.

Unfreezing is the stage at which a situation is prepared for change.

Unplanned change occurs spontaneously and without a change agent's direction.

Valence is the value to the individual of various work outcomes.

Validity is the degree of confidence one can have in the results of a research study.

Value congruence occurs when individuals express positive feelings upon encountering others who exhibit values similar to their own.

Values can be defined as broad preferences concerning appropriate courses of action or outcomes.

Variable is a measure used to describe a real-world phenomenon.

Vertical specialization is a hierarchical division of labor that distributes formal authority.

Virtual groups work together via computer networks.

Virtual organization is an ever-shifting constellation of firms, with a lead corporation that pools skills, resources, and experiences to thrive jointly.

Virtual team convenes and operates with members linked together via networked computers and information technologies.

Wikis are collaborative web sites to which individuals contribute material and edit previous postings by others.

Work stressors are the things that arise at work to create stress.

Workforce diversity describes how people differ in age, race, ethnicity, gender, physical ability, and sexual orientation.

Notes

Chapter 1

ENDNOTES

[1] Information and quotations from "Stern Willing to Listen to Complaints About Ball," *Columbus Dispatch* (December 6, 2006); "Spalding NBA Basketball," *Business Week* (December 18, 2006), p. 94; Roscoe Nance, "Bounced: NBA Scraps New Ball," *USA Today* (December 12, 2006), pp. 1c, 3c.

[2] Brian Mahoney, "Now That's an Odd Bounce: Stern Reverts to Leather Ball," *Columbus Dispatch* (December 12, 2006).

[3] For a general overview. See Jay W. Lorsch (ed.), *Handbook of Organizational Behavior* (Englewood Cliffs. NJ: Prentice Hall, 1987).

[4] Jeffrey Pfeffer and Robert I. Sutton, "Management Half-Truths and Nonsense. How to Practice Evidence-Based Management," *California Management Review*, 48 (Spring, 2006), pp. 77–100.

[5] Geert Hofslede. "Cultural Constraints in Management Theories," *Academy of Management Executive* 7 (1993):81–94.

[6] John Huey, "Managing in the Midst of Chaos," *Fortune* (April 5,1993). pp. 38–18. See also Tom Peters, *Thriving on Chaos* (New York Knopf. 1991): Jay R. Galbraith, Edward E. Lawler III, and Associates. *Organizing for the Future: The New Logic for Managing Organizations* (San Francisco: Jossey-Bass, 1993); William H. Davidow and Michael S. Malone. *The Virtual Corporation: Structuring and Revitalizing the Corporation of the 21st Century* (New York HarperBusiness 1993): Charles Handy, *The Age of Unreason* (Boston: Harvard Business School Press, 1994); Peter Drucker, *Managing in a Time of Great Change* (New York: Truman Talley. 1995). Peter Drucker, *Management Challenges for the 21st Century* (New York: Harper, 1999).

[7] Based on Jay A. Conger, *Winning 'Em Over: A New Model for Managing in the Age of Persuasion* (New York: Simon & Schuster 1998), pp 180–181: Stewart D. Friedman, Perry Christensen, and Jessica DeGroot, "Work and Life: The End of the Zero–Sum Game," *Harvard Business Review* (November/December 1998): 119–129. C. Argyris, "Empowerment: The Emperor's New Clothes," *Harvard Business Review* (May/June 1998); 98–105.

[8] Reported in Eric Schmidt and Hal Varian, "Google: Ten Golden Rules," *Newsweek* (December 2, 2005); reported on msnbc.com (retrieved September 17, 2006).

[9] Robert B. Reich, "The Company of the Future," *Fast Company* (November 1998): p. 124ff.

[10] For more on mission statements see Patricia Jones and Larry Kahaner. "Say It and Live It: The 50 Corporate Mission Statements that Hit the Mark" (New York: Currency/Doubleday, 1995); John Graham and Wendy Havlick, *Mission Statements: A Guide to the Corporate and Nonprofit Sectors* (New York: Garland, 1995).

[11] James C. Collins and Jerry I. Porras, "Building Your Company's Vision," *Harvard Business Review* (September/October 1996): 65–77.

[12] Information from Ken Parish Perkins, "Inclusive TV," *Southwest Airlines Spirit* (December 2006), pp. 62–64.

[13] These mission statements and others are found on corporate websites.

[14] See Michel E. Porter, *Competitive Strategy Techniques for Analyzing Industries and Competitors* (New York: Free Press, 1980); *Competitive Advantage: Creating and Sustaining Superior Performance* (New York: Free Press, 1986); Gary Hamel and C.K. Prahalad. "Strategic Intent." *Harvard Business Review* (May/June 1989):63–76, Richard A. D'Aveni, *Hyper Competition: Managing the Dynamics of Strategic Managing* (New York: Free Press, 1994).

[15] Edgar Schein, *Organizational Culture and Leadership*, 2nd ed. (San Francisco: Jossey-Bass, 1997); Edgar Schein, *The Corporate Culture Survival Guide* (San Francisco: Jossey-Bass, 1999). See also Terrence E. Daeal and Alan A. Kennedy, *Corporate Cultures: The Rites and Rituals of Corporate Life* (Reading, MA: Addison Wesley, 1982).

[16] James Collins and Jerry Porras, *Built to Last* (New York: Harper Business, 1994).

[17] See the OCI and other resources at www.humansynergistics.com.

[18] Robert A. Cooke and J. L Szurnal, "Measuring Normative Beliefs and Shared Behavioral Expectations in Organizations: The Reliability and Validity of the Organizational Culture Inventory," *Psychological Reports* 72 (1993): 1299–1330.

[19] Ibid; Robert A. Cooke and J. L. Szumal, "Using the Organizational Culture Inventory to Understand the Operating Cultures of Organizations," in N. M. Ashkanasy, C. P. M. Wilerom, and M.F. Peterson (eds.), *Handbook of Organizational Culture and Climate* (Thousand Oaks, CA: Sage, 2000), pp. 147–162.

[20] The foundation report on diversity in the American workplace is *Workforce 2000: Work and Workers in the 21st Century* (Indianapolis: Hudson Institute 1987). For comprehensive discussions see Martin M. Chemers, Stuart Oskamp, and Mark A. Costanzo. *Diversity in Organization: New Perspectives for a Changing Workplace* (Beverly Hills: Sage, 1995): Robert T. Golembiewski *Managing Diversity in Organizations* (Tuscaloosa: University of Alabama Press, 1995).

[21] See Taylor Cox Jr., "The Multicultural Organization," *Academy of Management Executive* 5 (1991): 34–47; *Cultural Diversity in Organizations: Theory, Research and Practice* (San Francisco: Bernett-Koehler, 1993).

[21A] Alice H. Eagley, Mary C. Johannesen-Smith, and Marloes L. van Engen, "Transformational, Transactional and Laissez-Faire Leadership Styles: A Meta-Analysis Comparison," *Psychological Bulletin* 124.4(2003):569–591.

[22] R. Roosevelt Thomas Jr., *Beyond Race and Gender* (New York: AMACOM, 1992), p. 10; see also R. Roosevelt Thomas Jr., "From 'Affirmative Action' to 'Affirming Diversity,'" *Harvard Business Review* (November/December 1990): 107-17; R. Roosevelt Thomas Jr., with Marjorie I. Woodruff, *Building a House for Diversity* (New York: AMACOM, 1999).

[23] *Workforce 2000: Work and Workers for the 21st Century*, op. cit.

[24] Dean Treftz, "Women Post Job Gains, Data Show," *The Wall Streets Journal* (February 20, 2007), p. A8.

[25] For current information, see U.S. Census Bureau reports at www.factfinder.census.gov.

[26] Cox, op. cit.; Thomas, 1990, 1992, op. cit.

[27] Thomas and Woodruff (1991).

[28] See Thomas and Woodruff, op. cit; Thomas, 1990, 1992, op. cit.

[29] Treftz, op. cit., and, Francesco Guerra and Andrew Ward, "Women on March to Top of U.S. Companies," *Financial Times* (March 28, 2007), pp. 13,14.

[30] For more on the management process, see John R. Schermerhorn Jr., *Management*, 9th ed. (New York: Wiley, 2008).

[31] The review is from Henry Mintzberg, *The Nature of Managerial Work* (New York: Harper & Row, 1973). For related and further developments, see Morgan W. McCall Jr.,

Ann M. Morrison, and Robert L. Hannan. *Studies of Managerial Work: Results and Methods*, Technical Report No. 9 (Greensboro, NC: Center for Creative Leadership, 1978); John P. Kotter, *The General Managers* (New York: Free Press, 1982): Fred Luthans, Stuart Rosenkrantz, and Harry Hennessey, "What Do Successful Managers Really Do?" *Journal of Applied Behavioral Science* 21(2) (1985): 255–270; Robert E. Kaplan, *The Warp and Woof of the General Manager's Job*, Technical Report No. 27 (Greensboro, NC: Center for Creative Leadership, 1986); Fred Luthans, Richard M. Hodgetts, and Stuart A. Rosenkrantz, *Real Managers* (New York: HarperCollins, 1988).

[32] Mintzberg (1973). See also Henry Mintzberg, *Mintzberg on Management* (New York: Free Press, 1989); "Rounding Out the Manager's Job." *Sloan Management Review* (Fall 1994): 11–26.

[33] Kotter (1982). "What Effective General Managers Really Do," *Harvard Business Review* 60 (November/December 1982): 161. See Kaplan (1986).

[34] Herminia Ibarra, Managerial Networks. Teaching Note: 9-495-039. Harvard Business School Publishing, Boston, MA.

[35] Robert L. Katz, "Skills of an Effective Administrator, *Harvard Business Review* 52 (September/October 1974):94. See also Richard E. Royatzis, *The Competent Manager: A Model for Effective Performance* (New York: Wiley, 1982).

[36] Daniel Goleman, *Emotional Intelligence* (New York: Bantam, 1995); Daniel Goleman, *Working with Emotional Intelligence* (New York: Bantam, 1998). See also Daniel Goleman "What Makes a Leader," *Harvard Business Review* (November/December 1998): 93–102; and "Leadership That Makes a Difference," *Harvard Business Review* (March/April 2000): 79–90, quote from p. 80.

[37] Archie B. Carroll, "In search of the Moral Manager," *Business Horizons* (March/April 2001):7–15.

[38] Mahzarin R. Banagji, Max H Bazerman, and Dolly Chugh, "How (Un)ethical are You?" *Harvard Business Review* (December 2003).

[39] Terry Thomas, John R. Schermerhorn Jr., and John W. Dinehart, "Strategic Leadership of Ethical Behavior in Business," *Academy of Management Executive* (2004).

[40] Information and quotations from the *Associated Press*, "Oprah Opens School for Girls in S. Africa. Lavish Leadership Academy Aims to Give Impoverished Chance to Succeed," msnbc.com (January 2, 2007); "Oprah Winfrey Leadership Academy for Girls—South Africa Celebrates Its Official Opening," www.oprah.com/about/press/releases/200701/press_releases_20070102.jhtml.

[41] See Peter Senge, *The Fifth Discipline* (New York: Harper, 1990); D. A. Garvin, "Building a Learning Organization," *Harvard Business Review* (November/December 1991): 78–91; Chris Argyris, *On Organizational Learning*, 2nd ed. (Malden, MA: Blackwell, 1999).

[42] For a discussion of experiential learning, see D. Christopher Kayes, "Experiential Learning and its Critics: Preserving the Role of Experience in Management Learning and Education," *Academy of Management Learning and Education.* 1(2). (2002): pp. 137–149.

MARGIN PHOTOS
Human Rights Campaign—Information from "More U.S. Companies Promote Gay-Friendly Policies," *Messenger*, Athens, OH (October 22, 2006), p. C6.
Digg.com—Information from Sarah Lacy and Jessi Hempel, "Valley Boys," *Business Week* (August 4, 2006), pp. 40–41.
Source: Developed with permission from "The Organizational Culture Inventory," published by Human Synergistics International (Plymouth, Michigan).

Primer

ENDNOTES
[1] C. William Emory, *Business Research Methods*, rev. ed. (Homewood, IL: Irwin, 1980).
[2] John B. Miner, *Theories of Organizational Behavior* (Hillsdale: Dryden Press, 1980).
[3] See Richard L. Daft, "Learning the Craft of Organizational Research," *Academy of Management Review* Vol. 8 (October 1983), pp. 539-546; Eugene Stone, *Research Methods in Organizational Behavior* (Santa Monica, CA: Goodyear, 1978), p. 21.
[4] Stone op. cit. (1978), p. 26.
[5] Duane Davis and Robert M. Casenza, *Business Research for Decision Making* (Belmont, CA: Wadsworth, 1993), p. 134.
[6] Davis and Casenza, op. cit. (1993), Ch. 5.
[7] Davis and Casenza, op. cit. (1993).
[8] Davis and Casenza, op. cit. (1993), p. 174.
[9] Davis and Casenza, op. cit. (1993), p. 125

Chapter 2

ENDNOTES
[1] Adapted from Maxmilian Wechsler, "Black Forest Charm on Sukhumvit," *Bangkok Post* (March 5, 2006), P2.
[2] See P. E. Jacob, J. J. Flink, and H. L. Schuchman, "Values and Their Function in Decisionmaking," *American Behavioral Scientist* 5, suppl. 9 (1962), pp. 6–38.
[3] Based on Alex Taylor III, "Double Duty," *Fortune* (March 7, 2005), pp. 104–110
[4] See M. Rokeach and S. J. Ball Rokeach, "Stability and Change in American Value Priorities, 1968–1981," *American Psychologist* (May 1989), pp. 775–784.

[5] Milton Rokeach, *The Nature of Human Values* (New York: Free Press, 1973).
[6] See W. C. Frederick and J. Weber, "The Values of Corporate Managers and Their Critics: An Empirical Description and Normative Implications," pp. 123–144 in *Business Ethics Research Issues and Empirical Studies*, ed. W. C. Frederick and L. E. Preston (Greenwich, CT: JAI Press, 1990).
[7] Gordon Allport, Philip E. Vernon, and Gardner Lindzey, *Study of Values* (Boston: Houghton Mifflin, 1931).
[8] Adapted from R. Tagiuri, "Purchasing Executive: General Manager or Specialist?" *Journal of Purchasing* (August 1967), pp. 16–21.
[9] Bruce M. Maglino and Elizabeth C. Ravlin, "Individual Values in Organizations: Concepts, Controversies and Research," *Journal of Management* 24 (1998), pp. 351–389.
[10] Maglino and Ravlin, 1998.
[11] Daniel Yankelovich, *New Rules! Searching for Self-Fulfillment in a World Turned Upside Down* (New York: Random House, 1981); Daniel Yankelovich, Hans Zetterberg, Burkhard Strumpel, and Michael Shanks, *Work and Human Values: An International Report on Jobs in the 1980s and 1990s* (Aspen, CO: Aspen Institute for Humanistic Studies, 1983); William Fox, *American Values in Decline: What We Can Do* (Gainesville, FL: 1st Books Library, 2001).
[12] See D. Jamieson and Julia O'Mara, *Managing Workplace 2000* (San Francisco: Jossey-Bass, 1991), pp. 28–29.
[13] Geert Hofstede, *Culture's Consequences: International Differences in Work-Related Values*, 2nd ed. (Beverly Hills, CA: Sage, 2001); Fons Trompenaars and Charles Hampden-Turner, *Riding the Waves of Culture: Understanding Cultural Diversity in Global Business*, 2nd ed. (New York: McGraw-Hill, 1998). For an excellent discussion of culture, see also "Culture: The Neglected Concept," in *Social Psychology Across Cultures*, 2nd ed., Peter B. Smith and Michael Harris Bond (Boston: Allyn & Bacon, 1998). See also Michael H. Hoppe, "An Interview with Geert Hofstede," *Academy of Management Executive* 18 (2004), pp. 75–79; Harry C. Triandis, "The Many Dimensions of Culture," *Academy of Management Executive* 18 (2004), pp. 88–93.
[14] Geert Hofstede, *Culture and Organizations: Software of the Mind* (London: McGraw-Hill, 1991).
[15] Hofstede, 2001; Geert Hofstede and Michael H. Bond, "The Confucius Connection: From Culture Roots to Economic Growth," *Organizational Dynamics* 16 (1988), pp. 4–21.
[16] Hofstede, 2001.
[17] Chinese Culture Connection, "Chinese Values and the Search for Culture-Free Dimensions of Culture," *Journal of Cross-Cultural Psychology* 18 (1987), pp. 143–164.
[18] Hofstede and Bond, 1988; Geert Hofstede, "Cultural Constraints in Management Theories," *Academy of Management Executive* 7 (1993), pp. 81–94. For a further dis-

cussion of Asian and Confucian values, see also Jim Ro-hwer, *Asia Rising: Why America Will Prosper as Asia's Economies Boom* (New York: Simon & Schuster, 1995).

[19] For an example, see John R. Schermerhorn Jr. and Michael H. Bond, "Cross-Cultural Leadership Dynamics in Collectivism + High Power Distance Settings," *Leadership and Organization Development Journal* 18 (1997), pp. 187–193.

[20] Adapted from "Corruption Cases 'Overwhelming Chinese Judges'" *Bangkok Post* (March 12, 2006).

[21] R. Jacob, "The Resurrection of Michael Dell," *Fortune* (August 1995), pp. 117–128.

[22] See N. Brody, *Personality: In Search of Individuality* (San Diego, CA: Academic Press, 1988), pp. 68–101; C. Holden, "The Genetics of Personality," *Science* (August 7, 1987), pp. 598–601.

[23] See Geert Hofstede, 1984.

[24] Chris Argyris, *Personality and Organization* (New York: Harper & Row, 1957); Daniel J. Levinson, *The Seasons of a Man's Life* (New York: Knopf, 1978); Gail Sheehy, *New Passages* (New York: Ballantine Books, 1995).

[25] Viktor Gecas, "The Self-Concept," p. 3 in *Annual Review of Sociology,* Vol. 8, ed. Ralph H. Turner and James F. Short Jr. (Palo Alto, CA: Annual Review, 1982). Also see Arthur P. Brief and Ramon J. Aldag, "The Self in Work Organizations: A Conceptual Review," *Academy of Management Review* (January 1981), pp. 75–88; Jerry J. Sullivan, "Self Theories and Employee Motivation," *Journal of Management* (June 1989), pp. 345–363.

[26] Compare Philip Cushman, "Why the Self Is Empty," *American Psychologist* (May 1990), pp. 599–611.

[27] Based in part on a definition in Gecas, 1982, p. 3.

[28] Suggested by J. Brockner, *Self-Esteem at Work* (Lexington, MA: Lexington Books, 1988), p. 144; John A. Wagner III and John R. Hollenbeck, *Management of Organizational Behavior* (Englewood Cliffs, NJ: Prentice-Hall, 1992), pp. 100–101.

[29] M. R. Barrick and M. K. Mount, "The Big Five Personality Dimensions and Job Performance: A Meta Analysis," *Personnel Psychology* 44 (1991), pp. 1–26; M. R. Barrick and M. K. Mount, "Autonomy as a Moderator of the Reltionships between the Big Five Personality Dimensions and Job Performance," *Journal of Applied Psychology* (February 1993), pp. 111–118.

[29A] Adapted from Sampo V. Paunonen, Jan-Erik Lonngvist, Markku Verkasalo, Sointa Leikas, and Vesa Nissinen, "Narcissism and Emergent Leadership in Military Cadets," *The Leadership Quarterly* 17 (2006), pp. 475–486.

[30] See Jim C. Nunnally, *Psychometric Theory*, 2nd ed. (New York: McGraw-Hill, 1978), chapter 14.

[31] See David A. Whetten and Kim S. Cameron, *Developing Management Skills*, 3rd ed. (New York: HarperCollins, 1995), p. 72.

[32] Raymond G. Hunt, Frank J. Kryzstofiak, James R. Meindl, and Abdalla M. Yousry, "Cognitive Style and Decision Making," *Organizational Behavior and Human Decision Processes* 44.3 (1989), pp. 436–453. For additional work on problem-solving styles, see Ferdinand A. Gul, "The Joint and Moderating Role of Personality and Cognitive Style on Decision Making," *Accounting Review* (April 1984), pp. 264–277; Brian H. Kleiner, "The Interrelationship of Jungian Modes of Mental Functioning with Organizational Factors: Implications for Management Development," *Human Relations* (November 1983), pp. 997–1012; James L. McKenney and Peter G. W. Keen, "How Managers' Minds Work," *Harvard Business Review* (May–June 1974), pp. 79–90.

[33] Some examples of firms using the Myers-Briggs Type Indicators are given in J. M. Kunimerow and L. W. McAllister, "Team Building with the Myers-Briggs Type Indicator: Case Studies," *Journal of Psychological Type* 15 (1988), pp. 26–32; G. H. Rice Jr. and D. P. Lindecamps, "Personality Types and Business Success of Small Retailers," *Journal of Occupational Psychology* 62 (1989), pp. 177–182; B. Roach, *Strategy Styles and Management Types: A Resource Book for Organizational Management Consultants* (Stanford, CA: Balestrand, 1989).

[34] J. B. Rotter, "Generalized Expectancies for Internal versus External Control of Reinforcement," *Psychological Monographs* 80 (1966), pp. 1–28.

[35] Don Hellriegel, John W. Slocum Jr., and Richard W. Woodman, *Organizational Behavior*, 5th ed. (St. Paul, MN: West, 1989), p. 46.

[36] See Wagner and Hollenbeck (1992), chapter 4.

[37] Niccolo Machiavelli, *The Prince*, trans. George Bull (Middlesex, UK: Penguin, 1961).

[38] Richard Christie and Florence L. Geis, *Studies in Machiavellianism* (New York: Academic Press, 1970).

[39] See M. Snyder, *Public Appearances/Private Realities: The Psychology of Self-Monitoring* (New York: Freeman, 1987).

[40] Snyder, 1987.

[41] Adapted from R. W. Bonner, "A Short Scale: A Potential Measure of Pattern A Behavior," *Journal of Chronic Diseases* 22 (1969). Used by permission.

[42] See Meyer Friedman and Ray Roseman, *Type A Behavior and Your Heart* (New York: Knopf, 1974). For another view, see Walter Kiechel III, "Attack of the Obsessive Managers," *Fortune* (February 16, 1987), pp. 127–128.

[43] Arthur P. Brief, Randall S. Schuler, and Mary Van Sell, *Managing Job Stress* (Boston: Little, Brown, 1981).

[44] See Orlando Behling and Arthur L. Darrow, *Managing Work-Related Stress* (Chicago: Science Research Associates, 1984).

[45] Behling and Darrow, 1984.

[46] M. J. Burke, A. P. Brief, and J. M. George, "The Role of Negative Affectivity in Understanding Relations between Self-Reports of Stressors and Strains: A Comment on the Applied Psychology Literature," *Journal of Applied Psy-*

chology 78 (1993), pp. 402–412; D. Watson and L. A. Clark, "Negative Affectivity: The Disposition to Experience Aversive Emotional States" *Psychological Bulletin* 96 (1984), pp. 465–490.

47 A review of research is available in Steve M. Jex, *Stress and Job Performance* (Thousand Oaks, CA: Sage, 1998).

48 "Couples Dismayed at Long Workdays, New Study Finds," *Columbus Dispatch* (January 23, 1999), p. 5A.

49 See H. Selye, *The Stress of Life*, rev. ed. (New York: McGraw-Hill, 1976).

50 Jeffrey Pfeffer, *The Human Equation: Building Profits by Putting People First* (Boston: Harvard Business School Press, 1998).

51 Quotations are from Alan M. Webber, "Danger: Toxic Company," *Fast Company* (November 1998), p. 152.

52 See John D. Adams, "Health, Stress and the Manager's Life Style," *Group and Organization Studies* 6 (1981), pp. 291–301.

53 Information from Mike Pramik, "Wellness Programs Give Businesses Healthy Bottom Line," *Columbus Dispatch* (January 18, 1999), pp. 10–11.

54 Pramik, 1999.

55 Pfeffer, 1998.

56 J. Laabs, "Interest in Diversity Training Continues to Grow," *Personnel Journal* (October 1993), p. 18.

57 L. R. Gomez-Mejia, D. B. Balking, and R. L. Cardy, *Managing Human Resources* (Englewood Cliffs, NJ: Prentice-Hall, 1995), p. 154.

58 John P. Fernandez, *Managing a Diverse Workforce* (Lexington, MA: Heath, 1991); Jamieson and O'Mara, 1991.

59 Howard N. Fullerton Jr. and Mitra Toosi, "Labor Force Projections to 2010: Steady Growth and Changing Composition," *Monthly Labor Review* (November 2001), pp. 21–30.

60 Linda A. Krefting and Frank J. Kryzstofiak, "Looking Like America: Potential Conflicts between Workplace Diversity Initiatives and Equal Opportunity Compliance in the U.S." Working paper (Lubbock, TX: Texas Tech University, 1998), p. 10.

61 Krefting and Kryzstofiak, 1998.

62 See L. Gardenswartz and A. Rowe, *Managing Diversity: A Complete Desk Reference and Planning Guide* (Homewood, IL: Business One Irwin, 1993), p. 405.

63 See E. Macoby and C. N. Jacklin, *The Psychology of Sex Differences* (Stanford, CA: Stanford University Press, 1974); G. N. Powell, *Women and Men in the Management* (Beverly Hills: Sage, 1988); T. W. Mangione, "Turnover—Some Psychological and Demographic Correlates," in *The 1969–70 Survey of Working Conditions*, R. P. Quinn and T. W. Mangione, eds. (Ann Arbor: University of Michigan Survey Research Center, 1973); R. Marsh and H. Mannan, "Organizational Commitment and Turnover: A Predictive Study," *Administrative Science Quarterly* (March 1977), pp. 57–75; R. J. Flanagan, G. Strauss, and L. Ulman, "Worker Discontent and Work Dis-

content and Work Place Behavior," *Industrial Relations* (May 1974), pp. 101–123; K. R. Garrison and P. M. Muchinsky, "Attitudinal and Biographical Predictions of Incidental Absenteeism," *Journal of Vocational Behavior* (April 1977), pp. 221–230; G. Johns, "Attitudinal and Non-attitudinal Predictions of Two Forms of Absence from Work," *Organizational Behavior and Human Performance* (December 1978), pp. 431–444; R. T. Keller, "Predicting Absenteeism from Prior Absenteeism, Attitudinal Factors, and Non-attitudinal Factors," *Journal of Applied Psychology* (August 1983), pp. 536–540.

64 Gomez-Mejia, Balkin, and Cardy, 1995, p. 171.

65 "The Growing Influence of Women," *Workplace Visions* (September–October 1998), p. 2.

66 This discussion is summarized from Alice H. Eagly in Marloes Goethals, Georgia J. Sorenson, and James McGregor Burns, eds. *Encyclopedia of Leadership*, vol. 4. (Great Barrington, MA/Thousand Oaks, CA: Berkshire/Sage 2004), pp. 1657–1663; Alice H. Eagly and Linda L. Carli, "Women and Men as Leaders," pp. 279–302 in *The Nature of Leadership*, John Antonakis, Anna T. Cianciolo, and Robert J. Sternberg, eds. (Thousand Oaks, CA: Sage, 2004); Alice H. Eagly and Linda L. Carli, "The Female Leadership Advantage: An Evaluation of the Evidence," *Leadership Quarterly* 14.6 (2003), pp. 807–834; Robert Vecchio, "Leadership and Gender Advantage," *The Leadership Quarterly* 6.13 (2002), pp. 643–671.

67 Fullerton and Toosi, 2001, p. 22.

68 Nina Monk, "Finished at Forty," *Fortune* (February 1, 1999), pp. 50–58.

69 "Diversity News: Age Discrimination Unrest in Britain," *Mosaics* 3.2 (March–April 1997), p. 3.

70 Paul Mayrand, "Older Workers: A Problem or the Solution?" *AARP Textbook Authors' Conference Presentation* (October 1992), p. 29; G. M. McEvoy and W. F. Cascio, "Cumulative Evidence of the Relationship between Employee Age and Job Performance," *Journal of Applied Psychology* (February 1989), pp. 11–17.

71 Fernandez (1991); Patrick Digh, "Finding New Talent in a Tight Market." *Mosaics* 4.3 (March–April, 1998), pp. 1, 4–6.

72 See Fernandez, 1991, p. 236; "Diversity News: Age Discrimination Unrest in Britain," *Mosaics* 4.2 (March–April 1998), p. 4.

73 See Taylor H. Co and Stacy Blake, "Managing Cultural Diversity: Implications for Organizational Competitiveness," *Academy of Management Executive* 5.3 (1991), p. 45.

74 Literature covering this topic is reviewed in Stephen P. Robbins, *Organizational Behavior*, 8th ed. (Englewood Cliffs, NJ: Prentice-Hall, 1998), chapter 2.

75 Robbins, 1998.

76 Krefting and Kryzstofiak, 1998, p. 14.

77 Larry L. Cummings and Donald P. Schwab, *Performance in Organizations: Determinants and Appraisal* (Glenview, IL: Scott, Foresman, 1973), p. 8.

[78] See J. Hogan, "Structure of Physical Performance in Occupational Tasks," *Journal of Applied Psychology* 76 (1991), pp. 495–507.

[79] H. W. Lane and J. J. DiStefano, eds., *International Management Behavior* (Scarborough, Ontario: Nelson Canada, 1988), pp. 4–5; Z. Abdoolcarim, "How Women Are Winning at Work," *Asian Business* (November 1993), pp. 24–29.

[80] Gardenswartz and Rowe, 1993, p. 405; Michelle N. Martinez, "Equality Effort Sharpens Bank's Edge," *HR Magazine* (January 1995), pp. 38–43.

[81] Based on Ernst & Young, "Delivering on Diversity: A Firm Commitment" (2006) www.ey.com/us/about; Kriengsak Niratpattanasai, "Diversity in Action at a Progressive Bank," *Bangkok Post* (April 10, 2006), p. B5.

[81A] Adapted from Cheryl Hall, "Deloitte Keeps its 'Step-outs in the Fold'." *Dallas Morning News* (August 2, 2005), pp. 1D, 7D.

MARGIN PHOTOS

The Aging of America—Adapted from "Graying Work Force Puts Experience on the Line," *Lubbock-Avalanche Journal* (May 29, 2005), p. D6.

The Kids Under Stress—Adapted from "Millions of Thai Kids Under Stress," *Bangkok Post* (April 11, 2006), p. L2.

Chapter 3

ENDNOTES

1 Alan Shipnuck, "Master of the Elements," *Sports Illustrated* (April 16, 2007), p. 37.

2 Based on J. A. Fuller, J. M. Stanton, G. G. Fisher, C. Spitzmuller, S. S. Russell, and P. C. Smith, "A Lengthy Look at the Daily Grind: Time Series Analysis of Events, Mood, Stress, and Satisfaction," *Journal of Applied Psychology* 88 (2003), pp. 1019–1033; C. J. Thoreson, S. A. Kaplan, A. P. Barsky, C. R. Warren, and K. de Chermont, "The Affective Underpinnings of Job Perceptions and Attitudes; A Meta-Analytic Review and Integration," *Psychological Bulletin* 129 (2003), pp. 914–925.

3 These concept definitions and discussions based on J. M. George, "Trait and State Affect," p.45 in *Individual Differences in Behavior in Organizations,* ed. K. R. Murphy (San Francisco: Jossey-Bass, 1996); N. H. Frijda, "Moods, Emotion Episodes and Emotions," pp. 381–403 in *Handbook of Emotions,* ed. M. Lewis and J. M. Haviland (New York: Guilford Press, 1993); H. M. Weiss and R. Cropanzano, "Affective Events Theory: A Theoretical Discussion of the Structure, Causes, and Consequences of Affective Experiences at Work," pp. 17–19 in *Research in Organizational Behavior,* Vol. 18, eds. B. M. Staw and L. L. Cummings (Greenwich, CT: JAT Press, 1996); P. Ekman and R. J. Davidson, eds., *The Nature of Emotions: Fundamental Questions* (Oxford, UK: Oxford University Press, 1994); Frijda, 1993, p. 381.

4 See L. Cosmides and J. Tooby, "Evolutionary Psychology and the Emotions," pp. 91–115 in *Handbook of Emotions,* 2nd ed., M. Lewis and J. M. Haviland-Jones, eds. (New York: ed. Guilford Press, 2000).

5 Weiss and Cropanzano, 1996, pp. 1–74.

5A Susan Casey, "Eminence Green," *Fortune* (April 2, 2007), pp. 62–68.

6 J. P. Tangney and K. W. Fischer, eds., *Self-conscious Emotions: The Psychology of Shame, Guilt, Embarrassment and Price* (New York: Guilford Press 1995); J.L. Tracy and R.W. Robbins, "Putting the Self into Self-Conscious Emotions: A Theoretical Model," *Psychological Inquiry* 15 (2004), pp. 103–125; D. Keltner and C. Anderson. "Saving Face for Darwin: The Functions and Uses of Embarrassment," *Current Directions in Psychological Science* 9 (2000), pp. 187–192; J. S. Beer, E. A. Heery, D. Keltner, D. Scabini, and R. T. Knight, "The Regulatory Function of Self-Conscious Emotion: Insights from Patients with Orbitofrontal Damage," *Journal of Personality and Social Psychology* 85 (2003), pp. 594–604; R. P. Vecchio, "Explorations of Employee Envy: Feeling Envious and Feeling Envied," *Cognition and Emotion* 19 (2005), pp. 69–81; C. F. Poulson II. "Shame and Work," pp. 490–541 in *Emotions in the Workplace: Research, Theory, and Practice,* eds. N. M. Ashkanasy, W. Zerby, and C. E. J. Hartel (Westport, CT: Quorum Books).

7 R. E. Lucas, A. E. Clark, Y. Georgellis, and E. Deiner, "Unemployment Alters the Set Points for Life Satisfaction," *Psychological Science* 15 (2004), pp. 8–13; C. Graham, A. Eggers, and S. Sukhtaner, "Does Happiness Pay?: An Exploration Based on Panel Data from Russia," *Journal of Economic Behaviour and Organization* (in press, 2006); C. J. Howell, R. T. Howell, and K. A. Schwabe, "Does Wealth Enhance Life Satisfaction for People Who Are Materially Deprived?: Exploring the Association among the Orang Asli of Peninsular Malaysia," *Social Indicators Research* (in press, 2006); G. L. Clore, N. Schwartz, and M. Conway, "Affective Causes and Consequences of Social Information Processing," pp. 323–417 in *Handbook of Social Cognition,* Vol. 1, eds. R. S. Wyer Jr. and T. K. Srull (Hillsdale, NJ: Erlbaum, 1994); K. D. Vohs, R. F. Baumeister, and G. Lowenstein, *Do Emotions Help or Hurt Decision Making?* (New York: Russell Sage Foundation Press, in press 2006); H. M. Weiss, J. P. Nicholas, and C. S. Daus, "An Examination of the Joint Effects of Affective Experiences and Job Beliefs on Job Satisfaction and Variations in Affective Experiences over Time," *Organizational Behavior and Human Decision Processes* 78 (1999), pp. 1–24; N. M. Ashkanasy "Emotion and Performance," *Human Performance* 17 (2004), pp. 137–144.

8 H. M. Weiss and R. Cropanzano, "An Affective Events Approach to Job Satisfaction," pp. 1–74 in *Research in Organizational Behavior,* Vol. 18, ed. B. M. Staw and

L. L. Cummings (Greenwich, CT: JAI Press, 1996); N. M. Ashkanasy and C. S. Daus, "Emotion in the Workplace: New Challenges for Managers," *Academy of Management Executive* 16 (2002), pp. 76–86.

[9] A. G. Miner and C. L. Hulin, *Affective Experience at Work: A Test of Affective Events Theory*. Poster presented at the 15th annual conference of the Society for Industrial and Organizational Psychology, 2000.

[10] A. Grandey, "Emotional Regulation in the Workplace: A New Way to Conceptualize Emotional Labor," *Journal of Occupational Health Psychology* 5.1 (2000), pp. 95–110; R. Cropanzano, D. E. Rupp, and Z. S. Byrne, "The Relationship of Emotional Exhaustion to Work Attitudes, Job Performance and Organizational Citizenship Behavior," *Journal of Applied Psychology* (2003), pp. 160–69.

[11] S. M. Kruml and D. Geddes, "Catching Fire without Burning Out: Is There an Ideal Way to Perform Emotional Labor?" pp. 177–188 in *Emotions in the Workplace,* eds. N. M. Ashkanasy, C. E. J. Hartel, and W. J. Zerby (New York: Quorum, 2000).

[12] A. A. Grandey, "When 'The Show Must Go On': Surface Acting and Deep Acting as Determinants of Emotional Exhaustion and Peer-Rated Service Delivery," *Academy of Management Journal* (2003), pp. 86–96.

[13] For a composite definition, see Jennifer M., George and Gareth R. Jones. *Understanding and Managing Organizational Behavior*, pp. 59–60 (Upper Saddle River, NJ: Person Prentice Hall, 2008).

[14] K. S. Law, C. Wong, and L. J. Song "The Construct and Criterion Validity of Emotional Intelligence and Its Potential Utility for Management Studies," *Journal of Applied Psychology* 89 (2004), pp. 483–496.

[15] In Davies, L. Stankow and R.D. Roberts "Emotion and Intelligence: In Search of an Elusive Construct," *Journal of Personality and Social Psychology* 75 (1998), pp. 989–1015.

[16] I. Greenstein *The Presidential Difference: Leadership Style from FDR to Clinton* (Princeton, NJ: Princeton University Press, 2001).

[17] I. Lorenz. "Seven Tips for Combating Desk Rage," CNN.com/CareerBuilder.com, http//www.cnn.com/2004/US/Careers/08/13/boss.spying/index.html.

[18] B. M. Bass, *A New Paradigm of Leadership* (Alexandria, VA: U.S. Army Research Institute for the Behavioral and Social Sciences, 1996).

[19] B. E. Ashforth and R. H. Humphrey, "Emotions in the Workplace: A Reappraisal," *Human Relations* (1995), p. 110.

[20] W. Tasl and Y. Huang, "Mechanisms Linking Employee Affective Delivery and Customer Behavioral Intentions," *Journal of Applied Psychology* 87 (2002), pp. 1001–1008.

[21] Adapted from Daniel Goleman, "Can You Raise Your Social IQ?" (*Parade*, September 3, 2006), pp. 10–11.

[22] P. A. Simpson and L. K. Stroh, "Gender Differences: Emotional Expression and Feelings of Personal Inauthenticity," *Journal of Applied Psychology* 89.4 (2004), pp. 715–721.

[23] M. Eid and E. Diener, "Norms for Experiencing Emotions in Different Cultures: Inter-and Intranational Differences," *Journal of Personality & Social Psychology* 81.5 (2001), pp. 869–885.

[24] Eid and Diener, 2001.

[25] B. Mesquita, "Emotions in Collectivist and Individualist Contexts," *Journal of Personality and Social Psychology* 80.1 (2001), pp. 68–74.

[26] D. Rubin, "Grumpy German Shoppers Distrust the Wal-Mart Style," *Seattle Times* (December 30, 2001), p. a15; A. Rafaeli, "When Cashiers Meet Customers: An Analysis of Supermarket Cashiers," *Academy of Management Journal* (1989), pp. 245–273.

[27] Compare Martin Fishbein and Icek Ajzen, *Belief, Attitude, Intention and Behavior: An Introduction to Theory and Research* (Reading, MA: Addison-Wesley, 1973).

[28] See A. W. Wicker, "Attitude Versus Action: The Relationship of Verbal and Overt Behavioral Responses to Attitude Objects," *Journal of Social Issues* (Autumn 1969), pp. 41–78.

[29] L. Festinger, *A Theory of Cognitive Dissonance* (Palo Alto, CA: Stanford University Press, 1957).

[30] See W. E. Wymer and J. M. Carsten, "Alternative Ways to Gather Opinions," *HR Magazine* 37.4 (April 1992), pp. 71–78.

[31] The Job Descriptive Index (JDI) is available from Dr. Patricia C. Smith, Department of Psychology, Bowling Green State University; the Minnesota Satisfaction Questionnaire (MSQ) is available from the Industrial Relations Center and Vocational Psychology Research Center, University of Minnesota.

[32] B. M. Staw, "The Consequences of Turnover," *Journal of Occupational Behavior* 1 (1980), pp. 253–273; J. P. Wanous, *Organizational Entry* (Reading, MA: Addison-Wesley, 1980).

[33] C. N. Greene, "The Satisfaction-Performance Controversy," *Business Horizons* 15 (1972), pp. 31–41; M. T. Iaffaldano and P. M. Muchinsky, "Job Satisfaction and Job Performance: A Meta-Analysis," *Psychological Bulletin* 97 (1985), pp. 251–273; D. Organ, "A Reappraisal and Reinterpretation of the Satisfaction-Causes-Performance Hypothesis," *Academy of Management Review* 2 (1977), pp. 46–53; P. Lorenzi, "A Comment on Organ's Reappraisal of the Satisfaction-Causes-Performance Hypothesis," *Academy of Management Review* 3 (1978), pp. 380–382.

[33A] See endnote 35 and Benjamin Schneider, Paul J. Hanges, D. Brent Smith, and Amy Salvaggio, "Which Comes First: Employee Attitudes or Organizational, Financial, and Market Performance?" *Journal of Applied Psychology*, 88.5 (2003), pp. 836–851.

[34] L. W. Porter and E. E. Lawler III, *Managerial Attitudes and Work Performance* (Homewood, IL: Irwin, 1968).

34A Benjamin Schneider, Paul. J. Hanges, D. Brent Smith, and Amy Nicole Salvaggio, "Which Comes First: Employee Attitudes or Organizational Financial and Market Performance?" *Journal of Applied Psychology* 88.5 (2003), pp. 836–851.

35 Richard Busch, "Turning Inward," *AARP Bulletin* (December 2006) p. 39.

MARGIN PHOTOS

Let's Have Fun!—"Is This the Year? (No, but....)," *Sports Illustrated* (February 26, 2007), p. 42.

Optimism Because Optimism Makes You Live Longer—Monica Hesse, AARP Bulletin, March and April, 2007, p. 86.

Chapter 4

ENDNOTES

1A Gretchen C. Kovach, "Girls Commanding Attention in JROTC," *Dallas Morning News* (December 11, 2005), p. 1B.

1 "Clark's Catch Engraved in NFL Lore," *Lubbock Avalanche-Journal* (January 11, 1992), p. D5.

2 H. R. Schiffmann, *Sensation and Perception: An Integrated Approach*, 3rd ed. (New York: Wiley, 1990).

3 Example from John A. Wagner III and John R. Hollenbeck, *Organizational Behavior*, 3rd ed. (Upper Saddle River, NJ: Prentice-Hall, 1998), p. 59.

3A Linda Rhoades Shannock and Robert Eisenberger, "When Supervisors Feel Supported: Relationships with Subordinates' Perceived Supervisor Support, Perceived Organizational Support, and Performance," *Journal of Applied Psychology* 91. 3 (2006), pp. 689–695.

4 See Georgia T. Chao and Steve W. J. Kozlowski, "Employee Perceptions on the Implementation of Robotic Manufacturing Technology," *Journal of Applied Psychology* 71 (1986), pp. 70–76; Steven F. Cronshaw and Robert G. Lord, "Effects of Categorization, Attribution, and Encoding Processes in Leadership Perceptions," *Journal of Applied Psychology* 72 (1987), pp. 97–106.

5 See Robert G. Lord, "An Information Processing Approach to Social Perceptions, Leadership, and Behavioral Measurement in Organizations," pp. 87–128 in *Research in Organizational Behavior,* vol. 7, eds. B. M. Staw and L.L. Cummings, (Greenwich, CT: JAI Press, 1985); T. K. Srull and R. S. Wyer, *Advances in Social Cognition* (Hillsdale, NJ: Erlbaum, 1988); U. Neisser, *Cognitive and Reality* (San Francisco: Freeman, 1976), p. 112.

6 See J. G. Hunt, *Leadership: A New Synthesis* (Newbury Park, CA: Sage, 1991), ch. 7; R. G. Lord and R. J. Foti, "Schema Theories, Information Processing, and Organizational Behavior," pp. 20–48 in *Thinking Organization,* ed. H. P. Simms Jr. and D. A. Gioia (San Francisco: Jossey-Bass, 1986); S.T. Fiske and S. E. Taylor, *Social Cognition* (Reading, MA: Addison-Wesley, 1984).

6A Marc Gunther, "Will Success Spoil Rick Warren?" *Fortune* (October 31, 2005), pp. 108–120.

7 D. Bilimoria and S. K. Piderit, "Board Committee Membership Effects of Sex-Based Bias," *Academy of Management Journal* 37 (1994), pp. 1453–1477.

8 Dewitt C. Dearborn and Herbert A. Simon, "Selective Perception: A Note on the Departmental Identification of Executives," *Sociometry* 21 (1958), pp. 140–144.

9 J.P. Walsh, "Selectivity and Selective Perception: An Investigation of Managers' Belief Structures and Information Processing," *Academy of Management Journal* 24 (1988), pp. 453–470.

10 J. Sterling Livingston, "Pygmalion in Management," *Harvard Business Review* (July–August 1969), pp. 81–89.

11 D. Eden and A. B. Shani, "Pygmalion Goes to Boot Camp," *Journal of Applied Psychology* 67 (1982), pp. 194–199.

12 See B. R. Schlenker, *Impression Management: The Self-Concept, Social Identity, and Interpersonal Relations* (Monterey, CA: Brooks/Cole, 1980); W. L. Gardner and M. J. Martinko, "Impression Management in Organizations," *Journal of Management* (June 1988), p. 332; R. B. Cialdini, "Indirect Tactics of Image Management: Beyond Banking," pp. 45–71 in *Impression Management in the Organization,* eds. R. A. Giacolini and P. Rosenfeld (Hillsdale, NJ: Erlbaum, 1989).

13 See H. H. Kelley, "Attribution in Social Interaction," in *Attribution: Perceiving the Causes of Behavior,* ed. E. Jones et al. (Morristown, NJ: General Learning Press, 1972).

13A David Dudley, "Curing a Clinic Shortage," *AARP* (January–February, 2007), p. 43.

14 See "Obese Women Finding Business Just Doesn't Pay," *Lubbock Avalanche-Journal* (January 28, 2001) p. 2D.

15 See Terence R. Mitchell, S. G. Green, and R. E. Wood, "An Attribution Model of Leadership and the Poor Performing Subordinate," pp. 197–234 in *Research in Organizational Behavior,* eds. Barry Staw and Larry L. Cummings (New York: JAI Press, 1981); John H. Harvey and Gifford Weary, "Current Issues in Attribution Theory and Research," *Annual Review of Psychology* 35 (1984), pp. 427–459.

16 R. M. Steers, S. J. Bischoff, and L. H. Higgins, "Cross Cultural Management Research," *Journal of Management Inquiry* (December 1992), pp. 325–326; J. G. Miller, "Culture and the Development of Everyday Causal Explanation," *Journal of Personality and Social Psychology* 46 (1984), pp. 961–978.

17 A. Maass and C. Volpato, "Gender Differences in Self-Serving Attributions about Sexual Experiences," *Journal of Applied Psychology* 19 (1989), pp. 517–542.

18 See J. M. Crant and T. S. Bateman, "Assignment of Credit and Blame for Performance Outcomes," *Academy of Management Journal* (February 1993), pp. 7–27; E. C. Pence, W. E. Pendelton, G. H. Dobbins, and J. A. Sgro, "Effects of

Causal Explanations and Sex Variables on Recommendations for Corrective Actions Following Employee Failure," *Organizational Behavior and Human Performance* (April 1982), pp. 227–240.

[19] See F. Fosterling, "Attributional Retraining: A Review," *Psychological Bulletin* (November 1985), pp. 496–512.

[20] For good overviews of reinforcement-based views, see W. E. Scott Jr. and P. M. Podsakoff, *Behavioral Principles in the Practice of Management* (New York: Wiley, 1985); Fred Luthans and Robert Kreitner, *Organizational Behavior Modification and Beyond* (Glenview, IL: Scott, Foresman, 1985).

[21] For some of B. F. Skinner's work, see his *Walden Two* (New York: Macmillan, 1948); *Science and Human Behavior* (New York: Macmillan, 1953); *Contingencies of Reinforcement* (New York: Appleton-Century-Crofts, 1969).

[22] E. L. Thorndike, *Animal Intelligence* (New York: Macmillan, 1911), p. 244.

[23] Adapted from Luthans and Kreitner, 1985.

[24] This discussion is based on Luthans and Kreitner (1985).

[25] Both laws are stated in Keith L. Miller, *Principles of Everyday Behavior Analysis* (Monterey, CA: Brooks/Cole, 1975), p. 122.

[26] This example is based on a study by Barbara Price and Richard Osborn, "Shaping the Training of Skilled Workers," working paper (Detroit: Department of Management, Wayne State University, 1999).

[27] "Making the Grade," *Lubbock Avalanche Journal* (October 29, 2005), p. B3.

[28] These have been used for years; see K. M. Evans, "On-the-Job Lotteries: A Low-Cost Incentive That Sparks Higher Productivity," *Compensation and Benefits Review* 20.4 (1988), pp. 63–74.

[29] A. R. Korukonda and James G. Hunt, "Pat on the Back Versus Kick in the Pants: An Application of Cognitive Inference to the Study of Leader Reward and Punishment Behavior," *Group and Organization Studies* 14 (1989), pp. 299–234.

[30] See "Janitorial Firm Success Story Started with Cleaning Couple," *Lubbock Avalanche-Journal* (August 25, 1991), p. E7.

[31] Edwin A Locke, "The Myths of Behavior Mod in Organizations," *Academy of Management Review* 2 (October 1977): pp. 543–553. For a counterpoint, see Jerry L. Gray, "The Myths of the Myths About Behavior Mod in Organizations: A Reply to Locke's Criticisms of Behavior Modification," *Academy of Management Review* 4 (January 1979), pp.121–129.

[32] Robert Kreitner, "Controversy in OBM: History, Misconceptions, and Ethics," in Lee Frederiksen (ed.), *Handbook of Organizational Behavior Management* (New York: Wiley, 1982), pp. 71–91.

[33] W.E. Scott Jr. and P.M. Podsakoff, *Behavioral Principles in the Practice of Management* (New York: Wiley, 1985);

also see W. Clay Hamner, "Reinforcement Theory and Contingency Management in Organizational Settings," in Richard M. Steers and Lyman W. Porters (eds.), *Motivation and Work Behavior*, 4th ed. (New York: McGraw-Hill, 1987), pp. 139–165; Luthans and Kreitner (1985); Charles C. Manz and Henry P. Sims Jr., *Superleadership* (New York: Berkeley, 1990).

[34] A. Bandura, *Social Learning Theory* (Englewood Cliffs, NJ: Prentice-Hall, 1977).

[35] See, for example, A. M. Morrison, R. P. White, and E. Van Velsor, *Breaking the Glass Ceiling* (Reading, MA: Addison-Wesley, 1987); J. D. Zalesny and J. K. Ford, "Extending the Social Information Processing Perspective: New Links to Attitudes, Behaviors and Perceptions," *Organizational Behavior and Human Decision Processes* 47 (1990), pp. 205–246; M. E. Gist, C. Schwoerer, and B. Rosen, "Effects of Alternative Training Methods of Self-Efficacy and Performance in Computer Software Training," *Journal of Applied Psychology* 74 (1989), pp. 884–91; D. D. Sutton and R. W. Woodman, "Pygmalion Goes to Work: The Effects of Supervisor Expectations in a Retail Setting," *Journal of Applied Psychology* 74 (1989), pp. 943–950; M. E. Gist, "The Influence of Training Method on Self-Efficacy and Idea Generation among Managers," *Personnel Psychology* 42 (1989), pp. 787–805.

[36] See M. E. Gist, "Self Efficacy: Implications in Organizational Behavior and Human Resource Management," *Academy of Management Review* 12 (1987), pp. 472–485; A. Bandura, "Self-Efficacy Mechanisms in Human Agency," *American Psychologist* 37 (1987), pp. 122–147.

[36A] Adapted from: "Gaining Perspective–A Discussion [with Rushworth M. Kidder] on the Topic of Ethical Business Leadership," *BGS International Exchange* (Vol. 5, number 3, Fall 2006), pp. 6–8.

MARGIN PHOTOS

Ivan Seidenberg—Based on Janine Latus, "Ivan: The Charitable," *Continental* (July 2003), pp. 51–53.

Goeffrey Orsak—Based on Cheryl Hall, *Dallas Morning News*, April 3, 2005, page 1D, 4D.

Chapter 5

ENDNOTES

[1] Information from Carol Hymowitz, "Women Tell Women: Life in the Top Jobs Is Worth the Effort," *Wall Street Journal* (November 20, 2006), p. B1.

[2] See John P. Campbell, Marvin D. Dunnette, Edward E. Lawler III, and Karl E. Weick, Jr., *Managerial Behavior Performance and Effectiveness* (New York: McGraw-Hill, 1970), ch. 15.

[3] Geert Hofstede, "Cultural Constraints in Management Theories," *Academy of Management Executive* 7 (February 1993):81–94.

[4] Geert Hofstede, *Culture's Consequences: International Differences in Work-Related Values*, abridged ed. (Beverly Hills: Sage, 1984).

[5] Abraham Maslow, *Eupsychian Management* (Homewood, IL: Irwin, 1965); Abraham Maslow, *Motivation and Personality*, 2nd ed. (New York: Harper & Row, 1970).

[6] Lyman W. Porter, "Job Attitudes in Management: II. Perceived Importance of Needs as a Function of Job Level," *Journal of Applied Psychology* 47 (April 1963):141–148.

[7] Douglas T. Hall and Khalil E. Nougaim, "An Examination of Maslow's Need Hierarchy in an Organizational Setting," *Organizational Behavior and Human Performance* 3 (1968):12–35; Porter (1963); John M. Ivancevich, "Perceived Need Satisfactions of Domestic Versus Overseas Managers," *Journal of Applied Psychology* 54 (August 1969):274–278.

[8] Mahmoud A. Wahba and Lawrence G. Bridwell, "Maslow Reconsidered: A Review of Research on the Need Hierarchy Theory," *Academy of Management Proceedings* (1974):514–520; Edward E. Lawler III and J. Lloyd Shuttle, "A Causal Correlation Test of the Need Hierarchy Concept," *Organizational Behavior and Human Performance* 7 (1973):265–287.

[9] Nancy J. Adler, *International Dimensions of Organizational Behavior*, 2nd ed. (Boston: PWS-Kent, 1991), p. 153; Richard M. Hodgetts and Fred Luthans, *International Management* (New York: McGraw-Hill, 1991), ch. 11.

[10] Clayton P. Alderfer, "An Empirical Test of a New Theory of Human Needs," *Organizational Behavior and Human Performance* 4 (1969):142–175; Clayton P. Alderfer, *Existence, Relatedness, and Growth* (New York: Free Press, 1972); Benjamin Schneider and Clayton P. Alderfer, "Three Studies of Need Satisfaction in Organization," *Administrative Science Quarterly* 18 (1973):489–505.

[11] Lane Tracy, "A Dynamic Living Systems Model of Work Motivation," *Systems Research* 1 (1984):191–203; John Rauschenberger, Neal Schmidt, and John E. Hunter, "A Test of the Need Hierarchy Concept by a Markov Model of Change in Need Strength," *Administrative Science Quarterly* 25 (1980):654–670.

[12] Information from Jerry Harkavy, "New Book Details Evolution of L. L. Bean," *Columbus Dispatch* (December 4, 2006), p. E6. See also, Leon Gorman, *L. L. Bean: The Making of an American Icon* (Boston, MA: Harvard Business School Publishing, 2006).

[13] Sources pertinent to this discussion are David C. McClelland, *The Achieving Society* (New York: Van Nostrand, 1961); David C. McClelland, "Business, Drive and National Achievement," *Harvard Business Review* 40 (July/August 1962):99–112; David C. Mc Clelland, "That Urge to Achieve," *Think* (November/December 1966):19–32; G. H. Litwin and R. A. Stringer, *Motivation and Organizational Climate* (Boston: Division of Research, Harvard Business School, 1966), pp. 18–25.

[14] George Harris, "To Know Why Men Do What They Do: A Conversation with David C. McClelland," *Psychology Today* 4 (January 1971):35–39.

[15] David C. McClelland and David H. Burnham, "Power Is the Great Motivator," *Harvard Business Review* 54 (March/April 1976):100–110; David C. McClelland and Richard E. Boyatzis, "Leadership Motive Pattern and Long-Term Success in Management," *Journal of Applied Psychology* 67 (1982):737–743.

[16] P. Miron and D. C. McClelland, "The Impact of Achievement Motivation Training in Small Businesses," *California Management Review* (Summer 1979):13–28.

[17] The complete two-factor theory is well explained by Herzberg and his associates in Frederick Herzberg, Bernard Mausner, and Barbara Bloch Synderman, *The Motivation to Work*, 2nd ed. (New York: Wiley, 1967); Frederick Herzberg, "One More Time: How Do You Motivate Employees?" *Harvard Business Review* 46 (January/ February 1968):53–62.

[18] From Herzberg (1968).

[19] See Robert J. House and Lawrence A. Wigdor, "Herzberg's Dual-Factor Theory of Job Satisfaction and Motivation: A Review of the Evidence and a Criticism," *Personnel Psychology* 20 (Winter 1967):369–389; Steven Kerr, Anne Harlan, and Ralph Stogdill,

[20] Adler (1991), ch. 6; Nancy J. Adler and J. T. Graham, "Cross Cultural Interaction: The International Comparison Fallacy," *Journal of International Business Studies* (Fall 1989):515–537; Frederick Herzberg, "Workers Needs: The Same Around the World," *Industry Week* (September 27, 1987), pp. 29–32.

[21] See, for example, J. Stacy Adams, "Toward an Understanding of Inequality," *Journal of Abnormal and Social Psychology* 67 (1963):422–436; J. Stacy Adams, "Inequity in Social Exchange," in L. Berkowitz (ed.), *Advances in Experimental Social Psychology* (Vol. 2) (New York: Academic Press, 1965), pp. 267–300.

[22] Adams, op cit., 1965.

[23] These issues are discussed in C. Kagitcibasi and J. W. Berry, "Cross-Cultural Psychology: Current Research and Trends," *Annual Review of Psychology* 40 (1989):493–531.

[24] See Blair Sheppard, Roy J. Lewicki, and John Minton, *Organizational Justice: The Search for Fairness in the Workplace* (New York: Lexington Books, 1992); Jerald Greenberg, *The Quest for Justice on the Job: Essays and Experiments* (Thousand Oaks, CA: Sage, 1995); Robert Folger and Russell Cropanzano, *Organizational Justice and Human Resource Management* (Thousand Oaks, CA: Sage, 1998); Mary A. Konovsky, "Understanding Procedural Justice and Its Impact on Business Organizations, " *Journal of Management* 26 (2000):489–511.

[25] Interactional justice is described by Robert J. Bies, "The Predicament of Injustice: The Management of Moral Outrage, " in L. L. Cummings & B. M. Staw (eds.), *Research in*

Organizational Behavior (Vol. 9) (Greenwich, CT: JAI Press, 1987), pp. 289–319. The example is from Carol T. Kulik and Robert L. Holbrook, "Demographics in Service Encounters: Effects of Racial and Gender Congruence on Perceived Fairness, " *Social Justice Research*, Vol. 13 (2000), pp. 375–402.

26 Information from Sally Beatty, "Big Green Investment," *Wall Street Journal* (September 22, 2006), p. W2; Stanley Holmes, "Nike Goes for the Green," *Business Week* (September 25, 2006), pp. 106, 108; Jeffrey Gangemi, "Giving Goes Green," *Business Week* (November 27, 2006), p. 84; and Pete Engardio, "Beyond the Green Corporation," *Economic Times Bangalore* (January 28, 2007), p. 5.

27 Victor H. Vroom, *Work and Motivation* (New York: Wiley, 1964).

28 See ibid.

29 See Terence R. Mitchell, "Expectancy Models of Job Satisfaction, Occupational Preference and Effort: A Theoretical, Methodological, and Empirical Appraisal," *Psychological Bulletin* 81 (1974):1053–1077; Mahmoud A. Wahba and Robert J. House, "Expectancy Theory in Work and Motivation: Some Logical and Methodological Issues," *Human Relations* 27 (January 1974):121–147; Terry Connolly, "Some Conceptual and Methodological Issues in Expectancy Models of Work Performance Motivation," *Academy of Management Review* 1 (October 1976):37–47; Terrence Mitchell, "Expectancy-Value Models in Organizational Psychology," in N. Feather (ed.), *Expectancy, Incentive and Action* (New York: Erlbaum & Associates, 1980).

30 See Adler (1991).

31 Boris Groysberg, Andrew N. McLean, and Nitin Nohria, "Are Leaders Portable?" *Harvard Business Review* (May, 2006).

32 Edwin A. Locke, Karyll N. Shaw, Lise M. Saari, and Gary P. Latham, "Goal Setting and Task Performance: 1969–1980," *Psychological Bulletin* 90 (July/November 1981): 125–152; Edwin A. Locke and Gary P. Latham, "Work Motivation and Satisfaction: Light at the End of the Tunnel," *Psychological Science* 1(4) (July 1990):240–246; Edwin A. Locke and Gary Latham, *A Theory of Goal Setting and Task Performance* (Englewood Cliffs, NJ: Prentice Hall, 1990).

32A Alexander D. Stajkovic, Edwin A. Locke, and Eden S. Blair, "A First Examination of the Relationships Between Primed Subconscious Goals, Assigned Conscious Goals, and Task Performance," *Journal of Applied Psychology*, 91,5 (2006), pp. 1172–1180

33 Gary P. Latham and Edwin A. Locke, "Goal Setting—A Motivational Technique That Works," *Organizational Dynamics* 8 (Autumn 1979): 68–80; Gary P. Latham and Timothy P. Steele, "The Motivational Effects of Participation Versus Goal-Setting on Performance," *Academy of Management Journal* 26 (1983):406–417; Miriam Erez and Frederick H. Kanfer, "The Role of Goal Acceptance in Goal Setting and Task Performance," *Academy of Management Review* 8 (1983):454–463; R. E. Wood and E. A. Locke, "Goal Setting and Strategy Effects on Complex Tasks," in B. Staw and L. L. Cummings (eds.), *Research in Organizational Behavior* (Greenwich, CT: JAI Press, 1990).

34 See E. A. Locke and G. P. Latham, "Work Motivation and Satisfaction," *Psychological Science* 1(4) (July 1990):241.

35 Ibid.

36 For a good review of MBO, see Anthony P. Raia, *Managing by Objectives* (Glenview, IL: Scott, Foresman, 1974).

37 Ibid. Steven Kerr summarizes the criticisms well in "Overcoming the Dysfunctions of MBO." *Management by Objectives* 5(1), 1976.

MARGIN PHOTOS

JL Lane— Information from Raymund Flandez, "An Education in Itself," *Wall Street Journal* (September 23, 2006), p. R10; see also www.jllane.com.

Blue Man Group—See www.blueman.com/about_bmg/whatisBMG.shtml.

Chapter 6

ENDNOTES

1 Information and quotes from Michelle Conlin, "Smashing the Clock," *Business Week* (December 11, 2006), pp. 60–68; and "The Pros and Cons of Flex-Time," *Business Week* (January 8, 2007), p. 19.

2 Frederick W. Taylor, *The Principles of Scientific Management* (New York: Norton, 1967).

3 Information from Reuters, "Coming to Work Sick Afflicts Biz," *Economic Times Bangalore* (January 28, 2007), p. 14; and www.webmd.com/content/article/86/98895.htm.

4 Frederick Herzberg, "One More Time: How Do You Motivate Employees?" *Harvard Business Review* 46 (January/February 1968): 53–62.

5 Paul J. Champagne and Curt Tausky, "When Job Enrichment Doesn't Pay," *Personnel* 3 (January/February 1978): 30–40.

6 For a complete description, see J. Richard Hackman and Greg R. Oldham. *Work Redesign* (Reading, MA: Addison-Wesley, 1980).

7 See J. Richard Hackman and Greg Oldham, "Development of the Job Diagnostic Survey," *Journal of Applied Psychology* 60 (1975): pp. 159–170.

8 Information from Andrew Ward, "Spanx Queen Firms up the Bottom Line," *Financial Times* (November 30, 2006), p. 7.

9 Hackman and Oldham (ibid). For forerunner research, see Charles L. Hulin and Milton R. Blood, "Job Enlargement, Individual Differences, and Worker Responses,"

Psychological Bulletin 69 (1968): 41–55: Milton R. Blood and Charles L. Hulin. "Alienation, Environmental Characteristics and Worker Responses," *Journal of Applied Psychology* 51 (1967):284–290.

[10] Gerald Salancik and Jeffrey Pfeffer, "An Examination of Need-Satisfaction Models of Job Attitudes," *Administrative Science Quarterly* 22 (1977): 427–456: Gerald Salancik and Jeffrey Pfeffer, "A Social Information Processing Approach to Job Attitude and Task Design." *Administrative Science Quarterly* 23 (1978):224–253.

[11] George W. England and Itzhak Harpaz, "How Working Is Defined: National Contexts and Demographic and Organizational Role Influences." *Journal of Organizational Behavior* (July 1990):253–266.

[12] William A. Pasmore, "Overcoming the Roadblocks to Work-Restructuring Efforts." *Organizational Dynamics* 10 (1982):54–67; Hackman and Oldham. op. cit. (1975).

[13] See William A. Pasmore, *Designing Effective Organizations: A Sociotechnical Systems Perspective* (New York: Wiley, 1988).

[14] "Robots," *The Economist* (October 17, 1998). p. 116.

[15] Peter Senker, *Towards the Automatic Factory: The Need for Training* (New York: Springer-Verlag, 1986).

[16] See Ramchandran Jaikumar. "Postindustrial Manufacturing," *Harvard Business Review* (1986):69–76.

[17] Michael Hammer, "Reengineering Work: Don't Automate, Obliterate," *Harvard Business Review* (July/August 1990):104–112.

[18] See Thomas M. Koulopoulos, *The Workflow Imperative: Building Real World Business Solutions* (New York: Van Nostrand Reinhold, 1995).

[19] For a good overview, see Michael Hammer and James Champy, *Reengineering the Corporation* (New York: HarperBusiness, 1993); Michael Hammer, *Beyond Reengineering* (New York: HarperBusiness, 1997).

[20] For overviews, see Allan R. Cohen and Herman Gadon, *Alternative Work Schedules: Integrating Individual and Organizational Needs* (Reading, MA: Addison-Wesley, 1978); and Jon L. Pearce, John W. Newstrom, Randall B. Dunham, and Alison E. Barber, *Alternative Work Schedules* (Boston: Allyn & Bacon, 1989). See also Sharon Parker and Toby Wall, *Job and Work Design* (Thousand Oaks, CA: Sage, 1998).

[21] B. J. Wixom Jr., "Recognizing People in a World of Change," *HR Magazine* (June 1995):7–8; "The Value of Flexibility," *Inc.* (April 1996):114.

[22] Information from Alan Krueger and Alexandre Mas, "Strikes, Scabs and Tread Separations: Labor Strife and the Production of Defective Bridgestone/Firestone Tires," Working Paper, Princeton University Industrial Relations Section (January 9, 2002); "The Hidden Cost of Labor Strife," *Wall Street Journal* (January 30, 2002), p. 1.

[23] C. Latack and L. W. Foster, "Implementation of Compressed Work Schedules: Participation and Job Redesign as Critical Factors for Employee Acceptance," *Personnel Psychology* 38 (1985): 75–92.

[24] Information from Sue Shellenbarger, "The Mommy Drain: Employers Beef up Perks to Lure New Mothers Back to Work," *Wall Street Journal* (September 28, 2006), p. D1.

[25] *Business Week* (December 7, 1998), p. 8.

[26] "Aetna Life & Casualty Company," *Wall Street Journal* (June 4, 1990), p. R35 (June 18, 1990), p. B1.

[27] Getsy M. Selirio, "Job Sharing Gains Favor as Corporations Embrace Alternative Work Schedule," *Lubbock Avalanche-Journal* (December 13, 1992), p. 2E.

[28] Ibid.

[29] "Making Stay-at-Homes Feel Welcome," *Business Week* (October 12, 1998), pp. 153–155.

[30] T. Davenport and K. Pearlson. "Two Cheers for the Virtual Office," *Sloan Management Review* (Summer 1998): 51–64.

[31] "Making Stay-at-Homes Feel Welcome" (1998).

[32] Daniel C. Feldman and Helen I. Doerpinghaus, Missing Persons No Longer: Managing Part-Time Workers in the "90s," *Organizational Dynamics* (Summer 1992): pp. 59–72.

MARGIN PHOTOS

Job Sharing Duo—Information from Susan Berfield, "Two for the Cubicle," *Business Week* (July 24, 2006), pp. 88–92. Time Zone Warriors—Information from Sue Shellenbarger, "Time-Zone Warriors Work around a Global Schedule," *Wall Street Journal* (February 16–18, 2007), p. 27.

Chapter 7

ENDNOTES

[1] Information from Steve Hamm, "A Passion for the Plan," *Business Week* (August 21, 2B 2006), pp. 92–94.

[2] For complete reviews of theory, research, and practice see Edward E. Lawler III, *Pay and Organizational Effectiveness* (New York: McGraw-Hill, 1971); Edward E. Lawler III, *Pay and Organizational Development* (Reading, MA: Addison-Wesley, 1981): Edward E. Lawler III. "The Design of Effective Reward Systems." in Jay W. Lorsch (ed.), *Handbook of Organizational Behavior* (Englewood Cliffs, NJ: Prentice-Hall, 1987), pp. 255–271.

[3] "Reasons for Pay Raises," *Business Week* (May 29, 2006), p. 11.

[4] As an example, see D. B. Balkin and L. R. Gómez-Mejia (eds.), *New Perspectives on Compensation* (Englewood Cliffs, NJ: Prentice-Hall, 1987).

[5] Jone L. Pearce, "Why Merit Pay Doesn't Work: Implications from Organization Theory," in Balkin and Gómez-Mejia (1987), pp. 169–178; Jerry M. Newman, "Selecting Incentive Plans to Complement Organizational Strategy," in Balkin and Gómez-Mejia (1987), pp. 214–224; Edward E.

Lawler III, "Pay for Performance: Making It Work," *Compensation and Benefits Review* 21 (1989):55–60.

[6] See Daniel C. Boyle, "Employee Motivation That Works," *HR Magazine* (October 1992):83–89; Kathleen A. McNally, "Compensation as a Strategic Tool," *HR Magazine* (July 1992):59–66.

[7] Information from "Win-Win Situations for Those at the Top," *Financial Times* (January 4, 2007), p. 16; "CEO's Fatal Flaw: Failing to Understand New Demands," *Wall Street Journal* (January 4, 2007), pp. A1, 12.

[8] See Brian Graham-Moore, "Review of the Literature," in Brian Graham-Moore and Timothy L. Ross (eds.), *Gain sharing* (Washington, DC: Bureau of National Affairs, 1990), p. 20.

[9] S. E. Markham, K. D. Scott, and B. L. Little, "National Gainsharing Study: The Importance of Industry Differences," *Compensation and Benefits Review* (January/February 1992):34–45.

[10] L. R. Gómez-Mejia, D. B. Balkin, and R. L. Cardy, *Managing Human Resources* (Englewood Cliffs, NJ: Prentice-Hall, 1995), pp. 410–411.

[11] Ibid., pp. 409–410.

[12] S. Caudron, "Master the Compensation Maze." *Personnel Journal* (June 1993):640–648.

[13] N. Gupta, G. E. Ledford, G. D. Jenkins, and D. H. Doty, "Survey Based Prescriptions for Skill-Based Pay," *American Compensation Association Journal* 1(1) (1992):48–59; L. W. Ledford, "The Effectiveness of Skill-Based Pay," *Perspectives in Total Compensation* 1(1) (1991):1–4.

[14] C. O'Dell and J. McAdams, "The Revolution in Employee Benefits," *Compensation and Benefits Review* (May/June 1987):68–73.

[15] Information from Monica Langley, "Inside Mulally's 'War Room'": A Radical Overhaul of Ford," *Wall Street Journal* (December 22, 2006), pp. A1, A10; and, "Mulally's First Impressions," *Wall Street Journal* (December 22, 2006).

[16] For more details, see G. P. Latham and K. N. Wexley, *Increasing Productivity through Performance Appraisal* (2nd ed.); Stephen J. Carroll and Craig E. Schneier, *Performance Appraisal and Review Systems* (Glenview, IL: Scott, Foresman, 1982).

[17] See George T. Milkovich and John W. Boudreau, *Personnel/Human Resource Management: A Diagnostic Approach*, 5th ed. (Plano, TX: Business Publications, 1988).

[18] Mark R. Edwards and Ann J. Ewen, *360-Degree Feedback: The Powerful New Tool for Employee Feedback and Performance Improvement* (New York: Amacom, 1996).

[19] For discussion of many of these errors, see David L. Devries, Ann M. Morrison, Sandra L. Shullman, and Michael P. Gerlach, *Performance Appraisal on the Line* (Greensboro, NC: Center for Creative Leadership, 1986), ch. 3.

[20] E. G. Olson. "The Workplace Is High on the High Court's Docket," *Business Week* (October 10, 1988), pp. 88–89.

[20A] Joseph M. Stauffer and M. Ronald Buckley, "The Existence and Nature of Racial Bias in Supervisory Ratings," *Journal of Applied Psychology* 90 (2005), pp. 586–591. Also cited: K. Kraiger and J. K. Ford, "A Meta-analysis of Ratee Race Effects in Performance Ratings," *Journal of Applied Psychology* 70 (1985), pp. 56–65; and, P. R. Sackett and C. L. Z. DuBois, "Rater-Ratee Race Effects on Performance Evaluations: Challenging Meta-Analytic Conclusions," *Journal of Applied Psychology* 76 (1991), pp. 873–877.

[21] Based on J. J. Bernardin and C. S. Walter. "The Effects of Rater Training and Diary Keeping on Psychometric Error in Ratings," *Journal of Applied Psychology* 61 (1977):64–69: see also R. G. Burnask and T. D. Hollman, "An Empirical Comparison of the Relative Effects of Sorter Response Bias on Three Rating Scale Formats," *Journal of Applied Psychology* 59 (1974):307–312.

MARGIN PHOTOS

Women Trail Men in Rewards—Information from "Women Lag Men in Corporate Leadership," *Columbus Dispatch* (February 22, 2007), p. D1; and David Leonhardt, "Smart Women, Smarting Salaries," *New York Times* (December 24, 2006), p. B5.

Microsoft Sheds Pounds—Information from Michele Conlin, "More Micro, Less Soft," *Business Week* (November 27, 2007), p. 42.

Chapter 8

ENDNOTES

[1] Information from David Kirkpatrick, "The Second Coming of Apple, *Fortune* (November 9, 1998), pp. 86–92. See also Owen Linzmeyer and Owen W. Linzmeyer, *Apple Confidential 2.0: The Definitive History of the World's Most Colorful Company* (San Francisco: No Starch Press, 2004); and Jeffrey L. Cruikshank, *The Apple Way* (New York: McGraw-Hill, 2005).

[2] For a good discussion of groups and teams in the workplace, see Jon R. Katzenbach and Douglas K. Smith, "The Discipline of Teams," *Harvard Business Review* (March/April 1993):111–120; and Greg L. Stewart, Charles C. Mane, and Henry P. Sims, *Team Work and Group Dynamics* (New York: John Wiley & Sons, 1999).

[3] Harold J. Leavitt and Jean Lipman-Blumen, "Hot Groups," *Harvard Business Review* (July/August 1995): 109–116.

[4] See, for example, Edward E. Lawler III, *High-Involvement Management* (San Francisco: Jossey-Bass, 1986).

[5] Marvin E. Shaw. *Group Dynamics: The Psychology of Small Group Behavior*, 2nd ed. (New York: McGraw-Hill, 1976).

[6] Bib Latané, Kipling Williams, and Stephen Harkins, "Many Hands Make Light the Work: The Causes and Consequences of Social Loafing." *Journal of Personality and*

Social Psychology 37 (1978):822–832; E. Weklon and G. M. Gargano, "Cognitive Effort in Additive Task Groups: The Effects of Shared Responsibility on the Quality of Multi-Attribute Judgments," *Organizational Behavior and Human Decision Processes* 36 (1985):348–361; John M. George, "Extrinsic and Intrinsic Origins of Perceived Social Loafing in Organizations," *Academy of Management Journal* (March 1992):191–202; W. Jack Duncan, "Why Some People Loaf in Groups While Others Loaf Alone," *Academy of Management Executive* 8 (1994):79–80.

[7] D. A. Kravitz and B. Martin. "Ringelmann Rediscovered," *Journal of Personality and Social Psychology* 50 (1986): 936–941.

[8] A classic article is by Richard B. Zajonc. "Social Facilitation," *Science* 149 (1965):269–274.

[9] Rensis Likert, *New Patterns of Management* (New York: McGraw-Hill, 1961).

[10] Information from "MBAs 'Cheat Most,'" *Financial Times* (September 21, 2006), p. 1; "The Devil Made Me Do It," *Business Week* (July 24, 2006), p. 10; Karen Richardson, "Buffett Advises on Scandals: Avoid Temptations," *Wall Street Journal* (October 10, 2006), p. A9.

[11] For a good discussion of task forces, see James Ware, "Managing a Task Force," Note 478–002, Harvard Business School, 1977.

[12] See D. Duarte and N. Snyder, *Mastering Virtual Teams: Strategies, Tools, and Techniques That Succeed* (San Francisco: Jossey-Bass, 1999).

[13] See, for example, Leland P. Bradford. *Group Development*, 2nd ed. (San Francisco: Jossey-Bass, 1997).

[14] J. Steven Heinen and Eugene Jacobson, "A Model of Task Group Development in Complex Organization and a Strategy of Implementation." *Academy of Management Review* 1 (October 1976):98–111: Bruce W. Tuckman, "Developmental Sequence in Small Groups," *Psychological Bulletin* 63 (1965):384–399; Bruce W. Tuckman, and Mary Ann C. Jensen, "Stages of Small Group Development Revisited." *Group & Organization Studies* 2 (1977):419–427.

[15] See J. Richard Hackman. "The Design of Work Teams," in Jay W. Lorsch (ed.), *Handbook of Organizational Behavior* (Englewood Cliffs. NJ: Prentice Hall, 1987), pp. 343–357.

[16] David M. Herold, "The Effectiveness of Work Groups," in Steven Kerr (ed.), *Organizational Behavior* (New York: Wiley, 1979), p. 95; see also the discussion of group tasks in Stewart, Manz, and Sims, op. cit. (1999), pp. 142–143.

[17] Daniel R. Ilgen, Jeffrey A. LePine, and John R. Hollenbeck, "Effective Decision Making in Multinational Teams," in P. Christopher Earley and Miriam Erez (eds.), *New Perspectives on International Industrial/Organizational Psychology* (San Francisco: New Lexington Press, 1997); Warren Watson, "Cultural Diversity's Impact on Interaction Process and Performance," *Academy of Management Journal* 16 (1993).

[18] L. Argote and J. E. McGrath, "Group Processes in Organizations: Continuity and Change," in C. L. Cooper and I. T. Robertson (eds.), *International Review of Industrial and Organizational Psychology* (New York: Wiley, 1993), pp. 333–389.

[19] See Ilgen. Le Piner, and Hollenbeck (1997), pp. 377–409.

[20] William C. Schultz, *FIRO: A Three-Dimensional Theory of Interpersonal Behavior* (New York: Rinehart, 1958).

[21] William C. Schultz, "The Interpersonal Underworld," *Harvard Business Review* 36 (July/August 1958):130.

[22] Katzenbach and Smith (1993).

[23] F. J. Thomas and C. F. Fink, "Effects of Group Size," in Larry L. Cummings and William E. Scott (eds.), *Readings in Organizational and Human Performance* (Homewood, IL: Irwin, 1969), pp. 394–408.

[24] Shaw (1976).

[25] George C. Homans, *The Human Group* (New York: Harcourt Brace, 1950).

[25A] Kenneth H. Price, David A. Harrison, and Joanne H. Gavin, "Withholding Inputs in Team Contexts: Member Composition, Interaction Processes, Evaluation Structure, and Social Loafing," *Journal of Applied Psychology,* 91.6 (2006), pp. 1375–1384.

[26] Information from "Cirque du Balancing Act," *Fortune* (June 12, 2006), p. 114; www.cirquedusoleil.com.

[27] For a discussion of intergroup dynamics, see Edgar H. Schein, *Process Consultation,* Volume I (Reading, MA: Addison-Wesley, 1988), pp. 106–115.

[28] "Producer Power." *The Economist* (March 4, 1995), p. 70.

[29] The concept of interacting, coacting, and counteracting groups is presented in Fred E. Fiedler, *A Theory of Leadership Productivity* (New York: McGraw-Hill, 1967).

[30] Research on communication networks is found in Alex Bavelas, "Communication Patterns in Task-Oriented Groups," *Journal of the Acoustical Society of America* 22 (1950):725–730. See also "Research on Communication Networks," as summarized in Shaw (1976), pp. 137–153.

[31] The discussion is developed from Schein (1988), pp. 69–75.

[32] Ibid., p. 73.

[33] Developed from guidelines presented in the classic article by Jay Hall, "Decisions, Decisions, Decisions," *Psychology Today* (November 1971):55–56.

[34] Norman R.F. Maier, "Assets and Liabilities in Group Problem Solving," *Psychological Review* 74 (1967):239–249.

[35] Irving L. Janis, "Groupthink," *Psychology Today* (November 1971):33–36; Irving L. Janis. *Groupthink,* 2nd ed. (Boston: Houghton Mifflin, 1982). See also J. Longley and D. G. Pruitt, "Groupthink: A Critique of Janis' Theory," in L. Wheeler (ed.). *Review of Personality and Social Psychology* (Beverly Hills, CA: Sage, 1980); Carrie R. Leana, "A Partial Test of Janis's Groupthink Model: The Effects of Group Cohesiveness and Leader Behavior on Decision Processes," *Journal of Management* 1:(1) (1985):5–18. See

also Jerry Harvey, "Managing Agreement in Organizations: The Abilene Paradox," *Organizational Dynamics* (Summer 1974):63–80.

[36] Janis (1982).

[37] Gayle W. Hill, "Group Versus Individual Performance: Are Two Leads Better Than One?" *Psychological Bulletin* 91 (1982):517–539.

[38] These techniques are well described in George P. Huber. *Managerial Decision Making* (Glenview, IL: Scott, Foresman, 1980): Andre L Delbecq, Andrew L. Van de Ven, and David H. Gustafson, *Group Techniques for Program Planning: A Guide to Nominal Groups and Delphi Techniques* (Glenview, IL: Scott, Foresman. 1975): William M. Fox, "Anonymity and Other Keys to Successful Problem-Solving Meetings," *National Productivity Review* 8 (Spring 1989):145–156.

[39] Delbecq, Van de Ve, and Gustafson al., op. cit. (1975): Fox. op. cit. (1989).

[40] R. Brent Gallupe and William H. Cooper, "Brainstorming Electronically," *Sloan Management Review* (Fall 1993):27–36.

[41] Information from Jessi Hempel, "Big Blue Brainstorm," *Business Week* (August 7, 2006), p. 70.

Chapter 9

ENDNOTES

[1] Information from Jena McGregor, "Game Plan: First Find the Leaders," *Business Week* (August 21, 28, 2006), pp. 102–103.

[2] Jon R. Katzenbach and Douglas K. Smith, "The Discipline of Teams," *Harvard Business Review* (March/April 1993a):111–120; Jon R Katzenbach and Douglas K. Smith, *The Wisdom of Teams: Creating the High-Performance Organization* (Boston: Harvard Business School Press, 1993b).

[3] Jay A. Conger, *Winning 'Em Over: A New Model for Managing in the Age of Persuasion* (New York: Simon & Schuster, 1998).

[4] Ibid., p. 191.

[5] Katzenbach and Smith (1993a and 1993b).

[6] See also Jon R. Katzenbach, "The Myth of the Top Management Team," *Harvard Business Review* 75 (November/December 1997):83–91.

[7] Katzenbach and Smith (1993a and 1993b).

[8] For a good overview, see Greg L. Stewart, Charles C. Manz, and Henry P. Sims, *Team Work and Group Dynamics* (New York: Wiley, 1999).

[9] Katzenbach and Smith (1993a), p. 112.

[10] Developed from ibid. (1993a), pp. 118–119.

[11] See Stewart, Manz., and Sims (1999), pp. 43–44.

[12] See Daniel R. Ilen, Jeffrey A. LePine, and John R. Hollenbeck, "Effective Decision Making in Multinational Teams," in P. Christopher Earley and Miriam Erez (eds.), *New Perspectives on International Industrial/Organizational Psychology* (San Francisco: New Lexington Press, 1997), pp. 377–409.

[13] Ibid., Warren Watson, "Cultural Diversity's Impact on Interaction Process and Performance," *Academy of Management Journal* 16 (1993).

[14] For an interesting discussion of sports teams see Ellen Fagenson-Eland, "The National Football League's Bill Parcells on Winning, Leading, and Turning Around Teams," *Academy of Management Executive* 15 (August 2001):48–57; Nancy Katz, "Sport Teams as a Model for Workplace Teams: Lessons and Liabilities," *Academy of Management Executive* 15 (Agust 2002): 56–69.

[15] For a good discussion of team building, see William D. Dyer, *Team Building*, 3rd ed. (Reading, MA: Addison-Wesley, 1995).

[16] Jeanne Brett, Kristan Behfar, and Mary C. Kern, "Managing Multicultural Teams," *Harvard Business Review* (November 2006), pp. 84–91.

[17] Developed from a discussion by Edgar H. Schein, *Process Consultation* (Reading, MA: Addison-Wesley, 1969), pp. 32–37; Edgar H. Schein, *Process Consultation* (Vol. 1) (Reading, MA: Addison-Wesley, 1988), pp. 40–49.

[18] The classic work is Robert F. Bales, "Task Roles and Social Roles in Problem-Solving Groups," in Eleanor F Maccoby, Theodore M Newcomb, and E. L. Hartley (eds.), *Readings in Social Psychology* (New York: Holt, Rinehart & Winston, 1958).

[19] For a good description of task and maintenance functions, see John J. Gabarro and Anne Harlan, "Note on Process Observation," Note 9-477-029 (Harvard Business School, 1976).

[20] See Daniel C. Feldman, "The Development and Enforcement of Group Norms," *Academy of Management Review* 9 (1984):47–53.

[20A] Dora C. Lau and J. Keith Murnighan, "Interactions within Groups and Subgroups: The Effects of Demographic Faultlines," *Academy of Management Journal* 48 (2005), pp. 645–659; and "Demographic Diversity and Faultlines: The Compositional Dynamics of Organizational Groups," *Academy of Management Review* 23 (1998), pp. 325–340.

[21] See Robert F. Allen and Saul Pilnick, "Confronting the Shadow Organization: How to Select and Defeat Negative Norms," *Organizational Dynamics* (Spring 1973):13–17; Alvin Zander, *Making Groups Effective* (San Francisco: Jossey-Bass, 1982), ch. 4: Feldman (1984).

[22] Information from Ken Gordon, "Tressel's Way Transforms OSU into 'Model Program,'" *Columbus Dispatch* (January 5, 2007), pp. A1, A4.

23 For a summary of research on group cohesiveness, see Marvin E. Shaw, *Group Dynamics* (New York: McGraw-Hill, 1971), pp. 110–112, 192.

24 Information from Stratford Shermin, "Secrets of HP's 'Muddled' Team," *Fortune* (March 18, 1996), pp. 116–120.

25 See Jay R. Galbraith and Edward E. Lawler III, "The Challenges of Change: Organizing for Competitive Advantage," in Mohrman, Galbraith, Lawler, et al. (1998).

26 See Kenichi Ohmae, "Quality Control Circles: They Work and Don't Work," *Wall Street Journal* (March 29, 1982), p. 16; Robert P. Steel, Anthony J. Mento, Benjamin L. Dilla, Nestor K. Ovalle, and Russell F. Lloyd, "Factors Influencing the Success and Failure of Two Quality Circles Programs," *Journal of Management* 11(1) (1985):99–119; Edward E. Lawler III and Susan A. Mohrman, "Quality Circles: After the Honeymoon," *Organizational Dynamics* 15(4) (1987):42–54.

27 See Jay R. Galbraith, *Designing Organizations* (San Francisco: Jossey-Bass, 1998).

28 Jerry Yoram Wind and Jeremy Main, *Driving Change: How the Best Companies Are Preparing for the 21st Century* (New York: Free Press, 1998), p. 135.

29 Jessica Lipnack and Jeffrey Stamps, *Virtual Teams: Reaching Across Space, Time, and Organizations with Technology* (New York: Wiley, 1997).

30 For a review of some alternatives, see Jeff Angus and Sean Gallagher, "Virtual Team Builders—Internet-Based Teamware Makes It Possible to Build Effective Teams from Widely Dispersed Participants," *Information Week* (May 4, 1998).

31 R. Brent Gallupe and William H. Cooper, "Brainstorming Electronically," *Sloan Management Review* (Fall 1993):27–36.

32 Information from Robert D. Hof, "Amazon's Risky Bet," *Business Week* (November 13, 2006), pp. 52+.

33 Ibid.

34 See Guido Hertel, Susanne Geister, and Udo Konradt, "Managing Virtual Teams: A Review of Current Research," *Human Resource Management Review* 15 (March 2005), pp. 69–95; and Luis L. Martins, Lucy L. Gilson, and M. Travis Maynard, "Virtual Teams: What Do We Know and Where Do We Go from Here?" *Journal of Management* 30 (December 2004), pp. 805–835.

35 For early research on related team concepts, see Richard E. Walton, "How to Counter Alienation in the Plant," *Harvard Business Review* (November/December 1972):70–81: Richard E. Walton, "Work Innovations at Topeka: After Six Years," *Journal of Applied Behavior Science* 13 (1977):422–431; Richard E. Walton, "The Topeka Work System: Optimistic Visions, Pessimistic Hypotheses, and Reality," in Zager and Rosow (eds.), *The Innovative Organization*, ch. 11.

36 For an overview see Linda Moran, Jack Orsburn, Jack D. Orsburn, and John H. Zenger, *The New Self-Directed Work Teams: Mastering the Challenge* (New York: McGraw-Hill, 1999).

MARGIN PHOTO

Nucor's inspring boss—Information from "Most Inspiring Steel Boss," *Business Week* (December 18, 2006), p. 61.

Chapter 10

ENDNOTES

1 www.cisco.com.

2 While several scholars emphasize interdependence, such as W. Richard Scott and Gereal F. Davis in *Organizations and Organizing: Rational, Natural and Open Systems Perspectives* (Upper Saddle River , NJ: Pearson-Prentice Hall, 2007), the most extensive early work was done by Jeffrey Pfeffer, *Organizations and Organization Theory* (Boston: Pitman, 1983) and by Jeffrey Pfeffer and Gerald R. Salancik, *The External Control of Organizations* (Englewood Cliffs, NJ: Prentice Hall, 1978).

3 Rosabeth Moss Kanter, "Power Failure in Management Circuit," *Harvard Business Review* (July–August 1979), pp. 65–75.

4 John R. P. French and Bertram Raven, "The Bases of Social Power," in *Group Dynamics: Research and Theory*, ed. Dorwin Cartwright (Evanston, IL: Row, Peterson, 1962), pp. 607–623.

5 Pfeffer, 1983; Pfeffer and Salancik, 1978.

6 Stanley Milgram, "Behavioral Study of Obedience," in *The Applied Psychology of Work Behavior*, ed. Dennis W. Organ (Dallas: Business Publications, 1978), pp. 384–398. Also see Stanley Milgram, "Behavioral Study of Obedience," *Journal of Abnormal and Social Psychology* 67 (1963), pp. 371–378; "Group Pressure and Action Against a Person," *Journal of Abnormal and Social Psychology* 69 (1964), pp. 137–143; "Some Conditions of Obedience and Disobedience to Authority," *Human Relations* 1 (1965), pp. 57–76; *Obedience to Authority* (New York: Harper and Row, 1974).

6A Information from www.northwestmutual.com; www.rwbarid.com/news/currentnewsrelese049.

7 Chester Barnard, *The Functions of the Executive* (Cambridge, MA: Harvard University Press, 1938).

8 Ibid.

9 See Joseph R. DesJardins, *Business Ethics and the Environment: Imagining a Sustainable Future* (Upper Saddle River, NJ: Pearson-Prentice Hall, 2007); Steven N. Brenner and Earl A. Mollander, "Is the Ethics of Business Changing?" *Harvard Business Review* 55 (February 1977), pp. 57–71; Barry Z. Posner and Warren H. Schmidt, "Values and the American Manager: An Update," *California Management Review* 26 (Spring 1984), pp. 202–216.

10 French and Raven, 1962.

11 We have added process, information, and representative power to the French and Raven list.

[12] We have added coalition power to the French and Raven list.

[13] See Jean-Jacques Herings, Gerald Van Der Lean, and Doif Tallman, "Social Structured Games," *Theory and Decision* 62.1 (2007), pp. 1–30 and William Matthew Bowler, "Organizational Goals Versus the Dominant Coalition: A Critical View of the Value of Organizational Citizenship Behavior," *Journal of Behavior and Applied Management* 7.3 (2006), pp. 258–277.

[14] For an interesting but different take on power, networks, and visibility see Calvin Morrill, Mayer N. Zold, and H. Roa, " Covert Political Conflict in Organizations: Challenges from Below," *American Sociological Review* 29 (2003), pp. 391–416.

[15] David Kipinis, Stuart M. Schmidt, Chris Swaffin-Smith, and Ian Wilkinson, "Patterns of Managerial Influence: Shotgun Managers, Tacticians, and Bystanders," *Organizational Dynamics* 12 (1984), pp. 60–69.

[16] Ibid; David Kipinis, Stuart M. Schmidt, and Ian Wilkinson, "Intraorganizational Influence Tactics: Explorations in Getting One's Way," *Journal of Applied Psychology* 65 (1980), pp. 440–452.

[16A] Based on Gerald Cavanagh, Dennis Moberg, and Manuel Velasquez, "The Ethics of Organizational Politics," and Manuel Velasquez, Dennis J. Moberg, and Gerald Cavanagh, "Organizational Statesmanship and Dirty Politics: Ethical Guidelines for the Organizational Politician," pp. 65–79 in *Organizational Dynamics*, vol. 11 (1983).

[17] Warren Schilit and Edwin A. Locke, " A Study of Upward Influence in Organizations," *Administrative Science Quarterly* 27 (1982), pp. 301–316.

[18] Ibid; see Amil Somech and Anat Drach-Zahavy, "Relative Power and Influence Strategy: The Effect of Agent-Target Organizational Power on Superiors' Choices of Influence Strategies," *Journal of Organizational Behavior* 23.2 (2002), pp. 167–194.

[19] For a discussion of empowerment see Scott E. Seibert, Seth R. Silver, and W. Allan Randolph, " Taking Empowerment to the Next Level: A Multiple-level Model of Empowerment, Performance and Satisfaction," *Academy of Management Journal* 47.3 (2004), pp. 37–53; John E. Mathieu, Lucky L. Gibson, and Thomas M. Ruddy, "Empowerment and Team Effectiveness: An Empirical Test of an Integrated Model," *Journal of Applied Psychology* 91.1 (2006), pp. 1–10; Jean M. Bartunek and Gretchen M. Spreitzer, "The Interdisciplinary Career of a Popular Construct Used in Management: Empowerment in the Late 20th Century," *Journal of Management Inquiry* 15.3 (2006), pp. 255–274.

[20] Jeffery Pfeffer, " Producing Sustainable Competitive Advantage through the Effective Management of People," *Academy of Management Executive* 19.4 (2005), pp. 85–115.

[21] Useful reviews include a chapter in Robert H. Miles, *Macro Organizational Behavior* (Santa Monica, CA: Goodyear, 1980); Bronston T. Mayes and Robert W. Allen, "Toward a Definition of Organizational Politics," *Academy of Management Review* 2 (1977), pp. 672–677; Dan Farrell and James C. Petersen, "Patterns of Political Behavior in Organizations," *Academy of Management Review* 7 (1982), pp. 403–412; D. L. Madison, R. W. Allen, L. W. Porter, and B. T. Mayes, "Organizational Politics: An Exploration of Managers' Perceptions," *Human Relations* 33 (1980), pp. 92–107.

[22] Pfeffer, 1981.

[23] For a discussion, see Christopher Gresov and Carroll Stephen, " Context of Interunit Influence Attempts," *Administrative Science Quarterly* 38.2 (1993), pp. 252–304.

[23A] Gerald Ferris, Sherry Davidson, and Pamela Perrewe. *Political Skill at Work* (Mountain View, CA: Davies-Black, 2005).

[24] See Craig Furfine, "The Costs and Benefits of Moral Suasion: Evidence from the Rescue of Long Term Capital Management," *Journal of Business* 79.2 (2006), pp. 593–623; Mark Stein "Unbounded Irrationality: Risk and Organizational Narcissism at Long Term Capital Management, *Human Relations* 56.5 (2003), pp. 523–549. For a conceptual discussion see R. N. Osborn and D. H. Jackson, "Leaders, Riverboat Gamblers, or Purposeful Unintended Consequences in Management of Complex Technologies," *Academy of Management Journal* 31 (1988), pp. 924–947.

[25] Warren K. Schilit and Edwin A. Locke, "A Study of Upward Influence in Organizations," *Administrative Science Quarterly* 27 (1982), pp. 304–316.

[26] Mayes and Allen, 1977, p. 675; James L. Hall and Joel L. Leldecker, "A Review of Vertical and Lateral Relations: A New Perspective for Managers," pp. 138–146 in *Dimensions in Modern Management,* 3rd ed., ed. Patrick Connor (Boston: Houghton Mifflin, 1982); John P. Kotter, "Power, Success, and Organizational Effectiveness," *Organizational Dynamics* 6 (1978), pp. 27–43.

[27] See Susan William and Rick Wilson, "Group Support Systems, Power, and Influence in an Organization: A Field Study," *Decision Sciences* 28.4 (1997), pp. 911–938.

[28] B. Ashforth and R. T. Lee, "Defensive Behavior in Organizations: A Preliminary Model," *Human Relations* (July 1990), pp. 621–648; personal communication with Blake Ashforth, March 2006; Pfeffer, 1983.

[29] For discussion of attribution theory see Simon Tagger and Michell Neubert, "The Impact of Poor Performers on Team Outcomes: An Empirical Examination of Attribution Theory," *Personnel Psychology* 57.4 (2004), pp. 935–979; Robert G. Lord and Karen Maher, "Alternative Information-Processing Models and Their Implications," *Academy of Management Review* 15.1 (1990), pp. 9–29.

[30] For more extensive discussions see Richard Ritte and Steven Levy, *The Ropes to Skip and the Ropes to Know:*

Studies in Organizational Behavior, 7th ed. (Hoboken, NJ: John Wiley and Sons, 2006); Gerry Griffin and Ciaran Parker, *Games Companies Play: An Insider's Guide to Surviving Politics* (Hoboken, NJ: John Wiley and Sons, 2004).

[31] See J. M. Ivancevich, T. N. Deuning, J. A. Gilbert, and R. Konopaske, "Deterring White-Collar Crime," *Academy of Management Executive* 17.2 (2003), pp. 114–128.

[32] See J. P. O'Connor Jr., R. Priem, and K. M. Gilly, "Do CEO Stock Options Prevent or Promote Fradulent Financial Reporting?" *Academy of Management Journal* 49.3 (2006), pp. 483–500; D. Dalton, C. Daily, A. E. Ellstrand, and J. L. Johnson, "Meta-Analysis of Financial Performance and Quality: Fusion or Confusion," *Academy of Management Journal* 46.1 (1998), pp. 13–26.

[33] Ibid.

[34] Ibid.

[35] See David Henry, "Worker vs. CEO Pay: Room to Run," *Business Week* (October 30, 2006), pp. 13–14; Takao Kato and Katsuyuii Kubo, "CEO Compensation and Firm Performance in Japan, Evidence from New Panel Data on Individual CEO Pay," *Journal of the Japanese and International Economics* 20.1 (2006), pp. 1–31; Jeffery Moriarty, "Do CEOs Get Paid Too Much?" *Business Ethics Quarterly* 15.15 (2005), pp. 257–266.

[36] O'Connor, Priem, and Gilly, 2006; C. Daily, D. Dalton, and A. A. Cannella Jr., "Corporate Governance: Decades of Dialog and Data," *Academy of Management Review* 28 (2003), pp. 114–128.

[37] See Pfeffer, 1983.

[38] Richard N. Osborn, "Strategic Leadership and Alliances in a Global Economy," working paper, Department of Business, Wayne State University, 2007.

[39] The notion of a dominant coalition was a key concept in James D. Thompson, *Organizations in Action* (New York: McGraw-Hill, 1967). Also see Rony Simons and Randall S. Peterson, "When to Let Them Duke It Out," *Harvard Business Review* 84.6 (2006), pp. 23–49; M. Firth, P. M. Y. Fund, and O. M. Rui, "Firm Performance, Governance Structure, and Top Management Turnover in a Transition Economy," *Journal of Management Studies* 43.6 (2006), pp. 1289–1299; John A. Pearce, "A Structural Analysis of Dominant Coalitions in Small Banks," *Journal of Management* 21.6 (1995), pp. 1075–1096.

Chapter 11

ENDNOTES

[1] Barry Yeoman, "Foreign Service," *AARP Bulletin*, February 2007, 33.

[2] Arthur G. Bedeian and James G. Hunt, "Academic Amnesia and Vestigial Assumptions of Our Forefathers," *The Leadership Quarterly* 17 (2006), 190–205.

[3] See J.P. Kotter, *A Force for Change: How Leadership Differs from Management* (New York: Free Press, 1990).

[4] Gary Yukl, *Leadership in Organizations*, 6th ed. (Upper Saddle River, NJ: Prentice Hall, 2006), 8.

[5] See Bernard M. Bass, *Bass and Stogdill's Handbook of Leadership*, 3rd ed. (New York: Free Press, 1990).

[6] See Alan Bryman, *Charisma and Leadership in Organizations* (London: Sage, 1992), ch. 5; Ralph M. Stogdill, *Handbook of Leadership* (New York: Free Press, 1974).

[7] Ralph M. Stogdill, *Handbook of Leadership* (New York: Free Press, 1974

[8] Based on information from Robert J. House and Ram Aditya, "The Social Scientific Study of Leadership: Quo Vadis?" *Journal of Management* 23 (1997); 409–474; Shelley A. Kirkpatrick and Edwin A. Locke, "Leadership: Do Traits Matter?" *The Executive* 5(2) (1991); 48–60; Gary Yukl, *Leadership in Organizations*, 3rd ed. (Upper Saddle River, NJ: Prentice-Hall, 1998), ch. 10.

[9] Rensis Likert, *New Patterns of Management* (New York: McGraw-Hill, 1961).

[9A] L. Jon Wertheim, "Do College Athletics Corrupt?" *Sports Illustrated* (March 5, 2007), p. 67.

[10] Bass (1990), ch. 24.

[11] Robert R. Blake and Jane S. Mouton (Houston: Gulf Publishing Co., 1991.), p. 29.

[12] See M.F. Peterson, "PM Theory in Japan and China: What's in It for the United States?" *Organizational Dynamics* (Spring 1988); 22–39; J. Misumi and M.F. Peterson, "The Performance-Maintenance Theory of Leadership: Review of a Japanese Research Program," *Administrative Science Quarterly*, 30 (1985); 198–223; P.B. Smith, J. Misumi, M. Tayeb, M.F. Peterson, and M. Bond, "On the Generality of Leadership Style Measures Across Cultures," paper presented at the International Congress of Applied Psychology, Jerusalem, July 1986.

[13] House and Aditya (1997).

[14] Kirkpatrick and Locke (1991); Yukl (1998), ch. 10; J.G. Hunt and G.E. Dodge, "Management in Organizations," *Handbook of Psychology* (Washington, DC; American Psychological Association, 2000).

[15] This section is based on Fred E. Fiedler and Martin M. Chemers, *Leadership* (Glenview, IL: Scott, Foresman, 1974).

[16] This discussion of cognitive resource theory is based on Fred E. Fiedler and Joseph E. Garcia, *New Approaches in Effective Leadership* (New York: Wiley, 1987).

[17] See L.H. Peters, D.D. Harke, and J.T. Pohlmann, "Fiedler's Contingency Theory of Leadership: An Application of the Meta-Analysis Procedures of Schmidt and Hunter," *Psychological Bulletin* 97 (1985); 274–285.

[18] Yukl (2006).

[19] F.E. Fiedler, Martin Chemers, and Linda Mahar, *Improving Leadership Effectiveness: The Leader Match Concept*, 2nd ed. (New York: Wiley, 1984).

20 For documentation, see Fred E. Fiedler and Linda Mahar, "The Effectiveness of Contingency Model Training: A Review of the Validation of Leader Match," *Personnel Psychology* (Spring 1979); 45–62; Fred E. Garcia, Cecil H. Bell, Martin M. Chemers, and Dennis Patrick, "Increasing Mine Productivity and Safety Through Management Training and Organization Development: A Comparative Study," *Basic and Applied Social Psychology* (March 1984):1–18; Arthur G. Jago and James W. Ragan, "The Trouble with Leader Match Is That It Doesn't Match Fiedler's Contingency Model," *Journal of Applied Psychology* (November 1986); 555–559; Yukl (1998); R. Ayman, M. M. Chemers, and F.E. Fiedler, "The Contingency Model of Leadership Effectiveness: Its Levels of Analysis," *The Leadership Quarterly* (Summer 1995); 147–168.

21 See Yukl (1998); R. Ayman, M. M. Chemers, and F. E. Fiedler. "The Contingency Model of Leadership Effectiveness: Its Levels of Analysis," *The Leadership Quarterly* (Summer 1995); 141–188.

22 This section is based on Robert J. House and Terence R. Mitchell, "Path-Goal Theory of Leadership," *Journal of Contemporary Business* (Autumn 1977); 81–97.

23 House and Mitchell (1977).

24 C.A. Schriesheim and L.L. Neider, "Path-Goal Theory: The Long and Winding Road," *The Leadership Quarterly* 7 (1996); 317–321; M.G. Evans, "Commentary on R.J. House's Path-Goal Theory of Leadership Effectiveness," *The Leadership Quarterly* 7 (1996); 305–309.

25 R.J. House, "Path-Goal Theory of Leadership: Lessons, Legacy, and a Reformulated Theory," *The Leadership Quarterly* 7 (1996); 323–352.

26 See the discussion of this approach in Paul Hersey and Kenneth H. Blanchard, *Management of Organizational Behavior* (Englewood Cliffs, NJ: Prentice Hall, 1988); Paul Hersey, Kenneth Blanchard, and Dewey E. Johnson, *Management of Organizational Behavior*, 8th ed. (Upper Saddle River, NJ: Prentice Hall, 2001).

27 R.P. Vecchio and C. Fernandez, "Situational Leadership Theory Revisited," in M. Schnake (ed.), *1995 Southern Management Association Proceedings* (Valdosta, GA: Georgia Southern University, 1995), pp. 137–139; Claude L. Graeff, "Evolution of Situational Leadership Theory: A Critical Review," *The Leadership Quarterly* 8 (1997); 153–170.

28 Yukl (1998); George Graen, "Leader-Member Exchange Theory Development: Discussant's Comments," paper presented at the Academy of Management meeting, San Diego, August 1998.

28 Yukl (1998); Peter G. Northouse, *Leadership Theory and Practice* (Thousand Oaks, CA: Sage, 1997), ch. 7.

29 G.B. Graen and M. Uhl-Bien, "Relationship-Based Approach to Leadership: Development of Leader-Member Exchange (LMX) Theory of Leadership over 25 Years Applying a Multi Level Multi-Domain Perspective," *The Leadership Quarterly* 6 (1995); 219–247.

29A Based on Gary Yukl, "Leader-Member Exchange Theory." *Leadership in Organizations* (2006); pp. 117–120.

30 The discussion in this section is based on Steven Kerr and John Jermier, "Substitutes for Leadership: Their Meaning and Measurement," *Organizational Behavior and Human Performance* 22 (1978); 375–403; Jon P. Howell, David E. Bowen, Peter W. Dorfman, Steven Kerr, and Phillip M. Podsakoff, "Substitutes for Leadership: Effective Alternatives to Ineffective Leadership," *Organizational Dynamics* (Summer 1990); 21–38.

31 Phillip M. Podsakoff, Peter W. Dorfman, Jon P. Howell, and William D. Todor, "Leader Reward and Punishment Behaviors: A Preliminary Test of a Culture-Free Style of Leadership Effectiveness," *Advances in Comparative Management* 2 (1989); 95–138; T. K. Peng, "Substitutes for Leadership in an International Setting," unpublished manuscript, College of Business Administration, Texas Tech University (1990); P.M. Podsakoff and S.B. MacKenzie, "Kerr and Jermier's Substitutes for Leadership Model: Background, Empirical Assessment, and Suggestions for Future Research," *The Leadership Quarterly* 8(2) (1997); 117–132.

32 See J. Pfeffer, "Management as Symbolic Action: The Creation and Maintenance of Organizational Paradigms," in Cummings and Staw, *Research in Organizational Behavior* (Vol. 3) (Greenwich, CT. JAI Press, 1981), pp. 1–52.

33 James R. Meindl, "On Leadership: An Alternative to the Conventional Wisdom," in Staw and Cummings, *Research in Organizational Behavior* (Vol. 3) (Greenwich, CT. JAI Press, 1981), pp. 159–203. Compare with Bryman (1992); also see James G. Hunt and Jay A. Conger (eds.), *The Leadership Quarterly* 10(2) (1999), special issue.

34 D. Eden and U. Leviatan. "Implicit Leadership Theory as a Determinant of the Factor Structure Underlying Supervisory Behavior Scales," *Journal of Applied Psychology*, 60 (1975); 736–741.

35 See T.R. Mitchell, S.G. Green, and R.E. Wood, "An Attributional Model of Leadership and the Poor Performing Subordinate: Development and Validation," in L.L. Cummings and B.M. Staw (eds.), *Research in Organizational Behavior* (Vol. 3) (Greenwich, CT: JAI Press, 1981), pp. 197–234.

36 Robert Lord and Karen Maher, *Leadership and Information Processing* (Boston: Unwin Hyman); Jun Yan and James G. Hunt, "A Cross-Cultural Perspective on Perceived Leadership Effectiveness," *International Journal of Cross Cultural Management* (In press, 2006).

37 Yan and Hunt (2006 in press).

38 James G. Hunt, Kimberly B. Boal, and Ritch L. Sorenson, "Top Management Leadership: Inside the Black Box," *The Leadership Quarterly* 1 (1990); 41–65.

39 C.R. Gerstner and D.B. Day, "Cross-Cultural Comparison of Leadership Prototypes," *The Leadership Quarterly* (1994); 122–134.

40 Jun Yan and James G. Hunt (in press, 2006).

41 Olga Epitropaki and Robin Martin, "Implicit Leadership Theories in Applied Settings: Factor Structure, Generalizability, and Stability Over Time," *Journal of Applied Psychology*, 89 (2004); 293–310.

42 See R. J. House, "A 1976 Theory of Charismatic Leadership," in J.G. Hunt and L.L. Larson (eds.), *Leadership: The Cutting Edge* (Carbondale: Southern Illinois University Press, 1977), pp. 189–207.

43 R.J. House, W.D. Spangler, and J. Woycke, "Personality and Charisma in the U.S. Presidency," *Administrative Science Quarterly* 36 (1991); 364–396.

44 Pillai and E.A. Williams, "Does Leadership Matter in the Political Arena? Voter Perceptions of Candidates' Transformational and Charismatic Leadership and the 1996 U.S. Presidential Vote," *The Leadership Quarterly* 9 (1998); 397–416.

45 See Jane M. Howell and Bruce J. Avolio, "The Ethics of Charismatic Leadership: Submission or Liberation," *Academy of Management Executive* 6 (May 1992); 43–54.

46 Jay Conger and Rabindra N. Kanungo, *Charismatic Leadership in Organizations* (San Francisco: Jossey-Bass, 1998).

47 Conger and Kanungo (1998).

48 Boas Shamir, "Social Distance and Charisma: Theoretical Notes and an Exploratory Study," *The Leadership Quarterly* 6 (Spring 1995); 19–48.

49 See B.M. Bass, *Leadership and Performance Beyond Expectations* (New York: Free Press, 1985); Bryman (1992), pp. 98–99.

50 B.M. Bass, *A New Paradigm of Leadership* (Alexandria, VA: U.S. Army Research Institute for the Behavioral and Social Sciences, 1996).

50A Adapted from Jeffery S. Mio, Ronald E. Riggio Shana Levin, and Renford Reese, "Presidential Leadership Charisma: The Effects of Metaphor." *The Leadership Quarterly*, 16 (2005); 287–294.

51 Bryman (1992), ch. 6; B.M. Bass and B.J. Avolio, "Transformational Leadership: A Response to Critics," in M.M. Chemers and R. Ayman (eds.), *Leadership Theory and Practice: Perspectives and Directions* (San Diego, CA: Academic Press, 1993), pp. 49–80; Kevin B. Lowe, K. Galen Kroeck, and Nagaraj Sivasubramanium, "Effectiveness Correlates of Transformational and Transactional Leadership: A Meta-Analytic Review of the MLQ Literature," *Leadership Quarterly* 7 (1996); 385–426.

51A Greg Scott, "Á Leader Emerges," *Southern Alumni*, September, 2006; 23–24, 41.

52 Bass (1996); Bass and Avolio (1993).

53 See Jay A. Conger and Rabindra N. Kanungo, "Training Charismatic Leadership: A Risky and Critical Task," in Jay A. Conger, Rabindra N. Kanungo and Associates (eds.), *Charis-matic Leadership: The Elusive Factor in Organizational Effectiveness* (San Francisco: Jossey-Bass, 1988), ch. 11.

54 See J.R. Kouzas and B.F. Posner, *The Leadership Challenge: How to Get Extraordinary Things Done in Organizations* (San Francisco: Jossey-Bass, 1991).

55 Marshall Sashkin and Molly G. Sashkin, *Leadership That Matters* (San Francisco: Berrett-Koehler, 2003), ch. 10.

55A OB Savvy information from Jay A. Conger and Rabindra N. Kanungo, "Training Charismatic Leadership: A Risky and Critical Task," in J.A. Conger, R.N. Kanungo, et al. (eds.), *Charismatic Leadership: The Elusive Factor in Organizational Effectiveness* (San Francisco: Jossey-Bass, 1988), ch 11.

MARGIN PHOTOS

Curtis Simmons, Boot Camp Commander—"Boot Camp Commander Takes Unique Approach." *Lubbock Avalanche-Journal*, August 6, 2006, p. A-11.

Tailoring Education to the Child—Ray Westbrook, "YWCA's Woman of Excellence for 2007." *Lubbock Avalanche-Journal*, February 13, 2007, p. B1

SOURCE NOTES

Fiedler model based on F.E. Fiedler and M.M. Chemers, *Leadership and Effective Management* (Glenview, IL: Scott, Foresman, 1974).

Path-goal information adapted from Richard N. Osborn, James G. Hunt, and Lawrence R. Jauch, *Organizational Theory: An Integrated Approach* (New York: Wiley, 1980), p. 464.

From Paul Hersey and Kenneth H. Blanchard, *Management of Organizational Behavior* (Englewood Cliffs, NJ: Prentice Hall, 1988), p. 171. Used by permission.

Based on Steven Kerr and John Jermier, "Substitutes for Leadership: Their Meaning and Measurement," *Organizational Behavior and Human Performance 22* (1978); 387; Fred Luthans, *Organizational Behavior* 6th ed. (New York: McGraw-Hill, 1992), ch. 10.

Close and distant based on Boas Shamir, "Social Distance and Charisma: Theoretical Notes and an Exploratory Study," *The Leadership Quarterly* 6 (1995); 19–48.

Chapter 12

ENDNOTES

1 "Interview with Lieutenant General William J. Lennox, Jr., Superintendent of the U.S. Military Academy at West Point," *Leader to Leader: Leadership Breakthroughs from West Point,* Special Supplement (2005), pp. 85–92.

2 This discussion is built primarily upon John Antonakis, Bruce J. Avolio, and Nagaraj Sivasubramaniam, "Context and Leadership: An Examination of the Nine-Factor Full-Range Leadership Theory Using the Multi-factor Leadership Questionnaire," *The Leadership Quarterly* 14 (2003), pp. 261–296.

[3] Craig L. Pearce and Jay A. Conger, eds., *Shared Leadership* (Thousand Oaks, CA: Sage Publications, 2003), Chapter 1.

[4] This discussion relies heavily on that of Katrina A. Zalatan and Gary Yukl, "Team Leadership," in George R. Goethals, Georgia J. Sorenson, and James McGregor Burns, *Encyclopedia of Leadership* vol. A (Great Barrington, MA, Berkshire/Sage, 2004), pp. 1529–1552.

[5] Jeffery D. Houghton, Christopher P. Neck, and Charles C. Manz, "Self Leadership and Super Leadership," in *Shared Leadership*, ed. Craig L. Pearce and Jay A. Conger, pp. 123–140 (Thousand Oaks, CA: Sage Publications, 2003).

[6] This discussion is built primarily upon Robert J. House, Paul J. Hanges, Mansour Javidan, Peter W. Dorfman, and Vipin Gupta, eds., *Culture, Leadership, and Organizations* (Thousand Oaks, CA: Sage Publications, 2004); Mansour Javidan, Peter W. Dorfman, Mary Sully de Luque, and Robert J. House, "In the Eye of the Beholder: Cross Cultural Lessons in Leadership from Project GLOBE," *Academy of Management Perspectives* 20.1 (2006), pp. 67–90.

[7] This discussion of the multiple-level perspective is based primarily on James G. Hunt, *Leadership: A New Synthesis* (Thousand Oaks, CA: Sage Publications, 1991) and Ken Shepard, Jerry L. Gray, James G. (Jerry) Hunt & Sarah McArthur (eds.), *Organization Design, Levels of Work and Human Capability* (Ontario, Canada, Global Organization Design Society, 2007), p. 534.

[8] This discussion of top-management teams is based primarily on Amy C. Edmonson, Michael A. Roberto, and Michael D. Watkins, "A Dynamic Model of Top Management Team Effectiveness: Matching Unstructured Task Streams," *The Leadership Quarterly* 14 (2003), pp. 297–325.

[9] This discussion of Boal and Hooijberg's strategic leadership perspective is based primarily on Kimberly B. Boal and Robert Hooijberg, "Strategic Leadership Research: Moving On," *The Leadership Quarterly* 11 (2000), pp. 515–550.

[10] Robert E. Quinn, Sue R. Faerman, Michael P. Thompson, and Michael R. McGrath, *Becoming a Master Manager*, 4th ed. (Hoboken, NJ: Wiley, 2006).

[10A] David Kirkpatrick, "This PC Wants to Save the World," *Fortune* (October 30, 2006), p. 82.

[11] Michael E. Brown and Linda K. Trevino, "Ethical Leadership: A Review and Future Directions," *The Leadership Quarterly* 17 (2006), pp. 595–616.

[12] Based on Bruce J. Avolio and William L. Gardner, "Authentic Leadership Development: Getting to the Root of Positive Forms of Leadership," *The Leadership Quarterly* 16 (2005), pp. 315–338; William L. Gardner, Bruce J. Avolio, Fred Luthans, Douglas R. May, and Fred O. Walumba," 'Can You See the Real Me?' A Self-Based Model of Authentic Leader and Follower Development," *The Leadership Quarterly* 16 (2005), pp 343–372, Bill George, Peter Sims, Andrew N. McLean, and Diana Mayer, "Discovering Your Authentic Leadership," *Harvard Business Review* (February 2007), pp. 1–9.

[12A] Adapted from Karlene Grabner, "Giving Circles Bring People Together for Sake of Charity" (*Lubbock Avalanche-Journal* November 12, 2006), p. D6.

[13] Judith A. Ross, "Making Every Leadership Moment Matter," *Harvard Management Update* (September 2006), pp. 3–5.

[13A] Michael Silver, "The Top of His Game," *Sports Illustrated* March 12, 2007, pp. 69–77.

[14] James K. Dittmar, "An Interview with Larry Spears," *Journal of Leadership & Organizational Studies* 13 (2006), pp. 108–118.

[15] Based on Lewis W. Fry, "Toward a Paradigm of Spiritual Leadership," *The Leadership Quarterly* 16 (2005), pp. 619–622. Lewis W. Fry, Steve Vitucci, and Marie Cedillo, "Spiritual Leadership and Army Transformation: Theory, Measurement, and Establishing a Baseline," *The Leadership Quarterly* 16.5 (2005), pp. 835–862.

[16] Michael Beer and Nitin Mitra, "Cracking the Code of Change," *Harvard Business Review* (May–June, 2000), p. 133.

[17] See David Nadler and Michael Tushman, *Strategic Organizational Design* (Glenview, IL: Scott, Foresman, 1988); Noel M. Tichy, "Revolutionize Your Company," *Fortune* (December 13, 1993), pp. 114–118.

[18] Jerry I. Porras and Robert C. Silvers, "Organization Development and Transformation," *Annual Review of Psychology* 42 (1991), pp. 51–78

[19] The classic description of organizations on these terms is by Harold J. Leavitt, "Applied Organizational Change in Industry: Structural, Technological and Humanistic Approaches," in *Handbook of Organizations,* ed. James G. March (Chicago: Rand McNally, 1965). This application is developed from Robert A. Cooke, "Managing Change in Organizations," in *Management Principles for Nonprofit Organizations,* ed. Gerald Zaltman (New York: American Management Association, 1979). See also David A. Nadler, "The Effective Management of Organizational Change," pp. 358–369 in *Handbook of Organizational Behavior*, ed. Jay W. Lorsch (Englewood Cliffs, NJ: Prentice-Hall, 1987).

[20] Beer and Mitra, 2000, p. 133.

[20A] John P. Kotter, "Why Transformation Efforts Fail," *Harvard Business Review* (March–April 1995), pp. 59–67.

[21] Kurt Lewin, "Group Decision and Social Change," pp. 459–473 in *Readings in Social Psychology,* ed. G. E. Swanson, T. M. Newcomb, and E. L. Hartley (New York: Holt, Rinehart & Winston, 1952).

[22] Noel M. Tichy and Mary Anne Devanna, *The Transformational Leader* (John Wiley & Sons, 1986), p. 44.

[23] The change strategies are described in Robert Chin and Kenneth D. Benne, "General Strategies for Effecting Changes in Human Systems," pp. 22–45 in *The Planning of Change,* 3rd ed. Warren G. Bennis, Kenneth D. Benne,

Robert Chin, and Kenneth E. Corey (New York: Holt, Rinehart & Winston, 1969).

[24] Example developed from an exercise reported in J. William Pfeffer and John E. Jones, *A Handbook of Structural Experiences for Human Relations Training,* vol. II (La Jolla, CA: University Associates, 1973).

[24A] John Amis, Trevor Slack, and C. R. Hinings, "The Pace, Sequence, and Linearity of Radical Change," *Academy of Management Journal* 47.1 (2004), pp. 15–40.

[25] Pfeffer and Jones, 1973.

[26] Pfeffer and Jones, 1973.

[27] Donald Klein, "Some Notes on the Dynamics of Resistance to Change: The Defender Role," in Bennis et al., 1969, pp. 117–124.

[28] See Everett M. Roberts, *Communication of Innovations,* 3rd ed. (New York: Free Press, 1993).

[29] Everett M. Roberts, 1993.

[30] John P. Kotter and Leonard A. Schlesinger, "Choosing Strategies for Change," *Harvard Business Review* 57 (March–April 1979), pp. 109–112.

MARGIN PHOTOS

Big Sports: Big Business—Adapted from L. Jon Wertheim, "Portrait of a Powerhouse: The Athletic Director Gene Smith," *Sports Illustrated*; March 5, 2007, p.58.

Nathalie Sanchez—Olivia Munoz, "College Students Use Spring Break to Help Out-of-Work Farmworkers," *Lubbock Avalanche-Journal* (March 18, 2007), p. C9.

Fred Smith of FedEx on Change—Ellen Florian, "I Have a Cast-Iron Stomach," *Fortune* (August 1, 2006).

SOURCE NOTES

Note: H=high rank; M=medium rank; L=low rank when compared against the impact the culturally endorsed implicit leadership theory (CLT) has for each leadership dimension.

Chapter 13

ENDNOTES

[1] www.plantemorand.com.

[2] For concise overviews see Susan J. Miller, David J. Hickson, and David C. Wilson, "Decision-Making in Organizations," pp. 293–312 in *Handbook of Organizational Studies,* ed. Steward R. Clegg, Cynthia Hardy, and Walter Nord (London: Sage, 1996); George P. Huber, *Managerial Decision Making* (Glenview, IL: Scott, Foresman, 1980).

[2A] Information from www.nokia.com.

[3] Fons Trompenaars, *Riding the Waves of Culture: Understanding Cultural Diversity in Business* (London: Nicholas Brealey, 1993), p. 6.

[4] Ibid.

[5] For a good discussion of decision making in Japanese organizations see Min Chen, *Asian Management Systems* (New York: Routledge, 1995).

[6] Nancy J. Adler, *International Dimensions of Organizational Behavior,* 4th ed. (Boston: PWS-Kent, 2002).

[7] Ibid.

[8] We would like to thank Kristi M. Lewis for emphasizing the importance of identifying criteria and weighing criteria, and for urging us to include this section on ethics.

[9] For an expanded discussion of ethical frameworks for decision making see Joseph R. Desjardins, *Busines, Ethics and the Environment* (Upper Saddle River, NJ: Pearson Education, 2007); Linda A. Travino and Katherine A. Nelson, *Managing Business Ethics* (New York: Wiley, 1995); Saul W. Gellerman, "Why 'Good' Managers Make Bad Ethical Choices," *Harvard Business Review* 64 (July–August 1986), pp. 85–90; Barbara Ley Toffler, *Tough Choices: Managers Talk Ethics* (New York: Wiley, 1986).

[10] Stephen Fineman, "Emotion and Organizing," pp. 542–580 in *Handbook of Organizational Studies,* ed. Steward R. Clegg, Cynthia Hardy, and Walter Nord (London: Sage, 1996).

[11] This section stems from the classic work on decision making found in Michael D. Cohen, James G. March, and Johan P Olsen, "The Garbage Can Model of Organizational Choice," *Administrative Science Quarterly* 17 (1972), pp. 1–25; and James G. March and Herbert A. Simon, *Organizations* (New York: John Wiley, 1958), pp. 137–142.

[12] For an interesting historical discussion and international applications see Takahashi Nobuo, "A Single Garbage Can Model and the Degree of Anarchy in Japanese Firms," *Human Relations* 50.1 (1997), pp. 91–109.

[13] See KPMG, Enterprise Risk Management Services, www.kpmg.com.

[14] www.REI.com.

[14A] Information from Paul Nutt, "Decision Debacles and How to Avoid Them," *Business Strategy Review* 21.2 (2001), pp. 23–34.

[15] This traditional distinction is often attributed to Herbert Simon, *Administrative Behavior* (New York: Free Press, 1945), but an available source is Herbert Simon, *The New Science of Management Decision* (New York: Harper and Row, 1960).

[16] Ibid.

[17] For a historical review see Leight Buchanan and Andrew O'Connell, "Thinking Machines," *Harvard Business Review* 84.1 (2006), pp. 38–49. For recent applications see Jiju Antony, Raj Anand, Maneesh Kumar, and M. K. Tiwari, "Multiple Response Optimization Using Taguchi Methodology and Nero-Fuzzy Based Model," *Journal of Manufacturing Technology Management* 17.7 (2006), pp. 908–112.; Craig Boutilier, "The Influence of Influence Diagrams on Artificial Intelligence," *Decision Analysis* 2.4 (2005), pp. 229–232.

[18] Also see Mary Zey, ed., *Decision Making: Alternatives to Rational Choice Models* (Thousand Oaks, CA: Sage Publications, 1992).

[19] Simon, *Organizations,* 1958.

[20] For discussions see Cohen, March, and Olsen, 1972; Miller, Hickson, and Wilson, 1996; and Michael Masuch and Perry LaPontin; "Beyond Garbage Cans: An AI Model of Organizational Choice," *Administrative Science Quarterly* 34 (1989), pp. 38–67.

[21] Weston H. Agor, *Intuition in Organizations* (Newbury Park, CA: Sage, 1989).

[22] See Henry Mintzberg, "Planning on the Left Side and Managing on the Right," *Harvard Business Review* 54 (July–August 1976), pp. 51–63.

[23] See Weston H. Agor, "How Top Executives Use Their Intuition to Make Important Decisions," *Business Horizons* 29 (January–February, 1986), pp. 49–53; Agor, 1989.

[24] The classic work in this area is found in a series of articles by D. Kahneman and A. Tversky: "Subjective Probability: A Judgement of Representativeness," *Cognitive Psychology* 3 (1972), pp. 430–454; "On the Psychology of Prediction," *Psychological Review* 80 (1973), pp. 237–251; "Prospect Theory: An Analysis of Decision Under Risk," *Econometrica* 47 (1979), pp. 263–291; "Psychology of Preferences," *Scientific American* (1982), pp. 161–173; "Choices, Values, Frames," *American Psychologist* 39 (1984), pp. 341–350.

[25] Definitions and subsequent discussion based on Max H. Bazerman, *Judgement in Managerial Decision Making*, 3rd ed. (New York: John Wiley, 1994).

[26] See Cameron M. Ford and Dennis A. Gioia, *Creative Action in Organizations* (Thousand Oaks, CA: Sage, 1995).

[27] G. Wallas, *The Art of Thought* (New York: Harcourt, 1926). Cited in Bazerman, 1994.

[28] E. Glassman, "Creative Problem Solving," *Supervisory Management* (January 1989), pp. 21–26; B. Kabanoff and J. R. Rossiter, "Recent Developments in Applied Creativity," *International Review of Industrial and Organizational Psychology* 9 (1994), pp. 283–324.

[29] www.pella.com.

[30] I. L. Thompson and L. Brajkovich, "Improving Creativity of Organizational Work Groups," *Academy of Management Journal* 17 (2003), pp. 96–115.

[31] Ibid.

[32] For further discussion of these factors see R. W. Woodmand, J. E. Sawyer, and R. W. Griffin, "Toward a Theory of Organizational Creativity," *Academy of Management Review* 18 (2003), pp. 293–321; M. A. Glyn, "Innovative Genius: A Framework for Relating Individual and Organizational Intelligences to Innovation," *Academy of Management Review* 21 (1996), pp. 112–1134; C. M. Ford, "A Theory of Individual Creativity in Multiple Social Domains," *Academy of Management Review* 24 (1999), pp. 286–307.

[33] R. Drazen, M. Glenn, and R. Kazanijan, "Multilevel Theorizing about Creativity in Organizations: A Sensemaking Perspective," *Academy of Management Review* 21 (1999), pp. 286–307.

[34] Ibid.

[35] Ibid.

[36] For recent studies see J. Perry Smith and C. Shalley, "The Social Side of Creativity: A State and Dynamic Social Network Perspective," *Academy of Management Review* 28 (2003), pp. 89–101; S. Tagaar, "Individual Creativity and Group Ability to Utilize Individual Creative Resources: A Multilevel Model," *Academy of Management Journal* 45 (2002), pp. 315–330.

[37] Ibid.

[38] See, for instance, Peter M. Allen and Lia Varga, "A Coevolutionary Complex Systems Perspective on Information Systems," *Journal of Information Technology* 21.4 (2006), pp. 229–247.

[39] Ibid.

[40] James A. F. Stoner, *Management*, 2nd ed. (Englewood Cliffs, NJ: Prentice Hall, 1982), pp. 167–168.

[41] Information from www.gore.com. and www.gore.com/Gore CEO Terri Kelly featured in *Fastle Company* Magazine.

[42] They may also try and include too many others as shown by Phillip G. Clampitt and M. Lee Williams, "Decision Downsizing," *MIT Sloan Management Review* 48.2 (2007), pp. 77–89.

[43] Paul C. Nutt, "Surprising But True: Half the Decisions in Organizations Fail," *Academy of Management Executive* 13.4 (1999), pp. 75–90.

[44] Victor H. Vroom and Philip W. Yetton, *Leadership and Decision Making* (Pittsburgh: University of Pittsburgh Press, 1973); Victor H. Vroom and Arthur G. Jago, *The New Leadership* (Englewood Cliffs, NJ: Prentice Hall, 1988).

[45] Barry M. Staw, "The Escalation of Commitment to a Course of Action," *Academy of Management Review* 6 (1981), pp. 577–587; Barry M. Staw and Jerry Ross, "Knowing When to Pull the Plug," *Harvard Business Review* 65 (March–April 1987), pp. 68–74. See also Glen Whyte, "Escalating Commitment to a Course of Action: A Reinterpretation," *Academy of Management Review* 11 (1986), pp. 311–321.

[46] Joel Brockner, "The Escalation of Commitment to a Failing Course of Action: Toward Theoretical Progress," *Academy of Management Review* 17 (1992), pp. 39–61; J. Ross and B. M. Staw, "Organizational Escalation and Exit: Lessons from the Shoreham Nuclear Power Plant," *Academy of Management Journal* 36 (1993), pp. 701–732.

[47] See Brockner, 1992; Ross and Staw, 1993; J. Z. Rubin, "Negotiation: An Introduction to Some Issues and Themes," *American Behavioral Scientist* 27 (1983), pp. 135–147.

[48] G. McNamara, H. Moon, and P. Bromiley, "Banking on Commitment: Intended and Unintended Consequences of

Organizations' Attempt to Attenuate Escalation of Commitment, *Academy of Management Journal* 45 (2002), pp. 443–452.

MARGIN PHOTOS

Decentralized Decision Making at Sterling Bank—www.sterlingbank.com.

Innovation and Decision Daking at Jack in the Box—www.jackinthebox.com.

Chapter 14

ENDNOTES

[1] Information from Jane Spencer, "To Sell PCs, Lenovo CEO Hits the Sky," *Wall Street Journal* (November 21, 2006), pp. B1, B4; "Bill Amelio, CEO of Lenovo," www.cnn.worldnews (February 26, 2007).

[2] Surveys reported online at the American Management Association Web site (www.amanet.org): "The Passionate Organization" (September 26–29, 2000) and "Managerial Skills and Competence" (March/April 2000).

[3] See Angelo S. DeNisi and Abraham N. Kluger, "Feedback Effectiveness: Can 360-Degree Appraisals Be Improved?" *Academy of Management Executive* 14 (2000): 129–139.

[4] Networking is considered an essential managerial activity by Kotter (1982).

[5] Thomas J. Peters and Robert H. Waterman, Jr., *In Search of Excellence* (New York: Harper & Row, 1983).

[6] Patricia Kitchen, "Businesses Beginning to See Benefits of Employing Wikis," *The Columbus Dispatch* (March 26, 2007), pp. C1,C2.

[7] See Robert H. Lengel and Richard L. Daft, "The Selection of Communication Media as an Executive Skill," *Academy of Management Executive* (August 1998): 225–232.

[8] *Business Week* (May 16, 1994), p. 8.

[9] "Sun Power: Is the Center of the Computing Universe Changing?" *Business Week* (January 18, 1999).

[10] See Axelrod (1996).

[11] Information from "Chapter 2," *Kellogg* (Winter 2004), p. 6; "Room to Read," *Northwestern* (Spring 2007), pp. 32–33.

[12] See Richard L. Birdwhistell, *Kinesics and Context* (Philadelphia: University of Pennsylvania Press, 1970).

[13] Edward T. Hall, *The Hidden Dimension* (Garden City, NY: Doubleday, 1966).

[14] See D. E. Campbell, "Interior Office Design and Visitor Response," *Journal of Applied Psychology* 64 (1979):648–653; P. C. Morrow and J. C. McElroy, "Interior Office Design and Visitor Response: A Constructive Replication," *Journal of Applied Psychology* 66 (1981):646–650.

[15] M. P. Rowe and M. Baker, "Are You Hearing Enough Employee Concerns?" *Harvard Business Review* 62 (May/June 1984): 127–135.

[16] This discussion is based on Carl R. Rogers and Richard E. Farson, "Active Listening" (Chicago: Relations Center of the University of Chicago).

[17] Modified from an example in ibid.

[18] N. Shivapriya, "Accenture All Set to Venture into Corporate Training," *Economic Times* (February 17, 2007), p. 5.

[19] See C. Bamum and N. Woliansky, "Taking Cues from Body Language," *Management Review* 78 (1989):59; S. Bochner (ed.), *Cultures in Contact: Studies in Cross-Cultural Interaction* (London: Pergamon, 1982); A. Furnham and S. Bochner, *Culture Shock: Psychological Reactions to Unfamiliar Environments* (London: Methuen, 1986); "How Not to Do International Business," *Business Week* (April 12, 1999); Yon Kagegama, "Tokyo Auto Show Highlights," Associated Press (October 24, 2001).

[20] Edward T. Hall, *Beyond Culture* (New York: Doubleday, 1976).

[21] Quotes from "Lost in Translation," *Wall Street Journal* (May 18, 2004), pp. B1, B6.

[22] See Gary P. Ferraro. "The Need for Linguistic Proficiency in Global Business," *Business Horizons* 39 (May/June 1966):39–46.

[23] Information from Chad Terhune and Joann S. Lublin, "Pepsi's New CEO Doesn't Keep Her Opinions Bottled Up," *Wall Street Journal* (August 15, 2006), pp. B1, B7; William Kay, "Pepsico's New CEO Adds Fizz to U.S. Female Elite," *Sunday Times* (August 30, 2006), p. 3.22; "Nooyi Elected Pepsi Board Chairman," *Economic Times* (February 6, 2007), p. 8.

[24] This example is from Richard V. Farace, Peter R. Monge, and Hamish M. Russell, *Communicating and Organizing* (Reading, MA: Addison-Wesley, 1977), pp. 97–98.

[25] The statements are from *Business Week* (July 6, 1981), p. 107.

[26] See A. Mehrabian, *Silent Messages* (Belmont, CA: Wadsworth, 1981).

[26A] *Reference:* Kimberly D. Elsbach, "Interpreting Workplace Identities: The Role of Office Décor," *Journal of Organizational Behavior* 25 (2004), pp. 99–128.

[27] This research is reviewed by John C. Athanassiades, "The Distortion of Upward Communication in Hierarchical Organizations. " *Academy of Management Journal* 16 (June 1973):207–226.

[28] F. Lee, "Being Polite and Keeping Mum. How Bad News Is Communicated in Organizational Hierarchies," *Journal of Applied Social Psychology* 23 (1993):1124–1149.

[29] Waterman (1983).

[30] Information from Old 26; Lewis, 2007.

[31] Diane Brady, "*!@the E-Mail. Can We Talk?" *Business Week* (December 4, 2006), pp. 109–110.

[32] See Daniel Goleman, *Social Intelligence: The New Science of Human Relationships* (New York: Bantam Books, 2006).

[33] Katherine Reynolds Lewis, "Digital Debris," *Columbus Dispatch* (February 26, 2007), p. B1.

[34] Reported in "Big Brother Inc.," www.pecomputing.com (March 2000), p. 88. See "My Boss, Big Brother," *Business Week* (January 22, 1996), p. 56.

[35] Deborah Tannen, *Talking 9 to 5* (New York: Avon, 1995).

[36] Deborah Tannen, *You Just Don't Understand: Women and Men in Conversation* (New York: Ballantine, 1991).

[37] Deborah Tannen, "The Power of Talk: Who Gets Heard and Why," *Harvard Business Review* (September/October, 1995): 138–148.

[38] Reported by *Working Woman* (November 1995), p. 14.

[39] Ibid.

[40] For an editorial opinion, see Jayne Tear, "They Just Don't Understand Gender Dynamics." *Wall Street Journal* (November 20, 1995), p. A14.

SOURCE NOTES

Information from "Entrepreneurs Speak at HBS." *Harvard Business School Bulletin* (February 1999):6; corporate Web site: www.virgin.com.

Monsanto: Information from Timothy D. Schellhardt, "Monsanto Best on Box Buddies," *Wall Street Journal* (February 23, 1999), p. 131.

Information from "How They Feel," *Columbus Dispatch* (February 20, 2004), p. D1.

MARGIN PHOTOS

Online Communities Are Big Business—Information from David Enrich, "Turning an Online Community into a Business," *Wall Street Journal* (February 27, 2007), p. B8.

No e-mail Fridays—Information from Brady, 2006.

Chapter 15

ENDNOTES

[1] Information from "From 'Blank Looks' to Blank Checks," *Business Week Enterprise* (December 7, 1998), pp. 18–20: www.capitalacrossamerica.org; and www.boovers.com.

[2] See, for example, Henry Mintzberg, *The Nature of Managerial Work* (New York: Harper & Row, 1973); John R. P. Kotter, *The General Managers* (New York: Free Press, 1982).

[3] One of the classic discussions is by Richard E. Walton, *Interpersonal Peacemaking: Confrontations and Third-Party Consultation* (Reading, MA: Addison-Wesley, 1969).

[4] Kenneth W. Thomas and Warren H. Schmidt, "A Survey of Managerial Interests with Respect to Conflict," *Academy of Management Journal* 19 (1976): 315–318.

[5] For a good overview, see Richard E. Walton, *Managing Conflict: Interpersonal Dialogue and Third Party Roles*, 2nd ed. (Reading, MA: Addison-Wesley, 1987); Dean Tjosvold,

The Conflict-Positive Organization: Stimulate Diversity and Create Unity (Reading, MA: Addison-Wesley, 1991).

[6] Walton (1969).

[7] Ibid.

[8] Information from Michael M. Phillips, Marcus Walker, and Mark Whitehouse, "Financial Pioneer of 'Microloans' Wins Nobel Prize," *Wall Street Journal* (October 14–15, 2006), pp. B1, B5; "A Big Stage Set for Small Loans," *Business Week* (November 27, 2006), p. 82; Jay Greene, "Taking Tiny Loans to the Next Level," *Business Week* (November 27, 2006), pp. 76–79.

[9] Information from Hal Lancaster, "Performance Reviews: Some Bosses Try a Fresh Approach," *Wall Street Journal* (December 1, 1998), p. B1.

[10] Richard E. Walton and John M. Dutton, "The Management of Interdepartmental Conflict: A Model and Review," *Administrative Science Quarterly* 14 (1969): 73–84.

[11] Information from Stanley Reed, "The Opening of Libya," *Business Week* (March 12, 2007), pp. 54–57.

[12] Geert Hofstede. *Culture's Consequences: International Differences in Work-Related Values* (Beverly Hills, CA: Sage Publications, 1980), and Geert Hofstede, "Cultural Constraints in Management Theories," *Academy of Management Executive* 7 (1993): 81–94.

[13] Information from "Capitalizing on Diversity: Navigating the Seas of the Multicultural Workforce and Workplace," *Business Week,* Special Advertising Section (December 4, 1998).

[14] These stages are consistent with the conflict models described by Alan C. Filley, *Interpersonal Conflict Resolution* (Glenview. IL: Scott, Foresman, 1975); and Louis R. Pondy, "Organizational Conflict. Concepts and Models," *Administrative Science Quarterly* (September 1967): pp. 269–320.

[15] Information from Ken Brown and Gee L. Lee. "Lucent Fires Top China Executives," *The Wall Street Journal* (April 7, 2004), p. A8.

[16] Walton and Dutton (1969).

[17] Rensis Likert and Jane B. Likert. *New Ways of Managing Conflict* (New York: McGraw-Hill, 1976).

[18] See Jay Galbraith, *Designing Complex Organizations* (Reading, MA: Addison-Wesley, 1973); David Nadler and Michael Tushman, *Strategic Organizational Design* (Glenview, IL: Scott, Foresman, 1988).

[19] E. M. Eisenberg and M. G. Witten, "Reconsidering Openness in Organizational Communication," *Academy of Management Review* 12 (1987): 418–426.

[20] R. G. Lord and M. C. Kernan, "Scripts as Determinants of Purposeful Behavior in Organizations," *Academy of Management Review* 12 (1987): 265–277.

[21] See Filley (1975); L. David Brown, *Managing Conflict at Organizational Interfaces* (Reading, MA: Addison Wesley, 1983).

[22] Ibid., pp. 27, 29.

[23] For discussions, see Robert R. Blake and Jane Strygley Mouton, "The Fifth Achievement," *Journal of Ap-*

plied Behavioral Science 6 (1970): 413–427; Kenneth Thomas, "Conflict and Conflict Management," in M. D. Dunnett (ed.), *Handbook of Industrial and Organizational Behavior* (Chicago: Rand McNally, 1976), pp. 889–935; and Kenneth W. Thomas, "Toward Multi-Dimensional Values in Teaching: The Examples of Conflict Behaviors," *Academy of Management Review 2* (1977): 484–490.

[24] See, for example, Valerie Patterson, "How to Negotiate Pay in a Tough Economy," *The Wall Street Journal* (March 29, 2004), p. R7.

[25] For an excellent overview, see Roger Fisher and William Ury. *Getting to Yes: Negotiating Agreement Without Giving In* (New York: Penguin, 1983). See also James A. Wall Jr., *Negotiation: Theory and Practice* (Glenview, IL: Scott, Foresman, 1985).

[26] Roy J. Lewicki and Joseph A. Litterer, *Negotiation* (Homewood, IL: Irwin, 1985), pp. 315–319.

[27] Ibid., pp. 328–329.

[28] For a good discussion, see Michael H. Bond, *Behind the Chinese Face* (London: Oxford University Press. 1991); and Richard D. Lewis, *When Cultures Collide*, Ch. 23 (London: Nicholas Brealey Publishing, 1996).

[29] Information from Robert Moskowitz, "How to Negotiate Increase," www.worktree.com (retrieved March 8, 2007); Mark Gordon, "Negotiating What You're Worth," *Harvard Management Communication Letter* 2.1 (Winter 2005); Dona DeZube, "Salary Negotiation Know-How," www.monster.com (retrieved March 8, 2007).

[30] The following discussion is based on Fisher and Ury (1983); and Lewicki and Litterer (1985).

[31] This example is developed from Max H. Bazerman, *Judgment in Managerial Decision Making,* 2nd ed. (New York: Wiley, 1991), pp. 106–108.

[32] For a detailed discussion, see Fisher and Ury (1983); and Lewicki and Litterer (1985).

[33] Developed from Bazerman (1991), pp. 127–141.

[34] Fisher and Ury (1983), p. 33.

[35] Lewicki and Litterer (1985), pp. 177–181.

[35A] Timothy D. Golden, John F. Veiga, and Zeki Simsek, "Telecommuting's Differential Impact on Work-Family Conflict: Is There No Place Like Home?" *Journal of Applied Psychology* 91.6 (2006), pp. 1340–1350.

MARGIN PHOTOS

Boeing builds for a white-collar and blue-collar togetherness—Information from "Mixing White and Blue Collar," *Fortune* (February 19, 2007), p. 74.

Native Americans Pursue Outsourcing—Information from Jena McGregor, "The Other Indian Outsourcer," *Business Week* (November 6, 2006), p. 40.

Chapter 16

ENDNOTES

[1] This description and quote were provided by Marcus B. Osborn.

[2] For a recent treatment see Ali Danisman, C. R. Hinnings, and Trevor Slack, "Integration and Differentiation in Institutional Values: An Empirical Investigation in the Field of Canadian National Sport Organizations," *Canadian Journal of Administrative Sciences* 23.4 (2006), pp. 301–315. This and many analyses of corporate culture are based on Edgar Schein, "Organizational Culture," *American Psychologist* 45 (1990), pp. 109–119; and Edgar Schein, *Organizational Culture and Leadership* (San Francisco: Jossey-Bass, 1985).

[3] www.cantor.com/heritage/.

[4] Schein, 1990.

[4A] Information from www.cantor.com/heritage/.

[5] See www.dellapp.us.dell.com.

[6] This example was reported in an interview with Edgar Schein, "Corporate Culture Is the Real Key to Creativity," *Business Month* (May 1989), pp. 73–74.

[7] See Schein, 1985.

[8] Jeffery Pfeffer, *The Human Equation: Building Profits by Putting People First* (Boston: Harvard Business School Press, 1998).

[9] For an extended discussion, see J. M. Beyer and H. M. Trice, "How an Organization's Rites Reveal Its Culture," *Organizational Dynamics* (Spring 1987), pp. 27–41.

[10] A. Cooke and D. M. Rousseau, "Behavioral Norms and Expectations: A Quantitative Approach to the Assessment of Organizational Culture," *Group and Organizational Studies* 13 (1988), pp. 245–273.

[11] Mary Trefry, "A Double-edged Sword: Organizational Culture in Multicultural Organizations," *International Journal of Management* 23 (2006), pp 563–576; J. Martin and C. Siehl, "Organization Culture and Counterculture," *Organizational Dynamics* 12 (1983), pp. 52–64.

[12] www.apple-history.com

[13] For a recent discussion of the clash of corporate cultures see George Lodorfos and Agyenim Boateng, "The Role of Culture in the Merger and Acquisition Process: Evidence from the European Chemical Industry," *Management Decision* 44 (2006), pp. 1405–1410.

[14] See R. N. Osborn, "The Aftermath of the Daimler and Detroit," working paper, Department of Management, Wayne State University 2005.

[15] Ibid.

[16] Ibid.

[16A] Information from www.flowserve.com.

[17] Taylor Cox Jr., "The Multicultural Organization," *Academy of Management Executive,* 2.2 (May 1991), pp. 34–47.

[18] For early work see T. Deal and A. Kennedy, *Corporate Culture* (Reading, MA: Addison-Wesley, 1982); T. Peters and R. Waterman, *In Search of Excellence* (New York: Harper & Row, 1982). More recent studies are summarized in Joanne Martin and Peter Frost, "The Organizational Culture War Games: The Struggle for Intellectual Dominance," pp. 599–621 in *Handbook of Organization Studies*, ed. Stewart R. Clegg, Cynthia Hardy, and Walter R. Nord (London: Sage, 1996).

[19] See Schein, 1985, pp. 52–57; Schein, 1990.

[20] For a discussion from a different perspective see Anat Rafaeli and Michael G. Pratt, eds., *Artifacts and Organizations: Beyond Mere Symbols* (Mahwah, NJ: Lawrence Erlbaum Associates, 2006).

[21] Schein, 1990.

[22] www.montereypasta.com.

[23] H. Gertz, *The Interpretation of Culture* (New York: Basic Books, 1973).

[24] See Rafaeli and Pratt, 2006; Beyer and Trice, 1987.

[25] H. M. Trice and J. M. Beyer, "Studying Organizational Cultures through Rites and Ceremonials," *Academy of Management Review* 3 (1984), pp. 633–669.

[26] J. Martin, M. S. Feldman, M. J. Hatch, and S. B. Sitkin, "The Uniqueness Paradox in Organizational Stories," *Administrative Science Quarterly* 28 (1983), pp. 438–453; *Business Week* (November 23, 1992), p. 117.

[27] For a recent study see John Barnes, Donald W. Jackson, Michael D. Hutt, and Ajith Kumar, "The Role of Culture Strength in Shaping Sales Force Outcomes," *Journal of Personal Setting and Sales Management* 26.3 (2006), pp. 255–269. This tradition of strong cultures goes back to work by Deal and Kennedy, 1982, and Peters and Waterman, 1982.

[28] Trice and Beyer, 1984.

[29] R. N. Osborn and D. Jackson, "Leaders, River Boat Gamblers or Purposeful Unintended Consequences," *Academy of Management Journal* 31 (1988), pp. 924–947.

[30] For an interesting twist see John Connolly, "High Performance Cultures," *Business Strategy Review* 17 (2006), pp. 19–32; a more conventional treatment may be found in Martin, Feldman, Hatch, and Sitkin, 1983.

[31] This section is based on R. N. Osborn and C. C. Baughn, *An Assessment of the State of the Field of Organizational Design* (Alexandria, VA: U.S. Army Research Institute, 1994).

[32] www.cisco.com.

[33] www.sherwinwilliams.com.

[33A] Information from www.sherwinwilliams.com.

[34] J. Kerr and J. Slocum, "Managing Corporate Culture through Reward Systems," *Academy of Management Executive* 19.4 (2005), pp. 130–138.

[35] Martin and Frost, 1996.

[36] See G. Hofstede and M. H. Bond, "The Confucius Connection: From Cultural Roots to Economic Growth," *Organizational Dynamics* 16 (1991), pp. 4–21.

[36A] J. Karpoff, D. S. Lee, and G. Martin (2007); "A company's reputation is what gets fried when its books are cooked." www.uwnews.org.

[37] Warner Burke, *Organization Development* (Reading, MA: Addison-Wesley, 1987); Wendell L. French and Cecil H. Bell Jr., *Organization Development*, 4th ed. (Englewood Cliffs, NJ: Prentice-Hall, 1990); Edgar F. Huse and Thomas G. Cummings, *Organization Development and Change*, 4th ed. (St. Paul, MN: West, 1989).

[38] Warren Bennis, "Using Our Knowledge of Organizational Behavior," in Lorsch J. W. (ed), *Handbook of Organizational Behavior* (Englewood Cliffs, NJ: Prentice-Hall, 1987), pp. 29–49.

[39] Excellent overviews are found in Huse and Cummings, 1989, pp. 32–36, 45; and French and Bell, 1990.

[40] Richard Beckhard, "The Confrontation Meeting," *Harvard Business Review* 45 (March–April 1967), pp. 149–155.

[41] See Jacsalyn Sherriton and James Stern, "HR's Role in Culture Change," *HR Focus* 74.4 (1997), pp. 27–29; Dale Zand, "Collateral Organization: A New Change Strategy," *Journal of Applied Behavioral Science* 10 (1974), pp. 63–89; Barry A. Stein and Rosabeth Moss Kanter, "Building the Parallel Organization," *Journal of Applied Behavioral Science* 16 (1980), pp. 371–386.

[42] J. Richard Hackman and Greg R. Oldham, *Work Redesign* (Reading, MA: Addison-Wesley, 1980).

MARGIN PHOTOS

Herman Miller—Courtesy Herman Miller, Inc.

Core Values at LAM—Information from www.lamrc.com

Chapter 17

ENDNOTES

[1] The bulk of this chapter was originally based on Richard N. Osborn, James G. Hunt, and Lawrence R. Jauch, *Organization Theory: Integrated Text and Cases* (Melbourne, FL: Krieger, 1985). For a more recent but consistent view see Lex Donaldson, "The Normal Science of Structural Contingency Theory," pp. 57–76 in *Handbook of Organizational Studies*, ed. Stewart R. Clegg, Cynthia Hardy, and Walter R. Nord (London: Sage, 1996). For a more advanced treatment see W. Richard Scott and Gerald F. Davis, *Organizations and Organizing: Rational and Open Systems* (Englewood Cliffs, NJ: Prentice-Hall, 2007).

[2] For more information about Cummins Inc. and its CEO see www.cummins.com.

[3] Ibid.

[4] H. Talcott Parsons, *Structure and Processes in Modern Societies* (New York: Free Press, 1960).

[5] See B. Bartkus, M. Glassman, and B. McAfee, "Mission Statement Quality and Financial Performance," *European Management Journal* 24.1 (2006), pp. 66–79; J. Peyrefitte and F. R. David, "A Content Analysis of the Mission Statements of United States Firms in Four Industries," *International Journal of Management* 23.2 (2006), pp. 296–305; Terri Lammers, "The Effective and Indispensable Mission Statement," *Inc.* 7.1 (August 1992), p. 23; I. C. MacMillan and A. Meshulack, "Replacement Versus Expansion: Dilemma for Mature U.S. Businesses," *Academy of Management Journal* 26 (1983), pp. 708–726.

[6] Anonymous, "Making Vision Statements Meaningful," *British Journal of Administrative Management* (April–May 2006), p. 17; L. Larwood, C. M. Falbe, M. Kriger, and P. M. Miesing, "Structure and Meaning of Organizational Vision," *Academy of Management Journal* 38:4 (1995), pp. 740–770.

[7] See Scott and Davis, 2007; Stewart R. Clegg and Cynthia Hardy, "Organizations, Organization and Organizing," pp. 1–28 in *Handbook of Organizational Studies*, ed. Clegg, Hardy, and Nord, 1996; William H. Starbuck and Paul C. Nystrom, "Designing and Understanding Organizations," in *Handbook of Organizational Design: Adapting Organizations to Their Environments*, ed. P. C. Nystrom and W. H. Starbuck (New York: Oxford University Press, 1981).

[8] See Jeffery Pfeffer, "Barriers to the Advance of Organization Science," *Academy of Management Review* 18.4 (1994), pp. 599–620; Richard M. Cyert and James G. March, *A Behavioral Theory of the Firm* (Englewood Cliffs, NJ: Prentice-Hall, 1963). A historical view of organizational goals is also found in Charles Perrow, *Organizational Analysis: A Sociological View* (Belmont, CA: Wadsworth, 1970), and in Richard H. Hall, "Organizational Behavior: A Sociological Perspective," pp. 84–95 in *Handbook of Organizational Behavior,* ed. Jay W. Lorsch (Englewood Cliffs, NJ: Prentice-Hall, 1987).

[9] See Osborn, Hunt, and Jauch, 1985, for the historical rates; for differences in survival rates by time of formation in the development of a technology see R. Agarwal, M. Sarkar, and R. Echambadi, "The Conditioning Effect of Time on Firm Survival: An Industry Life Cycle Approach," *Academy of Management Journal* 25 5 (2002), pp. 971–985.

[10] Janice Beyer, Danta P. Ashmos, and R. N. Osborn, "Contrasts in Enacting TQM: Mechanistic vs. Organic Ideology and Implementation," *Journal of Quality Management* 1 (1997), pp. 13–29; for an early treatment, see Paul R. Lawrence and Jay W. Lorsch, *Organization and Environment* (Homewood, IL: Irwin, 1969).

[10A] Information from www.53.com.

[11] Chandler, A. D. op. cit. *The Visible Hand: The Managerial Revolution in American Business* (Cambridge, MA: MIT Press, 1977).

[12] For reviews, see Scott and Davis, 2007; Osborn, Hunt, and Jauch, 1985; Clegg, Hardy, and Nord, 1996.

[12A] Information from Anne L. Davis and Hannah R. Rothstein. "The Effects of the Perceived Behavioral Integrity of Managers on Employee Attitudes: A Meta-analysis," *Journal of Business Ethics* 67.4 (2006), pp. 407–426.

[13] See www.nucor.com.

[14] For instance, see J. Gao, R. Kishore, K. Nam, H. R. Rao, and H. Song, "An Investigation of the Factors That Influence the Duration of IT Outsourcing Relationships," *Decision Support Systems* 42.4 (2007), pp. 21–37; J. E. M. McGee, M. J. Dowling, and W. L. Megginson, "Cooperative Strategy and New Venture Performance: The Role of Business Strategy and Management Experience," *Strategic Management Journal* 16 (1995), pp. 565–580; James B. Quinn, *Intelligent Enterprise: A Knowledge and Service Based Paradigm for Industry* (New York: Free Press, 1992).

[15] F. T. Rothaemel, M. A. Hitt, and L.A. Jobe, " Balancing Vertical Integration and Strategic Outsourcing: Effects on Product Portfolio, Product Success, and Firm Performance," *Strategic Management Journal* 27.11 (2006), pp. 1033–1049. See L. F. Cranor and S. Greensteing, eds., *Communications Policy and Information Technology: Promises, Problems and Prospects* (Cambridge, MA: MIT Press, 2002); P. Candace Deans, *Global Information Systems and Technology: Focus on the Organization and Its Functional Areas* (Harrisburg, PA: Ideal Group, 1994); Osborn, Hunt, and Jauch, 1985.

[16] Haim Levy and Deborah Gunthorpe, *Introduction to Investments,* 2nd ed. (Cincinnati, OH: South-Western, 1999); L. F. Cranor and S. Greensteing, 2002.

[17] William G. Ouchi and M. A. McGuire, "Organization Control: Two Functions," *Administrative Science Quarterly* 20 (1977), pp. 559–569.

[18] This discussion is adapted from W. Edwards Deming, "Improvement of Quality and Productivity through Action by Management," *Productivity Review* (Winter 1982), pp. 12, 22; W. Edwards Deming, *Quality, Productivity and Competitive Position* (Cambridge, MA: MIT Center for Advanced Engineering, 1982).

[19] For related reviews see Scott and Davis, 2007; Osborn, Hunt, and Jauch, 1985; Clegg, Hardy, and Nord, 1996.

[20] See C. Bradley, "Succeeding by (Organizational) Design,": *Decision: Ireland's Business Review* 11:1 (2006), pp. 24–29. See Osborn, Hunt, and Jauch, 1985, pp. 273–303, for a discussion of centralization/decentralization.

[21] Ibid.

[22] For reviews of structural tendencies and their influence on outcomes see also Scott and Davis, 2007; Clegg, Hardy, and Nord, 1996.

[23] Ibid.

[24] For a good discussion of the early use of matrix structures, see Stanley Davis, Paul Lawrence, Harvey Kolodny,

and Michael Beer, *Matrix* (Reading, MA: Addison-Wesley, 1977).

[25] See P. R. Lawrence and J. W. Lorsch, *Organization and Environment: Managing Differentiation and Integration* (Homewood, IL: Richard D. Irwin, 1967).

[26] See Osborn, Hunt, and Jauch, 1985; Scott and Davis, 2007.

[26A] Beth A. Bechky, "Gaffers, Gofers, and Grips: Role-based Coordination in Temporary Organizations, *Organization Science* 17.1 (2006), pp. 3–23.

[27] Max Weber, *The Theory of Social and Economic Organization,* translated by A. M. Henderson and H. T. Parsons (New York: Free Press, 1947).

[28] These relationships were initially outlined by Tom Burns and G. M. Stalken, *The Management of Innovation* (London: Tavistock, 1961).

[29] See Henry Mintzberg, *Structure in Fives: Designing Effective Organizations* (Englewood Cliffs, NJ: Prentice-Hall, 1983).

[30] Ibid.

[31] Ibid.

[32] See Osborn, Hunt, and Jauch, 1984, for an extended discussion.

[33] See Peter Clark and Ken Starkey, *Organization Transitions and Innovation—Design* (London: Pinter 1988).

MARGIN PHOTOS

Noble Drilling—Courtesy Noble Corporation
At Amgen it is high touch to get effective high tech—www.Amgen.com
Land O'Lakes—Lend O' Lakes

Chapter 18

ENDNOTES

[1] See www.generalmills.com.

[2] This view of strategy was drawn from several sources, including, David Simon, Michael Hitt, and Duane Ireland, "Managing Firm Resources in Dynamic Environments to Create Value: Looking Inside the Black Box," *Academy of Management Review* 32 (2007), pp. 273–292. Alfred D. Chandler, *The Visible Hand: The Managerial Revolution in America* (Cambridge, MA: Belnap, 1977); Michael E. Porter, *Competitive Strategy* (New York: Free Press, 1980); L. R. Jauch and R. N. Osborn, "Toward an Integrated Theory of Strategy," *Academy of Management Review* 6 (1981), pp. 491–498; B. Wernefelt, "A Resource-based View of the Firm," *Strategic Management Journal* 5 (1984), pp. 171–180; J. B. Barney, "Firm Resources and Sustained Competitive Advantage," *Journal of Management* 17 (1991), pp. 99–120; Russ Marion, *The Edge of Organization: Chaos and Complexity Theories of Formal Social Systems* (London, Sage, 1999); Arie Lewin, Chris Long, and Timothy Caroll,

"The Coevolution of New Organizational Forms," *Organization Science* 10 (1999), pp. 535–550; Michael A. Hitt, R. Duane Ireland, and Robert E. Hoskisson, *Strategic Management: Competition and Globalization* (Cincinnati, OH: Southwestern, 2001).

[3] See www.generalmills.com.

[4] For the classic popular work see Peter F. Drucker, *Innovation and Entrepreneurship* (New York: Harper, 1985); Edward B. Roberts, "Managing Invention and Innovation," *Research Technology Management* (January–February 1989), pp. 1–19 provides a practitioner perspective, and an interesting extended case study is provided by John Clark, *Managing Innovation and Change* (Thousand Oaks, CA: Sage, 1995).

[5] The terms "exploration" and "exploitation" were popularized by James G. March. See James G. March, "Exploration and Exploitation in Organizational Learning," *Organization Science* 2.1 (1991), pp. 71–87.

[6] For a recent review see Sung-Choon Kang, Shad S. Morris, and Scot A. Shell, "Relational Archetypes, Organizational Learning, and Value Creation: Extending the Human Resource Architecture," *Academy of Management Review* 32 (2007), pp. 236–256.

[7] See Justin J. P. Jansen, Frans A. J. Van Den Bosh, and Henk W. Volberda, "Exploratory Innovation, Exploitive Innovation and Performance: Effects of Organizational Antecedents and Environmental Moderators," *Management Science* 52.11 (2006), pp. 197–226.

[8] G. Huber, "Organizational Learning: The Contributing Process and the Literature," *Organization Science* 2.1 (1991), pp. 88–115.

[9] J. W. Myer and B. Rowan, "Institutionalized Organizations: Formal Structure as Myth and Ceremony," *American Journal of Sociology* 83 (1977), pp. 340–363.

[10] M. Mumford, "The Leadership Quarterly Special Issue on Leading Innovation," *Leadership Quarterly* 14 (2003), pp. 385–387; M. Mumford, G. Scott, B. Gaddis, B. Strange, and J. Strange, "Leading Creative People: Orchestrating Expertise and Relationships" *Leadership Quarterly* 13 (2002), pp. 705–750.

[11] See Bjame Espedal, "Do Organization Routines Change as Experience Changes?" *Journal of Applied Behavior Science,* 42.4 (2006), pp. 468–491.

[12] See Raji Srinivasan, Pamela Haunschild, and Rajdeep Grewal, "Vicarious Learning in Product Development Introductions in the Early Years of a Converging Market," *Management Science* 53.1 (2007), pp. 16–29.

[13] James G. March, *Decisions and Organizations* (Oxford: Basil Blackwell, 1988).

[14] For an illustration with dire consequences see R. N. Osborn and D. H. Jackson, "Leaders, Riverboat Gamblers, or Purposeful Unintended Consequences in the Management of Complex Technologies," *Academy of Management Journal* 31 (1988), pp. 924–947.

[15] O. P. Walsch and G. R. Ungson, "Organization Memory," *Academy of Management Review* 16.1 (1991), pp. 57–91.

[16] Jansen, Van Den Bosh, and Volberda, 2006.

[17] Simon, Hitt, and Ireland, 2007.

[18] This discussion of organizational design was initially based on R. N. Osborn, J. G. Hunt, and L. Jauch, *Organization Theory Integrated Text and Cases* (Melbourne, FL: Krieger, 1984), pp. 123–215. For a more advanced treatment see W. Richard Scott and Gerald F. Davis, *Organizations and Organizing: Rational and Open Systems* (Englewood Cliffs, NJ: Prentice-Hall, 2007).

[19] Simon, Hitt, and Ireland, 2007; Marion, 1999; Jauch and Osborn, 1981.

[20] Porter, 1980.

[21] For example, Simon, Hitt, and Ireland, 2007.

[22] Jeffery Pfeffer, "Producing Sustainable Competitive Advantage through the Effective Management of People," *Academy of Management Executive* 19.4 (2005), pp. 85–115.

[23] Marion, 1999.

[23A] See, Samuel J. Palmisano, "The New CIO: Setting the Innovation Agenda," speech for the first IBM CIO Leadership Forum, Monte Carlo, www.IBM.com.

[24] See Henry Mintzberg, *Structure in Fives: Designing Effective Organizations* (Englewood Cliffs, NJ: Prentice-Hall, 1983).

[25] This inertia may result from fixed routines as well as from resources issues; see Gilbert Clark, "Unbundling the Structure of Inertia: Resource Versus Routine Rigidity," *Academy of Management Journal* 48.6 (2005), pp. 741–763.

[26] See R. Lord and M. Kernan, "Scripts as Determinants of Purposeful Behavior in Organizations," *Academy of Management Review* 12 (1987), pp. 265–278; A. L. Stinchcombe, *Economic Sociology* (New York, Academic Press, 1983).

[27] Osborn and Jackson, 1988.

[28] Ibid.

[29] See Scott and Davis, 2007; Osborn, Hunt, and Jauch, 1984.

[30] Ibid.

[31] See Peter M. Blau and Richard A. Schoenner, *The Structure of Organizations* (New York: Basic Books, 1971); Joan Woodward, *Industrial Organization: Theory and Practice* (London: Oxford University Press, 1965).

[32] Gerardine DeSanctis, "Information Technology," in *Blackwell Encyclopedic Dictionary of Organizational Behavior*, pp. 232–233 in Nigel Nicholson, ed. (Cambridge, MA: Blackwell Publishers, 1995).

[33] James D. Thompson, *Organization in Action* (New York: McGraw-Hill, 1967).

[34] Woodward, 1965.

[34A] See www.millennium.com.

[35] For an updated review see Scott and Davis, 2007; this discussion also incorporates Osborn, Hunt, and Jauch, 1984. Also see Louis Fry, "Technology-Structure Research: Three Critical Issues," *Academy of Management Journal* 25 (1982), pp. 532–552.

[36] Mintzberg, 1983.

[37] See Henry Mintzberg and Alexandra McHugh, "Strategy Formulation in an Adhocracy," *Administrative Science Quarterly* 30.2 (1985), pp. 160–193.

[38] Halit Keskis, Ali E. Akgun, Ayse Gunsel, and Salih Imamoglu, "The Relationship between Adhocracy and Clan Cultures and Tacit Oriented KM Strategy," *Journal of Transnational Management* 10.3 (2005), pp. 39–51.

[39] DeSanctis, 1995.

[40] Prashant C. Palvia, Shailendra C. Palvia, and Edward M. Roche, *Global Information Technology and Systems Management: Key Issues and Trends* (Nashua, NH: Ivy League Publishing, 1996).

[41] DeSanctis, 1995.

[42] Osborn, Hunt, and Jauch, 1984.

[43] Jaana Woiceshyn, "The Role of Management in the Adoption of Technology: A Longitudinal Investigation," *Technology Studies* 4.1 (1997), pp. 62–99; Melissa A. Schilling, "Technological Lockout: An Integrative Model of the Economic and Strategic Factors Driving Technological Success and Failure," *Academy of Management Review* 23.2 (1998), pp. 267–284.

[44] David Lei, Michael Hitt, and Richard A. Bettis, "Dynamic Capabilities and Strategic Management," *Journal of Management* 22 (1996), pp. 547–567.

[45] See M. L. Markus, B. Manville, and C. E. Agres, "What Makes a Virtual Organization Work," *MIT Sloan Management Review* 42 (2002), pp. 13–27; Janice Beyer, Danta P. Ashmos, and R. N. Osborn, "Contrasts in Enacting TQM: Mechanistic vs. Organic Ideology and Implementation," *Journal of Quality Management* 1 (1997), pp. 13–29.

[45a] Markus, Manville, and Agres, 2002.

[46] Jack Veiga and Kathleen Dechant, "Wired World Woes: www.help," *Academy of Management Executive* 11, 3, (1997), pp. 73–79.

[47] Michael A. Hitt, R. Duane Ireland, and Robert E. Hoskisson, *Strategic Management: Competitiveness and Globalization* (Cincinnati, OII: South-Western College Publishing, 2007).

[48] See www.amazon.com.

[49] While this form is known under a variety of names, we emphasize the information technology base that makes it possible. See Peter Senge, Benjamin B. Lichtenstein, Katrin Kaeufer, Hilary Bradbury, and John S. Carol, "Collaborating for Systematic Change," *MIT Sloan Management Review* 48.2 (2007), pp. 44–59; Josh Hyatt, "The Soul of a New Team," *Fortune*, 153.11 (2006), pp. 134–145. Markus, Manville, and Agres, 2002; B. Hedberg, G. Hahlgren, J. Hansson, and N. Olve, *Virtual Organizations and Beyond*

(New York: John Wiley and Sons, 2001); Beyer, Ashmos, and Osborn, 1997.

[50] This section is based on R. N. Osborn, *The Evolution of Strategic Alliances in High Technology,* working paper (Detroit: Department of Business, Wayne State University, 2007); R. N. Osborn and J. G. Hunt, "The Environment and Organization Effectiveness," *Administrative Science Quarterly* 19 (1974), pp. 231–246; and Osborn, Hunt, and Jauch, 1984. For a more extended discussion see P. Kenis and D. Knoke, "How Organizational Field Networks Shape Interorganizational Tie-formation Rates," *Academy of Management Journal* 27 (2002), pp. 275–294.

[51] See R. N. Osborn and C. C. Baughn, "New Patterns in the Formation of U.S. Japanese Cooperative Ventures," *Columbia Journal of World Business* 22 (1988), pp. 57–65.

[52] This section is based on R. N. Osborn, "International Alliances: Going Beyond the Hype," *Mt. Eliza Business Review* 6 (2003), pp. 37–44; S. Reddy, J. F. Hennart, and R. Osborn, "The Prevalence of Equity and Non-equity Cross-border Linkages: Japanese Investments in the U.S.," *Organization Studies* 23 (2002), pp. 759–780.

[53] Ibid.

[53A] Wepin Tsai, "Knowledge Transfer in Interorganizational Networks: Effects of Network Position and Absorptive Capacity on Business Unit Innovation and Performance," *Academy of Management Journal* 44.5 (2001), pp. 996–1004.

[54] Ibid.

[55] Warner-Lambert Annual Report (1997), p. 24.

[56] This treatment of the boundaryless organization is based on R. Ashkenas, D. Ulrich, T. Jick, and S. Kerr, *The Boundaryless Organization: Breaking the Chains of Organizational Structure* (San Francisco: Jossey-Bass, 1995). For an earlier discussion also see R. Golembiewski, *Men, Management and Morality* (New Brunswick, NJ: Transaction, 1989). For a critical review see R. Golembiewski, "The Boundaryless Organization: Breaking the Chains of Organizational Structure, A Review," *International Journal of Organizational Analysis* 6 (1998), pp. 267–270.

[57] S. Kerr and D. Ulrich, "Creating the Boundaryless Organization: The Radical Reconstruction of Organization Capabilities," *Planning Review* 23 (1995), pp. 41–46.

[58] See Scott and Davis, 2007; David A. Nadler and Michael L. Tushman, *Competing by Design: The Power of Organizational Architecture* (New York: Oxford University Press, 1997); Veiga and Dechant, 1997.

[59] A. A. Marcus, *Business and Society: Ethics, Government and the World of Economy* (Homewood, IL: Richard D. Irwin, 1993).

Self-Test Answers

Chapter 1

MULTIPLE CHOICE
1. b **2.** d **3.** c **4.** c **5.** c **6.** c **7.** a **8.** a **9.** d **10.** d
11. a **12.** c **13.** c **14.** c **15.** b

SHORT RESPONSE

16. OB as a scientific discipline has the following characteristics: a) It is an interdisciplinary body of knowledge, drawing upon insights from such allied social sciences as sociology and psychology. b) OB researchers use scientific methods to develop and test models and theories about human behavior in organizations. c) OB focuses on application, trying to develop from science practical insights that can improve organizations. d) OB uses contingency thinking, trying to fit explanations to situations rather than trying to find "one best" answer that fits all situations.

17. The term "valuing diversity" is used to describe behavior that respects individual differences. In the workplace this means respecting the talents and potential contributions of people from different races and of different genders, ethnicities, and ages, for example.

18. An effective manager is one who is able to work with and support other people so that long-term high performance is achieved. This manager is able to maintain an environment for sustainable high performance by creating conditions for job satisfaction as well as high task performance.

19. Mintzberg would say that the executive would be very busy throughout the day and would work long hours. He would note that the day would be fragmented as the executive worked on many different tasks while subject to interruptions. He would point out that the day would be very communication intensive, with the executive interacting with other people in a variety of scheduled and unscheduled meetings and communicating by telephone and other electronic media.

APPLICATION ESSAY

20. Carla is about to lead an important discussion since the world of work will certainly be different by the time these sixth graders are ready to enter the workforce. As they look ahead, she should encourage them to consider the following points:

- Commitment to ethical behavior
- Importance of knowledge and experience in the form of "human capital"
- Less emphasis on boss-centered "command and control"
- Emphasis on teamwork
- Emphasis on use of computers and information technology
- Respect for people and their work expectations
- More people working for themselves and more job/employer shifting by people; fewer people working a lifetime for one organization

Of course, one of Carla's greatest challenges will be to express these concepts in words and examples that sixth graders will understand. Your answer should reflect that use of language and examples.

Chapter 2

MULTIPLE CHOICE
1. c **2.** b **3.** d **4.** a **5.** a **6.** d **7.** a **8.** a **9.** d **10.** c
11. c **12.** b **13.** c **14.** b **15.** c

SHORT RESPONSE

16. The dimension of individualism-collectivism reflects different cultural emphases, and it appears in both the Hofstede and Trompenaars frameworks. As pointed out by Hofstede, for example, individualistic cultures tend to emphasize individual reward systems, whereas collectivist cultures emphasize teamwork. OB should help us become more aware of how cultural differences may affect the management of individuals and groups in various settings.

17. In high-power distance cultures managers are likely to be respected by subordinates and expected to exercise authority in their assigned roles. In low-power distance cultures the distinction between manager and subordinate may be more casual, and subordinates will expect to be more involved in decisions affecting them and their work.

18. Demographic characteristics are important for a number of reasons: (1) they serve as the basis for managing diversity; (2) there are various nondiscrimination laws affecting them; (3) they are often erroneously used stereotypically to categorize individuals; and (4) they can form the basis of a bio-data approach to help select employees.

19. Stress can be both constructive and destructive. Up to a certain point, stress is beneficial to performance because it helps to stimulate effort and even creativity. Beyond that point, stress becomes harmful because anxiety and other problems detract from performance. Thus the relationship between stress and performance is curvilinear; too little or too much stress has a negative effect on performance, whereas moderate stress has a positive effect on performance. The problem is finding the "friction" point where stress can be maintained for any given individual at the moderate level.

APPLICATION ESSAY

20. Your boss needs to use selected demographic, aptitude and ability, personality, and value and attitude characteristics of individuals to help match specific job and organizational requirements. Along with this, your boss can use the kinds of accountability, development, and recruitment practices designed to manage a diverse, nontraditional workforce effectively.

Chapter 3

MULTIPLE CHOICE

1. a **2.** a **3.** c **4.** b **5.** a **6.** a **7.** d **8.** a **9.** a **10.** d
11. b **12.** d **13.** d **14.** c **15.** a

SHORT RESPONSE

16. See Figure 3.1.

17. Anger: often bad, stops someone from being taken advantage of; empathy: often good, encourages being taken advantage of.

18. (1) Work itself: responsibility, interest, and growth; (2) Quality of supervision: technical and social support; (3) Relationships with co-workers: social harmony and respect; (4) Promotion opportunities: chances for further advancement; (5) Pay: adequacy and perceived equity vis-à-vis others. Although it depends on the individual and the context, in general each of these can be considered equally important.

19. Cognitive dissonance describes a state of inconsistency between an individual's attitudes and his or her behavior. Such inconsistency can result in changing attitudes, changing

future behavior, or developing new ways to explain the inconsistency. The amount of control an individual has over the situation and the magnitude of the reward tend to influence which of these actions will be chosen.

APPLICATION ESSAY

20. The heart of the issue rests with something called the "satisfaction-performance controversy" in our textbook. The controversy involves a core issue in this discussion—whether or not satisfaction causes performance. It appears that satisfaction alone is no guarantee of high-level job performance. Although a satisfied worker is likely not to quit and to have good attendance, his or her performance still remains uncertain. In the integrated model of motivation, performance is a function not only of motivation and effort, but also of individual attributes and organizational support. Thus I would be cautious in focusing only on creating satisfied workers and high-performing ones. I would try to make sure that the rewards for performance create satisfaction. I would also try to make sure that the satisfied worker has the right abilities, training, and other support needed to perform a job really well. Assuming that satisfaction alone will always lead to high performance seems risky at best; it leaves too many other important considerations left untouched, an example of which is described in the study of satisfaction in groups across time.

Chapter 4

MULTIPLE CHOICE

1. b **2.** c **3.** b **4.** b **5.** c **6.** d **7.** d **8.** b **9.** a **10.** d
11. d **12.** b **13.** a **14.** a **15.** b

SHORT RESPONSE

16. A model similar to that in Figure 4.4 should be drawn to include a brief discussion of its components and the sub-components discussed in the chapter.

17. There are six perceptual distortions listed and discussed; you may select any two and briefly note how they distort the perceptual process.

18. Figure 4.7 summarizes the underlying similarities and differences between classical and operant conditioning. Elaborate on the summary shown in the figure and use and explain different examples than those in the figures or the Pavlov's dog example.

19. Reinforcement learning is a function of its consequences as is social learning theory. However, the latter emphasizes observational learning and the importance of perception and attribution. Thus, people respond to how their perceptions and attributions help define consequences, and not to the objective consequences as emphasized in reinforcement learning. Social learning theory may be elaborated through an explanation of Figure 4.11 and contrasted with reinforcement as shown through the different reinforcement strategies in Figure 4.10.

APPLICATIONS ESSAY

20. Your boss needs to understand that attribution is a form of perception that focuses on how people attempt to understand: the causes of an event; assess responsibility for the event's outcomes; and evaluate the personal qualities of the people involved in the event.

A good example to illustrate attribution is the fundamental attribution error as opposed to the self-serving bias. You should explain the fundamental attribution error as the tendency to underestimate the influence of situational factors and to overestimate the influence of personal factors in evaluating someone else's behaviors. In contrast, the self-serving bias is the tendency to deny personal responsibility for performance problems but accept personal responsibility for performance success. Then follow up with an example of each and implications for managing the department.

Chapter 5

MULTIPLE CHOICE

1. a **2.** d **3.** b **4.** d **5.** d **6.** d **7.** b **8.** a **9.** c **10.** c
11. b **12.** d **13.** a **14.** a **15.** b

SHORT RESPONSE

16. Basically, this principle states that when one level of need is unsatisfied (or frustrated) the individual can revert back (or regress) to seek further satisfaction of a lower-level need. For example, if a need for psychological growth in one's job is frustrated, the person may regress back to place more emphasis on satisfying relatedness needs.

17. According to Herzberg, the job content or satisfier factors are what really motivate people to work hard. They include such things as feelings of responsibility, opportunities for advancement and growth, and job challenges. To make jobs more motivational Herzberg recommends job enrichment—that is, adding job content factors by moving into a job things traditionally done by higher levels, such as planning and controlling responsibilities.

18. Distributive justice is when everyone is treated by the same rules, with no one getting special favors or exceptions; procedural justice is when all rules and procedures are properly followed.

19. Expectancy theory states that Motivation = Expectancy $\times$ Instrumentality $\times$ Valence. The presence of multiplication signs creates the "multiplier effect." This means that a "0" in expectancy or instrumentality or valence creates a "0" for motivation. In other words, the multiplier effect is that all three factors—expectancy, instrumentality, valence—must be positive in order for motivation to be positive.

APPLICATION ESSAY

20. The issue in this case boils down to motivation to work hard. Person A is arguing that satisfying needs will do this. However, a job might provide a lot of satisfaction—relationships, good pay, etc.—but an employee may not work hard because there is no link between receiving the need satisfactions and doing a really good job every day. To apply the needs theories of motivation, managers need to link opportunities for need satisfaction with tasks and activities that are important to getting the job done well. In this case, as perhaps Person B would be suggesting, individuals will work hard because they are satisfying important needs by doing important job-relevant tasks.

Chapter 6

MULTIPLE CHOICE

1. c **2.** d **3.** c **4.** d **5.** d **6.** a **7.** d **8.** b **9.** b **10.** a
11. b **12.** a **13.** d **14.** b **15.** d

16. Job depth is increased when the individual is allowed to do more of the tasks traditionally done by supervisors or managers. For example, allowing the individual to plan how the work is to be done, set the schedules, and organize the needed resources increases depth. Allowing the individual to measure results, check quality, and make decisions to correct things for the better also adds depth. All of these are examples of things that can "enrich" a job.

17. It is a moderator variable. In other words, it sets the condition under which an individual will or will not respond positively to the job characteristics. When an individual is high in growth-need strength, the prediction is that he or she will respond positively to a job high in the core characteristics and therefore largely enriched. However, when the individual has low-growth-need strength, the prediction is that he or she will not respond positively to high core characteristics and may be dissatisfied and less productive in such enriched job conditions.

18. The compressed workweek, or 4–40 schedule, offers employees the advantage of a three-day weekend. However, it can cause problems for the employer in terms of ensuring that operations are covered adequately during the normal five-day workweek. Also, the compressed workweek will entail more complicated work scheduling. In addition, some employees find that the schedule is tiring and can cause family adjustment problems.

19. Job sharing is when two or more individuals share the same job. Work sharing is when employees agree to cut back on the number of hours worked to save jobs that would otherwise be cut—basically, everyone agrees to work fewer hours so that everyone gets to have a job.

APPLICATION ESSAY

20. Using the job characteristics model, I might start by having the job of salesperson evaluated based on each of the core characteristics. Ideally, this evaluation would be done by managers and by the salespersons themselves. Then we could have a discussion about how the job could be redesigned to emphasize core characteristics that would be motivational to the salespersons. Also, we could discuss possible ways alternative work schedules, such as flexible hours, compressed work weeks, and job sharing, might be used to make the jobs more appealing.

Chapter 7

MULTIPLE CHOICE
1. d **2.** b **3.** c **4.** d **5.** b **6.** a **7.** a **8.** b **9.** a **10.** a **11.** b **12.** c **13.** b **14.** d **15.** d

16. An ESOP is an employee stock ownership plan. The basic idea is to give employees an ownership stake in the company so that they will have a personal financial incentive to work hard so that the company performs well and its stock prices increase in the future. If the stock price goes up, employees benefit financially and this sense of "ownership" and "financial stake" in the firm's success should be motivational.

17. In a traditional evaluation the employee's performance is evaluated by the supervisor. In the 360° evaluation the employee's performance is evaluated by those with whom he or she works, including supervisor, peers, subordinates, and perhaps even customers. The 360° evaluation also typically includes a self-evaluation. When the results of all evaluations are analyzed and compared, the employee has a good sense of his or her accomplishments and areas for improvement. This evaluation can then be discussed with the supervisor.

18. The major problem with the standard graphic rating scale is that the items included on the scale may not be a good reflection of important job behaviors. Although it is easy to rate someone's performance on such a scale, unless the scale is solidly based on a job analysis it is of little actual value as a performance measure.

19. A halo error in performance appraisal occurs when one attribute or behavior inappropriately influences the overall appraisal. For example, an individual may have a unique style of dress but be a very high performer. If the evaluator lets his or her distaste for the dress style negatively bias the overall performance evaluation, a halo error has occurred. A recency error occurs when a performance appraisal is biased due the influence of recent events. In other words, the performance appraisal is based on most recent performance and may not be an accurate reflection of performance for a full evaluation period. For example, I might have a very bad week just prior to an evaluation due to family problems. If my supervisor uses that week's performance to negatively bias the evaluation even though for the prior six months

I had been a very strong performer, recency error would have occurred.

APPLICATION ESSAY
20. There are many things that can be done to use rewards and performance management well in the context of student organizations. On the reward side the most appropriate thing is to make sure that those who get the benefits from the organization are the ones who do the work. For example, if there is a fund-raiser to support a student trip, only those who actively raise the money should get financial support for the trip. And possibly, the financial support should be proportionate to the amount of time and effort each person contributed to raising the funds. Also it is probably quite common that little or no evaluation is done of how people perform in offices and special assignments in the student organizations. Many possible ways of creating and using more formal evaluation systems could be established. For example, officers could be rated on a BARS scale developed by the membership to reflect the desirable officer behaviors. These ratings could take place every month or two, and individuals who perform poorly can be counseled or removed, while those who perform while can be praised and continued.

Chapter 8

MULTIPLE CHOICE
1. a **2.** b **3.** d **4.** c **5.** b **6.** a **7.** c **8.** a **9.** a **10.** c **11.** b **12.** c **13.** d **14.** c **15.** c

16. Groups are potentially good for organizations for several reasons. Groups are good for people, they can improve creativity, they sometimes make the best decisions, they gain commitment to decisions, they help control the behavior of their members, and they can help to counterbalance the effects of large organization size.

17. Permanent formal groups appear on organization charts and serve an ongoing purpose. These groups may include departments, divisions, teams, and the like. Temporary groups are created to solve a specific problem or perform a defined task and are then disbanded. Examples are committees, cross-functional task forces, and project teams.

18. Required behaviors are formally expected of group members. They are part of the group's formal structure and represent conditions of membership that are "required" to be exhibited. Emergent behaviors are not formally required of members. They "emerge" spontaneously as members work and relate together. They are part of the informal structure of the group.

19. Intergroup competition can create problems in the way groups work with one another. Ideally, an organization is a cooperative system in which groups are well integrated and help one another out as needed. When groups get competitive, however, there is a potential dysfunctional side. Instead of communicating with one another, they decrease communication. Instead of viewing one another positively, they develop negative stereotypes of one another. Instead of viewing each other as mutual partners in the organization, they become hostile and view one another more as enemies. Although intergroup competition can be good by adding creative tension and encouraging more focused efforts, this potential negative side should not be forgotten.

APPLICATION ESSAY

20. I would tell Alejandro that consensus and unanimity are two different, but related, things. Consensus occurs through extensive discussion and much "give and take," in which group members share ideas and listen carefully to one another. Eventually, one alternative emerges that is preferred by most. Those who disagree, however, know that they have been listened to and have had a fair chance to influence the decision outcome. Consensus, therefore, does not require unanimity. What it does require is the opportunity for any dissenting members to feel they have been able to speak and be sincerely listened to. A decision by unanimity that generates 100 percent agreement on an issue may be the ideal state of affairs, but it is not always possible to achieve. Thus, Alejandro should always try to help the force members work intensively together, communicate well with one another, and sincerely share ideas and listen. However, he should not be concerned for complete unanimity on every issue. Rather, consensus should be the agreed-upon goal in most cases.

Chapter 9

MULTIPLE CHOICE

1. d **2.** a **3.** d **4.** a **5.** b **6.** b **7.** c **8.** b **9.** d **10.** c **11.** b **12.** a **13.** a **14.** b **15.** b

16. Team building usually begins when someone notices that a problem exists or may develop in the group. Members then work collaboratively to gather data, analyze the situation, plan for improvements, and implement the plan. Everyone is expected to participate in each step, and the group as a whole is expected to benefit from continuous improvement.

17. To help build positive norms, a team leader must first act as a positive role model. She or he should carefully select members for the team and be sure to reinforce and reward members for performing as desired. She or he should also hold meetings to review performance, provide feedback, and discuss and agree on goals.

18. A basic rule of group dynamics is that members of highly cohesive groups tend to conform to group norms. Thus, when group norms are positive for performance, the conformity is likely to create high-performance outcomes.

When the norms are negative, however, the conformity is likely to create low-performance outcomes.

19. Self-managing teams take different forms. A common pattern, however, involves empowering team members to make decisions about the division of labor and scheduling, to develop and maintain the skills needed to perform several different jobs for the team, to help train one another to learn those jobs, and to help select new team members.

APPLICATION ESSAY

20. My answer to the Internet call for "help" follows. Dear Galahad. Greetings from Brighton. Saw your message and wanted to respond. Don't worry. There is no reason at all that a great design engineer can't run a high-performance project team. Go into the job with confidence, but try to follow some basic guidelines as you build and work with the team. First off, communicate high-performance standards right from the beginning. Set the tone in the first team meeting and even create a sense of urgency to get things going. Be sure that the members have the right skills, and find ways to create some early "successes" for them. Don't let them drift apart; make sure they spend a lot of time together. Give lots of positive feedback as the project develops and, perhaps most importantly, model the expected behaviors yourself. Go for it!

Chapter 10

MULTIPLE CHOICE

1. d **2.** a **3.** d **4.** d **5.** c **6.** b **7.** a **8.** c **9.** d **10.** a **11.** b **12.** a **13.** d **14.** a **15.** d

SHORT ANSWER

16. For the first part of the question, you should consider the notions of reward and coercive, legitimate, expert, and referent power. The response should recognize the difference between position sources and personal sources. The second part of the question concerns the power of lower-level participants in organizational settings. Link the sources of power with Bernard's acceptance theory of authority.

17. The text introduces five basic guidelines for increasing position power. They are (1) increase your centrality and criticality in the organization; (2) increase the personal discretion and flexibility of your job; (3) build into your job tasks that are difficult to evaluate; (4) increase the visibility of your job performance; (5) increase the relevance of your tasks to the organization. The text also identifies three basic guidelines for acquiring personal power. They are: (1) increase your knowledge and information as it relates to the job; (2) increase your personal attractiveness; (3) increase your effort in relation to key organizational tasks.

18. The text identifies seven basic strategies of managerial influence: reason, friendliness, coalition, bargaining, assertiveness, higher authority, and sanctions. You should be able to express them in everyday language and provide an example for each one. Each of these strategies is available to the manager in the downward influence attempt; however, the choices in upward attempts may be more limited. In the exercise of upward influence, influence attempts can frequently be expected to include assertiveness, friendliness, and reason.

19. *Organizational politics* is formally defined as "the management of influence to obtain ends not sanctioned by the organization or to obtain sanctioned ends through nonsanctioned means." Yet it can also be viewed as the art of creative compromise among competing interests. You should be able to express these apparently conflicting views in everyday language that communicates a sense of understanding. It is important that politics not be viewed as an entirely dysfunctional phenomenon that can result in people becoming dissatisfied and feeling emotionally distraught or estranged from the organizational situation. The functional aspects of organizational politics include helping managers overcome personal inadequacies, cope with change, channel personal contacts, and substitute for formal authority.

APPLICATION ESSAY

20. While the financial implications to stockholders from merger and acquisition seems to vary considerably, one lesson is quite clear: the senior executive of the acquiring firm gains power and influence. Further, a chief reason for senior executives involuntarily leaving firms is that the organization is being taken over by another corporation. Thus, some executives believe that it is "merge or be merged," so they would rather be on the acquiring end.

Chapter 11

MULTIPLE CHOICE

1. a   **2.** b   **3.** b   **4.** b   **5.** c   **6.** c   **7.** a   **8.** d   **9.** b   **10.** a
11. c   **12.** a   **13.** b   **14.** a   **15.** c

SHORT RESPONSE

16. Leadership is the process of influencing others and facilitating effort in order to accomplish shared objectives. Leadership tends to emphasize adaptive or useful change, whereas management is designed to promote stability or to enable the organization to run smoothly.

17. Leader trait and behavior approaches assume that, in a given setting, leadership (as opposed to other variables) is central to task performance and satisfaction-related outcomes.

18. Situational contingency approaches to leadership assume that leader traits or behaviors act in conjunction with situational contingencies (other important aspects of the leadership situation) to determine outcomes.

19. Implicit leadership is in the mind of the respondent and is discussed in the text in two forms: Leadership as attribution (inference-based) and leadership prototypes. Leadership as attribution argues that followers tend to describe a leader of a high performing group or organization favorably; in other words, they infer good leadership or real leadership to such an individual and if the group is not performing well, poor leadership is inferred. In the leadership prototype approach, people are seen as having a mental image of the characteristics that make a good or real leader in a given situation. This is sometimes termed recognition-based (you know a good leader when you see one). The characteristics range from specific to general for different kinds of leaders and across different cultures.

APPLICATION ESSAY

20. You are asked to respond to the point that leadership is not real and is only a figment of peoples' imaginations. You might start by arguing there is some truth to the argument, but it neglects the fact that leadership can also be real, where if it had not been exhibited certain outcomes would not have occurred. So the argument here, as in many cases, would be one of moderation—leadership can be real but it also can be inference- or recognition-based. That is, leadership can be seen as a mixture of both. The report can also use some examples of inference- and recognition-based leadership and how these relate to the more traditional treatment of leadership as a real phenomenon. One also could extend the discussion to leadership and management differences and similarities and how they relate to this point.

Chapter 12

MULTIPLE CHOICE

1. c   **2.** d   **3.** a   **4.** a   **5.** c   **6.** d   **7.** c   **8.** b   **9.** b   **10.** d
11. b   **12.** d   **13.** c   **14.** b   **15.** a

SHORT RESPONSE

16. Three ways in which shared leadership can be used in self-directed work teams are (1) behavior-focused strategies that tend to increase self-awareness, leading to the behaviors involving necessary but not always pleasant tasks; (2) self rewards in conjunction with behavior-focused strategies; and (3) constructive thought patterns that focus on the creation or alteration of cognitive thought processes. The student should then elaborate on each of these along the lines of the discussion in the chapter.

17. The multiple-level approach argues that organizations comprise three domains from bottom to top, with two managerial levels within each domain. The domains from bottom to top are production, organization, and systems. Each domain and level gets more complex in terms of managerial and leadership requirements. Managerial leader cognitive and behavioral complexity should match the additional complexity requirements at each domain and level. The Boal and Hooijberg approach essentially builds absorptive capacity, capacity to change, and managerial wisdom around charismatic, transformational, and vision leadership and their interaction with behavioral, social, and cognitive complexity. These characteristics are argued to be related to strategic leadership effectiveness and organizational effectiveness. Essentially, the student should elaborate and provide examples for the above frameworks and then do a compare and contrast treatment.

18. Not all change in organizations is planned. Unplanned change—that which occurs spontaneously or by surprise—can be useful. The appropriate goal in managing unplanned change is to act immediately once the change is recognized to minimize any negative consequences and maximize any possible benefits. The goal is to take best advantage of the change situation by learning from the experience.

19. External forces for change are found in the relationship between an organization and its environment. Examples are the pressures of mergers, strategic alliances, and divestitures. Internal forces for change include those found in different lifecycle demands as the organization passes from birth through growth and toward maturity. Internal forces also include the political nature of organizations as reflected in authority and reward systems.

APPLICATION ESSAY

20. Jorge may begin his attempts to deal with resistance to change by using education and communication. Through one-on-one discussions, group presentations, and even visits to other centers he can better inform his staff about the nature and logic of the changes. He should also utilize participation and involvement by allowing others (for example, in a series of task forces) to help choose the new equipment and design the new programs. In all this he should offer enough facilitation and support to help everyone deal with any hardships the changes may cause. He should be especially alert to listen to any problems and complaints that may arise. On certain matters, Jorge might use negotiation and agreement to exchange benefits for staff support. In the extreme case, manipulation and cooperation through covert attempts to influence others might be used to achieve needed support, although this is not advisable. Similarly, explicit or implicit coercion would use force to get people to accept change at any cost. My advice would be to stick with the first four strategies as much as possible and avoid the latter two.

Chapter 13

MULTIPLE CHOICE

1. c **2.** b **3.** a **4.** c **5.** b **6.** d **7.** a **8.** c **9.** a **10.** a **11.** b **12.** b **13.** a **14.** b **15.** c

SHORT RESPONSE

16. Heuristics are simplifying strategies, or "rules of thumb," that people use to make decisions. They make it easier for individuals to deal with uncertainty and limited information, but they can also lead to biased results. Common heuristics include availability-making decisions based on recent events; representativeness-making decisions based on similar events; and anchoring and adjustment-making decisions based on historical precedents.

17. Individual, or authority, decisions are made by the manager or team leader acting alone based on information that he or she possesses. Consultative decisions are made by the manager or team leader after soliciting input from other persons. Group decisions are made when the manager or team leader asks others to participate in problem solving. The ideal form of the group decision is true consensus.

18. Escalating commitment is the tendency to continue with a previously chosen course of action even though feedback indicates that it is not working. This can lead to waste of time, money, and other resources, in addition to the sacrificing of the opportunity to pursue a course of action offering more valuable results. Escalating commitment is encouraged by the popular adage, "If at first you don't succeed try, try, again." Another way to look at it is "throwing good money after bad."

19. Most people are too busy to respond personally to every problem that comes their way. The effective manager and team leader knows when to delegate decisions to others, how to set priorities, and when to abstain from acting altogether. Questions to ask include: Is the problem easy to deal with? Might the problem resolve itself? Is this my decision to make? Is this a solvable problem within the context of the organization?

APPLICATION ESSAY

20. Dilbert is popular because it is funny and it has a ring of truth. It reflects the so-called "garbage can" model of decision making in which the main components of the choice process—problems, decisions, solutions, participants, choice situations—are all mixed together in strange and wonderful ways.

Chapter 14

MULTIPLE CHOICE

1. d **2.** b **3.** a **4.** b **5.** a **6.** d **7.** a **8.** d **9.** a **10.** a **11.** b **12.** c **13.** a **14.** d **15.** a

16. Channel richness is a useful concept for managers because it describes the capacity of a communication channel to convey and move information. For example, if a manager wants to convey basic and routine information to a lot of people, a lean channel such as the electronic bulletin or written memorandum may be sufficient.

However, if the manager needs to convey a complicated message and one that may involve some uncertainty, a richer channel such as the face-to-face meeting may be necessary. Simply put, the choice of channel may have a lot of impact on the effectiveness of a communication attempt.

17. Informal communication channels are very important in today's organizations. The modern workplace places great emphasis on cross-functional relationships and communication. Employee involvement and participation in decision-making are very important. This requires that people know and talk with one another, often across departmental lines. Progressive organizations make it easy for people to interact and meet outside of formal work assignments and relationships. When people know one another, they can more easily and frequently communicate with one another.

18. Status effects can interfere with the effectiveness of communication between lower and higher levels in an organization. Lower-level members are concerned about how the higher-level members will respond, especially if the information being communicated is negative or unfavorable. In such cases, a tendency exists to filter or modify the information to make it as attractive as possible to the recipient. The result is that high-level decision makers in organizations sometimes act on inaccurate or incomplete information. Although their intentions are good, they just aren't getting good information from their subordinates.

19. There may be a gender difference in communication styles. Some research suggests that the socialization of women makes them more sensitive to others, whereas men are socialized to be more aggressive and individualistic. Women may be more inclined to behave in ways that make them perceived as interested in others, willing to communicate with others, and willing to work with others in empowering ways. Questions have also been raised regarding how well women and men communicate with one another. It is suggested men may communicate to advance their positions, whereas women communicate to make connections. As these possibilities are considered, however, the tendency to use inappropriate gender stereotypes should be avoided.

APPLICATION ESSAY

20. Organizations depend on communication flowing upward, downward, and laterally. Rapid developments in technology have led to a heavy reliance on computers to assist in the movement of this information. E-mail is one part of an electronic organizational communication system. Research suggests that people may fall prey to the "impersonality" of computer-based operations and that the personal or face-to-face side of communication may suffer. Rather than eliminate e-mail and other forms of computer-

mediated communication, however, the managing director should work hard to establish proper e-mail protocols and provide many other avenues for communication. The managing director can serve as a role model in his or her use of e-mail, in being regularly available for face-to-face interactions, by holding regular meetings, and by "wandering around" frequently to meet and talk with people from all levels. In addition, the director can make sure that facility designs and office arrangements support interaction and make it less easy for people to disappear behind computer screens. Finally, the director must actively encourage communication of all types and not allow himself or herself to get trapped into serving as a classic example of the "e-mail boss."

Chapter 15

MULTIPLE CHOICE

1. c **2.** a **3.** b **4.** b **5.** d **6.** b **7.** a **8.** c **9.** d **10.** c
11. a **12.** c **13.** c **14.** a **15.** b

16. Managers can be faced with the following conflict situations: vertical conflict—conflict that occurs between hierarchical levels; horizontal conflict—conflict that occurs between those at the same hierarchical level; line-staff conflict—conflict that occurs between line and staff representatives; role conflict—conflict that occurs when the communication of task expectations is inadequate or upsetting.

17. The major indirect conflict management approaches include the following: appeals to common goals—involves focusing the attention of potentially conflicting parties on one mutually desirable conclusion; hierarchical referral—using the chain of command for conflict resolution; organizational redesign—including decoupling, buffering, linking pins, and liaison groups; use of myths and scripts—managing superficially through behavioral routines (scripts) or to hide conflict by denying the necessity to make a tradeoff in conflict resolution.

18. You should acknowledge that different styles may be appropriate under different conditions. Avoidance is the extreme form of nonattention and is most commonly used when the issue is trivial, when more important issues are pressing, or when individuals need to cool off. An accommodation strategy is used when an issue is more important to the other party than it is to you, or to build social credits.

19. Distributive negotiation focuses on staking out positions and claiming portions of the available "pie." It usually takes the form of hard negotiation—the parties maximize their self-interests and hold out to get their own way—or soft negotiation—one party is willing to make concessions in order to reach an agreement. Distributive negotiation can lead to competition, compromise, or accommodation, but it tends to be win-lose oriented in all cases. Integrative negotiation focuses on the merits of an issue and attempts to enlarge the available "pie." It may lead to avoidance, compromise, or collaboration. It tends to be more win-win oriented and seeks to satisfy the needs and interests of all parties.

APPLICATION ESSAY

20. When negotiating the salary for your first job, you should attempt to avoid the common pitfalls of negotiation. These include falling prey to the myth of the "fixed pie"; nonrational escalation of conflict, such as trying to compare the proposed salary to the highest offer you have heard; overconfidence; and ignoring other's needs (the personnel officer probably has a fixed limit). While the initial salary may be very important to you, you should also recognize that it may not be as significant as what type of job you will have and whether you will have an opportunity to move up in the firm.

Chapter 16

MULTIPLE CHOICE

1. c **2.** a **3.** b **4.** a **5.** d **6.** d **7.** a **8.** a **9.** b **10.** c
11. b **12.** a **13.** d **14.** d **15.** a

SHORT RESPONSE

16. Cox's theory is designed for organizations that are located in the United States. His ideas may not be easily applied to multinational corporations headquartered in other cultures. Cox believes that it is important for culturally divergent groups within an organization to communicate and educate one another. This helps subgroups become more tolerant and interactive with other portions of the organization. In addition, the organization needs to make sure that one type of cultural group is not segregated into one type of position. When cultural subgroups are spread throughout the organization, interaction increases as stereotyping decreases. Companies may also need to restructure many informal lines of communication. When informal communication is encouraged, subgroups become more involved with one another. An organization must also ensure that no one group is associated with the company's outside image. A company that is perceived to be uniform in its culture attracts individuals who are from a similar culture. Finally, Cox states that interpersonal conflict based on group identity needs to be controlled.

17. Groups first need to define who is in the group and who is not. Criteria for both formal and informal groups need to be established to provide a framework for membership. Second, the group needs to set standards of behavior. These standards should consist of a series of informal rules that describe proper behavior and activities for

the members. Finally, group members need to identify the friends and adversaries of the group. The identification process helps the group build alliances throughout the organization when they attempt to get projects and ideas completed.

18. If you have not had full-time employment, think seriously about this question because it is designed to help you appreciate the importance of organizational rules and roles. Formal rules should be covered to show that they help dictate procedures individuals use. Informal interaction should be discussed as well. Such questions as "How are subgroups treated?" "Do different instructors have different rules?" and "Are Seniors treated differently from Sophomores in this system?" could all be potential subtopics.

19. The first element is the need for a widely shared philosophy. Although this first element seems vague, an effective company philosophy is anything but abstract. Members of the organization need to be exposed to what the firm stands for. The firm's mission needs to be articulated often and throughout the organization. Organizations should put people ahead of rules and general policy mandates. When staffers feel included and important in a system they feel more loyal and accepting of the culture. Every company has heroes or individuals who have succeeded beyond expectations. Companies with strong company cultures allow the stories of these individuals to become well known throughout the organization. Through these stories, workers need to make sure that they understand the rituals and ceremonies that are important to the company's identity. Maintaining and enhancing these rituals helps many organizations keep a strong corporate culture. Informal rules and expectations must be evident so that workers understand what is expected of them and the organization. Finally, employees need to realize that their work is important; their work and knowledge should be networked throughout the company. The better the communication system in the company, the better the company's culture.

APPLICATION ESSAY

20. The OD process has three stages: (1) diagnosis—gather and analyze data to assess a situation and set appropriate change objectives; (2) intervention—change objectives pursued through a variety of specific activities; and (3) reinforcement—changes are monitored, reinforced, and evaluated. The diagnostic foundations of OD encompass three levels: (1) organizational effectiveness understood with respect to external environment and major organizational aspects; (2) group effectiveness viewed in a context of forces in the internal environment of the organization and major group aspects; and (3) individual effectiveness considered in relation to the internal environment of the work group and individual aspects.

Chapter 17

MULTIPLE CHOICE
1. b 2. b 3. b 4. c 5. d 6. a 7. a 8. d 9. b 10. d

TRUE/FALSE
11. True 12. False 13. True 14. False 15. True

SHORT RESPONSE

16. Output goals are designed to help an organization define its overall mission and to help define the kind of business it is in. Output goals can often help define the types of products and the relationships the company has with its consumers. Output goals often help demonstrate how a company fits into society. The second kind of organizational goal is the systems goal. A systems goal helps the company realize what behaviors it needs to maintain for its survival. The systems goal provides the means for the ends. It is important to recognize the importance of systems goals for day-to-day operations.

17. Control is the set of mechanisms used to keep action or outputs within predetermined limits. Two types of controls are often found in organizations. Output controls focus on desired targets to allow managers discretion in using different methods for reaching these targets. Process controls attempt to specify the manner in which tasks are accomplished. Policies, procedures, and rules as well as formalization and standardization can be seen as types of process controls. Total Quality Management can be seen as a systemic way of managing processes within the firm and thus be viewed as a control mechanism.

18. The first advantage is that functional specialization can yield clear task assignments that replicate an individual's training and experience. Functional specialization also provides the ability for departmental colleagues to build upon one another's knowledge and experience. The functional approach also provides an excellent training ground for new managers. Finally, this system is easy to explain because managers can understand the role of each group even thought they do not understand a particular individual's function. There are some major disadvantages to the system as well. The system may reinforce overspecialization. Many jobs within the system may become boring and too routine. The lines of communication within the organization may become overly complex. Top management is often overloaded with too many problems that should be addressed at a lower level. Many top managers spend too much time dealing with cross-functional issues. Finally, many individuals look up in the hierarchy for reinforcement instead of focusing their attention on products, services, and clients.

19. A matrix combines the strengths of both the functional and divisional forms. For instance, divisional specialization provides the organization with adaptability and flexibility

to meet important demands of key external groups. With the matrix, this emphasis is blended with a stress on technical affairs found under functional departmentation. Unfortunately, there is a cost for this blending. Unity of command is lost. The authority and responsibilities of managers may overlap, causing conflict. In addition, this form may be expensive.

APPLICATION ESSAY

20. The notion that the United States Postal Service is a mechanistic bureaucracy is important because it suggests that there are already many controls built into the system by the division of labor. You should recognize several primary side effects that are exhibited when control mechanisms are placed on an individual in an organization such as the Postal Service. There is often a difficulty in balancing organizational controls. As one control is emphasized, another may be neglected. Controls often force managers to emphasize the "quick fix" instead of long-term planning. Often, controls lead to solutions that are not customized to specific problems (i.e., "across the board cuts"). Planning and documentation can become burdensome and limit the amount of action that actually occurs. Managers often become more concerned with internal paperwork than with problem solving or customers. And there are far too many supervisors and managers. Controls that are vaguely designed are often ineffective and unrealistic. As a result, the manager may interpret the control as he or she wants. The "do the best you can" goal that is commonly given to managers in the Postal Service is an example of this concept. Controls that are inserted drastically and harshly often cause panic among managers and administrators. A swift change in the territories of postal delivery clerks is an example. Finally, many goals and controls are inserted without the appropriate resources. This practice can make the attainment of goals difficult, if not impossible.

Chapter 18

MULTIPLE CHOICE
1. d 2. d 3. d 4. a 5. d 6. d 7. c 8. c 9. c 10. d

TRUE/FALSE
11. False 12. True 13. False 14. False 15. False

SHORT RESPONSE

16. There are a number of ways to answer this question. Actually, a very large firm could use a simple structure but its chances of reaching its goals and surviving would be small. As the firm grows so does the complexity inside, and individuals become overwhelmed if the firm does not evolve into a bureaucracy. Recall that a bureaucracy involves labor that is divided so that each worker is special-

ized. Every worker has well-defined responsibilities and authorities. To complement this specialization, the organization should be arranged hierarchically. Authority should be arranged from the bottom up. A worker should be promoted only on the basis of merit and technical competence. Most importantly, employees work under rules and guidelines that are impersonal and applied to all staffers equally.

17. Information technology is the combination of machines, artifacts, procedures, and systems used to gather, store, analyze, and disseminate information for translating it into knowledge. It can be used as (a) a partial substitute for some operations as well as some process controls and impersonal methods of coordination, (b) a capability for transforming information to knowledge for learning, and (c) a strategic capability.

18. James Thompson believed that technology could be divided into three categories: intensive, mediating, and long linked. An intensive technology occurs when uncertainty exists as to how to produce the desired outcomes. Teams of specialists are brought together to pool knowledge and resources to solve the problem. An interdependence among specialists develops because all parties need one another to complete the project successfully. This technology often occurs in the research and development portion of organizations. A mediating technology allows various parties to become interdependent. For example, the ATM network that most banks utilize allows customers to bank at other institutions and still be tied to their home bank, automatically. Without this technology, the banking industry would not be so well linked. The technology helps determine the nature of the banks' relationships with one another. Finally, Thompson believed that long-linked technologies had a unique effect on organizations as well. Long-linked technology is more commonly known as industrial technology. This type of knowledge allows organizations to produce goods in mass quantities. The assembly line designed by Henry Ford is one of the early examples of long-linked technology. Thompson uses these distinctions to highlight the various impacts that technology has on organizations. His approach differs greatly from Joan Woodward's approach, which focuses more on the mode of production. Woodward divides technology into three areas: small-batch manufacturing, mass production, and continuous-process custom goods. Crafts persons are often characterized as small producers who must alter production to fit the needs of each client. Mass production technology deals with production of uniform goods for a mass market. The production design is altered to maximize speed while limiting product styles. The last type of technology deals with continuous-process technology. Oil refineries and chemical plants are classic examples of this type of technology. These industries are intensely automated and produce the same products without variation.

19. We define environmental complexity as an estimate of the magnitude of the problems and opportunities in an organization's environment as influenced by three main factors: degree of richness, degree of interdependence, and degree of uncertainty. The first factor, environmental richness, is shown by an environment that is improving around the company. The economy is growing, and people are investing and spending money. Internally, the company may be growing, and its employees may be prospering as well. In a rich environment, organizations can succeed despite their poor organizational structure. An environment that is not rich allows only well-organized companies to survive in the long run. The second major factor in environmental complexity is the level of interdependence. This factor focuses on the relationships an organization needs to develop to compete in a certain setting. How free is that organization to conduct business? Uncertainty and volatility are the final factors that make up complexity. Organizations must decide how to react to markets and environments that are continually changing.

APPLICATION ESSAY

20. In the design and development of cars and trucks, Ford must recognize both the voice of the customer and a whole series of extremely complex technical requirements. If the company violates either the customer requirements or the technical requirements, it will not be able to develop a profitable vehicle. In the product and assembly plants these conflict forces are not as prominent, and the firm may opt for a simpler structure.

Photo Credits

Chapter 9

Page 190: Streeter Lecka/Reportage/Getty Images, Inc. **Page 192:** Andy Mead/Icon SMI/NewsCom. **Page 196:** Mike Fuentes/Bloomberg News /Landov LLC. **Page 197:** Bob Mahoney/Time & Life Pictures/Getty Images, Inc. **Page 201:** Amy Sancetta/©AP/Wide World Photos. **Page 204:** Color-Blind Images/Iconica/Getty Images, Inc. **Page 205:** © Dan Lamont/Corbis Images. **Page 206:** Bruce Ayres/Stone/Getty Images, Inc.

Chapter 10

Page 212: Nathan Bilow/Allsport Concepts/Getty Images, Inc. **Page 214:** ©AP/Wide World Photos. **Page 216:** Courtesy of Robert W. Baird & Company. **Page 219:** Blend Images LLC/Getty Images, Inc. **Page 225:** Photodisc Green/Getty Images, Inc. **Page 230:** Courtesy of Little Caesar Enterprises, Inc. **Page 231:** Comstock/Picture Quest/Jupiter Images Corp.

Chapter 11

Page 240: White Packert/Iconica/Getty Images, Inc. **Page 242:** Misty Keasler/Renee Rhyner & Company. **Page 245:** Kevork Djansezian/©AP/Wide World Photos. **Page 246:** Mark Sterkel/Odessa American. **Page 251:** Jim Watkinns/Lubbock Avalanche-Journal. **Page 261:** Courtesy of Oksana Parylo, MS in Ed, SIUC, BS from Ukraine.

Chapter 12

Page 266: Bambu Productions/Iconica/Getty Images, Inc. **Page 268:** Stephan Savoia/©AP/Wide World Photos. **Page 277:** Will Shilling/©AP/Wide World Photos. **Page 279:** Walter Bieri/©AP/Wide World Photos. **Page 281:** File Photo/©AP/Wide World Photos. **Page 283:** Reed Saxon/©AP/Wide World Photos. **Page 284:** Rogelio Solis/©AP/Wide World Photos.

Chapter 13

Page 296: Microzoa/Stone/Getty Images, Inc. **Page 300:** Roslan Rahman/AFP/Getty Images, Inc. **Page 304:** Antonio M Rosario/The Image Bank/Getty Images. Inc. **Page 305:** JGI/Blend Images/Getty Images, Inc. **Page 308:** Courtesy of Pella Windows and Doors. **Page 310:** Courtesy of W. L. Gore & Associates, Inc.; photo by Eric Crossan. **Page 311:** Courtesy of Jack in the Box Restaurants.

Chapter 14

Page 318: Stockbyte/Getty Images, Inc. **Page 320:** Vincent Yu/©AP/Wide World Photos. **Page 323:** Manfred Rutz/Photodisc Red/Getty Images, Inc. **Page 325:** Courtesy of Quentin English, quentinsfriends.com. **Page 326:** AFP/NewsCom. **Page 330:** Manpreet Romana/AFP/Getty Images, Inc. **Page 333:** Patrick Molnar/The Image Bank/Getty Images, Inc.

Chapter 15

Page 340: Jakob Helbig/Riser/Getty Images, Inc. **Page 342:** Index Stock Imagery/Picture Quest/Jupiter Images Corp. **Page 343:** ©Everett Kennedy Brown/Corbis. **Page 346:** Mahmud Turkia/AFP/Getty Images, Inc. **Page 347:** Jen Petreshock/Getty Images, Inc. **Page 349:** John Froschauer/©AP/Wide World Photos. **Page 353:** Jose Azel/Aurora/Getty Images, Inc.

Chapter 16

Page 362: Chris Bradley/Axiom Photographic Agency/Getty Images, Inc. **Page 364:** Courtesy of R & R Parners, Las Vegas. **Page 366:** Courtesy of Herman Miller, Inc. **Page 368:** Courtesy of Flowserve. **Page 372:** Courtesy of Lam Research Corporation. **Page 375:** Courtesy of Sherwin-Williams.

Chapter 17

Page 386: Sam Royds/Riser/Getty Images, Inc. **Page 388:** Courtesy of Cummins. **Page 391:** Al Behrman/©AP/Wide World Photos. **Page 393:** Courtesy of Springer Science and Business Media. **Page 396:** Courtesy of Noble Corporation. **Page 398:** Jeff Greenberg/Age Fotostock America, Inc. **Page 408:** Courtesy of Land O Lakes, Inc.

Chapter 18

Page 414: Justin Guariglia/National Geographic/Getty Images, Inc. **Page 416:** Al Behrman/©AP/Wide World Photos. **Page 421:** Courtesy of Corning, Inc. **Page 423:** Dibyangshu Sarkar/AFP/Getty Images, Inc. **Page 427:** Michael Melford/The Image Bank/Getty Images, Inc. **Page 428:** Courtesy of Monster.com. Copyright 2006, Monster, Inc. All rights reserved. www.monster.com. **Page 431:** ©AP/Wide World Photos.

Organizations Index

Name Index

Ringlemann, Max, 172
Rokeach, Milton, 35, 36, 56
Rollo, Kathy, 251
Roosevelt, Franklin D., 66
Rose, Kevin, 15
Rotter, J. B., 45

S
Sackett, P. R., 164
Salancik, Gerald, 137
Salvaggio, Amy Nicole, 72
Sanchez, Nathalie, 283
Sanger, Stephen W., 416
Sashkin, Marshall, 261
Sashkin, Molly G., 261
Schaefer, George A., Jr., 391
Scharer, Kevin, 398
Schein, Edgar, 183, 197
Schermerhorn, John R., Jr., 17
Schneider, Benjamin, 72
Schultz, William, 178
Schutzman, Charlotte, 142
Scott, George C, 259
Seidenberg, Ivan, 89
Seifert, George, 281
Shamir, Boas, 258
Sheehy, Gail, 41
Simmons, Curtis, 246
Simon, Herbert, 303, 304
Simsek, Zeki, 143

Skinner, B. F., 95, 96
Slack, Trevor, 288
Smith, Antonio, 201
Smith, D. Brent, 72
Smith, Fred, 284
Smith, Gene, 277
Smoot, P. J., 344
Solso, Tim, 388
Stajkovic, Alexander D., 122
Staubach, Roger, 80
Stauffer, Joseph M., 164
Stern, David, 4
Stoll, Sharon, 245
Sully de Luque, Mary, 274

T
Tannen, Deborah, 335
Taylor, Frederick, 131
Thomas, John, 347
Thomas, R. Roosevelt, 12
Thomas, Terry, 16, 17
Thompson, J. T., 130
Thompson, James D., 426, 427
Thorndike, E. L., 95
Tressel, Jim, 201
Trevino, Linda K., 278

V
van Engen, Marloes L., 12
Vassiliadis, Billy, 364
Veiga, John F., 143

Velasquez, Manuel, 224
Vitucci, Steve, 282
Vroom, Victor, 118–120, 125, 311, 312, 315

W
Wachtmeister, Erick, 325
Wade, J., 233
Walsh, Bill, 280, 281
Warren, Rick, 86
Weber, Max, 406
Welch, Jack, 86
Wells, Mark, 130
Wepin, Tsai, 435
West, Tim, 173
White, Danny, 80
Willis, Randall L., 353
Winfrey, Oprah, 17, 136
Wood, John, 326
Woods, Tiger, 62
Woodsmall, Jennifer, 117
Woodward, Joan, 426, 427

Y
Yankelovich, Daniel, 37
Yetton, Phillip, 311, 315
Yunus, Mohammad, 343

Z
Zore, Edward, 215, 216

Subject Index

Leaders:
    charismatic, 257–258
    women as, 52, 53
Leader match training, 249
Leader-member exchange (LMX)
        theory, 253–254
Leadership, 242–246
    as attribution, 255–256
    behavioral theories of, 244–246
    change, 283–291
    charismatic, 67, 257 258, 260
    defined, 243
    distributed, 198
    and emotions, 67
    formal vs. informal, 243
    implicit, 255–257
    inspirational, 257–262
    integrative, 268–278
    management vs., 242–243
    moral, 278–283
    path-goal theory of, 249–251
    romance, 255
    shared, 269–271
    and situational contingencies,
        246–255
    substitutes for, 254–255
    trait theories of, 243 244
    transformational/transactional,
        258–260
    by women, 12
Leadership grid, 246
Leading, and management
        process, 13–14
Learning, 18–19, 94–102
    organizational, 18, 418–421
    and punishment, 215, 216
    and reinforcement, 94 101
    social, 94, 101–102
    vicarious, 419–420
Least preferred co-worker (LPC)
        scale, 247–249
Legitimate power, 218
Leniency error, 163
Libya, 279, 346
Life cycle, organizational, 284
Lifelong learning, 18
Life stressors, 49
Line-staff conflict, 348
Line units, 394–395
Linking-pin roles, 349

Listening, active, 327–328
LMX, see Leader-member ex-
        change theory
Locus of control, 45
Long-linked technology, 426
Long Term Capital Management
        (LTCM), 227
Long-term/short-term orientation,
        38
Lose-lose conflict, 350
Low-context cultures, 329
Low-differentiation errors, 163
Lower-order needs, 112–113
LPC scale, see Least preferred co-
        worker scale
LTCM (Long Term Capital Man-
        agement), 227
Lump-sum increases, 154

M
Machiavellianism, 45–46
Mach scales, 46
Maintenance activities, 198
Malaysia, 178
Management, 13–17
    activities of, 14–15
    leadership vs., 242–243
    moral, 16, 17
    of organizational culture,
        374–377
    performance, 155–157
    process of, 13–14
    skills needed for, 15–16
    virtual, 142
Management by objectives
        (MBO), 123–124
Management philosophy, 374–375
Managers, 13
    activities of, 14
    decision making by, 310–313
    effective, 13
    responsibilities of, 392, 393
    roles of, 14–15
Managerial scripts, 425
Managerial wisdom, 277
Manifest conflict, 348
Manufacturing:
    computer-aided, 429
    flexible manufacturing systems,
        138

Masculinity-femininity, 38
Mass production, 427
Matrix departmentation, 401–403
Maturity, emotional, 244
Maturity-immaturity continuum,
        41, 42
MBA programs, cheating in, 173
MBO, see Management by objec-
        tives
MBTI (Myers Briggs Type Indica-
        tor), 45
MBWA, 333
Meanings, shared, 373
Mechanistic type bureaucracy
        (machine bureaucracy),
        406–407
Mediating technology, 426
Mediation, 359
Meetings, confrontation, 380
Merit pay, 152
Meta analyses, 6
Mexico, 38, 41, 87, 113, 121, 255
Mimicry, 418–419
Minnesota Satisfaction Question-
        naire (MSQ), 71
Mission statements, 8, 9, 389, 390
Mixed messages, 331
MNCs (multinational corpora-
        tions), 119
Models, 5
Moderator variables, 26
Moods, 62–63
Moral leadership, 278–283
    and authentic leadership,
        279–281
    and ethical leadership, 278–279
    and servant leadership,
        281–282
    and spiritual leadership,
        282–283
Moral management, 16, 17
Moral managers, 16
Motivating potential score (MPS),
        135
Motivation, 110–111
    across cultures, 111
    content vs. process theories of,
        111
    defined, 111
    and emotions, 67